DYNASTIES *and* INTERLUDES

PAST AND PRESENT IN CANADIAN ELECTORAL POLITICS

LAWRENCE LEDUC | JON H. PAMMETT | JUDITH I. MCKENZIE | ANDRÉ TURCOTTE

DUNDURN PRESS
TORONTO

Copy Editor: Allison Hirst
Design: Jesse Hooper
Printer: Transcontinental

Library and Archives Canada Cataloguing in Publication

Dynasties and interludes : past and present in Canadian electoral politics / by Lawrence LeDuc ... [et al.].

Includes bibliographical references and index.
Also issued in electronic format.
ISBN 978-1-55488-796-5 (pbk.). ISBN 978-1-55488-886-3 (bound)

1. Canada--Politics and government. 2. Elections--Canada--History. 3. Politics, Practical--Canada--History. I. LeDuc, Lawrence

JL65.D96 2010 320.971 C2010-902427-3

1 2 3 4 5 14 13 12 11 10

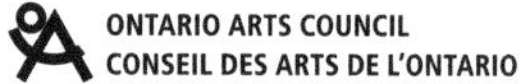

We acknowledge the support of the **Canada Council for the Arts** and the **Ontario Arts Council** for our publishing program. We also acknowledge the financial support of the **Government of Canada** through the **Canada Book Fund** and **The Association for the Export of Canadian Books**, and the **Government of Ontario** through the **Ontario Book Publishers Tax Credit program**, and the **Ontario Media Development Corporation**.

Care has been taken to trace the ownership of copyright material used in this book. The author and the publisher welcome any information enabling them to rectify any references or credits in subsequent editions.

J. Kirk Howard, President

Printed and bound in Canada.
www.dundurn.com

Dundurn Press
3 Church Street, Suite 500
Toronto, Ontario, Canada
M5E 1M2

Gazelle Book Services Limited
White Cross Mills
High Town, Lancaster, England
LA1 4XS

Dundurn Press
2250 Military Road
Tonawanda, NY
U.S.A. 14150

For Philip Converse, John Meisel, Maurice Pinard, Peter Regenstreif, and Mildred Schwartz — principal investigators of the first (1965) Canadian National Election Study

CONTENTS

LIST OF FIGURES

LIST OF TABLES

PREFACE

The research and writing of this book has taken place over a substantial period of time and we have accumulated many debts, intellectual and otherwise, in the course of that work. We dedicate the volume to the group of pioneering scholars who carried out the first major survey of the Canadian electorate following the 1965 federal election. But we have also relied on similar studies conducted in all but one of the federal elections since that time, involving the work of many new generations of scholars.

These studies were supported by the Social Sciences and Humanities Research Council of Canada, and by its predecessor, the Canada Council, without whose funding they would never have been possible. Taken together, this body of social science research, spanning nearly half a century, provides a comprehensive picture of the changing nature of the Canadian electorate, in addition to critical insights into the attitudes and behaviour of voters in specific elections.

While this large body of survey material was central to our research, it is not the only evidence employed herein. For more than 20 years before the 1965 study, the Canadian Institute of Public Opinion (the Gallup affiliate in Canada) polled Canadians on a regular basis regarding their attitudes toward a variety of political and social issues.

Together with the election studies, archives of these data provide a valuable window on the politics of that earlier time.

In the period before public opinion polling and survey research became established, we have relied more heavily on memoirs, biographies, and historical treatments of elections. John Meisel's study of the 1957 election, for example, was described by its author as "an exercise in contemporary history." This and other works contemporary to the various periods of Canadian political life that we seek to analyze in this book help us to better understand the evolution of our politics, and the social, political, and economic forces which drove the larger processes of change that we examine here.

Works on particular elections have proved invaluable to us in this research. From 1974 to 1984, Canada was included in the comparative series of books on elections edited by Howard Penniman and published by the American Enterprise Institute. Beginning in 1984, scholars based at Carleton University have published books on each election involving a collaboration between journalists and political scientists, bringing the unique insights of each field to bear on the election process and outcome. Since 1997, this series has been published by Dundurn Press, and has greatly expanded in its coverage of each successive election. Some of the work found in the 2006 and 2008 volumes of this series reflects ideas that were beginning to develop in the writing of this book.

We are grateful to the staff at Dundurn for helping us to bring this project to fruition, particularly Kirk Howard, Michael Carroll, and editor Allison Hirst. We also wish to thank Library and Archives Canada for providing some of the material for early chapters in this book, and for making it possible to include photographs of past electoral campaign activities. Thanks as well to Jean-Marc Carisse for making available to us a number of his photographs from later periods. We are likewise grateful to Dan Hilton of the Conservative Party of Canada who helped us immensely in obtaining some of the more contemporary photos.

We owe a special debt to Allan Kornberg, Peter Russell, and Dennis Pilon, who read an earlier draft of this manuscript and provided much helpful feedback. We happily absolve them from any responsibility for errors of fact or interpretation that may remain in spite of their best efforts. That there are some, we have no doubt.

The goal of this project from the beginning has been to develop a broader theoretical understanding of the ebb and flow of Canadian electoral politics as it has evolved over a century and a half of Canadian democracy. The electorate has changed greatly over that period, as women gained the vote and the technology of electoral campaigns evolved markedly. Politicians of the nineteenth century would barely recognize the electoral campaigns of today. Yet, if they looked more closely, they would undoubtedly see similarities in the framing of economic issues, the concern with aspects of national unity, the reliance on party leaders, or the importance of Canada's relations with the United States.

As we argue in the first chapter of the book, many of these themes were advanced by André Siegfried in 1907, and continue to be of relevance today. Our objective in the writing of this book is to develop a better understanding of current electoral politics in Canada, as well as that which is yet to occur. But part of the key to that understanding remains firmly rooted in the past.

CHAPTER 1

CONTINUITY AND CHANGE IN FEDERAL ELECTIONS

Elections are markers in a nation's political history. They provide occasions, both practical and symbolic, when a collective political decision is rendered by the citizenry. Long after they occur, they also provide important reference points for significant political events or periods of political, social or economic change. The 1896 and 1968 elections that inaugurated the Laurier and Trudeau eras were two such major political turning points. Election results can sometimes be decisive, as in the "landslide" elections that occasionally thrust one party into a dominant position. Canada has experienced this type of outcome in elections such as those of 1940, 1958, and 1984 (see Table 1.1).

Such decisive victories are often interpreted at the time as a clear expression of the national will, but they do not always inaugurate a long era of dominance for the winning party. In reality, they sometimes owe as much to the operation of our electoral system as to the wishes of the voters. In the most recent of these dramatically one-sided elections (1984), the winning Progressive Conservatives received barely half of the total votes cast.[1] And nine years later, the Parliamentary caucus of the PCs was reduced to two members.

TABLE 1.1
An Overview of Canadian Federal Elections, 1867–2008

Election		Total seats	Ballots Cast	Turnout	Winning Party	Vote (%)	Seats	Prime Minister
1867	7 August–20 September	181	268,387	73.1	Lib.-Cons.	50.1	108	John A. Macdonald
1872	20 July–12 October	200	318,329	70.3	Lib.-Cons.	49.9	104	John A. Macdonald
1874	22 January	206	324,006	69.6	Liberal	53.8	138	Alexander Mackenzie
1878	17 September	206	534,029	69.1	Conservative	52.5	142	John A. Macdonald
1882	20 June	211	508,496	70.3	Conservative	50.7	139	John A. Macdonald
1887	22 February	215	724,517	70.1	Conservative	50.2	126	John A. Macdonald
1891	5 March	215	778,495	64.4	Conservative	51.1	121	John A. Macdonald
1896	23 June	213	912,992	62.9	Liberal	46.1	118	Wilfrid Laurier
1900	7 November	213	958,497	77.4	Liberal	51.2	133	Wilfrid Laurier
1904	3 November	214	1,036,878	71.6	Liberal	52.0	138	Wilfrid Laurier
1908	26 October	221	1,180,820	70.3	Liberal	50.4	135	Wilfrid Laurier
1911	21 September	221	1,314,953	70.2	Conservative	50.9	134	Robert L. Borden
1917	17 December	235	1,892,741	75.0	Unionist	57.0	153	Robert L. Borden
1921	6 December	235	3,139,306	67.7	Liberal	40.7	116	W.L. Mackenzie King
1925	29 October	245	3,168,412	66.4	Conservative	46.5	116	W.L. Mackenzie King*
1926	14 September	245	3,273,062	67.7	Liberal	46.1	128	W.L. Mackenzie King
1930	28 July	245	3,922,481	73.5	Conservative	48.8	137	R.B. Bennett
1935	14 October	245	4,452,675	74.2	Liberal	44.8	173	W.L. Mackenzie King
1940	26 March	245	4,672,531	69.9	Liberal	51.5	181	W.L. Mackenzie King

1945	11 June	245	5,305,193	75.3	Liberal	40.9	125	W.L. Mackenzie King
1949	27 June	262	5,903,572	73.8	Liberal	49.5	193	Louis St. Laurent
1953	10 August	265	5,701,963	67.5	Liberal	48.8	171	Louis St. Laurent
1957	10 June	265	6,680,690	74.1	P.C.	38.9	112	John Diefenbaker
1958	31 March	265	7,357,139	79.4	P.C.	53.6	208	John Diefenbaker
1962	18 June	265	7,772,656	79.0	P.C.	37.3	116	John Diefenbaker
1963	8 April	265	7,958,636	79.2	Liberal	41.7	129	Lester B. Pearson
1965	8 November	265	7,796,728	74.8	Liberal	40.2	131	Lester B. Pearson
1968	25 June	264	8,217,916	75.7	Liberal	45.5	155	Pierre Elliott Trudeau
1972	30 October	264	9,974,661	76.7	Liberal	38.5	109	Pierre Elliott Trudeau
1974	8 July	264	9,671,002	71.0	Liberal	43.2	141	Pierre Elliott Trudeau
1979	22 May	282	11,541,000	75.7	P.C.	35.9	136	Joe Clark
1980	18 February	282	11,015,514	69.3	Liberal	44.3	147	Pierre Elliott Trudeau
1984	4 September	282	12,638,424	75.3	P.C.	50.0	211	Brian Mulroney
1988	21 November	295	13,281,191	75.3	P.C.	42.9	169	Brian Mulroney
1993	25 October	295	13,863,135	69.6	Liberal	41.3	177	Jean Chrétien
1997	2 June	295	13,174,698	67.0	Liberal	38.4	155	Jean Chrétien
2000	27 November	301	12,997,185	61.2	Liberal	40.8	172	Jean Chrétien
2004	28 June	308	13,683,570	60.9	Liberal	36.7	135	Paul Martin
2006	23 January	308	14,908,703	64.7	Conservative	36.3	124	Stephen Harper
2008	14 October	308	13,929,093	58.8	Conservative	37.6	143	Stephen Harper

* Replaced by Arthur Meighen (Conservative) on June 29, 1926.

Sources: Elections Canada [www.elections.ca]; Scarrow, Canada Votes; Feigert, Canada Votes: 1935–1988; Beck, Pendulum of Power.

Election outcomes can also be indecisive, sometimes making the formation of a government difficult and creating an atmosphere of political uncertainty. Minority governments such as those elected in 1957, 1962, 1979, or 2004 lasted only a short time before the public was asked to render a verdict in another election. In the past, minority results have sometimes paved the way for majorities, as in 1925, 1957, and 1972. At other times, they have led to reversals of electoral fortune, as happened after the 1979 and 2004 elections.

The electoral system plays a role in producing these minority outcomes as well. The Progressive Conservatives, for example, who formed a minority government following the 1979 election, received four percent *fewer* votes in that election than did the Liberals, but substantially more seats.[2] In the 2006 federal election, Stephen Harper's Conservative Party of Canada received about the same percentage of votes (36.3 percent) as Joe Clark's Progressive Conservatives in 1979 (35.9 percent). In both instances, the party that assumed office held the confidence of barely more than a third of the Canadian electorate, but formed a minority government nevertheless.

Over the course of Canadian history, electoral patterns have sometimes become established that persisted over several consecutive elections. Typically, these elections have ushered in long periods of relative political stability, which we will refer to throughout this book as political dynasties.

There have been a number of instances in Canadian political history when the same party held power for a considerable length of time, often under the same prime minister. But these long periods of dominance by one party, so significant to historians today, would not necessarily have been regarded as imminent at the time they began. The 1993 election, for example, brought about one of the greatest political upheavals in Canadian history, devastating the then governing Progressive Conservatives and thrusting two new political parties — Reform and the Bloc Québécois — onto the federal scene (see Chapter 11). As it happened, the period following 1993 proved to be one of remarkable political stability, with Jean Chrétien winning three consecutive majority governments before yielding power to Paul Martin in 2003. Similarly, Mackenzie King's tenure in office began during a period of turmoil following the First World War, a time of great social change both in Canada and in many other countries.

King first gained power with a minority government in 1921, an election which also saw the Progressives win 64 seats — one of the most successful "third party" surges in Canadian history. Winning fewer seats and substantially fewer votes than the Conservatives in the following election of 1925, King nevertheless clung to power, yielding office briefly to Arthur Meighen, but recovering to win a majority of seats in the election that took place less than a year later.[3] Despite that victory, few would have predicted at that time that King would go on to lead the most successful political dynasty in Canadian history. But, when he finally retired in 1948, King had served a total of 22 years as prime minister, his long tenure in office interrupted only by the three months that Meighen served as prime minister in 1926 and by R.B. Bennett's single term in office (1930–35).

Brief departures from long periods of political stability, such as the Bennett government, we refer to here as *interludes*. Political scientist Peter Regenstrief first used this term in the Canadian context when he titled his analysis of the Diefenbaker years "The Diefenbaker Interlude."[4] At the height of Diefenbaker's success in 1958, it was not generally anticipated that the Liberals would be back in power only a few years later. It is only with the benefit of hindsight that analysts of that period of Canadian politics were able to recognize the Diefenbaker regime as an interlude in an otherwise long period of Liberal hegemony, first under King and St. Laurent, and later under Pearson and Trudeau.[5] In the aftermath of his 1958 landslide, Diefenbaker's political prospects would have appeared very different to his contemporaries (see Chapter 4).

In this book, we will advance the thesis that Canadian politics has repeatedly followed these patterns — long periods of political hegemony under successful political leaders, punctuated by short, sharp interludes that disrupted what seemed at the time to be a one-dimensional political success story. Nearly all of Canada's successful political leaders have had this experience. Macdonald lost power to Mackenzie's Liberals in the election of 1874, but regained it in the following election and continued on to head Canada's first political dynasty until his death in 1891. Laurier, who became prime minister in the transformative election of 1896 and retained his majority in each of the next three (1900, 1904, and 1908), lost an election to Borden in 1911. Mackenzie King's political dynasty was interrupted twice over a long period, by the Meighen and Bennett interludes, respectively. Having passed power on to Louis St. Laurent in 1948, the Liberal dynasty begun by King continued until Diefenbaker upset it in 1957. But Diefenbaker's landslide victory in the election a year later proved to be short lived, in spite of the size of his parliamentary majority. Reduced to a minority government in 1962, Diefenbaker was out of office in 1963, replaced by the two successive minority governments of Lester Pearson. Pearson's successor, Pierre Trudeau, consolidated a new Liberal dynasty with a decisive electoral victory in 1968 but suffered a setback in the near defeat of 1972.

Trudeau went on to lead one of the more successful political dynasties in modern Canadian history. Regaining a majority government in 1974, Trudeau's tenure in office was also punctuated by a short interlude of defeat in 1979 (see Chapter 8). But the minority government of Joe Clark itself went on to electoral defeat only nine months later, placing Trudeau once again at the head of a majority government. When he retired from office in 1984, Trudeau had served a total of 15 years as prime minister, a tenure equivalent to that of Laurier and surpassed only by King (22 years) and Macdonald (18 years).

Chrétien's dynasty lasted 11 years, and might conceivably have continued further had Paul Martin and his supporters not pushed him out of office in 2003.[6] Martin's two years in office can be thought of now primarily as an extension of the Chrétien dynasty, of which Martin was a key part until the onset of the "civil war" between these two camps within the Liberal Party (see Chapter 13).

Library and Archives Canada.

Sir Wilfrid Laurier campaigning in Exeter, Ontario, 1904 election.

TABLE 1.2

Five Elections That Established New Political Dynasties

	Macdonald	Laurier	King	Trudeau	Chrétien
ESTABLISHING	**1867**	**1896**	**1921**	**1968**	**1993**
TESTING	1872	1900	1925	1972	1997
↓	1874[1]				
	1878				
CONFIRMING	1882	1904	1926	1974	2000
	1887	1908	1930[2]	1979[3]	2004[4]
	1891		1935	1980	
			1940		
			1945		
			1953[5]		
			1949[5]		

1. Mackenzie interlude
2. Bennett interlude
3. Clark interlude
4. Liberal Party led by Paul Martin
5. Liberal Party led by Louis St. Laurent

TABLE 1.3

Six Elections That Failed to Establish New Dynasties

	Mackenzie	Borden	Bennett	Diefenbaker	Clark	Mulroney
ESTABLISHING	1874	1911	1930	1957–58	1979	1984
TESTING	**1878**	1917[1]	**1935**	1962	**1980**	1988
NOT CONFIRMING		**1921**[2]		**1963**		**1993**[3]

1. Union government
2. Conservative Party led by Arthur Meighen
3. Progressive Conservative Party led by Kim Campbell

The election in 2006 of a minority Conservative government under Stephen Harper could ultimately prove to be either an interlude (albeit one including two election victories), or the beginning of a new dynasty, depending upon Harper's continued success in repositioning his party along the key issue dimensions of Canadian federal politics — an enduring characteristic of all successful dynasties that we will discuss in some detail throughout this book.[7]

In the chapters following, we will highlight the rise and fall of five major political dynasties: those of John A. Macdonald and Wilfrid Laurier, who shaped so much of Canada's early political history; William Lyon Mackenzie King, whose dynasty continued for another nine years through the succession of Louis St. Laurent; Pierre Trudeau, representing a long period of Liberal governance begun by Lester Pearson in 1963 and punctuated only by the short-lived Clark government of 1979–80; and Jean Chrétien, whose three consecutive election victories beginning in 1993 extended a period of Liberal dominance with a fourth election won by Paul Martin in 2004.

The establishment of these dynasties was not a simple matter. While each of the periods described above started with a decisive election victory, the new pattern established in that election was tested in the one following. Often, given the inherent volatility of Canadian electoral politics, the existence of the dynasty could not be confirmed until a third election demonstrated the staying power of both the party and its leader (see Table 1.2).

In the cases of both Mackenzie King and Pierre Trudeau, the test that occurred after their initial election was a dramatic one. King lost the election of 1925, but managed to remain in power for eight months before yielding to Arthur Meighen, whom he defeated more decisively in the subsequent election (1926). Trudeau's election victory in 1968 was followed by near defeat in 1972 (see Chapters 6 and 7). Only after his political recovery in the 1974 election would it have been possible to discern the shape and durability of a "Trudeau dynasty."

Such patterns suggest that to understand electoral politics in Canada, it is essential not to put too much emphasis on the interpretation of a single election. Instead, it is important to place elections within the context of a somewhat longer and more complex process of political and social change and of the evolution of political leadership.

The *interludes* to which we refer throughout this book also contain many elements of complexity. A few, such as the single-term governments of Alexander Mackenzie (1874–78) or R.B. Bennett (1930–35) are readily demarcated. Likewise, the nine-month administration headed by Joe Clark (1979–80) represents a typical interlude, with Pierre Trudeau being returned to power decisively in the election of 1980. But others are not so readily classified. The Borden government elected in 1911 might not have lasted so long had its term not first been extended by the war and then subsequently by the election of a wartime Unionist government in 1917. Historically, it now appears as an extended interlude, in spite of the decisiveness of the 1911 and 1917 elections, both of which we will examine in greater detail in Chapter 2.

The Diefenbaker and Mulroney periods are likewise complicated segments of Canadian electoral history. Given their one-sided election victories (Diefenbaker in 1958, Mulroney in 1984), both of these leaders had the potential to establish new political dynasties. Mulroney in particular had the clear determination to do so. But, for a number of reasons that we will explore in greater detail in Chapters 5 and 11 respectively, neither Diefenbaker nor Mulroney was able to translate his dramatic election victory into the type of lasting political success attained by King or Trudeau (see Table 1.3). Despite the 1958 landslide, Diefenbaker failed a crucial electoral test in the election of 1962, and his government was defeated a year later. Mulroney, in contrast, won a difficult re-election in 1988, but was ultimately unable to either hold on to power himself or to pass the leadership on to a successor who could do so.

Had the political and economic events of the early 1990s unfolded differently, there could well have been a "Mulroney dynasty." We could argue that the 2008 election likewise represented a crucial electoral test for Stephen Harper. But the continuation of minority government and the persistent strength of the Bloc Québécois makes the possible emergence of a "Harper dynasty" doubtful. However, judgments about a "Harper interlude" are equally suspect, or at least premature.

Of course, we should not consider elections only in the context of political leaders, important as these may be, both in establishing dynasties and in interrupting them. Elections can also be critical or watershed events, representing major societal turning points and reflecting deep-seated processes of political and social change. "Critical" elections, as they are sometimes called by political scientists, reflect deep underlying patterns of social and economic change. Such elections often bring with them both new issues and new ways of thinking about politics. They also create realignments in the support base of the parties.

The American scholar V.O. Key, examining the important U.S. election of 1932, which ushered in the "New Deal" era of American politics, argues that the patterns of social and demographic change that could be observed in America in the previous decade of the 1920s had as much or more to do with the election of Roosevelt as did the actual political events of 1932.[8] The enduring effect in American politics was to bring working class voters to the Democratic side of the American political spectrum.

The federal election of 1917 was a traumatic event in Canada, in which the campaign generated unprecedented levels of ethnic antagonism, opening deep wounds which, some might say, never fully healed.[9] But it was the changing social and political environment of the time that precipitated these developments, as much as any of the issues, candidates and events associated directly with the election itself. And many Unionist voters that sustained the Borden government in 1917 did not continue thereafter to support the Conservatives.

The election of 1945 saw the Co-operative Commonwealth Federation (CCF) make a major electoral breakthrough, winning 28 seats, mainly in the Prairie provinces. The CCF, which had been founded in Regina in 1933 as a farmer-labour based socialist movement, forced the other parties to come to terms with the reality of social class relations.[10]

Occurring at the same time as Labour's accession to power under Clement Attlee in Britain, the 1945 election drew attention to important patterns of post-war social change that were occurring both in Europe and North America. In that same election in Canada, the strong showing of the Bloc populaire in Quebec (two seats with 12 percent of the Quebec vote) provided an early indication of the future growth of Quebec nationalism.[11] Later events, such as Quebec's "Quiet Revolution" of the 1960s and René Lévesque's unexpected provincial victory in 1976, demonstrated that some of these early signs of change in the old political alignments were more than transient phenomena, and that they would have enduring consequences in the evolution of federal politics.

We do not explicitly employ a "critical elections" framework of analysis in this book, in part because we believe that this approach tends to place undue emphasis on the issues and events associated with a single election. Also, when connected explicitly to concepts such as "realignment," as is done in some of the American studies cited above, it can imply a degree of partisan stability that is absent in Canadian federal politics.[12] Even though one party has sometimes been able to hold power for long periods of time, this success has not been based on solid groups of supporters voting for the party time after time. Nevertheless, we would have no difficulty in recognizing important elections such as those of 1896 or 1993 as "critical" elections within the traditional meaning of this particular theoretical approach.[13] Such elections represented major turning points in Canada's politics, even if the underlying causes of some of the changes that they embodied lay well beyond the confines of the election campaign.

Parties and Party Systems

Elections can also be examined for their role as important reference points for changes in the party system, which in turn determines the types of choices that are available to citizens when they vote in an election. Canada's first party system, which lasted into the early part of the twentieth century, was a largely two party affair reflecting both the characteristics of early Canadian society and the constraints imposed by the electoral system, which makes it difficult for minor parties or new political movements to gain parliamentary representation. Canada evolved under this basic structure of a two-party system during the first 50 years after Confederation. Conservatives and Liberals reflected in part the ethnic and sectarian divisions of early Canadian society, and also developed strengths in particular regions of the country. As we will show in this book, the Conservatives advocated protection of Canadian industries during much of this period, while the Liberals supported various versions of free trade with the United States.

While there were sporadic "third party" interventions in elections as early as 1896,[14] the 1920s and 1930s saw a series of new movements and parties contest Canadian federal elections. The first of these was the Progressive Party, a Western farmers' movement which elected 64 members in 1921. Later the CCF and Social Credit became major political players in Canadian elections. As a result, there existed a "two-and-a-half" party system for most of the next 70 years, although the Liberals were dominant throughout much of that time.

The established pattern of "two and a half" party politics survived the events of the 1958 landslide, in which John Diefenbaker swept away much of the basis of the old party system, firmly anchoring the Progressive Conservatives to Western Canadian support. It also survived the phenomenon of "Trudeaumania" in 1968, when Trudeau brought the country into what seemed to be a "new politics" during the period of rapid social and cultural change now commonly associated with the 1960s. The competition in the dramatic election of 1988, focused around the historic Free Trade Agreement with the United States, was also between the Conservatives, the Liberals and the NDP. Things were to change shortly thereafter. The "earthquake" election of 1993 all but destroyed the old Progressive Conservative party, and brought two newcomers — the Bloc Québécois and Reform — to the political scene in its place.

The effects of that dramatic election still reverberate in the political life of Canada today. Kenneth Carty divides the historical patterns into three distinct periods — the first party system before 1921, the second that began with the election of King and the rise of the Progressives in the 1920s, and a third configuration which commenced with the defeat of the Liberals in 1957–58.[15] According to this interpretation, Canada in the 1990s may have begun to evolve into a "fourth" party system, beginning with the collapse of the Conservatives in 1993 and the rise of the Bloc and Reform.

This new party system, if it is indeed distinctive from those of the past, may eventually become more like some of the multi-party systems found in many European countries. Alternatively, it may represent only part of a transition to something quite different, as it goes through an extended process of "rebuilding" following the 1993 cataclysm.[16] However, the events of elections from 2004 onward suggest that the merger of the Canadian Alliance with the remnants of the old Progressive Conservatives has been at least partially successful in replicating some previously successful Conservative electoral strategies. If the new Conservative Party of Canada should increasingly come to resemble previous Conservative alignments, and the Bloc eventually begins to recede, we may well come to question how different this "new" party system really is from those of a somewhat more distant past. There are, in other words, elements of continuity as well as change that are clearly visible in today's system of political parties.

Over the course of Canadian history, there have been relatively few occasions where the political parties have chosen to form and fight along the territorial, ethnic, linguistic, religious, or class cleavages that have long been a part of the Canadian social fabric. In the Canadian federal state, the composition of the nation and the relative power of the provinces, have been issues of continuing importance which still are not settled. Some analysts have suggested that the Canadian preoccupation with issues of national unity, ethnic relations, and federal–provincial negotiation has inhibited the emergence of an electoral politics of social class or ideology.[17]

Canadian political parties have traditionally been brokerage parties.[18] Lacking stable support groups in the electorate, and avoiding clear ideological differentiation from their competitors, political parties approach each election anew, hoping to put together a coalition of support across the entire electorate. Brokerage parties do not seek to appeal in election campaigns on the basis of long-standing principles, or on a commitment to fundamental projects to restructure the economy or society, even if they have these. They are not bound by positions or actions they have taken in the past. Electoral platforms are typically put together from a short-term point of view, offering a mixture of assurances of general competence to deal with the major problems of the day, commitments to prosperity and social security, specific promises designed for instant appeal, and an assertion that only *they* can provide creative leadership.

Certain types of regional and ideological divisions have become more apparent over the past two decades, as the political parties became more regionalized and, in the process, less competitive outside their own core areas of support. Today, it remains uncertain whether political parties will be able to continue the historic pattern of acting as "brokers" between the diverse elements of Canada's multicultural society, or whether they will continue to fragment into narrower expressions of specific regional, linguistic, or ideological interests.

Not all scholars writing about Canadian political parties agree that Canadian political parties are brokerage parties, either in the political world of the past or in the present day. For Political Scientist David Smith, the arrival on the scene of John Diefenbaker, Lester Pearson and Pierre Trudeau marked a new "pan-Canadian approach" which transformed the

Liberals and Conservatives more into parties of principle, in the process becoming both more leader oriented and more programmatic.[19] Kenneth Carty likewise sees the period of the late 1950s and early 1960s as one of significant departure from these earlier traditions of Canadian party politics, but characterizes it somewhat differently. In his view, the period after 1963 emphasized "electronic politics" (with the rise of television) and gave greater prominence to the role of the party leader ("personal parties").[20]

Our position in this book is that recent electoral campaigns such as those run by the Mulroney Conservatives (1984–93) and the Chrétien and Martin Liberals (1993–2004), or even the Harper Conservatives in 2006 and 2008, continue to fit the brokerage model quite well, although there are some contradictory trends that are also in evidence. The Reform Party in the late 1980s (with its slogan "the West wants in") and the Bloc Québécois, which now routinely casts itself as *the* party of Quebec,[21] appeared to emphasize regional interest above all else. As the Reform Party transformed itself into the Canadian Alliance prior to the 2000 election, it began to place ideology above region in its quest to "unite the right." Both instances would seem to run strongly counter to the tradition of brokerage parties as it has existed through much of Canadian history. In the 2004 election, the newly formed Conservative party, created from the 2003 merger of the Alliance and Progressive Conservatives, showed signs of returning to the brokerage tradition more associated with its predecessors. The result of the 2004 election suggested that this initial attempt failed, as the new party at that time seemed largely unable

Conservative Party of Canada. Herman Cheung, photographer.

Stephen Harper and Laureen Harper with campaign plane, 2008 election.

to escape its regional and ideological past (see Chapter 13). However, the 2006 and 2008 elections yielded a new and more electorally successful turn, with the Conservatives winning both of those elections with a more centrist strategy.

While there is still considerable uncertainty about the future of the Canadian party system in this new political environment, the fact remains that it has more often than not demonstrated a tendency to revert to the brokerage model — a characterization that extends back through much of Canadian electoral history. In part, the reason for this tendency is that brokerage has long been associated with electoral success, while parties and leaders that have attempted to emphasize region, ideology or class interests have not been nearly as successful over time, or have enjoyed a degree of political success only during brief interludes.

The Keys to Victory

The main argument in this book centres around the various ways that Canadian political parties structure the choices available to the voter in an election.[22] In Canada, the parties have had considerable freedom in this regard because they have typically tended to eschew long-term ideological commitments and are thus better able to manoeuvre strategically in choosing issues and emphases in any given election campaign. The particular ways in which parties attempt to structure the voting choice in any given election are often dependent on short-term strategic choices of issues and the appeal of the current party leaders. However, the parties are not totally free to structure electoral choice in any way that they wish. They are constrained by a set of factors traditionally associated with the Canadian political landscape, and which commonly recur in electoral appeals.[23] They must be well positioned on the key economic questions of the time, have public confidence on issues of national integration, and, since the Depression, be in favour of expanding or at least preserving the welfare state.

Lest we think these factors are of recent vintage, consider the views of André Siegfried, writing at the beginning of the twentieth century about elections in Canada:

> In all electioneering programmes [in Canada] there are certain points upon which the politicians lay stress, instinctively as it were, because they know them to be calculated to impress public opinion; and nothing throws more light upon the real spirit of a constituency than the kind of language addressed to it by the candidates, its licensed flatterers. In this chapter we shall study the arguments of a general character which the Canadian election organizers are most given to invoking, and which ensure victory to their party when they can make out their claim with sufficient plausibility. They are four in number: the defence of one of the two races or of one of the two religions against the other; the prosperity of the country; the promise of public works or material local advantages; and the personal prestige of the party leader.[24]

The "prosperity of the country," the need to promote economic growth and a pledge to attack any problems that may appear to be threatening it, has always been an important part of Canadian electoral discourse. In any election, parties will attempt to structure choices to their advantage around economic issues. To some extent, they are free to espouse specific economic policies which they consider advantageous, as the Conservative Party did with the National Policy under Macdonald in 1878, the Little New Deal under Bennett in 1935, Wage and Price Controls under Stanfield in 1974, and the Free Trade Agreement under Mulroney in 1988. In many cases, however, these were responses to larger economic problems which have thrust their way onto the electoral stage. American domination, recession or depression, inflation, unemployment, government debt — whatever the threat to Canadian economic prosperity — political parties promise solutions, whether specific or general, in order to persuade the public that they are the ones who should be trusted to deal with the complex matters of economic policy.

"The defence of … race … or … religion" identifies a second constraint on Canadian electoral politics, though not necessarily in the way invoked in the quotation. Siegfried saw a communal appeal as a kind of "ultimate weapon" of Canadian politics, one which "fortunately, though … always latent, does not always manifest itself in outbreaks of anger."[25] We can conceptualize this constraint, then, as a necessity for parties to decide whether to appeal along, or across, racial, ethnic, religious or regional lines. Often in the past, the parties, whether defending their principles or seeking short-term electoral advantage, have opted to structure their appeal *across* cleavage lines, in particular to accommodate Quebec. The accommodation of Quebec has provided some vestiges of internal structuring in Canadian parties, placed constraints on cabinet selection, and influenced strategic decisions on election issues. For a considerable part of Canadian electoral history, the success of one party in appealing to Quebec as part of a national community (first the Conservatives, then the Liberals) has structured important elements of federal electioneering. The appeal of the Bloc Québécois to represent the province (or at least the francophone majority thereof) along cleavage lines in elections since 1993 reversed this historic pattern, and caused other parties to react by making strategic decisions of their own to deal with ethnic and linguistic relations, either in an accommodating manner or in a more antagonistic one.

Attempts by the major parties to accommodate the West have over time been less successful than with Quebec, and that region has spawned several new parties which have from time to time altered or disrupted the Canadian party system. Starting in 1921 with the Progressives, then in 1935 with the CCF and Social Credit, and later in 1993 with Reform, several new political parties have arisen as representatives of the West, and structured their appeals along regional lines. The strategic question of whether to continue to act as a regional party or to aspire to become a national entity has bedeviled all of these parties.

The Canadian Alliance's attempt to break out of this pattern in the 2000 election was only marginally successful. Its Conservative successor did better in this regard in the elections after 2004, but still faced the dilemma of balancing its desire to act as a true representative of western grievances with its ambition to form a national government. The decision to act solely as a regional party is a momentous one, since it would appear to involve abandoning the ultimate ambition of forming a government. In fact, such political movements of the past (e.g. Social Credit, the Progressives) have generally faded over time, or been absorbed by the major parties. Reform's quest to find a "united alternative," beginning in 1997 and continuing under the Alliance banner in 2000 and the Conservative one after the 2003 merger, eventually came to display an awareness of the fact that even successful regional parties in Canada must grow and change in order to survive. Whether the Bloc can prove the exception to this strong historical pattern remains one of the most intriguing questions of the current political era, since the Bloc, unlike the Alliance, does not have the option of transforming itself into a Canadian "national" party.

A third important factor in the electoral campaigns of all major Canadian parties is the need to extend, maintain, improve, or defend the welfare state. This factor represents a more modern extension of the emphasis that Siegfried in the era in which he was writing placed on "public works." The modern variation on this theme stems from the policy consensus which developed after the Great Depression of the 1930s establishing that it was a responsibility of the state to provide a "social safety net."

During and after the Second World War, a number of programs were put in place to create such a framework for social policy — unemployment insurance, welfare, health insurance, medicare, and pensions. Not all of these were established by the federal government, and their implementation often involved controversy. However, their popularity with the public meant that their acceptance needs to be stated with assurance by political parties during election campaigns, regardless of any desires they might harbour for substantially changing or even replacing such programs. Brian Mulroney's reference to social programs as a "sacred trust" during the 1984 election campaign provided such assurance to voters at the time, but came back to haunt him later when he sought to implement changes in pension and welfare policies. The accusation by the Liberals in the 2004 election campaign that the new Conservatives under Stephen Harper had a "hidden agenda" favouring tax cuts at the expense of social programs was in part directed toward this same end. Any attack on the welfare state that might be in the policy plans of politicians cannot easily be acknowledged in elections, even in the name of financial prudence, without serious repercussions.[26] The incorporation of welfare state measures into their electoral programs is the price that mainstream parties have had to pay to prevent sharp class divisions from arising in Canadian elections.[27]

Canadians have not, at least in more recent times, tended to be constrained in their voting choices by powerful social or ideological cleavages, or by strong partisanship. This has allowed the parties to appeal to voters across lines of ethnicity, regionalism, or social class as noted earlier, even though such appeals are not always successful in any given election.

Since the time of the first major surveys in 1965, scholars have observed that the Canadian electorate as a whole has tended to exhibit relatively weak ties to political parties and therefore exhibits considerable volatility in elections.[28] Unhindered by past feelings of party loyalty, many voters feel free to choose which party to support on the basis of such short-term factors as the particular issues of the day, their assessment of the state of the economy, the characteristics of the party leaders, or the likelihood of effective representation from a local candidate.

Such a pattern contrasts quite markedly with some of the more ideologically driven party systems of European countries or with the more party-identified electorate of the United States. In their study of the 1974 Canadian electorate, Clarke et al. classified only about a third of the Canadian electorate as *durable* partisans, whose support could generally be relied upon by their party of choice in any given election. The remaining two-thirds were *flexible* partisans, whose support in a given election could in many instances be won or lost on the basis of shorter-term factors.[29]

Of course, the actual movement of voters between elections may often be less than these figures would seem to imply. But given the implications of a weakly aligned electorate, political parties have long

TABLE 1.4

Images of Canadian Political Parties, 1974–1984

(percent)*

	1974	1979	1980	1984
Policy/issue	61	51	60	51
Style/performance	47	50	60	53
Leader/leadership	38	37	51	23
Parties/general	35	42	40	41
Area/group	28	27	31	34
Ideology	14	15	18	16
N =	2,445	2,670	928	3,380

* Multiple response to open-ended questions. Canadian National Election Studies, 1974–1984. For more information on these measures, see Clarke, Jenson, LeDuc, and Pammett, ***Political Choice in Canada***, Chapter 6.

been well aware that they cannot count on the continued support of a loyal band of followers in order to win elections. The sudden reversals of party fortunes that have occurred in elections such as 1972, 1979, 1984, 1993, or 2006 demonstrate this point convincingly. The relative freedom from sociodemographic constraints that Canadian parties enjoy is thus a mixed blessing for them. On the one hand, political parties are able to fashion new appeals and seek new sources of support as opportunities arise. But they also know that even many seemingly "loyal" supporters can quickly turn against them if they become disillusioned.[30] This explains both the periodic tendency toward sudden and sharp electoral reversals, but also the ability of parties over time to recover from adversity and adapt to new political circumstances.

Data on the types of images which Canadians hold of the political parties (See Table 1.4) shows why it is possible for parties to reinvent themselves from time to time in this way. Relatively few voters hold images of the parties that are tied to ideology, group or regional alignments, or simple partisanship. Many more form their images of the parties based on the particular policies or issues that they embrace at a given time, party performance (particularly when in office), and feelings about the party leaders. Thus, a change in leadership is often instrumental to a party in renewing its image with the electorate. The period of change that occurred in both major parties in the late 1960s demonstrates this strategy clearly. As the Diefenbaker–Pearson era came to an end, voters gradually wearied of their entrenched personal and partisan rivalry which had played out over the course of four elections. With the ouster of Diefenbaker and the selection of Robert Stanfield as leader in 1967, the Conservatives quickly gained electoral advantage, as evidenced by the public opinion polls of the time (see Chapter 6). But this advantage proved to be short-lived, as the Liberals soon began their own period of renewal with the selection of Pierre Trudeau as leader in 1968. Within a period of barely more than a year, both major parties had acquired entirely new images to present to the electorate.

The set of issue constraints on political parties introduced in this section provides a framework that will be used throughout this book in explaining why political parties win or lose elections. In addition, sustained mastery of the three issue areas of economic, national unity, and social welfare issues provides the key to the reasons why some political leaders and their parties have been able to establish dynasties that stand the test of time, while others have not.

Electoral Rules and Structures

Two other important dimensions of electoral contests in Canada are that they are *parliamentary* elections, and that the Canadian government is a *party* government. The votes cast in federal elections are for individual candidates within constituencies, sometimes called "ridings," the number of which has risen from 181 in 1867 to 308 in 2008. No matter how popular or unpopular the party leaders may be, the *real* electoral contest is the one between the parties to obtain a majority of seats in the House of Commons. Political parties as organizations are essential to the Canadian electoral process, and they form the structural backbone of Canadian government.

Canadian elections are not "presidential," as in the United States or France.[31] Party leaders, no matter how prominent, must organize teams of candidates to fight elections throughout the country if they hope to form the government. A national organization must be sustained and put into full operation at regular intervals. Parties attempt to nurture a positive public image for themselves, which they can later draw upon at election time. Leaders play a role in this process, but they are not the sole actors. Nevertheless, in a television age, the leader often defines much of a party's image. Sometimes, this can be a deliberate part of a party's electoral strategy, as exemplified by the Liberals' characterization of their campaign as "Team Martin" in the 2004 election. During the Trudeau years, many felt that the leader himself personified the Liberal party. In more recent years, leaders have been less often cited as the primary reasons for voting choice.[32]

The electoral system is vital to the operation of this process. Although Canadian electoral procedures have changed over time, and the electorate has expanded, this has occurred for the most part within the context of the single member electoral district, "first past the post" framework.[33] The basic form of our electoral system was inherited from Britain and, in spite of extensive criticisms of it, has remained in place throughout our entire history.[34] These electoral rules have had a number of important effects on the outcome of elections and, since they are well-known to parties and politicians, they have also affected the way in which campaigns are organized.[35] The most clearly identifiable effect has been the tendency of the system to produce governments with large parliamentary majorities but narrower electoral pluralities.[36] Prominent examples of "majority" governments elected with relatively modest proportions of the total vote, all of which will be discussed later in this book, include the federal elections of 1945, 1974, 1993, and 1997.

In the most recent of these (1997), the Liberals formed a majority government with just over 38 percent of the vote, the lowest such total in Canadian history. In Canada, single member plurality (SMP) also distorts regional representation, and gives an electoral advantage to political parties that are able to concentrate their votes in one province or region of the country, generally at the expense of parties with a broader national appeal. In recent elections, the Bloc Québécois has been a clear beneficiary of this characteristic of the electoral system, and the NDP has been repeatedly disadvantaged by it. Parties such as Reform in 1997 or the Canadian Alliance in 2000 have experienced both the advantages and disadvantages of this distortion of representation. They have swept disproportionate numbers of seats within their own dominant region, but have been unable to win seats in other parts of the country even when gaining a significant percentage of votes. In 2000, for example, the Alliance won 24 percent of the popular vote in Ontario, but managed to win only two of the province's 103 seats in that election. As a result, it continued to be perceived as a largely "western" party, in spite of what otherwise might have been interpreted as a relatively strong performance in Canada's largest province.

In principle, the SMP electoral system simplifies political choice for the voter. Canadian voters under this system cast only a single vote for a local candidate. Since smaller parties can rarely break through to win in many constituencies, the tendency is for voters to shy away from "wasting their votes" by casting ballots for them, and thus for fewer such parties to be sustained over long periods of time. The Green Party fielded candidates in 303 of the 308 constituencies in the 2008 election, obtaining 6.8 percent of the total vote but no parliamentary seats. The larger political parties in Canada have frequently capitalized on public awareness of the tenuous position of smaller parties, urging voters to make a clear choice between those parties that have the potential to form a government instead of supporting smaller or newer parties.

Such appeals for "strategic voting" may have made some difference in the 2004 election when it was evident to many voters that a vote cast for the NDP or the Greens might have the perverse effect of electing a Conservative government.[37] It is also not uncommon for a major party to make "majority government" into an election issue, as the Liberals did in 1965 and 1974, in each case following two years of a minority administration.

Whatever the electoral context, Canadian voters, unlike their American, German, or French counterparts, have only a single vote to cast, and in the end they must decide whether to cast it sincerely or strategically, and whether to place the emphasis on the party as a whole, the party leader, or the local candidate. There is no such thing in a Canadian election as a "split ticket."

The thesis of the supposed "simplification" of the party system produced by the electoral system runs into difficulty, however, when the regional nature of Canadian politics is taken into account. Rather than being disadvantaged, regionally based smaller parties have sometimes taken advantage of the ability to win disproportionate numbers of seats by concentrating their appeal in a particular province or region. Two Quebec examples of this have been the Créditistes, which emerged with surprising strength in the House of Commons in 1962 because of concentration in one geographical area of the province, and the Bloc Québécois, which became the Official Opposition after the 1993 election, despite contesting the election only in Quebec. Thus, rather than maintaining a national party system by discouraging smaller parties, the electoral system may actually be partly responsible for producing the opposite effect in Canada — a more regionalized party system.

Some political parties in recent years have chosen to appeal to the electorate as representatives of geographical or territorial cleavages in the country, and have been rewarded with substantial numbers of parliamentary seats for so doing. In contrast, parties with a broader national following, such as the NDP, or the Progressive Conservatives after 1993, have been severely disadvantaged by the operation of the electoral system. However, the regional nature of the Canadian system extends beyond such extreme cases. Even under more normal electoral circumstances, parties have at times depended on large regional blocks to form government. This was certainly the case with Diefenbaker who won 42 seats in the Prairie provinces in 1962, or Trudeau, who won 74 out of the 75 Quebec seats in 1980, or more recently with Chrétien who won 101 of 103 Ontario seats in 1997.

The Composition of the Electorate

Another important consideration when studying elections in Canada is the changing composition of the electorate. The post-Confederation electorate was a relatively restricted one. Until 1885, the franchise was under the control of the provinces. Most provinces followed the doctrine that the right to vote should be restricted to those *men* who had acquired a certain amount of property or wealth. However, there were some differences in electoral qualifications. For example, New Brunswick required a man to have $400 in annual income in order to qualify, but did not link this to the ownership of property. Nova Scotia, however, required the ownership of property worth $150, but no minimum annual income. Ontario required both a minimum annual income of $250, and ownership of property worth $200 in the cities and $100 in rural areas. Only British Columbia imposed no property or income requirements.[38]

British Columbia, while egalitarian on the income dimension, led the way in the imposition of racial restrictions on voting eligibility. That province banned not only Indians (as did Ontario and Manitoba) but also immigrants of Chinese origin. It was also common to deny the vote to certain categories of provincial government employees, such as judges, sheriffs, land registrars, and tax collectors. But here again there were inconsistencies. In Nova Scotia workers in the post office were specifically prohibited from voting while in British Columbia they were specifically included in the electorate. In Quebec and Ontario, rural postal workers could vote whereas those working in cities and town could not.

In 1885, the Conservative government of John A. Macdonald succeeded in passing a bill giving the federal government control of the franchise, ostensibly in order to eliminate the kinds of inequities described above. In fact however, this legislation contained a potpourri of income and property qualifications, which differentiated urban from rural areas and owners from tenants of property.[39] It raised the levels of such qualifications in Nova Scotia and Manitoba, and imposed them for new voters entering the electorate in British Columbia and Prince Edward Island, where they had heretofore been absent. Macdonald's self-described "greatest triumph" was a piece of legislation intended largely to benefit his own party through the property qualifications, favouritism to rural areas, and the continued exclusion for racial reasons of virtually all Indians and Chinese.[40] After the Liberal party won the 1896 election, they promptly gave the franchise determination back to the provinces again, prohibiting them "from excluding a citizen, otherwise qualified to vote, from exercising the right to vote on the grounds that he practiced a particular profession or carried on a particular occupation, worked for the federal government or a provincial government, or belonged to any class of persons."[41] This last clause was intended to provide voting rights to Canadians of Asian origin, but British Columbia attempted to get around it by enacting a provision that voters had to be able to read the *Elections Act* in English. Discrimination by British Columbia against voters of Asian origin was reimposed in 1920, and was not finally ended until 1948.

The Canadian electorate has increased from a few hundred thousand eligible voters in the years after Confederation to well over twenty million in 2008.[42] The pattern was one of gradual growth commensurate with the increase in population until the elections of 1917 and 1921. Prime Minister Robert Borden, heading a Unionist coalition government of Conservatives and non-Quebec Liberals, made two strategic moves to enhance his chances of winning the 1917 election. The first was to count separately the votes of the military who were overseas fighting the First World War and allow the government to assign their votes to any place they had previously resided or failing that to a riding chosen by the government — all this to be done a month after the election.[43] The second was to grant the vote to all spouses and female relatives of servicemen.

The 1917 act also removed the power to enumerate voters and construct the voters' lists from the provinces and gave it back to the federal government. While Borden sought to gain political advantage through extension of the franchise, the changes in the electorate and electoral laws that took place in this period reflected more than mere political calculation. In particular, the strength of the suffrage movement made voting rights for women all but inevitable after the end of the war. Following its victory in the 1917 election, the Borden government introduced the *Dominion Elections Act*, which enfranchised all female citizens, resulting in the doubling of the size of the electorate. In the 1921 federal election, Agnes Macphail became the first woman to be elected to the House of Commons. The *Dominion Elections Act* of 1920 also provided for the appointment of the first Chief Electoral Officer, and established many of the norms for the conduct of elections in the modern era. The next large jump in the composition of the electorate came with the extension of the vote to 18–21 year olds, which came into force with the federal election of 1972. Immigration has also contributed over time to changes in both the size and composition of the Canadian electorate, as has internal movement of the population between cities and provinces.

In the period between 1867 and 2008, Canadians went to the polls in national elections 40 times, plus another three times in referendums — a total of 43 occasions in all. The average turnout in federal elections was 70.1 percent of eligible voters, although this figure conceals a substantial amount of dispersion around it.

The zenith of Canadian electoral participation came during the Diefenbaker and Pearson years, with a 79 percent turnout registered in the elections of 1958, 1962, and 1963. For the most part, turnout in elections during the Trudeau and Mulroney years was also well above average, leading to a general expectation that about three-quarters of eligible voters would cast their ballots at any given election. A study done for the Royal Commission on Electoral Reform and Party Financing made optimistic projections regarding electoral participation suggesting that, with some administrative changes to make the actual voting process easier, turnout could well rise above the 80 percent mark.[44]

Ironically, however, despite the implementation of some minor measures toward this end, voting turnout has been declining steadily in recent years, dropping to 67 percent of registered voters in the election of 1997 and recording an historic low of less than 59 percent in 2008. Although turnout rebounded slightly to just under 65 percent in the 2006 election, evidence suggests that it remains unlikely to return to the levels of the 1970s and 1980s, and could well decline further in future elections in spite of new efforts on the part of the electoral authorities and other interested groups to stimulate greater participation in elections.

According to recent research, the decline in voting turnout that has taken place over the past two decades is attributable largely to the failure of newly eligible young voters to enter the active electorate in numbers commensurate with their proportion of the total population.[45] In contrast, older voters continue to participate in about the same proportions as in the past, and are also living longer and remaining more active in social and political affairs. Taken together, these two trends suggest an electorate that is growing older and shrinking in size (at least as a proportion of the total population). Political parties are thus encouraged to target their appeals more directly to those segments of the population most likely to participate in elections. The emphasis in recent elections on the issue of health care shows that parties tend to target their electoral appeals toward those Canadians who are the most likely to vote, rather than to the population at large.

The fact that such a large proportion of eligible voters fails to cast a ballot in any particular election also means that there is considerable movement into and out of the electorate from one election to the next. In spite of the sustained decline in turnout of recent years, there have in the past been relatively few Canadians who *never* voted in elections. Rather, many non-voters were in reality "transient" voters, who could be mobilized on some occasions but not others. In crafting their campaign strategies, parties thus sought to appeal across the broader electorate — to persuade their previous supporters to trust them again, to woo those people who voted for their opponents, and to try to attract back into the electorate many less-interested voters who did not cast a ballot last time. This necessity to appeal across the board contributes to the amorphous and insubstantial nature of many party campaign strategies. And that in turn risks discouraging some previous voters who may come to feel that voting is not meaningful.

Campaigns

In Canadian elections, there is little doubt that campaigns matter. Since parties cannot rely on cadres of supporters to come out and vote for them time after time, they must assemble at least partly new coalitions on each occasion. Much strategic thinking goes into the choice of which issues to emphasize in a campaign. Big economic problems facing the country force themselves onto the electoral agenda, and necessitate a response from the parties. However, most major parties prefer to treat such problems on a high level of generality and stress their capacity to tackle them rather than to announce a specific program to implement a solution. Policies that are too specific have the potential to alienate as many voters as they attract. The fate of parties proposing specific policy responses like Reciprocity in 1911, the Little New Deal in 1935, Wage and Price Controls in 1974, or the Green Shift in 2008 has not been a happy one. In the 1988 election, the Mulroney Conservatives attempted to define the campaign issue, not as the just-negotiated Free Trade Agreement with the United States, but as "managing change," a vacuous phrase which appeared to mean nothing much more than "trust us." Over the course of the campaign however, the continuing controversy over the Free Trade Agreement forced it to the centre of the campaign agenda of all of the parties (See Chapter 10).

When it comes to smaller scale issues, party promises can have an impact, as exemplified by the Liberal Red Book in the 1993 election campaign. Strategically, this package of detailed policy proposals allowed the Liberals to argue that after nine years in government, the Conservatives did not have any plan for the future, in contrast to themselves. As a policy manifesto, the Red Book strategy had many shortcomings, but as a campaign strategy, it was highly effective (See Chapter 11). A similar observation can be made about the Conservatives' Five Point Program in 2006.

Techniques of electoral persuasion have changed dramatically in the years since Confederation. As implied in the quotation from Siegfried (see page 36), "the promise of public works or material local advantages" was an important element in the campaign strategy of governing parties for many years. Once political leaders in the pre-Confederation colonies had wrested control of the state away from the officers of the British Crown, they fell heir to all of the techniques of manipulation and patronage that went with their positions and gained control of the resources to implement them.[46]

Historian Gordon Stewart identifies Macdonald and Laurier as the great masters of patronage politics. Both established elaborate clientelist networks whereby local notables competed for material benefits for their areas, and dispensed gifts or "treats" to entice voters. The electoral politics of personal gain and group gain provided the lens through which policy proposals like the National Policy and Reciprocity were viewed.[47]

Early techniques of electoral influence involved personal contact with local patrons and subsidiary brokers. For those who could read, the print medium provided a powerful source of electoral persuasion.

Newspapers were invariably partisan, and exhorted their readers to support one or another of the competing parties or candidates. Pamphlets and posters, often with graphic illustrations, helped the parties to get their points across. As the twentieth century unfolded, techniques of political campaigning evolved as well. With the filling out of the geographical shape of the country, the growth of population and the increased size of cities, came a change in the operating procedures of political parties. It was no longer possible for elaborate networks of local operators to mobilize votes to the same extent. Although patronage did not disappear as a means of attracting voters, it was on a larger scale, favouring regions rather than localities. In particular, the governments of Mackenzie King created a system of regional ministers who distributed patronage in order to attract votes in all areas of the country for the Liberal party.[48] More and more voters were being reached directly through the communications media instead of indirectly through local operatives. Newspapers increased their circulation and their professionalism and were no longer as closely identified with partisan positions on the news pages.[49] The new medium of radio was used for the first time in the election campaign of 1930 by Mackenzie King and R.B. Bennett. From that time forward, leaders could make direct oratorical appeals to the Canadian public at large.

Media politics took a gigantic leap in 1957 with the first election campaign in which television played a key role. The main beneficiary was Progressive Conservative leader John Diefenbaker who, unlike Liberal leader Louis St. Laurent, "took well to the new medium."[50] The early television broadcasts were free-time allocations to the parties, generally featuring a talk by the leader. From this point on, television gradually took over the major role in linking the public with the campaign, with free-time broadcasts fading in importance in comparison with appearances on nightly news programs and interview shows, together with carefully crafted campaign advertisements. The activities of professional behind-the-scenes campaign strategists were a novelty when Alistair Grosart ran the Conservative campaign of 1957 and Keith Davey the Liberal campaign of 1963, but these have since become commonplace. Teams of strategists now direct election campaigns, supported by extensive public opinion polling to test prospective messages before they are introduced and to monitor their effectiveness along the way. Where election campaigns were once fought at the constituency level between groups of party workers, today they are fought largely on television, between leaders who are advised by campaign professionals.

Leaders have played an important role in Canadian electoral politics, as Siegfried also noted at the dawn of the previous century.[51] Not only have they been the primary spokespersons for their parties during the campaign, but they have directed the strategy of the parties in planning the themes of the campaign. In large part, this has been because of the nature of the parties themselves. Those wishing to form a national government have had to tie together a broad organization capable of campaigning throughout the country without the "glue" of a distinctive ideology. By default, the glue has been the personal appeal of the party leader, together with the power that a successful leader would inherit if victorious in the election — power to distribute offices and favours to those working alongside. Party leaders have also become an important part of a party's identity in the minds of voters. Lacking strong ideological or policy driven images, the personality of a leader imprints itself easily on that of the party. One important side effect of this tendency toward a leader driven politics is that parties have been better able to adapt to adversity by merely changing the leader. Such a strategy of course has not always been successful. While the Liberals revived their flagging electoral fortunes with the selection of Pierre Trudeau in 1968, their attempt to do the same with John Turner in 1984 proved disastrous for the fortunes of the party.

Although party leaders have been central to shaping the images of their parties, the appeal of the leader to the electorate has been a complex one. A few prominent prime ministers with a claim to the adjective "charismatic" (Macdonald, Laurier, Diefenbaker, Trudeau) have attracted large numbers of votes through the force of their own personalities. For many others, however, it is more likely to have been the content of a leader's message that produced the votes rather than the personality of the messenger. The advent of leaders' debates in the 1968 election campaign and their institutionalization since the 1984 campaign has given leaders greater campaign exposure, and has also meant that the leaders are well briefed on current issues, and well rehearsed in the techniques of presenting their points of view.[52] Debates have plenty of "content," and leaders are able to use these occasions to advance their parties' strategic plan for the campaign.[53] In modern election campaigns, the leader debates have become the centrepiece of the campaign, and one of its principal events. But, as the dramatic events of 1988 demonstrated, other campaign factors above and beyond the leader debates can also play a critical role in determining election outcomes.

In Canada, as in other democratic countries, the structure of election campaigns continues to evolve, driven both by new technologies and changing styles of political communication.[54] In recent campaigns, the internet has begun to play an important role in the process of communication between parties, candidates, and voters. Over time, such changes will undoubtedly have significant effects on the nature of electoral campaigns, as have those of the past involving the advent of radio and television, or the use of campaign debates or negative election advertising.[55] Yet many of the fundamental principles of election campaigning remain the same. Political parties and their leaders compete for the votes of the citizens, and their success or failure is determined in the course of that process of competition. Politicians who take Canadian voters for granted do so at their peril.

Issues, Policies, and Mandates

In every election, "the people speak." But in the aftermath of the vote, a voice can often be heard to whisper: "but what did they say?" How can a myriad of individual voting decisions ever be interpreted as a collective act? This question has always been a thorny one for democratic theorists.[56] Representative democracy sees elections primarily as a mechanism for choosing leaders and rendering public officials accountable for their actions. While elections can sometimes provide a certain degree of policy direction to those in charge of the machinery of government, rarely if ever does an election serve as a "referendum" on a detailed program of public policy, either established or proposed. The choice of one party or another to form a government implies only in a very limited way a collective decision on the substance of what that party stands for. Policy mandates have been difficult to achieve in Canadian elections, even when the campaign discourse has dealt with important issues regarding the country's economic, social, or constitutional future.[57] For this reason, advocates of more direct forms of democracy often argue in favour of holding separate referendums on major questions of public policy, viewing elections as too imperfect a tool to provide true policy choices.[58] Many commentators of the time, for example, considered the election of 1988 to be the equivalent of a "referendum" on the Free Trade Agreement, which had been negotiated in the year preceding the election by the Mulroney government. But had the Agreement been put to an actual referendum, it almost certainly would have been defeated (see Chapter 10). Thus, while elections can have policy implications and consequences, they cannot always be interpreted in issue terms. Voters, in the end, cast their votes for a party and candidate, and not for a policy agenda. In modern election campaigns, avoiding specific policy commitments is as likely to be a part of a party's electoral strategy as embracing them.

Voting in elections is often "retrospective" — i.e. looking to the recent past rather than the future.[59] Canadian voters are adept at "throwing the rascals out" when they have become disillusioned with those in power. Many of the *interludes* referred to in this book have come about in this way, when voters opted to punish a governing party by defeating it in an election. Such electoral interludes were often read at the time as major turning points, but they sometimes proved to be nothing more than a timely rebuke to a party in power. Opposition parties that have benefited from such circumstances have sometimes misread the mood of the electorate as conferring a larger policy mandate, as the short-lived Clark government did in 1979. But such mandates, even when they appear to exist, can be fleeting endorsements. Canadian voters have only a single weapon at their disposal, and they tend to deploy it against any government that fails to perform up to their expectations.

Political parties play this electoral game from the other side, seeking whatever formula may seem to promise victory. Issues become vehicles through which to appeal to the voters rather than commitments to be turned into policies. It seemed not to bother the Liberals in their 2004 campaign that they promised to initiate a daycare program that had originally been promised in the 1993 Red Book. Similarly, the Conservative campaign took little heed of criticisms that its promised program of tax cuts appeared to be at variance with its commitment to sharply increased spending on health care and defence.

In Canadian election campaigns, shuffling the issue agenda is sometimes the only way that parties can avoid being trapped in their own inconsistencies on policy matters. Yet, it is also true that the most successful political parties and leaders over the course of Canadian history — those that have been able to construct dynasties rather than being rejected by the voters after a short interlude — have been those best able to navigate the constraints imposed by the underlying realities of the Canadian polity. To be successful over time, they must master the demands imposed by the need to foster economic prosperity, maintain national unity, and sustain a modern welfare state. Leaders such as R.B. Bennett or John Diefenbaker, who failed on one or more of these fundamentals, were confined by the voters to rather short periods in office, in spite of their initial electoral successes. The circumstances of the time may also play a role in determining success or failure. Brian Mulroney, who following his 1984 electoral landslide appeared to understand the constraints imposed in all three of these areas, nevertheless eventually fell victim to both the recession of the early 1990s and the failure of his two bold constitutional initiatives — the Meech Lake and Charlottetown accords. What might have been a new political dynasty instead became an interlude, and in the process his party was destroyed as well.

Adaptation and Change

In the remaining chapters of this book, we will explore the evolution of Canadian party politics through an examination of the 40 federal elections that have taken place since Confederation. These elections can be grouped into several distinct periods of Canadian political history, demarcated by particular configurations of party hegemony, specific issues, or dominant leaders. Remarkably, two of the political parties that contest federal elections today have the same names as the ones that fought Canada's first elections, although today's Conservatives are clearly not the same party that John A. Macdonald led in the years following Confederation. The Liberals also have undergone extensive changes in their approach to politics over the years, yet they have survived in spite of severe electoral setbacks such as those of 1958 or 1984. The story of party politics in Canada, as we will see, is in many respects one of adaptability and change. As Peter Mair has observed, political parties in the established western democracies have often shown a remarkable capacity to adapt to new political and social circumstances, as well as a keen instinct for political survival.[60] An electorate with fundamentally weak ties to parties and a demonstrated high degree of electoral volatility such as the Canadian one will always contain within itself the potential for sudden and dramatic change. Yet, despite a high degree of electoral turnover, the major Canadian parties have for the most part adapted and survived. Even the Conservatives, following the disastrous election of 1993, found new political life through their merger with the Canadian Alliance and returned to power with a minority government in 2006.

In previous work, we have noted that there is considerable issue volatility from one election to the next.[61] Political parties are often able to reshuffle the issue agenda in any given election in an effort to put together a winning political coalition in the short term. Yet it is also true that the same *types* of political issues — economic prosperity, national unity, social welfare — recur with considerable regularity over time. Parties or leaders that fail in one of these policy areas can sometimes recover and adapt, as King did in 1935 or Trudeau in 1980. But electoral circumstances, or the electorate itself, are not always forgiving of failure on the part of a party or leader to balance these sometimes competing interests. It was often said of them at the time that Diefenbaker never *really* understood Quebec, or Trudeau the West.[62] Yet one leader was able to overcome a major political setback and return to power, while the other was not.

Just as Canada's old parties adapt and change, new players have appeared from time to time on the political scene that did not exist in the early years of Confederation. But there is continuity even here. In part because of the tendency of the major parties to occupy the same political turf by representing similar sets of political ideas at any given time, the door has often been opened to "third" parties of both the left and right, or to parties expressing regional discontent. While movements of the past such as the Progressives, Social Credit, CCF, or Bloc populaire may appear to bear only superficial similarity to the NDP, Reform, or Bloc Québécois, it is clear that certain basic clusters of ideas and interests have recurred in varying forms throughout the history of Canadian electoral politics. As Maurice Pinard noted in his classic study of the rise of Social Credit in Quebec, the emergence of "third" parties in Canada has often been related to the weakness of the traditional opposition party in particular parts of the country.[63] In Quebec prior to 1984, the weakness of the Conservatives was largely a function of that party's traditional identification with "English Canada," creating electoral opportunities first for the Bloc populaire and later for Social Credit. In the West, support for the wartime Union government blurred the distinction between the major parties, opening the door to the rise of the Progressive, CCF, and Social Credit movements. In recent years, the weakness of one of the major parties in Quebec and in the West created similar opportunities for the Reform party and the Bloc Québécois. The new parties, as they have arisen, have sometimes served as vehicles of political protest, but they have also been a source of renewal and change.

The 1993 election, which we will consider in more detail in Chapter 11, appeared to pose a fundamental challenge to our traditional understanding of a party system which seemed over the years to exhibit a remarkable capacity to survive and adapt. In this watershed election, the forces of volatility and discontent evident within the Canadian electorate in recent years suddenly manifested themselves in an entirely new way. The Conservative party, which only five years earlier had succeeded in winning a second consecutive majority government, was not only defeated in its bid for a third term but thoroughly decimated. The two new parties which rose to prominence in that election seemed overnight to have transformed the Canadian political world into something very different. Yet as we view that election with the benefit of over a decade of additional hindsight, it is clear that the process of adaptation is already well advanced. The 1993 election was after all won, not by any of the new parties, but by the Liberals, who over the course of the twentieth century have been Canada's most successful political party. Only twenty years ago, the Liberal Party itself seemed to teeter on the edge of the political precipice. But today, in spite of recent electoral setbacks, it remains highly competitive. At the same time, the 2003 merger of the seemingly moribund Progressive Conservatives with the Canadian Alliance has created a political entity which is both new and old, and has restored the fortunes of the political grouping in Canada that can trace its roots back to John A. Macdonald. As the analyses in this volume will demonstrate, the past can provide important keys to understanding both the present and future shape of party politics in Canada. "Change" is a fact of everyday life, but the underlying continuities and the fundamental characteristics of the political world in which it occurs, are often equally important.

Notes

1. The highest of these three elections was 1958, in which the winning Progressive Conservatives received 53.6 percent of the total votes cast.
2. The Progressive Conservatives won 136 seats on 35.9 percent of the vote in the 1979 election. The Liberals obtained only 114 seats while gaining 40.1 percent of the total votes cast.
3. Although King's parliamentary majority rested on the support of a dozen members elected as "Liberal-Progressives" in 1926. See Chapter 3.
4. Peter Regenstreif, *The Diefenbaker Interlude* (Toronto: Longman's, 1965).
5. Often our dynasties as defined here involve more than one leader, e.g. King/St. Laurent, Pearson/Trudeau, Chrétien/Martin, etc.
6. On the Martin–Chrétien "civil war," see John Gray, *Paul Martin: The Power of Ambition* (Toronto: Key Porter, 2003) and Susan Delacourt, *Juggernaut: Paul Martin's Campaign for Chrétien's Crown* (Toronto: McClelland & Stewart, 2003). See also the more extensive discussion of this period in Chapter 13.
7. Of course, it is also possible that we have entered an entirely new political era, in which the creation of a "dynasty" similar to those of the past may no longer be achievable. We will consider this possibility in greater detail in Chapter 14. On the prospect that minority government may endure for some time under current conditions, see Peter Russell, *Two Cheers for Minority Government: The Evolution of Canadian Parliamentary Democracy* (Toronto: Emond Montgomery, 2008). See also the analysis and evaluation of the October 2008 parliamentary crisis in Peter Russell and Lorne Sossin (eds.), *Parliamentary Democracy in Crisis* (Toronto: University of Toronto Press, 2009).
8. V.O. Key, "A Theory of Critical Elections," *Journal of Politics*, 17 (1955), 3–18. See also Geoffrey Evans and Pippa Norris, *Critical Elections: British Parties and Voters in Long-Term Perspective* (London: Sage, 1999), and Walter Dean Burnham, *Critical Elections and the Mainsprings of American Politics* (NY: Norton, 1970).
9. See John English, *The Decline of Politics: The Conservatives and the Party System, 1901–1920* (Toronto: University of Toronto Press, 1977).
10. On the founding and growth of the CCF, see Walter Young, *The Anatomy of a Party: The National CCF, 1932–61* (Toronto: University of Toronto Press, 1969).
11. Founded in 1942 in reaction to the national plebiscite on conscription, the Bloc populaire canadien ran candidates in both federal and Quebec provincial elections until 1949. In the 1944 provincial election in Quebec, it won 4 seats with 14 percent of the vote.
12. On the treatment of these issues in the United States, see James L Sundquist, *Dynamics of the Party System: Alignment and Realignment of Political*

Parties in the United States (Washington D.C.: Brookings, 1983). See also Byron Shafer (ed.), *The End of Realignment?: Interpreting American Political Eras* (Wisconsin: University of Wisconsin Press, 1991).

13. See, for example, Donald L. Blake, "1896 and All That: Critical Elections in Canada," *Canadian Journal of Political Science* 12 (1979), 259–80.
14. The 1896 elections saw two such political movements based in Ontario. One was led by D'Alton McCarthy, and was dedicated to the proposition that English should be the sole language of speech and education for Canada. The second, the Patrons of Industry, came into Canada from the United States, and championed the interests of the agrarian sector in co-operation with industrial workers.
15. "Three Canadian Party Systems," in R.K. Carty, ed., *Canadian Political Party Systems: A Reader* (Toronto: Broadview Press, 1982), 563–86.
16. R. Kenneth Carty, William Cross, and Lisa Young, *Rebuilding Canadian Party Politics* (Vancouver: University of British Columbia Press, 2000).
17. See Robert Alford, *Party and Society* (Chicago: Rand McNally, 1963), and John Porter, *The Vertical Mosaic* (Toronto: University of Toronto Press, 1965), for some of the classic academic statements of these themes. On the weakness of class politics in Canada, see Jon H. Pammett, "Class Voting and Class Consciousness in Canada," *Canadian Review of Sociology and Anthropology* 24 (1987), 269–90.
18. On this theme, see Harold D. Clarke , Jane Jenson, Lawrence LeDuc, and Jon H. Pammett, *Absent Mandate: Canadian Electoral Politics in an Era of Restructuring* (Toronto: Gage, 1996), 15–21. See also Janine Brodie and Jane Jenson, *Crisis, Challenge and Change: Party and Class in Canada Revisited* (Ottawa: Carleton University Press, 1988).
19. David E. Smith, "Party Government, Representation and National Integration in Canada," in Peter Aucoin, ed., *Party Government and Regional Representation in Canada* (Toronto: University of Toronto Press, 1985).
20. Carty, "Three Canadian Party Systems," 576–84.
21. In the 2004 campaign, the Bloc's slogan was *"un parti propre au Québec."* In its 2006 campaign advertising, it used the phrase *"ici, c'est le Bloc"* to convey the message of its identity with Quebec interests.
22. On this theme, see especially Peter Mair, "Party Systems and Structures of Competition," in Lawrence LeDuc, Richard G. Niemi, and Pippa Norris (eds), *Comparing Democracies: Elections and Voting in Global Perspective* (Thousand Oaks, CA: Sage. 1996), and Leon Epstein, *Political Parties in Western Democracies* (New Brunswick, NJ: Transaction Books, 1980).
23. On the topic of constraints on political parties, see William L. Miller and Richard G. Niemi, "Voting Choice, Conditioning, and Constraint," in Lawrence LeDuc, Richard G. Niemi, and Pippa Norris (eds), *Comparing Democracies 2: New Challenges in the Study of Elections and Voting* (London: Sage, 2002), 169–88.

24. André Siegfried, *The Race Question in Canada* (London: Eveleigh Nash, 1907), 207.
25. *Ibid.*, 169.
26. See Raymond Blake, Penny Bryden, and J. Frank Strain (eds), *The Welfare State in Canada: Past, Present and Future* (Concord, ON: Irwin, 1997).
27. Brodie and Jenson, *Crisis, Challenge and Change.*
28. See Fred Engelman and Mildred A. Schwartz, *Political Parties and the Canadian Social Structure* (Scarborough, ON: Prentice-Hall, 1967), and John Meisel, *Working Papers on Canadian Politics* (Montreal: McGill-Queen's Press, 1975).
29. Harold D. Clarke, Jane Jenson, Lawrence LeDuc, and Jon H. Pammett, *Political Choice in Canada* (Toronto: McGraw-Hill Ryerson, 1979), 301–19. For a comparison of patterns of partisan attachment in Canada, Britain, and the United States, see Lawrence LeDuc, "Partisan Change and Dealignment in Canada, Great Britain, and the United States," *Comparative Politics* 17 (1985), 379–98.
30. For example, Clarke et al. estimate the extent of switching between the parties in the 1984 election at 28 percent. In 1993, however, with the collapse of the Progressive Conservatives and the rise of the new parties, the comparable figure rises to 51 percent. *Absent Mandate: Canadian Electoral Politics in an Era of Restructuring*, 105–09.
31. On the significance of this seemingly obvious point in the contemporary political environment, see Jennifer Smith, "Parliamentary Democracy versus Faux Populist Democracy," in Peter Russell and Lorne Sossin, eds., *Parliamentary Democracy in Crisis* (Toronto: University of Toronto Press, 2009), 175–88.
32. In 2006, for example, 23 percent said that party leaders were the most important factor in voting, while 24 percent chose local candidates, and 53 percent cited parties taken as a whole. See André Turcotte, "After Fifty-Six Days ... the Verdict," in Jon H. Pammett and Christopher Dornan, eds., *The Canadian Federal Election of 2006* (Toronto: Dundurn Press, 2006), 292.
33. The exceptions have been dual-member ridings in Prince Edward Island, Nova Scotia, and British Columbia. In all of these, voters were given the same number of votes as there were members to be elected. On the electoral system more generally, see Dennis Pilon, *The Politics of Voting* (Toronto: Emond Montgomery, 2007). See also J. Paul Johnston and Harvey E. Pasis, eds., *Representation and Electoral Systems: Canadian Perspectives* (Toronto: Prentice-Hall, 1990).
34. The recent experiment in New Zealand, in which the traditional SMP model was replaced by a system of mixed member proportional (MMP) representation is of particular interest to Canadians who have been critical of some of the effects of the SMP model in Canada. For a discussion and synthesis of some of these arguments, see Henry Milner, *Making Every Vote Count: Reassessing Canada's Electoral System* (Toronto: Broadview Press,

1999).

35. See Alan Cairns, "The Electoral System and the Party System in Canada," *Canadian Journal of Political Science* 1 (1968), 55–80, for the classic statement of this argument.
36. André Blais, "The Debate Over Electoral Systems," *International Political Science Review* 12 (1991), 239–60, and André Blais and Louis Massicotte, "Electoral Systems," in LeDuc, Niemi and Norris, *Comparing Democracies 2: New Challenges in the Study of Elections and Voting* (Toronto: Sage, 2002).
37. See Chapter 13. See also Jon H. Pammett and Christopher Dornan (eds), *The Canadian General Election of 2004* (Toronto: Dundurn Press, 2005).
38. On the history and evolution of the Canadian electorate, see Elections Canada, *A History of the Vote in Canada* (Ottawa: Minister of Public Works and Government Services, 1997).
39. Elections Canada, *A History of the Vote in Canada*, 49.
40. Gordon T. Stewart, "John A. Macdonald's Greatest Triumph," *Canadian Historical Review* 33 (1982), 3–33.
41. Elections Canada, *A History of the Vote in Canada*, 52.
42. The number of eligible voters in the 2008 election was 23,677,639. Elections Canada. Accessed at *www.elections.ca.*
43. Elections Canada, *A History of the Vote in Canada*, 58.
44. Jon H. Pammett, "Voting Turnout in Canada," in Herman Bakvis (ed), *Voter Turnout in Canada* (Toronto: Dundurn Press, 1991).
45. For an analysis of this recent trend, see Jon H. Pammett and Lawrence LeDuc, *Explaining the Turnout Decline in Canadian Federal Elections: A New Survey of Non-Voters* (Ottawa: Elections Canada, 2003). See also Lawrence LeDuc and Jon H. Pammett, "Voter Turnout in 2006: More Than Just the Weather," in Jon H. Pammett and Christopher Dornan, eds., *The Canadian General Election of 2006* (Toronto: Dundurn Press, 2006).
46. See Gordon T. Stewart, *The Origins of Canadian Politics: a Comparative Approach* (Vancouver: University of British Columbia Press, 1986), and S.J.R. Noel, *Patrons, Clients and Brokers: Ontario Society and Politics, 1791–1896* (Toronto: University of Toronto Press, 1990).
47. Jon H. Pammett, "A Framework for the Comparative Analysis of Elections Across Time and Space," *Electoral Studies* 7 (1988), 125–42.
48. Herman Bakvis, *Regional Ministers: Power and Influence in the Canadian Cabinet* (Toronto: University of Toronto Press, 1991).
49. W. H. Kesterton, *A History of Journalism in Canada* (Toronto: McClelland & Stewart, 1967).
50. John Meisel, *The Canadian General Election of 1957* (Toronto: University of Toronto Press, 1962).
51. André Siegfried, *The Race Question in Canada*, 168–77.
52. There were no televised debates in 1972, 1974, or 1980. However, televised debates between the leaders, both in English and French, have been held continuously since 1984.

53. Lawrence LeDuc, "The Leaders' Debates ... (And the Winner Is ...)," in Alan Frizzell and Jon H. Pammett (eds), *The Canadian General Election of 1997* (Toronto: Dundurn Press, 1997).
54. On this issue, see Pippa Norris, *On Message: Communicating the Campaign* (London: Sage, 1999). See also David Farrell, "Campaign Strategies and Tactics," in LeDuc, Niemi and Norris, *Comparing Democracies.*
55. Ann Dale and Ted Naylor, "Dialogue and Public Space: An Exploration of Radio and Information Communication Technologies," *Canadian Journal of Political Science* (2005), 203–25.
56. See, among other sources on this point, David Held, *Models of Democracy* (Stanford: Stanford University Press, 1987), and C.B. Macpherson, *The Life and Times of Liberal Democracy* (Oxford: Oxford University Press, 1977).
57. Clarke et al., *Absent Mandate: Canadian Electoral Politics in an Era of Restructuring.*
58. See, for example, Patrick Boyer, *The People's Mandate: Referendums and a More Democratic Canada* (Toronto: Dundurn Press, 1992).
59. On this theme, see Morris Fiorina, *Retrospective Voting in American National Elections* (New Haven: Yale University Press, 1981).
60. Peter Mair, "Myths of Electoral Change and the Survival of Traditional Parties," *European Journal of Political Research* 24 (1993), 121–33.
61. Clarke et al., *Absent Mandate: Canadian Electoral Politics in an Era of Restructuring.*
62. See, for example, Peter C. Newman, *Renegade in Power* (Toronto: McLelland & Stewart, 1963), and Richard Gwyn, *The Northern Magus* (Toronto:McLelland & Stewart, 1980).
63. Maurice Pinard, *The Rise of a Third Party: A Study in Crisis Politics* (Englewood Cliffs, NJ: Prentice Hall, 1971).

CHAPTER 2

THE MACDONALD AND LAURIER DYNASTIES

Two political dynasties founded and sustained the Canadian dominion, established the country's first party system, and produced the expectation by the voting public that strong leaders would emerge to control the nation's affairs. These two political dynasties also established the building blocks around which subsequent elections would be won and lost. John A. Macdonald (prime minister from 1867–74, and 1878–91) fashioned the Conservative Party (then called the Liberal-Conservative Party) into the main vehicle for national government during the whole period from Confederation to 1896. During Macdonald's lifetime, Conservatives had strength in all regions of the country and among all classes of voters, though they were particularly dependent for their finances on manufacturing, railway, and banking interests. Wilfrid Laurier (prime minister from 1896–1911) created a mastery over the Canadian political system, and established the dominance of the Liberal Party which continued for much of the twentieth century. Laurier did this by virtue of his sweeping personal appeal in Quebec, and his mollification of commercial interests, together with appeals to traditional Liberal support among farmers and working class voters who were entering the eligible electorate in greater numbers with the expansion of the suffrage. Even though the Laurier

Liberals were defeated in 1911, the basis of the Liberal dynasty had been laid so well that it survived the party's ill fortunes during the First World War. Conservatives, starting with Borden and continuing with Meighen, Bennett, Diefenbaker, Clark, and Mulroney, produced only interludes, despite election victories, sometimes decisive ones. King (followed by St. Laurent), Trudeau (following Pearson) and Chrétien (with Martin), on the other hand, established and maintained Liberal dynasties.

Legitimating the new Canadian Confederation was no easy task. For the architects of the agreement, led by Macdonald and his Quebec lieutenant, George-Étienne Cartier, the job had to be undertaken without a cohesive national political party to rely on. The first three elections — 1867, 1872, and 1874 — took place separately in the different provinces, in different months of the year. John A. Macdonald skillfully exploited his position as the popular architect of the Confederation agreement (popular at least in Ontario and Quebec) to obtain early victories in elections which established the legitimacy of the new state. His goal was to solidify a popular commitment to the Confederation gamble. Economic growth, railway building, and regional development were important reasons for supporting the Macdonald Conservatives. The Liberal opposition was initially in disarray. The fact that their leaders, including George Brown and Edward Blake, had joined with Macdonald and his Conservative colleagues to support Confederation had removed a major issue that might have allowed them to distinguish themselves and their party from the Tories.

The main issue of national unity at that period was support for Confederation itself, and the main battleground was in the Maritimes. The success of anti-Confederate forces in the first elections in New Brunswick and Nova Scotia undermined the opposition's ability to present a united front to the electorate. It also meant that the Liberals had to rely more on economic policy to distinguish themselves from the Conservatives. Attempts to do this by emphasizing free trade within North America were largely unsuccessful, as we shall see in this chapter.

Canada's First Elections

Not only did the first Canadian elections not take place on the same date, but the electoral rules for their conduct also varied among provinces. This was because there was no uniform Canadian elections act; rather, there was simply a continuation of the electoral provisions from the colonial period in each province. This meant variation in two main aspects of electoral management: how voting was conducted, and who was eligible to vote. In the first of these, New Brunswick took the lead. There, the provincial electoral law of 1855 provided for both the compilation of an electoral register, and a version of the secret ballot in which a voter deposited the written name of his choice in a ballot box.[1]

In Canada East and Canada West, voting registers based on municipal assessment rolls had been established by 1861, but the secret ballot was only adopted after the Liberals came to power in 1874. The Liberals, however, had been campaigning for the secret ballot since the beginning, believing that the Conservatives were bribing and intimidating voters. In Nova Scotia, as elsewhere, defenders of open voting argued that secrecy merely promoted deception, and that electors should have the courage to declare their choice to all, as was done in Britain. However, in Nova Scotia there was no open voting after 1870, in part because forces seeking to elect Joseph Howe in Hants County had used questionable tactics.[2]

Eligibility to vote was restricted somewhat differently in the provinces, but in general property or income qualifications were imposed. For example, in Ontario, an owner or tenant would have to hold property worth $200 in an urban area, or $100 in a rural area.[3] Although this meant in practice that anyone on the property tax rolls was enrolled on the electoral register, it is estimated that 16.5 percent of the population was enfranchised in Ontario in 1867.[4] Women were not eligible to vote, and there was a list of other exclusions. In all provinces, those employed by the government in positions we would today refer to as the "civil service" were excluded, as were magistrates, judges, police and prosecutors. In the event that male Indians managed to meet the property qualifications, most provinces specifically excluded them from voting if they received any benefit paid by the government. As new provinces entered Confederation, and various adjustments were made in the criteria, the percentage of eligible voters gradually increased. By 1882, for example, it was estimated that 20 percent of the Ontario adult population was eligible to cast a ballot.[5]

By 1872, the Liberals had positioned themselves to present more of a challenge as a credible alternative government, and Macdonald had to go all out to secure a narrow victory. His efforts to build a Conservative Party free of links to the colonial past meant that many loosely organized factions, and independent members of Parliament, had to be organized into a group that would support him in power.[6] The expansion of the electorate, gradual though it was, meant that many more 'ordinary voters' were eligible to cast ballots. Macdonald spent an extraordinary amount of his time "micro-managing" the distribution of favours and positions, since patronage was the glue that tied supporters to the early political parties.[7] Patronage was overt and ubiquitous; supporters were promoted and accommodated, and opponents were ignored. As a by-product, the party itself was built as an institution, and the public's evaluation of it as an entity eventually outlasted any personal benefits that trickled down to the populace.

Macdonald struggled mightily to win the 1872 election. Plead as he might for "four more years" to finish the job of consolidating Confederation, opposition was plentiful. Macdonald's personal popularity could not overcome the effects of some of the events of his first administration. Macdonald had been made part of the British delegation in negotiations with the Americans to settle a variety of outstanding differences between them. During the course of these talks, the United States was given access to fishing rights in eastern Canadian waters, with only some limited payment from Britain in return.[8] Neither was there to be access to American markets for Canadian goods, nor some kind of reciprocity or free trade provision. This issue was especially telling in Ontario, where the Liberals, by Beck's estimate, ended up with 8 more seats and 10 percent more of the vote than the Conservatives.[9] The Liberal provincial government of Ontario campaigned against Macdonald, and in the farming areas of Western Ontario, the Grits maintained their established strength. And in the new Western provinces of Manitoba and British Columbia, Macdonald was not seen as moving fast enough on his promise to build the transcontinental railway within a decade. Among the desperate actions that Macdonald took in order to win the 1872 election was an acceptance of large sums of money from Montreal financier Sir Hugh Allan, who in turn was granted the rights to build the Canadian Pacific Railway. Faced with the ensuing scandal and the desertion of some members of his own caucus when these secret contributions were revealed, Macdonald resigned in 1873 and retreated to opposition.[10]

The 1874 election solidified a two-party system in Canada, since elected Liberals had to support the government of Alexander Mackenzie, and those Conservatives elected were mainly the hard core of the party. Public morality was the central issue for the upright Scottish stonemason who led the Liberals. Their economic platform consisted of promises to manage the public finances responsibly and without corruption. Overall economic growth was, of course, the underlying goal, but caution was the watchword, and railway building would have to be slowed to maintain control of the public finances.

The 1878 Election

This was the first modern election in Canadian history. Despite its plodding, fiscally conservative conduct of the nation's business, the Mackenzie government, in office since 1874, had introduced a number of measures that changed the electoral landscape forever. The first was the secret ballot, which was extended nationwide. The second was the simultaneous conduct of the election in all provinces east of the Manitoba–Ontario border. September 17 was election day, marking the end of the previous electoral practice whereby the government chose to hold elections first in places where they felt they were strong in order to gauge the extent of their support and also to try to generate a bandwagon effect. Such tactics had been mainstays of John A. Macdonald's electoral kitbag.

The Mackenzie Liberal government had pledged to do politics differently. They had won the 1874 election because of the demonstrated corruption of the Macdonald administration which had governed Canada since Confederation. They were going to let contracts through public tender rather than favouritism, not make extravagant promises they couldn't keep (such as building the transcontinental railway to British Columbia within a decade, as the Conservatives had pledged to do) and have ministers take personal charge of their departments, to ensure honest and prudent administration. At the time, it was common practice for the prime minister to appoint himself to a cabinet position, partly because there was a salary attached. Macdonald had been minister of justice before his defeat, and would later take the position of minister of the interior when he returned to power. Mackenzie, however, decided to appoint himself minister of the department of public works — the largest and most complex government department of the time, in charge of all public undertakings, starting with railways and canals. With *this* prime minister personally standing guard, something like the "Pacific Scandal" could never recur.

Judgments on Mackenzie's decision to administer this particular department personally were unanimously scathing, from colleagues and opponents alike. Sir Charles Tupper, the former and future Conservative minister of finance, said, "Mackenzie meant well, but he devoted too much time to supervising the departments of his colleagues, and doing work which should have been performed by subordinates."[11]

Sir Richard Cartwright, Mackenzie's own minister of finance, said in his memoirs:

> Had Mr. Mackenzie but devoted four hours a day to studying how he could best keep his party together, and to the grave questions of state policy with which he had to deal, he would have done infinitely more both for himself and for the country than by slaving, as he very often did, for fourteen hours at his desk at details which any second-class clerk in his Department could have done as well.[12]

Although these two judgments were rendered well after the fact, there is also ample evidence from the time that Mackenzie's decision to try to micro-manage the state apparatus was ill advised.[13]

The 1878 election was the first modern Canadian election in another sense as well; it was the first to be dominated by economic issues. The general economic climate was negative, and had been so almost from the time that Mackenzie took office. A worldwide depression, which affected exports, incomes, and government revenues, had been triggered in the United States by a series of bank failures caused by risky loans defaulted on by railway builders.[14] With work suspended on the railways, and widespread layoffs, there was a collapse of demand in the United States. Canada was caught up in the wake of the economic storm. Six years of stagnation followed, with effects on Canadian shipping, the lumber industry, and small retailers.[15] The government's reaction was caution.

There were cutbacks to expensive projects like the railway to the West Coast, and cutbacks to public expenditures of all sorts. To the Liberals, the depression was a general problem, to be endured with stoicism, not a condition susceptible to policy tinkering. "Stay the course" was the Liberal policy.

The Conservatives, in opposition, decided to propose a new policy — a policy of protection of Canadian industries, a "National Policy." Although the idea of protective tariffs had been discussed for many years, it was by no means a foregone conclusion that the party would adopt this policy. Macdonald, however, saw an opportunity to distinguish his party from a floundering Liberal government, and regain the support of organized manufacturing interests at the same time. If international markets were weak or closed to Canadian producers, an enhanced domestic market was a plausible solution. In Parliament, the major business of the 1877 session (the longest session to date, at three months of the year) centred on Macdonald's attempts to debate the tariff issue, by introducing amendments to financial resolutions in which he proposed higher protective tariffs. By 1878, the amendments had sharpened into the wording, "That the welfare of Canada requires the adoption of a National Policy ... by a judicious readjustment of the tariff."[16]

The term "National Policy" (often shortened at the time to NP) has a disputed origin. Tupper in his memoirs claims authorship of the term. He points to a speech in Parliament in 1870, when he was the lone Conservative member from Nova Scotia, in which he proposed "this Canadian policy — this national policy, this rational policy ... a national policy which shall encourage the industries of our country."[17] Macdonald's biographer Donald Creighton feels that, although the term may have had some previous use, it was Macdonald's decision to adopt it in preference to the term "protection" that was the key to its success.[18] Historian Peter Waite emphasizes the broad appeal of the term:

> [Macdonald] never intended it for one class in society. Protective duties would be made to help everyone, farmers (who can be as protectionist as anyone when it's in their interest) workers and manufacturers. Macdonald had adopted it in 1876 to apply to all three. The tariff was to be "adjusted" rather than raised. Macdonald kept the

> name "National Policy" — that was a stroke of genius by someone — and added in 1878 the battle cry "Canada for the Canadians.[19]

This Conservative campaign slogan, "Canada for the Canadians," added to the economic appeal the second major area of party struggle, national unity. The National Policy for Macdonald was simultaneously a nation-building policy within Canada, and a nationalistic statement of the country's retaliation against American tariffs. The Americans had had success in protecting, for example, their sugar industry through an increased tariff, to the detriment of Canadian sugar refineries.[20] The patriotic element of the National Policy enabled the Conservatives to campaign with the underlying implication that those opposing them were slightly disloyal to the country.

For the Liberals' part, they were unwilling to cede the national unity battleground to their opponents. High tariffs, they said, would *destroy* national unity by setting region against region. Ontarians would have to buy their coal from Nova Scotia instead of cheaper foreign sources, and in return Ontario would gain the Maritime market for grain. In both cases, though, the result would be higher prices, creating regional friction and resentment which would more than offset any gains in employment resulting from industrial expansion. And as far as the Conservative slogan "Canada for the Canadians" went, Mackenzie riposted "I not only believe in having Canada for the Canadians, but the United States, South America, the West Indies, and our share of the European and Australasian trade."[21] In addition, protectionism meant the end of the British Imperial Preference, and thus disloyalty to the mother country. Freedom of trade was the only way to assure exports and future prosperity.

Furthermore, according to Mackenzie, class antagonism would rise along with regionalism under a Tory government. Speaking to an association of workingmen in Toronto, Mackenzie professed himself surprised to hear that some workers were supporting the Conservatives:

> The power of the workingman is made manifest only when a country becomes civilized and powerful. The power of a workingman is nothing in a state of semi-barbarism. The Tory party in England were but the

> followers or the successors of those who oppressed the workingman in times gone by. Protectionism and restrictions of trade are a way to control workers, and exploit them by paying them starvation wages. Protective tariffs are taxes on workers, which operate by raising prices.[22]

Later in the summer, on a hastily arranged visit to Saint John to attempt to shore up Liberal fortunes in New Brunswick, Mackenzie returned to this theme:

> Now sir, what is the National Policy. So called. No policy can be called thoroughly national which proposes to protect a certain class of the community, and leave all the others unprotected, and this is precisely what a system of protection means. It is a system which in the course of a few years will ensure a much larger percentage of poverty than exists at the present time. It is a system which would build up a few great firms or individuals in some particular manufacturing business and make them millionaires, but for every dollar that is added to the coffers of the rich manufacturers there are two dollars extracted from those who earn their bread by the sweat of their brow.[23]

The Conservatives, however, were having none of these arguments — the NP would bring all sectors of society together since it would protect everyone, and the expansion of Canadian industry would create a stronger country.

Tariff policy was not the only issue which played out along a national–regional dimension. Foremost among the other issues was the railway policy. The Conservatives knew that their solid base of support in British Columbia was dependent on promises to quickly complete the line, and they hoped that seats in Manitoba would result from it also. The Liberals, besides arguing that all regions would benefit from the financial prudence of a slow construction policy, were not above implying to easterners that the West was getting favoured treatment through the proposed Conservative commitment of resources for rapid railway building.

Different kinds of divisive issues were operating in Ontario and Quebec. The Mackenzie government, codifying the strong moralistic tone which dominated its rhetoric, had passed the *Canada Temperance Act*, providing for local option votes on the prohibition of liquor. This, according to Cartwright, set the government "against the entire tavern and liquor interest in Ontario. I think at the time there were some five or six thousand hotel and tavern keepers in Ontario, and ... each one of them personally controlled quite a number of votes."[24] The Liberal partiality toward prohibition also went a long way toward alienating Irish Catholic voters in Ontario, blunting potential gains that the party might have made due to the support of the Orange Order in the province for the Conservatives.

In Quebec, the Liberal Party was also in trouble. The stigma of anticlericalism still hung over it, as the party that had traditionally opposed the dominance of the Church over secular affairs. On the positive side for the party, the young Wilfrid Laurier had entered the cabinet in 1877, but was too inexperienced to play a major role in the campaign. The question of leadership was a factor which tilted heavily in the Conservative direction by 1878. Prime Minister Mackenzie was overworked and surrounded by allies of dubious political value. Foremost among these were *Toronto Globe* editor George Brown, seen as dictating Mackenzie's views; the mercurial Edward Blake, seeking to replace him as leader; and Richard Cartwright, a former Conservative who had joined the Liberals to become finance minister and who had his own leadership ambitions. On the hustings, Mackenzie displayed a certain dry wit, as when he likened the protectionists to Robinson Crusoe,

> building his own house, and with a knife made out of bone, whittling a weed out of which he made cloth, and with needles of bone stitching it into articles of clothing. That was protection to home industry with a vengeance; and most undoubtedly Robinson Crusoe was the leader of the Protectionist Party of Juan Fernandez [island] at that time. [Loud laughter and cheers.][25]

More common, however, was his straightlaced introduction to another speech, this time to a political picnic:

> I feel somewhat as Paul felt when he was permitted to speak for himself, because I believe (as he believed) that I am at least before an upright judge; and I am quite sure that the words I address to you, and which are addressed generally to the people of Canada, will find a hearty response among a vast majority of the people of this country.[26]

In contrast, Macdonald was healthy, rested and relatively sober. He depended on a substantial reservoir of public trust from his Confederation-building activities and previous governments, and he had more dependable allies (Tupper, Tilley, Chapleau) than Mackenzie. Contrast Mackenzie's dour approach with Macdonald's jocular introduction to a speech in Montreal:

> Gentlemen, I feel bound to follow the example set me by the Premier of Canada — by the Honourable Alexander Mackenzie — for we must be careful to speak of him as the Hon. Alexander Mackenzie in the future. [Laughter.] We all got a lesson lately, which I know you will take to heart, in politeness and deportment. We were told that no more must he be styled Sandy Mackenzie [renewed laughter] ... I didn't know, gentlemen, before I read that speech, what a deeply injured man I was myself; I didn't know that the people of Canada, from the Atlantic to the Pacific, had been insulting me for thirty years by calling me "John A." [Laughter and Cheers] And then I could not but reflect when that speech will be re-echoed, as such a speech deserves to be re-echoed, across the Atlantic, how Mr D'Israeli and Mr Lowe will feel, when their attention is called to the fact that they, great statesmen as they are, one of them Premier, have allowed themselves to be called plain Dizzy and Bob Lowe. [Laughter.] Now gentlemen, I know that every one of

> you are F.F.Cs [of the first families of Canada] and so remember that while you are quite at liberty to address one another as Tom, Dick or Harry, you must always speak to and of Mr. Mackenzie as "the Honourable Alexander Mackenzie."[27]

The picnic grounds of Ontario towns were the scene of many political meetings after some early Conservative successes with such venues in 1876. Macdonald's entertaining speaking style was a natural fit for summer afternoons in the parks. Not to be left behind, however, Mackenzie and other Liberals mounted a grueling picnic schedule in 1877. Starting in Kingston on June 27, the speaking tour hit six additional locations in southern Ontario ending on July 9. Again in September, seven towns were visited in eight days (Orangeville, Brampton, Galt, Simcoe, Aylmer, Teeswater, Port Elgin), but partway through, Mackenzie fell ill and the tour had to be completed by others. The picnics were highly partisan affairs, crowded (reports put attendance between 6,000 and 20,000 at each) with supporters; the speakers were several (two or three at least); the speeches were lengthy (up to three hours) and filled with detail. Furthermore, the speeches were all different (though of course they dealt with many of the same subjects); this was not the repetition of a "standard stump speech" so common with leaders' tours in the present day. Oratory was a required skill in the electoral politics of the nineteenth century. It is likely that such large and enthusiastic crowds at the political picnics gave the Liberals a false sense of optimism that they would win re-election. Certainly, the Liberals found it hard to believe that any intelligent person would prefer protectionism over free trade. As for Macdonald's commitment to protection, the Liberals felt it was pure expediency. In Fergus, Ontario, on July 2, 1877, Mackenzie said,

> There is no more principle in the demand of Sir John Macdonald for protection than there would be if he should all at once demand a republic. No, Sir John Macdonald is as much as I am a thoroughly free trade man. It is simply impossible that a man like him should have gone through as long and as distinguished a course of public service as he has, and spent almost

> thirty years in Parliament, without having imbibed the ideas of progress so prevalent in our age. But I know at the same time that there has never been a principle he advocated that he was not willing to set aside and trample in the dust if he could thereby climb over its ruins into office.[28]

And Cartwright, who was Macdonald's friend and colleague until 1873, says, "prior to 1873 I had many conversations with him on that subject, and I found him not only theoretically but practically even more averse to anything like protection than I was myself."[29]

Cartwright believed that up until 1876 it was unclear what position the Conservatives would adopt on protection. Even if some of the protestations that Macdonald had expressed protectionist sentiments earlier are to be believed,[30] it is likely that the National Policy was only the first of a series of major Canadian economic policy issue positions adopted for short-term electoral gain rather than any deep abiding economic philosophy. For the Conservatives, the policy provided a potential relief from the depression, and gained them support and financing from the manufacturing interests.

Conservative electoral strategy consisted of more than promoting the National Policy. The party gave considerable attention to blunting the Liberal edge on the honesty and corruption issue. Mackenzie was very defensive of the government's reputation for honesty, and devoted large portions of his speeches to detailed refutation of Conservative allegations about improprieties following the Liberal assumption of power in 1874. The Tories, for their part, published numerous attacks on the Liberals, charging hypocrisy. For example, the Toronto *Mail* published a 77-page campaign broadside with sections on Mackenzie's "Record of Extravagance and Corruption."[31] It contained sections on the "steel rails transaction" (a government purchase of unneeded rails at an inflated price from a Liberal supporter); "The Nebbing Hotel" (sold at an inflated price to the government, who needed the land for an ill-advised railway line); "The Fort Frances Lock" (a useless waste of a quarter of a million dollars), and many other examples of Liberal incompetence and dishonesty. The Liberals, for their part, were reluctant to let go of the Pacific Scandal; on the picnic trail, Mackenzie commented "I hear some one say that that story is worn out. I don't think it is."[32] But, simply by virtue of having taken the reins of government, the Liberals had lost the high moral ground, even if their transgressions were minor in comparison to those of their predecessors.

The election of 1878 was a triumph for Macdonald. The Conservatives won majorities of seats in every province except New Brunswick, and their total of 140 was more than twice that achieved by Mackenzie's Liberals (see Table 2.1). For the third election in a row, British Columbia gave all its seats to the Tories. More important, however, was the turnaround for Macdonald's party in Ontario and Quebec. The seats won by the Conservatives in those two provinces combined were enough for a majority in themselves. Macdonald was back in office, and he stayed there until his death soon after the election of 1891. By winning four straight elections — six in total — the Macdonald dynasty set the pattern for other periods of one-party dominance to come. His, however, was to be the only Conservative Party dynasty in the nation's history. The Mackenzie interlude was important, since the remnants of the Liberal Party which survived the 1878 defeat eventually rebounded, united by their taste of power, to coalesce behind Wilfrid Laurier.

In the subsequent elections of 1882, 1887, and 1891, the Conservatives continued their commitment to the policy of protectionism, which was claimed to be responsible for good economic times when these existed (1882) and to be the best hope for recovery when they did not (1887). The Liberals became increasingly strident in their commitment to free trade. National unity gathered strength as a divisive political issue after Louis Riel was hanged in 1885. The Liberals failed to capitalize on public anger in Quebec about the hanging of the Western francophone rebel in 1887, but began to do so in 1891, when Wilfrid Laurier had been chosen as leader. In the 1891 election, the Liberals and Conservatives fought to a relatively even split in Ontario and Quebec, but the Conservatives dominated the periphery.

In 1885, Macdonald engineered passage of the *Franchise Act*, transferring control over voting eligibility from the provinces to the federal government. This piece of legislation, which Macdonald referred to as the greatest triumph of his political life, was in part a move to head off the widening of the franchise in ways being contemplated by provinces like Ontario. The Ontario provincial government desired to extend the franchise in the province to those owning less or even no property and Macdonald feared an influx of Liberal voters onto the federal electoral rolls. The franchise qualification adopted in 1885 retained the property qualification to vote, but created a bewildering set of exceptions and provincial and occupational variations.[33] Even so, Ward calculates that the proportion of the population eligible to vote in 1885 increased somewhat, for example to 26 percent in Ontario.[34] After the Liberals won the 1896 election, they turned the provision of the federal franchise back to the provinces.

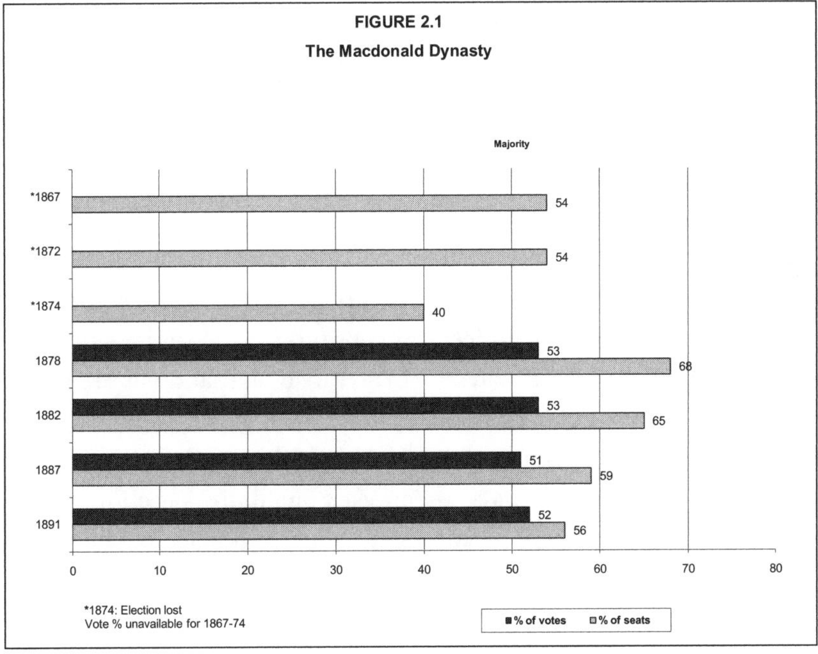

The 1896 Election

This federal election changed the course of Canadian politics, ended the Macdonald dynasty and began, not only the Laurier dynasty but a succession of periods of Liberal dominance. Many factors favoured the Liberals in 1896, particularly that of leadership. Macdonald had died in 1891, and the most promising of his successors, John Thompson, had also died, prematurely and suddenly in 1894, just as the party was organizing for the next election. An interim leader, Mackenzie Bowell, was appointed, but the party was thrown into disarray by internal cabinet disputes over how to respond to the Manitoba school crisis (see pages 80-82). In desperation, the Conservatives turned to their old stalwart, Sir Charles Tupper, to lead them in the parliamentary session of 1895, and subsequently into the election of 1896. In his memoirs, Tupper says "When a majority of the members of the Bowell Cabinet had resigned and the party had been broken into pieces, I was reluctantly induced to come to the rescue."[35] At 75 years of age, and out of politics (not to mention out of Canada) since 1888, Tupper campaigned as best he could. "He ... conjured up in the minds of distraught Conservatives a vision of the grand old days under Macdonald; he was a link with a happier past which they hoped would come to life again."[36] But neither on the hustings nor in the creation of political strategy was he the match of Wilfrid Laurier.

One of Laurier's biographers notes that, at this period in the country's political history, he "stood alone on the Canadian landscape as a potential and respectable leader."[37] It was a remarkable achievement. Unlike Macdonald on the Conservative side, and Mackenzie and Edward Blake for the Liberals, Laurier was by no means an obvious choice as party leader. When Blake, the great orator and advocate of free trade, fell ill in 1887, it was only because of his personal decision that Laurier, not an Ontario Liberal like Premier Oliver Mowat or former finance minister Richard Cartwright, was anointed leader by the caucus. Laurier was very reluctant to accept, sensing a future of tedious work and financial ruin. His Liberal colleagues were hesitant to accept the first French Canadian to lead a federal political party. But Laurier, a member of Parliament since 1874, had served the kind of apprenticeship that was expected of leaders in that era. His appeal in Quebec was well recognized, and he had prepared his ground well by condemning the Riel hanging a decade earlier. His popularity was such that it began to transcend the opposition of the Roman Catholic Church to the Liberal party, and to give the church pause in its anti-Grit rhetoric. In the rest of the country, acceptance was more grudging, but Laurier's stature was recognized. His stance in favour of national unity as the main purpose of his politics, and his willingness to compromise, allowed alliances to be made and gave voters reason to favour him. His magnificent oratorical skill served him well, but policy compromises were necessary on the free trade issue.

From 1878 onward, the Liberal Party tied itself to the banner of Free Trade, inveighing against the protective tariffs of the National Policy as being antithetical to the interests of farmers and workers, and consumers of all sorts. As recently as 1891, the Liberals had advocated "unrestricted reciprocity" as their economic and trade policy, arguing that such a deal with the United States would accelerate the economic growth of the country. In that election, this position had allowed Macdonald to campaign on the slogan "The Old Flag, the Old Policy, the Old Leader." He was the "Old Leader"; the National Policy of tariff protection was the "Old Policy": and the reference to the "Old Flag" was a none-too-subtle inference that the Liberals were willing to sell Canada out to the United States. With Free Trade would come annexation, and the old (Canadian, formerly British) flag would be flown no more.

Laurier, having little interest in economic questions, was quite willing to modify the party's trade position.[38] While he might have personally preferred the policy of reciprocity, or even some type of commercial union with the United States, he was sensitive to the pleas of Canadian business and was prepared to water down trade policy by 1895. And it turned out that to do so was relatively simple. No great policy "flip-flop" need be acknowledged; it was simply a matter of the purpose of tariffs. The Liberal position, as it appeared in their subsequent campaign literature, was that,

> though it should be our misfortune for many years to come to have to raise a revenue by customs duties, these duties should be levied only so far as is necessary to carry on the business of the Government ... no duty should be levied for protection's sake ... [or to support] a private and privileged class.[39]

This was, the Liberals said, the way free trade was practised in England. Thus, the continuation of tariffs could be justified as a necessary revenue measure. The Liberals could say that their opposition to protection was still in force, and that they would work toward the

Library and Archives Canada.

"The Old Flag, the Old Policy, the Old Leader." An 1891 campaign poster.

diminution of tariffs and their gradual elimination. A revenue tariff, it was stated, would not line the pockets of millionaire businessmen, but rather ensure the efficient operation of government for all citizens. And the revenue source that would eventually replace the customs duties was never revealed.

The Conservatives professed to be outraged at the Liberal shift. Laurier, one pamphlet opined, was a "gyrating tariff weathercock" who has supported at various times protection, free trade, different degrees of reciprocity, and now this "as exists in Britain" policy. "As a political economist and statesman in a business country [Laurier is] absurd!"[40] As far as the Tories were concerned, their policy of protection had enriched the country and aided its independence by building up Canadian industries. It had benefited the people because foreign producers, not local consumers, paid taxes. Furthermore, the stimulation of local industry offered by protection kept production high and drove down prices to levels lower than foreign products would cost. There was no need, in their view, to revise the National Policy, which had served the country so well.

But once again the economy had slipped into a depression, and the Conservative "stay the course" policy seemed an inadequate response to the economic circumstances in which the country now found itself.[41] Despite the Conservative tariffs and the reciprocation of these by other countries, Canada relied on exports of natural products for economic growth. Canadian farm produce, fish, grain, minerals, and lumber were now running into competition. As economist O.D. Skelton observed:

> The world over production seemed to have outrun consumption. In the United States, in Australia, in Argentina and Chile, in Russia, in India, tens of millions of new acres were growing grain, or pasturing countless flocks and herds. The improvement of railroad and steamship facilities poured this embarrassing abundance quickly and cheaply on the common markets of the world. The sudden expansion of the supply of food and raw materials, coinciding with the failure of the world's gold supply to increase in proportion, and the demonetization of silver, brought a fall in prices, world-wide and world-disturbing.[42]

In the West, in particular, conditions were poor, especially once construction of the Canadian Pacific Railway had been completed in 1885. The conditions were right for public acceptance of a change in economic policy, and the Liberals were primed to take advantage.

The Liberal decision to move to a less confrontational economic strategy made it easier for some groups of voters to shift their support. Those who, in previous elections, had been deterred by Conservative charges that free trade would lead to eventual annexation by the United States, or at least to a diminution of Canadian independence and the abandonment of Britain, were reassured. But there were not many vote-catching economic promises from the Liberals. Rather, it was the symbolism of standing for change that propelled the Liberal bandwagon — change, however undefined, that might improve the economy, as well as change in the techniques of French–English relations, and federal–provincial relations.

These latter elements were by no means injected into a federal election campaign for the first time in 1896. Being the party, and the leader, who could get along with both French and English Canadians, and who could bring the provincial governments into line, was a major part of Macdonald's appeal. But by 1896, the Conservatives had managed to get themselves into the position of being part of the national unity problem rather than the engine of continued harmony. It was in this area that the Old Man (Macdonald) was most missed by the Tories. It is hard to believe that Macdonald would ever have allowed the party to be put into the position in which it now found itself under Tupper.

Twenty years after the *Manitoba Act* of 1870 had provided for separate Protestant and Catholic school systems, the Liberal provincial government, led by Thomas Greenway, passed an act abolishing the religious basis of schools and setting up one public school system. Pressure from Quebec immediately began to build on the federal government to take action to disallow the legislation, using its constitutional powers to do so. The federal Conservative government delayed for several years, hoping that the courts would declare the provincial act unconstitutional, and therefore spare it the decision to reinstate Catholic schools in Manitoba, and with it the possibility of raising the wrath of militant Protestant elements in Ontario. Eventually, in 1895, the final court of appeal, the Judicial Committee of the Privy Council in Britain, decided that the province had had the power to pass the *Manitoba Schools Act*, but also that the federal government had the power to disallow it and replace it with legislation of its own. So, when it could delay no longer, the Conservatives brought in a "remedial bill" to re-establish the separate school system in Manitoba.

> The bill provided for the establishment of a system of separate schools in Manitoba, supervised by a Roman Catholic board of education, supported by the local rates of such Catholics as did not declare themselves public-school supporters, with exemption from public-school local rates, and entitled to receive whatever provincial grant the legislature might allot; the bill, while declaring such a grant a right and privilege of the minority, would not … specifically command the province to make it.[43]

The omission in the Federal Remedial Bill providing for Catholic schools in Manitoba of a directive to the province to actually provide a grant to the schools allowed the Liberals to argue that the bill did not really establish a minority system at all, but was a fraud. The Conservatives, however, initially believed that their action had given them an advantage on the issue, since they could appeal to Quebec as defenders of the Catholic minority, and explain to English areas of Canada that they were merely following the requirements of the courts. The support of the Catholic clergy in Quebec, they thought, would cement the victory.[44] And the Church did respond, with some bishops speaking from the pulpit in favour of the Conservative bill and against the Liberals, though, as Neatby points out, the amount of action undertaken by the Quebec clergy was an indication of the weakness of the Conservative leadership in the province.[45]

The instructions of the bishops were not limited to Quebec; the Bishop of Antigonish, Nova Scotia, said that "to vote for a Liberal in the present crisis is in reality to vote against the justice which must be rendered to the Manitoba minority."[46] However, there were indications of some hesitancy for the church to take too strong a stand. The Bishop of Montreal instructed his clergy not to speak from the pulpit on this matter. And in the end, the dictates of the Church against the Liberals were fewer and less effective than might originally have been estimated.

Laurier and the Liberals had been responsible for preventing the passage of the remedial bill before the election by extending debate until time ran out. In the Liberal campaign, major strategic decisions had to be taken about what image to present, since his opposition was charging that Laurier was a traitor to his own people. Fortunately for him, the omission of the requirements for provincial funding of the separate schools in the bill (because the provincial budget was under its own control) allowed him to take the position that his goal was the establishment of French rights, and that he could do it as prime minister by negotiation rather than legislation, and could do a better job of it. This approach was the handiwork of the Quebec Liberal strategist Israel Tarte. Once the Manitoba school question was presented as an issue of the future of the French race in Canada, rather than as a religious or an educational issue, electing Laurier as prime minister was presented as the best hope for the protection of the French race.[47]

Outside Quebec, the Liberals played their opposition to the Remedial Bill as respect for provincial autonomy.[48] To appeal to Catholic voters, they also pointed to the deficiencies in the bill, and to the benefits of co-operation. For example, a pamphlet issued by a Catholic Liberal candidate from Halifax argued that

> good tempered appeals to the generosity and sense of justice of our Protestant fellow citizens will nearly always gain recognition for our reasonable claims and due regard for our conscientious convictions; while on the other hand, anything in the nature of aggression or coercion is almost certain to lead to resistance and failure.[49]

In Prince Edward Island and Nova Scotia, much of the campaign debate revolved around either economic or specific local issues, and avoided the Manitoba school issue.[50]An analysis of the election in New Brunswick, however, gives the Manitoba issue an important role in solidifying the Acadian vote in the northern part of the province for the Conservatives.[51] In Manitoba itself, the school question was not the main issue, according to a detailed analysis, because "most Manitobans did not come in contact with separate schools," although it undoubtedly was important to French Catholics in particular areas.[52] Only half of the eligible Manitoba voters went to the polls, and the Conservatives, supposedly the ones attacking the autonomy of the provincial government as well as maintaining the

National Policy, which was hated by farmers because it raised prices for manufactured goods, maintained their seat total.

The 1896 election showed how the Liberals were able to successfully appeal to the public as the party most likely to solve the problems of slow economic growth, and to do so without making drastic changes in economic policy. They also, for the first time, established their credentials on the national unity dimension as the party of compromise and accord between French and English, despite the fact that they campaigned against a piece of legislation designed to guarantee French rights. It was Laurier's personal qualities and persuasive ability which allowed them to do this. In maneuvering his party to the publicly popular side of both the economic and national unity issue dimensions, Laurier took up the mantle of the fallen Macdonald.

Victories in three successive elections, 1900, 1904, and 1908, solidified the Laurier dynasty. The Liberals benefited enormously from the fact that boom economic conditions followed shortly after their accession to power in 1896, and continued through the first decade of the twentieth century. Although the Liberals made some minor changes to the tariff structure,

Library and Archives Canada.

Sir Wilfrid Laurier campaigning in Berlin, Ontario, 1908 election.

the economic prosperity occurred with the same basic economic policies in place that they inherited from the Conservatives. Nevertheless, the Liberals became established in the public mind as the party associated with both economic growth and harmonious ethnic relations. In the latter area, Laurier exerted his mastery to the point where Tupper attacked him as being "too English."[53] His campaign slogan in 1900 was "Union, Peace, Friendship and Fraternity." In 1904, the Liberals fused national unity with economic development by promoting their support for a second transcontinental railway, and also for the "opening" of the West to settlement. As Figure 2.2 indicates, the Liberals won majorities of the popular vote, and over 60 percent of the parliamentary seats, in all three elections of 1900, 1904, and 1908.

An important political event of the period which would also have broad implications for the future was the Prohibition Plebiscite of 1898. Held only two years after he had assumed office, the plebiscite demonstrated Laurier's skill and resourcefulness in managing a thorny and nearly unsolvable problem. The *Canada Temperance Act*, enacted by the Mackenzie government in 1878, had effectively removed prohibition as an issue from the national political stage by providing for "local option" in banning the manufacture and sale of liquor. But local option also guaranteed that the issue would be kept alive, albeit at a different level of government. A royal commission appointed by the Conservative government in 1892 rejected a proposal for outright national prohibition, in effect entrenching the status quo. As the temperance movement, many of whose activists were women who were also involved in the fight for womens' suffrage, grew into one of Canada's first important social movements, lobbying from both sides for a more consistent national policy became more intense. The 1896 change of government had created new political opportunities, and Laurier was known to be receptive to the idea of a national referendum.[54] The Women's Christian Temperance Union, in particular, which had been active in many local and provincial prohibition campaigns, aggressively lobbied the new government. In 1898, Parliament enacted the *Prohibition Plebiscite Act*, and the date of Canada's first national direct vote on an issue was set for September 29. The question put to voters was, "Are you in favour of the passing of an Act prohibiting the importation, manufacture or sale of spirits, wine, ale, beer, cider and all other alcoholic liquors for use as beverages?" While many of the organizations that had pressed for the referendum argued that women should be permitted to vote in it, Parliament opted to maintain the same voting franchise that existed at the time for federal elections. In other words, women were not allowed to vote.

Turnout in the plebiscite was a modest 44 percent and, as expected, the vote was close, with just over 51 percent voting YES. But the vote was close *only* because Quebec had voted overwhelmingly against prohibition, while the rest of the country had voted solidly in favour of it (see Table 2.2). The narrow national majority, however, along with the deep divide between Quebec and English Canada, allowed Laurier to avoid any further action. The issue would be left to the provinces, several of which already had large dry areas outside the major cities. But the concept of a direct vote of the people on an important public issue had been established in Canadian politics, and Laurier would later (in opposition) also advocate holding a referendum to deal with another divisive issue — conscription.[55]

At the outset of the Laurier dynasty, the Conservatives believed that they were in a good position for a comeback. In the election of 1896, the two parties were virtually tied in public support, outside Quebec. Initially, the Tories stayed with Tupper as their leader, asking him to fight the election of 1900 at the age of 79. When it became clear that new leadership was necessary, the Conservative caucus turned to another Nova Scotian, Robert Borden, who had been heavily promoted to them by Tupper. The Conservatives, however, could make no inroads into Liberal strength in Quebec, and their cautious approach to railway building and immigration was out of step with the expansionist mood of the time. Laurier laid the basis for a Liberal predominance in Canadian electoral politics that remained, but for several short interludes, for much of the twentieth century.

TABLE 2.1

Results of the 1878 and 1896 Elections, by Province

		Conservative*		Liberal		Other	
		1878	1896	1878	1896	1878	1896
Prince Edward Island	votes (%)	57	49	43	51	-	-
	seats (#)	5	3	1	2	-	-
Nova Scotia	votes (%)	52	50	44	49	4	X
	seats (#)	14	10	6	10	1	-
New Brunswick	votes (%)	45	49	55	44	-	7
	seats (#)	5	9	11	5	-	-
Quebec	votes (%)	56	46	40	54	3	X
	seats (#)	45	16	20	49	-	-
Ontario	votes (%)	52	45	47	40	X	15
	seats (#)	62	43	26	43	-	6
Manitoba	votes (%)	50	49	50	35	-	18
	seats (#)	3	4	1	2	-	1
Sask/Alta (NWT)	votes (%)	-	44	-	46	-	10
	seats (#)	-	1	-	3	-	0
British Columbia	votes (%)	89	51	-	49	11	-
	seats (#)	6	2	-	4	-	-
TOTAL CANADA	votes (%)	53	46	45	45	12	9
	seats (#)	140	88	65	118	1	7

* Includes 49 candidates elected as Liberal-Conservative in 1878. In both elections, a few candidates elected as Independent Conservative, Nationalist Conservative, or Independent Liberal are included with their respective parties. "Other" includes unaffiliated independents, as well as some candidates whose party affiliation is unknown.

X less than 1 percent

TABLE 2.2

Results of the 1898 Prohibition Plebiscite, by Province

	% voting YES
Prince Edward Island	89.2
Nova Scotia	87.2
New Brunswick	72.2
Quebec	18.5
Ontario	57.3
Manitoba	80.6
Saskatchewan/Alberta (N.W.T.)	68.8
British Columbia	54.6
TOTAL CANADA	51.2

FIGURE 2.2

The Laurier Dynasty

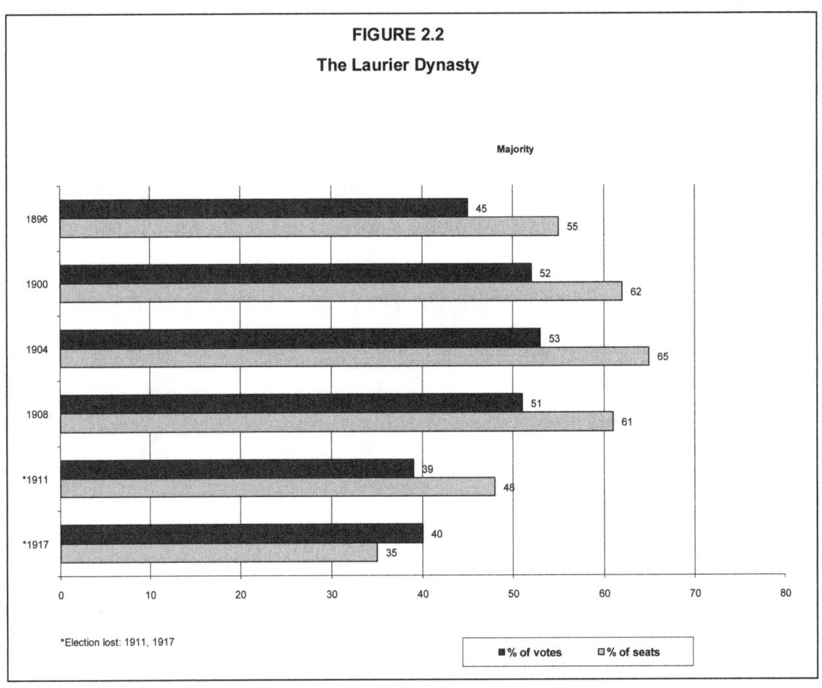

The 1911 Election

The 1911 federal election closed the Laurier era, and brought the Conservatives back to power. This result would have been difficult to foresee even a year before the election, but in this short period the Liberals managed to adopt policies which suddenly put them on the unpopular side of both the economic and national unity dimensions of Canadian election issues. These events, coupled with more effective Conservative leadership, nationalist activity in Quebec, and decay in the Liberal Party's electoral organization, spelled defeat for Laurier. Conservative leader Robert Borden was a serious, restrained, and methodical figure, with a far-from-colourful political style. According to John English, "He could not accept that his role was simply to please the electorate, to play to its prejudices and fancies."[56] It took him a full decade, and many missteps, to position himself and his party as a serious alternative government.

We have already seen the longstanding underlying support within Liberal ranks for free trade, especially as it manifested itself in proposals for reciprocity with the United States. An unexpected American receptivity to such an agreement, on terms which seemed favourable to Canada, led the Liberals to conclude that their opportunity was finally at hand, and that the time was right to sign a draft treaty months before the 1911 election. Though the opposition managed to hold up passage of the Reciprocity Treaty in Parliament, the Liberals felt confident enough to call the election to acquire a "mandate" to complete it. Their confidence perhaps stemmed from public satisfaction with their economic stewardship for over a decade. After all, why would this not manifest itself in public trust that a new direction in trade policy would be the right step? Their miscalculation became quickly apparent, as the economic policy arena became an electoral battleground with regional, class and loyalty dimensions unanticipated by the normally astute Laurier and his advisers.

In defending the treaty in Parliament, Laurier presented reciprocity as a progressive step which Canada needed to take to advance to future prosperity. The old National Policy and its focus on protection was the only means possible in its day, he said, because earlier Canadian proposals for reciprocity had been spurned. Now, Canada was mature enough to compete for markets in the United States, and the long-awaited opportunity to do so on equal terms was at hand.[57] The general Liberal argument was focused on benefits to consumers, as manifested in lower prices. Specific arguments were directed to sectors of the economy. And it was to Western farmers that the policy had its greatest appeal. As J.W. Scallion, honorary president of the Manitoba Grain Growers Association, was quoted as saying, "No trade arrangements which the Canadian government would enter into with any country would meet with greater favor or stronger support from the farmers of this country than a wide measure of reciprocal trade with the United States."[58] The removal of duty on agricultural crops like wheat and oats would make these crops more profitable. And the Liberals trumpeted the support of the provincial Conservative leader in Saskatchewan for the "western man" over his party's and leader's position.[59] Similar arguments were made by the Liberals for the benefits of reciprocity for the forest industries. But making so many specific predictions of sectoral benefits left the Liberals vulnerable to attack on a number of different fronts.

Almost from the beginning, the Liberal campaign was forced to adopt a defensive tone. In Laurier's speech referred to above, he dealt at length with four opposition arguments: trade will be channelled through the United States rather than Canada; Canadian natural resources will be exploited and destroyed; industry will be threatened; and Canada will be annexed to the United States. At least half of the speech was devoted to fending off these criticisms. Other Liberal campaign literature spent a lot of time on the defensive. In *Reciprocity: A Good Thing for Canada*, it is argued strenuously that the "loyalty cry" against the policy was false, because Britain was said to favour reciprocity for Canada.[60] And the awkwardly titled *Bigger Markets, Better Conditions: Are Creators of Contentment, not Breeders of Disloyalty* tried to use American statements about the benefits of the Treaty in such a way as to reduce the implications of future political union which some of them contain.[61] Conservative leader Robert Borden moved quickly to establish an interpretation of the Reciprocity treaty as having set out on the road to American annexation. He found it very suspicious that the United States was making these proposals now, after many years of rejecting the idea. His conclusion: "Mr. Taft [the American president] wants our resources … [because] their own resources [are] nearly exhausted." On the contrary, "we want to develop them ourselves." His watchword was: "Keep Canada for the Canadians,"[62] a slogan reminiscent of John A. Macdonald's in the 1878 election.

The Conservative campaign message proceeded on two fronts, the economic and the patriotic. Economically, reciprocity was bad policy, because it would not bring benefits to many sectors. Speaking about the threats to British Columbia, Conservative premier Richard McBride maintained that the treaty would subject the fruit growing industry to greater competition from Washington, Oregon, and California, areas where the industry was well established and where labour costs were cheaper.[63] Another pamphlet took on other agricultural products, and argued that the implementation of the treaty would cut Canada out of the British market, without any guarantees that Canada's prices would allow it to compete with the United States.[64] Furthermore, Americans would be free to fish in Canadian waters after depleting their own.[65] We might be able to sell our pulp wood, but the Canadian paper manufacturing industry will suffer. And so on; sector after sector was analysed and predicted to suffer from the agreement. At times, efforts were made to bring the arguments home to average people. For example, removing the protective duty of three cents per dozen would flood the Canadian market with American eggs and "take money out of the purses of [Canadian farm] women-folk … [causing] disappointment among the women in farm homes and the consequent lack of former comforts and bright adornments."[66]

It was the Conservatives' ability to shift the ground of discussion away from the purely economic to the consequences for Canadian nationhood that proved pivotal in turning the reciprocity treaty issue to their advantage. The United States, they said, is bent on annexation of Canada, and saw its opportunity in the willingness of naive Canadian negotiators to sign this agreement. Trade will lead to demands for Canada's water and Canada's forests. It has happened elsewhere: "Big nations get their way."[67] Other Conservative literature carried titles like *An Appeal to the British Born* and *The Road to Washington*. For the United States, reciprocity offers have not been made for economic, but rather for political reasons. In the past, Hawaii, Cuba, Puerto Rico, and Alaska have been brought into the American orbit this way.[68] Canada was next.

In Quebec, another nationalistic issue took shape, with both sides endeavouring to portray themselves as the champions of a true Canadian nationality. Canada needed to respond to pressure from Britain to support it in the face of a growing European threat from Germany. As Laurier saw it, it was preferable to do this on Canadian rather than British terms, by developing a Canadian navy, which could then fight alongside Britain if war came.[69] As it turned out, this position satisfied very few people. In English-speaking Canada, particularly the parts with a British heritage, the aid for Britain did not appear direct enough. Conservative leader Robert Borden's proposal to contribute two ships ("dreadnoughts") to the British navy, was more like it. In Quebec, the implication that the Canadian navy would be sent to the assistance of Britain was too much, even if the ships did remain under Canadian control.

The nationalist Henri Bourassa, editor of *Le Devoir* since its founding in 1910, organized a movement/party to fight the 1911 election. His philosophical position was one of Canadian nationalism, with the underlying stipulation that such independence for the country would best serve francophone and Quebec interests. Bourassa himself professed to support the Liberal economic policy of reciprocity, because the treaty represented a "good blow to imperialism."[70] At the same time, the Liberal naval policy had to be opposed, since it promised, at least as he interpreted it, the lending of the Canadian navy to Britain in times of war, thus promoting imperialism. Again and again, Bourassa described his nationalistic position in pan-Canadian terms, with his ideal situation being where all citizens are working "on the building up of Canada and the creation of a truly national sentiment throughout the Dominion."[71] Bourassa's Parti autonomiste ran candidates in Quebec in co-operation with the Conservatives, who supported and financed them, and did not run against them. We see here the initial use of a co-operative, anti-Liberal strategy that was to emerge several more times in the future, particularly in the Diefenbaker–Duplessis era.

The Liberals tried to make the most of Laurier's personal appeal, which had by no means totally faded despite his 70 years. A Quebec campaign document has 42 subject headings, starting with Laurier's character traits: eloquence, liberalism, character, tact, studies and work, love of Canada, conviction, simplicity, and magnetism. This is followed by a longer list of his policy accomplishments, and the final question *"Pourquoi changer?"*[72]

But plenty of voters saw a reason to change, particularly those in Ontario and Quebec. As with any election, there were numerous factors to consider for a complete explanation, besides the two issues examined here. In Ontario, scholars have noted the decline of the Liberal party organization, still controlled by Allen Aylesworth, the aging minister of justice, and not yet by the young Mackenzie King.[73] Aylesworth refused to embrace the prohibitionist positions demanded by fundamentalist Protestant churches and temperance movements in the province. In British Columbia, the Liberals were denounced for inadequately limiting immigration from Asia.[74] But most of these factors were secondary to the importance of the Reciprocity Treaty, in both its economic and nationalistic manifestations. Aside from Western grain growers and perhaps exporters of forest products, many other economic interests believed that they would be losers under the treaty.[75] In Quebec, 27 autonomistes were elected on the tide of Bourassa's anti-imperialistic message. And in Ontario, Stephen Leacock regarded the rejection of reciprocity as an "earnest wish for an enduring union with the Empire."[76] While this was undoubtedly true to some extent, as important to the Ontario Conservative victory was the influx of support and money from industrial interests, whose self-interest in maintaining existing tariff policy coincided nicely with their professed patriotism.[77] The Liberal Party had lost popular advantage on both the economic and the national unity issue areas. The Laurier dynasty was over.

The 1911 triumph was a long time in coming for Robert Borden, the earnest Halifax lawyer who had become Conservative leader back in 1901. Even though the losses in Quebec contributed to the Liberal defeat, Bourassa's support was not needed for a majority in Parliament, as the Conservatives had won a massive victory in Ontario. British Columbia was also strongly for Borden, aided by his stated intention to keep Canada "white." And in other areas, appeals to the British connection, national feeling, and doubts about American intentions led to Conservative victories.

Following his 1911 victory, Borden had only a couple of short years before his troubles began. Conservative support in Quebec, never solid to begin with, fell away as Bourassa's nationalists deserted the party over Borden's plan to build warships for the British navy. In addition, the Senate, full of Laurier Liberals, refused to pass the naval legislation. By 1914, a period of good economic times had given way to a depression; railways were in need of bailouts and unemployment rose. Quickly, the Conservative advantage in the economic and national unity areas turned into a disadvantage. Laurier, still leading the Liberals, waited for the next election opportunity, confident that he could re-establish himself in power. And he might well have, if not for the outbreak of the First World War.

The election was put off in 1916, because of the war, and the following year Borden created a Union government, asking Liberals to join him. His invitation was accepted by many, but rejected by Laurier, Liberal members from Quebec, and a handful of others. The next election, when it finally came, would be fought under a very different set of political circumstances.

The 1917 Election

The 1917 federal election was held during wartime because Laurier would not give consent for the further continuance of Parliament, which had already exceeded its constitutional limit. The government he was facing, the Union government, contained a substantial number of his own MPs elected in 1911, particularly in areas outside Quebec. Prime Minister Sir Robert Borden proposed to bring in conscription to fill out the ranks of the Canadian forces participating in the war. Forcing an election was Laurier's way of bringing the issue of conscription into the electoral arena, as his proposal for a national referendum on the issue had been rejected. The strength of national feeling on the issue, and the ethnic divisions which it inflamed, ensured that it would be at the centre of the election campaign.

The Conservative/Union appeal was made on several levels. In his formal election manifesto, Borden took the high road, emphasizing that a military draft through conscription was only being implemented out of military necessity. Described in Borden's election manifesto issued to the Canadian people, it was "a democratic measure, calling the rich as well as the poor"; it was impartial, with "no preferences for groups, classes, sections or interests"; it "paid no attention to provincial boundaries or racial groupings." Canada's democratically elected Parliament had taken the decision to participate in the war in support of Great Britain, and the Union government had allowed both parties to work together to "abolish trading in patronage, to fill public offices by merit and not by favoritism, and to establish honest and open competition in awarding contracts and buying supplies." Plans are already afoot so that after the war, soldiers can be "re-educated" and "re-established on the land or in other pursuits."[78] For the good of the country, it argued that voters should support Borden and the Unionists.

But the references to conscription "pay[ing] no attention to provincial boundaries or racial groupings" would not have been lost on English Canadians. Conscription was directed at French Canada, whose young men had not signed up in large numbers to defend Britain. And to drive the message home, the Union government campaign used more visceral appeals. A special *Wartime Elections Act* gave the vote to wives and other female relatives of servicemen, on the government's assumption that they would support it. While clearly self-serving, this innovation also implicitly recognized the growing strength of the women's suffrage movement:

> Why should the women of Canada vote for the Union Government? Because they are vitally interested in seeing that the war against Germany and all Germany represents is carried on to the bitter end ... Germany's attitude to women is that of the uncivilized savage.... [Germans are] brutal ... fiendish ... inhuman.... [In Belgium] lustful and cruel, they violated women and girls, murdered their husbands, tortured and mutilated children, and murdered babies.[79]

By the time of this election, Henri Bourassa and his nationalist followers in Quebec had abandoned the alliance with the Conservatives that had been so important to the Liberal defeat in 1911 and joined with Laurier to campaign against conscription. This alliance allowed the Conservatives a much larger target than would have been the case if Laurier alone was the opposition. In their appeal to English-speaking voters, the Conservatives charged that Laurier had capitulated to Bourassa, who "is anti-British and pro-German and ... has a bitter hatred for the English-Speaking people of Canada ... [Bourassa's words are] little short of treason and sedition."

The unionist message concluded,

> The teachings of Bourassa and the failure of Laurier to rally his race in the war are bearing fruit in a wave of race bigotry and desire for French Canadian domination and A SOLID ENGLISH SPEAKING CANADA, DETERMINED TO MAINTAIN BRITISH IDEALS AND BRITISH TRADITIONS IN

CANADA WILL SUCCESSFULLY COPE WITH A SITUATION PREGNANT WITH PERIL.[80]

No matter what they say, the Conservatives trumpeted, the Liberals want to "quit the war."[81]

Faced with this onslaught, the Liberal campaign in English Canada, doomed as it might have been, attempted to sustain a tone of moderation. Laurier's election manifesto, widely used in the Liberal campaign, is a calm, reasoned document which gives every appearance of being personally written. It begins with a number of mild criticisms of the government — they should do more to reduce prices and tariffs and to stop anyone profiteering from the war. On conscription, he proposes instead a "strong appeal for voluntary recruiting" together with a referendum. Laurier denies that he wants to quit the war, citing the rejection of conscription in Australia, a country which has continued to fight. The problem of enlistment in Quebec, says Laurier, was something the government brought on themselves by their alliance with the nationalists in 1911 and their rejection of his own proposal for a Canadian navy. Now, when they ask for Quebec volunteers, "they reaped what they had sown."[82]

Toward the end of his manifesto, Laurier strikes another note. It is only conscription of men which is being implemented by the government, not conscription of wealth.[83] This theme, echoed by Bourassa in Quebec[84] was an effort to shift the ground from an ethnic conflict to one of equality of classes and wealth. The Liberals made the most of this point. In a major campaign document the headings tell the story: Who Shall Rule? The People or the Big Interests? —Democracy and a Free People or Autocracy and Organized Privilege — On Which Side Are You? The Soldier, the Worker , the Consumer, the Taxpayer, or the Profiteer, the Trusts, the Food Manipulators, the Pork Barons? — Read the War Record of Canada's New Rulers.[85] This amazing campaign document goes on for over 200 pages, documenting scandals of the Borden government in excruciating detail. But the Liberal attempt to turn conscription into a class issue was not successful; patriotism was the trump card.

In Quebec, Bourassa's arguments maintained a "Canada First" theme and were isolationist in tone. In terms of the military effort, he said,"Canada has done enough." He felt that the nation had sent proportionately more soldiers than other countries, despite the fact that we were poorer. Bankruptcy was on the horizon, not to mention famine. Rather than sending them to Europe, he felt the "slackers" should be on the land, producing food. Furthermore, Bourassa believed that conscription was exacerbating the "race problem" in Canada, and was a threat to harmony between French and English. French Canadians would defend Canada — their own country — but not France, and certainly not Britain. In his mind they were the real patriots.[86] But some of the Quebec campaign material points to an inwardness and fear of being caught up in an alien war in unknown circumstances. One telling drawing shows a small Quebec conscript looking at a worker who has presumably taken his job, with the caption *"Et quand nous serons partis les 'blokes' viendront prendre nos places, nos foyers, nos femmes."*[87]

As we have already seen, the conscription issue had an economic dimension. The "conscription of wealth" position espoused by the Liberals and Quebec nationalists was to some extent simply positioning; Laurier's taxation policy was never spelled out in detail. It was also, however, an appeal to segments of society that would be hardest hit by conscription, namely farm families and urban working families where the absence of a labourer might make a real difference in their ability to maintain a way of life.[88] The Conservatives, taking note of the opposition, proposed to exempt "only sons" of farm families from conscription, and also proposed to increase the taxes paid by the wealthy. Borden's manifesto proposes that "Wealth will be conscripted by adequate taxation of war profits and increased taxation of income."[89] This was the origin of what was to become the major taxation instrument of modern times in Canada — the income tax.

The discontent aroused in agricultural and urban working areas by the 1917 election resulted in independent political movements in both sectors. Twenty-two Labour candidates ran in the election,[90] and the Progressive movement in the West was on the horizon. In 1917, the "Farmers' Program," proposed by the combined farm organizations, made no mention of conscription and concentrated on economic issues, such as lowering the tariff, taxing income and idle land, and nationalizing the railways and telegraphs.[91]

Election day editorial opinion raised the rhetoric even higher. The *London Free Press* opined that "EVERY VOTE CAST FOR A LAURIER CANDIDATE IS A VOTE CAST FOR THE KAISER,"[92] and the Toronto *Mail and Empire* told its readers

> that a vote for a Laurier candidate was a vote for Bourassa and against the Canadian army at the front; it was a vote against the British connection and the Empire and a vote for Germany, the Kaiser, Hindenburg, von Tirpitz, and the German soldier who sank the *Lusitania*. The man who had a son overseas was told that a vote for Laurier meant that he was ready to betray that son.[93]

Ontario, to whom the bulk of the negative campaigning on the part of the government was directed, responded with a turnout of 79 percent of registered voters, higher than the national turnout of 75 percent, and a figure unmatched in the past and not to be matched again until the election of 1958. The Union government won 63 percent of the votes in Ontario, and 90 percent of the seats there. The other anglophone provinces produced similar results (see Table 2.3). Only one Liberal of 15 was elected in Manitoba, where the erstwhile Liberal newspaper, the *Winnipeg Free Press*, told its readers, "December 17 will be Doomsday. The Contest is not an election but a destiny and beyond all reasonable doubt it is a contest for the soul of this nation."[94] Only Quebec was left to Laurier, where the Liberals won 73 percent of the vote and 62 of 65 seats.

The *Wartime Elections Act* helped the government in other ways beyond the mobilizing of votes of supportive women voters. Anyone born in a country at war with Canada and Britain who had become a citizen after 1902 was disenfranchised, thus robbing the Liberals of many potential votes in the West of Germanic origin.[95] An accompanying piece of legislation, the *Military Voters Act*, allowed servicemen to have their vote assigned by the party they voted for to any riding in the country. This service vote was counted and assigned a month after the election. "The Conservatives won at least 14 additional seats by redistributing the military vote to ridings where the opposition candidates had a slight lead."[96] This use of the *Military Voters Act* had the potential of creating bad publicity for the Conservatives, however, once the occasion had passed. A local Liberal Association president in Ontario published the following after an investigation:

> There was a conspiracy of fraud in England to influence the result of the elections, involving perjury, forgery,

> personation, repeaters in voting, double ballots, unqualified voting, ballot stuffing, replacing of ballots, opening of ballot boxes.... I am prepared to prove, under sworn testimony, that more than a score [men] were either sent into the fighting line because they declined to vote for the Government or were threatened with immediate return to the trenches if they would not mark their ballots to the Government in the presence of commanding officers.[97]

Having manipulated the electoral franchise to their benefit in 1917, Borden and Arthur Meighen (who was to succeed Borden as prime minister in July of 1920) went on to introduce the *Dominion Elections Act* of 1920. This piece of legislation, which was in place for the federal election of 1921, established federal control over the eligibility for federal voting, and extended it to most of the adult population. Women were finally granted the vote, and all property qualifications were removed (some had remained in the individual provinces). The post of Chief Electoral Officer was created and given a status independent of the government of the day. Some restrictions remained; rural voters' lists were created by door-to-door canvassers, but urban voters not already on existing provincial lists had to apply to be added. Nevertheless, universal suffrage had, for all intents and purposes, arrived in Canada.

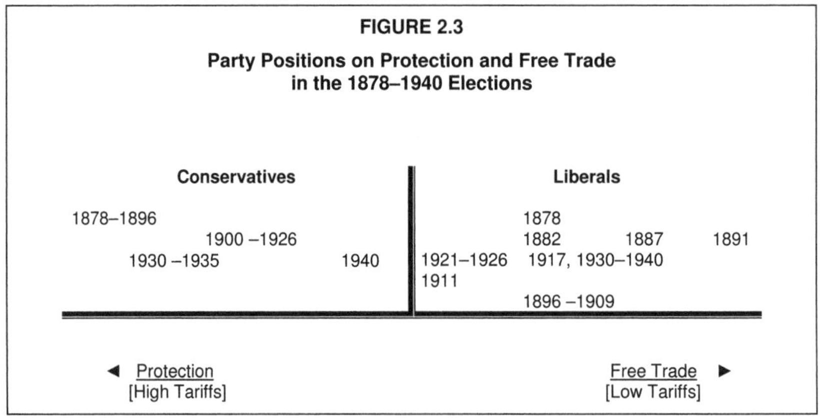

TABLE 2.3

Results of the 1911 and 1917 Elections, by Province

		Conservative/ Unionist		Liberal/ Opposition		Other	
		1911	1917	1911	1917	1911	1917
Prince Edward Island	votes (%)	51	50	49	50	-	-
	seats (#)	2	2	2	2	-	-
Nova Scotia	votes (%)	49	48	51	46	X	6
	seats (#)	9	12	9	4	-	-
New Brunswick	votes (%)	49	59	51	41	-	-
	seats (#)	5	7	8	4	-	-
Quebec	votes (%)	49	25	51	73	X	2
	seats (#)	27	3	38	62	-	-
Ontario	votes (%)	56	62	43	34	X	4
	seats (#)	73	74	13	8	-	-
Manitoba	votes (%)	52	80	45	20	3	-
	seats (#)	8	14	2	1	-	-
Saskatchewan	votes (%)	39	74	59	26	2	-
	seats (#)	1	16	9	-	-	-
Alberta	votes (%)	43	61	53	36	4	4
	seats (#)	1	11	6	1	-	-
British Columbia	votes (%)	59	68	38	26	4	6
	seats (#)	7	13	-	-	-	-
Yukon Territory	votes (%)	61	54	39	46	-	-
	seats (#)	1	1	-	-	-	-
TOTAL CANADA	votes (%)	51	57	48	40	1	3
	seats (#)	134	153	87	82	-	-

X less than 1 percent

The Early Dynasties

In the period between Confederation and the end of the First World War, and certainly as exemplified by the four elections that we have examined in detail here, the Conservative and Liberal parties competed on two major issue dimensions. The first was economic. On the most general level, this involved the question of which party could be trusted to pursue economic growth most successfully. After Confederation, the initial period of public trust given to Macdonald allowed him to establish the Conservatives as custodians of economic responsibility, particularly in the period after the 1878 election. The National Policy, fortuitously coinciding with a period of economic growth, became the economic orthodoxy, and established the paramountcy of the Tories on this issue dimension. The policy content of the economic issue debate was defined along a dimension leading from protectionism to free trade (see Figure 2.3). By establishing the National Policy, the Conservatives equated economic protectionism with national unity. Although this equation was disputed in agricultural sections of the country, it maintained government support in substantial parts of the central and eastern regions, and gave them financial aid from the industrialists whom the policy was designed to protect. The Liberals maneuvered at the free trade end of the dimension from 1878 to 1896. By 1896, "unrestricted reciprocity" had turned into "free trade as practiced in Britain" with the acceptance of a "tariff for revenue, not protection." At the same time, the economic growth associated with the National Policy came to an end, and the depression of the 1890s allowed the Liberals to parlay their modified economic policy into public acceptance of their accession to government in the election of 1896. Once in power, the economic good times, and the reluctance of Laurier to pursue more extreme free trade options allowed the Liberals to sustain a run of four successive election victories. Laurier, in turn, donned the mantle of the protector of the national economy and amicable relations between the races. In 1911, the sudden lurch toward reciprocity, coupled with the accumulated dissatisfaction with an aging Liberal government, allowed the Conservatives once again to claim that they were the custodians of the national economic policy, and make good their insinuations that the Liberals were being disloyal by attempting to sell out the country.

The second dimension involved national unity versus particularistic representation of regions. The secret of the two long-serving prime ministers in this period was that they were able to position themselves and their parties toward the national unity end of this continuum, though they were certainly not above regional appeals. It was Macdonald's base in Ontario, and Laurier's in Quebec, that led to their success in bringing the other region onside, together with their general mastery of compromise and patronage, and a large dose of personal charm. Macdonald established his credentials through his brokering of the Confederation agreement, and cemented it by his partnership with Cartier. Laurier managed to get a satisfactory agreement on the Manitoba schools, while still keeping anglophone opinion on his side. Even in the election of 1917, when animosity toward French Canadians was at its peak, his goal was to try to soothe relations, first by arguing for persuasion, then suggesting a referendum, and finally insisting on an election so that a national decision would be rendered to make the conscription policy more palatable. Laurier's death in 1919 and Meighen's assumption of office in 1920 brought the Borden interlude to a close. The passions aroused by the war and the formation of the Union government had extended it by several years, but the conditions for the establishment of a second Conservative dynasty never really existed. It was not long before the Liberals were able to engineer another election victory, with another leader at the helm.

Notes

1. The discussion of early electoral arrangements in this paragraph is sourced from John Garner, *The Franchise and Politics in British North America, 1755–1867* (Toronto: University of Toronto Press, 1969), 68, 112; Norman Ward, *The Canadian House of Commons Representation* (Toronto: University of Toronto Press, 1950), 157–58; Elections Canada, *A History of the Vote in Canada* (Ottawa: Ministry of Public Works and Government Services Canada, 1997), 16.
2. J. Murray Beck, *The Government of Nova Scotia* (Toronto: University of Toronto Press, 1957), 265.
3. *History of the Vote in Canada*, op. cit., 46.
4. Ward, *op. cit.*, 212.
5. Ward, *op. cit.*, 214.
6. Escott M. Reid, "The Rise of National Parties in Canada," in Hugh G. Thorburn and Alan Whitehorn, eds., *Party Politics in Canada*, 8th

edition (Toronto: Prentice Hall, 2001), 9–15 (article originally published in 1932).

7. Gordon T. Stewart, *The Origins of Canadian Politics* (Vancouver, University of British Columbia Press, 1986), 86–87. See also Michael Bliss, *Right Honourable Men* (Toronto: HarperCollins, 1994), Chapter 1.
8. George F.G. Stanley, "The 1870s," in J.M.S. Careless and R. Craig Brown, *The Canadians, 1867–1967* (Toronto: Macmillan, 1967), 48–50.
9. J. Murray Beck, *Pendulum of Power* (Toronto: Prentice-Hall, 1968) 21.
10. Donald Creighton, *John A. Macdonald: The Old Chieftain* (Toronto: Macmillan, 1955), Chapter 5. See also Donald Swainson, *Sir John A. Macdonald: The Man and the Politician* (Kingston: Quarry Press, 1989), 95–97.
11. W.A. Harkin, ed., *Political Reminiscences of the Right Honourable Sir Charles Tupper* (London: Constable & Co., 1914), 135–36.
12. Sir Richard Cartwright, *Reminiscences* (Toronto: William Briggs, 1912), 146.
13. Dale C. Thomson, *Alexander Mackenzie: Clear Grit* (Toronto: Macmillan, 1960), 300.
14. H.M. Hyndman, *Commercial Crises of the Nineteenth Century* (London: Swan Sonnenschein, 1892), 115.
15. See O.D. Skelton, *General Economic History of the Dominion: 1867–1912* (Toronto: Publishers Association of Canada, 1913), 137, and Peter B. Waite, *Canada 1874–1896* (Toronto: McClelland & Stewart, 1971), 75.
16. House of Commons, *Debates 1878*, 854.
17. Harkin, *op. cit.*, 142–43.
18. Creighton, *op. cit.*, 120.
19. Peter B. Waite, *Macdonald: His Life and World* (Toronto: McGraw-Hill Ryerson, 1975), 135.
20. *Results of Five Years Grit-Rouge Rule in Canada: The National Policy and How It Will Affect the Future of Canada* (T & R White, *The Gazette*, Montreal, 1878), 4, National Library of Canada (henceforth NLC).
21. Alexander Mackenzie, *Speech to the Workingmen's Demonstration* (Toronto: supplement to the *Freeholder*, May 30, 1878), 11. NLC.
22. *Ibid.*, 1–2.
23. Alexander Mackenzie, *Speech in Saint John* (*St. John Daily News*, August 22, 1878), 7. NLC.
24. Cartwright, *op. cit.*, 168–69.
25. Alexander Mackenzie, *Speech to the Workingmen's Demonstration*, 11.
26. Alexander Mackenzie, *Political Points and Pencillings* (Toronto: Grip, 1878) NLC.
27. Sir John A. Macdonald, *Grits in Office: Profession and Practice*. Speech at Montreal (Ottawa: Conservative Association for the Dominion, 1876), 5. NLC.
28. The Liberal speeches for 1878 are collected in *Reform Government in the Dominion: The Pic-Nic Speeches* (Toronto: Globe Publishing, 1878) NLC.

The quote is from page 102. The schedule in the previous paragraph is derived from this document.

29. Cartwright, *op. cit.*, 155.
30. Sir Joseph Pope, *Sir John A. Macdonald Vindicated: A Review of the Right Honourable Sir Richard Cartwright's Reminiscences* (Toronto: Publishers Association of Canada, 1912), 16–17.
31. *A Summary of the Public Records of the Past Five Years for the Use of the People* (Toronto: *The Mail*, 1878) NLC.
32. *Pic-Nic Speeches, op. cit.*, 5.
33. Elections Canada, *op. cit.*, 49.
34. Ward, *Canadian House of Commons*, op. cit., 221. Macdonald originally proposed to extend the franchise to women of property, whom he expected to vote Conservative, but agreed to the removal of this section from the bill.
35. Sir Charles Tupper, Bart, *Recollections of Sixty Years in Canada* (London: Cassell, 1914), 308.
36. Allan Wallace Macintosh, "The Career of Sir Charles Tupper in Canada, 1864–1900" (Ph.D. dissertation, University of Toronto: 1960), 464. NLC.
37. Joseph Schull, *Laurier: The First Canadian* (Toronto: Macmillan, 1965), 294.
38. Paul Douglas Stevens, "Laurier and the Liberal Party in Ontario" (Ph.D. dissertation, University of Toronto: 1966), 14. NLC. See also Jack Macleod, "The Political Thought of Sir Wilfrid Laurier: A Study in Canadian Party Leadership" (Ph.D. dissertation, University of Toronto: 1965), 197. NLC.
39. Ontario Liberal Association, *Facts for the People, 3: Tariff Reform, Freer Trade, Reduced Taxation* (Toronto: 1896), 14. NLC.
40. Conservative Party of Canada, *Information for the Electors*, 6, 1896, 16. NLC. See also Conservative Party, *Political Pointers for the Campaign of 1896* (Ottawa, 1896) NLC.
41. John Saywell, "The 1890s," in J.M.S. Careless and R. Craig Brown, eds., *The Canadians* (Toronto: Macmillan, 1967), 108–35.
42. O.D. Skelton, *op. cit.*, 179.
43. O.D. Skelton, *Life and Letters of Sir Wilfrid Laurier*, Vol. 1, Carleton Library Edition (Toronto: McClelland & Stewart, 1965), 159. On the Manitoba school question, Skelton acidly comments, "it was not really an educational question; rarely is the public roused to a lively interest in the genuine problems of education. The school was merely the arena where religious gladiators displayed their powers, and the occasion for stirring the religious convictions and religious prejudices of thousands, and of demonstrating how little either their education or their religion had done to make them tolerant citizens.": 150.
44. J.W. Dafoe, *Laurier: A Study in Canadian Politics* (Toronto: Thomas Allan, 1922), 40–42.
45. Blair Neatby, *Laurier and a Liberal Quebec: A Study in Political Management*, Carleton Library Edition (Toronto: McClelland & Stewart, 1973), 73.
46. L.A. Paquet, *The Manitoba School Question: The Bishops' View and Mr. Laurier's View* (no publication information, 1896), 27. NLC.

47. Laurier Lapierre, "Politics, Race and Religion in French Canada: Joseph Israel Tarte" (Ph.D. dissertation, University of Toronto, 1962), 286–87. NLC.
48. Skelton, *Life and Letters of Sir Wilfrid Laurier, op. cit.*, 159. See also André Siegfried, *The Race Question in Canada* (New York: Appleton, 1907), 82.
49. Lawrence Geoffrey Power, *The Remedial Bill from the Point of View of a Catholic Member* (Ottawa, March 3, 1896), 21. NLC.
50. Harold Leard, "The 1896 Federal Election in Prince Edward Island" (M.A. thesis, University of New Brunswick, 1972), 189. NLC. See also K.M. McLaughlin, "The Canadian General Election of 1896 in Nova Scotia" (M.A. thesis, Dalhousie University, 1967), 148. NLC.
51. John Irvine Little, "The Federal Election of 1896 in New Brunswick" (M.A. thesis, University of New Brunswick, 1970), 232. NLC.
52. Ellen Gillies Cooke, "The Federal Election of 1896 in Manitoba" (M.A. thesis, University of Manitoba, 1943), 203. NLC. See also Donald E. Blake, "1896 and All That: Critical Elections in Canada," *Canadian Journal of Political Science* XII: 2 (June, 1979), 259–80, especially 265.
53. Owen D. Carrigan, *Canadian Party Programs, 1867–1968* (Toronto: Clark, 1968), 41.
54. Joseph Schull, *Laurier: The First Canadian* (Toronto: Macmillan, 1965), 339–40.
55. Patrick Boyer, *Direct Democracy in Canada: The History and Future of Referendums* (Toronto: Dundurn Press, 1992), 31–32.
56. John English, *The Decline of Politics: The Conservatives and the Party System, 1901–1920* (Toronto: University of Toronto Press, 1977), 56.
57. Sir Wilfrid Laurier, *Speech to the House of Commons, March 7, 1911* (Liberal Party pamphlet, 1911), 7. NLC.
58. Liberal Party of Canada, *The Grain Grower and Reciprocity*, 1911 pamphlet, 1. NLC.
59. Liberal Party of Canada, *Haultain and Reciprocity*, 1911 pamphlet (Regina) NLC.
60. Liberal Party of Canada, *Reciprocity: A Good Thing for Canada*, 1911 pamphlet, 10. NLC.
61. Liberal Party of Canada, *Bigger Markets, Better Conditions: Are Creators of Contentment, not Breeders of Disloyalty*, 1911 pamphlet. NLC.
62. Sir Robert Borden, *Speech to the House of Commons, February 9* (Conservative Party pamphlet, 1911), 7–9, 14. NLC.
63. Conservative Party, *Speech of Premier Richard McBride to the B.C. Legislature*, 1911 pamphlet, 5. NLC.
64. Conservative Party, *Reciprocity and the Canadian Farmer: Which Will Reciprocity Bring Him the Most of?New Markets or New Competitors?* 1911 pamphlet. NLC.
65. Conservative Party, *Our Fisheries and Our Forests: Two of Our National Monopolies, Two Matchless National Resources. Shall We Keep them or Shall We Lose Them?* 1911 pamphlet, 2. NLC.

66. Conservative Party, *Egg Money: The Rightful Perquisite of the Women on the Canadian Farms*, 1911 pamphlet, 1, 4. NLC.
67. Conservative Party, *Results of Reciprocity: Evils the Taft–Fielding Agreement Will Bring: "By Canadians, for Canadians, About Canada,"* 1911 pamphlet, 4. NLC.
68. E.B. Biggar, *The Political Side of Reciprocity* (Montreal: Canadian Century, 1911), 2. NLC.
69. La Nation Canadienne, *Autonomie: victoires autonomistes de Sir Wilfrid Laurier* (1911) NLC.
70. Henri Bourassa, *The Reciprocity Agreement and its consequences as Viewed from the Nationalist Standpoint* (Montreal, *Le Devoir*, 1911),. 23, NLC
71. John Boyd, *The Nationalist Movement* (Montreal, *The Canadian* magazine, 1911), 9. NLC.
72. Liberal Party of Canada, *Sir Wilfrid Laurier: Chef du parti liberal*, 1911 pamphlet, sections 3–12, 14–42, and 51. NLC.
73. Paul Stevens, "Laurier, Aylesworth and the Decline of the Liberal Party in Ontario," *Historical Papers of the Canadian Historical Association* (1968), 94–113.
74. J. Murray Beck, *Pendulum of Power* (Toronto: Prentice-Hall, 1968), 127.
75. John Allen, "Economic Self-Interest and Voting in the 1911 Election" (M.A. thesis, Department of Economics, Queen's University, 1971) NLC.
76. Stephen Leacock, "The Great Victory in Canada," *National Review* (London, England, 1911), 12. NLC.
77. Canadian National League, *Campaign of 1911 Against Reciprocity with USA* (1911) NLC.
78. Robert Borden, *Manifesto of Sir Robert Borden to the Canadian People* (Ottawa: Union Government Publicity Bureau, 1917), 4, 6, 7.
79. Union Government Publicity Bureau, *German Atrocities*, 1917 pamphlet, 1. NLC.
80. Union Government Publicity Bureau, *Plain Facts for English-Speaking Electors*, 1917 pamphlet, 4, 7. NLC. Emphasis in the original.
81. Union Government Publicity Bureau, *English Canadians and the War*, 1917 pamphlet, 2. NLC.
82. Sir Wilfrid Laurier, *Manifesto to the Canadian People*, 1917 pamphlet, 7, 11. NLC.
83. *Ibid.*, 9.
84. Henri Bourassa, *Conscription* (Montreal, *Le Devoir*, 1917), 19. NLC.
85. Liberal Party, *Who Shall Rule? The People or the Big Interests?* (Ottawa: Central Information Office, 1917) NLC.
86. Henri Bourassa, *Conscription, op. cit.*, 12–13, 17–22.
87. J. Charlebois, *La Conscription: Tristes Dessins et Légendes Tristes* (Montreal, *Le Devoir*, 1917) NLC.
88. Janine Brodie and Jane Jenson, *Crisis, Challenge and Change* (Ottawa: Carleton University Press, revised edition, 1988), 94.

89. Borden, *Manifesto*, *op. cit.*, 7.
90. Beck, *op. cit.*, 146.
91. Canadian Council of Agriculture, *The Farmers' Platform* (Winnipeg, 1917), adopted by the UFA, SGGA, MGGA, UFO. 3–5. NLC.
92. Patrick Ferraro, "English Canada and the Election of 1917" (M.A. Thesis, Department of History, McGill University, 1971), 50. NLC.
93. Elizabeth Armstrong, *The Crisis of Quebec, 1914–1918* (Toronto: McClelland & Stewart, 1974), 207 (first published in 1937).
94. Ferraro, *op. cit.*, 102.
95. Elections Canada, *op. cit.*, 59–60.
96. *Ibid.*, 60.
97. W.T.R. Preston, *Startling Exposures of Overseas Military Election Frauds* (speech to Durham Liberal Association).

Selected Reading

Beck, J. Murray. *Pendulum of Power* (Toronto: Prentice-Hall, 1968).

Carrigan, Owen D. *Canadian Party Programs, 1867–1968* (Toronto: Clark, 1968).

Creighton, Donald. *John A. Macdonald* (2 volumes) (Toronto: Macmillan, 1955).

Elections Canada. *A History of the Vote in Canada* (Ottawa: Elections Canada, 1997).

English, John. *The Decline of Politics: The Conservatives and the Party System, 1901–1920* (Toronto: University of Toronto Press, 1977).

Neatby, Blair. *Laurier and a Liberal Quebec: A Study in Political Management* (Toronto: McClelland & Stewart, 1973).

Stewart, Gordon T. *The Origins of Canadian Politics* (Vancouver: University of British Columbia Press, 1986).

Schull, Joseph. *Laurier: The First Canadian* (Toronto: Macmillan, 1965).

Skelton, O.D. *The Life and Letters of Sir Wilfrid Laurier* (Toronto: McClelland & Stewart, 1965).

Thomson, Dale. *Alexander Mackenzie: Clear Grit* (Toronto: Macmillan, 1960).

Waite, Peter B. *Canada 1874–1896* (Toronto: McClelland & Stewart, 1971).

CHAPTER 3

A NEW LIBERAL DYNASTY: THE MACKENZIE KING ERA

William Lyon Mackenzie King was an unlikely candidate to become Canada's longest-serving and electorally most successful prime minister. Not physically prepossessing, and an indifferent speaker in an age when people still expected great oratory from their leaders, King relied for his appeal on an ability to stake out the middle ground on issues, bring people and parts of the country together into a governmental coalition through the Liberal Party, and above all to tread cautiously and not offend major interests. King was a tireless worker (despite many complaints to his *Diary* of being tired) and showed a keen sense of attention to detail. A lifelong bachelor, he spent many hours a day alone, engaged in reading (including "the little books," as he called them, which were of a religious nature), note taking, diary writing, and correspondence. He read a great deal of meaning into his dreams and visions, and his predilection for the spirit world is well known (though it was not during his lifetime).[1]

King had parlayed a background in labour relations into the civil service position of deputy minister of labour by 1900, ran for election successfully in 1908, and became minister of labour in the last Laurier cabinet. When both he and the party were defeated in 1911, King was out of a job and out of politics. Because he was not in the House of Commons during the war, but rather had taken a position with the American industrialist John D. Rockefeller as adviser on labour matters, King was spared the decision faced by many prominent Liberals on whether to enter the Borden Union government. He ran unsuccessfully once again in 1917 in his old constituency of Waterloo North (Ontario) as a Liberal, and always maintained that he had been loyal to Laurier, and that Laurier considered him his heir and trusted him above all other advisers. Biographers Ferns and Ostry take a different view of King in 1917:

> In this contest Mackenzie King made his political fortune. Laurier doubted his loyalty. In the election he had pushed a line so like that of the Government that only in refinements of emphasis could the differences be detected. He refused to travel to Western Canada or to Quebec with Laurier lest the people see him with his leader and he be obliged to say too much. But, in spite of all this, he appeared to have been loyal to Laurier.[2]

Nevertheless, his loyalty to Laurier was a common theme in King's own thoughts, speeches, and (later) actions.

Mackenzie King's work for Rockefeller not only provided him with a steady income, but it allowed him to hone his skills in personal and public relations, and to further develop his ideas about labour–management relations. King was in some ways a reformer, since he genuinely was appalled at labour conditions in many places, and believed that workers deserved good treatment, fair wages and representation. At the same time, his sense of caution meant that he opposed strikes to secure union accreditation as official representatives of labour, a position which endeared him to Rockefeller, who was fighting just such a strike in Colorado. King's compromise position on industrial relations revolved around the establishment of a "company union" where representatives of workers consulted with the management on a regular basis regarding grievances, and bargained with them over wage agreements.[3] As expounded in his book, *Industry and Humanity*,[4] King felt that the great potential for a clash between labour and management could be headed off by a limited amount of collective bargaining between people of good faith on both sides. He favoured compulsory arbitration to end disputes, a principle embodied in the *Industrial Disputes Investigations Act*, a piece of legislation enacted while he was minister of labour.[5] Some writers, however, have read *Industry and Humanity* to be a radical document.[6] Perhaps put off by its length and turgid style, delegates to the 1919 convention that elected King as Liberal leader likely had not read it at all.[7]

Mackenzie King was chosen leader of the Liberal Party in the first leadership convention to be held in this country. These conventions quickly became established as the preferred way to perform this task, incorporating as they did a moderate amount of intra-party democracy and an opportunity for the party to raise its profile across the country and gather publicity. In 1919, the Liberal gathering was originally intended to be a policy convention, called by Laurier to revive the party after the bruising 1917 campaign and associated events. However, Laurier's death transformed the meeting into one which would choose the next leader.[8] The convention played a major role in solidifying the postwar Liberals, conciliating some of those who had strayed from the fold to the Unionists during the war. It reinforced the party's traditional position on tariff reduction, and adopted a number of resolutions designed to appeal to farmers, workers and industry, some of them under the guidance of Mackenzie King.[9]

King adopted a low-key approach in seeking the leadership, absenting himself from Canada for a long period before the convention met. Though he professed doubts about his suitability as leader, and was doubtless tempted by the lucrative possibility of continued employment by Rockefeller or an equivalent high-profile post in the United States, King confided to his diary, to his brother, and to his longtime friend and executive assistant Fred McGregor, that God and his destiny called him to be party leader and prime minister.[10] And King was in a strong position to pick up delegate votes in Quebec because of his association with Laurier, and elsewhere because of his association with labour and industrial issues. His main competitor, William Fielding, had the experience of having been minister of finance on his side, but had favoured conscription and furthermore had already attained the age of 70. At a decisive moment in the convention, King seized the opportunity to give an effective speech praising Laurier and attacking the Borden government.[11] He was chosen leader on the third ballot.

Organized labour was a new force which had to be incorporated into politics in the early decades of the twentieth century, and was the initial focus of King's concern. However, it was a second force, organized farmers, which was to dominate the politics of the 1920s. In the early years of the decade, United Farmers' movements took power in three provinces — Ontario, Alberta, and Manitoba — and were also politically important in Nova Scotia and a strong influence behind the Liberals in Saskatchewan. Opposition to the Borden Union government during the war had caused the Farmers' movement to dissociate itself from both of the traditional parties. The farmers' discontent proved to be stronger and more lasting with the federal Conservatives, partly because that party was still committed to a high tariff policy, and partly because the new Conservative leader, Arthur Meighen, was associated with elite industrial interests. To King, the goal was to unite farmers and labour with the Liberal Party. According to biographer R. MacGregor Dawson, he regarded the farmer and labour movements as allies of the liberal side of politics, all the components of which opposed the conservative forces. King's task was to get them into the Liberal Party alongside him.[12]

In his pragmatic and flexible approach to politics, only Macdonald, in the judgment of Canadian historians and political scientists, rivalled King.[13] A later Conservative leader, R.J. Manion, when rating the prime ministers in a memoir, said, "Mackenzie King was [note the past tense in a book published in 1936] the best politician — if by that term one implies a skill in winning elections."[14] According to Jack Pickersgill, his former executive assistant and speech writer, King was "not a thinker … was not at home in the world of ideas and had no coherent political faith."[15] Except, of course, his faith in the principle of conciliation, and the confidence that he was the only leader who could accomplish it. And, as biographer Blair Neatby points out, he did just that:

> In 1919 King had become leader of a party with almost no parliamentary representation from English Canada, and in which the personal animosities of the conscription crisis and the acid test of loyalty to Sir Wilfrid Laurier still coloured every issue. Only three decades later the Liberal party had not only been in office for more than twenty years, but it was also so firmly established that the talk was of one-party government. As party leader, King's achievement was even more remarkable. He left to his successor a united party which remained in office

> for almost another decade, something which not even John A. Macdonald had been able to do.[16]

King was eager, at least early in his career, to look to the West for new Liberal support. For one thing, the Western commitment to the principle of free trade matched his own. He was also attracted to farming as the rural equivalent of industrial labour, which had been his cause. Once he became leader, he "convinced himself that he was particularly suited to represent the West.... [His attitude was] a complex mixture of genuine sympathy, self-deception and political expediency. King's western sympathies served a definite pragmatic purpose, but it must be understood that he believed them to exist."[17] King thought that the Farmer and Labour movements in the West were his natural allies, but underestimated the degree to which they were alienated from all the traditional parties.[18] An additional problem for him was the fact that many Western Liberals had joined the Union government, and on returning to the Liberal fold were suspicious of him because of his loyalty to Laurier and his Ontario base. These Liberal problems on the Prairies paved the way for not only the rise of the Progressives in 1921, but also the CCF and Social Credit in the 1930s.[19]

National unity was a prominent theme, not only of King's first campaign as leader in 1921, but of every subsequent campaign, even in the 1930s, when the economic problems of the Depression were so dominant in the public mind. To him, as Neatby points out, national unity extended the ideal principles of labour–management relations; it was a matter of bringing different sides together and finding common interests.[20] Capital and labour, farming and urban interests, Quebec and English Canada, the West and the East, all of these elements of the nation needed to be included in the grand representational coalition of the Liberal Party. Patience was necessary, and long periods of discussion. The Liberal Party needed to be brought around to accepting compromise solutions and half measures in order to preserve national unity.

With King's natural caution and with the necessity for coalition building to occur largely behind the scenes, national unity was continually defined in his public speeches as a general principle and goal. Early in the 1921 campaign, King arrived in Pictou, Nova Scotia, and wrote in his diary:

> Was met at the station by an immense crowd, & procession with pipers band formed to exhibition grounds. Quite a large crowd was assembled there. I spoke from a motor to the "assembled multitude" on National Unity and Good-Will. Felt in good shape and know that I succeeded in making a good impression.[21]

It is indicative of King's positive state of mind that he could take so much pride in speaking so often on this theme.[22] He was well aware that he was not popular with the public, had little or no charisma, and was often sneered at as a purveyor of platitudes. But, as Neatby contends, "King could not change his personality or his style of leadership. He was sure that his approach was the only way to keep the party united and to respond responsibly to national needs."[23]

The 1921 Election

The Conservative government that sought re-election in 1921 was led by Borden's successor, Arthur Meighen. Meighen had been the architect of the methods used by the Union government to implement conscription and win the election of 1917. Frequently described as brilliant, a great orator, a debater used to destroying his opponents, and a master of Parliamentary procedure, he is just as frequently called self-deluded, cold, arrogant, and ruthless. Historian John Williams notes: "To Meighen there were only two sides to every question, his and the wrong side."[24] Liberal cabinet minister "Chubby" Power, who claimed to admire Meighen in debate, remarked that when questioned in Parliament by Mackenzie King

> Meighen's answers were almost invariably couched in terms of almost frigid contempt. Meighen never seemed to attempt either to charm or to persuade; his efforts were aimed at confirming in his own people the belief that the course of conduct he was advocating was the only one that was sound, reasonable, and just.[25]

TABLE 3.1

Party Leadership Conventions1919–1948

DATE	PARTY	LOCATION	WINNER	# CANDIDATES*	# BALLOTS	RUNNER-UP**
1919 08 05	Liberal	Ottawa	W.L. Mackenzie King	4	3	William Fielding
1927 10 10	Conservative	Winnipeg	R.B. Bennett	6	2	Hugh Guthrie
1938 07 05	Conservative	Ottawa	R.J. Manion	5	2	M.A. MacPherson
1942 12 09	Conservative	Winnipeg	John Bracken	5	2	M.A. MacPherson
1948 08 07	Liberal	Ottawa	Louis St. Laurent	3	1	James Gardiner
1948 09 30	Conservative	Ottawa	George Drew	3	1	John Diefenbaker

* On first ballot

** On final ballot

Meighen was so devoted to principle that he despised anyone who was not, particularly Mackenzie King. He became obsessed with criticizing King, to the point where his supporters urged him to ignore the Liberal leader or treat him more reasonably, lest the public sympathize with him.[26] Needless to say, there was no love lost toward Meighen on the part of King. Following the election, he confided to his diary the remark "Meighen defeated in his own riding gave me real satisfaction. He has been so contemptible in his attitude toward me."[27]

The political party that Meighen led in 1921 was not the same party that won the 1917 election. The Union government coalition had for the most part been dissolved, but an effort was made to retain the image of unity by adopting the name National Liberal and Conservative Party. But the "National" label fooled no one. The old Conservative Party had no support in Quebec, and little support in the West. The former was dominated by the Liberals, and the latter was being contested by the newly formed Progressive Party, as the provincial farmers' organizations had agreed to call themselves.[28] Although loosely organized, and dedicated to ideas of local constituency autonomy, the Progressives were united on one thing, their commitment to the principle of removal of protective tariffs.[29] The Progressives saw the tariff structure, the pillar of Conservative economic policy since the time of Macdonald, as the foe of competition, farmers, and workers, and the friend only of Big Business.[30] T.A. Crerar, the Progressive leader (and former member of the Union government), recognized, however, that tariffs would have to be phased out gradually rather than suddenly abolished, in order to provide a period of adjustment for Canadian industry.[31] This position provided an opening for King, who emphasized the Liberals' free trade position, avoided confrontation with the Progressives and regarded them as just "Liberals in a hurry." Meighen, however, attacked the Progressives as radicals, socialists, and worse, who were out to destroy the existing social order.[32]

The Progressives, and their provincial cousins, the United Farmers parties, were by no means an isolated phenomenon in the Western regions of North America. In the United States and Canada, these movements, often tied to farm organizations, protested the adoption of economic policies designed to benefit eastern manufacturers, bankers, and other elite groups at the expense of ordinary producers. Always uneasy at the prospect of acting like a conventional political party, forming a government or an opposition, creating formal organizations, compromising their positions and diversifying their programs, the Progressives gradually lost momentum and dissolved, with a certain amount of their support being picked up by the Liberals, just as King had planned. But the Depression of the 1930s produced heirs to the Progressives in the form of the Social Credit Party and the Co-operative Commonwealth Federation, which spread beyond the West in their search for support and their challenge to the conventional party system.[33] And in contrast to the Progressives, later parties like the CCF and its successor, the New Democratic Party, became committed to the creation of strong party organizations and were willing to bargain in the legislature to achieve their policy goals.[34]

The post-war period was one of dislocation and restlessness throughout Canadian society, not only on the farms. Price increases had occurred after the war, a situation not matched by rises in wage levels.[35] Returning troops often opted for life in the cities rather than rural areas, but jobs were not plentiful. Discontent with the cost and standard of living for workers boiled over in Winnipeg in 1919, when the army had to be mobilized to put down a general strike, with attendant loss of life. Ideas about alternative social systems, if not revolution, were in the air — in North America as well as on the Continent. The British Labour Party formed a government in 1924, and socialist and communist movements were expanding in Germany, Russia, France, and elsewhere throughout Europe. Various groups of new Canadian immigrants looked back to homelands in which new political ideas and movements were rising. It was not a time when an established Canadian political party could hope to sweep the country with a message of complacency and generality.

It was the Progressive commitment to free trade that led King and the Liberals to believe that they could divert such support to themselves. The Liberal policy supporting free trade was a longstanding one, to the extent of having proposed reciprocity with the United States during their losing campaign in 1911. And what of the tariff issue in 1921? The official Liberal position stated:

> The tariff issue today is not between free trade and protection, or between farmers and manufacturers or urban workers. The issue is whether the tariff shall be framed at the dictation of a few great interests or revised in accordance with the will of the people working in

> stores and offices, in fields and factories. Is there to be a real democracy or a sham democracy, camouflaging plutocracy? It is for the people of Canada to say.[36]

In the past, there had been no "Farmers Parties" during Liberal administrations, because the Liberals were on the farmers' side over the tariff issue.[37] According to a 1921 National Liberal Committee pamphlet, "Liberals and Farmers worked together in the past. They should work together now.... Both opposed to [the] Meighen government. Their platforms and policies afford ground for common action."[38] In other words, the Liberals were not about to abolish tariffs, but gave the impression they were intent on lowering them and somehow making them serve the common people.

However successful King may have ultimately been in enticing Progressive support toward the Liberal Party, this strategy was not successful in the 1921 election. In part, he overestimated the degree to which Western and Ontario discontent channelled toward the Progressives was based simply on the tariff policy. As Morton points out, the discontent was aimed toward the existing party system in general, and included considerable skepticism regarding the promises of King and the Liberals.[39] The Liberals, after all, had been campaigning as the champions of free trade and tariff reduction since Confederation, with little, so farmers thought, to show for it. They had come to power in 1896 by hedging on their low tariff platform, and had not succeeded in carrying the country on reciprocity in 1911. If Laurier, with all his popularity and political skill, could not significantly lower the tariff, how could King, the prevaricator, do it? He certainly would not do it, thought many farmers, without pressure from representatives of a different party in Parliament. Despite the fact that there were two distinct "wings" to the Progressive movement — moderates from Manitoba and Ontario and more ideological advocates of "group government" from Alberta — and despite the lack of much organization beyond the constituency level, the Progressives were poised to make a major impact in 1921.

King began a campaign tour pattern which was to persist throughout his career as leader. Using a railway car (later called "car 100") leased from the CPR, King embarked on two lengthy trips, one through the Maritimes and one to the West. He visited important constituencies, met with local and regional leaders and candidates, and made at least one speech per day to a political meeting held in a theatre, hockey rink, or armoury. As the campaign wound into November, King began to complain about the rallies in hockey rinks. He wrote in his diary: "At 8 went to meeting in Rideau rink [in Ottawa] — a cold cheerless dismal place, spoke with hat & coat on not to good effect."[40] In general, during this campaign, however, King was self-assured and upbeat about his speeches, and enjoyed his travels. His diary contains a number of lyrical descriptions of the fall colours and splendid scenery he encountered along the way. Sometimes there was dancing at the post-speech parties, an activity the bachelor King enjoyed.[41] His confidence was buoyed by an encounter with Conservative leader Meighen at a mid-campaign stop in the Maritimes:

> Went to the train at 2, met Meighen at the station. I was shocked at his appearance & voice. He had hardly any voice left, & has a bad cough. He looks to me to be in an advanced stage of tuberculosis.... I should not be surprised to see a complete collapse any moment & I shall be surprised if he finishes out the campaign. He looks to me done.[42]

Meighen may or may not have been "done" by his brutal schedule of 250 speeches in two months,[43] but the Conservative campaign was certainly going nowhere. Lectures to the West and Quebec about the benefits of protective tariffs were falling on deaf ears. "Many Farmers are Protectionists," proclaimed one publicity leaflet directed to the West; it gives the example of the British Columbia fruit growers, whose industry would be submerged in a tide of Washington state apples if not protected.[44] "Cotton Employs 7,000 Quebec Workers" was another leaflet giving a cautionary tale of the potential dangers of free trade to labour: "In a word, support the Tariff that protects your industries, that protects your own pocket."[45]But Quebec was lost to the Conservatives because of conscription, and the West was lost because of the economic situation. The latter is summed up in a letter Meighen received shortly before the election from a party official in Manitoba:

> I do not know how close you are in touch with Western conditions at the present time but it seems to me that the election will be won or lost East of the Great Lakes. I do not think you can count on many seats West of there. Unfortunately, this Fall is the worst possible time you could have chosen for an election. The crops suffered from various drawbacks including grasshoppers in some districts, extensive drought and an unusual amount of hail; then the especially wet weather in September and October did more damage than all the other causes.... I am told the railway companies are refusing to accept oats for shipment east unless the freight is prepaid being afraid that the grain will not sell for enough to pay the freight charges.... In view of these conditions, the farmer is strongly antagonistic to the existing government and desires a change without considering the merits of your policy as compared to Mr. Crerar or Mr. King.[46]

Meighen replied, "Your letter ... bears out exactly what I have heard respecting the condition of a large number of farmers in the West."[47]

All of the Conservative campaign literature adopts a stiff, lawyer-like tone — as if it were personally written by Meighen himself (as perhaps it was). The party proposes "the carrying out of policies that are nation-wide in their application or effect and that look toward the growth and the development of the whole of Canada and the prosperity and happiness of all of its people." Then we have the "fullest development of natural resources," "efficient, expert management and operation of the entire railway system," "the inauguration of policies conceived with a view of increasing the agricultural production of Canada," and "continued thorough study by competent experts of foreign markets and the opportunities therein for the development and extension of Canadian trade," and the "energetic promotion of immigration of desirable classes of persons who wish to establish homes in Canada and become loyal Canadian citizens."[48] These elements of the party program were translated into additional pamphlets with uninspiring titles such as: *Crerar and Redistribution. Facing Both Ways*; *The Depreciation of Our Dollar in the United States*; and *Some Reasons Why the Government of the National, Liberal and Conservative Party Should be Upheld.*[49]

The 1921 contest was the first Canadian federal election that provided full suffrage for women. The partial suffrage given to women in 1917 (see Chapter 2) to replace male electors in the armed services was not only criticized for being manipulative but also led to widespread demands for the extension of this right to *all* women over 21. Both traditional parties attempted to take advantage of this development by making special appeals to women. The Conservatives pointed out that it was their government that gave women the vote while the Liberals maintained that it was their intention to do so and that several provincial governments under their control had already implemented female suffrage.[50]

The Conservative literature *A Word to the Woman Voter* warned gravely, "It may well be that the future of the entire race is to be henceforth in women's hands. If this be so, then there is one thing that the woman voter cannot escape — her responsibility." It went on to describe all sorts of wild social experiments being implemented in Russia, which were advocated by certain forces in Canada, and went on to warn that these should be avoided at all costs, since it was women's role to keep traditional society together.[51] The Liberal pamphlet, *Women and Politics*, noted that on election day,

> Every woman will, on that day, determine by her vote what Party or **set of men** [emphasis added] will administer the Government of Canada for the next five years.... Women are more concerned with the home life of the Nation than with any other interest. The real questions, therefore, for them are — How can a Political Party affect the Home — The Cost of Living?[52]

Four women stood as candidates in 1921, and one, Agnes Macphail, was elected as a Progressive in Ontario.[53] Macphail was a high-profile M.P., but few women were elected in subsequent elections: there were only two in 1935, and one in 1940, when Macphail herself was defeated by a Liberal.

The result of the 1921 federal election was a Liberal victory, but one that fell one seat short of a majority. The Meighen-led Conservative Party was deserted by much of the country, winning no seats at all in six provinces and falling to third place in the party standings.

The Progressives not only won the bulk of the seats in the West, but also elected 24 members in Ontario. The United Farmers of Ontario had formed a minority provincial government since 1919, and gave campaign support to the Progressives. Also, the Liberals in some cases did not run candidates against the Progressives in Ontario; they ran only 65 candidates in the 82 Ontario ridings, while the Progressives ran in 71 and the Conservatives in 79.[54] The absence of three-way contests in a number of Ontario ridings allowed the Progressives to directly confront the Conservatives, emphasizing not only their opposition to protective tariffs but also pointing out that the Conservatives had reneged on their 1917 promise to exempt farmers' sons from conscription. In addition, two Labour candidates were elected, including the future leader of the CCF — J.S. Woodsworth. In terms of party support, the country now had a more complex series of sectional divisions than ever before, and the old two-party system was shattered.

The Progressives, the second-largest group in Parliament (with 64 seats to the Conservatives' 50), refused the role of Official Opposition, just as they refused King's overtures to join the Liberals in a coalition and take cabinet positions.[55] They attempted to exercise leverage where they could on specific issues, but were not willing to act as a bloc. In addition, they were divided between a Manitoba-based wing led by Crerar which was mainly concerned with the tariff and an Alberta group led by Henry Wise Wood that rejected the whole nature of centrist political parties. Faced with this delicate situation, King proceeded slowly. Uncertain as to whether there might be challenges to his leadership position, and fearful of introducing measures which did not get Progressive support, King did very little on the domestic front. William Fielding, reinstalled in the Finance portfolio, felt economic conditions were too precarious to risk reducing the tariff in the 1923 budget, whereupon the Progressives voted en masse against it.[56] The 1924 budget made some changes but did not go far enough to please the Progressives. On the key question of keeping freight rates low, King faced opposition from the railways that claimed they could not make money. King delayed. But all the attention to Upper Canadian and Western issues was eroding Liberal support in the Maritimes, where a sudden stroke removed Fielding (of Nova Scotia) from politics. Old-age pension legislation was defeated in the Senate, whereupon King propounded the need for Senate reform.[57] But little was getting done.

The 1925 Election

By early 1925, King felt the time had come to improve his standing in Parliament, and judged the cards were falling his way. As he noted in his diary:

> I made a decision today ... which will shape my actions more or less from now on —viz — to go to the country this year. First there is the uncertainty of waiting to the bitter end — & the unknown and all that may then develop. Next there is the present weak position of our opposing forces, Tories and farmers alike, especially the former. Meighen's leadership is at a very low ebb. Third there is the present position of our party before the country. It is stronger than it has been since we took office. Fourth there is the fairly prosperous condition of the country and relatively settled conditions of politics, no question likely to sweep people off feet.[58]

Though the year's diary entries reveal that King became more and more committed to the idea of an October election, he began to worry that his troops were not up to the task: "I felt the Cabinet was very weak, lamentably weak in fact — really nothing to grip to. Many like barnacles rather than fighters. I felt, however, determined whatever the outcome to adhere to decision to bring on an election this fall. To wait is to be surrounded by intrigue for months, to have life made a sort of hell by almost impossible situations and to lose ground."[59]

However, the omens looked worse for the Liberals as time progressed. The Liberal provincial government in Ontario fell to the Conservatives in 1923, and in 1925, Nova Scotia and New Brunswick followed suit. All of these provincial premiers campaigned for Meighen. In the Maritimes, economic conditions were poorer than in the rest of Canada, and sentiment ran high against the King government for failing to do anything meaningful about it.[60] In Ontario, the Meighen promise of higher tariffs to help industry and create jobs began to have more resonance than it did at the beginning of the decade.

The Liberal campaign platform of 1925 attempted to make a lot of very little. Everything, according to the Liberals, was much better than before they took over: "In the short time that we have been in office ... we have reduced the public debt. We have reduced the taxation of this country. We have reduced the cost of the public service. We have reduced the cost of living.... We are able to point to a vast increase in the trade of the country ... "[61]

The Liberal campaign tried to emphasize policies designed to address the main pillars of Canadian electoral success but had little substance to offer. On the economic front, fiscal responsibility and trade expansion were emphasized. Moreover, the Conservative high-tariff position was categorically rejected. To begin to address issues related to social welfare and the disruption created by the influx of new Canadians, moderate immigration was to be pursued. And a new spirit of national unity was to be extended. Once again, King relied on his commitment to consensus and compromise. But inaction and caution had been taken to an extreme. As Beck says, "The Government could not point to a single conspicuous achievement. It had lasted for four years under difficult circumstances, but the mere act of survival would hardly win votes. It had tinkered with economic problems, but the country was just beginning to recover from the long postwar recession."[62] Meighen was scathing in his condemnation of Liberal inaction.

Though he had his moments of doubt, King expected to win the 1925 election with a majority.[63] He didn't, as the Conservatives outpolled the Liberals by a considerable margin and won 17 more seats (See Table 3.2). Although the overall Liberal vote percentage declined by less than 1 percent, their seat total was only 99 of the 245 in the House of Commons. The Progressive vote was cut severely, but they still elected 24 members. There were again Labour candidates in several provinces that also siphoned off votes, and two of these were elected in Manitoba. The Conservatives, on the other hand, increased their support almost everywhere in the country, picking up the bulk of the seats in Ontario and the Maritimes. In fact, the Conservative percentage of the Ontario vote — 57 percent — has never been equalled.

King lost his own seat and was forced to seek election the following February in a by-election in Prince Albert, Saskatchewan, there being no Ontario Liberal seat considered safe enough to ensure his victory.[64] Meighen would have had the seats to form a government but for one region — Quebec. The Quebec Liberals had found their future leader in Ernest Lapointe, later to become King's minister of justice. In 1925, Meighen was an easy target for the Liberals in Quebec. His willingness to apply conscription to the youth of Quebec during the First World War allowed them to portray him as a murderer, despite the fact that no Quebec conscripts were actually killed.[65] The Liberal Quebec campaign was merciless, portraying Meighen as the advocate of war, with his hands soaked in blood.[66] It was the Liberals' revenge for the Unionist campaign of 1917.

Things were so bad for the Tories in Quebec that the party made the decision to turn over the campaign in the province to Esioff-Léon Patenaude. Patenaude was elected to the House of Commons in 1908 as a Conservative, and joined the Borden Cabinet in 1915, but retired from politics in 1917 because he could not support conscription.[67] After a long courtship, Patenaude finally agreed to lead the Quebec campaign in 1925, but he did so under the condition that he be given independence from Meighen. As a result, Meighen never appeared in the province at all, creating a very confusing situation not conducive to electoral success. "In 1925," says "Chubby" Power, "there was not a single Meighen candidate in the province. They were all Patenaude candidates, and Patenaude, in his own words, was independent of both King and Meighen. Thus, the most reputable Conservative of that day, E.L. Patenaude, refused to take responsibility for Meighen and his sins of omission and commission."[68] The Conservatives elected only four candidates from Quebec in 1925, none of them francophone, although the Conservative share of the popular vote in the province nearly doubled.[69]

The period after the 1925 election established King's reputation as a wily politician who managed to snatch victory from the jaws of defeat. Faced with a situation where he had 17 fewer members of Parliament than the Conservatives (achieved with almost 7 percent less of the popular vote overall) King at no point considered tendering the resignation of the government, despite constant demands on the part of Meighen and much of the press.

The day after the election, he wrote, "It looks like a heavy road ahead, but the Progressives may come in with us. The times will continue to improve — fears to be allayed — and we may get thro a session in which event we will be able to carry on. I have 'faith and courage' — will take this refining in the furnace of affliction as it is meant, and seek to rise into a nobler and higher manhood through it all."[70] God and Sir Wilfrid Laurier were speaking to King, urging him to carry on. Only *he* could preserve national unity. Meighen in power would be a disaster for the country.

King's strategy was to hold on to power by persuading the Progressives to support the government, since with their votes a bare majority could be secured. To appeal to the Progressives, he made another series of promises to reduce tariffs and to reintroduce legislation providing for old-age pensions, familiar moves from the previous session of Parliament. He counted, however, on the reluctance of the Progressives to provoke another election, after their vote had plummeted to 9 percent from its high of 23 percent in 1921, and with predictions of their imminent demise in the air. King survived for six months in this situation. He continued to fend off increasingly blunt suggestions from the governor general, Lord Byng, that he resign and allow the plurality winner of the election — Meighen — to form a government. Eventually faced with imminent defeat over a scandal brewing in the Customs Department, King requested a dissolution of Parliament and a new election. The governor general denied this request, King resigned, and Byng asked Meighen to form a government. Finally, after what they saw as their 1925 election victory, the Conservatives were in power.

It is ironic that the denial of the dissolution of Parliament to King likely saved his career, and that the acceptance of power ruined Meighen's. Pickersgill remarks, "Perhaps it was only hindsight, but [King] told me one day over twenty years later that, if Byng had given him the dissolution, he believed Meighen would have won the election and his own political career would have ended."[71]

In the three days of the abortive Conservative government, King aggressively attacked them in a series of speeches, and embarrassed the Progressives by forcing them to take positions of support for the Conservatives in order to avoid an election and continue the session. Several Progressives decided they could not continue to do so, and defeated a second government within days. Once again, Arthur Meighen was able to lead a Conservative government into an election, and once again he led them to defeat.

TABLE 3.2

Results of the 1925 and 1926 Elections, by Province

		Conservative		Liberal*		Progressive		Other	
		1925	1926	1925	1926	1925	1926	1925	1926
Prince Edward Island	votes (%)	48	47	52	53	-	-	-	-
	seats (#)	2	1	2	3	-	-	-	-
Nova Scotia	votes (%)	56	54	42	44	-	-	2	3
	seats (#)	11	12	3	2	-	-	-	-
New Brunswick	votes (%)	60	54	40	46	-	-	X	1
	seats (#)	10	7	1	4	-	-	-	-
Quebec	votes (%)	34	34	59	62	-	-	7	4
	seats (#)	4	1	59	60	-	-	2	1
Ontario	votes (%)	57	54	31	39	9	4	3	3
	seats (#)	68	53	11	26	2	2	1	1
Manitoba	votes (%)	41	42	20	38	27	11	11	9
	seats (#)	7	-	1	11	7	4	2	2
Saskatchewan	votes (%)	25	28	42	57	32	16	1	-
	seats (#)	-	-	15	18	6	3	-	-
Alberta	votes (%)	32	32	28	24	32	39	9	5
	seats (#)	3	1	4	3	9	11	-	1
British Columbia	votes (%)	49	54	35	37	6	-	10	9
	seats (#)	10	12	3	1	-	-	1	1
Yukon Territory	votes (%)	59	56	41	44	-	-	-	-
	seats (#)	1	1	-	-	-	-	-	-
TOTAL CANADA	votes (%)	47	45	40	46	9	5	5	3
	seats (#)	116	91	99	128	24	20	6	6

* Liberal total in 1925 and 1926 includes one Independent Liberal; in 1926 it also includes 11 Liberal-Progressives and one Liberal-Labour.

The 1926 Election

The circumstances of the 1926 election were such that both major parties campaigned with a sense of self-righteous outrage against the other. For the Tories, the election was an opportunity to lecture the public about the perfidies of King, who "demeaned himself" by asking for a dissolution of Parliament while a motion of censure against the government was being debated. They claimed he "sought to abrogate responsible government" by so doing, and that this had never happened "in the history of Parliamentary Government."

Once the opportunity for an election had been denied, King refused to confer with Meighen to hand over power. The Conservatives stated that the governor general had acted perfectly properly in dissolving Parliament when Meighen asked him to, since King had been censured by Parliament and could not form another government.[72] As for the Progressives, "[they] have placed a stigma upon themselves that can not be eradicated. They have demonstrated their utter untrustworthiness and their unfitness to be intrusted [sic] with the affairs of the people."[73] Having established their position on the constitutional issue, the Conservatives emphasized Liberal corruption in the Customs Department during their administration. Officials in the Department were found by a Parliamentary inquiry to have been in league with smugglers bringing in goods from the United States, and the former minister, Jacques Bureau, was accused of knowing about it.[74]

King was delighted at the turn of events which granted Meighen the dissolution of Parliament that he had been denied by the governor general:

> I replied Thank you, that is fine! I came to my room and on entering proposed three cheers. I said now we have the issue in a manner that permits of no mistaking it.... Then the caucus came at 2:30 with a demand to go there and speak. I was given a great reception when I went in, but found it very difficult to speak as I would have liked. I cld only say our whole position had been vindicated, that we had a first-class issue, thanked them for their confidence in me during the years I had been the leader — urge moderation of language in the campaign ahead,

> and to focus attack on Meighen as advisor of crown of such a course, to prepare at once for battle, organize their constituencies.[75]

As can be noted here, King had the good sense to focus his attacks on Meighen rather than the governor general, and was helped in this by Meighen's willingness to accept responsibility for the course of action undertaken.[76] King was urged by a number of officials in his party to avoid extensive discussion of such an "academic" question as the Constitution, but the pages of his diary make clear that he knew his audiences were responding when he inveighed against his opponents' attempt to thwart what he asserted was the will of the people and Canadian parliamentary principles. Observers who remark on King's pedestrian and ineffective speaking style make an exception for the "unforgettable" speeches in the 1926 election campaign.[77] King had found his issue. Meighen was proposing to return Canada to the status of a colony, where the representative of the Crown dictated who was in power.

King had found another kind of issue as well. The 1926 election campaign saw a much greater emphasis on the third type of electoral issue which, along with national unity and the economy, dominated the campaigns of the twentieth century in Canada — the social security or welfare issue. King spoke frequently in this campaign of social justice. In particular, he was promising an old-age pension of 20 dollars per month for workers over 70 who could demonstrate need. During his long railway-car tours of the West and East, King found that the old-age pension issue resonated with voters, and he further persuaded himself that this measure was a mission he must fulfill. He wrote the following about his address in Yarmouth, Nova Scotia:

> There has been a great loss of life of fisher folk which brings home to one the sacrifice that industry entails. I made a feature of this in my address tonight, seeking to develop the thought of industry as social service, & the old age pension a reward in the nature of social justice, to those who give of their energy & strength, & bear the burden in the heat of the day.[78]

The pension bill, as eventually passed in 1927, required a matching contribution from the provincial governments and went into effect only when they had passed similar legislation; it took until 1936 before all provinces were participating.[79]

The Conservative vote in 1926 remained similar to that of 1925 (see Table 3.2). However, the Liberals increased their vote to 46 percent, and made seat gains particularly in Ontario and Manitoba. In both provinces, arrangements were made with the Progressives in a number of constituencies to mutually withdraw competing candidates and run unified "Liberal-Progressive" candidates. Thus, the number of three-way contests was reduced, and a unified opponent to the Conservatives presented. The distribution of the vote proved particularly important in Manitoba — the Conservatives increased their vote slightly, yet lost all 7 of their seats, including Meighen's.[80] In Ontario, the Liberals managed to increase their vote by 8 percent and win 15 more seats. Along with their continued dominance in Quebec, the centre of the country went a long way toward giving King a majority government. In the Prince Albert (Saskatchewan) constituency, King himself successfully won election in a race against a young Conservative named John Diefenbaker.

The 1930 Election

There was to be one more interlude before the consolidation of the King dynasty. In the latter years of the 1920s, the Conservative Party chose a new leader — R.B. Bennett. Bennett possessed some similarities to King. Both were lifelong bachelors and both suffered periods of intense loneliness, though apparently not depression.[81] More important, however, were the differences. Bennett was extremely wealthy, to the point where he personally financed the Conservative Party organization for his entire decade as leader. And in terms of personal style, Bennett was anything but a clone of the cautious King. He was energetic, full of bombast, bravado, and bluster, a magnetic personality on the hustings, to a degree that King considered unseemly: "I really blushed as I listened to him — such demagoguery, declamation and ranting there was nothing constructive."[82] In the election of 1930, however, the times called more for Bennett's passion than King's reserve.

Bennett was chosen leader on the second ballot of a leadership convention in 1927 (see Table 3.1). The Conservatives had been impressed with the electoral boost which appeared to be given the federal Liberals after their 1919 convention, and the Ontario Conservatives after they had selected Howard Ferguson in 1920 at a convention. Both parties had gone on to electoral victories.

Shortly after he was selected leader, Bennett embarked on an extensive tour of Quebec in order to try to reestablish the party's credentials. In contrast to Meighen, he tried to be modest and friendly, and he also took positions which he felt would be positively received in Quebec.[83] Foremost among these was a position critical of Canadian reliance on imports from the United States. Canada should stop the "drain of money and resources to the South."[84] Efforts to link Liberal policies with subservience to the United States paid dividends when, in response to the Depression, the American government raised tariffs on some Canadian exports, such as milk and dairy products. In addition, Liberal adherence to British Commonwealth preference on tariffs allowed imports of butter from New Zealand, which undercut production from local dairy farmers in Quebec and elsewhere in the country.

In preparation for the 1930 election, the two parties engaged in a curious reversal of their traditional positions on trade relations and national autonomy. In a pre-election budget, the King Liberals reduced preferential tariffs on many items from Britain, and raised them on items from the United States. As they explained in their election literature, the idea was to create "the double object of diverting large proportions of existing Canadian imports from the United States to Great Britain and of assisting the Canadian consumers to the greater advantage of the lower scale of duties under the British Empire Preference."[85]

On the face of it, this position seems dubious in its logic. Not buying American might punish them for their high tariff, but what does it do for exports? And doesn't it support the Conservative policy of protecting Canadian industry so that Canada would not need so many imports at all? Supposedly, the increase in British imports envisioned here would lead the British to buy more Canadian wheat and other Canadian products, since in 1930 Canadian exports to Britain had dramatically declined, ostensibly because of the trade imbalance in Canada's favour.[86] The Liberals subsequently portrayed Bennett and the Conservatives as not favouring the British preference, but quoting

Bennett to the effect that he stands for "Canada first" seems hardly to have put him in a bad light.[87]

In their responses to the deepening Depression, the Conservatives seized the Liberal mantle of the party of national autonomy. They gave their policies for economic recovery a nationalistic twist, as headlines in their party magazine for June 16, 1930, attest: "Bennett's First Concern is Canada," "Look to Our Own People," "Canada Will Win Through," "Consider Canadian Interests," "This is Canada!" "King Government Unfair to Canadians."[88] While these magazine segments were very short on specifics, the message was that the Liberals were still free traders at heart, and anxious to sell out the country to the United States, or even Britain. In distinction to the Liberal stand-pat approach, Bennett pledged quick action on unemployment — his pledge on June 25, 1930, being AN END TO UNEMPLOYMENT AND WORK FOR ALL. A special session of Parliament was to be called as soon as they were elected, to receive his program of work for all.[89]

The Liberal attempts to appeal to the public in the realm of growth and prosperity were not successful. As usual, King wanted to take a low-key approach, relying on their "Outstanding Record of Achievement: MACKENZIE KING GOVERNMENT BRINGS ORDER OUT OF FINANCIAL CHAOS OF CONSERVATIVE ADMINISTRATION," referring to the Meighen government of 1921.[90] This had led to unprecedented prosperity for Canada.

A subsequent pamphlet, entitled *Did You Know?*, tells us that "during the past seven years Canada has been wonderfully prosperous, more prosperous than ever before; more prosperous than any other country in the world? ... **There was a larger increase in the Total Number Employed in the Six Years between 1922 and 1928 than in the Previous Thirty-Two Years.**"[91]

Unfortunately for the Liberals, the election was being held in 1930, when many of these same people were facing unemployment once more.

An uncharacteristically careless statement in Parliament shortly before dissolution was used by the Conservatives to taunt King throughout the campaign. Facing opposition suggestions that the provinces should be given relief money to fight unemployment, and reacting to the fact that many of these provincial governments were run by Conservatives, King stated that he "wouldn't give a five-cent piece" to any Conservative government.

He realized immediately that he had made a mistake; he had meant only to denigrate the sincerity of his opponents in claiming that they had been working on unemployment relief while the federal government had not.[92] However, the Conservatives lost no opportunity to point to his insensitivity to the plight of the unemployed. In an effort to deal with the "five-cent" issue, the Liberals issued a pamphlet saying this comment was only directed at some particularly ridiculous Conservative proposals, and through "political trickery" the opposition was trying to make it a general slur against the Conservative provincial governments, including Ontario. Their strategy was then to give "the real story," whereby plenty of cash goes to the provinces, and to show that "the record stands" and tell people that they shouldn't be taken in by "a flimsy trick."[93]

Back on their heels from their defensive positions on two issue areas, growth and prosperity and sovereignty/nationalism, the Liberals proposed an extension of their pension legislation to try to salvage the social security/welfare state domain. Trumpeting that "Canada's War Pension Legislation is the Most Advanced in the World," the Liberals bragged that they were "The Soldiers' Friend" in that they brought in legislation providing for pensions for veterans over 60 (though there was a means test, with married veterans not allowed to have an income over $250 a year to get it, and the unmarried $125). Then, in 1927, they provided for a general old-age pension after age 70 of $20 a month for those making less than $365 a year.[94] Not to be outdone, the Conservatives claimed to have initiated the idea of old-age pensions under the Borden government by establishing a Royal Commission in 1919, and indicated that they had been prepared to bring in a national pension plan based on the recommendations of this commission, but that King had implemented only a pale version of it. They documented their motions in Parliament to use 65 as the pension age, to increase the amount allowed, and to add coverage for unemployment and illness.[95]

The 1930 election saw an innovation in campaign technology, which was to change campaigns forever. It was the first "electronic campaign," meaning that the new medium of radio allowed the leaders to make instant contact with national audiences rather than simply make personal contact with those attending political rallies, or an impersonal impact through the next day's newspaper reports. King was very conscious of the opportunity that radio presented, but found the speeches an ordeal:

> Tonight I made what I believe has been the greatest effort of my life. I spoke for nearly two hours over the radio … to an unseen audience from coast to coast.… I prayed very earnestly as I faced the microphone, thinking of the people of Canada as a whole. I found everything went well once I started, save only that I was far from covering all the ground I had laid out. I had to speak rapidly and I had to condense, leave out parts.[96]

Not only was Bennett's animated speaking style more interesting for radio audiences, but the colourful content of an opposition leader on the attack, promising to use the tariff to "blast Canada into the markets of the world," made a real impact. From this point on, leaders' campaign speeches would need to become shorter, crisper, more tailored to the medium on which they were delivered.

The Conservatives won a clear majority in the 1930 election, even to the extent of picking up 24 seats in Quebec.[97] King listed the factors that contributed to the Liberal loss: "Our defeat is owing primarily to lack of organization, next lack of propaganda, third delay in meeting situation arising out of importation of New Zealand butter, the extent of unemployment counted for very much, my 'five-cent speech' was a bad beginning."[98]

But, as many commentators have pointed out, and as King himself recognized, this was an election he was very lucky to lose. The Conservative program in 1930 was a recipe for defeat five years later, since providing unemployment relief, "guaranteeing" an end to unemployment, balancing the budget, and providing old-age pensions could not be done. Public disappointment was bound to result. By 1933, "the Prime Minister who had confidently guaranteed recovery … was now an object of public derision, his name used to describe shanty towns (Bennett boroughs), horse-drawn cars (Bennett buggies), abandoned farmsteads (Bennett barnyards), and a boiled grain brew (Bennett coffee)."[99]

For Bennett's part, he had appointed his brother-in-law, W.D. Herridge, Ambassador to Washington, and as the Depression continued, Herridge had become convinced that the New Deal being constructed by President Franklin Roosevelt was the way to pull the economy out of its tailspin.

Early in 1935, Herridge persuaded Bennett to put forward a series of reforms, which would be a platform for re-election, either as pieces of enacted legislation or as campaign proposals. In a series of shocking radio speeches, the arch-capitalist Bennett announced the end of laissez-faire and the advent of government controls. He "promised federal legislation to set minimum wage and maximum hours of work standards; establish an insurance plan for unemployment, sickness, and accidents; increase taxation on the idle rich; strengthen the Farm Loan Board; broaden the *Natural Products Marketing Act*, implement the Price Spreads recommendations, and amend the *Companies Act* to protect investors."[100] Though far from radical in an absolute sense, this program was a major departure for the Conservative Party, and also a surprise to Bennett's colleagues, who had not been consulted about it.

The 1935 Election

When the campaign finally came, Bennett started out with a version of the New Deal agenda, but soon reverted to more familiar Conservative themes.

> This process reached a climax at a large rally in Maple Leaf Gardens on October 9, when Bennett laid out his prescription for economic recovery — rigid government economy, a balanced budget, no repudiation on contracts, a solution to the railway debt problem, and vigorous prosecution of Communist agitators. It was a program to gladden the heart of any capitalist. Over six weeks, Bennett had marched the party from left to right, and seemingly repudiated some of his own reforms.[101]

In part, Bennett was attempting to distance himself from H.H. Stevens, a former member of his cabinet, who had broken with him over what he saw as the lack of genuine relief for those suffering from depressed economic conditions.[102] Stevens had headed the Royal Commission on Price Spreads in the pre-election years, and founded the Reconstruction Party to fight the election, on a program of putting the recommendations of that commission into effect and ending profiteering against consumers.

The Reconstruction Party was essentially a one-man show for Stevens, and it succeeded in electing only their leader in 1935. However, campaigning mostly in the eastern part of the country, and the cities of Ontario, they took enough votes from the Conservatives, several observers say, to cost them a number of seats. In Nova Scotia, the Reconstruction Party polled 13.5 percent of the vote, and by one estimate cost the Conservative Party five seats, as the Liberals ended up winning all 12 of the seats in the province.[103] In part, the Reconstruction Party did so well in Nova Scotia because neither of the other new parties campaigned there, allowing it to concentrate the protest vote.[104] However, despite its lack of elected members, the party polled almost as many votes as the CCF (which elected seven), and considerably more than Social Credit (which elected 17 by concentrating its vote in Alberta and Saskatchewan).

While Stevens' Reconstruction Party merits little discussion in the electoral history of Canada, the 1935 election saw the emergence of two enduring political parties that reshaped electoral politics for decades. The Co-operative Commonwealth Federation was founded in Regina in 1933 as an alliance of farm organizations, former Progressives, labour groups, and socialist thinkers.[105] Its founding manifesto stated:

> We aim to replace the present capitalist system, with its inherent injustice and inhumanity, by a social order from which the domination and exploitation of one class by another will be eliminated, in which economic planning will supersede unregulated private enterprise and competition, and in which genuine democratic self-government, based upon economic equality will be possible.[106]

Although the directness of the attack on capitalism was to cause problems for the party, it represented the frustrations of both farmers and labour at the inability of existing parties and elites to significantly alleviate the effects of the Depression on them. These frustrations were most strongly felt in the West, and the party's support was strongest in British Columbia, Saskatchewan, and Manitoba.

Social Credit was the federal wing of the party that had come to power in the province of Alberta earlier in 1935, displacing the United Farmers' government. The radical element in Social Credit was not a denunciation of capitalism per se, but rather a set of monetary theories which proposed to allow government to take control of the financial system.[107] In their concern for populist mechanisms of referendum, recall, and the delegate, rather than representative roles assigned to MPs, Social Credit could claim to be the genuine heir of the Alberta wing of the Progressive movement. Although they elected more members to the House of Commons in the 1935 and 1940 elections than the CCF did, this was a result of the concentration of their support in Alberta. They were the heirs of the Progressives in another sense, as well: they were less interested in acting like a conventional political party, with strong party organizations and leaders brokering their interests in Parliament, than they were in promoting their ideas. The CCF, on the other hand, relished the parliamentary life. Ultimately, Social Credit did not last as a political party and eventually met the same fate as the Progressives. The CCF, through its successor, the New Democratic Party, survives — and occasionally thrives — in the current Canadian party system.

Both the CCF and Social Credit parties campaigned primarily in the West in 1935. Their main target was the Bennett Conservative government, but to them the King Liberals were not likely to provide much of an improvement. Both of the "old line parties" were committed to riding out the Depression without disrupting existing financial and state institutions in any fundamental manner, despite Bennett's rhetorical outbursts in his radio broadcasts. A few small-scale relief programs would not cure the root problems whereby ordinary people were left destitute by the collapse of their employment prospects or their agricultural markets. An overhaul of the economic system was needed.

King met the initial announcement of the Bennett New Deal with a strategy of withholding extensive general comment and asking to see the actual legislation. When very little of it appeared, King was able to implement his preferred campaign strategy of running a low-key campaign, without dramatic promises of change and reform.[108] But by now King had positioned the Liberal Party to gain from all three issue elements of a successful Canadian election campaign.

First, the Liberals had simply to point to the dire economic situation and pledge to do their best to improve it, particularly by alleviating unemployment.

Second, there was national unity, King's favourite theme. In speech after speech, King maintained that "Bennett had almost destroyed national unity and ... only the Liberal Party could restore it.... Instead of offering magical nostrums, the Liberal Party would stress the necessity of co-operation, of working together in a common cause."[109]

Finally, King offered attention to the social security area. In a radio address a month before the election he pledged to set up

> a representative national commission to co-operate with the provinces and municipalities in the administration of unemployment relief and in an endeavour to provide work for the unemployed. It is pledged to the enactment of a constitutionally valid system of unemployment insurance and, as rapidly as the financial position of the country warrants, its expansion into a general scheme of social insurance, including health insurance as well as old-age pensions.[110]

The Liberal campaign slogan summed it all up: "It's King or Chaos."

Faced with this choice, the people opted for King. The Conservatives were reduced to 40 seats, most of them in Ontario. It would take the party two decades, and five changes in leadership, to regain power in Ottawa. The Liberals, however, did not increase their vote from that registered in 1930; in fact, the party received a slightly lower percentage. The difference was the substantial shares of the vote registered by the CCF, Reconstruction, and Social Credit parties, as well as a variety of independent candidates and those representing other smaller parties. Overall, these "third force" candidates accumulated over one-quarter of all votes cast, and the rejection of the traditional parties was much higher than that in the West.[111]

The 1940 Election

The Liberal victories in the elections of 1940 and 1945 were heavily influenced, as in 1935, by the nature of world events. Just as being calm, reasonable, and experienced in response to the Depression had stood Mackenzie King in good stead, so, too, did acting in the same manner in the early and the final stages of the Second World War. Wartime was no time, the Liberals pointed out, to be changing the captain of the ship of state. The Conservatives were not helped in this regard by the public perception that the gate to their leadership had become something of a revolving door.

After the 1935 defeat, R.B. Bennett stayed on for a time as leader, but approved few new policies, seemingly regarding the treatment of his New Deal legislation in the courts (much was ruled unconstitutional) as a personal negative judgment on him. He did not make peace with Stevens, and he did not continue to be generous with funds to support the party organization. The Conservative Party essentially marked time until 1938, when Bennett finally resigned and retired to rural England.[112]

He was succeeded as leader by Robert J. Manion, the former minister of railways and canals in the Bennett administration who had been defeated in 1935 due to, his biographer says, neglect of his constituency.[113] Though perhaps seen as a "lightweight,"[114] Manion campaigned as best he could against long odds:

> He was further handicapped by the fact that in Quebec he was identified by the French Canadians as a Liberal who had deserted Laurier to become a Conservative, and in Ontario Manion was not accepted by Protestant Orangemen because he was a Roman Catholic married to a French Canadian wife.[115]

To the convention that elected him, his Catholicism and the fact that his wife was French Canadian gave some hope that the party might make inroads in Quebec.[116] However, the fact that the same convention heard a keynote speech from Arthur Meighen advocating unswerving loyalty to Britain in time of war meant that such an appeal was impossible.

King confided to his diary a dim view of his new opponent: "Manion is making a buffoon of himself. His performance at the Walker theatre on Saturday night was that of a jackass. The Tory party are disgusted with him and are almost in despair."[117] After the election, however, King took pity on the impoverished Manion, and offered him a wartime job. King was a pallbearer at his funeral; Conservative leaders were not present.[118]

More serious than any of Manion's personal characteristics, however, were the general reputation of the Conservative Party a few short years after the Bennett government, and the inability of the party to compete with the Liberals in any of the issue areas important to electoral victory. In the "growth and prosperity" area, the economy had improved in the latter part of the 1930s, and the wartime situation in the country reduced the pressures of unemployment.

To preserve national unity, King promised that conscription would not be invoked in this war, in contrast to the First World War. The Conservatives, as might be expected, were divided over the ultimate need for conscription. In 1940, their policy was, if elected, to create a national government to conduct the war. Such a proposal, however, evoked the Union government that was constructed during the First World War, and further ensured that the Conservatives would get no support in Quebec, especially as the Tories had no counterpart to Ernest Lapointe. Moreover, it was not clear how such a government could be constructed if the other parties would not join it, and neither the CCF nor the Liberals had any intention of doing so. King drove the point home: "I can only conclude that Dr. Manion ... sees no possibility whatever of the election of a Conservative Government."[119]

The Liberals were not content with merely dismissing the national government idea — they brought out the sledgehammer. Here is the complete text of a Liberal pamphlet issued in Saskatchewan in 1940:

> ***An Affront to Canadians***
>
> Dr Manion has thrown the historic Conservative Party overboard.... Has appointed himself leader of a mythical "National Government" movement.
>
> WHO DOES HE REPRESENT?
>
> WHO ARE HIS SPONSORS?
>
> WHO ARE HIS SUPPORTERS?
>
> Is he secretly acting for railway amalgamationists? Or vested interests intent upon reviving the old Bennett policy of "National self-sufficiency"?

> There must be someone behind his costly coast-to-coast campaign for so-called "national government"
>
> BUT WHO?
>
> NEVER BEFORE HAVE THE CANADIAN ELECTORS TOLERATED AN UNSPONSORED CANDIDATE FOR THE PRIME MINISTERSHIP. WHY SHOULD THEY DO SO TODAY?
>
> Dr Manion's attempt to foist himself upon the Canadian electors under the masquerade of "national government" is an affront to the people ...
>
> To assure sound administration by known leaders — in Canada's united wartime effort.
>
> VOTE FOR THE **MACKENZIE KING CANDIDATE**[120]

The National Liberal Federation also produced a set of electoral brochures on the economic front relating to Liberal economic policies, all of which were detailed with tables and statistics about the improvement of conditions under the King administration after the 1935 victory. These had titles such as: *Liberal Methods of Diminishing the Unemployment Problem*; *Growth of Canada's External Trade Under the Encouragement of Liberal Policies*; *Improvement in Dominion Public Finance Under Liberal Management*; *Meeting Canada's Transportation Problems the Liberal Way*; and *The Canada–United States Trade Agreements: A Great Canadian Ambition Achieved by the Mackenzie King Government.*[121]

Unspectacular, and actually rather boring, this literature was designed to reinforce an image of quiet competence on the part of King and his cabinet. Finally, on the social welfare front, King was ready to move ahead with unemployment insurance, even though it had been mentioned in previous Liberal campaigns. All three bases were covered.

Against this deliberate attempt by the Liberals to run a campaign emphasizing their competence in running a wartime government, the other parties had difficulty settling on issues of emphasis. Aside from his national government proposal, Manion pointed to a variety of areas in which the Liberals were engaging in wasteful or ineffective expenditures, or were not getting proper equipment to the troops. He also offered a variety of subsidies for farmers, miners, and other groups, to create a social agenda.[122] The CCF had problems of a different sort, since their leadership was divided over whether or not to support the war. J.S. Woodsworth was a pacifist, whereas M.J. Coldwell felt the war needed to be won to create the conditions for the establishment of socialism. Conditions in 1940 were certainly not ripe for a major advance of the left-wing party.

By the time of the 1940 campaign, radio broadcasting had become the main vehicle for the leaders' appeals to the country. Whether it was an excuse or not, King used the necessity of being in Ottawa at the helm of a wartime government to avoid his usual heavy schedule of campaign visits by train to all parts of the country. There was only a short Western trip this time, to Winnipeg, Prince Albert (his constituency), and Saskatoon, with a final rally in Toronto. But in reality, the time that was saved with the truncation of travels was spent in writing and endlessly revising the texts of the radio broadcasts. Historian Jack Granatstein notes:

> [F]or his opening radio address of the campaign, scheduled for February 7th, fully seven revisions were prepared over five days, all but one by the prime minister himself. The starting point, almost invariably, was a long dictated memorandum, often little more than points to be stressed or countered and intended ordinarily for Pickersgill, who would sketch out the first draft. To flesh out the speech the prime minister's office maintained its own ready-reference file, a compendium of newspaper articles, Hansard speeches, pamphlets, and the like, all designed to bolster King's recollections of his record — and of the follies of the opposition parties.[123]

When the speeches were delivered, however, there was still the problem of making them fit the time available. King records in his diary the nerve-wracking experience of being signalled to read faster or slower depending upon the estimated end of the time period. When the signal to speed up was given, King worried that he might not finish and have the conclusion of his speech cut off, but then when he read faster he worried that he was going too fast for audience comprehension, and furthermore that he would finish too soon, creating a bad impression. The whole process tired him out.[124]

The 1940 election was another Liberal triumph, the size of which was the apex of King's career. An absolute majority of the popular vote, 51.5 percent, brought 181 of the 245 seats and substantial numbers of Liberals were elected from every province in the Dominion. The Conservatives once again only had 40 seats, with sparse representation from all provinces except Ontario. The CCF vote declined to 8.5 percent. Social Credit gave way in Alberta (temporarily as it turned out) to a slate of candidates under the leadership of W.D. Herridge, the architect of the Bennett New Deal. They elected 10 members under the banner of New Democracy. King had a mandate to run the war effort, and the country, in his methodical, consensus-seeking manner. But there was a problem on the horizon.

Conscription had been banished from the Liberal lexicon, but conscription was apparently necessary, according to the advice the government was getting from the military. In 1941, the Conservatives chose Arthur Meighen as their leader once again, and he advocated conscription. King brought Louis St. Laurent into the cabinet as his Quebec lieutenant, replacing Lapointe, and he argued against it. But pressure built, both from within his party, from the opposition, and from the provinces, and King decided on a referendum. There was discussion of its wording, but King decided that the safest course was to ask for release from the government's commitment not to implement conscription. They could then reassure Quebec that there was no imminent plan to bring in conscription. The wording was as follows:

TABLE 3.3

Results of the 1942 Conscription Plebiscite, by Province

	% voting YES
P.E.I.	82.9
Nova Scotia	77.1
New Brunswick	69.8
Quebec	27.9
Ontario	84.0
Manitoba	80.3
Saskatchewan	73.1
Alberta	71.1
British Columbia	60.4
Yukon Territory	74.4
Military vote	80.5
TOTAL CANADA	64.5

"Are you in favour of releasing the Government from any obligations arising out of any past commitments restricting the methods of raising men for military service?" King's pledge, in the famous phrase, was "conscription if necessary, but not necessarily conscription."

Many forces in Quebec organized to oppose conscription such as the *Ligue pour la défense du Canada*, led by André Laurendeau. When the vote came, large majorities in the English provinces supported it, but the Quebec vote in favour was less than 28 percent (See Table 3.3).

King felt that the negative Quebec vote helped the conscription movement, as it seemed to indicate that Quebec voters thought it meant that conscription would be brought in if it passed. King had hoped that Quebec would vote to trust the government, implying they *didn't* think it would be brought in.[125] Despite the potential for division, King managed to keep the majority of his Quebec caucus with him by delaying the implementation of conscription. However, Chubby Power, one of King's most dependable Quebec lieutenants, resigned over the issue, and was only persuaded to run in the 1945 election as the leader of a slate of "Independent Liberals."

The forces in Quebec opposed to conscription were also organized as a political party to fight the provincial and federal elections of 1945. The federal wing of the Bloc populaire was led by Maxime Raymond and espoused conservative Québécois nationalistic beliefs, drawing on the ideas of Abbé Groulx and Henri Bourassa, professing loyalty to Canada as a preference, but hinting that separatism might be a future option if conscription was imposed.

In a parody of King's rhetoric, Raymond said the Bloc was "not necessarily separatist, but separatist if necessary."[126] Their organization was never very strong, and most of its potential election campaign funds were expended fighting the 1942 referendum and publishing the party newspaper, *Le bloc*. They had to fight the federal election of 1945 only eight months after the provincial election, where they came a distant third behind the Union Nationale and the Liberals. In the 1945 federal election, the Bloc populaire got 12.8 percent of the Quebec votes (21.8 percent of the vote in constituencies where they had candidates) but only elected two members.[127] The Liberal sweep of Quebec with over half the vote was a testament to King's ability to portray himself as the prisoner of events beyond his control, not wanting conscription, and doing the minimum when he had to implement it.

The 1945 Election

The Conservatives, meanwhile, were changing their leader again, as Meighen had been defeated in a by-election by a CCF candidate (the Liberals did not run a candidate). Abandoning temporarily thoughts of appealing to Quebec, the party moved its sights westward. This time they opted for a man who was not a traditional Conservative at all, but was considered a nonpartisan figure, if anything closer to the Liberals.[128]

John Bracken had led the Progressive provincial government of Manitoba since 1922, and had enjoyed good relations with both federal Liberal and Conservative administrations without becoming committed to either.[129] Bracken was honest, plain-spoken, and full of concern for all working sectors of society. "I want to know how the low-salaried, unorganized, white-collared worker is getting along," he said. "I want to know how the unorganized labourer is faring."[130]

Even though he entered the race at the leadership convention at the last minute, and was facing four other candidates with better party credentials, Bracken was the clear choice, almost winning on the first ballot (see Table 3.1). With his election as leader, the party accepted a name change, becoming the Progressive Conservative Party of Canada. This change of name was only the latest in a long series of complicated party names, the most frequent being Liberal Conservative. In a speech justifying what today would be called "re-branding," Bracken stated that the double-barrelled name stands for "the preservation of what was best from the world of yesterday and the adoption of what is best in the world of today."[131]

The speech in general was an attack on socialism, and the position taken was that the basic choice was between two different paths to progress: one which will work and one which won't. The Progressive Conservative way was presented as a way that rewards free enterprise, and avoids "excessive taxation" of business.[132]

But the Progressive Conservative way, according to Bracken, was also one that recognized the rights contained in a "People's Charter." These rights are such principles as:

> [The] right of every man to have a job … the right of every worker to a fair day's pay for a fair day's work … the right of farmers and other primary producers to a

> fair share of the nation's income … the right of private enterprise to a fair return on the investment it risks in providing employment … the right of every child and youth to equal opportunity for health and the maximum education and training suited to its capacity that the State can afford … the right of every citizen to security against loss of income arising from accident, sickness, loss of employment, old-age or other disability … the right of future generations to a world of plenty … and the right of future generations to a world of peace.[133]

These principles of a welfare state without socialism were restated in much of the Conservative publicity in 1945. Their vagueness was the subject of a certain amount of pointed questioning; one such exchange with Blair Fraser in *Maclean's* magazine elicited the admission from Bracken that "the so-called People's Charter was but a homely statement of objectives that the State should set out deliberately to achieve for its people."[134]

And while the objectives were doubtless highly laudable, it is unclear how seriously the public took the Conservative program and strategy, considering that it came from a party that had changed leaders and direction so many times, and that had so little credibility remaining from its last period in government. The attempts to position the Conservatives as social reformers to siphon votes from the CCF stood little chance of success as long as the Liberals were doing the same thing. Bracken did not help matters by deciding not to seek a seat in Parliament from the time of his selection as party leader in 1942 until the general election of 1945. He toured the country, attempting to raise support for the party, but was criticized for not being in the House of Commons to confront the Liberals.

King's strategy in 1945 was to let the five-year time period run to its end before calling the election, thus showing that he only interrupted work when it was unavoidable. He mused in his diary about his different philosophy of leadership from those who urged him to "show leadership" by calling an election earlier: "This is a common failing with many men that leadership consists in showing that one has power rather than in getting one's end by means that lead to the agreement of all. Only the latter to my mind is a true kind of leadership."[135]

Also integral to leadership was acting as a statesman. King spent almost an entire month of the election campaign on a long train trip to San Francisco for a conference on post-war reconstruction that led to the founding of the United Nations, and then took the train back up to Vancouver and across the Prairies. When he spoke, he praised the soldiers, advocated international co-operation in the post-war world, and talked of expanding trade to ensure economic growth and prosperity.

The election of 1945 was Mackenzie King's last. Its result showed that, after a temporary retreat at the beginning of the war, the CCF and to a lesser extent Social Credit had emerged as genuine third parties in a multi-party system. When the Gallup poll at the beginning of 1945 asked "What kind of government would you like to see leading the country in the period following the war?" public opinion was quite dispersed: Liberal 28 percent, Progressive Conservative 21, CCF 17, Other 13, with 21 percent undecided.[136]

As the war approached its end, the CCF benefited, not only from the agrarian and industrial discontent which had led to its founding, but also from a public optimism about a new social and economic order that could follow the end of fighting, an outlook that fit the party's idealistic message. The argument that business was profiting from the war struck a responsive chord, particularly in the West: "The CCF insists that war profiteering must cease. Fortunes must not be made out of the blood and agony of war."[137]

In their 1945 campaign, the CCF called for a broad program of assistance to returning service personnel, together with substantial expenditures on public works, and some expansion of state control, though the party was careful not to be too specific about government takeovers or the taxation required to pay for these endeavours.[138] Unfortunately for the CCF, the 1945 federal election came only a week after the Ontario provincial election, in which the party was unable to make the breakthrough they expected. Here, the anti-capitalist message of the CCF occasioned a highly effective propaganda campaign launched against it, which equated the party with communists.[139] Ironically, the party was also attacked from the left by the real communists (called the Labour Progressive Party of Canada) which fielded 70 candidates and, it was estimated, cost the CCF a number of seats they might otherwise have won.[140] The vote for the CCF doubled, to almost 16 percent, and their seat total rose to 28, but they elected no one east of Manitoba. The anticipated breakthrough for the party in Ontario never materialized.

With the CCF, the Progressive Conservatives, Social Credit, and others claiming to speak for the common people against the big interests, King and the Liberals needed to orient their campaign appeal in this direction as well. King promised economic recovery through full employment, together with measures of social security which would support the high standard of living he envisioned for all Canadians. Their slogan, "Vote Liberal and Keep Building a New Social Order for Canada," captures the spirit of their appeal to the clientele of the moderate left.[141] "If the Liberals were re-elected, there would be farm improvement loans, more homes, better labour conditions, reduced taxation, veterans' benefits, and, above all, family allowances."[142]

Library and Archives Canada. Nicholas Morant, photographer

Mackenzie King delivering radio address, VE Day, 1945.

TABLE 3.4

Reasons for Voting in the 1945 Election

(column percentages)

	Liberal	Conservative	CCF
Good record	29%	-	-
Policies / Platform	24	33%	50%
Calibre of candidates	25	23	13
Tradition	12	11	1
Time for a change / Keep others out	3	25	28
Other / None	7	8	8

The Gallup Report, July 18, 1945.

TABLE 3.5

Second Choice Party, 1948

(column percentages)

	Conservatives	Liberals	CCF
Conservatives	3%	45%	15%
Liberals	54	4	35
CCF	10	16	3
Social Credit	5	7	11
Labour-Progressive	-	1	6
Other	2	2	2
Undecided/NA	22	25	28

The Gallup Report, November 10, 1948.

By choosing the Liberals, the voter could have all the benefits the other parties were promising, together with an experienced administrative team to carry them out. And to add to the economic and social welfare appeals, there was King's traditional emphasis on national unity, including a new national flag.[143] The key elements of the Liberal appeal in 1945 may be seen from Table 3.4, the first public release of an open-ended "reasons for vote" poll question in Canada. More than 40 percent of Liberal voters said they supported the party because of the party's record in government or because they had always been Liberal. However, the Liberal platform was also important, as was the quality of the Liberal candidates. In contrast, half of the reasons for voting CCF had to do with the party platform. Conservative voters cited similar reasons to the CCF, with somewhat more attention being given to the party's candidates. Interestingly, Gallup did not code reasons having to do with the party leadership; in the Liberal case this illustrates King's ability to fuse his own image with that of the party itself in the public mind.

Gallup polls were appearing in the press with increasing frequency as the war went on, gauging public opinion on such events as the 1942 conscription plebiscite, and the 1944 Quebec election.[144] At the same time, the Liberal Party began to use private polls for their own information.

The Liberal politician in charge of polls was Brooke Claxton, and the main advertising agency that organized them was Cockfield, Brown, using as a consultant the prominent American social psychologist and survey pioneer Hadley Cantril.[145] After rejecting an ambitious but overly costly plan to survey each riding in the country, Cockfield, Brown used the market research company Canadian Facts to survey Toronto-area ridings in 1944, revealing to the party the extent to which the CCF was making inroads into their support base.[146] Shortly after that, polling was curtailed for financial reasons, but there was speculation that the polls helped to create a more sophisticated Liberal appeal in 1945, as compared to the other parties.[147]

The 1949 Election

In 1948, the Mackenzie King era came to an end in an orderly succession by Quebec corporation lawyer, and former minister of justice and external affairs in King's governments, Louis St. Laurent.

St. Laurent possessed many of the same negotiating skills displayed by King, to the extent that Jack Pickersgill, who knew and served both of them, regarded St. Laurent as the one who was more adept at governing the country.[148]

Calm and dignified, "Uncle Louis" was the focus of the Liberal campaign in 1949; Liberal strategists finally had a leadership figure who was personally extremely popular, and they made the most of him.[149] Buttressed by a variety of supportive media, abundant financial resources, and a set of efficient regional campaign organizations under the national direction of Brooke Claxton, the Liberals held most of the cards. They were firmly situated as the "Government Party."[150]

Library and Archives Canada.

Louis St. Laurent, campaigning for the 1949 election.

The Liberals were able to run in 1949 a campaign that they were themselves quoted as saying was "issueless."[151] Rather, the government's successful record was the issue; why would voters want to turn their backs on that? This position is illustrated by an examination of *Unity, Security, Freedom: The Record of a Great Party*, a nicely produced 48-page pamphlet, with a red-and-white cover and a picture of a benign Louis St. Laurent on the title page.[152]

Unity comes first, with the claim that the Liberals have led Canada to full independence and "a proud place among nations." Only after the Liberals took over from the Conservatives in 1921 was a foreign service established, and under the party the country met "the challenge of war." Liberals supported the establishment of the United Nations and may be counted on to keep up a strong defence policy: "As in the past, Liberalism stands on guard!"

In the *economic* arena, "Liberal Policy aims to Maintain High Income; Full Employment," stable fiscal policy, "new and sounder arrangements with provincial governments," and, when it comes to trade, "Liberal Policies have Made Canada the third Trading Nation of the World." It is implied that post-war liberal trade relations, accepted by other countries, were a Liberal idea. Finally, Liberals have provided *social security* by way of old-age pensions, unemployment insurance, and family allowances.

Next on the way is health insurance, which has already begun even though this is an area of provincial jurisdiction. The rights of labour are protected, and in housing, "Building of new homes exceeds all previous records as Liberals meet challenge." There are no attacks on the opposition in the Liberal literature; in fact, the existence of an opposition is never mentioned. Rather, the St. Laurent Liberals identified themselves with the advancement of the country, with economic prosperity and tolerance of minorities, human rights, and social welfare. They were truly all things to all people.

To counter the avuncular appeal of Louis St. Laurent, the Conservatives turned to George Drew, a man who had had a successful career as premier of Ontario. Drew had led the Ontario Conservatives to three straight majority victories, the latest being in 1948, though there was a slight tarnish on his image stemming from the loss of his own seat. Conservative journalist Grattan O'Leary, a Drew supporter, describes the scene: "Arriving in Ottawa for the 1948 leadership convention, Drew came on like a conquering hero, greeted by the kind of hyperbole usually reserved by the cynics in the Press Gallery for visiting movie stars."[153]

Drew had a military background, and was sometimes referred to by the title of Colonel Drew. His main convention opponent, the prairie populist John Diefenbaker, running unsuccessfully for the second time at a Tory leadership convention, thought Drew was very much the establishment choice. Aside from his own personal appeal and his "coattails" in Ontario, Drew was seen as a potential key to the revival of Conservative fortunes in Quebec because he had made common cause with Premier Maurice Duplessis in asserting provincial rights against the federal government of Mackenzie King.[154]

But Drew's abrasive style made an unfortunate contrast with "Uncle Louis" in Quebec and elsewhere. A Gallup poll after the 1949 election asked respondents which leader "did the best job for his party"; the result was that 62 percent chose St. Laurent, with only 9 percent choosing Drew, and the rest undecided or picking the CCF leader, M.J. Coldwell (6 percent).[155]

The campaign for Drew was a continuing search for an issue that would capture the public imagination. In his initial campaign speech he announced the start of "the fight to save Confederation" by working with the provinces, rather than centralizing like the Liberals. The next day, continued appeals to curb centralization were followed by a plea to curb "creeping socialism" being brought in by the Liberals. Then, suddenly, Drew's speech shifted to the economic area, talking of problems with export trade and loss of markets: "I am sure that this problem can be solved.... When called upon to assume the responsibility of government, we will immediately take vigorous steps, not only to recapture those Canadian export markets which we held before, but also to find new markets."

On May 26, in a national radio broadcast, Drew chose to compete with the Liberals in the social security area, by proposing a national health program, old-age pensions at 65 without a means test, and family allowances for every child, as well as extended unemployment insurance. Another national radio broadcast, on June 9, was devoted to how Canadair of Montreal "passed out of Canadian control as a result of secret negotiations conducted by Mr. Howe."

And then back to general statements in the final national radio speech:

> The basic issue in this election is whether or not we are going to have a return to responsible government with the members of parliament free to exercise their rights on behalf of the people who elected them.... You will be called upon to decide whether you think that this country can develop its great human and material resources to the best advantage under the federal system or under centralized power at Ottawa.... The vote on Monday will decide whether our public affairs are to be directed by an irresponsible bureaucracy or whether we are to return to the democratic principle of government of the people, by the people themselves through their elected representatives.[156]

As Figure 3.1 shows, a poll published in mid-campaign was not encouraging for Drew. Also not encouraging for the PCs were the findings of a 1948 poll question asking about voters' second choice party (see Table 3.5). The poll showed that the Liberals were an acceptable second choice for a majority of Conservatives, and also that CCF voters, if forced to make a second choice, were much more likely to pick the Liberals than the Conservatives. The general acceptability of the Liberal Party indicated that it was placed firmly in the middle ground of Canadian politics, able to draw support from all the opposition parties if their supporters became disenchanted with them.

The 1949 election showed this Liberal dynasty in full flower. Under St. Laurent, the party elected almost three-quarters of the members of the House of Commons with almost half the popular vote, while the Conservatives were reduced once again to 41 seats and less than 30 percent of the popular vote. The CCF and Social Credit challenges were beaten back everywhere except in their strongholds in Saskatchewan and Alberta respectively. The Conservatives had counted on making gains in Quebec, since Premier Maurice Duplessis was tacitly supporting them, but these gains did not materialize. Historian John Williams writes,

> In some respects Duplessis' assistance was more of a handicap than an asset in Quebec. Although the Union Nationale had won an overwhelming victory in the

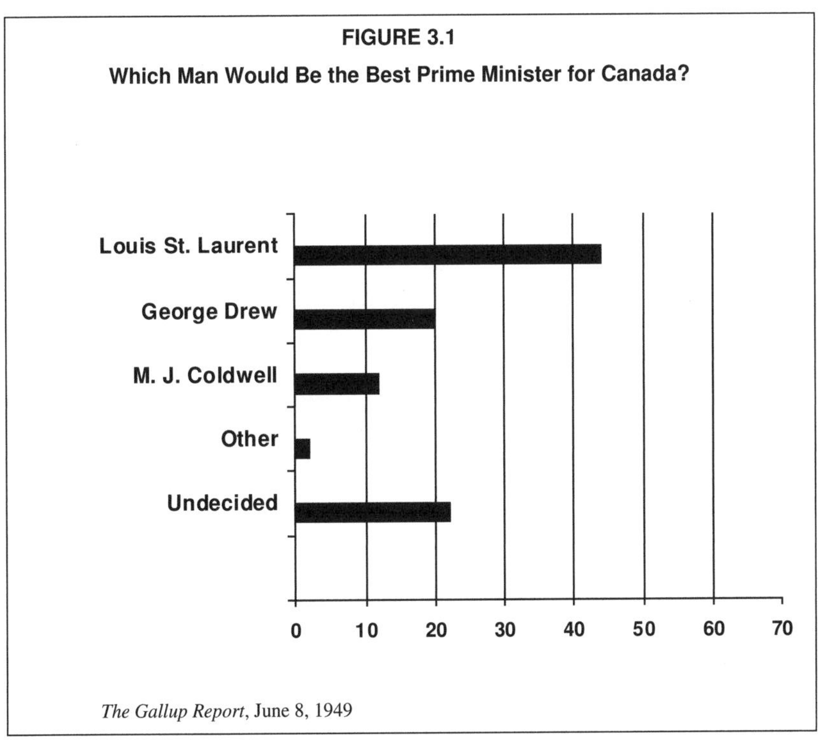
FIGURE 3.1
Which Man Would Be the Best Prime Minister for Canada?
Louis St. Laurent
George Drew
M. J. Coldwell
Other
Undecided
0
10
20
30
40
50
60
70
The Gallup Report, June 8, 1949

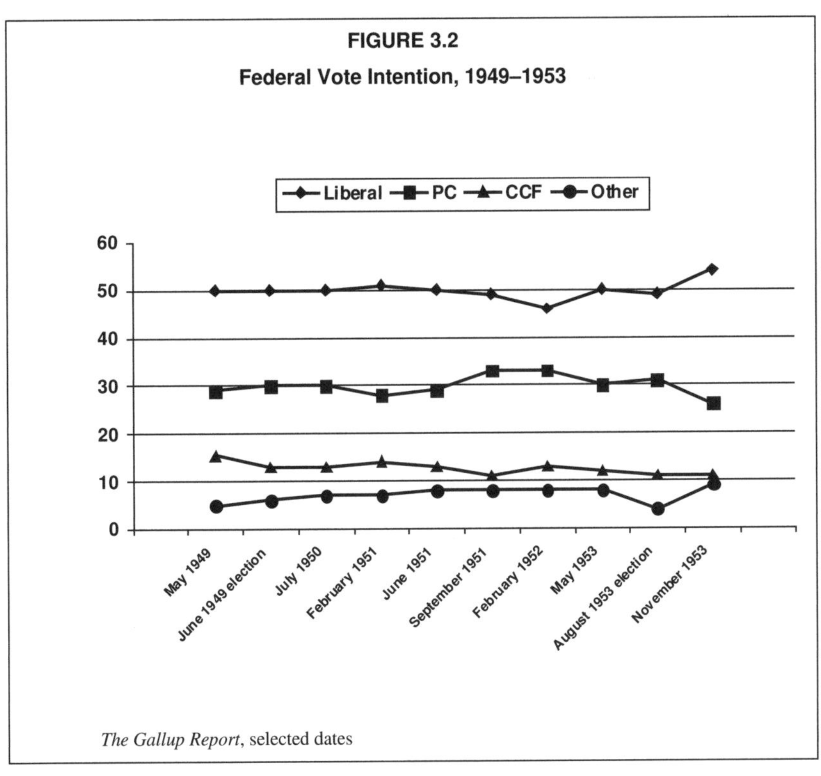
FIGURE 3.2
Federal Vote Intention, 1949–1953
Liberal
PC
CCF
Other
60
50
40
30
20
10
0
May 1949
June 1949 election
July 1950
February 1951
June 1951
September 1951
February 1952
May 1953
August 1953 election
November 1953
The Gallup Report, selected dates

TABLE 3.6

Results of the 1953 Election, by Province

		Liberal	PC	CCF	SC	Other	Liberal Net Gain/ Loss from 1949
Newfoundland	votes (%)	67	28	1	-	4	-
	seats (#)	7	-	-	-	-	+2
Prince Edward Island	votes (%)	51	48	1	-	-	-
	seats (#)	3	1	-	-	-	-
Nova Scotia	votes (%)	53	40	7	-	X	-
	seats (#)	10	1	1	-	-	-
New Brunswick	votes (%)	53	42	3	X	2	-
	seats (#)	7	3	-	-	-	-1
Quebec	votes (%)	61	29	2	-	8	-
	seats (#)	66	4	-	-	5	-2
Ontario	votes (%)	47	40	11	X	1	-
	seats (#)	51	33	1	-	-	-5
Manitoba	votes (%)	40	27	24	6	3	-
	seats (#)	8	3	3	-	-	-4
Saskatchewan	votes (%)	38	12	44	5	1	-
	seats (#)	5	1	11	-	-	-9
Alberta	votes (%)	35	15	7	41	3	-
	seats (#)	4	2	-	11	-	-1
British Columbia	votes (%)	31	14	27	26	2	-
	seats (#)	8	3	7	4	-	-3
Yukon / NWT	votes (%)	54	27	-	14	6	-
	seats (#)	2	-	-	-	-	+1
TOTAL CANADA	votes (%)	49	31	11	5	3	-
	seats (#)	171	51	23	15	5	-22

X less than 1 percent

provincial election of 1948, there had been growing dissatisfaction with Duplessis' administration because of higher taxes and generally autocratic behavior. This alliance with Duplessis hurt the Conservatives in the rest of the country as well, as Drew was called upon to defend his friendship with a man of dubious reputation outside Quebec.[157]

The 1953 Election

The 1953 federal election bore many similarities to 1949. The Liberals disdained to make promises, and once again campaigned on their record as a government, and on the personal appeal of Louis St. Laurent. The election was called for August 10 by St. Laurent, who knew the desperate state of the Progressive Conservative Party (the only Canadian federal election ever to be held in that month).

As Dalton Camp, working in the Conservative party's central office in Ottawa, remembered, "The prospect of an August election appalled [the PCs] ... the Tory vote would be secluded in summer cottages; the cities would be insufferable; campaign audiences would be small and distracted by the heat; the farmers would be tending their crops."[158]

In an effort to come up with a winning platform, Conservative Party strategists decided to promise a half-billion-dollar tax cut: "Drew Pledges Drastic Slash in Taxation. George Drew, Progressive Conservative leader, said tonight that taxes can be reduced by $500,000,000 a year by ending over-taxation and increasing efficiency in government."[159]

According to Camp, "The effect on the Tory Party and upon its candidates and workers was instant consternation. In the Liberal Party, as it reacted intuitively and almost immediately, the effect was satisfaction enhanced by incredulity."[160]

Strategically, this move prevented Tory candidates from making promises of increased spending in local areas, and was particularly unpopular in the Maritimes, since lower taxes meant lower interprovincial transfer payments and affected that area both federally and provincially.

FIGURE 3.3
The King/St. Laurent Dynasty

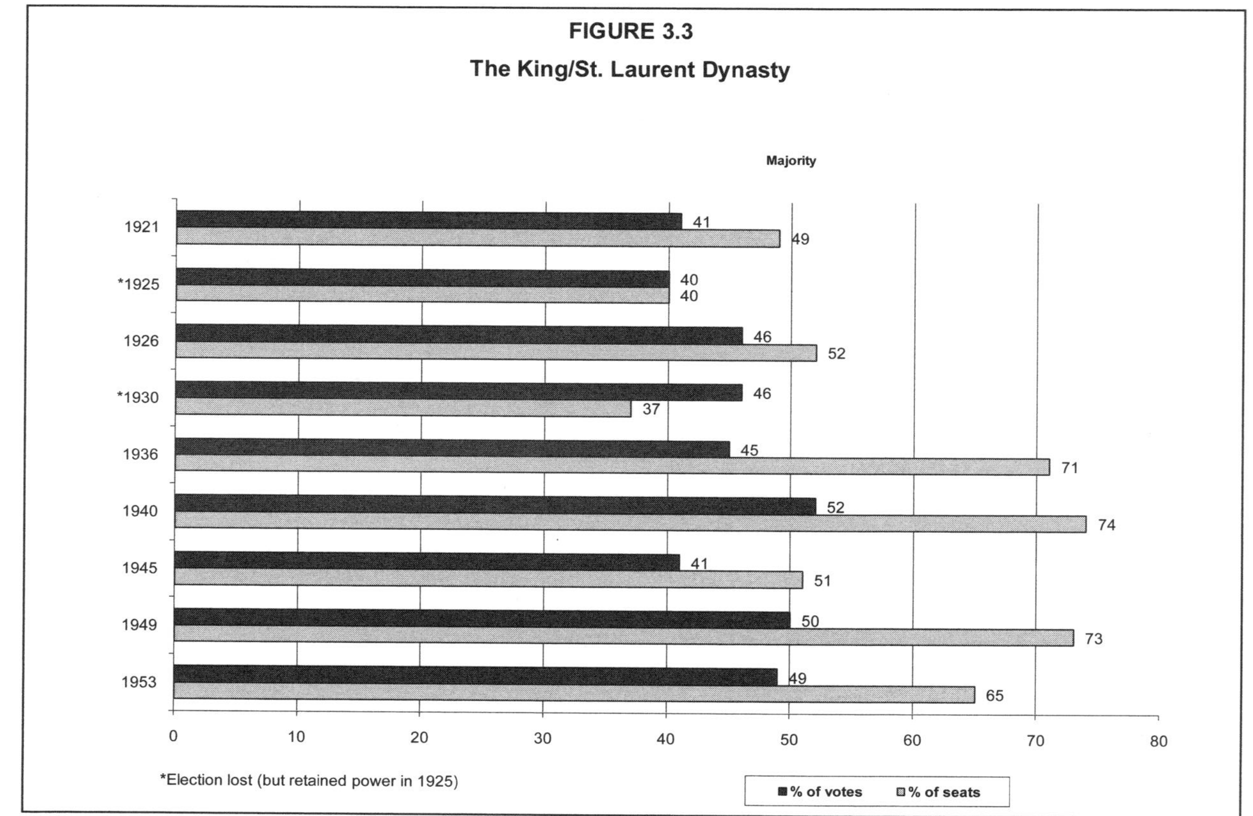

Camp went on to say, "Drew's election manifesto was intended to be a bombshell, and it was, bursting over the heads of the unsuspecting party candidates and organization."[161] As well as the tax cut, there were such proposals as an exemption for municipal councils and school boards from sales taxes, a proposed federal–provincial conference, a contributory health insurance scheme, aid to people with small incomes to buy homes, action on waste in government, the re-establishment of the supremacy of Parliament, a committee to reform the Senate, and this pledge: "We will introduce legislation to amend the Criminal Code which will make it an offence punishable by due process of law to engage in Communist or other subversive activities designed to destroy our democratic system."[162]

Drew's campaign denunciations of the "reds," however, did not seem to have any more effect than the rest of his campaign. The public was satisfied with St. Laurent (58 percent in July 1952 thought he was doing a "good job" as prime minister; even 47 percent of PC supporters thought so).[163] The Liberal Party was highly popular (see Figure 3.2). Who was to predict that four years later it would all come crashing down?

Conclusion

The Liberal dynasty that began with King and ended with St. Laurent spanned over three decades, with the interlude of Conservative control at the beginning of the Depression. It was established and maintained by two of the most successful political leaders Canada has ever had. Individually (and for a period together) they positioned the Liberal Party in the centre of the political spectrum, bending one way or the other as the times warranted.

As heirs to the party of the Laurier dynasty, they campaigned as the champions of national unity, the party which could accommodate Quebec in Canada. As the stewards of economic prosperity, they contrasted themselves with untried socialism on the one hand and deference to the demands of industry bosses on the other. And they were the ones that gradually introduced on the national scene the fundamental elements of the Canadian welfare state. Despite differences in style, the two men sought to develop consensus on acceptable solutions to common problems. Jack Pickersgill, sitting with St. Laurent during one of his periods of depression following his 1957 defeat, told the old man,

> Mackenzie King, when he saw a problem that looked almost insoluble, did nothing whatever about it until he was quite sure everybody in the country realized there was a problem. Then he found a solution that was not always first-rate but, because it was a solution, people said he was a great statesman. When you [St. Laurent] saw a problem on the horizon, you almost always found a solution before the public knew there was a problem.... And what was the verdict of the Canadian people? [It] ...was that Canada was an easy country to govern, and that anybody could govern Canada, and they decided to let anybody try.[164]

Notes

1. For a book-length treatment of King's explorations in the spirit world, see C.P. Stacey, *A Very Double Life: The Private World of Mackenzie King* (Toronto: Macmillan, 1976). Stacey, like most other King biographers, rejects suggestions that public decisions were made by King on the basis of séances. His reliance on advice from beyond was particularly evident during his period in opposition, 1930–35, but during the War Stacey entitles his chapter "The Prime Minister Swears Off."
2. Henry Ferns and Bernard Ostry, *The Age of Mackenzie King* (Toronto: Lorimer, 1976), 242.
3. H. M. Gitelman, *Legacy of the Ludlow Massacre: A Chapter in American Industrial Relations* (Philadelphia: University of Pennsylvania Press), 44–52. See also Stephen Scheinberg, "Rockefeller and King: the Capitalist and the Reformer," paper presented to the Mackenzie King Centennial Colloquium, University of Waterloo, December 16, 1974.
4. William Lyon Mackenzie King, *Industry and Humanity* (Boston: Houghton Mifflin, 1918).
5. Ferns and Ostry, *op. cit.*, 72.
6. R. MacGregor Dawson, *William Lyon Mackenzie King, a Political Biography Vol 1* (Toronto: University of Toronto Press, 1958), 251, feels it showed a concern for workers' welfare that was far from traditional liberalism. Bruce Hutchison, *The Incredible Canadian* (Toronto: Longmans, Green, 1952), calls the book "an indictment of modern industrial society possibly more penetrating than the indictment of Marx" (page 40).

7. Hutchison says, "Fortunately, nobody seemed to have grasped the meaning of *Industry and Humanity*," *op. cit.*, 45. Dawson agrees that "It seems impossible to doubt the soundness of his [Hutchison's] conclusion that when the Liberal party came to choose Laurier's successor a few months later, it obtained an unorthodox leader, and eventually a welfare state, largely because it had not troubled to find out where that leader stood or anything beyond his political suitability as a young man with a promising record and a somewhat engaging personality." Dawson, *op. cit.*, 251.
8. John C. Courtney, *Do Conventions Matter?: Choosing National Party Leaders in Canada* (Montreal: McGill-Queen's University Press, 1995), 9.
9. Dawson, *op. cit.*, 302–03.
10. . F.A. McGregor, *The Fall and Rise of Mackenzie King: 1911–1919.* (Toronto: Macmillan, 1962), 331.
11. Dawson, *op. cit.*, 305–6.
12. Dawson, *op. cit.*, 317.
13. Elizabeth Jean Ballard, "Characteristics of Canadian Prime Ministers: Ratings of Historians and Political Scientists" (M.A. thesis, Department of Psychology, University of British Columbia, 1982). Throughout this survey, the degree of commonality between the judgments of Macdonald and King is striking. Both are rated as top political operators, practical and flexible, and considered strong, effective leaders, but low in honesty and principle.
14. R.J. Manion, *Life is an Adventure* (Toronto: Ryerson Press, 1936), 289. The National Library of Canada owns the copy Manion presented to King, inscribed "To the Rt Hon Mackenzie King, with sincere and friendly personal regards." According to Manion, King resembles Borden in terms of style "yet King lacks Borden's sound logic" (290). "He has never been very popular either in the House or in the country, but he has been both very successful and very lucky, an opportunist par excellence." His oratorical problem is "prolixity speaking at far too great a length and often burying his argument in wordy detail." "Personally, he lacks many of Laurier's qualities, such as the … ability to mix with and attract his followers, nor is his sense of humour so highly developed, though he is a very kindly companion in society, and shows no ill will indeed consistently shows real friendliness to his political opponents" (290–91).
15. J. W. Pickersgill, "Mackenzie King's Political Attitudes and Public Policies: A Personal Impression," in John English and J.O. Stubbs, eds., *Mackenzie King: Widening the Debate* (Toronto: Macmillan, 1977), 16.
16. H. Blair Neatby, "Mackenzie King and the Historians," in English and Stubbs, *op. cit.*, 5.
17. Robert A. Wardhaugh, *Mackenzie King and the Prairie West* (Toronto: University of Toronto Press, 2000), 34–35.
18. *Ibid.*, 46.
19. David E. Smith, *The Regional Decline of a National Party: Liberals on the Prairies* (Toronto: University of Toronto Press, 1981).

20. H. Blair Neatby, *William Lyon Mackenzie King, 1932–1939: The Prism of Unity* (Toronto: University of Toronto Press, 1976), 5–16.
21. Diary, PAC, September 28, 1921.
22. John C. Courtney, "Prime Ministerial Character: An Examination of Mackenzie King's Political Leadership," *Canadian Journal of Political Science* (9:1, March 1976), 99.
23. Neatby, *Prism of Unity*, 15.
24. John R. Williams, *The Conservative Party of Canada, 1920–1949* (Durham, N.C., Duke University Press, 1956), 47.
25. Norman Ward, ed., *A Party Politician: The Memoirs of Chubby Power* (Toronto: Macmillan, 1966), 72.
26. Roger Graham, *Arthur Meighen, A Biography* : Volume II (Toronto: Clarke, Irwin, 1963), 11.
27. *Diary, PAC, December 6, 1921.*
28. W.L. Morton, *The Progressive Party in Canada* (Toronto: University of Toronto Press, 1950).
29. *The New National Policy (as adopted by the Organized Farmers of Canada in The Farmers' Platform)* Canadian Council of Agriculture, 1918, 12–17.
30. *Ibid.*, 16.
31. Morton, *op. cit.*, 116.
32. Morton, *op. cit.*, 104.
33. Frederick C. Engelmann and Mildred A. Schwartz, *Canadian Political Parties: Origin, character, Impact* (Scarborough, Prentice-Hall, 1975). 30–39.
34. Walter D. Young, *Democracy and Discontent*, second edition (Toronto: McGraw-Hill Ryerson, 1978). Alan Whitehorn, *Canadian Socialism: Essays on the CCF-NDP* (Toronto: Oxford University Press, 1992).
35. Roger Graham, "Through the First World War," and W.L. Morton, "The 1920s" in J.M.S. Careless and R. Craig Brown, *The Canadians 1867–1967* (Toronto: Macmillan, 1967).
36. National Liberal Committee *The Liberal Point of View* (Ottawa, 1921), 14.
37. National Liberal Committee *Liberals and Farmers* (Pamphlet #10) (Ottawa, 1921), 4.
38. *Ibid.*, 3.
39. Morton, *op. cit.*, 105.
40. *Diary, PAC, November 7, 1921.* The political meetings held in armouries were often subject to the opposite condition, becoming hot and stuffy as the evening progressed.
41. For examples, see *Diary* entries for September 27, 30, and October 1, 1921.
42. *Diary, PAC, October 14, 1921.*
43. Williams, *op. cit.*, 152.
44. *Many Farmers are Protectionists* (Ottawa: National Liberal Conservative Party Publicity Bureau, 1921) NLC, 2.
45. *Cotton Employs 7,000 Quebec Workers* (Ottawa: National Liberal Conservative Party Publicity Bureau, 1921) NLC, 4.

46. *Letter to Meighen from J. Roy Colwill, Barrister of Portage La Prairie, Manitoba*. November 3, 1921, *PAC*, Meighen papers, series 2, Vol. 25, page D14834.
47. *Meighen to Colwill, Ibid.*, D14835.
48. *Platform of the National Liberal and Conservative Party* (Ottawa: NLCP Publicity Bureau, 1921) various pages.
49. Ottawa, National Liberal Conservative Party Publicity Bureau, 1921.
50. Catherine Lyle Cleverdon, *The Woman Suffrage Movement in Canada* (Toronto: University of Toronto Press, 1950),138.
51. *A Word to the Woman Voter* (Ottawa: NLCP Publicity Bureau, 1921), 6.
52. *Women and Politics* (Ottawa: National Liberal Committee, 1921), 2.
53. Terry Crowley, *Agnes Macphail and the Politics of Equality* (Toronto: Lormier, 1990).
54. J.M. Beck, *Pendulum of Power: Canada's Federal Elections* (Toronto: Prentice-Hall, 1968), 160.
55. Morton, *Progressive Party*, *op. cit.*, 130–31.
56. Dawson, *op. cit.*, chapters 14 and 15.
57. H. Blair Neatby, *William Lyon Mackenzie King, 1924–1932 The Lonely Heights* (Toronto: University of Toronto Press, 1963), chapters 1 and 2.
58. *Diary, PAC, March 7, 1925.*
59. *Diary, PAC, August 18, 1925.*
60. J.M. Beck, *op. cit.*, 169.
61. *Progress and Achievement* (Ottawa: National Liberal Committee, 1925), 1. The quote is from a speech King gave in the House of Commons in April.
62. Beck, *op. cit.*, 164.
63. *Diary, PAC, October 29, 1925.*
64. Neatby, *op. cit.*, 112–13.
65. Lita-Rose Betcherman, *Ernest Lapointe: Mackenzie King's Great Quebec Lieutenant* (Toronto: University of Toronto Press, 2002), 90.
66. Roger Graham, *Arthur Meighen, Vol II And Fortune Fled* (Toronto: Clarke Irwin, 1963), 338–43.
67. Nelson Michaud, *L'Enigme du Sphinx: Regards sur la vie politique d'un nationaliste (1910–1926)* (Québec: Les Presses de l'Université Laval, 1998).
68. Power, *op. cit.*, 76.
69. From 18 percent in 1921 to just under 34 percent in 1925.
70. *Diary, PAC, October 29, 1925.*
71. J.W. Pickersgill, "Mackenzie King's Political Attitudes and Public Policies: A Personal Impression," in English and Stubbs, *op. cit.*, 21.
72. *The Constitutional Crisis* (Ottawa: Publicity Committee of the Liberal-Conservative Party, 1926). Note the party had dropped the "National" from the party name, but retained the "Liberal."
73. *Why We Have an Election: Story of the Last Ten Days in Parliament* (Ottawa: Liberal-Conservative Party Organization Committee, 1926), 7.
74. Neatby, *op. cit.*, 131–42.

75. *Diary, PAC, July 2, 1926.*
76. Neatby, *op. cit.*, 160.
77. Paul Martin, "King, the View from the Backbench and the Cabinet Table," in English and Stubbs, *op. cit.*, 31.
78. *Diary, August 27, 1926.*
79. Neatby, *op. cit.*, 219.
80. Beck, *op. cit.*, 185.
81. Neatby's biography of King in the 1920s is subtitled *The Lonely Heights*, while P.B. Waite's series of character sketches of Bennett is titled *The Loner* (Toronto: University of Toronto Press, 1992).
82. *Diary, June 9, 1930.*
83. T.C. Nesmith, "R.B. Bennett and the Conservative Party in Quebec, 1927–1930" (M.A. thesis, Queen's University, 1975) NLC, 112.
84. *Ibid.*, 90.
85. *Canada's Future is in Your Hands* (Ottawa: Liberal Party of Canada, 1930) NLC, 28
86. *Ibid.*, 58.
87. *Ibid.*, 63.
88. *The Canadian* (Ottawa: Confederation Publishing, 1930) compiled into the Liberal Conservative Party *Speakers" Guide*. NLC.
89. *Ibid.*
90. *Canada's Future is in Your Hands, op. cit.*, 5.
91. *Liberal Speakers Handbook* (Ottawa: Liberal Party of Canada, 1930) NLC, 24. Emphasis in original.
92. Neatby, *op. cit.*, 318.
93. *Liberal Speakers Handbook*, op. cit., 221–22.
94. *Ibid.*, 85.
95. *Liberal Conservative Speakers' Guide, op. cit.*, June 28, 1930.
96. *Diary, June 16, 1930.*
97. Ernest Lapointe, King's main Quebec lieutenant, was sent to campaign in northern Ontario and the West in 1930, reflecting Liberal over-confidence that Quebec was secure. See Betcherman, *op. cit.*, 176–78.
98. *Diary, July 29, 1930.*
99. Larry A. Glassford, "Canadian Conservatism in Crisis: A Study of the Federal Conservative Party during the R.B. Bennett Years" (Ph.D. dissertation, York University, 1985), 139.
100. *Ibid.*, 208.
101. *Ibid.*, 240–41.
102. Richard Wilbur, *H. H. Stevens* (Toronto: University of Toronto Press, 1977).
103. Carman V. Carroll, "The Influence of H.H. Stevens and the Reconstruction Party in Nova Scotia, 1934–35" (M.A. thesis, University of New Brunswick, 1972) NLC, 216.
104. *Ibid.*, 33.

105. Walter D. Young, *Anatomy of a Party* (Toronto: University of Toronto Press, 1977); Seymour Martin Lipset, *Agrarian Socialism* (Garden City, NY: Doubleday Anchor edition, 1968, originally published in 1950), Alan Whitehorn, *Canadian Socialism* (Toronto: Oxford, 1992).
106. Regina Manifesto, Appendix to Kenneth McNaught, *A Prophet in Politics: A Biography of J.S. Woodsworth* (Toronto: University of Toronto Press 1959). A former Progressive, Woodsworth was one of the founders of the CCF.
107. C.B. Macpherson, *Democracy in Alberta: Social Credit and the Party System* (Toronto: University of Toronto Press, 1953), Chapter 4.
108. Neatby, *Prism of Unity*, 94–120.
109. *Ibid.*, 115.
110. *Mr. King Replies to Mr. Bennett, September 17th, 1935.* (Ottawa: National Liberal Federation) NLC Transcript of King's radio address, p 13.
111. Janine Brodie and Jane Jenson, *Crisis, Challenge and Change* (Ottawa: Carleton University Press, second edition, 1988), 181.
112. John M. Beatty, "The Decline of the Conservative Party, 1935–1938" (M.A. thesis, Carleton University, 1971).
113. Roy H. Piovesana, *Robert J. Manion, Member of Parliament for Fort William, 1917–1935* (Thunder Bay, Thunder Bay Historical Museum Society, 1990), 65.
114. Beatty, *op. cit.*, 176.
115. John R. Williams, *The Conservative Party of Canada: 1920–1949* (Durham, NC, North Carolina University Press, 1956), 166.
116. George Perlin, *The Tory Syndrome: Leadership Politics in the Progressive Conservative Party* (Montreal: McGill-Queen's press, 1980), 47.
117. *Diary, February 27, 1940.*
118. Piovesana, *op. cit.*, 69.
119. *Canada's War Effort: How Best Promoted* (Ottawa: National Liberal Federation, 1940), 13.
120. *Manion's National Government Proposal* (Regina: Saskatchewan Liberal Association, 1940).
121. All pamphlets NLC (Ottawa: National Liberal Federation, 1940).
122. Beck, *op. cit.*, 227; Perlin, *op. cit.*, 47.
123. J.L. Granatstein, *Canada's War: The Politics of the Mackenzie King Government, 1939–1945* (Toronto: Oxford University Press, 1975), 85.
124. *Diary, February 7, 1940.*
125. Granatstein, *Canada's War*, 228.
126. Paul-André Comeau, *Le Bloc Populaire, 1942–1948* (Québec, Boréal, 1998. Originally published in 1982), 146–53.
127. *Ibid.*, 327–9.
128. John Kendle, *John Bracken: A Political Biography* (Toronto: University of Toronto Press, 1979), 183.
129. Morton, *op. cit.*, 229–31.
130. "A New National Policy" in *John Bracken Says* (Toronto: Oxford University Press, 1944), 98.

131. "Canada Must Choose" in *Ibid.*, 54.
132. "What Makes Politics Tick," Bracken Clubs of Canada, NLC, 1944.
133. "The People's Charter" in *John Bracken Says*, 4–8.
134. "What Do the Progressive Conservatives Stand For?" *Maclean's Magazine*, May 1, 1944.
135. *Diary, April 3, 1945.*
136. *Gallup Report* (Toronto: Canadian Institute of Public Opinion, February 7, 1945).
137. *C.C.F. Election Program* (Ottawa: CCF National Office, 1940) NLC.
138. Ivan Avakumovic, *Socialism in Canada: A Study of the CCF-NDP in Federal and Provincial Politics* (Toronto: McClelland & Stewart, 1978) 132.
139. Whitehorn, *op. cit.*, 197.
140. Avakumovic, *op. cit.*, 132.
141. Beck, *op. cit.*, 248.
142. Gerald L. Caplan, *The Dilemma of Canadian Socialism: The CCF in Ontario* (Toronto: McClelland & Stewart, 1973), 156.
143. Beck, *op. cit.*, 249.
144. Daniel J. Robinson, *The Measure of Democracy: Polling, Market Research, and Public Life, 1930–1945* (Toronto: University of Toronto Press, 1999), 74–76.
145. *Ibid.*, 127–49.
146 *Ibid.*, 152–53.
147. *Ibid.*, 155. Reginald Whitaker, *The Government Party: Organizing and Financing the Liberal Party of Canada, 1930–1958* (Toronto: University of Toronto Press, 1977). Chapter 6 explores the financial relationship the party had with its advertising agencies, beginning with Cockfield Brown.
148. J.W. Pickersgill, *My Years with Louis St. Laurent: a Political Memoir* (Toronto: University of Toronto Press, 1975), 328.
149. Dale Thomson, *Louis St. Laurent, Canadian* (Toronto: Macmillan, 1967), 286–272.
150. Whitaker, *The Government Party*, 204–07.
151. Beck, *op. cit.*, 264, quoting the *Halifax Chronicle-Herald*, May 12, 1949.
152. *Unity, Security, Freedom: the Record of a Great Party* (Ottawa: National Liberal Federation of Canada, May 1949) NLC.
153. Grattan O'Leary, *Recollections of People, Press and Politics* (Toronto: Macmillan, 1977), 101.
154. Perlin, *op. cit.*, 53.
155. Canadian Institute of Public Opinion, *News Release*, July 30, 1949.
156. All references and citations from Drew's speeches are from the collection in the *George Drew Papers*, PAC, Series 3B, Vol. 313.
157. John R. Williams, *The Consevative Party of Canada: 1921–1949* (Durham, NC: Duke University Press), 182.
158. Dalton Camp, *Gentlemen, Players and Politicians* (Toronto: McClelland & Stewart, 1970), 133.

159. *Montreal Gazette*, June 23, 1953.
160. Camp, *op. cit.*, p 136.
161. *Ibid.*
162. *Progressive-Conservative Speakers Handbook* (Ottawa: Progressive-Conservative Party of Canada, 1953) NLC.
163. CIPO, Release, July 1952.
164. Pickersgill, *My Years with Louis St. Laurent, op. cit.*, 328.

Selected Reading

Camp, Dalton. *Gentlemen, Players and Politicians* (Toronto: McClelland & Stewart, 1970).

Dawson, R. MacGregor. *William Lyon Mackenzie King: A Political Biography* (Toronto: University of Toronto Press, 1958).

Ferns, Henry, and Bernard Ostry. *The Age of Mackenzie King* (Toronto: Lormier, 1976).

Graham, Roger. *Arthur Meighen: A Biography* (Toronto: Clarke Irwin, 1963).

Macpherson, C.B. *Democracy in Alberta, Social Credit and the Party System* (Toronto: University of Toronto Press, 1953).

Morton, W.L. *The Progressive Party of Canada* (Toronto: University of Toronto Press, 1950).

Neatby, H. Blair. *William Lyon Mackenzie King, 1924–1932: The Lonely Heights* (Toronto: University of Toronto Press, 1963).

Pickersgill, J.W. *My Years with Louis St. Laurent: A Political Memoir* (Toronto: University of Toronto Press, 1975).

Robinson, Daniel J. *The Measure of Democracy: Polling, Market Research and Public Life, 1930–1945* (Toronto: University of Toronto Press, 1999).

Thomson, Dale. *Louis St. Laurent, Canadian* (Toronto: Macmillan, 1967).

Whitehorn, Alan. *Canadian Socialism: Essays on the CCF-NDP* (Toronto: Oxford University Press, 1992).

Williams, John R. *The Conservative Party of Canada, 1920–1949* (Durham, NC: Duke University Press, 1956).

Young, Walter D. *Anatomy of a Party* (Toronto: University of Toronto Press, 1977.

CHAPTER 4

THE DIEFENBAKER INTERLUDE

If prosperity and tranquility were critical keys to the enduring popularity of a government, the St. Laurent Liberals should have been easily re-elected in 1957. The prime minister enjoyed an approval rating of 65 percent, according to a Gallup poll published in July 1956.[1] The economy appeared to be robust for much of the period and the Liberal government continued to report a budget surplus. But the King/St. Laurent dynasty had run its course and had not rejuvenated itself. The total dominance of the economic, national unity, and social welfare elements of the issue agenda, which sustained them in power and had enabled them to win elections since 1935, had slipped away. Lester Pearson — who would become Liberal leader after the 1957 election — talked of the malaise that beset the Liberal Party:

> We were coming to the end of our career as a Liberal Party in power. We had been the government for over twenty years; people were getting tired of us, which was inevitable and natural.... We were vulnerable to any pressure against us; we were more likely to be hurt by our mistakes than if we had made them ten or fifteen years earlier.[2]

At the same time, the Conservatives were invigorated by the election of a new leader.

John Diefenbaker as Party Leader

In late 1956, the Conservative leader, George Drew, fell seriously ill, and potential successors began to line up. Among them was John Diefenbaker. Described by Historian J.L. Granatstein as a "lonely Westerner and an advocate of increased social welfare," Diefenbaker's relations with party leaders from 1942 to 1956 were often cool, and he had little support within his own parliamentary caucus, despite the fact that he had sought the leadership twice before.[3]

He had, however, acquired a Canada-wide reputation for consistently and publicly defending civil rights and minority groups, and developed a vision of "one Canada" which departed from some of the previous assumptions of the basic nature of Canadian society. According to Diefenbaker, "there should be no German-Canadians, no Jewish — or French-Canadians, only Canadians, pure and simple."[4]

Despite the fact that his notion of "unhyphenated" Canadianism ran counter to the historical and constitutional identification of Canada as a

Library and Archives Canada. Duncan Cameron, photographer.

John Diefenbaker, campaigning in Edmonton, 1965 election.

nation of two founding peoples — French and English — Diefenbaker never departed from this vision during his entire political career. And, at least initially, his pan-Canadian vision appeared to capture the nation's imagination.

In a number of important respects, John Diefenbaker was unique in his quest for the leadership of the Progressive Conservative Party. Between 1927 and 1993, a majority of its leaders (five of nine) had not been members of Parliament when they were selected, and two-thirds had no national ministerial experience at the time they were chosen by convention. Diefenbaker, on the other hand, was an experienced parliamentarian who had sought the leadership on two previous occasions (1942 and 1948), finishing second to Drew in 1948 (see Chapter 3).

At the convention held on December 12–14, 1956, Diefenbaker threw his hat into the leadership ring once again and was successful on the first ballot (see Table 4.1).

John Diefenbaker was the most controversial of the three leadership candidates. He was not trusted by the Toronto and Montreal financial circles on which the party had traditionally depended for its funding. According to a 1969 interview, outgoing leader George Drew recalled how he reacted to the selection of Diefenbaker as leader: "The party's finished. It won't be more than three months before Diefenbaker has lost control. He gets his eye on one thing, and he concentrates on it, and he gets up and makes a speech on it. Then he goes away for two weeks to recover. The party needs people around to pick up the pieces afterwards."[5]

TABLE 4.1

Party Leadership Conventions, 1956–1961

DATE	PARTY	LOCATION	WINNER	# CANDIDATES*	# BALLOTS	RUNNER-UP**
1956 12 12	PC	Ottawa	John Diefenbaker	3	1	Donald Fleming
1958 01 14	Liberal	Ottawa	Lester Pearson	3	1	Paul Martin
1961 07 31	NDP	Ottawa	T.C. Douglas	2	1	Hazen Argue

* On first ballot

** On final ballot

Despite these criticisms, there is no question that Diefenbaker had his admirers,[6] even among his opponents for the leadership. Donald Fleming considered him a "front-rank" parliamentary debater and Davie Fulton described him in the following way:

> He was a brilliant performer in the House of Commons, a terrific debater, a man who attracted a following not only because of his personal qualities but because of his public personality. The way he shone just made him a very attractive man. A man of generous instincts, a man who befriended me, guided me, whose door was always open to somebody seeking advice.[7]

It remained to be seen whether Diefenbaker's evangelical style of oratory, combined with the tactics of a criminal lawyer, could counteract the personal popularity of Louis St. Laurent and M.J. Coldwell of the CCF.

The Liberals were actually pleased that Diefenbaker had won the leadership because he was far from popular in Conservative circles in Ontario, practically unknown in the Atlantic provinces, and unacceptable to Quebec Conservatives. Many at the time saw Diefenbaker as being anti-Quebec and, while the reality of this is unclear, he often left the impression that he neither understood nor appreciated the province and its aspirations.[8] As a fervent civil libertarian, Diefenbaker had been highly critical of several of Quebec premier Maurice Duplessis' policies, including the infamous Padlock Law.[9]

There were also some concerns that Diefenbaker was too old, in poor health, and too difficult to get along with. Given all of these obstacles, how was it that John Diefenbaker was able to end the Liberal dynasty?

First, Diefenbaker assembled one of the savviest campaign teams yet seen in Canadian federal politics. And second, the campaign put together by this group was highly effective in persuading disgruntled Liberals, new voters, and undecided voters to try something new. Once it began, momentum carried the Diefenbaker campaign along, taking full advantage of Liberal vulnerabilities. As will be noted later in this chapter, Diefenbaker has been described as the first "television era" leader. In a sense, the so-called modern era in Canadian party politics began with him.

The Liberal Collapse

The Liberals were so confident of victory in 1957 that they went into the election without filling 16 existing vacancies in the Senate. After 22 consecutive years in power, a sense of complacency within the Liberal Party that the Conservatives could never recapture Ottawa again was pervasive. Liberal government was characterized by a managerial style, and the party seemed unable or reluctant to recognize the changing nature of the country's population base. Where previously Canadians of only French or English extraction had predominated, now other ethnic groups — eastern and southern Europeans, for example — were becoming increasingly important in the electorate. Party organization had also been neglected during the St. Laurent years, and relations with the press were frequently poor, as the governing party saw little need for improvement of its organization or image. Finally, in Parliament itself, there occurred several political disputes and incidents that damaged the Liberals' democratic credentials.

Much had changed at the provincial level, as well. During the party's long tenure in Ottawa, there had been a significant swing away from the Liberals at the provincial government level. In 1935, when the Liberals had taken over the federal government, all provincial governments, with the exception of Alberta, were Liberal. Only Newfoundland, Prince Edward Island, and Manitoba remained under Liberal control by early 1957. This was important because the essential organizational and administrative help that a provincial party in power can lend to its federal allies was no longer available to the Liberals, and federal campaign organizations were virtually non-existent in Manitoba and Saskatchewan.[10] The Liberal Party had become organizationally moribund throughout the West, and the Liberals had failed to stay in close touch with their prairie constituents. The overwhelming majorities captured by the Liberals during the King/St. Laurent era did not necessarily reflect a deeply felt partisan commitment. Rather, many voters felt they simply had nowhere else to go or that the Liberals were a safe choice.[11]

Associated with this pattern was a widely held belief that had been successfully cultivated by the Liberals that they were the *only* party capable of governing the country.

The Liberals' fall from power cannot be explained solely by the renaissance of the Progressive Conservatives under their new populist leader, although there is little doubt that Diefenbaker and his advisers ran a strategically successful campaign. Initially, the Conservatives had such limited support in some important regions of the country that the party at first appeared to be heading toward another humiliating defeat. In March 1957, Gallup reported that the Liberals had the support of 48 percent of the electorate compared to 31 percent for the Conservatives — almost exactly the same figures as in the 1953 election (see Figure 4.1).

The collapse of the Liberal dynasty had a variety of causes, ranging from the lack of leadership shown by an aging leader, the absence of a clear successor from within the Liberal caucus, and a series of missteps on policy issues, including immigration, the Trans-Canada Pipeline, the Suez crisis, and farm subsidies that had angered particular constituencies across the country. None of these issues by itself galvanized widespread disillusionment and opposition, but, in a cumulative sense, all worked to plant questions and doubts in the minds of Canadian voters that the Liberals were the only party that could govern the country.

Another important factor was the retirement of several key cabinet ministers shortly after the 1953 election, which left a vacuum of leadership at the top. Included among these ministers were Brooke Claxton (Defence), Douglas Abbott (Finance), and Lionel Chevrier (Transport). All had been long-serving members of Parliament and cabinet ministers in both the King and St. Laurent governments. All were in their mid-50s when other opportunities lured them away from political life. Douglas Abbott received an appointment to the Supreme Court in 1954, Lionel Chevrier was named president of the St. Lawrence Seaway Authority, and Brooke Claxton went to a prestigious position in the private sector as Canadian vice president of the Metropolitan Insurance Company. According to J.W. Pickersgill, "there was no question that Abbott was the favourite to succeed St. Laurent as the leader of the Liberal Party both in Parliament and in the country."[12]

These changes had serious effects on the character and reputation of the St. Laurent cabinet. Historian Robert Bothwell noted that "at a blow, half of the cabinet's middle generation, men with ten years in the ministry, were wiped out, including the most acceptable choice for the next leader."[13]

Prior to the 1957 election, other cabinet changes were made that attempted to address some criticisms about representation and leadership. The Toronto area — at long last — was given its first cabinet representative in the St. Laurent administration, when 33-year-old

Paul Hellyer was promoted from his post as parliamentary assistant to associate minister of national defence. But the talent pool was thinner than in the past, since many backbenchers had decided not to spend their lives waiting for a cabinet post. Liberal arrogance, poor recruitment practices, and the absence of new ideas all contributed to the Liberal defeat. Writing in 1953, even C.D. Howe acknowledged that the government and its leader had stayed too long:

> I had an understanding with our leader that we would both retire after a year or two in office and give the new leader time to get organized. Unfortunately, our leader changed his mind about retiring, which was a mistake for him and for the party. The plain fact is that the Liberal dynasty had run out of ideas.[14]

Over and above the malaise within the Liberal Party itself, there were some disquieting signs that the economy, one of the pillars of electoral success in Canada, was weakening. Among these were indications that investment intentions for 1957 would be lower than in previous years, as well as a significant increase in unemployment over the previous year. In June 1954, an estimated 221,000 Canadians were unemployed compared to 115,000 in 1953.[15] In addition, the collapse of world prices for wheat resulted in more than a 50 percent drop in the net incomes of prairie farmers between 1953 and 1955. The Liberals were blamed for the plight of prairie farmers in the midst of general prosperity across the country. In the pre-election budget, the finance minister, who was managing a budget surplus, was cautious in handing out benefits. Although a $10 per month increase in old-age pensions had been predicted, only a six-dollar increase was proposed, earning the minister the unfortunate nickname "Six-buck Harris."

The government's mastery of the national unity area was affected by its contentious policy on immigration. The Liberals had long followed a British preference and selective system of immigration. Pickersgill — the minister of immigration in the St. Laurent Cabinet — defended this policy by saying that the selective system of immigration was based not upon race or creed, but on a "preference for immigrants we considered most likely to adapt themselves to Canadian society."[16] Between the end of November 1956 and the end of February 1957, an estimated 15,000 Hungarians came to Canada in the wake of the 1956 uprising in that country. The government defended its actions by claiming that this was the only practical and humane position to be taken in the face of the Hungarian tragedy. But the Conservatives raised the possibility that the country's traditional ethnic balance could be upset. And, behind closed doors, a whispering campaign had begun in which St. Laurent was accused of encouraging Hungarian immigration because the refugees were predominantly Catholic.[17] In addition to their weakening hold on the economic and national unity areas generally, the Liberals faced two specific policy crises which contributed to their collapse.

The Pipeline Debate

When the idea of a natural gas pipeline from Alberta to Montreal was first advanced in the early 1950s, there was little thought that it would precipitate the most serious parliamentary upheaval since the conscription crisis in 1944. The proposed trans-Canada pipeline was greater in cost and magnitude than the St. Lawrence Seaway and, with the passage of time, some analysts have compared it to the original transcontinental railway in terms of its importance to economic expansion and development. The controversy over the pipeline,[18] however, was not primarily about its scope, proposed ownership, and organization, but rather the way that the government spirited the enacting legislation through Parliament. Even a minister in St. Laurent's cabinet agreed that errors were made in the debate that surrounded the pipeline discussions. According to Pickersgill, "the fundamental mistake of the St. Laurent government in 1956 was to commit itself to the support of the construction of the longest pipeline in the world without a campaign explaining to the public both the difficulties and the advantages of this great national undertaking."[19] Many of the technicalities of the pipeline construction were far too complex for public discussion. What voters did understand, however, was that the government of the day was curtailing debate in the House of Commons in an aggressive and somewhat undemocratic manner. It was the government's image that was most deeply affected by the pipeline affair.

By means of a merger of existing firms, a new company called TransCanada PipeLines was created; however, the new company was not able to raise enough capital from private sources to build the entire line across Canada. Although the government wanted the pipeline to further Canadian economic development, it also understood that unless Canada moved reasonably quickly to make Canadian natural gas available to states in the Midwest and the Pacific Northwest, pipelines from Texas would be built into the area and this market would be denied to Canadian producers.

The government was conflicted. It wanted an American market to make Canadian pipelines economically viable, with construction entirely within Canada as a secondary objective. But it was caught in a dilemma — to give too much financial aid to a private company with predominantly foreign interests was undesirable and politically inexpedient, but to allow the project to fail for want of financial support was also not in the national interest or that of the government.[20] John Diefenbaker engaged the issue when "he invited his listeners to contemplate the government's 'touching solicitude' for American big business and for a company which 'would take for itself the profitable end of the project and pile the unprofitable on the backs of the Canadian taxpayers.' Such surrender of our natural resources to the Americans would make Canada 'a virtual economic 49th state.'"[21] This nationalistic tone would later become a common theme of the Diefenbaker-led Conservatives, and helped the party in the election neutralize any Liberal credit they might have expected for creating a national pipeline.

By the beginning of May, all hope of private financing was exhausted and the government faced the alternatives of indefinite postponement of the pipeline or financial rescue of the project by the public treasury. The news that cabinet was considering the loan leaked out, and the opposition harassed the government daily with embarrassing questions in Parliament. The decision was finally made and announced by C.D. Howe in Parliament on May 8 that the government had decided to loan up to 90 percent of the cost of constructing the western part of the line in order to make a 1956 start possible. The money was to come from a Crown corporation established for this purpose and was to be repaid by March 31, 1957, or else the government would take over the pipeline. It was this rather complex arrangement that was embodied in the Northern Ontario Pipeline Crown Corporation Bill, the bill over which such acrimonious debate took place. The resolution preceding the presentation of this bill came before the House on May 10, 1956. The Conservatives and CCF had made it clear that they intended to use whatever delaying and obstructionist tactics were available to prevent the construction of the pipeline by TransCanada. The pipeline debate lasted from May 14 to June 5, 1956, when St. Laurent moved for closure.[22] Public opinion on both the pipeline and the use of closure was sharply divided, as seen in Table 4.2.

TABLE 4.2

Public Opinion on the Trans Canada Pipeline and the Pipeline Debate, 1956

A. **Pipeline Funding**

Private Canadian Investors	33
Partly government, partly private funding	13
Built, financed, administered by government	21
Other	1
Don't Know/ No Answer/Not heard of pipeline	33

The Gallup Report, March 1956. Question read (those who had heard of pipeline): ***Which of these ways of financing do you think should be followed: Pipeline built and run by private Canadian investors; Pipeline built partly by the Government and partly by private investors from Canada and the U.S.; Pipeline built, financed and administered by the Government.***

B. **Use of Closure**

Justified	36
Not justified	38
No Opinion / not heard of closure	27

The Gallup Report, July 1956. Question read (those who had heard of use of closure): ***Do you feel that, just from what you have heard, that the Government was justified, or not justified, in using closure?***

When asked, nearly a third of Canadians polled believed that the pipeline should be built and run by Canadian investors. Just over 20 percent thought it should be built, financed, and run by the government. A lower number opted for a mixed option, and a third of the public had never heard of the pipeline issue (see Table 4.2A). While many people knew little about the technical details of pipeline financing, there is no mistaking a general desire that the transmission line be controlled by Canadians. On the issue of closure, Canadians were equally divided between those who felt the use of closure was justified and those who held the opposite view (see Table 4.2B). More time was spent debating issues of procedure than the bill itself. The bill was carried through all stages — resolution, second reading, committee, and third reading — under closure. This had never occurred before in Canadian parliamentary history, and the parliamentary debate was filled with insults coming from both sides of the House.[23] The bill went on to the Senate, passed quickly without acrimony in that House, and received Royal Assent on June 7, 1956, the day the option on the steel pipe would have expired.

Parliamentary experts have long debated whether closure was necessary in order to secure passage of the pipeline bill. Given that it had never been introduced before the debates began, it was an unusual choice of procedure. Denis Smith has argued that its use was all about the ego of C.D. Howe, who "was determined to defy the opposition and revenge a parliamentary humiliation of the previous year — all in the service of his national vision."[24] As evident in the polling figures described earlier, there was no public consensus on the pipeline issue. What was clear was that the Conservatives and the CCF had succeeded in transforming the debate from a discussion of the need for a super pipeline project into a battle over parliamentary rights. St. Laurent tried to downplay this 'spin' on the pipeline debate when he referred to the debate as having been "nearly as long as the pipeline itself, and quite as full of another kind of natural gas,"[25] but damage had clearly been done to the image of the Liberals as competent governmental managers. And seeds of doubt had been planted in many people's minds by John Diefenbaker that the Liberals really had Canadian interests at heart.

The Suez Crisis

The 10 years when Lester Pearson served as secretary of state for external affairs are often thought of as a "golden decade" for Canadian foreign policy. While Britain, France, Germany, and Japan had been devastated by the Second World War, Canada's economy was strengthened by the war effort, and it began to emerge as a significant world power. Although King had insisted on maintaining prime ministerial control of foreign policy, St. Laurent had great respect for Pearson and gave him free rein in most areas.

While foreign policy rarely creates serious divisions among Canadians, the Suez crisis in 1956 aroused deeply felt emotions and was politically divisive. The origins of the crisis were confusing and complex. There had been an uneasy truce in the Middle East since 1949 when the state of Israel was created. During the next six years, both Israel and the Arab countries conducted raids and reprisals. The United States, Canada, France, and other NATO countries had supplied Israel with weapons, while the Soviet Union had agreed to supply Egypt with arms. To many observers, there was growing concern that a conflict between Egypt and Israel might escalate into a world war between East and West.[26]

Egyptian president Nasser sought financial support from the United States and Britain to construct the Aswan Dam, and those negotiations were completed in July 1956. However, just a few days later, the U.S. secretary of state, John Foster Dulles, withdrew American support for the project. This reversal was largely driven by concerns relating to the growth in friendly relations between Egypt and the Soviet Union, as well as Egypt's recognition of Communist China. On July 26, President Nasser announced that the Egyptian government had nationalized the Suez Canal, thereby threatening British and French financial interests in the canal. The matter went to the United Nations, but Israeli forces moved into Egypt toward the Suez Canal. Britain and France gave Egypt an ultimatum — both the Egyptians and Israelis must cease fire and withdraw from the canal. If they did not, Britain and France would move in and occupy key points in order to keep shipping traffic moving. Egypt rejected this ultimatum.

Britain, France, and the United States then mounted a series of retaliations against Egyptian monetary interests, and the situation escalated. Canadian public opinion was sharply divided about what position should be taken against Egypt, but fewer than a quarter of Canadians surveyed by Gallup in September 1956 were prepared to risk a war (see Table 4.3).

TABLE 4.3

Public Opinion Regarding Action to Be Taken if Egypt Refuses Plan for Control of Suez

Risk war	23
Allow Egypt control	36
Qualified opinion	13
Don't know / no opinion / Not heard of Suez dispute	28

The Gallup Report, September 1956. Question read (for those who had heard of Suez dispute): ***If Egypt refuses all plans for international control of the Suez, do you think we should risk a war over it, or allow Egypt to control the canal?***

The prospects for war escalated, however, when, on October 29, the Israelis invaded Egypt and moved toward the canal. Two days later, British and French bombers began attacking certain points in the canal zone, precipitating the greatest international crisis since the Korean War. The Canadian government was conflicted by these actions, in part because of the implied presumption that Canada would automatically support Britain's action. The prime minister had not been advised of the Anglo-French ultimatum to Egypt, and Canada had received no prior warning of British intentions. Moreover, given that Britain and France had launched an attack while the Security Council of the United Nations was in the process of examining the dispute, there was grave concern that the legitimacy of the United Nations would be undermined. In his memoirs, Pearson makes it clear that he thought the Anglo-French course of action was not justifiable and that other factors were involved. Pearson also claims that France and England unilaterally decided that the use of force was the only solution and appeared to have little desire to find a peaceful resolution to the crisis:

> Throughout the crisis we had tried to persuade the British against the use of force. But the small group who planned the invasion were not to be persuaded, not by the United States, which they felt had badly let them down, and evidently not by Canada. In fact, we were

> told by a British official that their bitterness towards us was as great as that towards the Americans, because we had negotiated a wheat sale to Egypt in October. This, the British leaders regarded, in their almost irrational isolation, as a "stab in the back."[27]

Pearson first raised the idea of an international police force at a cabinet meeting on November 1, and Prime Minister St. Laurent urged him to go to New York. Upon arriving in New York, Pearson discovered that there were 21 speakers on the list ahead of him. The UN was debating an American proposal that called for a ceasefire and a withdrawal of all invading forces. Pearson concluded that the American resolution was inadequate because it did not contain a provision for supervising or enforcing the ceasefire. It was also apparent that Britain and France would not support the proposal. Pearson and some of his colleagues canvassed the views of a number of delegates, and by midnight that day it became clear that a resolution for a UN peacekeeping force would be well supported. Early the next morning, the U.S. resolution was voted on and Pearson, on Canada's behalf, abstained but asked for the floor in order to explain the abstention, as was allowed by the UN's rules of procedures. Before retiring that night, Pearson talked with UN Secretary General Dag Hammarskjold, whose support was essential if the idea of a peacekeeping force was to get off the ground. Pearson flew back to Ottawa to brief the prime minister and returned to New York for the November 3 meeting of the General Assembly. That day, Pearson learned that the United States, Egypt, Britain, and France would support the resolution. Pearson rose and introduced the Canadian resolution: "The General Assembly … requests, as a matter of priority, the secretary general to submit to it within 48 hours a plan for the setting up, with the consent of the nations concerned, of an emergency international United Nations force to secure and supervise the cessation of hostilities."[28]

The resolution was passed 57 to 0 with 19 nations abstaining. This was the diplomatic triumph of Lester Pearson's career, and on December 11, 1957, Pearson received the Nobel Peace Prize for his efforts during the Suez Crisis.

This international achievement might be thought to have bolstered the appeal of the Liberal government, but there was some political controversy back home. Conservatives generally supported the British position, but many Liberals viewed the British attack as an act of aggression contrary to the United Nations Charter. The emotions of many Canadians were aroused by the Conservatives' open appeal to their traditional British loyalties. There was also dissension within the Liberal Party itself as several ministers were concerned about such an open disagreement with the United Kingdom at a time of severe international tensions.[29]

The three major political events described here all took place in 1956 within a tightly compressed period of time, as the St. Laurent government was nearing the end of its second mandate. The acrimonious pipeline debate was concluded in June, and the Suez crisis came to a resolution in November. The next month, John Diefenbaker was chosen as the new leader of the Progressive Conservative Party. As the new year, 1957, dawned, attention quickly began to turn to the probability of a spring election — an election for which the Liberal Party would prove to be woefully unprepared. At the age of 76, still a popular and respected figure, St. Laurent would be fighting his third election as prime minister. Few could foresee that the weak and fragmented opposition parties posed any real threat to the Liberal dynasty. Peter C. Newman colourfully describes the prevailing psychology on the eve of the 1957 election campaign:

> The coterie of Liberal armchair strategists, gently rumbling in the palmy reaches of Ottawa's Rideau Club, smugly reminded each other of the hoary epithet that the Conservative Party's problems were, as always, insurmountable, its policies insufferable, and its prospects invisible. After twenty-two fat years, they could not know how wrong they were.[30]

The 1957 Campaign

There were three key figures in the 1957 Conservative campaign team. Diefenbaker's chief policy adviser during the election campaign was Merril W. Menzies, an economist who had done his doctoral dissertation on Canadian wheat policy. Prior to joining the campaign, he had undertaken an intensive study of national economic policies and problems for the Conservative Party as a researcher. For all intents and purposes, Menzies became Diefenbaker's idea man, creating the phrases and slogans that the party leader needed in order to convey his passionate vision to the country. By casting Diefenbaker as a new nation-builder, Menzies tried to inspire comparisons to John A. Macdonald.

Also on the campaign team were Allister Grosart and Dalton Camp, two of the most competent public relations experts in Canada. Grosart, who assumed the post of campaign manager and national director just prior to the election call, was, according to both admirers and detractors, brilliant and manipulative. As a political image maker, he was clearly a man ahead of his time, inviting comparisons to later practitioners of the craft, like Keith Davey and Allan Gregg. In *Renegade in Power*, Peter C. Newman notes that "the expression 'Grosart tactics' became either a sneer or a compliment, depending on the political persuasion of the speaker."[31] Camp, a Toronto advertising executive, directed the campaign in the Atlantic provinces, and would go on to become a stalwart of many subsequent Conservative campaigns.

Although Grosart evoked mixed reactions both from within his own party and from outside, he had absolute authority in the operation of the party machine. One of Grosart's key roles was to advise Diefenbaker on his approach to television. Television was used extensively in the 1957 election for the first time in Canada. Realizing that the new medium was going to be important in the campaign, the Liberals engaged a television expert, converted a garage attached to headquarters into a studio, and set up a closed-circuit television workshop. The premises were used to give "illustrated" talks on the new medium, to which Liberal members of Parliament were invited.[32] Despite having this facility, only one Liberal minister availed himself of the opportunity to perfect his television technique.

Because the Liberals were largely banking on St. Laurent's popularity in their campaign, it was critical that he adapt to the new medium of communication. This proved to be a major problem, according to Pickersgill:

> Right from the start I realized the Liberal campaign was unexciting. This was the first federal election with television coverage, and St. Laurent did not like the medium. I watched his opening broadcast on television at a friend's house. He delivered an indifferent text without animation and when the broadcast ended my friend

> said it had been a poor show and reflected how far out of touch with the people the government was.[33]

Other observers came to the same conclusion about the prime minister's television appearances as being the weakest aspect of his campaign. Although he had quickly adapted to radio on first entering public life, St. Laurent took an immediate dislike to television. He considered paraphernalia such as teleprompters and makeup as theatrical devices designed to deceive the public. On the three occasions that he made television broadcasts during the 1957 campaign, he read the text with scarcely a glance at the camera, and he looked older than usual.[34] While Diefenbaker's television manner was rather restless, exhibiting numerous personal mannerisms, it did not seem to detract from the effectiveness of his speeches. There is little question that he appeared more relaxed than the prime minister, and that his television broadcasts seemed as convincing to his viewers as his personal appearances were at meetings. M.J. Coldwell's biographer, Walter Stewart, agrees that Diefenbaker's 1957 campaign style was effective, and that television played a key role:

> This was Canada's first television election, and the camera loved Diefenbaker, with his broad gestures, rumbling voice and flawless timing. It was not a Conservative campaign but a Diefenbaker jubilee, and very few minutes of the free-time broadcasts allotted to the party were meted out to lesser lights; it was Diefenbaker who led the charge, from start to finish.[35]

The indifference of both the press and the public to the lacklustre Liberal campaign was countered by a growing interest in the Diefenbaker campaign. At long last, there was something exciting to write about, and many of them pictured the Progressive Conservative leader as David fighting Goliath against great odds. Worried about the situation, the Liberal campaign team began to turn to more negative strategies. But Liberal attacks on the new Conservative leader quickly backfired. As political scientist John Meisel observed, it would probably have been more effective "to have spoken well of Mr. Diefenbaker, but to have portrayed him as the prisoner of the Old Tory party."[36]

Another factor that contributed to the Conservative victory in 1957 was the poor health of the CCF leader, M.J. Coldwell. He had suffered a heart attack in February of 1957 and was not his usual self on the campaign hustings. Potential CCF voters may have considered that the party was even less likely to form a government with an ailing leader, and handed their votes to Diefenbaker — a harbinger of the type of "strategic voting" seen in more recent Canadian federal elections. In a plurality electoral system such as Canada's and with a multi-party system, many voters feel compelled to vote "strategically" — not necessarily for their first choice of candidate but for one who appears more competitive.

Conservative strategists believed that the key to success in 1957 was to attract disaffected Liberals, new voters, and undecided voters. The Conservatives calculated that their base of popular support was around 30 percent, sometimes even a little lower. In order to gain the necessary parliamentary representation to form a government, they had to appeal to the "uncommitted" voter and to individuals unhappy with their own parties. In order to attract these voters, it was deemed necessary to develop a distinction between Diefenbaker and his party in the minds of voters. Grosart decided to sell his movement not as the Conservative Party (which Canadians had been rejecting with regularity since 1935) but as a dynamic new political force under the leadership of a vital and fresh personality. Everything in the 1957 campaign was directed toward promoting this image, including its main slogan, "It's time for a Diefenbaker Government," which was frequently (but mistakenly) attributed to Dalton Camp.

According to Camp:

> I knew it was right. It was positive. It echoed what we took to be the greatest common denominator of the campaign — the belief that the Liberals had been in office too long, that it was time for a change. But "time for a change" begged a question — change to what? The answer ought not to be "change to the Conservatives," which invoked partisan loyalties and repelled Liberal sentiments. Better a soft answer: change to a Diefenbaker Government. Diefenbaker was obviously a better word than Conservative: it had no history; it was non-Wasp, more acceptable to Liberals.[37]

The party strategists believed that there were many people who wanted to vote against the Liberals, who liked Diefenbaker, but who would have preferred to overlook the fact that they were voting Conservative. By emphasizing the "Diefenbaker Party," it became possible for many to vote Conservative without feeling that they were doing so.

Diefenbaker was also the beneficiary of several well-oiled provincial Conservative election machines. In the Maritimes, provincial politics were dominated by the Conservatives, and even in Newfoundland, where a federal Liberal victory was taken for granted, Premier Smallwood was at best lukewarm about the federal government. Even in Quebec, which had long proven to be such a political wasteland for the Conservatives that they had elected only 21 members in the entire period since 1935, there was hope. This time the provincial Union Nationale government concentrated its opposition on several Liberal members who had campaigned actively against the Duplessis government in 1956.

Liberal organizers underestimated one significant factor, the feeling of animosity harboured by the Union Nationale leader against the only man capable of challenging his power. The by-elections of 1955 had demonstrated that his organization could counteract St. Laurent's personal influence without his even appearing in public; he decided to teach the prime minister a lesson by knocking out a few of the Liberal candidates.[38]

However, the most important provincial ally Diefenbaker had was Ontario's Conservative premier, Leslie Frost. While he had been only moderately supportive of Diefenbaker's predecessor, George Drew (who was a former Ontario premier), Frost supported Diefenbaker at election rallies all over the province in 1957, including the inaugural rally at Massey Hall in Toronto. This gave the Conservative campaign an aura of political legitimacy in Ontario. Although a number of Diefenbaker's ideas appealed to Frost, it was his promise for a more equitable division of tax revenues between the two levels of government that convinced him to throw his support and electoral machine squarely behind the new Conservative leader.[39]

While the PC campaign was gaining ground, the Liberal one was falling apart, despite spending an unprecedented four million dollars — nearly three times as much as the Conservatives. Rather than appealing to voters directly, St. Laurent appeared more than ever to be the chairman of an executive committee, exercising only a general supervision over his colleagues' activities. The Liberal campaign created the general impression that it was a competent but unspectacular government and that administrative considerations took priority over political ones. Increasingly the crowds were small at Liberal events. As the campaign progressed, St. Laurent abandoned more and more his prepared texts, and chatted amiably with his audiences. His speeches became largely anecdotal, interspersed with comments on newspaper articles or the benefits of Canadian democracy. The leader's dull performance and an unsympathetic media reinforced the perception that the party had become stale and bankrupt of ideas.

In contrast, Diefenbaker's meetings were increasingly well attended and his appeal was almost entirely an emotional one, focusing on Canadian nationalism and his love for the country. His campaign deftly mixed humour and righteous indignation with carefully calculated appeals to self-interest. One of the most significant aspects of the Diefenbaker campaign was that he spoke to constituencies outside of the traditional Conservative enclaves. He made direct campaign appeals to ethnic minorities and farm and low-income groups that had never been Conservative supporters. In outlining the legislative program that a Diefenbaker government would pursue, he offered intrinsic benefits to

FIGURE 4.1

Federal Vote Intention, 1953–1959

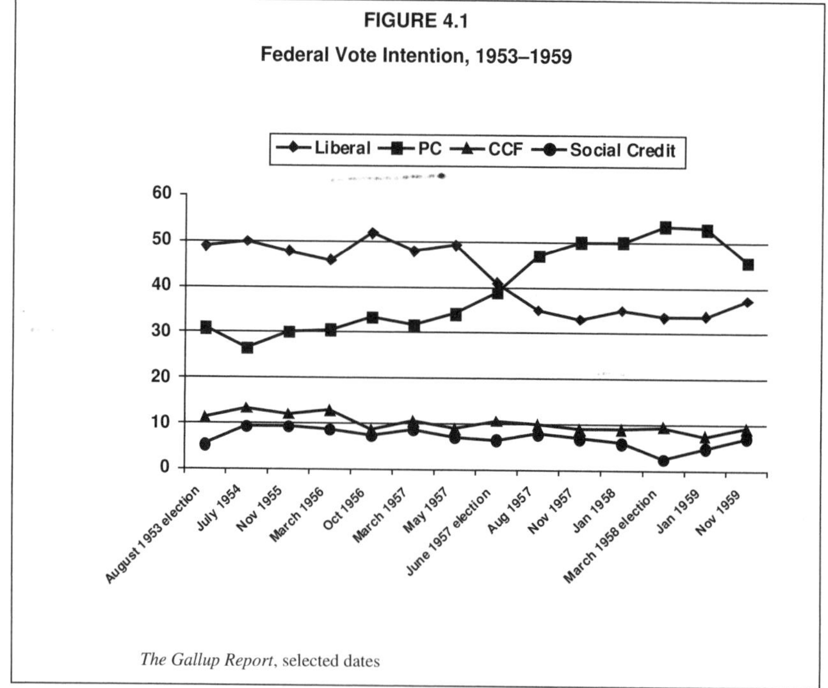

The Gallup Report, selected dates

these segments of society, such as increased old-age pensions, expanded welfare benefits, and subsidized wheat sales. Diefenbaker's campaign stressed a social program that was more welfare-oriented than that put forward by the Liberals, a marked departure from past Conservative campaigns. In doing this, he attempted to distance the party from its traditional image as a party that represented mainly the financial interests of St. James and Bay streets, and to better position his party around a winning configuration of issues, particularly those in the national unity and social welfare areas.

TABLE 4.4

Most Important Problem Facing Canada, 1954

	Percent (multiple responses) *
Economic Issues	
Unemployment	33
Cost of Living	4
Markets	7
Labour	4
Need of Industry	1
Social Issues	
War	10
Population	5
Communism	5
Housing	3
Youth	2
Government	2
Other Issues	
St. Lawrence Seaway	2
Personal faults	1
Traffic	1
Miscellaneous other	4

* *The Gallup Report*, July 1954.

TABLE 4.5

Results of the 1957 and 1958 Federal Election, by Province

		Liberal		PC		CCF		Social Credit		Other	
		1957	1958	1957	1958	1957	1958	1957	1958	1957	1958
Newfoundland	votes (%)	62	54	29	45	X	X	-	-	-	X
	seats (#)	5	5	2	2	-	-	-	-	-	-
Prince Edward Island	votes (%)	47	38	52	62	1	X	-	-	-	-
	seats (#)	-	-	4	4	-	-	-	-	-	-
Nova Scotia	votes (%)	45	38	50	57	4	5	X	-	X	-
	seats (#)	2	-	10	12	-	-	-	-	-	-
New Brunswick	votes (%)	48	43	49	54	1	2	1	1	1	-
	seats (#)	5	3	5	7	-	-	-	-	-	-
Quebec	votes (%)	58	46	31	50	2	2	X	1	9	2
	seats (#)	62	25	9	50	-	-	-	-	4	-
Ontario	votes (%)	37	33	49	56	12	11	2	X	X	X
	seats (#)	21	15	61	67	3	3	-	-	-	-

Manitoba	votes (%)	26	22	36	57	24	20	13	2	1	X
	seats (#)	1	-	8	14	5	-	-	-	-	-
Saskatchewan	votes (%)	24	20	18	51	36	28	11	X	X	2
	seats (#)	4	-	3	16	10	1	-	-	-	-
Alberta	votes (%)	28	14	18	60	6	4	38	22	X	X
	seats (#)	1	-	3	17	-	-	13	-	-	-
British Columbia	votes (%)	21	16	32	49	22	25	24	10	X	X
	seats (#)	2	-	7	18	7	4	6	-	-	-
Yukon / NWT	votes (%)	59	50	41	49	-	-	-	-	-	1
	seats (#)	2	1	-	1	-	-	-	-	-	-
TOTAL CANADA	votes (%)	41	34	39	54	11	10	7	3	3	1
	seats (#)	105	49	112	208	25	8	19	-	4	-

X less than 1 percent

Figure 4.1 displays responses to the standard Gallup vote intention question over an extended period following the August 1953 federal election. The Gallup data for the period show that support for the PC Party rose sharply in May 1957, and was generally on an uptrend. At this same time, there was also a sharp increase in the undecided category to more than 20 percent of all voters. The Liberals nevertheless remained in the lead in all of the pre-election polling. In the post-mortems that followed the 1957 election, Gallup claimed that one of the reasons that it underestimated the number of Conservative votes was a pronounced last-minute increase in Conservative support, suggesting a strong late-campaign effect.[40] Of course, it was also true that the Liberals won a narrow plurality of the popular vote, while the Conservatives won the larger number of seats. The PCs increased their support in all parts of the country. They did particularly well in Ontario and Atlantic Canada, somewhat less well in the West due to the strength of the CCF and Social Credit, and relatively poorly in Quebec, where they managed to capture only 8 of the 75 seats. Overall, there was an increase in the Conservative vote in every province, ranging from a high of +18.4 percent in British Columbia to a low of +1.7 percent in Quebec.

The election result shocked everyone, including the people closest to Diefenbaker. Dalton Camp speaks of this surprise in the following statement: "None of us ever thought of the possibility of minority government — a Diefenbaker minority government."[41] The Liberals not only lost the election, but a number of cabinet ministers; nine in total went down to defeat, including Howe, Harris, and Hellyer. The political forecasters had all been wrong. John Diefenbaker, who at times seemed alone in believing that he could win, had been right, with 112 Conservatives elected, 105 Liberals, and 48 from among the third parties. Many people believed that the explanation for the Conservative victory was the leader himself. His populist, anti-elitist rhetoric and his "One Nation" campaign theme resonated with many voters in English Canada. Others, however, credited Gordon Churchill's strategy of concentrating the party's focus and campaign spending on Ontario, Atlantic Canada, and the West, and not expending scarce resources on Quebec, where few electoral returns could be expected.

After the election, much credit for the Conservative victory was given to Ontario premier Leslie Frost, although Conservative support increased proportionately more in other provinces and regions than in

Ontario. But in Ontario, the 8 percent increase in the Conservatives' share of the vote yielded a dramatic increase in the number of seats — from 33 to 61. Turnout was also a factor. When turnout in the 1957 election is compared with that in 1953, it becomes apparent that the Prairies experienced the greatest resurgence in political interest. The turnout in this region increased by more than 10 percentage points. History would show that the resurgence of the Conservatives in the West was not just a short-lived shift, but one that would remain for the rest of the century and into the twenty-first. There was also a substantial increase in the support of farmers, as well as a significant shift away from the Conservatives' image as a British party to a multi-ethnic party. Diefenbaker's key legacy would be that he established a new and broader electoral base for the Conservative Party. Prior to the 1957 election, the party had won only 14 percent of Prairie seats in the five previous elections.[42] Not only did the Prairies become the new electoral base of the Conservative Party, it would become an electoral wasteland for the federal Liberals. But this development needed to await 1958 for its full flowering — in 1957 the Social Credit Party outpolled the PCs in Alberta, and the CCF did so in Saskatchewan (see Table 4.5).

Although the Liberals polled more votes than the Conservatives nationwide, nearly half their voting strength was in Quebec; 62 of the 105 Liberal members came from that province. The three-quarters of a million votes which they polled in Ontario were not used to best effect because of three- and four-cornered contests in single-member constituencies that took place in that province. When the traditional sources of Liberal support were diminished, as they were in 1957, the seeds of the drastic reversal of a year later were sown.[43]

The Diefenbaker Government

Shortly after his election victory, Diefenbaker attended the Commonwealth Prime Ministers' Conference in London. He was greeted with great fanfare — from a main headline in the *Daily Mail* that described him as "the new Strong Man of the Commonwealth" to Winston Churchill's statement that the 1957 Canadian election was "the most important event since the end of the war."[44] For 37 of his first 60 days in office, Diefenbaker traversed the country to acquaint the people with the new government. From officiating at the Calgary Stampede to addressing the Canadian Bar Association to receiving an honorary doctorate at Dartmouth College, he maintained a high public profile and a pace of vigorous activity.

Canadians also appeared to be impressed with the new Conservative cabinet that quickly dealt with implementing programs that had been promised in the election. Pay increases were approved for some federal employees, special assistance was given to the doom-ridden collieries at Springhill, Nova Scotia, and $150 million was allocated through the Central Mortgage and Housing Corporation for loans on low-cost homes. A grain-selling mission to the United Kingdom and continental Europe was dispatched. All of these measures were accomplished between July 11 and September 16.

Over the summer and into the autumn, the Gallup poll showed growing Conservative support across the country (see Figure 4.1). When Parliament was finally convened in October, Diefenbaker escorted Queen Elizabeth II to the inaugural ceremonies. This was the first time that the British monarch had ever been present for the opening of a Canadian Parliament and the visuals of the opening ceremonies gave the image of a prime minister in charge. In comparison to the Liberals, with St. Laurent remaining as the interim leader, the Tory performance looked impressive. They mounted a long and detailed legislative agenda. Old-age pensions were raised, western farmers were given cash payments for their crops, married women were included in the *Unemployment Insurance Act*, and improvements were made to old-age assistance, blind persons, disabled persons, and war veterans programs. In short, there appeared to be a little something for everyone. By the time the House adjourned for the Christmas recess, there was a widespread belief among Canadians that the Diefenbaker-led Conservatives had delivered what they had promised. Alvin Hamilton made the following statement of the 1957 government:

> I think, objectively, if you put a measuring scale of brand new legislation brought in and took all of the governments of Canada since 1867, there is only one period that would challenge the 1957 government and that would be the period from 1932 to 1935 under Bennett. There was a tremendous rush of brand new legislation then.[45]

The Liberals were nevertheless convinced that a leadership convention would restore their political fortunes. With his newly minted Nobel Prize in the background, there was little doubt that Lester Pearson would be chosen as leader. Even so, little was done to create a lively media event, and the convention was generally perceived as a dull affair. Pearson may have been the party's best hope, but his political experience was lacking.

On January 20, 1958, the newly elected Liberal leader was mulling over the wording of a supply motion that, if supported by all the opposition parties, could have led to the defeat of the government in the House. Pearson knew that the Liberals, as well as the other opposition parties, were tired, demoralized, and debt-ridden. However, at the urging of Pickersgill, St. Laurent, and Howe, Pearson agreed to put forward a motion that, in effect, would ask the Diefenbaker administration to resign and allow the Liberals to resume office. In support of his motion, Pearson stated, "I would be prepared, if called upon, to form a government to tackle immediately the formidable problem of ending the Tory pause and getting this country back on the Liberal highway of progress from which we have been temporarily diverted."[46]

What the motion was proposing was that a defeated and discredited party that was clearly slipping further in popularity wanted to be brought back to power without an election. As Denis Smith so aptly states, "Was

Library and Archives Canada. Bill Cadzow, photographer.

Lester B. Pearson speaking at 1968 Liberal convention, Ottawa.

there a more perfect demonstration of Liberal arrogance?"[47] In hindsight, Pearson himself describes this event by saying, "I have never regretted anything in my political career so much as my proposal that day.... I had made a spectacle of myself by coolly inviting the government to turn over their seals of office to those of us who had, a few months before, been rejected by the electorate."[48]

Reacting immediately, Diefenbaker accused the Liberals of concealing facts and numbers that showed that the economy was slipping. He produced a document called *The Canadian Economic Outlook*,[49] which had predicted higher levels of unemployment several months prior to the election. For almost two hours, Diefenbaker attacked the Liberals, whose only defence was that Diefenbaker was quoting from a confidential document offering advice to a previous government. Sensing his opportunity, Diefenbaker became convinced that he should go to the polls again shortly, particularly after a huge turnout at a Conservative event in Winnipeg one week later. Among the attendees was Mrs. Isabella Mary Gainsford, the granddaughter of Sir John A. Macdonald, who later told a friend, "He's got the punch."[50] On Saturday February 1, Diefenbaker recommended to Governor General Vincent Massey that Parliament be dissolved and a general election be called.

The 1958 Campaign

Building on the style and rhetoric that had been so successful in the 1957 contest, Diefenbaker opened his second campaign with references to his "Vision":

> This is the vision, One Canada. One Canada, where Canadians will have preserved to them the control of their own economic and political destiny. Sir John A. Macdonald saw Canada from East to West: he opened the West. I see a new Canada — a Canada of the North.... This is the vision![51]
>
> Canadians, realize your opportunities! This is the message I give you, my fellow Canadians. Not one of defeatism. Jobs! Jobs for hundreds of thousands of

> Canadians. A new Vision! A new hope! A new soul for Canada! We're going to call a national convention on conservation to map a national conservation policy to extend the principles of farm rehabilitation to all Canada, to maintain a continuing study of soils and land use, and a possible second Trans-Canada Highway route.[52]

There was little question that the "vision" struck a chord with many Canadians. It combined an expansion of economic opportunity with nationalism, reinforcing the party's appeal on those two key issue areas. When polled in 1956, nearly 45 percent of the public had expressed a preference to have the Liberal Party in power in the event that hard times were to come again. In the heat of the 1958 election campaign, only 25 percent responded in the same way, suggesting that nearly one-third of the electorate had experienced a change in opinion.[53] Diefenbaker's popularity was on the rise, with a majority of those sampled by Gallup indicating approval of his performance within three months of his assumption of the office of prime minister (see Figure 4.2). Lester Pearson, in contrast, had yet to establish himself as an effective alternative to the charismatic Conservative leader. Heading into the election, Gallup found that Diefenbaker enjoyed a margin of nearly two to one over Pearson as "the best man for the job" (see Figure 4.3). Economic issues also worked in favour of the Conservatives. By 1958, the rising level of unemployment had become the dominant issue facing the country (see Figure 4.4).[54] Diefenbaker's vision of a new powerhouse North full of job opportunities took advantage of that concern.

The Liberals had few areas they could count on, despite their dynastic status. Even support in Quebec was no longer assured, since the party was no longer led by a "native son" but by an English Canadian. Pearson was not only a unilingual Anglophone but also favoured a team approach to campaigning and was relatively shy about making grand leadership statements like those of his opponent. In addition, amidst concerns about American encroachment in the vital area of culture, Quebec nationalists were attracted to some of Diefenbaker's comments during the campaign about the dangers of American economic domination. Among French Canadians, particularly those in the lower economic and occupational strata, and even among trade union members, the Conservatives appealed convincingly for the first time in a generation.[55]

While Premier Duplessis had played a modest role for the Conservatives in the 1957 Quebec campaign, he was much more influential in 1958, particularly in constituencies along the south shore of the St. Lawrence River. Duplessis may have been retaliating for some actions of the federal Liberals in favouring his opponents in the previous provincial election, but in any case he saw the opportunity of sending a message to Ottawa about who really ran Quebec. According to Pierre Sévigny, who was to join the Diefenbaker Cabinet, Duplessis said, in 1958, "we are going to go all out for the Conservatives," committing the powerful provincial Union Nationale machine to the federal campaign.[56]

There were other factors at work in the 1958 election. The number of voters increased by nearly 700,000 over 1957, reflecting both natural population and immigration increases and higher overall turnout (79 percent versus 74 percent in 1957). The media interest in both the election and the Diefenbaker persona, along with the strong campaign waged by the Conservatives emphasizing the need for a majority government, captured the voters' attention. A steady flow of campaign contributions brought the Conservative campaign fund to $2.5 million — double the amount they had raised in 1957. Grosart was able to distribute $6,000 to each constituency in the country.[57]

FIGURE 4.2

Approval Ratings for Prime Minister Diefenbaker, 1957 and 1958

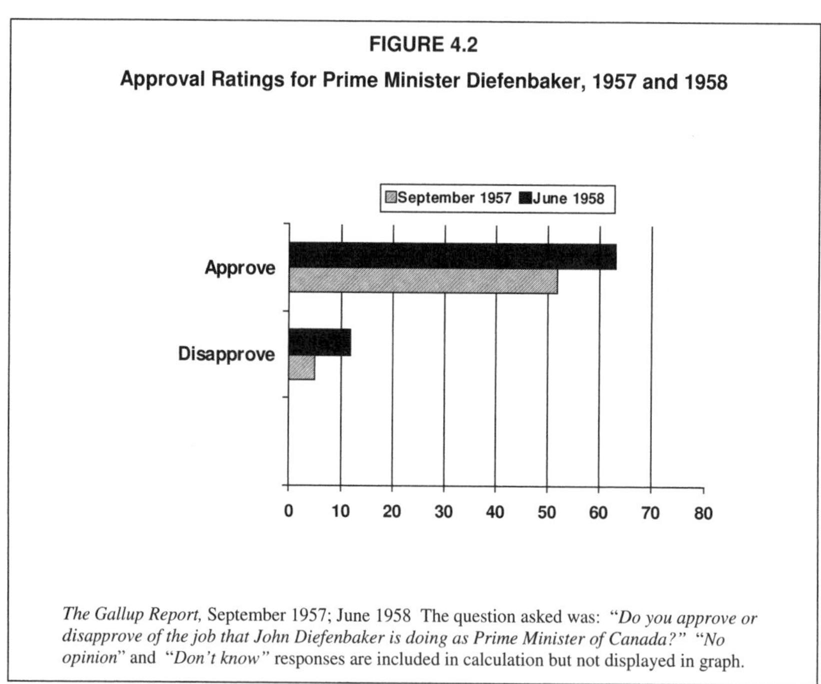

The Gallup Report, September 1957; June 1958 The question asked was: "*Do you approve or disapprove of the job that John Diefenbaker is doing as Prime Minister of Canada?*" "*No opinion*" and "*Don't know*" responses are included in calculation but not displayed in graph.

FIGURE 4.3

Best Man for Prime Minister – Diefenbaker or Pearson? March 1958

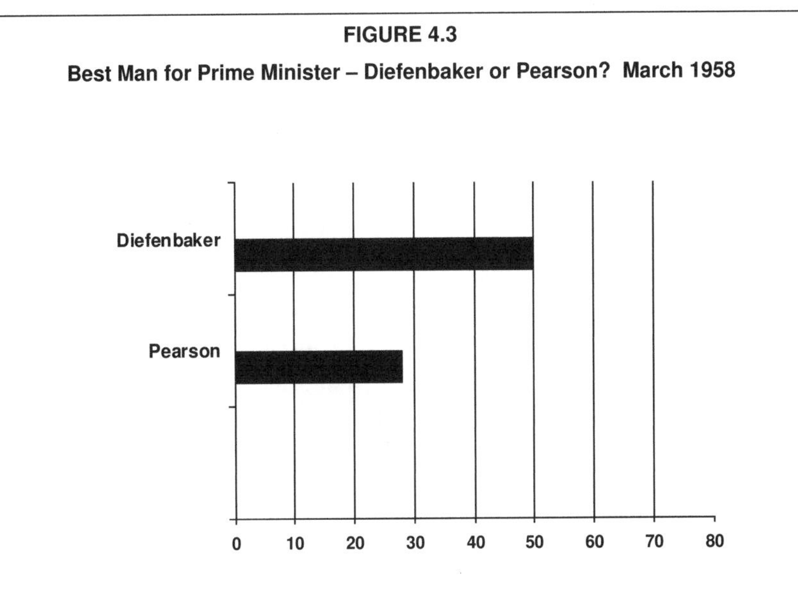

The Gallup Report, March 1958 The question asked was: "*Regardless of your own political feelings, which do you think would make the best prime minister for Canada – Lester B. Pearson or John Diefenbaker?*" "*Other*" mentions, "*No opinion*" and "*Both the same*" responses are included in calculation but not displayed in graph.

FIGURE 4.4

Most Important Problem Facing Canada, March 1958

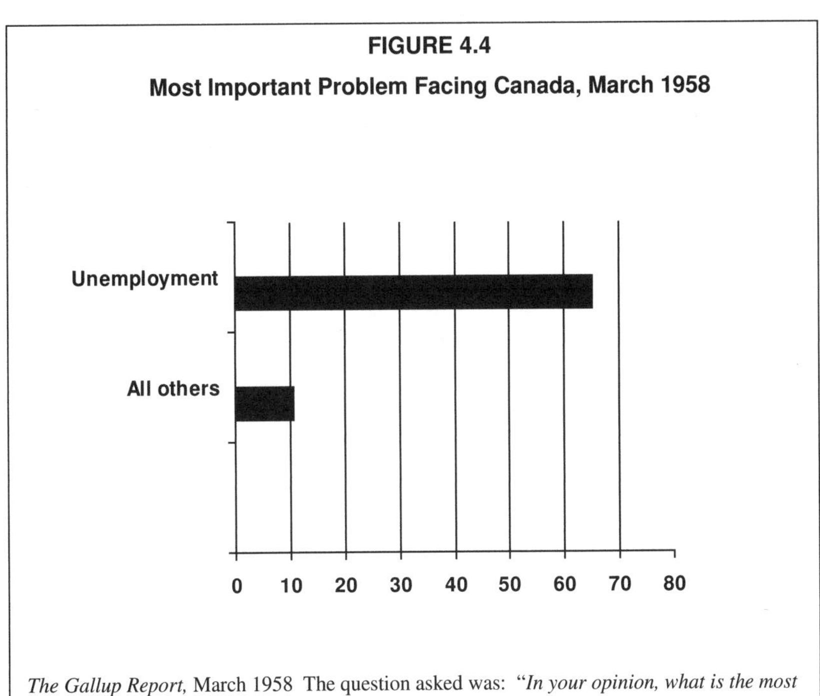

The Gallup Report, March 1958 The question asked was: "*In your opinion, what is the most important problem facing Canada today?*" "*No opinion*" and "*Don't know*" responses are included in calculation but not displayed in graph.

The Conservatives won the 1958 election in a landslide, their 208 out of the 265 seats in the Commons wiping out Liberal representation completely in four of the 10 provinces (see Table 4.5). Several former Liberal cabinet ministers went down to defeat, and the Social Credit Party was completely wiped out. The Social Credit provincial administrations in Alberta and British Columbia had been rocked by mismanagement charges and scandals, which contributed to significant discontent among Social Credit supporters. Their dislike for the Liberals was far more intense than it was for the Conservatives, and Diefenbaker's evangelical style was in keeping with what Socred supporters had been used to in their previous leaders. While the popular vote for the CCF declined by only 1 percent, their seat numbers plummeted from 25 to just 8. However, the most astonishing result was the Tory sweep in Quebec, something that had not happened since the days of John A. Macdonald. Also significant were the Ontario results. The Conservatives polled 56 percent of the vote to the Liberals' 33 percent, taking 67 of Ontario's 85 seats. Metropolitan and urban areas within Ontario supported the Diefenbaker-led Conservatives in both the 1957 and 1958 campaigns and in the process shattered the infrastructure of the Liberal Party.

New Intellectual Currents in Voting Behaviour and Election Analysis

The 1957 and 1958 elections marked the beginning of an emerging Canadian intellectual tradition in voting behaviour and election analysis. John Meisel's Ph.D. dissertation at the University of London, "The Canadian General Election of 1957," was a full-scale study of the 1957 election. Prior to 1957, Meisel had written an influential piece titled "Religious Affiliation and Electoral Behaviour" in *The Canadian Journal of Economics and Political Science*.[58] Meisel and other Canadian academics at that time were influenced by the rapid development of British and American studies of voting behaviour and elections. These studies were not restricted to voting alone, and were also aimed at examining the importance of issues, the tactics and strategies employed by parties, the structure of campaigns, and the role of the media. David Butler (under whom Meisel studied at the University of London) wrote

The British General Election of 1955, one of the many volumes on British elections which became known as the Nuffield Studies. In the United States, Berelson et al., *Voting: A Study of Opinion Formation in a Presidential Campaign* (1954), and Campbell et al., *The Voter Decides* (1954) and *The American Voter* (1960), likewise generated a powerful influence on the development of election studies in Canada. Other Canadian academics who joined this fledging tradition included Dennis H. Wrong, whose article, "Parties and Voting in Canada," appeared in *Political Science Quarterly* in 1958. Frank H. Underhill's classic work, *In Search of Canadian Liberalism*, was published in 1960, in part a response to the sea change in Canadian federal politics that had just taken place.

The technology of survey research was also evolving rapidly, providing scholars with new types of evidence on which to base their analyses of political events. The Canadian Institute of Public Opinion (the Canadian Gallup affiliate) had been surveying Canadians since 1942, but typically included only a few questions of interest to academics studying Canadian voting behaviour. Peter Regenstreif was an early researcher who used the Gallup data to study elections. In his book *The Diefenbaker Interlude* (1965) he employed Gallup data, together with some of his own polling conducted for the *Toronto Star*, to compare voting intentions prior to the 1962 and 1963 elections with the actual vote. Gallup data was the primary source for tracking public opinion until the first National Election Study was conducted by Meisel and his colleagues in 1965. These developments combined to increase the depth of our understanding of electoral behaviour in subsequent elections.

Conclusion

Looking back at the King/St. Laurent Liberal dynasty, the customary electoral pattern had been for the Liberals to win overwhelmingly in two regions of the country and to hold their own elsewhere. This template had allowed them to consistently put together majority governments, even though the components of that majority were not always the same, and the Liberals' share of the total vote rarely approached 50 percent. However, the 1958 Diefenbaker sweep had a different cast to it, as the Conservatives were able to poll very close to a majority of the vote in *every* region of the country, while winning 54 percent of the vote in the country as a whole. The Liberals, in contrast, had been reduced to a regional rump of 49 seats — heavily concentrated in Ontario and Quebec.[59] The regionally skewed Liberal caucus led John Meisel to raise the question, "Was something akin to the breakup of the Roosevelt coalition in the United States affecting the party once led by Mr. King and more recently by Mr. St. Laurent?"[60] Set alongside the re-election of Dwight Eisenhower in 1956, such speculation regarding the potential longer-term consequences of the Diefenbaker phenomenon appeared perfectly reasonable in the context of the times.

At long last, it seemed that federal politics in Canada had become nationalized and was no longer going to be characterized by regional differences and localisms. Observers began to sense the birth of a new era in Canadian federal politics in which elections would be based on pan-Canadian issues and campaigns rather than on appeals to specific groups or regions. Others pointed to the overwhelming Conservative victory of 1958 as a return to a two-party system in Canada, given that the CCF and Social Credit had fared so poorly. Certainly, the reduction of the influence of the minor parties in national politics held the potential to effect fundamental and lasting changes in Canadian politics. Ever since the sudden rise of the Progressives in 1921, "third" parties, based largely in the West, had played a pivotal role in federal politics. But with Diefenbaker's repositioning of the Conservatives around a strong western base, it appeared that parties such as Social Credit or the CCF might never regain their hold on western voters. In 1958, Canadians of every stripe had a host of reasons for voting Conservative. But, if the seeds of a new Conservative dynasty appeared to be present, events would soon show that it was not to be.

First, it became quickly evident that the Conservative landslide was not based on a lasting appeal on the three dimensions of economy, national unity, and social welfare. In particular, Diefenbaker's reluctance to move away from his "One Nation" concept led to a rapid erosion in his newly won support in Quebec. Moreover, while there were many Canadians who voted Conservative for the first time in 1958, their vote was cast primarily, as the party strategists had hoped, for Diefenbaker himself rather than for his party. The ties binding them to the party were weaker than ever and, as disillusionment with "the Chief" began to set in over the next few years, these voters were easily shaken loose. The sources of that disillusionment, and its consequences for the politics of the next decade, will be explored in Chapter 5.

Notes

1. Compared with 17 percent who disapproved of St. Laurent's performance, and 3 percent who expressed a "qualified" view. The balance of those sampled had no opinion. Canadian Institute of Public Opinion, *The Gallup Report*, July 1956.
2. Lester B. Pearson, *Mike: The Memoirs of the Right Honourable Lester B. Pearson* (Toronto: University of Toronto Press, 1973).
3. J.L. Granatstein, *Canada 1957–1967: The Years of Uncertainty and Innovation*. The Canadian Centenary Series. Ramsay Cook, ed., Vol. 19 (Toronto: McClelland & Stewart Limited, 1986), 16.
4. Diefenbaker as quoted in Granatstein, *Canada 1957–1967*, 16.
5. Denis Smith, *Rogue Tory* (Toronto: Macfarlane Waiter & Ross, 1995), 214.
6. One of those admirers was Brian Mulroney who cut his political teeth under Diefenbaker. See Brian Mulroney, *Memoirs* (Toronto: McClelland & Stewart, 2007), especially Chapter 4, 39–53.
7. Peter Stursberg, *Diefenbaker: Leadership Gained 1956–62* (Toronto: University of Toronto Press, 1975), 26.
8. Patrick Kyba, and Wendy Green-Finlay. "John Diefenbaker as Prime Minister: The Record Re-Examined," in D.C. Story and R. Bruce Shephard, eds., *The Diefenbaker Legacy: Canadian Politics, Law and Society Since 1957* (Regina: Canadian Plains Research Centre, 1998), 62.
9. This law allowed the Quebec government to shut down buildings that were being used for peaceful opposition purposes of any kind that were deemed to be communistic in nature.
10. Peter C.Newman, *Renegade in Power: The Diefenbaker Years* (Toronto: McClelland & Stewart, 1963), 47.
11. Peter Regenstreif, *The Diefenbaker Interlude: Parties and Voting in Canada* (Toronto: University of Toronto Press, 1965), 24.
12. J.W Pickersgill, *My Years with Louis St. Laurent — A Political Memoir* (Toronto and Buffalo: University of Toronto Press, 1975), 216.
13. Robert Bothwell, *C.D. Howe: A Biography* (Toronto: McClelland & Stewart, 1979).
14. Howe to Irvin Studer, May 23, 1958. Howe Papers, NAC.
15. Statistics Canada, *Historical Labour Force Statistics* (Ottawa, 1974).
16. Pickersgill, *op. cit.*, 238.
17. Pickersgill, *op. cit.*, 244. In fact, the statistical section of the Department of Citizenship and Immigration identified that a substantial number of Hungarian refugees were Jewish but were reluctant to declare their religion to immigration officials.
18. The pipeline debate was contentious for a number of reasons. While there was general support for the project itself, the policy, the pipeline's ownership, and the role of the federal government all became contested

by the various interests involved. The transport and sale of gas beyond the boundaries of a province was under federal jurisdiction and the pipeline carrying the gas out of Alberta could be built only by a company incorporated by Parliament. There was also opposition (primarily by the CCF) to a company with American interests being involved in the project and the preference was for a public company or Crown corporation. The CCF and other Canada-first supporters also opposed any sale of gas to the United States. Gas producers in the province of Alberta and the province itself supported the export of Alberta gas to the American Midwest, which would be more profitable than transporting it to Ontario and Quebec. See William Kilbourn, *Pipeline* (Toronto: Clark Irwin, 1970).

19. Pickersgill, *op. cit.*, 273.
20. Hugh Thorburn, "Parliament and Policy-Making: The Case of the Trans-Canada Gas Pipeline," *Canadian Journal of Economics and Political Science* 23 (1957), 521.
21. Bothwell, *op. cit.*, 305.
22. The closure rule had been adopted by the House of Commons in 1913 on the initiative of the Borden government to end a long and exhausting filibuster by the Liberal opposition led by Laurier. Closure then was denounced by the Liberals as a denial of freedom to debate and the tool of a tyrannical government. Although closure had been used on rare occasions since 1913, it was invariably applied by a Conservative government. The last time closure had been invoked was by the Bennett government in 1932. See Pickersgill, *op. cit.*, 276.
23. Canada, *Debates of the House of Commons*, 1956, Vol. 5, 4,463–75.
24. Smith, *Rogue Tory*, 201.
25. Newman, *Renegade in Power*, 54.
26. Bruce Thordarson, *Lester Pearson: Diplomat and Politician* (Toronto: Oxford University Press, 1974.), 85.
27. Pearson, *Mike: The Memoirs of the Right Honourable Lester B. Pearson*, Vol. 2, 242.
28. Thordarson, *Lester Pearson: Diplomat and Politician*, 89.
29. Dale C Thomson, *Louis St. Laurent: Canadian* (Toronto: Macmillan, 1967), 465.
30. Newman, *Renegade in Power*, 48.
31. Newman, *Renegade in Power*, 159.
32. John Meisel, *The Canadian General Election of 1957* (Toronto: University of Toronto Press, 1962), 70.
33. Pickersgill, *My Years with Louis St. Laurent*, 323–24.
34. Thomson, *Louis St. Laurent: Canadian*, 512.
35. Walter Stewart, *The Life and Times of M.J. Coldwell* (Toronto: Stoddart, 2000), 197–98.
36. Meisel, *The Canadian General Election of 1957*, 186.

37. In his book, Camp states that it was his colleague at Locke Johnson Advertising Agency, Hank Loriaux, who came up with the slogan "It's time for a Diefenbaker government." Dalton Camp, *Gentlemen, Players and Politicians* (Toronto: McClelland & Stewart, 1970), 279.
38. Thomson, *Louis St. Laurent: Canadian*, 510.
39. E. Bryden, "Money and Politics: Relations Between Ontario and Ottawa in the Diefenbaker Years," in D.D. Story and R. Bruce Shepard, eds., *The Diefenbaker Legacy*, 124–25.
40. Wilfrid Sanders, "How Polls Like That Happen," *Canadian Commentator*. Vol. 1, No. 6 (June 1957), 14–15.
41. Camp, *Gentlemen, Players and Politicians*, 339.
42. David Stewart, "Factions, Reviews and Reformers: Diefenbaker's Legacy to the Progressive Conservative Party," in D.C. Story and R. Bruce Shepard, eds., *The Diefenbaker Legacy*, 88.
43. Regenstreif, *The Diefenbaker Interlude*, 32.
44. Newman, *Renegade in Power*, 60–61.
45. Alvin Hamilton, as quoted in Peter Stursburg. *Diefenbaker: Leadership Gained 1956–62* (Toronto and Buffalo: University of Toronto Press, 1975), 78
46. Canada, *Debates of the House of Commons*, 1957–58, Vol. 6, 3,520.
47. Smith, *Rogue Tory*, 275.
48. Lester B. Pearson, *Mike: The Memoirs of the Right Honourable Lester B. Pearson*, Vol. 3 (1957–1968), 31, 33.
49. According to Denis Smith, this report was given to Diefenbaker by Patrick Nicholson. It was prepared in February and March 1957 as one of an annual series of confidential documents for ministers on the economic outlook. Nicholson had obtained it through some direct inquiries after Paul Martin had casually told him the previous summer that the Liberal government "had been warned of trouble ahead."
50. Newman, *Renegade in Power*, 68.
51. Diefenbaker, quoted in Smith, *Rogue Tory*, 280.
52. Diefenbaker, quoted in Newman, *Renegade in Power*, 70
53. Regenstreif, *The Diefenbaker Interlude*, 111.
54. Unemployment rose from an average of about 4.5 percent in 1957 to over 7 percent in 1958. Statistics Canada, *Historical Labour Force Statistics* (Ottawa, 1974).
55. Regenstreif, *The Diefenbaker Interlude*, 24.
56. Pierre Sevigny, as quoted in Peter Stursberg. *Diefenbaker: Leadership Gained, 1956–62*, 57.
57. Smith, *Rogue Tory*, 281.
58. John. Meisel "Religious Affiliation and Electoral Behaviour: A Case Study," *Canadian Journal of Economics and Political Science* 22 (1956), 481–96.
59. Although the party also won five of Newfoundlands's seven seats, polling 54.4 percent of the vote in that province. Newfoundland, along with the

Northwest Territories, were the only areas of the country that resisted the Diefenbaker sweep in 1958.

60. Meisel, *The Canadian General Election of 1957*, 252.

Selected Reading

Bothwell, Robert. *C.D. Howe: A Biography* (Toronto: McClelland & Stewart, 1979).

Fleming, Donald. *So Very Near: The Political Memoirs of the Honourable Donald M. Fleming. Volume One — The Rising Years* (Toronto: McClelland & Stewart, 1985).

Granatstein, J.L. *Canada 1957–1967. The Years of Uncertainty and Innovation.* The Canadian Centenary Series, Vol. 19 (Toronto: McClelland & Stewart 1986).

Meisel, John. *The Canadian General Election of 1957* (Toronto: University of Toronto Press. 1962).

Newman, Peter C. *Renegade in Power* (Toronto: McClelland & Stewart, 1963).

Pearson, Lester B. *Mike: The Memoirs of the Right Honourable Lester B. Pearson*, Vol. 2, 1948–1957, edited by John A. Munro and Alex I. Inglis (Toronto: University of Toronto Press, 1973).

Pickersgill, J.W. *My Years with Louis St. Laurent — A Political Memoir* (Toronto: University of Toronto Press, 1975).

Regenstreif, Peter. *The Diefenbaker Interlude: Parties and Voting in Canada* (Toronto: University of Toronto Press, 1965).

Smith, Denis. *Rogue Tory* (Toronto: MacFarlane Walter & Ross, 1995).

Thomson, Dale C. *Louis St. Laurent: Canadian* (Toronto: Macmillan of Canada, 1967).

CHAPTER 5

FORGING NEW STRUCTURES OF COMPETITION

In one blow, the outcome of the 1958 election shattered the party alignment that had been a fixture of federal politics for much of the twentieth century. With their huge majority, the Diefenbaker Conservatives towered above their rivals in all parts of the country, and the partisan landscape of Canadian federal politics had been completely rearranged. It looked as if a new era of Conservative ascendancy was about to begin, replacing the King/St.Laurent dynasty that had dominated federal politics since the 1920s. However, the partisan landscape that gradually took shape in the aftermath of the 1958 election was not to be the beginning of a new Conservative dynasty. Rather, a new and more competitive structure of partisan politics would be formed from the remnants of the old configuration. Each of the next three federal elections would produce minority governments, but some components of the 1958 Diefenbaker majority, such as the new strength of the PCs in the West, emerged as continuing characteristics of national politics for decades to come.

The sea change that 1958 initially appeared to represent was, in part, due to the natural tendency of single-member district systems of representation to overstate the true support of the winning party, especially when that party's vote total approaches a majority. Diefenbaker's massive parliamentary majority rested on just under 54 percent of the popular vote, an impressive total, but hardly a match for the 78 percent of the seats it yielded. In the same vein, although the CCF lost two-thirds of its parliamentary seats in the 1958 election, it nevertheless retained the support of about 1 in 10 voters, a total only slightly lower than its showing in the two previous elections.[1] Also, the Liberals retained the support of a third of the electorate, a decline to be sure from their previous levels, but not as precipitous as the drop in their parliamentary representation might appear to suggest.[2] Nevertheless, it was clear to most political observers of the time that an era had ended; what was less clear was the shape and sustainability of the new political era that had just begun.

The end of the King/St. Laurent dynasty was not the only significant change in the national political landscape. The Duplessis era in Quebec ended abruptly with the death of the long-time Quebec premier in 1959, unleashing a variety of long-repressed social and political forces.[3] No friend of Diefenbaker, Duplessis had nonetheless placed his powerful provincial Union Nationale machine behind the Tories in the 1958 election, largely for his own political reasons (see Chapter 4). New political opportunities might have been created when the widely respected Paul Sauvé succeeded Duplessis as premier. But Sauvé's sudden death from a heart attack at the age of 52, after fewer than four months in office, disrupted this seeming convergence of federal and provincial politics in Quebec. The provincial Union Nationale fell into disarray, and the Liberals under Jean Lesage won a narrow victory in the provincial election of the following year under the slogan "*maîtres chez nous.*"[4] Quebec's "Quiet Revolution" had begun. Although many of these events in Quebec were beyond his control, Diefenbaker demonstrated little understanding of them, thereby losing at the very beginning of his mandate one of the essential building blocks of any new dynasty that might have emerged from the 1958 Conservative victory.

In developing his Quebec strategy in both 1957 and 1958, Diefenbaker had followed the notorious "Churchill memorandum." Writing confidentially to Diefenbaker prior to the 1957 campaign, the PC's organizational director, Gordon Churchill, had advised the leader that Quebec should receive little strategic emphasis in the campaign. The Conservatives won only six seats in francophone Quebec in the 1957 election, and Diefenbaker appointed only one francophone minister to his first cabinet — Léon Balcer, who was named solicitor general. But even after 42 francophone Quebec members were elected in the 1958 sweep, Diefenbaker named only three to his next cabinet, in every instance placing them in minor portfolios. There was no Quebec lieutenant, as had been the case under previous anglophone prime ministers, nor any other strong Quebec minister. The few MPs who later emerged as potentially significant figures — Pierre Sévigny, Noël Dorion, or Balcer (promoted to Transport in 1960) — carried little weight in the cabinet and were not trusted by Diefenbaker. The heavy losses sustained by the Tories in Quebec in the elections of 1962 and 1963 would illustrate both the tenuous character of the 1958 result and Diefenbaker's lack of understanding of Quebec. The latter was perhaps the most obvious of the weaknesses that were to cause the newly dominant position of the Conservatives in federal politics to unravel so quickly.

The seeds of another major difficulty lay in Diefenbaker's own personality, and in the style of leadership that came to characterize his government. A charismatic politician, "the Chief" had led his party to power against all odds in 1957, and to a landslide election victory in 1958, with brilliant campaigns that caught the imagination of the electorate. A powerful orator, he performed effectively both in Parliament and on the newly emerging medium of television. But Diefenbaker proved unable to transfer these considerable skills to the art of governing. He continued to attack the Liberals, as if still the Leader of the Opposition rather than prime minister. Vain and autocratic, Diefenbaker often appeared more concerned with maintaining his personal popularity than with using his powerful majority to pursue specific policy goals. His suspicion of cabinet colleagues and civil servants led to paralysis and infighting, and he sometimes seemed to be presiding over a government that had little direction. Over the next four years, his administration would slowly come to be judged not on the rhetorical skills of its leader but on the more mundane policy issues of the day — a weakening economy, a currency crisis, and protracted disputes over foreign and defence policies. By mid-1960, four out of five Canadians identified unemployment or the economy as the most important problem facing the country (see Figure 5.1), and support for the Conservatives in public opinion polls had fallen to 38 percent, well behind the Liberals (see Figure 5.2). Bit by bit, and issue by issue, the public mood turned from adulation to disillusionment. Because his

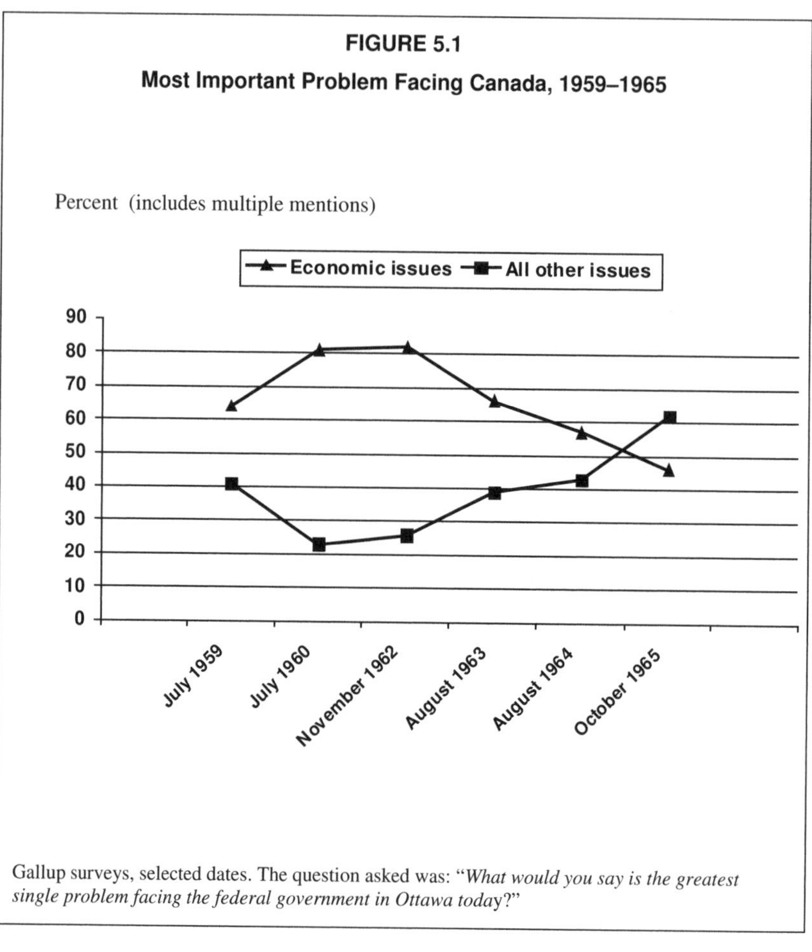

FIGURE 5.1
Most Important Problem Facing Canada, 1959–1965

Gallup surveys, selected dates. The question asked was: "*What would you say is the greatest single problem facing the federal government in Ottawa today?*"

government was so thoroughly identified with the personality of the man himself, Diefenbaker took the brunt of the blame for its failures.

Other changes that took place during this period also affected the electoral equation. The election of John F. Kennedy as president of the United States in 1960 generated a mood of change and renewal that quickly spilled over into Canada. The early sixties was a time of intense social and political change in America. Diefenbaker's style, however, was that of the rustic evangelical preacher, one which contrasted starkly with the glamour and sophistication of the Kennedy White House. Suddenly, the man who had injected a new sense of vision and excitement into Canadian politics in 1958 seemed old and out of touch — a throwback to a different time and place. It did not help matters that Diefenbaker loathed the Kennedys and was deeply suspicious of the Americans in general. A strong monarchist and supporter of the Commonwealth,

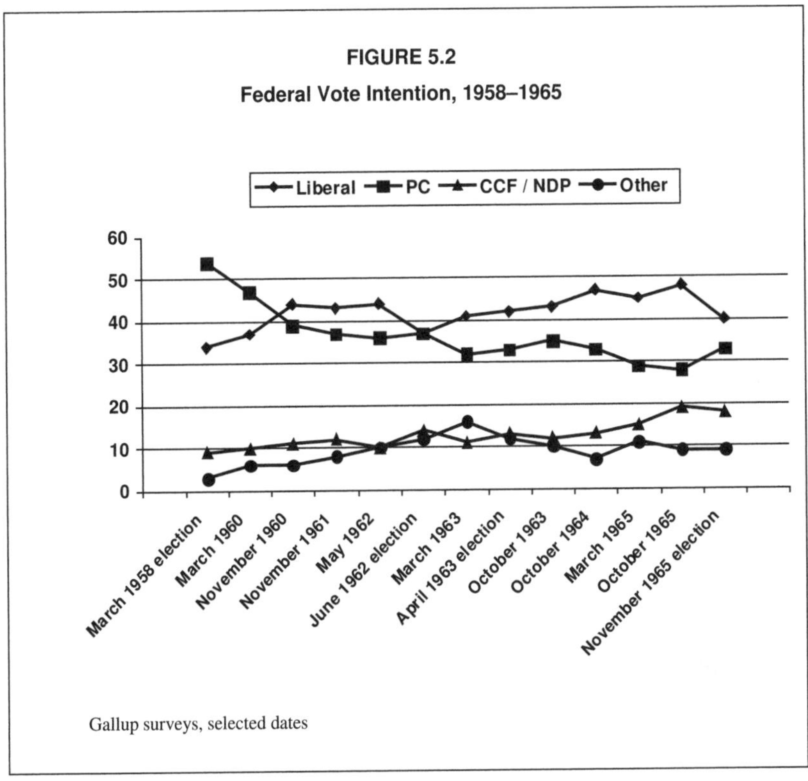

he talked vaguely and unrealistically about diverting more of Canada's trade to Britain, and opposed the idea of British entry into the European Common Market. President Kennedy's first (and only) visit to Ottawa, in May 1961, went badly, and relations between the two leaders soured rapidly afterward.[5] The new president's generally friendly relations with Lester Pearson fed Diefenbaker's suspicions and only made things worse. For these and other reasons having to do with the crisis over defence policy that began to develop at about the same time, the Diefenbaker years were a time of strained relations between Canada and the United States.

The defence policy crisis, which later formed the main backdrop to the 1963 election and contributed to the defeat of the Diefenbaker Conservatives, began to percolate in 1959. The starting point was the cabinet's decision to abandon support for a Canadian-built fighter aircraft, the AVRO Arrow, powered by the advanced Orenda Iroquois engine, both of which had been under development with government funding for a number of years. While this decision was made primarily on budgetary grounds, it had additional economic consequences because of the layoffs it precipitated in the fledgling Canadian aircraft industry, particularly in Toronto. In tandem with this decision the government agreed to accept American Bomarc missiles, because the Bomarcs were seen as both more cost-effective and in tune with changing North American defence requirements.

While it was never expressly stated that the Canadian Bomarcs would carry nuclear warheads, it was clear at the time that the missile had been designed for this purpose. Later, this fact was to raise a number of other more complicated issues in the area of defence policy, ranging from the prospect of joint control of such weapons to the more fundamental decision to abandon Canada's non-nuclear posture in international affairs.[6] The cabinet eventually split on these issues, precipitating the single greatest policy crisis of the Diefenbaker years, and instigating a cabinet revolt that came close to costing Diefenbaker his leadership.[7] The situation was not to reach a fever pitch until after the time of the Cuban Missile Crisis in October 1962, four months after the 1962 election had taken place. It would, however, be the issue on which the 1962–63 minority government suffered its parliamentary defeat, and the one that more than any other cost it the election in 1963.

Foreign and defence policy were not the only areas of government vulnerability in the period preceding the 1962 election. By 1959, the economy had already begun to approach recession conditions, a situation for which the prime minister largely blamed the previous Liberal government. Diefenbaker and his closest advisers tended to favour stimulative economic measures, both to deal with rising unemployment and in support of some of the social policies he had advocated during the 1958 campaign. But his cabinet contained a mixture of traditional and "Red" Tories, making economic policy a frequent internal battleground. His finance minister, Donald Fleming, had been Diefenbaker's principal opponent for the party leadership in 1956, and was clearly in the more traditional camp which favoured a "laissez-faire" economic agenda. Equally serious were conflicts arising between the government and the Bank of Canada, and particularly the governor of the Bank, James Coyne — a Liberal appointee. The situation eventually erupted into open conflict between the government and the Bank over its "tight money" policies — a long-festering dispute that gradually became more public and finally culminated in Coyne's dismissal in June 1961.[8] While there was ultimately no question that it was the government, not the Bank, that was responsible for the direction of federal economic policy, the "Coyne

Affair," as it came to be known, damaged Diefenbaker's reputation as much as Coyne's.

Around the same time, the Canadian dollar came under pressure in foreign exchange markets, in part because of a covert government policy favouring a cheaper dollar. Having declined to near parity from a level of US$1.03 a year earlier, the dollar fell more sharply in 1961 to a level of US$0.95, at which point the Bank of Canada, under its newly appointed governor, Louis Rasminsky, attempted to stabilize it (see Figure 5.3).

The "dollar crisis" might not have been as serious had not several cabinet ministers, including Fleming and Diefenbaker, given conflicting signals regarding the target value of the currency, thereby adding to its skittishness on the exchange markets. In 1962 it became necessary for Canada to obtain foreign exchange credits from Britain and the United States, as well as the International Monetary Fund, to support the currency, and Diefenbaker was forced to announce an economic austerity program. By the time the dollar was finally devalued and pegged at US$0.925 in May 1962, the issue had contributed substantially to the government's rapidly growing reputation for economic mismanagement, whatever the merits of the devaluation itself. The Liberals highlighted the currency crisis in their 1962 campaign, printing thousands of "Diefendollars" to distribute to voters (see Figure 5.4). But this was more a campaign tactic than a genuine dispute over monetary policy. When they eventually regained power in 1963, the Liberals made no effort to restore the dollar to its former value. Diefenbaker defended the devaluation to the end of his life, arguing that a cheaper dollar was beneficial to Canadian exports, and particularly to western farmers.[9] But the chaotic manner in which the policy had evolved, together with its unfortunate timing, did him considerable political damage and revitalized the opposition parties. The Tories were beginning to see the economic pillar of their success crumble.

For the Liberals, the period following the 1958 election was a time to regroup and rebuild. Initially stunned by the scale of their defeat, the Liberal parliamentary caucus appeared to be little more than a pale shadow of their seemingly invincible predecessors. Pearson, although secure in his leadership, was neither a strong parliamentary performer nor an experienced party organizer. With his slight lisp and unimposing style, he often seemed no match for the bombastic Diefenbaker in parliamentary debate. Having spent most of his political career in the

FIGURE 5.3

Trading Range of the Canadian Dollar on International Currency Markets, 1956–1966

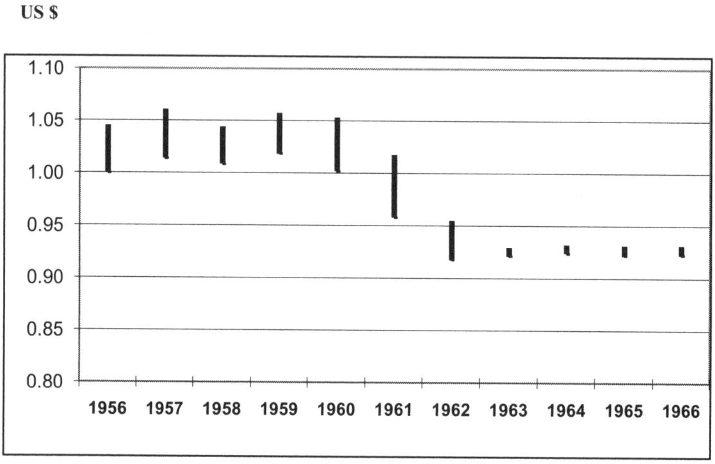

US $

1.10
1.05
1.00
0.95
0.90
0.85
0.80

1956 1957 1958 1959 1960 1961 1962 1963 1964 1965 1966

Statistics Canada

FIGURE 5.4

The "Diefendollar"

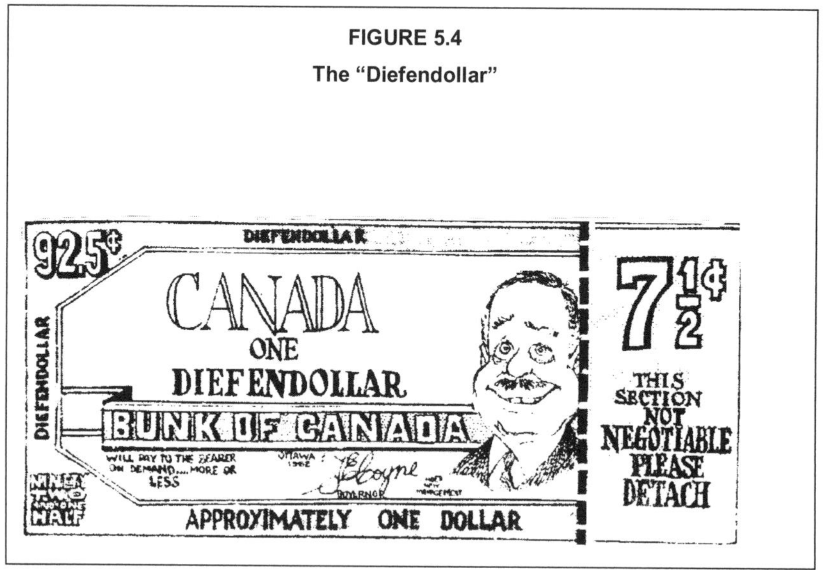

world of diplomacy rather than the rough and tumble of party politics, Pearson seemed at first to be the wrong person to undertake the enormous task of rebuilding the Liberal Party and positioning it for an eventual return to power. His general distaste for the world of partisan politics comes through clearly in his memoirs.[10] Pearson, however, was widely respected for the reputation he had gained in foreign affairs, including the Nobel Peace Prize for his work in defusing the Suez crisis in 1956 (see Chapter 4). He also had the good sense to surround himself with skilled political tacticians. As issues and events began to break in his favour during 1961 and 1962, the possibility that he might actually become prime minister seemed less implausible. To hasten their return to power, the Liberals first gave considerable attention to strengthening the party organization, which had atrophied under St. Laurent. Then they were determined to develop new policies and explore new ideas. As signs of party renewal, they held a high-profile "thinkers conference" in Kingston in 1960 and a party convention designed to produce a new platform and invigorate the party rank and file in 1961. Infatuated with the campaign strategies that had brought John F. Kennedy to power in 1960, Pearson's political advisers concentrated on modernizing the party's approach to electioneering, polling, and advertising, and developing the issue themes that would later guide the Liberal campaign.[11] All these efforts were designed with a view to return to power, as well as fighting off an emerging threat from the left.

The Birth of the NDP

The difficulties that the Conservatives would encounter in the 1962 election were presaged by the results of two important by-elections held in Ontario in the fall of 1960 — one in Niagara Falls and the other in Peterborough. The PCs lost both of these ridings by wide margins — Niagara Falls to the Liberal (Judy LaMarsh) and Peterborough to a candidate (Walter Pitman) running as the standard-bearer of the "New Party."

During the latter part of the 1950s, there had been much debate about the idea of forming a new party of the left, designed to replace the old CCF.[12] In the aftermath of its disastrous 1958 showing, a strong feeling had developed both within and outside the CCF that something had to be done. With strong support from organized labour, proponents of the new party hoped to transcend the Prairie base of the old CCF. A newly energized, more modern, more urban political movement would now emerge to take its place. Thus, the years following the 1958 election saw the reorganization and transition of the political left in Canada, culminating with the founding convention of the New Democratic Party held in Ottawa in July 1961. When Saskatchewan premier T.C. (Tommy) Douglas was elected as the new party's first leader, the prospect of a more potent national political force bridging East and West seemed within reach.[13] In 1961, the newly formed NDP had every reason to look to the political future with optimism. It felt that the economic issues facing the country were breaking its way. The provincial NDP government of Saskatchewan was about to launch a groundbreaking program of Medicare, putting the national party in the position of being a leader in the field of social policy. And the strong showing in the two Ontario by-elections provided hard evidence that the new national party of the left was on the right political track.[14]

Although the founding of the NDP guaranteed that the 1962 election would be more than a two-party contest, the full shape of the new competitive era of multi-party politics was not evident prior to the 1962 election. Social Credit, decimated in the 1958 vote, had little hope of a significant political revival in the West so long as Diefenbaker led the Conservatives. "Prairie populism" was by now a somewhat crowded political field. In

Library and Archives Canada. Horst Ehricht, photographer.

T.C. Douglas and David Lewis at NDP founding convention, 1961.

1960, Social Credit also held a national party convention intended to take stock of the party's position and set out new policy directions. Elected as its national leader at a convention a year later, Robert Thompson, criticizing Diefenbaker's brand of "Red Toryism," liked to say that his party was "the only *real* conservative party in Canada." Indeed, the provincial Social Credit administrations of E.C. Manning in Alberta and W.A.C. Bennett in British Columbia contained few remaining traces of the "funny money" days of "Bible Bill" Aberhart.[15] Although the provincial variations of Social Credit held a strong grip on politics in Alberta and British Columbia, the prospects of the federal party did not appear very bright. Almost unnoticed amid the new devotion of the party to fiscal discipline and the traditional conservatism espoused by Thompson was the party's new deputy leader, Réal Caouette, a car dealer from rural Quebec. The election of 26 Social Credit members from Quebec in 1962 would ultimately prove to be *the* story of the 1962 election. But few saw it coming.[16]

FIGURE 5.5

"Best Man for Prime Minister – Diefenbaker or Pearson?" 1957–1965

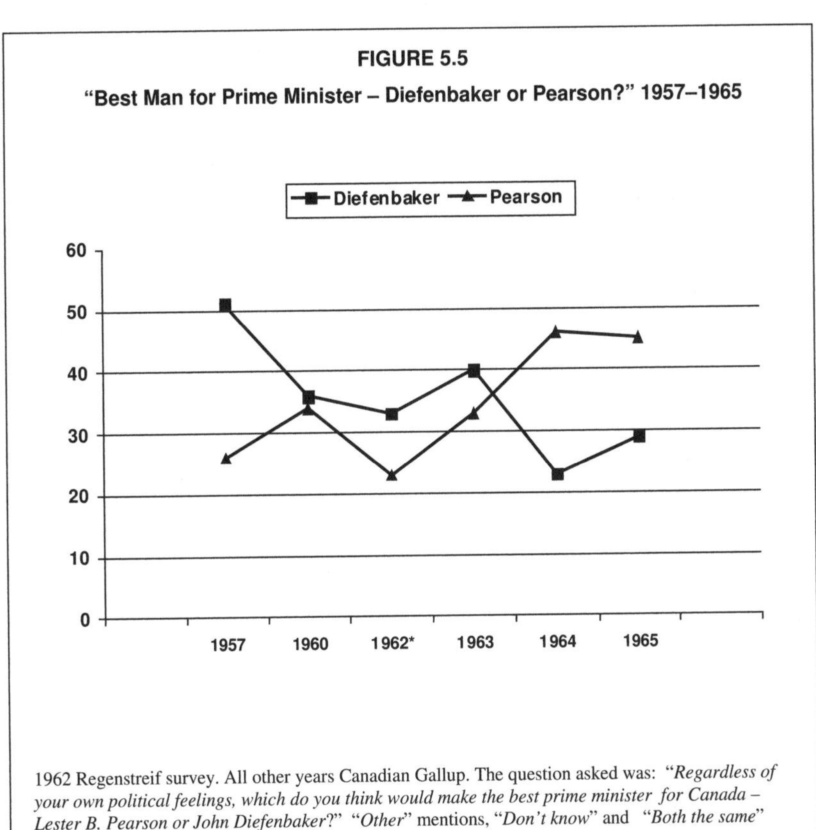

1962 Regenstreif survey. All other years Canadian Gallup. The question asked was: "*Regardless of your own political feelings, which do you think would make the best prime minister for Canada – Lester B. Pearson or John Diefenbaker?*" "*Other*" mentions, "*Don't know*" and "*Both the same*" responses are included in calculation but not displayed in graph.

The 1962 Election

The election took place more or less on schedule, four years and three months after that of 1958. The preceding year had been one of second-guessing regarding the timing and pre-election policy-making on the part of the government. The budget brought down by Fleming just a week before the election call had clearly been constructed as a centrepiece of the campaign, with an emphasis on increased pensions and public works projects. Although his party was behind the Liberals in the polls at the time of the election call, Diefenbaker had every reason to be optimistic. Canadians still believed that he was "a better man for the job of prime minister" than Pearson (see Figure 5.5), and he had won the two previous elections on the basis of a strong and highly personal campaign. As Regenstreif notes, "It was Diefenbaker's personality and personal qualities that attracted voters to him. In contrast, Pearson's support was more strongly party identified — that is, people preferring Pearson did so because he was the representative of the Liberal Party, rather than for any personal characteristics that differentiated him from his opponents."[17] This contrast suited Diefenbaker's campaign strategy well. He would campaign on the record of his four years in office, and portray his opponents as "the old Liberal crowd," the same bunch of aloof and arrogant Ottawa-based politicians that he had defeated in 1957 and 1958. Pearson's political advisers became a particular target of his invective — a bunch of "political fixers," "eggheads," "bureaucrats," and "back room boys" who had nothing but contempt for "the ordinary people."[18]

The 1962 campaign itself can be viewed, even by current standards, as a highly negative one. Diefenbaker was always at his most effective when on the attack, and he found plenty of targets in the Liberal Party backrooms, Bay Street, the American press, the Communists, and Pearson himself. Both parties sought the support of "ethnic" voters, particularly those of eastern European origin, by showcasing their anti-communist credentials. The Liberals for their part, sensing that the devaluation of the dollar could be portrayed as a symbol of economic mismanagement, distributed their "Diefendollars," and treated the matter as a subject for ridicule rather than an opportunity for a serious debate on economic policy. Because Diefenbaker's style, as well as many of his economic policies, ran counter to traditional conservative values, the Liberal campaign particularly stressed issues such as unemployment, deficits, and inflation — anything that could cast the governing party's economic stewardship in a negative light. Diefenbaker in turn, sensing that his strength lay in the small towns and rural areas rather than the big cities, portrayed himself constantly as the "little guy from rural Saskatchewan," standing up against "the big interests." The slickness of the Liberal campaign, which borrowed advertising techniques heavily from the 1960 American presidential campaign, made them easy targets for the prime minister. President Kennedy's pollster, Lou Harris, was brought in to advise the Liberal campaign.[19] Both major parties, of course, had a vested interest in attempting to portray the election as essentially a two-party affair.

The newly formed NDP, with its focus on organized labour, was an unknown quantity, but T.C. Douglas was himself a seasoned and effective campaigner. Few paid any attention to Social Credit, which was running two quite different (and rather unrelated) campaigns in the West and in rural Quebec. Réal Caouette also understood the ways in which the structure of political campaigning was changing in the 1960s. He had bought time on dozens of local television stations throughout rural Quebec to spread his message that Quebec voters had "nothing to lose" in voting Social Credit. Although attacking the competence of Diefenbaker and his government on economic issues dominated the Liberal campaign, social issues were also in the background. The Liberals, following their "thinkers" conference of 1960, were developing proposals for a national pension plan, which they would bring forth with more vigour in 1963. It was the NDP, however, which campaigned around the establishment of a medicare system similar to the one that had been implemented in Saskatchewan. In the short run, the issue did not appear to help the NDP; they elected nobody in Saskatchewan in 1962, and Douglas himself was defeated in his home constituency. But in the slightly longer run, medicare proposals as well as pensions were to contribute to the eventual victory of the Pearson Liberals, and the revived fortunes of the NDP.

Notably absent from the campaign rhetoric was attention given to national unity issues, and more specifically to Quebec's role in Confederation. With the three main party leaders all coming from outside "La Belle Province," the issue was largely ignored. In retrospect, we could easily question this decision. The Lesage government was preparing to call a snap election on its proposal to nationalize hydroelectricity in the province, and the Quebec government was becoming increasingly assertive and nationalistic under the stewardship of its high-profile natural resources minister, René Lévesque. Federal leaders demonstrated a lack of understanding of Quebec issues by simply ignoring one of the building blocks of their electoral success, a deficiency that likely contributed to the inconclusive election outcome.

By polling day, the election was widely seen as "too close to call," although polls continued to show the Liberals clinging to a narrowing lead. The Gallup poll of June 13, five days before the election, placed

Library and Archives Canada/ Social Credit Association of Canada.

Réal Caouette speaking, Quebec City area, 1963.

the Liberals at 38 percent and the Conservatives at 36. Only a few days earlier (June 6), the Liberal lead as measured by Gallup had been 10 points (42 percent to 32 percent).[20] But it was Quebec that provided the greatest surprise of the election as the results were tallied. The 26 seats won by Social Credit in Quebec, out of a total of 30 nationally, produced an entirely new political map — much as the Bloc Québecois would do in another election three decades later.[21] Although most of their seats were gains from Conservative incumbents who had been first elected in 1958, the Social Credit breakthrough in Quebec did the greatest damage to the Liberals, who had counted on Quebec returning to its previous partisan voting patterns. However, Pearson, like Diefenbaker, held little appeal for Quebec voters. The Liberals' net gain in Quebec amounted to only 10 seats over 1958, and this more than any single factor cost them the election. With only 100 Liberal seats compared to 116 for the Conservatives, Diefenbaker would be able to continue in power with a minority government for another 10 months.

As can be seen in Table 5.1, the results of the 1962 election were highly regionalized. The Conservative vote held up best in the Prairies, where Diefenbaker had the greatest personal following. Their support was also strong in Nova Scotia and Prince Edward Island, and in rural and small-town Ontario. In British Columbia, however, the PCs suffered heavy losses to the NDP, who took the largest share of the vote and almost half of B.C.'s 22 seats (Douglas was elected in Burnaby–Coquitlam in a subsequent by-election, and ran consecutively in that constituency until his retirement from politics in 1979). The election outcome exposed divisions in federal politics that reflected quite different perspectives in rural and urban Canada. These divisions were best understood within their provincial and/or regional context. Diefenbaker's appeal on the Prairies and in small-town Ontario and Nova Scotia did not extend to rural Quebec. The appeal of the Pearson Liberals to urban voters was confined largely to the East and excluded for the most part francophone Quebec and Western Canada. The new political map of Canada that the 1962 election produced was to be a much more complicated one than had previously existed, and it would take some time before its implications would be fully understood. The next six years would be a period not only of minority government, but also one in which no single political party would be able to dominate the federal political scene.

TABLE 5.1

Results of 1962, 1963, and 1965 Federal Elections, by Province

		PC			Liberal			NDP			Social Credit*		
		1962	1963	1965	1962	1963	1965	1962	1963	1965	1962	1963	1965
Newfoundland	votes (%)	36	30	32	59	65	64	5	4	1	-	-	2
	seats (#)	1	-	-	6	7	7	-	-	-	-	-	-
Prince Edward Island	votes (%)	51	52	54	43	46	44	5	2	2	-	-	-
	seats (#)	4	4	4	-	-	-	-	-	-	-	-	-
Nova Scotia	votes (%)	47	47	49	42	47	42	9	6	9	2	-	-
	seats (#)	9	5	10	2	7	2	1	-	-	-	-	-
New Brunswick	votes (%)	47	40	43	44	47	48	5	4	9	4	9	1
	seats (#)	4	4	4	6	6	6	-	-	-	-	-	-
Quebec	votes (%)	30	20	21	39	46	46	4	7	12	26	27	18
	seats (#)	14	8	8	35	47	57	-	-	-	26	20	9
Ontario	votes (%)	39	32	34	42	46	44	17	16	22	2	2	-

	seats (#)	35	27	25	44	52	51	6	6	9	-	-	-
Manitoba	votes (%)	42	42	41	31	34	31	20	17	24	7	9	4
	seats (#)	11	10	10	1	2	1	2	2	3	-	-	-
Saskatchewan	votes (%)	50	54	48	22	24	24	23	18	26	5	9	2
	seats (#)	16	17	17	-	-	-	1	-	-	-	-	-
Alberta	votes (%)	43	45	47	19	22	22	8	7	8	29	26	23
	seats (#)	15	14	15	-	1	-	-	-	-	2	2	2
British Columbia	votes (%)	27	23	-	27	32	-	31	30	-	14	13	-
	seats (#)	6	4	-	4	7	-	10	9	-	2	2	-
Yukon / NWT	votes (%)	48	54	45	46	42	52	-	-	3	6	4	-
	seats (#)	1	2	1	1	-	1	-	-	-	-	-	-
TOTAL CANADA	votes (%)	37	33	32	37	42	40	14	13	18	12	12	8
	seats (#)	116	95	97	99	129	132	20	17	21	30	24	14

*Includes Ralliement des Créditistes in 1965.

1962–63: The End of an Interlude

The 1962 election can now be clearly seen as the beginning of the end of the brief but turbulent Diefenbaker era in Canadian politics. The Conservatives' handling of the economy, together with the shortcomings of both Diefenbaker and Pearson in their approaches to Quebec, combined to assure that there was no new political dynasty yet in the making. But this period was also a time of transition and change. The Liberals had recovered from their devastating defeat of 1958, but it would be some years before they could again be a dominant force in federal politics. The NDP would remain a substantial third party for the next forty years, even though the new party's debut in the 1962 election was a relatively inauspicious one, with just under 14 percent of the vote and 19 parliamentary seats. Social Credit in Quebec, although its staying power in federal politics would ultimately prove to be more limited, was not to disappear from the scene quickly.[22] Even where some of the voting patterns of the 1962 election proved to be temporary, the changes that produced them were not. The next two elections, in 1963 and 1965, reconfirmed many of these patterns, even as they yielded different electoral outcomes. A new and quite different structure of party competition characterized federal politics in Canada for most of the decade.

The 1962 result could not be read as a victory by any of the parties, but the result quickly took its toll on the Diefenbaker Conservatives. A few days after the election, the prime minister was forced to announce an economic austerity program — part of the condition required in the move to stabilize the Canadian dollar during the pre-election period. It was no longer possible to pretend that the dollar devaluation had only positive economic consequences. Parliament did not reconvene until the end of September, and the brief session held prior to the Christmas recess attempted no new policy initiatives. The Conservatives quickly dropped a further four points in the Gallup poll. The difficulties of managing a minority government under the new partisan configuration soon became apparent, since the government was dependent on the support of Social Credit in order to remain in power.

By the time Parliament reconvened in late January, the defence policy crisis that would ultimately lead to the government's downfall was well underway. Douglas Harkness had been Diefenbaker's minister of national defence since 1960, and he had long been one of the strongest proponents in cabinet of the need for Canada to accept nuclear weapons to fulfil its defence commitments. Increasingly, his position clashed with the anti-nuclear views of the external affairs minister, Howard Green, and the cabinet split on this issue spilled into the open. Diefenbaker avoided taking a clear stand until events forced him to do so. The Cuban Missile Crisis in October 1962 refocused attention on the festering issue of North American defence.

The American position was that Canada was *already* committed to a nuclear role through its acquisition of the Bomarcs and its NORAD obligations. The retiring NATO commander, General Lauris Norstad, in a speech given in Ottawa in January 1963, stated this position forcefully.[23] The prime minister contradicted Norstad's view in a speech to the House of Commons shortly after Parliament reconvened at the end of January. Within a week, Harkness submitted his resignation, to be followed a short time later by the associate minister of defence, Pierre Sévigny, and the minister of trade and commerce, George Hees.[24] Meanwhile the Liberals, in a reversal of their previous position, announced that a Liberal government would "honour its commitments" by accepting nuclear warheads for the Bomarcs. Pearson moved a motion of non-confidence in the government that was carefully worded to attract the support of the other parties. There followed a brief flurry of behind-the-scenes activity, during which the possibility was held out that Social Credit might continue to support the government in exchange for Diefenbaker's resignation.[25] But the fate of the government was all but sealed. The Diefenbaker government was defeated in Parliament on February 5, 1963, by a vote of 142 to 111. The 1963 election campaign was underway, only eight months after the previous vote.

As the 1963 campaign unfolded, observers might have been forgiven for thinking that the outcome was a foregone conclusion. The Diefenbaker minority government had been a disaster. The Liberals held a solid lead among decided voters in the Gallup poll published at about the time of government's defeat.[26] Yet, the prime minister seemed almost relieved to be back on the campaign trail, able to once again take his case directly to the people. Freed of the problems of government and the strain of the cabinet crisis, Diefenbaker was able to replay the role that he loved best — the underdog fighting for his political life. Whistle-stopping through small-town Ontario, his campaign was reminiscent of that of U.S. President Harry Truman in 1948, a comparison in which Diefenbaker clearly delighted. The events of 1962 and 1963 had also handed him some new issues with which to fight the election — Liberal duplicity on the defence issue, American interference in Canadian affairs, and the obstruction of the minor parties in Parliament. It was much easier to spread the blame for the country's problems in the minority government atmosphere of 1963 than it had been when the Conservatives held a commanding majority in Parliament.

While a plurality of the electorate disapproved of his performance as prime minister, Diefenbaker was still narrowly preferred over Pearson as "the best man for the job."[27] Pearson's standing with voters was such that only 27 percent approved of his performance as Leader of the Opposition.[28] Furthermore, campaigning was Pearson's weakness, just as it was Diefenbaker's strength. But both major parties emphasized the need for majority government, hoping to pare back the gains made by the NDP and Social Credit in the election of the previous year. Pearson particularly campaigned on the theme of "a strong, decisive government," capable of dealing with the country's many challenges. Gradually hitting his stride as the campaign developed, Pearson promised "sixty days of decision" under a Liberal government. And the decisiveness theme did resonate with some; the final *Globe and Mail* editorial supporting the Liberals referred favourably to Pearson as the "Man of Decision."[29] But even that endorsement was faint in its praise: "Mr. Pearson is not a good speaker.... His words from election podiums may not inspire Canadians, but his actions in world crises have inspired the world."[30]

Unlike in 1962, national unity themes figured heavily in the 1963 campaign as the Liberals sought to improve their position in Quebec and to counter the Créditiste threat. Pearson, in a major policy statement six months earlier, had proposed the creation of a Royal Commission on Bilingualism and Biculturalism. In both 1962 and 1963, the Liberal platform had also called for the adoption of a new national flag, which Diefenbaker resolutely opposed. The defence issue, because of its implications for reversing Canada's traditional position on nuclear weapons, proved difficult for both parties. Diefenbaker accused the Liberals of caving in to American pressure, while at the same time avoiding any firm commitment to future action on the Bomarcs. An unflattering portrayal of Diefenbaker in *Newsweek* magazine encouraged Diefenbaker to play the nationalistic card with greater frequency during the campaign.[31] In contrast, Pearson attempted to articulate a more nuanced position on the issue that stressed "honouring our international commitments" but avoided much direct discussion of the nuclear issue itself, in part because the party's defence policy was something of a liability in Quebec, where the Liberals had the greatest hope of making gains at the expense of the Créditistes.[32]

In Quebec, the Liberals concentrated their fire on Social Credit, and courted the support of Premier Lesage who, while clearly indicating his preference for Pearson over Diefenbaker, maintained a cautious distance from the federal campaign. In Central and Eastern Canada, much of the political and economic establishment was already supporting the Liberals, a trend that Diefenbaker increasingly played upon in his campaign speeches in the small towns and rural areas, particularly in the West. Newspapers throughout the country overwhelmingly endorsed the Liberals.[33]

It was in the social policy area that the 1963 Liberal campaign sowed the important seeds of its dominance in the later governments run by Pearson and Trudeau. Pearson promised that a Liberal government would commence work on a list of social welfare measures, starting with pensions and following with medicare. Reminding voters that it was the St. Laurent government which had brought in an across-the-board old-age pension in 1951, Pearson proposed a new contributory pension plan, based on earnings of employed persons and portable if a person changed jobs. This pension plan was his "top priority."[34] Tying people to their jobs because private pension plan rights would be lost if they moved was "a form of 20th century feudalism," said Walter Gordon, the man who would become Pearson's minister of finance.[35] Extending his social policy commitment, Pearson promised that, within four years and in time for Canada's centennial in 1967, the Liberals would bring in a national health plan.[36] Struggling to keep up, Diefenbaker also promised a pension plan, but only if there were "increased revenues through extra productivity."[37] Douglas maintained that the NDP was the only party that would bring in comprehensive pension and medicare plans. But on balance, the Liberals were the ones to establish their credibility on these issues.

Looking at the election results, all of the party strategies worked to some degree (see Table 5.1). But, as had happened in 1962, the chance for a decisive electoral victory slipped from the Liberals' grasp in the final weeks of the campaign. Social Credit suffered a net loss of only six seats in Quebec, and its percentage of the total vote in the province actually rose slightly. The NDP declined by a net of two seats. Conservative losses were heaviest in Ontario (8 seats) and in Quebec (6 seats). Diefenbaker's support had again held up well throughout the West. Nevertheless, the modest Liberal gains in Ontario and Quebec were sufficient to give Pearson a minority government. With just under 42 percent of the popular vote, the Liberals had clearly won the election. In this regard, the polls had not been wrong, as they had consistently shown the Liberals leading throughout the campaign. But polls in Canada often do not provide accurate forecasts of constituency results, and these can become even more difficult to gauge when voting patterns are highly regionalized, as they were in both the 1962 and 1963 elections. Because of their weakness in the West and their failure to vanquish the Créditistes in Quebec, the Liberals ended up four seats short of a parliamentary majority. The period of minority government would continue, but under a new prime minister.

Prime Minister Pearson

The results of the 1963 election also confirmed that the new structure of party competition ushered in by the previous election was more than a transient phenomenon. While they had suffered small losses, both the NDP and Social Credit held on to most of the seats they had won in 1962, and both parties maintained nearly the same share of the vote. Caouette claimed the votes of more than a quarter of all Quebecers, indicating that the Créditiste phenomenon of 1962 amounted to more than mere short-term protest. The Conservatives' hold on western voters had stood up now through three consecutive elections, and would ultimately outlast Diefenbaker's leadership. The divisions which had opened up on Canada's political map in 1962 began to look both more permanent and more serious. Furthermore, national unity emerged as a central concern of the post-1963 period.[38] In the words of John Meisel, the party system appeared "stalled."[39] The results of the election to follow in less than three years time would reveal just how stalled it actually was. But it was incumbent on the newly elected prime minister to put a stamp on his first victory.

Pearson's "sixty days of decision" did not begin auspiciously. The very concept meant that the government was under pressure to deliver quickly on its campaign promises.[40] This proved difficult, since the Liberals were a minority government functioning in an acrimonious parliamentary setting. It was promising to be even more difficult considering the personality of the newly elected prime minister. The introduction of the Canada Pension Plan precipitated conflict with the provinces, particularly Ontario and Quebec. The appointment of the Royal Commission on Bilingualism and Biculturalism was hailed by many as a positive step, but it also served to draw attention to what was gradually becoming known as "the Quebec problem." The new national flag proposed by Pearson prompted a long and bitter parliamentary debate that dragged on for six months until closure was finally invoked. A string of scandals involving cabinet ministers generated a steady drumbeat of unfavourable publicity for the government, and Pearson's low-key style of leadership sometimes made it appear as if he was not fully in control. Diefenbaker adjusted to his new role of Leader of the Opposition with his former tenacity, and the government's missteps provided him with considerable scope for criticism. The resignation of the justice minister, Guy Favreau, in the wake of a a scandal in December 1964, represented the low point politically for the minority Liberal government.[41]

But the low point was not all that low. Liberal standing in the Gallup poll for the period declined only slightly, while support for the Conservatives had dropped even further. Diefenbaker faced continuing doubts from within his own party and caucus about his leadership, and it seemed only a matter of time before he might be replaced. A feeling began to develop among Liberal strategists that an early election, fought while Diefenbaker still led the Conservatives, might work to their advantage. Walter Gordon, the finance minister and one of Pearson's closest cabinet confidants, and Keith Davey, his chief election strategist, were known to hold this view. An early election might produce the majority that had eluded the Liberals in 1963. An improving economic climate began to give the governing party more confidence in its electoral prospects, and by-election victories in two Quebec ridings in February 1965 further boosted party morale. But there were obvious risks in an early election. Pearson's weaknesses as a campaigner were by now well known, and the absence of any clear issue on which to base an election call increased the possibility that an early election strategy might backfire. And, for all of his deficiencies as a party leader and prime minister, Diefenbaker remained a formidable force on the campaign trail. Eventually, the balance tipped in favour of the strategists. In September, Pearson announced that an election would be held on November 8. The governing party would campaign on its record of accomplishment in two and a half years in office, but would also stress the need for a majority government. "Our record in office has been a good one," Pearson stated, "but with a majority we could have done more."[42]

By this time, Pearson's political advisers were well aware of his limitations as a campaigner. Opting for a low-key "prime ministerial" strategy, which kept Pearson in Ottawa during much of the campaign, the Liberal election themes stressed the need for a "clear mandate" and a stable majority government. "National unity" was a continuing campaign theme, which the Liberals hoped would work to their advantage. For the Conservatives, party unity more than national unity was the compelling problem, and they resolved it (at least for the purposes of the campaign) more deftly than anyone who had witnessed the cabinet defections of 1963 could possibly have imagined. Dissidents such as George Hees and Davie Fulton returned to the fold (although Fulton proclaimed his intention to run for the leadership after the election), and powerful Tory premiers such as John Robarts of Ontario, Duff Roblin of Manitoba, and Robert Stanfield of Nova Scotia lined up solidly in support of what many believed would be Diefenbaker's last campaign. As in the previous election, whistle-stopping through the small towns again figured prominently in Diefenbaker's campaign strategy. Regaining his old energy and stamina as the campaign progressed, "the Chief" attacked the Liberals over and over again on every conceivable front, painting a picture of a government riddled through with corruption and arrogance. While the Conservative platform promised more money for universities, medical research, agriculture, old-age pensioners, as well as a variety of other projects,[43] Diefenbaker was more comfortable speaking of the "current mess in government." "We shall get to the bottom of this and assure Canadians that the cobwebs of the Mafia, the wrongdoings of the narcotics peddlers and the corruption of public officials does not become a way of life."[44] His "meet the people" campaign, charged with his innate energy and enthusiasm for politics, contrasted starkly with the Liberals' Ottawa-based strategy.

TABLE 5.2

Most Important Issues in the 1965 Election

	Percent (multiple response)*
Economic Issues	
Unemployment	6
Cost of living, inflation	4
Agriculture	2
Trade, commerce, development	2
Other economic	1
National Unity	
Ethnic relations, separatism	5
The flag	3
U.S. influence in Canada	2
Social Welfare	
Pensions, old age security	33
Health, medicare	15
Education	3
Social security, welfare	3
Family allowances	2
Other Issues	
Majority government	11
Corruption, scandals	5
Leadership	1
Other issues	6
None / Don't Know	29

* 1965 Canadian Election Study. N = 2,058.

Pearson's campaign stressed his party's record of accomplishment in its two and a half years in office, as well as the need for a majority government that could last for a full term. The latter, he said, was necessary in order to deal with the many difficult problems facing the country in the years ahead. Nevertheless, he stressed, the government had accomplished many of its objectives in the area of social security, and it presided over a strong and growing economy. Another major social policy objective — the extension of universal health insurance to cover doctors' services — was at the top of the government's priority list for the new Parliament. These issues appeared to resonate with a large segment of the electorate, which at this time ranked social issues well ahead of economic ones or national unity themes in their list of priorities (see Table 5.2). Liberal campaign rhetoric made frequent references to the "chaos" of the Diefenbaker years over the course of the campaign, attempting to draw a direct contrast between Pearson's record in office and Diefenbaker's. In his few campaign speeches, generally given in controlled settings in the larger cities, the prime minister repeatedly stressed the theme of majority government, which became for all practical purposes the central theme of the Liberal campaign: "We want a strong government, that can speak strongly with the provinces ... so the voice of Canada can be heard strong and clear in the councils of the world."[45] But Pearson continued to be undermined by his weaknesses as a campaigner and public speaker; his general dislike for the cut and thrust of partisan politics; and his inability to come across favourably on the then emerging critical medium of political campaigns — television. Putting the prime minister front and centre in the campaign was a strategy that had been proven in the past to be ineffective. But hiding him in Ottawa left too much of the field open to Diefenbaker. Gradually, the Liberal lead in the polls shrank. The *Globe and Mail* reluctantly endorsed the Conservatives, as did a number of other newspapers, often citing one or more scandals and Pearson's uneven record of leadership.[46]

In the end, the election of 1965 was to leave things pretty much as they were. Despite further modest gains in Quebec, the net Liberal improvement in the 1965 election was only two seats, still short of a majority. In Ontario, the Atlantic provinces, and particularly in the West, Diefenbaker's strong campaign had fought the Liberals to a virtual standstill. The "victory" that the Conservatives had won by denying the Liberals their majority was more than the effort of one man. Some of the scandals that had taken place during Pearson's administration, of which Diefenbaker reminded voters repeatedly in his campaign rhetoric, dogged the prime minister throughout the campaign. But more importantly, Pearson's leadership simply failed to generate any enthusiasm among voters outside the larger cities in Central Canada. In British Columbia, for example, the Liberals merely held on to the seven seats they had won in 1963. In Saskatchewan, Alberta, and Prince Edward Island they were shut out completely, losing the three seats that had been previously won by narrow margins in the latter two provinces.

As in the two previous elections, the minor parties also figured prominently in the 1965 result. The NDP improved its share of the total vote substantially in 1965 — to 18 percent compared with the 13 percent that it had won in 1963. However, this improvement netted it a total of only four additional seats — three in Ontario and one in Manitoba. The two halves of Social Credit had come apart in the period prior to the 1965 election.[47] But, in spite of the damaging split between the Thompson and Caouette wings of the party, the 1965 election was not a complete disaster for either group. The western wing of the party held on to its four seats, and won an additional one in British Columbia from the Conservatives. Caouette, although his star had faded considerably from the heady days of 1962, nevertheless won nine seats in Quebec under the banner of his Ralliement des Créditistes. All of the divisions that had characterized the Canadian political map prior to 1965 seemed to have remained in place.

Advances in Election Studies

The 1965 election also marked the beginning of large-scale, survey-based, academic studies of Canadian voting behaviour. While scholars such as Meisel, Regenstreif, and Mildred Schwartz had conducted earlier pioneering studies, the first truly national election study was conducted in 1965, permitting some of the voting patterns of this period to be investigated in a much more systematic manner than had been possible in previous elections.[48] Findings from this groundbreaking social survey painted an intriguing picture of the composition and behaviour of the Canadian electorate during this period in which new patterns of party competition had become established in federal politics. The study portrayed an electorate in which there was considerable volatility, but also one in which certain political and social patterns seemed to have the potential to endure over successive elections. About two-thirds of those surveyed in the 1965 study reported having supported the same party in both the 1963 and 1965 federal elections (see Figure 5.6), with the remainder moving either between parties or to or from non-voting.[49]

On the basis of his earlier surveys, Peter Regenstrief had characterized the political allegiances of Canadians as "remarkably unstable."[50] Yet, the 1965 data, together with the election outcomes themselves, appeared to disclose a considerable degree of continuity in voting patterns over the three elections. The issues that had been stressed by the Liberals over the course of the campaign, particularly those involving social policy, seemed to resonate with much of the electorate (see Table 5.2). Relatively few mentioned the various scandals that had plagued the Pearson government, and nearly 1 in 10 respondents placed majority government at the top of the list. Yet the Liberals had actually lost ground over the course of the campaign. Clearly, campaign dynamics were extremely important, perhaps more so than had conventionally been assumed.

FIGURE 5.6

Electoral Turnover, 1963–1965

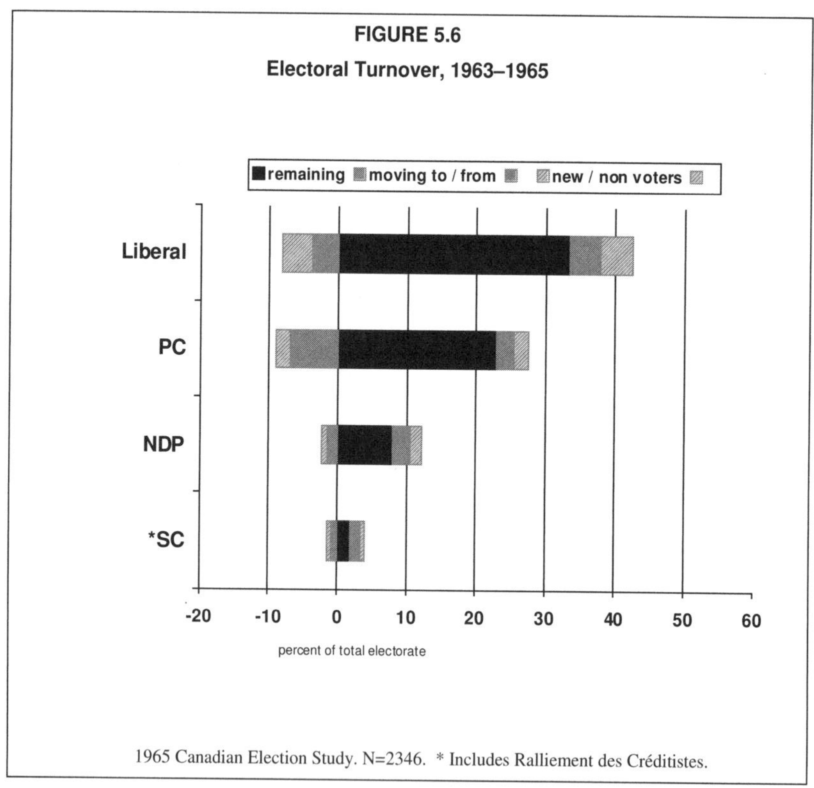

1965 Canadian Election Study. N=2346. * Includes Ralliement des Créditistes.

The findings of these early surveys of the Canadian electorate presented another puzzle for the scholars of the time, as the evidence gathered on peoples' feelings about political parties was subject to different interpretations. The early American voting studies, which had emphasized the importance of "party identification" in American politics, exerted an influence on this scholarly debate in Canada, as did findings from a number of European countries.[51] Some scholars believed that stable patterns of partisanship existed in Canada that were comparable to those often found in other countries. Sniderman et al., for example, later used the 1965 data to argue that identification with a party was the norm in Canada, as it was also in the United States, and that "the vote was marked by continuity, not volatility."[52] Indeed, the first reliable measure of partisanship, obtained in the 1965 study, appeared to portray an electorate with well-defined partisan attachments (see Figure 5.7). More than four out of every five Canadians surveyed in 1965 identified with a party, and within this group the Liberals appeared to hold a substantial

FIGURE 5.7
Federal Party Identification in 1965

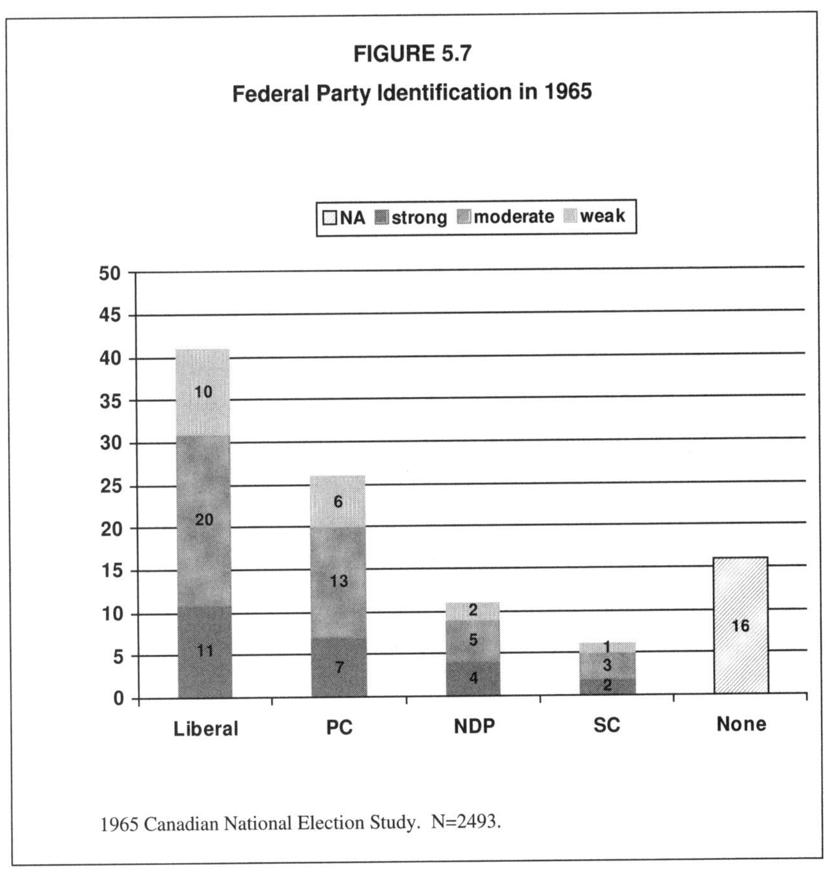

1965 Canadian National Election Study. N=2493.

advantage. But those allegiances also seemed to be relatively weak. Only 1 in 10 respondents to the 1965 survey thought of themselves as "very strong" Liberals, and the dependable partisan base of the other parties appeared even smaller. Jenson, Meisel, and others interpreted this same data differently, emphasizing both the weakness and the potential instability of Canadian partisan attachments.[53]

To some extent, the debate was not so much about partisanship as about its social and political underpinnings. In many other countries, notably in Europe, party systems reflected the cleavages that were most characteristic of the societies in which they existed — cleavages such as social class, religion, race, ethnicity, or region.[54] As a plural society, Canada was hardly immune from such cleavages. Yet they did not seem to possess the explanatory power often found elsewhere. Using the 1965 data, Mildred Schwartz found that a combination of "social structure" variables (including occupation, religion, and region) was able to explain only about 15 percent of the variation in voting behaviour in Canada — substantially lower than was found at around the same time in a comparable analysis of data from several European countries.[55] Among such factors, religion appeared to be more related to the vote in Canada than did other more likely candidates such as region or social class. This was puzzling to researchers, because the religious cleavage in Canada seemed in 1965 to be an artifact of the distant past rather than a meaningful contemporary basis of political division. An analysis by Irvine, again using the 1965 data, argued that religion was an intermediate variable, and that it was linked to partisanship only through other "cultural" factors such as language or ethnicity.[56] French-speaking Catholics, for example, were more likely to vote Liberal, not because they were Catholic but because they were francophones and resided in Quebec. But even at the time, the limits of such explanations of voting behaviour in Canada must have been apparent. John Diefenbaker, a western anglophone Protestant Conservative, had, after all, won nearly 50 percent of the popular vote (and 50 seats) in Quebec in the 1958 election. And Quebecers' historic leanings toward the Liberal Party, however well established, had not been strong enough to prevent the surge of the Caouette Créditistes in 1962, or to deliver Pearson his majority in 1965. The social and partisan cleavages that existed in Canada at the time, although real enough, were nevertheless vulnerable then, as now, to rather dramatic short-term swings driven by particular leaders, issues, or events. If a more stable pattern of party politics rooted in enduring social cleavages once existed in Canada, it belonged to a more distant past.

Conclusion

Although it was not obvious at the time, a new political dynasty was in the process of formation, aided by the outcome of the 1965 election. The Pearson government *had* been re-elected, despite the weaknesses of the leader and the shortcomings of the campaign. Pearson had managed to handle the social and economic issue areas with considerable success, and the national unity "problem," although persistent, was not yet a "crisis." Three strong new candidates had been recruited by the Liberals to run in safe Quebec ridings — Jean Marchand, Gérard Pelletier, and Pierre Trudeau — and they promptly became known as "the three wise men." All three were elected and became members of the cabinet during Pearson's second administration.[57] The ability to pass on power to a successor is as important an element in a successful dynasty as is the leadership question itself. Pearson's legacy, in spite of his failure to win a majority in 1965, would be favourably viewed by later historians and biographers.[58] The Trudeau dynasty, which we will explore in detail in the next three chapters, took its initial shape under Pearson's leadership.

Very soon after the 1965 election, attention began to focus on questions of leadership change in both major parties. Pearson and Diefenbaker now appeared as two aging chieftains, whose strengths and weaknesses were all too well known. Although his strong performance in the 1965 campaign could have given him the opportunity for a graceful retirement, Diefenbaker did not take it. He was eventually forced out of the leadership in a bitter internal party battle, to be succeeded in 1967 by the premier of Nova Scotia, Robert Stanfield, who was in many respects his complete opposite in terms of personality.[59] Diefenbaker's ouster from the leadership in 1967 established the practice of "leadership review," which would subsequently become institutionalized in both major parties. Pearson's exit was a more graceful one, securing the passage of the *Medical Care Act* in 1966 and presiding over Canada's 1967 centennial year. His new flag, which had been the subject of such divisiveness in the previous minority parliament, waved proudly over the Peace Tower.

The final reports of the Royal Commission on Bilingualism and Biculturalism were published over the next several years, leading, among other things, to the landmark passage of the *Official Languages Act* in 1969. But despite Pearson's policy accomplishments over five years of minority government, it would be his successor who generated the sense of excitement and renewal in Canadian federal politics that had been proven so elusive throughout much of the previous decade, and who would become the principal architect of the new Liberal dynasty that had taken root in the Pearson era.

Notes

1. The CCF won 10 percent of the popular vote in 1958 compared with 11 percent in 1957 and 1953.
2. The Liberal percentage in 1958 was 34 percent compared with 41 percent in 1957 and 49 percent in 1953.
3. On this topic, see Kenneth McRoberts and Dale Postgate, *Quebec: Social Change and Political Crisis* (Toronto: McClelland & Stewart, revised edition, 1980).
4. The Liberals won 51 seats with 51 percent of the total vote, to the Union Nationale's 43 seats and 47 percent in the provincial election of June 22, 1960.
5. For an account of this meeting, see Newman, *Renegade in Power*, 264–67. See also Arthur Schlesinger, *A Thousand Days: John F. Kennedy in the White House* (New York: Houghton Mifflin, 1965), 343–44.
6. One of the first major foreign and defence policy decisions of the Diefenbaker government in 1957 had been the decision to sign on to NORAD, this agreement having been concluded when the U.S. secretary of state, John Foster Dulles, visited Ottawa in July 1957, barely a month after Diefenbaker became prime minister.
7. See George Perlin, *The Tory Syndrome*, 61–71.
8. Coyne actually resigned in July 1961, following Diefenbaker's introduction of a bill in Parliament that would have declared the office "vacant."
9. *One Canada*, Vol. 3, 108–36.
10. *Mike: The Memoirs of the Right Honourable Lester B. Pearson*, Vol. 3, 4–57.
11. Keith Davey refers to Theodore White's book on the 1960 U.S. presidential campaign, *The Making of the President*, as his "textbook." Keith Davey, *The Rainmaker* (Toronto: Stoddart, 1986), 46.
12. See Desmond Morton, *The New Democrats 1961–1986: Years of Change*, 19–52.

13. Douglas was elected leader on the first ballot of the convention by a vote of 1,391 to 380 over then CCF leader Hazen Argue. See John C. Courtney, *The Selection of National Party Leaders in Canada*, 176–78.
14. The New Party candidate won 46 percent of the vote in the Peterborough by-election, compared with 7 percent for the CCF candidate in 1958. In Niagara Falls, the New Party candidate obtained 20 percent of the vote, more than double the total of the 1958 CCF candidate (10 percent). See Pauline Jewett, "Voting in the 1960 Federal By-Elections at Peterborough and Niagara Falls: Who Voted New Party and Why?" *Canadian Journal of Economics and Political Science*, Vol. 28 (1962), 35–53.
15. On the political transformation of Social Credit in the West at this time, see Peter Regenstreif, *The Diefenbaker Interlude*, 136–40. See also Frederick C. Engelmann and Mildred Schwartz, *Political Parties and the Canadian Social Structure*, 51–66.
16. Peter Regenstrief was among the first analysts of Canadian politics at the time to take note of the Caouette phenomenon in Quebec, through informal polling that he conducted primarily for the *Toronto Star* and other newspapers. See *The Diefenbaker Interlude*, ix–xii and 109–32.
17. Regenstrief, *The Diefenbaker Interlude*, 73.
18. J. Murray Beck, *Pendulum of Power* (Toronto: Prentice Hall, 1968), 332–33.
19. Keith Davey, *The Rainmaker*, 44–46.
20. CIPO #296 (June 1963).
21. On the characteristics of the Social Credit phenomenon in Quebec, see especially Maurice Pinard, *The Rise of a Third Party*, and Vincent Lemieux, "The Election in the Constituency of Levis," in John Meisel, *Papers on the 1962 Election*, 33–52.
22. The last of the Social Credit MPs from Quebec would not be defeated until the election of 1980. They were a factor, first in the support of, and later in the defeat of, the Clark government in 1979–80. See chapter 8.
23. See Newman, *Renegade in Power*, 351–54. See also Peyton Lyon, *Canada in World Affairs: 1961-63* (Oxford: Oxford University Press, 1968).
24. Hees and Sévigny submitted their resignations after the government's defeat in Parliament, and announced that they would not be candidates in the forthcoming election. Three other ministers — Davie Fulton, Donald Fleming, and Ernest Halpenny — later decided not to run again, but did not resign from the cabinet.
25. On these events, see *Renegade in Power*, 360–82.
26. The Liberals led 44 percent to 33 percent. CIPO #300 (February 1963).
27. Diefenbaker was preferred by the narrow margin of 33 percent to 31 percent. The balance had no opinion or rated both leaders equally. CIPO #301 (March 1963). See also Figure 5.5.
28. A total of 38 percent disapproved. The balance had no opinion. CIPO #301 (March 1963).
29. *Globe and Mail*, March 30, 1963: 6.

30. *Ibid.*
31. *Newsweek*, February 18, 1963.
32. Keith Davey, *The Rainmaker*, 64–65.
33. John Saywell (ed.), *Canadian Annual Review: 1963*: 17–18.
34. *Toronto Star*, March 16, 1963: 1; *Globe and Mail*, March 16, 1963: 3.
35. *Toronto Star*, March 21, 1963: 23.
36. *Toronto Star*, March 7, 1963: 1.
37. *Globe and Mail*, March 4, 1963: 1.
38. See J. Murray Beck, "The Election of 1963 and National Unity," *Dalhousie Review* 63. See also John Saywell (ed.), *Canadian Annual Review: 1963*, 41–42.
39. "The Stalled Omnibus: Canadian Parties in the 1960s," *Social Research* 30: 367–90.
40. The original suggestion of Keith Davey and Walter Gordon for a pledge of "one hundred days of decision" was altered by Pearson because he feared that "people would mix it up with the 'one hundred days' that preceded Napoleon's defeat at Waterloo!" Walter Gordon, *A Political Memoir* (Toronto: McClelland & Steward, 1977), 126. One hundred days would have given the government another month's grace.
41. At the centre of the scandal was Lucien Rivard, a businessman with Liberal Party connections, who was in the process of being extradited to the United States to face drug smuggling charges. See Saywell, *Canadian Annual Review: 1963.*
42. *Globe and Mail*, October 6, 1965.
43. *Globe and Mail*, November 2, 1965: 1.
44. *Globe and Mail*, October 8, 1965: 1.
45. *Globe and Mail*, November 6, 1965: 1.
46. *Globe and Mail*, October 30, 1965. See also Beck, *Pendulum of Power*, 381.
47. Réal Caouette and 12 other Quebec members left the Social Credit caucus in September 1963 and sat in Parliament as Le Ralliement des Créditistes. The other six Quebec members remained in the Social Credit Party under Robert Thompson's leadership.
48. The 1965 National Election Study was a single-wave post-election survey of 2,125 Canadians, conducted by Philip E. Converse, John Meisel, Maurice Pinard, Peter Regenstreif, and Mildred Schwartz. See John Meisel, *Working Papers in Canadian Politics* (Montreal, McGill-Queen's University Press, 1972).
49. Figure 5.6 provides a graphic display of reported patterns of movement among respondents to the 1965 Canadian Election Study. The solid bar represents those voters supporting the same party in both elections, while the shaded bars respectively show respondents who reported voting for different parties in 1963 and 1965 or those moving in to or out of the electorate (including previously ineligible voters and those who reported not voting in 1963 or 1965).

50. *The Diefenbaker Interlude*, 169. Regenstreif conducted more modest interview surveys of 210, 375, and 470 voters in the 1958, 1962, and 1963 elections. *Ibid.*, ix.
51. See especially Angus Campbell, Philip Converse, Warren Miller, and Donald Stokes, *The American Voter* (New York: Wiley, 1960).
52. Paul Sniderman, H.D. Forbes, and Ian Melzer, 1974, "Party Loyalty and Electoral Volatility: A Study of the Canadian Party System," *Canadian Journal of Political Science* 7: 286.
53. See Jane Jenson, "Party Loyalty in Canada: The Question of Party Identification," *Canadian Journal of Political Science* 8: 543–53, and John Meisel, "Cleavages, Parties and Values in Canada," *Sage Papers in Contemporary Political Sociology* (Beverley Hills, CA: Sage Publications, 1974).
54. See especially Seymour Martin Lipset and Stein Rokkan, eds., *Party Systems and Voter Alignments* (New York: Free Press, 1967).
55. Compared, for example, to 51 percent in the Netherlands or 37 percent in Sweden. Mildred Schwartz, "Canadian Voting Behaviour," in Richard Rose (ed.), *Electoral Behavior: A Comparative Handbook* (New York: Free Press, 1974). See also the introductory chapter by Rose, especially 16–18.
56. William Irvine, "Explaining the Religious Basis of Canadian Partisan Identity," *Canadian Journal of Political Science* 7: 560–63.
57. Although Trudeau did not become justice minister until April 1967.
58. See, for example, John English, *The Worldly Years: The Life of Lester Pearson, Vol. 2, 1949–72.*
59. See George Perlin, *The Tory Syndrome*, 71–107. Diefenbaker contested the leadership at the 1967 convention that resulted from this review process, and finished fourth in a field of 11 candidates. He withdrew from the contest after the first ballot (see Chapter 6).

Selected Reading

Courtney, John C., ed. *Voting in Canada* (Scarborough, ON: Prentice-Hall, 1967).

Diefenbaker, John G. *One Canada* (Toronto: Macmillan, 1977).

Gordon, Walter. *A Political Memoir* (Toronto: McClelland & Stewart, 1977).

Meisel, John, ed. *Papers on the 1962 Election* (Toronto: University of Toronto Press, 1964).

Meisel, John. "The Stalled Omnibus: Canadian Parties in the 1960s." *Social Research*, 30 (1963), 367–90.

Meisel, John. "The 1962 Election: Break-up of our Party System?" *Queen's Quarterly* 69 (1962), 329–46.

Newman, Peter C. *Renegade in Power* (Toronto: McClelland & Stewart, 1963).

Newman, Peter C. *The Distemper of Our Times* (Toronto: McClelland & Stewart, 1968).

Pearson, Lester B. *Mike: the Memoirs of the Right Honourable Lester B. Pearson* (Toronto: University of Toronto Press, 1975).

Pinard, Maurice. *The Rise of a Third Party: a Study in Crisis Politics* (Englewood Cliffs, NJ: Prentice-Hall, 1975).

Regenstreif, Peter. "Some Aspects of National Party Support in Canada." *Canadian Journal of Economics and Political Science* 29 (1963) 59–74.

Regenstreif, Peter. *The Diefenbaker Interlude: Parties and Voting in Canada.* (Toronto: University of Toronto Press, 1965).

Smiley, Donald V. "Canada's Poujadists: A New Look at Social Credit." *The Canadian Forum* 62 (1962) 121–23.

CHAPTER 6

TRUDEAUMANIA

"Prime Minister Pierre Elliott Trudeau speaking directly to the people of Canada, in the new Liberal Party approach to politics. The prime minister will freely and openly answer all questions."[1]

"He's new. He's frank." A shy smile as he talks directly to his interviewer.

"He's humorous." To a questioner from the Canadian Club in Kitchener who asked how he felt about creeping socialism: "I'm against creeping socialism, or any other kind of creep."

"He's a pragmatist, not bound by doctrine or rigid approaches. He is a seeker after solutions to problems, accepting the challenge of change." He believes we need to solve the French–English problem, the problem of regional disparity. He believes we need to balance the budget and be fiscally responsible. And he, emphatically, is not making promises, like conventional politicians. Pierre Trudeau is different. The signs behind him in the cheering crowd read: PIERRE FOR THE PEOPLE, COME WORK WITH ME. And finally, lingering on the television screen, there is just his picture.[2]

The 1968 campaign was unique in Canadian electoral history in that its main protagonist, Pierre Trudeau, was mobbed like a rock star wherever he travelled. Crowds and television audiences hung on his every word, to the extent that paid advertising was not necessary to get his message out to Canadians. Although some of his more celebrated exploits, like doing a pirouette behind the back of the Queen, were to come later, there were enough during the 1968 campaign to establish

Library and Archives Canada. Duncan Cameron, photographer

Pierre Trudeau at 1968 Liberal convention, Ottawa.

Trudeau's style as a truly different political leader. There were fancy dives into swimming pools, drives in his Mercedes convertible, kisses for pretty girls, signs that this shy intellectual had actually decided to make politics fun. When he visited Rideau Hall to advise the governor general to dissolve Parliament, he slid down the banister. The spirit of the early Trudeau period didn't last long, but it was fun while it lasted.

Pierre Trudeau, in victory and defeat, so dominated the era between 1967 and 1983 that it is sometimes difficult to recognize the fact that the developments that changed Canadian politics so thoroughly were only partly a product of Trudeau himself. His victory in the Liberal leadership convention of February 1968 followed an equally dramatic change in the leadership of the Progressive Conservative Party in September of 1967. With new leaders in both major parties, Canadian federal politics entered a new era.

A New Conservative Leader

John Diefenbaker's position as PC leader had been precarious as soon as the party lost power in 1963; it was generally accepted, at least in the academic and journalistic worlds, that a return of a Diefenbaker government was unlikely. Peter C. Newman's 1963 bestseller was a retrospective entitled *Renegade in Power: The Diefenbaker Years*, and Peter Regenstrief's pioneering empirical analysis of voting behaviour in 1965 was called *The Diefenbaker Interlude*.[3] These books and others essentially wrote off the prairie populist as a passing phenomenon, even though he was still the Leader of the Opposition. There were a number of attempts ("coup attempts," as Diefenbaker no doubt would have described them) to oust him from the party leadership. Quebec member Léon Balcer was convinced that with Diefenbaker at the helm, the party was doomed in Quebec, and he introduced a motion at a National Executive Committee meeting in February 1965 to hold a leadership convention. The motion was only narrowly defeated.[4]

The surprisingly strong showing of the Conservatives in the 1965 election (see Chapter 5) encouraged Diefenbaker to remain as Conservative leader, but it was not long before various elements in the party, led by national president Dalton Camp, began to manoeuvre to oust him. They felt that Diefenbaker's autocratic and unpredictable style would not allow the party to be rebuilt in such a way as to legitimately challenge for power again. Supported by the party's low standing in the polls as 1966 went on (see Figure 6.1), Camp campaigned for a "reassessment" of the leadership and the holding of a leadership convention. Without publicly mentioning the leader by name, Camp argued that the leader must show as much loyalty to the party as the party was expected to show to him.[5] At the party's annual meeting in November of 1966, Camp succeeded in securing re-election as party president, and in establishing the principle that a leadership convention would be held the next year. Diefenbaker loyalists were furious: "It was the night of the knives. It was the date on which the President of the Party assassinated the leader."[6]

For many Canadians inside and outside the Progressive Conservative Party, "The Chief" represented the past, while the whole country was looking ahead to the future. The centennial of Confederation was to be celebrated in 1967, and the celebration, symbolized by the new flag (which Diefenbaker strongly opposed), was widely anticipated. Support for the Tories in Quebec and Ontario showed no signs of recovery, and Diefenbaker appeared unconcerned about rebuilding the party in the centre of the country. Rather, he

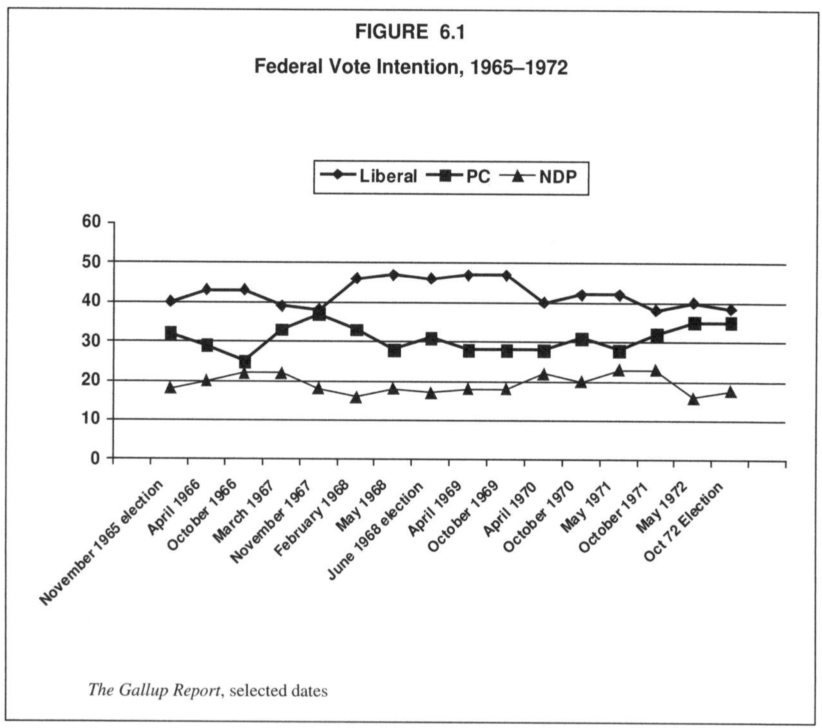

FIGURE 6.1
Federal Vote Intention, 1965–1972

The Gallup Report, selected dates

operated more and more in isolation from other Conservatives, and rejected any suggestion that it was time for him to retire. "Regularly, the pundits and prophets have predicted my demise. I allow the pundits and prophets to enjoy themselves while I continue to serve the Canadian people," he said.[7]

The division in the Conservative Party at this time was extremely bitter. For the pro- and anti-Diefenbaker forces respectively, Dalton Camp became a negative or positive symbol, standing either for the evil forces trying to rid the party of its most successful leader in the twentieth century, or for change and progress. Although he had been unsuccessful in his bid for election in a Toronto riding in 1965, Camp continued to work behind the scenes as a party strategist and national executive member and in public as national president. For his part, Camp was determined to ensure that a strong candidate emerge for the party leadership once the convention was called, because it was quite likely that Diefenbaker himself would enter the contest. His first choice was Nova Scotia Premier Robert Stanfield, a leader he had served in past provincial campaigns as a governmental adviser. But Stanfield procrastinated for such a long time that Camp made plans to run himself, despite the fact that such a move would badly split the party and would likely have been unsuccessful. Another possibility for the succession was Manitoba premier Duff Roblin, who also remained indecisive and undeclared. Both men were wary of their potential inability to unite the party, and fearful of inheriting the leadership of a party so divided as to doom its prospects in the next election.

As it happened, Stanfield did decide to contest the leadership, for the reason, some believe, that he feared the divisive effect on the party if Camp ran for the leadership. Roblin also eventually entered the race, as did a raft of former Tory cabinet ministers: Davie Fulton, George Hees, Wallace McCutcheon, Alvin Hamilton, Donald Fleming, and Michael Starr. Some of these candidates were partisans of Diefenbaker, later to be blindsided by "The Chief's" last-minute declaration of his own candidacy. With such a crowded field, a long multi-ballot convention became a virtual certainty. Indeed, five ballots were needed before a winner was produced. Roblin was handicapped by the dislike for him harboured by many of the other candidates; his late announcement that he was running had undercut their campaigns. Stanfield was initially handicapped by his association with Camp in his efforts to emerge as a consensus candidate between wings of the party, but he ultimately fared well with the ordinary constituency delegates, who formed the majority of those entitled to vote at the convention.[8]

TABLE 6.1

Party Leadership Conventions, 1967–1972

DATE	PARTY	LOCATION	WINNER	# CANDIDATES*	# BALLOTS	RUNNER-UP**
1967 09 05	PC	Toronto	Robert Stanfield	11	5	Duff Roblin
1968 04 04	Liberal	Ottawa	Pierre E. Trudeau	9	4	Robert Winters
1971 04 21	NDP	Ottawa	David Lewis	5	4	James Laxer

* On first ballot

** On final ballot

Stanfield, who later appeared slow-spoken and bumbling in comparison to Trudeau, was positively quick and snappy in comparison to Diefenbaker, and decisive in comparison to Lester Pearson. He espoused a centrist, cosmopolitan brand of conservatism, which relied little on the populism and rejectionism so vital to Diefenbaker. For example, at the outset of the 1968 election campaign, Stanfield attempted to counter Trudeau's theme of a "Just Society" with the promise of a guaranteed annual income for Canadians below the poverty line.[9] While this proposal was never fleshed out and was ultimately abandoned, it illustrates Stanfield's willingness to embrace a major social program. Such a stance of governmental activism was also to be found in the 1974 promise to enact wage and price controls to curb inflation. Robert Stanfield indeed appeared to embody the "progressive" side of Progressive Conservatism.

The public initially responded well to Stanfield's accession to the Tory leadership. As can be seen in Figure 6.1, by the end of 1967 the party had enjoyed a surge of popularity, to the point where they were running in a dead heat with the Liberals. If the Liberals under Pearson were to lose the confidence of the House (they were in a minority situation), it was distinctly possible that the Conservatives could find themselves back in government. The pressure for a renewal of leadership shifted suddenly to the Liberal Party. As Lester Pearson had been hinting that, once the centennial year was over, he would be prepared to leave the leadership, prospective candidates began to ponder their own futures as a potential prime minister.

A New Liberal Leader

As with the Conservatives, the list of potential Liberal successors was a long one. But unlike that party, the front-runners were cabinet ministers, not provincial premiers. Paul Martin, who had lost the leadership to Pearson a decade earlier, was confident it was his turn. Finance Minister Mitchell Sharp, Defence Minister Paul Hellyer, Health Minister Allan MacEachen, Registrar General John Turner, and eventually Trade and Commerce Minister Robert Winters, all decided to run for the job. As for Pierre Trudeau, first parliamentary secretary to the prime minister and then justice minister, a number of important figures in the Liberal Party, inside and outside Quebec, were intent on making him prime minister. Pearson himself was committed to the principle of alternation of French- and English-speaking leaders of the party, and wanted at least one strong francophone candidate. When Jean Marchand made it clear he would not run, Trudeau became Marchand's choice, and eventually Pearson's choice, as well. Pearson recalls in his *Memoirs:*

> As the campaign progressed, I came to the conclusion that he [Trudeau] and Sharp were the best candidates not only to succeed as Prime Minister but also to win elections. Trudeau created an immediate and exciting impression. He was the man to match the times, the new image for a new era. His non-involvement in politics became his greatest asset, along with his personal appeal, his charisma.[10]

Intellectual by nature, trained in law and economics, and vitally concerned with politics, Pierre Trudeau might well have set his sights on becoming a university professor, had the Quebec universities been open to adamant opponents of the Duplessis regime. Of the themes that marked his writing, the importance of individual liberty as a guarantee against oppression, and the need for a bill or charter of rights were most prominent.[11] A passionate democrat, he was prone to provocative statements, such as: "Historically, French Canadians have not really believed in democracy for themselves; and English Canadians have not really wanted it for others."[12] A fervent anti-nationalist, his diatribe against "Separatist Counter-Revolutionaries" begins, "I get fed up when I hear our nationalist brood calling itself revolutionary."[13] Though not explicitly a socialist, his writings were sympathetic to socialists, whom he urged to embrace federalism rather than centralism on the grounds that it provides numerous arenas for reform. In the periodical *Cité Libre*, which Trudeau founded with his friend Gérard Pelletier, he wrote political commentary and criticism on many subjects from 1950 onward. In 1956, a long and thoughtful analysis of the social, religious, economic, and political nature of Quebec society produced by Trudeau as the introduction to a book detailing the strike at Asbestos made his name more prominent as a commentator and analyst.[14]

By the mid 1960s, Trudeau had joined the Liberal Party, a party which had not escaped his critical pen and tongue. His view in 1960, for example, of the preceding Liberal dynasty was that: "Personally, I was convinced that King and St. Laurent had stayed too long in office and turned the Liberals into a party both arrogant and not democratic enough."[15] But his hopes that Diefenbaker would make substantive changes through, for example, introducing a meaningful Bill of Rights

Library and Archives Canada.

Robert Stanfield speaking at a dinner, Vancouver, 1971.

instead of one that cited good intentions but had no primacy as legislation, or outlawing the death penalty, were soon dashed. Trudeau's opinion of Lester Pearson's decision in the 1963 election campaign to accept nuclear warheads for missiles stationed in Canada was that: "Power beckoned to Mr. Pearson. He had nothing to lose but honour. He lost it. And his whole party lost it too."[16]

Despite these views, Trudeau was intellectually attracted to liberalism, and practically, he was attracted to power. The opportunity that beckoned in 1965 to him, Gérard Pelletier, and Jean Marchand, together with other Quebec colleagues like Marc Lalonde, to help fashion the Liberal Party's constitutional policies toward Quebec and toward individual rights, might never reappear. Trudeau justified his decision thusly: "Once the political critic decides to take action, he will inevitably join a political party he has already opposed," and, although it is fair for others to point this out, it is inevitable that compromises are made and important that action be taken.[17]

Once Trudeau was elected to Parliament in 1965, events moved quickly. He was appointed first parliamentary secretary to the prime minister, and then minister of justice. And then, in 1968, he sought the leadership of the party. Trudeau felt himself swept up in a tide not of his own making: "Running for the leadership seemed presumptuous for someone like me who had no deep roots in the Liberal Party, who barely knew the main party activists, and whose accomplishments to date were modest at best."[18] Some of Trudeau's biographers, like Richard Gwyn, take Trudeau's ostensible reluctance to seek the leadership at face value, though Gwyn also notes that he kept up the pretense of indecision even after he had decided.[19] It is true, though, that Trudeau's newness to the Liberal Party meant that he could not count on support from many longtime party activists.[20] He had to sell himself by virtue of his appeal to the public, which did not perceive him as a likely leadership candidate prior to the end of 1967,[21] and his possession of the aura of a likely election winner, which was rapidly given to him in the media.

Trudeau's candidacy for the Liberal leadership was helped along by his performance at a series of events that brought him more and more into the public eye. As minister of justice, he introduced, and eloquently defended, a bill that modernized legislation on divorce, abortion, and homosexuality, and in doing so uttering the memorable phrase, "the State has no business in the bedrooms of the nation." Trudeau biographers Stephen Clarkson and Christina McCall say that, while this phrase was not original with Trudeau, "Delivered by a minister of the Crown wearing a leather coat and sporting a Caesar haircut, it had an electrifying effect on the public imagination."[22]

In early 1968, Trudeau was the "star" of a federal–provincial First Ministers' meeting on the Constitution. During the televised proceedings, Trudeau entered into a confrontation with Quebec Premier Daniel Johnson over the place of Quebec in a federal Canada. Trudeau's defence of federalism at a time when separatist threats were looming, not only in Johnson's position but with the conversion of Quebec Liberal stalwart René Lévesque to the separatist cause, galvanized opinion in his favour, particularly in English Canada. Here was an attractive, highly intelligent federalist francophone who could "put Quebec in its place," or at least "deal with Quebec." That he based his opposition to Quebec nationalism on the position that Quebec should have a larger arena to operate in, as opposed to the narrow vision of the separatists, was a bonus.

"I tried to express simple and widely understandable ideas," wrote Trudeau later, "because I knew that if I became the leader those ideas would be the party platform in the general election that would follow. And so I based my campaign on the central theme of the Just Society."[23] Whatever the origins of the phrase "Just Society,"[24] Trudeau made it his own in 1968, in both his leadership campaign and the ensuing election. It was a brilliant organizing device, pointing as it did toward the future and committing the Liberal Party to leaving old prejudices and practices behind. It had relevance in all the issue areas that Trudeau wished to address. In reference to the liberalization of the Criminal Code and in moral areas like homosexuality, it promised justice under the law to all groups. In reference to national unity, it promised to "redress the Canadian state's traditional injustice towards French."[25] In reference to social welfare, it promised to support those in society who were in need. And in the economic realm, it called for attention to the development of poor regions like Atlantic Canada. In that one phrase of the "Just Society," Trudeau had established his mastery of all three essential issue areas for electoral success in Canada.

But the fine words would not have had the same effect if delivered by another speaker. It was Trudeau's personal charisma that put the message across. His style was full of seeming contradictions, shy yet forthright, playful yet serious, self-effacing yet arrogant, caring yet intolerant, serene yet impatient, tough yet vulnerable. His appeal to women was extraordinary, but female reaction to him did not appear to alienate males. Rather, Trudeaumania was a phenomenon which struck young and old, male and female. Pierre Trudeau seemed modern — the embodiment of the spirit of the country's second century. When Trudeau announced his candidacy for the Liberal leadership, he quickly became the odds-on favourite to win, despite the crowded field of candidates.

Aside from Pearson's covert approval, Trudeau had little establishment support before the convention itself. In part, this was because there were many ambitious ministerial candidates who had arranged for support bases within the caucus and party apparatus. In addition, there was a certain amount of resentment at the fact that Trudeau seemed to have come from nowhere to front-runner without paying his dues and earning the right to this status. One outspoken cabinet member, Judy LaMarsh, made no secret that she considered Trudeau an "arrogant bastard," even though she grudgingly admired many of his accomplishments as justice minister.[26]

A decisive development in the leadership race occurred when Mitchell Sharp withdrew from the race shortly before the convention and supported Trudeau, based on his self-assessment that he did not have a strong chance of winning. This was a sign of establishment approval that the finance minister would support the newcomer.[27] With Sharp came his parliamentary secretary, Jean Chrétien. At the convention, as the ballots went on, the contest became one between Trudeau and Robert Winters, a quintessential establishment candidate. This represented a left–right split within the party, as the old guard lined up behind Winters, except for John Turner, who refused to withdraw from the final ballot and thus maintained his neutrality. After four ballots, the verdict was narrowly in Trudeau's favour. The young people in the crowd were ecstatic. The Trudeau Era in Canadian politics had begun.

The 1968 Election

It is difficult in current political times to appreciate the atmosphere of hope and joy that surrounded the 1968 election campaign. "In a campaign that often seemed like a joyous coronation, crowds gathered by the tens of thousands ... simply to see [Trudeau]. Wherever he went, he was mobbed like a pop star."[28] It was remarked by many observers that Trudeau's speeches were often dull and boring, but this did not seem to matter; the crowds cheered them anyway. Trudeau's popularity was rated in the National Election Study 100-point thermometer scale measurement at 68, the highest score recorded for a Canadian political leader in these surveys before or since (see Figure 6.2). What is less often noted is that the thermometer ratings for the leaders of the two other major parties were also in positive territory, Stanfield at 56 and Douglas at 54. The 1968 election was conducted in a spirit of public benevolence and relative lack of animosity. It really did appear to be a "new politics."

"In the spring of 1968," wrote Ed Broadbent, later to lead the NDP, "we were prepared to vote for what we wanted to be rather than what we ought to be."[29]

If the Liberals initially proclaimed that, in a spirit of pragmatic realism, they were not going to make election promises, the other parties were not

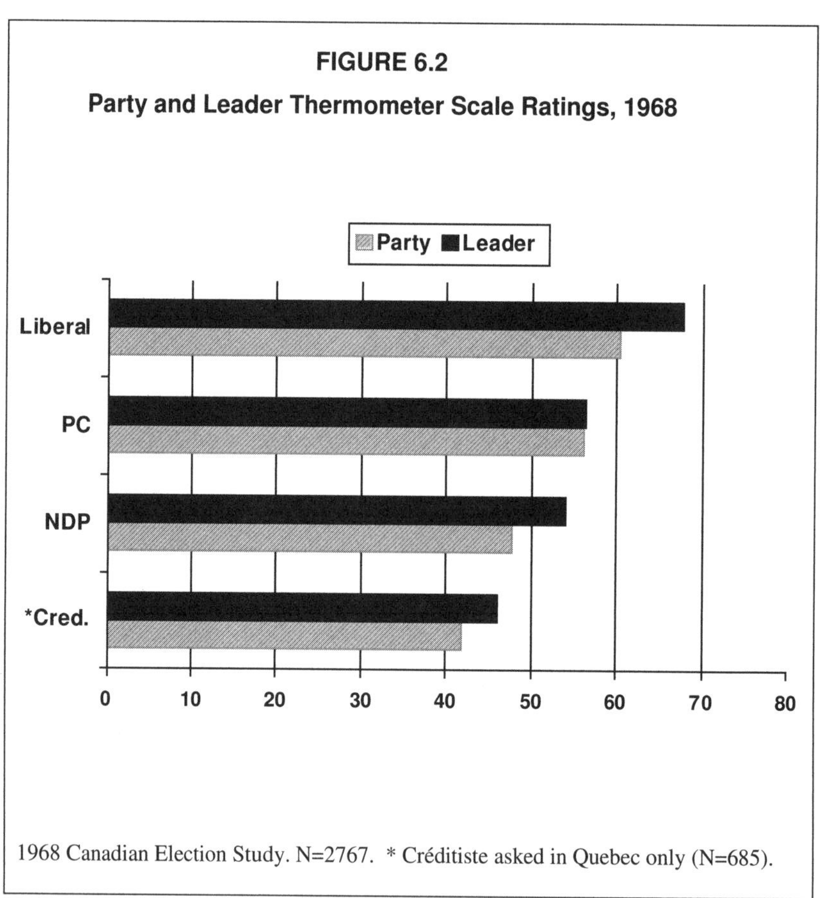

1968 Canadian Election Study. N=2767. * Créditiste asked in Quebec only (N=685).

similarly inhibited. Realizing that they could not compete on the basis of leader personality, the Conservatives began issuing policy statements early in the campaign, and continued for the duration. First, in early May, came the dramatic announcement that the Tories would bring in a guaranteed annual income for those living in poverty and unable to earn a living.[30] This was an effort designed to blunt the appeal of Trudeau's "Just Society," by allowing the Tories to claim they were actually going to do something to achieve equality. At the end of May, Conservative candidates received a blue leather-bound policy platform detailing 56 election proposals the party leadership was prepared to make. Many of these were early proposals of the party's policy advisory committee, headed by President Tom Symons of Trent University.

This document outlined a series of innovations in many areas besides that of social welfare. It focused on the state of Aboriginal life, and proposed to reorganize the Indian Affairs Department via a special task force. It promised to set up a special commission to control environmental pollution and develop a "national pollution abatement code." It proposed a complete foreign policy review, including the country's roles in NATO and NORAD. And in the agriculture area, improvements were promised in the creation of port facilities, farm credit, and crop insurance, with a special plan for development of eastern agriculture.[31] Added to these ideas was a promise by Stanfield in mid-June that, if the Tories formed a government, homeowners would be able to deduct mortgage interest over 7 percent from their income taxes.[32]

Not wanting to be outdone, the Liberals soon countered with a red leather-bound policy book containing their own platform. "The document is a dramatic attempt by the Liberals to counteract the image of Trudeau as the hero of a screaming cult of teenagers and to portray him instead as a Prime Minister with a carefully thought out program for his country," wrote Peter C. Newman.[33] The Liberal policy book, though vaguely worded and featuring few ideas with specific pricetags attached, did raise a number of issues that were to emerge at various times during Trudeau's tenure in office, such as an increase in federal government bilingualism, a charter of rights to be placed in the Constitution, a task force on the cities, and a reorganization of government departments.

The NDP ran an issue-based campaign, which began with a promise to raise the old-age pension. In addition, it took advantage of two prominent reports to propose implementing their recommendations.

One was the *Carter Report*, a Royal Commission on taxation, which proposed the implementation of a capital gains tax, among other reforms. The second was the *Watkins Report* on Canadian ownership of the economy, which proposed curbs on foreign ownership. NDP leader Tommy Douglas declared himself willing to accept the recommendations of both of these commissions in the interest of implementing genuine fairness throughout society.[34] However, the NDP's attempt to put a socialist class-based interpretation on Trudeau's call for a "Just Society" was lost in the wave of support for the Liberal leader.

FIGURE 6.3

Most Important Issues in the 1968 Election

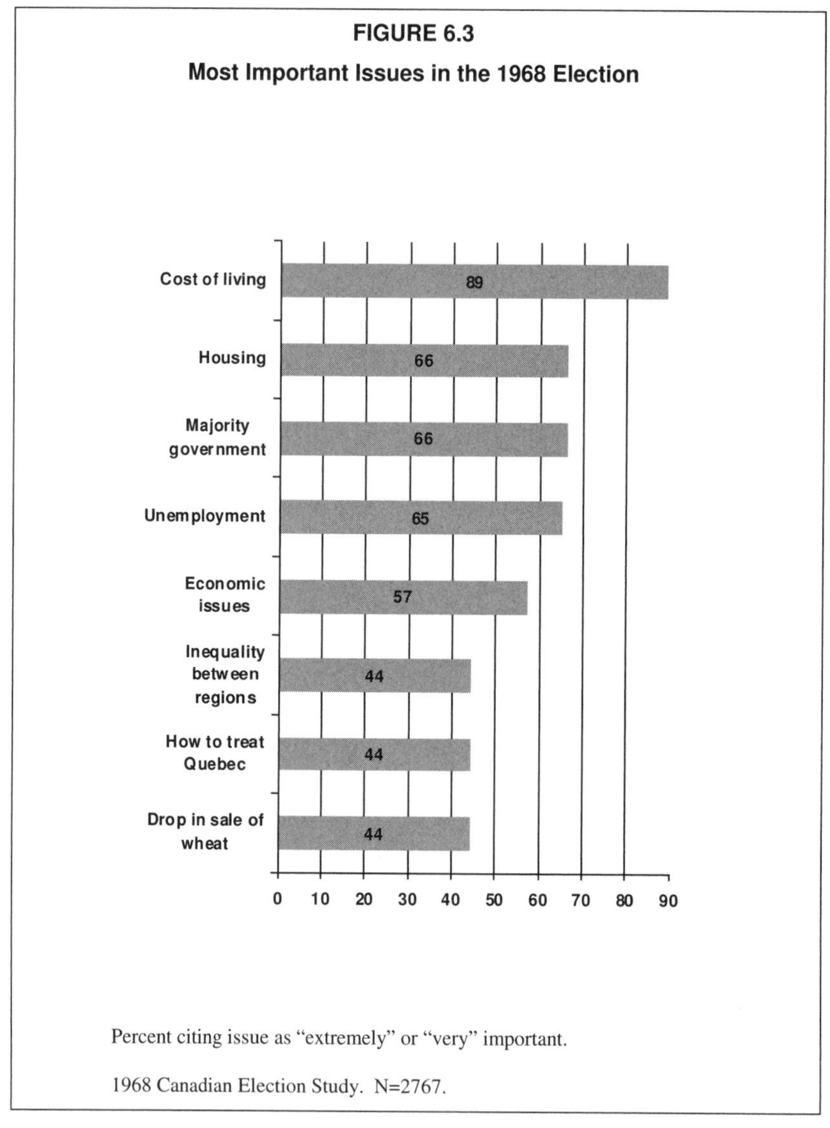

Percent citing issue as "extremely" or "very" important.

1968 Canadian Election Study. N=2767.

On paper, the number of issues in the electoral marketplace in 1968, and the detail with which they were delineated, was at least the equal of other Canadian elections. The importance of these issues, at least in their specific forms, is more problematic. Figure 6.3 gives the public rating from the National Election Study of the most important issues in the election. Taking them at their face value, we can see that several economic issues, particularly the "cost of living" and "unemployment," were cited as extremely or very important, along with "housing," which also has an important economic dimension. A variety of other issues, like those dealing with health and welfare and "how to treat Quebec" appeared less important to people. As we have already stressed, however, these latter subjects were very much a part of the Trudeau appeal, as encapsulated in his advocacy of the Just Society.

On the issue of Quebec, Trudeau proposed the extension of bilingualism, but explicitly rejected any special treatment for the province — a stance reminiscent of John Diefenbaker's "One Canada" position. The Liberal leader distinguished himself overtly from the approach recommended by the other two major parties. The NDP was in favour of special status for Quebec, a position, never clearly spelled out, which coexisted uneasily with the party's traditional commitment to a strong central government. The Progressive Conservatives, weakened substantially in the province after the dissolution of the Diefenbaker majority in the early 1960s, adopted a "two nations" policy toward Quebec at a policy convention in 1967. The party had intended this to be a simple and noncontroversial recognition of the existence of "two founding peoples" in Canada, in an effort to win back Quebec support. Through translating this idea from English to French and back again, the slogan of "two nations" took on the potential connotation of support for a Quebec state to match the separate nation.

The notion that the Tories were "soft on Quebec" was reinforced by the party's decision to appoint Marcel Faribault, a prominent adviser to Quebec Premier Daniel Johnson, as Quebec lieutenant for Stanfield.[35] Since one of the events that had led to Trudeau's rise to prominence was a widely publicized attack on Johnson for the Union Nationale's quasi-indépendentiste stance in constitutional affairs, the gauntlet was thrown down, and it was only a matter of time before Trudeau and the Liberals picked it up. In early June, Trudeau delivered a speech in British Columbia ridiculing the Conservatives for having "two voices on Quebec" — Faribault, and former justice minister Davie Fulton, who had claimed that Faribault did not speak for the party.[36] Then, as the campaign reached its conclusion, the Liberals published newspaper ads in the West attacking the Conservatives for supporting "two nations," implying that they were willing to break up the country. An indignant Stanfield accused Trudeau of a "smear campaign," while the latter replied that "he would have the ads withdrawn if Stanfield would state all over the country, including in Quebec, that he is opposed to the two nations concept."[37]

The Liberal exploitation of Trudeau's willingness to confront nationalist forces in Quebec came to a head on the day before the election. By coincidence or by design, the election date was set for June 25, one day after Quebec's St-Jean-Baptiste Day celebration. Trudeau had accepted an invitation to take part in a viewing of the traditional parade in Montreal from a reviewing stand downtown. At the parade, there was a violent clash between police and separatists, when the demonstrators attacked Trudeau with thrown bottles and other objects. Although urged to leave for his own safety, Trudeau remained firmly planted on the stand, clearly visible to the crowd, and the photographers. Conservative Party national president (and losing Toronto-area candidate) Dalton Camp was quoted as saying about the St-Jean-Baptiste Day riot, "The separatists made a supreme contribution to the achievement of our majority Government. When you are lucky in politics, even your enemies oblige you."[38] The election day headline in the *Toronto Star* was "Trudeau Defies Separatists."[39]

Camp's ironic reference to majority government echoes one of the Liberal themes of the campaign. After three elections in a row (1962, 1963, and 1965) that produced minorities of seats for the leading party in the House of Commons, there was a widespread feeling in the country that a majority was desirable this time to enable the government to be solidly in place for a normal term of office. Figure 6.3 shows that two-thirds of respondents to the National Election Study thought the issue of majority government was either "extremely" or "very" important. The tenor of the Liberal campaign, in particular, was designed to appeal to those wanting a stable majority. In his appearances, Trudeau continually urged Canadians to participate, to exchange ideas, to join him to work together for a great future. The implication was that he could be trusted to provide an environment for the carrying out of a great national leap forward to a better, more prosperous, more equal, more just society. All the talk of unity and togetherness may have masked the inevitable regional-, class-, and group-based conflicts in society, but it was extremely popular in the short run.

Trudeaumania appears to have overtaken the original strategic plans for the Liberal election campaign. A two-stage plan had been devised whereby, after the initial burst of enthusiasm for Trudeau had been satisfied by a whirlwind cross-country tour to let people see the leader and bask in his presence, he would become more serious and "prime ministerial" and produce more substance. This second stage was submerged by the waves of enthusiasm for Trudeau, which, to the astonishment of party officials, did not abate throughout the course of the campaign. "An examination of the party files suggests that Liberal strategists hardly understood Trudeaumania — let alone created it."[40] In part, this was because the wildest part of the passion for Trudeau was carried forward by young people, often those too young to vote.

The outpouring of enthusiasm for Pierre Trudeau overwhelmed Liberal organizers, and led to the establishment of a special youth wing of the Liberal campaign, called Action-Trudeau. Although there were four national coordinators, the structure called for the setting up of a separate Action-Trudeau group in each constituency, with a leader appointed by the campaign chairman.[41] The local leader recruited and trained the young workers in canvassing and phoning voters, and organized demonstrations and local entertainment. The national coordinators, and 10 provincial coordinators who worked under them, designed and supplied masses of promotional material, such as buttons, posters, and patterns for Trudeau mini-dresses and other clothing items. The existence of this separate campaign organization led by young people created substantial hostility on the part of the regular riding organizations, feelings which were only partly alleviated by the realization on their part that they could not handle the outpouring of young "Trudeau-workers."

Whatever their reservations, party officials had no wish to dampen the spirits of the wave of new supporters they had acquired. There is evidence, however, that as the campaign wore on, "Liberal strategists … started to get defensive and apprehensive about this new electoral phenomenon. Television was giving their leader all the exposure they felt they needed with regular news coverage, so the party decided not to purchase any television advertising."[42] When utilizing the slots of free broadcast time allocated to them, the Liberals ran long segments from Trudeau's speeches. Ironically, given his charismatic appeal, Trudeau was not a dynamic speaker, particularly when he stuck to a written text, as he often did.

In one free-time telecast, a half-hour was selected from a speech to a large outdoor crowd in Hamilton's Civic Stadium, normally used for football games. As usual, Trudeau's theme was the Just Society, but the subtopics were generalities: the importance of labour and management working together; the importance of the individual; the need to maintain social security; protection for consumers; the goal of a prosperous economy; the ideal of a peaceful world. He called on "all Canadians" to join him to solve these problems, and spoke of how "the Liberal Party is our party."[43] Over and over, these apparent platitudes were interrupted by applause. Cool in person, and cool on television, Trudeau exemplified the qualities of leadership. His friend Marshall McLuhan thought he was a perfect fit for the new electronic age.[44]

Not only was television campaign coverage important in 1968 to an unprecedented extent, but an event was staged which would later become a fixture in subsequent Canadian election campaigns — the leaders' debate. Held on June 9, two weeks before election day, the "National Debate" consisted of Pierre Trudeau, Robert Stanfield, and Tommy Douglas answering questions posed by a panel of journalists (Réal Caouette of the Créditistes joined the program for the last 40 minutes). Eighteen questions were posed during the two-hour program, with each of the three major party leaders having a limited time to answer each one.[45] Thus, the format was not so much a "debate" directly between the leaders as it was an extended "question and answer" session, where the leaders all addressed the same subjects. The topics ranged widely. The first question, stimulated no doubt by the recent assassination of Robert Kennedy in the United States, was about mandatory fingerprinting for those purchasing weapons. This was followed by a series of questions about the economic situation, including taxes, and later on by questions regarding the place of Quebec in Confederation, foreign policy, and other topics.

Both at the time, and subsequently, the verdict has been negative regarding the impact of the debate. The day after, the *Toronto Star* headlined "PM Admits It: Great Debate 'Pretty Dull' Stuff," and Peter Newman opined, "Nobody won it — but the audience lost."[46] In his history of the

Liberal Party, Joseph Wearing calls the debate "a disappointing bore."[47] But was there a winner? Two days later, Peter Regenstreif reported that a national survey had shown that NDP leader Tommy Douglas was chosen by 40 percent of viewers as having made "the best impression on you," with Trudeau second at 27 percent. A further question had established, however, that only 5 percent claimed that the debate had changed their vote intention.[48] Figure 6.4 shows the answers of the National Election Study sample to the questions of the winners and losers in the debate. The results are somewhat different from those reported at the time. In this survey done after the election, Trudeau clearly emerges as the one "who gained most in your eyes as a result of the debate," with Douglas

FIGURE 6.4

Perceived "Winners" and "Losers" in the 1968 Leaders Debate*

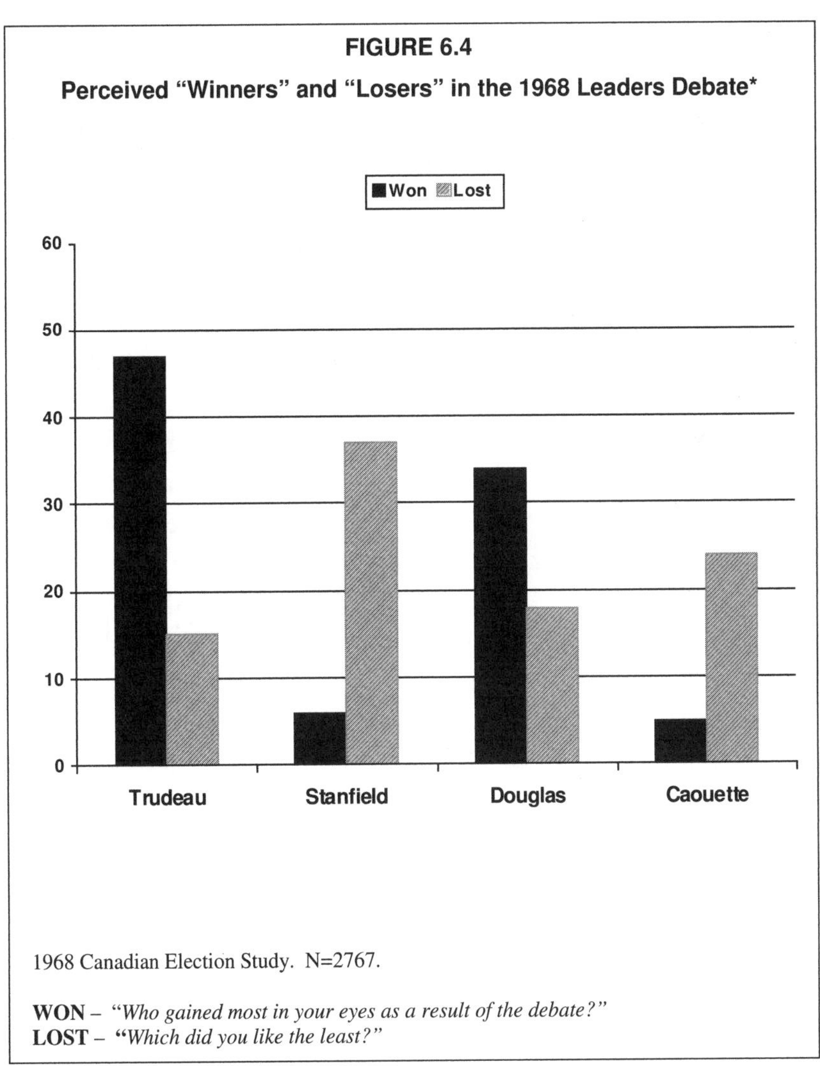

1968 Canadian Election Study. N=2767.

WON – *"Who gained most in your eyes as a result of the debate?"*
LOST – *"Which did you like the least?"*

in second place. It is clear, however, that Robert Stanfield suffered from his appearance in this television event. He appeared to be fumbling for answers at several points, and to be at a loss for words in determining his positions on some issues. Tommy Douglas was sure of himself and his answers, but sounded rather like the preacher he had once been. Suddenly joining the group near the end of the debate, Réal Caouette was at odds with all the others in terms of style, waving his hands, speaking quickly and passionately. And Trudeau was calm and almost above the fray, calling once again for the people to join him in searching for Canada's great future.

For all the assumptions that the election was over before it began, because Trudeaumania would sweep the country, the Liberal victory was modest in scope (see Table 6.2). The party's popular vote rose by about 5 percent nationwide, and the Conservative vote declined by only 1 percent. However, this shift in the popular vote produced 24 additional seats and a comfortable majority for the Liberals, whereas the Conservatives lost an equivalent number of seats. The Atlantic region went solidly for Stanfield, but the rest of the country was a different story. The Liberals held steady in Quebec and picked up seats in Ontario and the West to produce the result. The NDP won an additional seat, for a total of 22, but Tommy Douglas lost his riding by a handful of votes and shortly afterward announced his retirement as leader, a bitter reward for his success in the leadership debate. The Créditistes elected 14 members from ridings in rural Quebec, a minor success for leader Réal Caouette. Figure 6.5 shows that the electoral turnover was solidly in the Liberal direction, with twice as many voters moving from the PCs in 1965 to the Liberals in 1968 as moving from the Liberals to the PCs. In addition, those moving into the electorate in 1968, either from abstention or ineligibility, were more than twice as likely to choose the Liberals as any other party.

The post-election situation showed a decided "honeymoon effect" for Pierre Trudeau. Party identification (see Figure 6.6) measured after the election found that twice as many people considered themselves Liberals as Conservatives, a greater margin than the breakdown of votes for the two parties in the election. Having made so few specific promises during the election campaign, but promised so much in a general sense, expectations were bound to be sky high. Participatory democracy, social welfare, a new deal for cities, and above all a Just Society would be the heritage of the new era.

TABLE 6.2

Results of the 1968 Election

		Liberal	PC	NDP	Other	Liberal Net Gain/ Loss from 1965
Newfoundland	votes (%)	43	53	4	0	-
	seats (#)	1	6	0	0	-6
Prince Edward Island	votes (%)	45	52	3	0	-
	seats (#)	0	4	0	0	-
Nova Scotia	votes (%)	38	55	7	0	-
	seats (#)	1	10	0	0	-1
New Brunswick	votes (%)	44	50	5	1	-
	seats (#)	5	5	0	0	-
Quebec	votes (%)	54	21	8	18	-
	seats (#)	56	4	0	*14	-
Ontario	votes (%)	47	32	21	1	-
	seats (#)	64	17	6	1	+13
Manitoba	votes (%)	42	32	25	2	-
	seats (#)	5	5	3	0	+4
Saskatchewan	votes (%)	27	37	36	0	-
	seats (#)	2	5	6	0	+2
Alberta	votes (%)	36	50	9	5	-
	seats (#)	4	15	0	0	+4
British Columbia	votes (%)	42	19	33	6	-
	seats (#)	16	0	7	0	+9
Yukon / NWT	votes (%)	57	34	10	0	-
	seats (#)	1	1	0	0	-
TOTAL CANADA	votes (%)	46	31	17	6	-
	seats (#)	155	72	22	*14	+24

* Ralliement des Créditistes

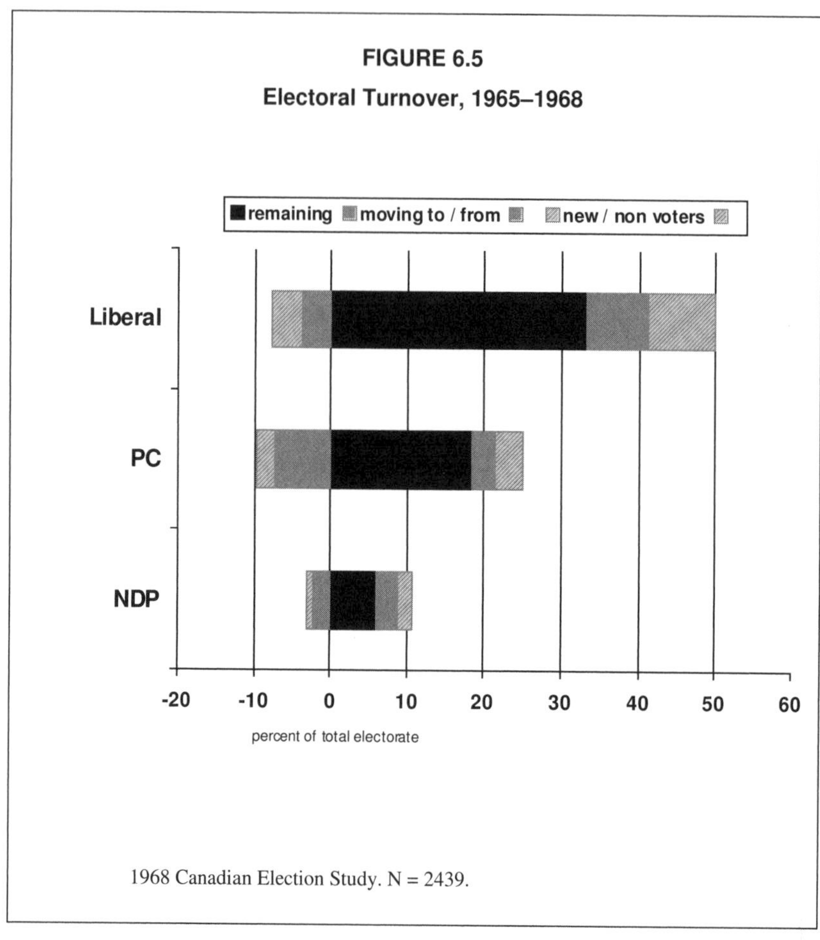

1968 Canadian Election Study. N = 2439.

As Trudeau set about governing, he placed his leadership rivals in the cabinet, but few experienced party operatives in positions of organizational power.[49] The unusual nature of the 1968 election campaign, where all the attention was focused on one leader and where the party itself seemed irrelevant, where the contact was directly between the leader and his adoring public, left Trudeau ill-prepared for the time-consuming and tedious work of implementing many of his "big ideas."

Trudeau In Power

During the 1968 to 1972 period, several factors led to a growing sense among Canadians that Pierre Trudeau was not the man they thought they had elected in 1968. The first problem was the seeming decline in the authority of cabinet, Parliament, and the Liberal Party itself as Trudeau surrounded himself with a new and powerful set of political advisers. Two figures in particular led the list. First as deputy clerk of the Privy Council and then as clerk, Michael Pitfield wielded extensive power over the bureaucracy. Only 32 years of age when given the clerk's office in 1970, his influence was based on his closeness to Trudeau. Pitfield was the architect of numerous organizational changes to the federal public service between 1968 and 1972, which included new ministries of state such as Urban Affairs and Science and Technology. He was also criticized for his politicization of the public service and some Ottawa commentators were convinced that the top ranks of the civil service had become indistinguishable from the Liberal Party.[50]

Marc Lalonde, a Montreal lawyer and member of Trudeau's original support group, was made head of the Prime Minister's Office; as the chief of staff, he dispatched orders to bureaucrats and cabinet ministers. In isolating Trudeau from the public, Parliament, and the party between 1968 and 1972, Lalonde came to illustrate the perception that Trudeau's personal staff had more influence with him than the cabinet. Indeed, according to biographer Richard Gwyn, "almost all Trudeau's ministers were intimidated by him and tailored their arguments to suit his style."[51] As if mesmerized by the fact that his personal appeal as leader had propelled his government to power, Trudeau allowed that personality to supersede both his cabinet and his party. In fact, some political commentators at the time claimed that he had, for all intents and purposes, replaced the Westminster-style parliamentary system with a quasi-presidential one. In most ways, the Liberal Party ceased to function between 1968 and 1972. Trudeau never consulted party president John Nicol, and the traditional intelligence-gathering function of the party and of backbench MPs was usurped by the new regional desks in his own office.

It was not long before things started to go wrong for the new government. Despite some initial indications from the provincial premiers that they would consider constitutional change, many of them began to grow suspicious or disinterested in entertaining proposals from Mr. Trudeau. For the first three years, federal–provincial negotiations on these matters had made little progress. In June of 1971, however, there appeared to be a breakthrough at the federal–provincial First Ministers'

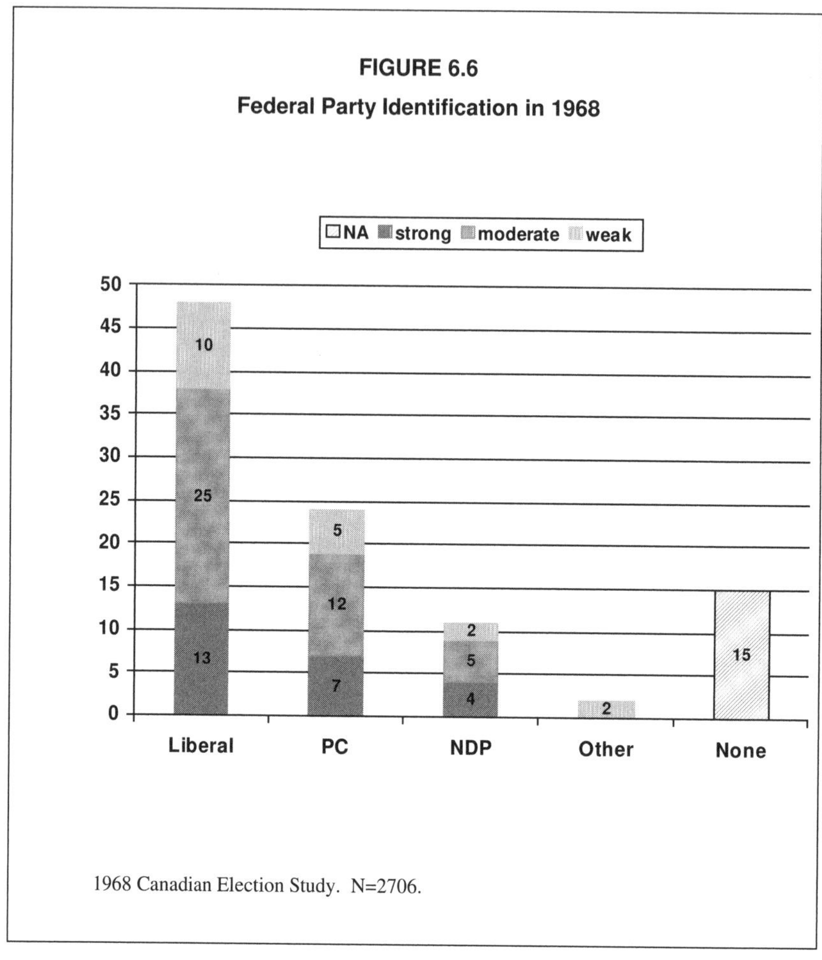

Conference in Victoria. After three days, Trudeau and the premiers emerged with an agreement that included a formula for amending the Constitution, a modest charter that guaranteed some rights, and language that would entrench the Supreme Court as well as ensure that any future judicial appointments would receive mandatory provincial approval. At last, Trudeau's obsession with constitutional renewal seemed to have been achieved. Within days, however, Robert Bourassa, the newly elected Liberal premier of Quebec, was subjected to a backlash of Quebec nationalists and trade unionists who were highly critical of the Victoria agreement. Soon he withdrew his consent to the deal and Trudeau was back at square one. There is little question that the energy he had put into the constitutional renewal project had been done at a cost to other planks in the domestic agenda. As Stephen Clarkson and Christina McCall concluded, "The public was tired of the subject. Canada's economic troubles were becoming serious, and arcane arguments over linguistic rights and amending formulas seemed irrelevant. Even Trudeau's closest allies in the constitutional wars thought the issue was dead."[52]

The most critical event in the national unity area that occurred during the Trudeau years, one that polarized the public more than any other, was the October Crisis of 1970. A small, revolutionary group promoting Quebec independence kidnapped Quebec's minister of labour, Pierre Laporte, on October 10, 1970, five days after they had seized James Cross, the British trade commissioner. Quebec nationalism, always Trudeau's bugbear, seemed to have taken a seriously violent turn. Trudeau was advised by his key political confidants that the only solution was to invoke the *War Measures Act*, a piece of legislation designed for wartime, when normal civil rights and legal procedures were suspended. The cabinet unanimously agreed to invoking the act on October 15, and it came into force the following morning.

Under this legislation, political rallies were banned and membership in the *Front de Libération du Québec* (FLQ) was made illegal, the legal right of *Habeas corpus* was suspended, and police were allowed to arrest, interrogate, and detain suspects without charge for up to ninety days. Many people were detained, particularly after Laporte's body was found. By early December 1970, the crisis was all but over but there was a great deal of political fallout. On one hand, Trudeau's "toughness" was admired in much of English Canada. On the other, the self-described champion of civil rights and liberties had imposed the *War Measures Act*, which suspended those very rights. Whether or not this was the right decision at the time has been debated for years. There is no doubt, however, that it emphasized the authoritarian side of Trudeau's "paradoxical" nature.[53]

While the idea that Trudeau would be the agent of Canadian national unity died a sudden death with the October Crisis of 1970, the decline of public confidence in his stewardship of the economy was more gradual. Expansion of the Canadian economy in the early and mid 1960s, though it had lowered the unemployment rate, produced an increase in inflation. By 1968, the inflation rate had reached 4.1 percent (after being, for example, 2.4 percent in 1965 and 1.8 percent in 1964) and rose to 4.5 percent in 1969.[54] This situation produced a substantial rise in public concern about inflation; in 1970 respondents to the Gallup poll reported it as the most important problem facing the country. The Bank of Canada reacted to the increase in inflation by curtailing the growth of the money supply, a policy that temporarily lowered the inflation rate but sharply increased unemployment.[55] Worried about the upcoming election, the government reintroduced an expansionary monetary policy that did almost nothing to the unemployment rate, but fuelled inflation once again. By the time of the 1972 election, the inflation rate was as high as it had been in 1969, and public concern about it had reached new heights.

Conclusion

The dramatic 1968 election victory set the stage for the Trudeau dynasty, the fourth in Canadian political history and the third to be organized by the Liberal Party. It became the most personalized Canadian dynasty, even allowing for the immense national appeal of Macdonald and Laurier. Unlikely as it seemed to those who knew him before he entered politics, Pierre Elliott Trudeau struck a responsive chord with much of the Canadian electorate. The Trudeau appeal was partly based on his ideas, especially individualism, with an emphasis on rights and accompanied with a splash of Canadian nationalism. It was also intimately tied up with the *way* these ideas were expressed; no previous leader had possessed the apparently effortless ability to give listeners a vision of the intellectual depth that lay beneath the words. Although close to 50 and just a little younger than his major opponent, many people referred to Trudeau as "young."[56] In relation to his two predecessors in office, of course, he *was* young. But it was primarily the dynamism and vigour with which he conducted himself that produced the image of youth.

The relatively contentless character of the 1968 election raised expectations very high for the Trudeau government. When these were not immediately fulfilled, and when the economic and national unity crises followed so shortly upon the election victory, the result was diminished popularity for the Liberals (see Figure 6.1). But despite the electoral setbacks of 1972 and 1979, Trudeau headed a Liberal government for all but nine months of the period between June 1968 and September 1984.

Though the negative aspects of his image — the aloofness, arrogance, and authoritarianism — had come to the fore by the end of his career, the forcefulness of his personality was such that, as his biographers put it, "He haunts us still."[57]

Notes

1. Liberal Party of Canada, free time broadcast, 5/31/1968. PAC V1 8805-0031.
2. Liberal Party of Canada, free time broadcast, 6/8/1968. PAC V1 8805-0015.
3. Peter C. Newman, *Renegade in Power: the Diefenbaker Years* (Toronto: McClelland & Stewart, 1963), and Peter Regenstrief, *The Diefenbaker Interlude* (Toronto: Longman's, 1965).
4. These are described in detail in George C. Perlin, *The Tory Syndrome: Leadership Politics in the Progressive Conservative Party* (Montreal, McGill Queen's Press, 1980), Chapter 4. For other accounts, see James Johnston, *The Party's Over* (Toronto: Longmans, 1971), 18; Geoffrey Stevens, *Stanfield* (Toronto: McClelland & Stewart, 1973), 162.
5. Camp delivered a speech to the Albany Club, a private gathering of influential Conservatives, in May of 1966, in which he argued, "the party is not the embodiment of the leader but rather the other way around; the leader is transient, the party permanent." Geoffrey Stevens, *The Player: The Life and Times of Dalton Camp* (Toronto: Key Porter, 2003), 168. This influential speech was never published.
6. Robert Coates, *The Night of the Knives* (Fredericton: Brunswick Press, 1969), 46. This book is full of inside accounts of the activity of the "Camp storm troopers" (57) as they accomplished their bloody deed.
7. John G. Diefenbaker, *One Canada: The Tumultuous Years, 1962 to 1967* (Toronto: Macmillan, 1977), 264.
8. On Roblin, see Perlin, *op. cit.*, 102–03. For an account of the convention, see Joseph Wearing, *Strained Relations: Canadian Parties and Voters* (Toronto: McClelland & Stewart, 1988), 208. Other substantial groups of delegates were party parliamentarians, and "delegates at large" from constituent groups within the party.
9. Jack Cahill, "Stanfield Promises Guaranteed Income for Nation's Poor," *Toronto Star*, May 6, 1968: 1.
10. Lester B. Pearson, *Mike*, Vol. 3 (Toronto: University of Toronto Press, 1975), 325.
11. Jacques Hebert, prefatory note to Pierre Elliott Trudeau, *Approaches to Politics* (Toronto: Oxford University Press, 1970).
12. This is the first sentence of Trudeau's essay "Some Obstacles to Democracy in Quebec," originally published in the *Canadian Journal of Economics and*

Political Science in 1958 and reprinted in Pierre Elliott Trudeau, *Federalism and the French Canadians* (Toronto: Macmillan, 1968), 103.

13. *Ibid.*, 204. Originally published in *Cite Libre* in 1964.
14. Pierre Elliott Trudeau and others, *The Asbestos Strike* (Toronto: James Lewis and Samuel, 1974), originally published as *La Greve de l'amiante* in 1956.
15. Pierre Elliott Trudeau, *Against the Current: Selected Writings, 1939–1996.*
16. Trudeau in *Cite Libre*, quoted by Stephen Clarkson and Christina McCall, *Trudeau and Our Times*, Vol. 1 (Toronto: McClelland & Stewart, 1990), 90.
17. Pierre Elliott Trudeau, *Cite Libre*, October 1965, in *Against the Current, op. cit.*, 25.
18. Pierre Elliott Trudeau, *Memoirs* (Toronto: McClelland & Stewart, 1993), 85.
19. Richard Gwyn, *The Northern Magus* (Toronto: McClelland & Stewart, 1980), 66.
20. Michel Vastel, *The Outsider: The Life of Pierre Elliott Trudeau* (Toronto: Macmillan, 1990), 129.
21. As late as December of 1967, *The Gallup Report* was not including Trudeau as a major contender for the Liberal leadership in its polls of public opinion on the matter, and the public was not raising him as a possibility either. Only 3 percent in that month mentioned any other contender than Paul Martin, Mitchell Sharp, Paul Hellyer, and John Turner.
22. Stephen Clarkson and Christina McCall, *Trudeau and Our Times*, Vol. 1 (Toronto: McClelland & Stewart, 1990), 107.
23. Trudeau, *op. cit.*, 85.
24. Clarkson and McCall say "it was a label Trudeau had appropriated from Frank Scott." *Op. cit.*, 115.
25. Trudeau, *op. cit.*, 85.
26. Judy LaMarsh, *Memoirs of a Bird in a Gilded Cage* (Toronto: McClelland & Stewart, 1969), 336–45.
27. Mitchell Sharp, *Which Reminds Me ... A Memoir* (Toronto: University of Toronto Press, 1994), 162.
28. George Radwanski, *Trudeau* (Toronto: Macmillan, 1978), 106.
29. Ed Broadbent, *The Liberal Rip-Off: Trudeauism vs the Politics of Equality* (Toronto: New Press, 1970), 3. As the title indicates, Broadbent argues that the 1968 confidence in the Trudeau Liberals was misplaced.
30. Jack Cahill, "Stanfield Promises Guaranteed Income for Nation's Poor," *Toronto Star*, May 6, 1968: 1.
31. Jack Cahill, "Tories Make 56 Promises ... And Its Only the Beginning," *Toronto Star*, May 31, 1968: 1,4.
32. Robert Miller, "Stanfield Promises Tax Relief to Ease High Mortgage Cost," *Toronto Star*, June 18, 1968: 1.
33. Peter Newman, "Now Non-Promising Trudeau Has 80 Promises to Make,"

Toronto Star, May 31, 1968: 1, 21.

34. Alan Whitehorn, *Canadian Socialism* (Toronto: Oxford, 1992), 88–89.
35. Andrew Salwyn, "Top Johnston Aide to Lead Quebec Tories," *Toronto Star*, May 13, 1968: 1.
36. Frank Jones, "Trudeau Hits Tories' Two Voices on Quebec," *Toronto Star*, June 4, 1968: 1.
37. Robert Miller, "Liberals Try to Exploit Anti-Quebec Feeling," and Frank Jones, "Trudeau Repudiates Ads Saying Tories Want Two Nations," *Toronto Star*, June 20, 1968: 1.
38. Camp quoted in Donald Peacock, *Journey to Power: The Story of a Canadian Election* (Toronto: Ryerson, 1968), 377.
39. *Toronto Star*, June 25, 1968: 1.
40. Joseph Wearing, *The L-shaped Party: The Liberal Party of Canada, 1958–1980* (Scarborough, ON: McGraw-Hill Ryerson, 1981), 190.
41. Jon H. Pammett, "Personal Identity and Political Activity: The Action-Trudeau Campaign of 1968," Ph.D. dissertation, University of Michigan, 1971. The account of Action-Trudeau in this paragraph is drawn from this study. A portion of this study, which does not concentrate on the political operations of Action-Trudeau, can be found in Jon H. Pammett, "Adolescent Political Activity as a Learning Experience: The Action-Trudeau Campaign of 1968," in Jon H. Pammett and Michael S. Whittington, eds., *Foundations of Political Culture: Political Socialization in Canada* (Toronto: Macmillan, 1976), 160–94.
42. Wearing, *op. cit.*, 190–91.
43. Liberal Party of Canada, free-time broadcast, 6/12/68, PAC V1 8805-0025.
44. Clarkson and McCall, *op. cit.*, 112, 126.
45. PAC V1 8210-0033/4.
46. *Toronto Star*, June 10, 1968: 1.
47. Wearing, *op. cit.*, 191.
48. *Toronto Star*, June 12, 1968: 1.
49. Christina McCall-Newman, *Grits: An Intimate Portrait of the Liberal Party* (Toronto: Macmillan, 1982), 120–28. See also Keith Davey, *The Rainmaker: A Passion for Politics* (Toronto: Stoddart, 1996), 159–63.
50. Gwyn, *op. cit.*, 78. Some Liberals who were awarded high-ranking civil service jobs were: ex-minister Bryce Mackasey, who was named Chairman of Air Canada; Bill Teron at the Central Mortgage and Housing Corporation; and Pierre Juneau at the National Capital Commission.
51. *Ibid.*, 87.
52. Clarkson and McCall, *op. cit.*, 277.
53. Anthony Westell, *Paradox: Trudeau as Prime Minister* (Toronto: Prentice-Hall, 1972).
54. Statistics Canada, *Main Economic Indicators.*
55. Frank Reid, "Unemployment and Inflation: An Assessment of Canadian Macroeconomic Policy," *Canadian Public Policy*, Vol. 6, No. 2, 1980: 291.

56. Jon H. Pammett, *Personal Identity and Political Activity*, *op. cit.*, 77. This observation was made frequently by young respondents when they were asked why voters in general were attracted to Trudeau.
57. Clarkson and McCall, *op. cit.*, 9.

Selected Reading

Clarkson, Stephen, and Christina McCall. *Trudeau and Our Times* (Toronto: McClelland & Stewart, 1990, 1994).

Gwyn, Richard. *The Northern Magus* (Toronto: McClelland & Stewart, 1980).

McCall-Newman, Christina. *Grits, an Intimate Portrait of the Liberal Party* (Toronto: Macmillan, 1982).

Peacock, Donald. *Journey to Power: The Story of a Canadian Election* (Toronto: Ryerson Press, 1968).

Perlin, George. *The Tory Syndrome: Leadership Politics in the Progressive Conservative Party* (Montreal: McGill-Queens Press, 1980).

Radwanski, George. *Trudeau* (Toronto: Macmillan, 1978).

Sullivan, Martin. *Mandate '68: The Year of Pierre Elliott Trudeau* (Toronto: Doubleday, 1968).

Stevens, Geoffrey. *Stanfield* (Toronto: McClelland & Stewart, 1973).

Stevens, Geoffrey. *The Player: The Life and Times of Dalton Camp* (Toronto: Key Porter, 2003).

Trudeau, Pierre Elliott. *Approaches to Politics* (Toronto: Oxford University Press, 1970).

Trudeau, Pierre Elliott. *Federalism and the French Canadians* (Toronto: Macmillan, 1968).

Trudeau, Pierre Elliott. *Memoirs* (Toronto: McClelland & Stewart, 1990).

Westell, Anthony. *Paradox, Trudeau as Prime Minister* (Toronto: Prentice-Hall, 1972).

CHAPTER 7

STUMBLING INTO A DYNASTY: 1972–74

Just four years after the excitement of the 1968 campaign and the national phenomenon of Trudeaumania had swept across the country, the very things that Canadians had admired about Pierre Trudeau in the 1968 campaign had become political liabilities. Trudeau's rhetorical embrace of participatory methods — his conversations with Canadians — that had played out so well in the 1968 election became meaningless musings. His intellectualism that was so appealing in the 1968 election was now perceived as arrogance or aloofness. Behaviour that was unlike that of a typical politician became less refreshing and more offputting. Trudeau's actions in the October Crisis of 1970 played no small part in this development. In short, the bloom was off the rose.

The day before Trudeau called the 1972 election, Robert Stanfield made the following comment about him:

> In 1968, Mr. Trudeau was accepted as the new spirit, above politics in the ordinary sense of the term. Now the people have seen him as prime minister for over four years. Some have seen him as a playboy who takes too many holidays. A great many doubt whether there

> is any warmth in his concern … I think he has difficulty in listening to people, difficulty in spending enough time with his caucus, keeping in touch with them and, through them, with the people of the country.… I have the impression Mr. Trudeau is pretty largely making the main decisions himself and relying mainly for advice on people he chooses. I don't think he suffers fools gladly. I don't want to sound patronizing to the Canadian people when I say this, but the prime minister has to be prepared to listen and to understand all kinds of people.[1]

As Opposition leader, Stanfield accomplished some impressive victories within his own party. He had brought peace within the party after the turbulent Diefenbaker years, and had subtly redirected the party's orientation from its outdated prairie populism to a more modern and more progressive approach to issues. However, although he was liked and respected as a man who was decent and dignified, the public had no clear sense of what he would be like as prime minister. And both Stanfield and his main adviser, Dalton Camp, knew that the widespread disillusionment with Trudeau did not mean that the Canadian people were automatically prepared to vote Tory. For one thing, Stanfield continued to be perceived in much the same way he had been in 1968, as "a nineteenth-century politician who had the ill luck to be born in the twentieth."[2] For another, the Conservatives had yet to come up with an alternate set of policy options which could be used as a platform for the next election.

The opposition was not helped in its pre-election planning by the fact that the economy was still in relatively good condition (see Figure 7.1). However, a number of signs of impending economic difficulties were in the air. Over the course of 1972, inflation began the steep rise that would dominate electoral discussion two years later. It had not yet been perceived as an imminent crisis, but by the fall, inflation numbers were reaching the point where it could be argued that the rate was nearly double that of the preceding year. Unemployment for the year 1972 was relatively steady at 6 percent, but seasonally adjusted figures issued at the end of the campaign put the September monthly rate at over 7 percent.[3] Economic growth was healthy, with the 1971 figure reading 6.4 percent rise in growth over the previous year, but by early 1972 figures were pointing to a slowdown (the year ended at 5.8 percent growth).

Library and Archives Canada. Duncan Cameron, photographer.

Robert Stanfield with photographers, Ottawa, 1967.

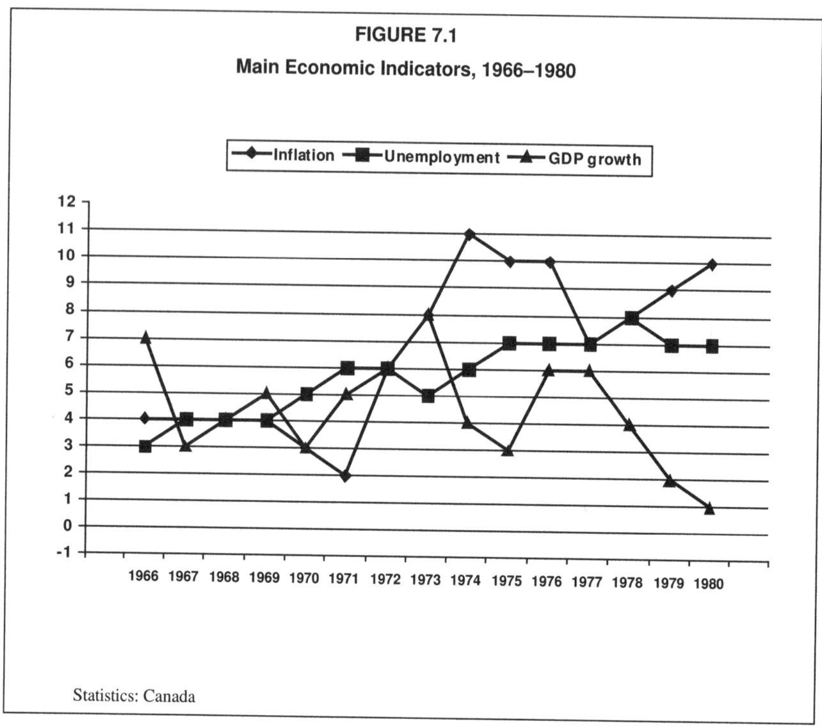

FIGURE 7.1
Main Economic Indicators, 1966–1980

Statistics: Canada

The public was uneasy about the economy, but undecided about the exact nature of the problem. Answers during 1972 to the Gallup poll opinion question "What is the most important issue facing Canada?" fluctuated between inflation and unemployment. In the June–July Gallup survey, 39 percent of those polled said that inflation/cost of living was the most important problem, followed by unemployment (36 percent). In the September survey, unemployment was identified by 58 percent as the most pressing problem with inflation/cost of living at only 9 percent. These fluctuations in public concerns meant that political parties did not have a clear target around which to develop their election platform. And as we will see, this, in turn, led to a perception that the politicians were not paying enough attention to economic policy.

The 1972 Election

Public opinion polls made it clear that the mood of the country was one that would be looking closely at where the parties stood on economic strategies and who the best leader would be in ensuring economic stability, despite the fact that it was not clear what the main economic problem was. While the economic vulnerabilities in Canada were similar to those faced by most advanced industrialized countries,[4] the government's ability to deal with the economy was weakened by the fact that more than two-thirds of trade was with the United States, and substantial levels of foreign ownership meant less national control of its economy.

A particular blow to the Canadian economy was a series of measures introduced by President Nixon in August 1971, including tax credits to corporations making investments in the United States and tax breaks on American exports. The fact that Canada no longer seemed to be a favoured trading partner of the United States, and the fact that Prime Minister Trudeau and President Nixon did not have close personal relations, did not help the Liberals when they tried to portray themselves as the most competent party to address the country's economic problems.

Despite the evidence that voters perceived economic problems to be the most important electoral issues facing the country, Trudeau and his advisers at MacLaren Advertising chose to adopt a very general theme, "The Land is Strong," as the centrepiece of the Liberal campaign. The intention of this slogan was to spread the message that, while there had been some problems over the past four years, Canadians had the will, the energy, and the ability to deal with them.[5] "The most important challenge facing Canada," Trudeau declared as he faced reporters after announcing the dissolution of Parliament, "is the preservation of its integrity."[6] Trudeau had been getting advice for some time that supported his inclination to run a different kind of election campaign, one focused not on confrontation with his opponents, but on "conversations with Canadians." It would be designed to emphasize the Liberals' unique ability to achieve national unity by appealing to all regions. Simultaneously, it would identify the weakness of the other parties, particularly the Conservatives in Quebec.

The Liberals anticipated that the opposition parties would make the economy and unemployment the primary issues, but did not believe that these would resonate with Canadian voters. Liberal strategists believed that most Canadians would either be satisfied that the economy was performing well or be tired of hearing the opposition parties talk of little else, or both. They counted on the Conservatives or the NDP having few new things to say on this issue. In retrospect, however, Trudeau himself was highly critical of the 1972 campaign slogan:

> Looking back on it, the errors I committed at the time seem startlingly clear to me. The campaign had gone badly from the beginning. The party had chosen an English slogan — "The Land is Strong" — that was both inept and untranslatable. As for me, I got off on the wrong foot by having a confused idea of my own role. I put myself at the head of the campaign, but I treated it not so much as an election battle as a simple appeal to the voters: "Here is the record of our four years in power; tell us what you think." I wanted to make a clean break between these elections and the emotionalism of Trudeaumania that had characterized the previous campaign.[7]

Initially, it was thought that the Liberals would unveil a "Liberal Charter" — a progressive series of ideas developed at a three-day policy convention in Ottawa to guide the decade of the seventies. However, by all accounts, it was not possible to forge a consensus in cabinet about what exactly would be contained in the charter. In particular, many cabinet ministers did not support the convention's resolutions on abortion, the guaranteed annual income, or an independent foreign investment review board.[8]

At the onset of the campaign, there was little evidence that the Tories were prepared to capitalize on the Liberals' poor start. Public opinion polls (see Figure 7.2) had shown the Conservatives to be gradually increasing their popularity in the period of time since the 1968 election, due to a combination of public unease with the economic future, mixed feelings about the Trudeau government's use of the *War Measures Act* in Quebec, and the increasingly divisive feelings that Trudeau himself had begun to inspire. The opportunity for opposition gains, if not outright victory, was present, but the Conservatives knew that they had to run a superior campaign to have any chance of winning the election. The Tory headquarters was in the Westbury Hotel on Yonge Street in Toronto, where Stanfield's senior assistant, Bill Grogan, and campaign manager Dalton Camp, set up shop. It was not clear, however, that their advice was being heeded. Surprisingly, rather than going after Trudeau and the Liberals on their economic and administrative record, Stanfield chose to emphasize his view that the overly generous provisions of the new

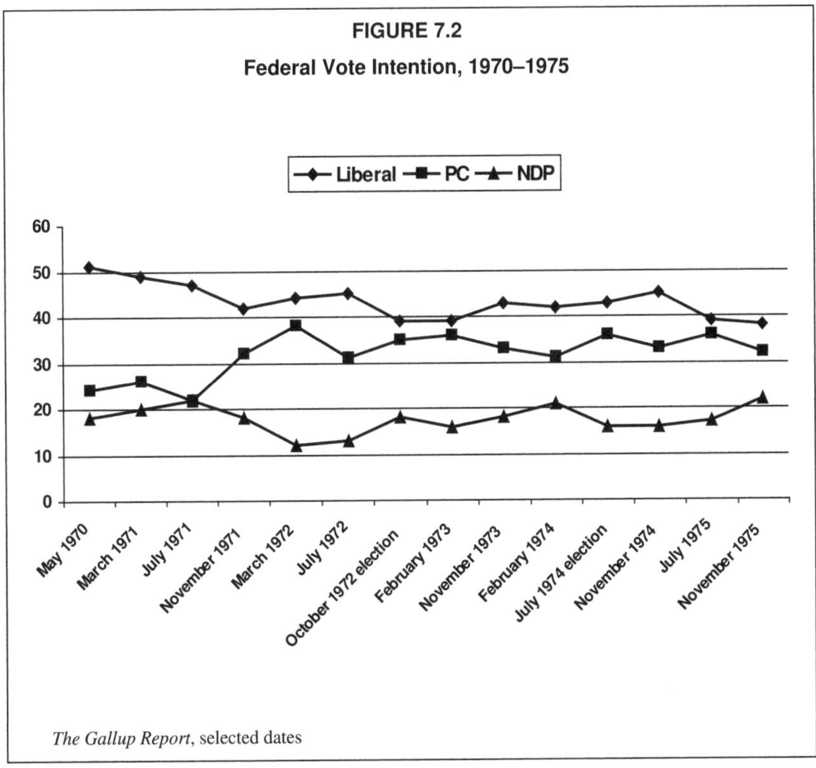

FIGURE 7.2
Federal Vote Intention, 1970–1975

The Gallup Report, selected dates

Unemployment Insurance Act which had come into force in June 1971 had weakened the work ethic of Canadian workers. The Conservative slogan, he said, would be "A Job for Canadians," meaning that Canada needed to be "a society that uses its human resources rather than wasting them."[9] Stanfield also had a major problem with the press, who perceived him as being very vague and frequently off-topic. According to his biographer, he "was accustomed to the gentle gopher balls served up by the docile Nova Scotia media and was … baffled by the low curves thrown by the national press."[10]

In a situation of lacklustre Liberal and Conservative campaigns, the NDP seized the initiative and the public imagination. David Lewis, the new leader of the New Democrats, did not accept the premise that the election campaign should be an abstract discussion of national priorities and strengths. Lewis decided to directly take on the business community that had been so critical of the welfare state. It was not the poor and unemployed who benefited most from government handouts, Lewis claimed — rather, it was business that reaped the rewards of economic policy. In speech after speech, Lewis criticized the "corporate welfare bums" that had benefited from government policies produced by both opponents, in that they were able to avoid taxes and maximize profits.

Realizing that his theme had struck a responsive chord in the public, Lewis and the NDP rushed into print *Louder Voices: The Corporate Welfare Bums*, a pocketbook that detailed charges against many corporations identified by name as having benefited from tax breaks that they had persuaded both Liberal and Conservative governments to enact. The book proclaimed, "government and big business are holding hands — in your pocket."[11]

Despite its successful theme, the NDP campaign was somewhat blunted in its impact by the friction within the party between the NDP establishment and the Waffle. The Waffle was a left-wing group that was promoting a return to its socialist roots — a "waffle to the left" — as they described it. In 1969, they released the *Waffle Manifesto*, which reflected the group's concern, among others, that the Canadian economy had been captured by American interests. They were highly critical of the NDP parliamentary caucus as having been co-opted by the centrist parties. The Waffle was expelled from the Ontario provincial NDP in 1972 but not without having hurt the NDP's electoral fortunes. On the eve of the 1972 election, polls indicated that the NDP had the support of only 15 percent of those surveyed.[12]

Despite the damage that the Waffle had done to the credibility of the NDP, there is no question that David Lewis ran the most successful campaign. Buoyed by the dramatic election victory of David Barrett and the NDP in the August 1972 British Columbia provincial election, Lewis campaigned where he knew the party had a chance — in the West, in northern Ontario, and in the industrialized areas of southern Ontario. Accepting the fact that they would not form the government, they campaigned on holding the *de facto* balance of power in Parliament with the clear if not-too-inspiring slogan "Canada Needs More New Democrats in Ottawa."

As the campaign progressed, leadership emerged as the factor that continued to favour the Liberals. Polls commissioned during the campaign showed that while the Liberals were slipping, Canadians, particularly younger ones, continued to believe that Trudeau was the preferred leader to Stanfield. This is important since the 1972 election was the first election held after the voting age was lowered to18 years of age. Despite the fact that both Trudeau and Stanfield had been opposed to lowering the voting age to 18 in the 1968 leaders' debate, the government announced its intention of introducing a bill to lower the voting age in the Speech from the Throne that was delivered on October 23, 1969.[13] Since many other countries were also lowering the voting age at this time (United Kingdom in 1968, Germany in 1970, the United States in 1971), this move was not particularly radical. Moreover, seven provinces had already lowered the voting age from 21. Between the 1968 and 1972 elections, the lists of electors produced by enumerations of the eligible population grew by over two million.[14] Interest in the 1972 election was high, partly for this reason. The turnout increased to 76.7 percent of registered voters, the highest since 1965 and much higher than the subsequent election of 1974.

Given that there was no National Election Study conducted in 1972, it is impossible to determine with precision which party this newly enfranchised 18–21-year-old cohort supported. Gallup poll leader preference data for voters 18–24 years and 25 years and older give some indications. Just under half of the voter cohort of 18–24 year olds surveyed felt that Trudeau would make the best prime minister compared to only 15 percent favouring Stanfield. Approximately 22 percent of older voters thought Stanfield would make the best prime minister compared to 36 percent who believed that Trudeau would make the best PM. Support for Lewis among younger and older voters was virtually the same at approximately 12 percent.[15]

Prominent cabinet ministers such as John Turner carried the issue of leadership across the country. At one point in the campaign, he was quoted as saying, "The election issue is leadership and that brings us to Mr. Trudeau. We don't have to compare him to the ideal. We don't have to compare him to the almighty. We have to compare him to the alternatives."[16] The Liberals entered the campaign certain of victory and confident that Trudeau still had the charisma to appeal to voters just as he had in 1968. However, the Trudeau of 1972 was not the Trudeau of 1968.

In Quebec, the political situation was evolving quickly. Trudeau's heavy-handed actions during the Cross and Laporte kidnappings in 1970 had two impacts. On the one hand, it galvanized the emerging nationalist factions in the province. Specifically, the Parti Québécois, an avowed separatist party, had been founded in 1968 and was gearing up to contest the provincial election of 1973. On the other hand, it had convinced the Conservatives that there were opportunities for them in Quebec — if they could find a prominent francophone to join Stanfield in the party's leadership team. Key people in the party doggedly pursued Claude Wagner, a former provincial Liberal cabinet minister who had left politics and was now a sitting judge. A survey that had been commissioned for the party suggested that Wagner's personal popularity within Quebec could result in winning a number of seats in that province. And, indeed, the Tory campaign literature in Quebec made scant mention of the Conservative Party at all. *"L'Equipe du Quebec Stanfield–Wagner"* toured the province with the message *"Wagner, C'Est Vrai,"* a slogan with the double meaning of "Wagner Is for Real" and "Wagner, it's True."[17]

In making the move to the Conservatives, Wagner claimed that joining the Tories could be defended given Trudeau's dismissal of Quebec nationalism. But his stock-in-trade was a "law and order" image, an appeal to those who, he said, were "searching for security, to be protected."[18] Honesty and straightforwardness were attributes associated with Claude Wagner. However, rather than becoming an asset for the Conservatives in Quebec, Wagner soon became a liability, as rumours began to swirl that he had been "bought" and had been guaranteed a huge cash settlement if he failed to win a seat. It turned out that Stanfield himself had authorized the establishment of a $300,000 trust fund in Wagner's interest to induce him to run.[19]

Considering the state of the respective campaigns, the election of 1972 not surprisingly ended in a virtual tie between the Liberals and Conservatives, at least in terms of seats in Parliament (see Table 7.1). The fact that the Liberals had two more seats (109 to 107) and four more percentage points in the popular vote, meant that they could carry on in power as a minority government without public disapproval, but the result ushered in a tense time of trial for Trudeau.

The key to the close outcome was the Ontario vote. In 1968 the Liberals had captured 64 of Ontario's 88 seats, but this dropped to 36 in 1972. The Conservatives captured 40 seats in Ontario, up from the 17 they had won four years earlier. The Conservatives also did well in the Atlantic provinces, the home region of Robert Stanfield, as well as in the West. If they had been able to couple these strong showings with gains in Quebec, where they had hoped to win between 8 and 10 seats, they would have formed a government, albeit a minority one. In fact, they only won two seats in Quebec, and slipped to third place in the popular vote behind the Liberals and Créditistes. The strategy of Claude Wagner as leader of a Quebec delegation of Conservatives had failed.

The near defeat of the Liberals in 1972, the resurgence of the Conservative Party in Ontario, and the surprising success of the NDP reflected an atmosphere of voter volatility not seen since 10 years earlier. The election result also led to much finger pointing and recrimination among the Liberals. While anti-Trudeau feelings were not seen as a significant factor in the near loss, there were many people who were blamed for the election outcome. Privately, the Prime Minister's Office (PMO) was accused of having been unrealistic and overly intellectual. The high philosophical ideals of the earlier Trudeau era simply did not work the second time around. Others blamed MacLaren Advertising and pollster Oliver Quayle for mismanaging the campaign. According to Liberal insider Jerry Grafstein, "the root of the problem was that MacLaren had become both 'judge and jury' of the entire media campaign."[20]

Yet others believed that Trudeau had failed to develop the extra-parliamentary wing of the party. One column quoted a Liberal insider as stating: "One of the failures of the Trudeau organization was the failure to bring along young people who came into the party in 1968 and to develop them in the organization."[21]

Much of the criticism that was launched at the PMO came from a group of Toronto MPs.[22] This group included some former operatives who had been influential during the Pearson era, as well as two defeated MPs, Martin O'Connell and John Roberts, who had joined the PMO as advisers. This group was influential for the better part of a year after the 1972 election. Their key recommendation was that Keith Davey be reinstated as federal campaign chairman.[23]

Trudeau was initially resistant to the appointment of Davey, as it seemed like a return to the days of cronyism and political professionals that he had always abhorred. However, it was evident by a series of early initiatives after the October 1972 election that efforts needed to be made to improve the party's electoral appeal, particularly in Ontario. In a cabinet shuffle that took place on November 27, 1972, almost all of the key economic portfolios — Finance, Industry Trade and Commerce, Labour, Energy, Mines and Resources, and National Revenue — were left with or handed over to men from Ontario, and "French power" was noticeably reduced in the cabinet.[24]

The real winners in the 1972 federal election were the New Democrats. As Desmond Morton has observed, not only did they hold the balance of power, but their 31-member caucus was likely the most

TABLE 7.1

Results of the 1972 and 1974 Federal Elections, by Province

		Liberal		PC		NDP		Social Credit	
		1972	1974	1972	1974	1972	1974	1972	1974
Newfoundland	votes (%)	45	47	49	44	13	10	-	-
	seats (#)	3	4	4	3	0	0	-	-
Prince Edward Island	votes (%)	41	46	52	49	8	5	-	-
	seats (#)	1	1	3	3	0	0	-	-
Nova Scotia	votes (%)	34	41	53	48	12	12	-	-
	seats (#)	1	2	10	8	0	1	-	-
New Brunswick	votes (%)	43	47	45	33	6	9	6	3
	seats (#)	5	6	5	3	0	0	-	-
Quebec	votes (%)	49	54	17	21	6	7	24	17
	seats (#)	56	60	2	3	0	0	15	11

Ontario	votes (%)	38	45	39	35	22	19	-	-
	seats (#)	36	55	40	25	11	8	-	-
Manitoba	votes (%)	31	27	42	48	26	24	1	1
	seats (#)	2	2	8	9	3	2	-	-
Saskatchewan	votes (%)	25	31	37	36	36	32	2	1
	seats (#)	1	3	7	8	5	2	-	-
Alberta	votes (%)	25	25	58	61	13	9	5	3
	seats (#)	0	0	19	19	0	0	-	-
British Columbia	votes (%)	29	33	33	42	35	23	3	1
	seats (#)	4	8	8	13	11	2	-	-
Yukon / NWT	votes (%)	30	28	39	39	30	33	-	-
	seats (#)	0	0	1	1	1	1	-	-
TOTAL CANADA	votes (%)	39	43	35	35	18	15	8	5
	seats (#)	109	141	107	95	31	16	15	11

able parliamentary representation they had ever had.[25] Pierre Trudeau moved to stabilize his precarious governmental position by making important concessions to the NDP in return for their support, though no formal coalition was offered or sought. Among other things, the Liberals raised the universal old-age pension by as much as $100 per month, and the NDP pushed the Liberals into passing Bill C-132, the government's new foreign investment legislation. There were also a number of other changes made in the pension field, and an income supplementation strategy was introduced. In fact, some claimed that the 29th Parliament marked a return to the government's preoccupation with social welfare policy, which had been the mantra of the Pearson era.[26]

Lewis and the NDP knew, however, that co-operating with the Liberals might cost them important political support, particularly in Western Canada. In the fall of 1973, at the NDP national convention, Lewis served notice that any future support of the Liberals would only be forthcoming if the Liberals made further concessions. By 1974, the initial popularity of the provincial NDP government of David Barrett in British Columbia was waning, a development which threatened the continued viability of the 11-member federal NDP contingent from B.C.

After the Liberals made known their intention to introduce their budget in May 1974, the NDP stated that three items must be contained in it in order to ensure their continued support. They demanded that there be a two-price system for Canadian commodities such as oil, gas, and lumber, that corporate taxes be substantially increased, and that the government introduce a subsidized 6-percent mortgage rate.[27] Refusing to make these concessions, the government was defeated on its budget and the campaign for the 1974 general election began. It is important to note that there had been 18 confidence votes in the House over the course of the session, and the government had endured numerous predictions of its impending defeat. The Trudeau government was in part able to survive because the Conservatives were ineffective as Her Majesty's Official Opposition in the post-72 parliamentary session. There is no question that they wanted the government to fall as quickly as possible.

However, it soon became clear that the Liberal minority government would not quickly collapse. Inflammatory attacks on the NDP by some members of the Conservative caucus did not help matters.[28] In their zeal to bring down the government, the Conservatives appeared to be more interested in achieving office than in presenting policy proposals to address the economic woes faced by the country. There were also a series of incidents that contributed to a decline in popularity of the Tories.

When the government introduced a motion to reaffirm support for the principles of official bilingualism, Stanfield could not command the unanimous support of his caucus and 16 members opposed the motion. This was seen as yet another indication of an anti-Quebec faction within the PC Party and further evidence that Stanfield did not have full control of his caucus, reinforcing perceptions that he was a weak leader. Rather than presenting itself as an alternative government or a government-in-waiting, the Stanfield Conservatives appeared to be fending off internal discord. The old rift between the pro-Diefenbaker camp and the Stanfield/Dalton Camp forces continued to simmer within the PC caucus.

A Gallup poll taken just before the government's defeat in May 1974 and published on June 5, showed the Liberals with 40 percent of the vote, and the Conservatives and NDP at 33 and 21 percent, respectively (see Figure 7.2). More importantly, a full one-third of those surveyed were undecided, which indicated that the campaign would be even more important than usual.

The 1974 Election Campaign

The widespread perception that the Liberal campaign in 1972 had been a disaster, together with the nearly equal parliamentary standing of the Liberals and Conservatives, resulted in careful and strategic planning for the upcoming campaign. The campaign period itself was likely to be decisive, and this time there were significant differences. Trudeau had now surrounded himself with astute political advisers and campaign professionals.

After the party had terminated MacLaren Advertising in the wake of the 1972 election debacle, they set up their own "in-house" advertising agency called Red Leaf Communications. This agency was under the command of Jerry Grafstein and was a consortium of highly partisan professionals from a variety of advertising firms across the country.[29] The Liberals also retained the services of Martin Goldfarb, who was widely viewed as Canada's premier pollster. Keith Davey and Jim Coutts managed the campaign on a tight leash, leaving nothing to chance. Their assignment was to identify policy issues and present ideas to the voters. According to Davey, "about thirty-five of us got together and finalized policies toward improved social security programs, easier home-buying, equality for women, and western freight-rate equalization."[30] Communicating these policy ideas to the voter was something that had been absent in the 1972 campaign. Davey and Coutts' approach to election planning was a far cry from the participatory methods espoused by Trudeau in 1968. Gone were the "Conversations with Canadians," marking the return to a more traditional elite-driven structure that has characterized the Liberals.

The Liberals were helped in their arguments by their ability to reference the proposed budget on which the government had been defeated. Trudeau kicked off the campaign by maintaining that he did not have to issue a platform (even though he said that a new one was coming imminently)[31] because his plans were all in the budget. "It's there; it's in the bills, it's written ... plans, not dreams.... These aren't campaign promises I'm giving you. They were written right there in the budget — and they voted against them!"[32] As the tone of the speech indicates, this was a more passionate, combative Trudeau than the country had seen before. As he had mentioned in an interview with the CBC's Patrick Watson in December of 1973, "next time around, I may be more impassioned and less rational. Who knows?"[33]

Convinced that the shift toward their party in the 1972 election was evidence of growing momentum, the Conservatives decided to take the offensive in the 1974 election campaign. By doing so they exposed themselves to attack.[34] By 1974, inflation had reached alarming proportions, and was dominating public discussion (see Figure 7.1). It was not difficult in this atmosphere for any of the parties to persuade the public of the importance of the issue and the desirability of taking action. To demonstrate their seriousness in the commitment to fight inflation, the Conservative Party proposed a system of wage and price controls. Although the details were not completely spelled out, the basic idea was to impose regulations on wage settlements and consumer prices. In taking this initiative, the Conservatives were gambling that their decisiveness would overcome a number of criticisms to which the policy was vulnerable. For one thing, inflation carries a variety of regional nuances. High grain prices may mean prosperity to the prairie wheat farmer, but may, at the same time, contribute to skyrocketing costs for Ontario livestock owners.[35]

The NDP response to this proposal was to argue that the Tory plan would in effect only be controls on wages, because wage settlements would have to be approved and prices would not be controlled at all. The Liberal response was to agree that inflation was a problem, but to maintain that it was a worldwide phenomenon, which would necessarily have to be alleviated on a more general basis. World oil prices, which were fuelling inflation, as well as other prices of imported goods such as food, could not be realistically subjected to domestic price controls. During the 50-day campaign, the PC wage and price control scheme came under attack from critics both outside and within the Conservative Party, and before long exceptions were being made:

> As the campaign progressed, the credibility of the simple, tough control policy was undermined by the Conservatives themselves. First, the leader kept adding qualifications to his initially strong policy: union contracts with built-in escalation clauses would still be valid; the price of farm produce would not be frozen; stock prices and interest rates would be exempted, and so on. Candidates' reservations were voiced with increasing volume as the concern about wage freezes rose.[36]

There was a lack of direction from the leader and the party's central campaign offices about the exact details of the policy, which left local candidates adrift when it came to explanations of its meaning on the doorsteps. And before long, Stanfield appeared to be downplaying the impact of the policy, leading to the May 27 headlines in the *Globe and Mail* "Stanfield Soft-Pedals on Price Freeze" and "Freeze on Prices and Incomes 'As Short As Possible' Stanfield Says." The final blow to the credibility of the Conservative wage and price control policy came when Trudean derisively depicted it as "Zap, you're frozen!"

To demonstrate their seriousness, the Conservatives decided to accompany their wage and price control policy with an austerity proposal regarding public expenditure. Stanfield maintained that a government run by the Conservatives would bring in a balanced budget (at a time when the Liberals were running a billion-dollar deficit) that would help to put the brakes on inflation.[37] While this pledge may have appeared persuasive in one way, it tied Stanfield's hands when he was asked about new spending or new programs. In contrast, there were promises made most days by Trudeau on such items as mortgage subsidies for low-income earners, a $500 cash grant for first-time homebuyers, a new policy for freight rates, a quarter of a billion dollars for urban mass transit, along with many others. These daily announcements put Stanfield on the defensive, forcing him to react and respond, but continue to avoid any commitments which would increase spending.

The media also took to competing with one another to publish unflattering photos of the awkward Stanfield. There were several embarrassing media shots of the Conservative leader, including one showing him fumbling a football, another wearing his trousers incorrectly inside cowboy boots and yet another showing him wearing a shirt with a Liberal sticker on his back.[38] Juxtaposed against these negative images of Stanfield was the debonair and newly energized Trudeau, moving through the campaign in a seemingly effortless manner.

Furthermore, Trudeau had at his side the "secret weapon" of his wife Margaret. Where Trudeau had previously insisted that his family life was separate from his political life, in the 1974 campaign his wife accompanied him to numerous events and delivered several impromptu speeches that praised him as a husband and father. She was successful in softening up his aloof and arrogant exterior by making statements like the following: "I want to speak of him as a person, as a loving human being who has taught me, in the three years we have been married and the few years before that, a lot about loving."[39]

As Table 7.2 shows, Canadians continued to be preoccupied with economic issues in 1974. Respondents to the 1974 National Election Study said that inflation was the most important issue (36.4 percent) followed by two other economic issues — the cost of living and unemployment at 7.6 and 7.3 percent respectively. This focus on economic issues was characteristic of the elections held during the Trudeau dynasty. National unity or confederation issues were pushed into the background, even though Trudeau maintained Liberal dominance in this area.

Not only did the Conservatives continue to struggle in Quebec, but this weakness was magnified by Stanfield's difficulties in French, and by internal disagreements within the party about the importance of bilingualism. One such example is found in Stanfield's decision to

TABLE 7.2

Most Important Issues in the 1974 Election

	Percent (multiple response)*
Economic Issues	
Inflation	38
Wage and Price Controls	8
The Economy (General)	5
Taxes / Government spending	4
Unemployment / Jobs	3
All other economic issues	5
National Unity	
Bilingualism / French language	3
Separatism / National unity	3
Foreign policy / Defence	2
Social Welfare	
Social programs / Social services	5
Pensions	5
Education / Health	1
Other social welfare	1
Other Issues	
The election / Majority government	7
The Leader / Leadership	6
Oil / Energy	2
Farm / Agricultural Issues	1
"Time for a change"	1
Other issues	3
No Important Issues	19
Don't Know	11

* 1974 Canadian National Election Study. N = 2,445.

refuse to recognize the candidacy of Leonard Jones in Moncton, New Brunswick, because Jones had been unwilling to endorse the party's support for official bilingualism. While Stanfield's decision was consistent with official Conservative policy, the fact that Jones had been nominated in the first place branded Conservatives as at least ambivalent about bilingualism. Jones's subsequent victory in the election as an independent further undermined the party's handling of the issue.

The NDP were strongly opposed to wage controls as unfair, but not as opposed to price controls, to the extent that they might prove workable. Leader David Lewis had been forced to adopt inflation as a key issue by the strong stance taken by the Canadian Labour Congress (CLC) at its convention shortly after the fall of the government. And while they blamed inflation on Liberal policies, the NDP spent almost as much time attacking the Conservatives on their wage and price control policy. In this sense, the NDP position added credibility to the Liberal attack. David Lewis and the NDP were also held responsible for the fall of the minority government and were resented by some for forcing yet another expensive — and in the eyes of many — unnecessary election. The conditions were thus set for strategic voting in 1974, primarily by NDP supporters who felt the necessity of choosing between the two major parties.

The Liberal brain trust knew that the Conservatives' biggest liability was its leader. Polls taken before the campaign had revealed that the public had retained a substantial amount of its confidence in the Liberal leader. To capitalize on this strength, the Liberals' strategy was to emphasize "leadership" as their core "issue" of the campaign. Although only 4.7 percent of Canadians stated that the leader or leadership was the most important issue in 1974 (see Table 7.2), Liberal strategists believed they could structure their response to inflation and other issues by maintaining that their superior leadership would provide the best response to growing economic problems. According to Clarkson, "the objective was to force the Conservatives to fight on the issue of leadership and back down from their issue of inflation."[40] The prime minister, always suspicious of the media, avoided them as much as he could during the 1974 campaign. In particular, the Liberals refused to participate in a leaders' debate, even though no debate had been held since 1968. Not only did this refusal to debate mean that Stanfield did not have the opportunity to make up the lost ground in leader comparisons that were occurring on the campaign trail, it also allowed Trudeau to escape being put on the spot about the cost of the Liberal campaign promises.

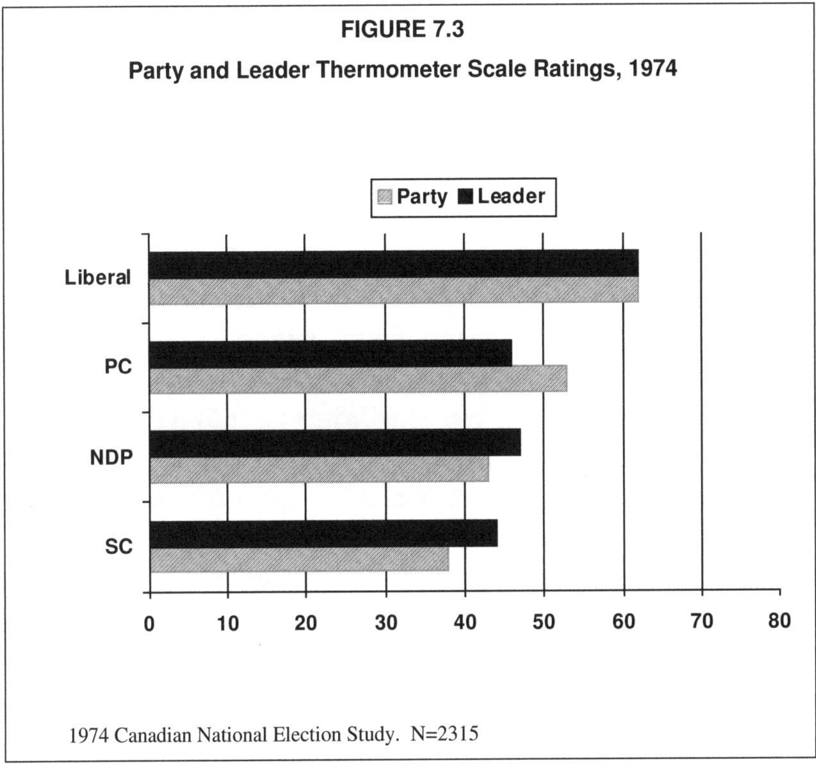

FIGURE 7.3
Party and Leader Thermometer Scale Ratings, 1974

1974 Canadian National Election Study. N=2315

Figure 7.3 highlights the mean party and party leader thermometer scores for the four main parties. For the Liberals, Trudeau and the Liberal Party were virtually synonymous in the public mind. Furthermore, their popularity scores were substantially higher than any of the others, exceeding the 60 mark out of 100. The Conservatives fared less well, and Stanfield lagged behind his party in popularity. To the extent that the Liberals could focus their attacks on Stanfield, and force a public evaluation of him rather than the party at large, they would benefit. For the NDP, on the other hand, and for the Créditistes in Quebec, leaders David Lewis and Réal Caouette were both more popular than the parties they led. In these cases, the Liberal campaign tactic was to criticize the NDP and Créditiste parties themselves, associating the former with too much state control and the latter with an outdated and problematic philosophy. In regional terms, Stanfield trailed behind Trudeau in every province of the country except his home province of Nova Scotia, and was well behind in the provinces of Quebec and Ontario, in particular.

The election of a Liberal majority government on July 8, 1974 was a surprise to just about everyone. Journalists had tended to discount the poll figures that showed the Liberals well ahead because they had been so inaccurate in 1972. The precarious situation of the Liberal minority government from October 1972 until the spring of 1974, and the media's daily reporting of the mood of the House, had attracted considerable negative attention. Although Gallup's pre-election figures proved highly accurate, other polls had placed the Liberals somewhat lower than Gallup. In fact, in its telecast on July 4, just a few days before the election, the CBC claimed that its polling suggested that a Progressive Conservative minority government was a distinct possibility.[41]

The Canadian National Election Study series of academic surveys resumed in 1974, under the direction of a new team. This allowed them, unlike in 1972, to look at the factors which influenced vote choice. The researchers published their main findings in *Political Choice in Canada*. The book analyzed voting behaviour in the 1974 election as part of a larger examination of the factors influencing the voting decisions of individuals. In addition to a new national post-election survey, the study included a content analysis of 21 major newspapers over 13 sampled dates. In total, there were 1,940 articles about the campaign, which represented an average of seven per issue. An estimated 78 percent of the newspaper coverage was national in scope compared to 18 percent that covered local races. An estimated 43 percent of the stories focused on the electioneering of the party leaders.[42] In addition, political issues and the parties were treated frequently in the context of the travels and pronouncements of the leaders. Because of the fixation on leaders, "the importance of their particular personalities was magnified, their family relationships became subjects of popular concerns, and extreme demands were placed on them and their speech writers to have something interesting and different to say on the same subjects several times a day."[43]

Table 7.3 compares both the positive and negative images of party leaders during the 1974 and 1968 elections. As shown in this table, Stanfield's negative image, in particular regarding his personality, was a clear liability when compared to 1968. Another interesting dynamic in this table is that Trudeau's positive images on the personality dimension in the 1974 election were only slightly below his "Trudeaumania" image of 1968. Moreover, his style and leadership images of 1974 were even higher than they had been in 1968. The Trudeau dynasty, despite the stumbles of the previous six years, was finally in place.

TABLE 7.3

Positive and Negative Images, by Leader, 1968, 1974

	Trudeau		Stanfield		Lewis	Douglas	Caouette	
	1974	1968	1974	1968	1974	1968	1974	1968
% of respondents mentioning								
Positive Images								
Personality	48	50	33	39	22	27	18	12
Style	36	25	12	16	19	26	21	17
Leadership	12	2	3	2	4	2	2	
Negative Images								
Personality	26	19	34	16	7	8	3	7
Style	17	22	24	30	10	8	8	11
leadership	7	1	2	3	2	1	1	1

Source: ***Political Choice in Canada***, 225

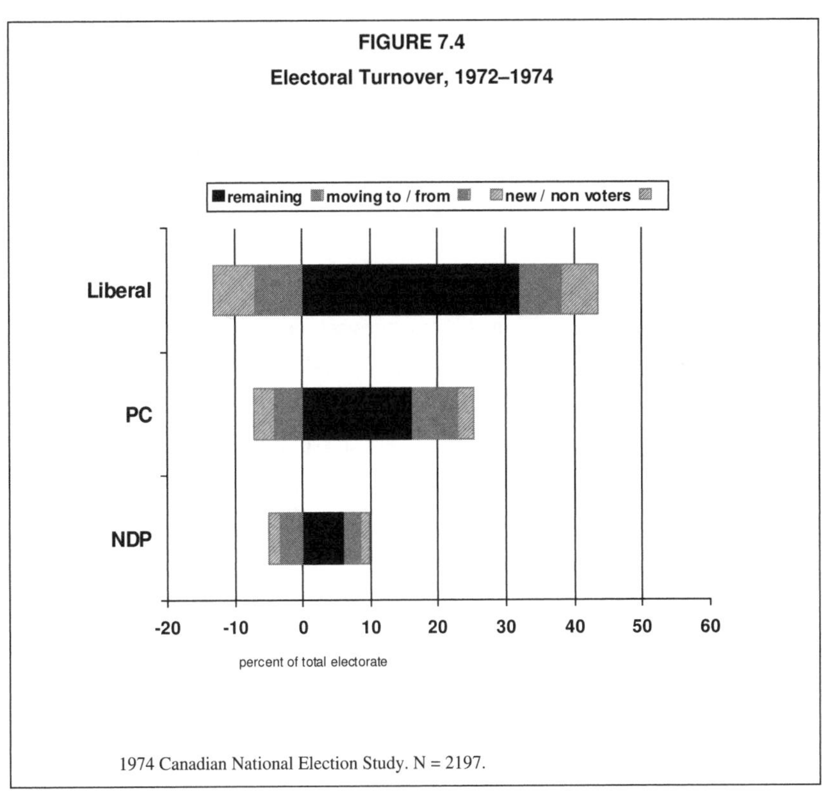

A glance at Figure 7.4 shows that the hesitation about predicting a Liberal victory may have been well-founded. These data from the 1974 election study show that the pattern of vote switching between those in the active electorate in both 1972 and 1974 was actually *away* from the Liberals. This is particularly apparent when direct switching between the Liberals and Conservatives is observed (5.2 percent of the entire electorate moving from a 1972 Liberal vote to the Conservatives as opposed to 3.4 percent going the opposite way). Offsetting this small net loss to the Liberals of their 1972 support, however, was an influx of previous non-voters and newly eligible voters who disproportionately chose the Liberal Party. In particular, the Liberals attracted an estimated 70 percent of the new voters in the 18–20 age bracket in Ontario.[44] The leader appeal to these groups played a major part in sustaining the Trudeau dynasty. Trudeau, with a little help from the media, was successful in shifting the focus of the electorate from inflation to leadership, and he took full advantage of his greater personal popularity among voters.

The New Democratic Party result in 1974 was as demoralizing to party officials and supporters as the 1972 result had been heartening. The overall national vote for the NDP dropped only 2 percent, from 17.7 percent in 1972 to 15.4 percent, but the party's representation in Parliament was virtually cut in half, from 31 to 16 seats. Particularly devastating were its losses in British Columbia, where the party lost 9 of its 11 seats. Leader David Lewis was defeated, and quickly announced his resignation.

As for the Social Credit Party, they had experienced some decline in Quebec and their leader, Réal Caouette, was in poor health. Some pundits were predicting the elimination of Social Credit, which had been a presence in federal politics in some form since 1935. Réal Caouette had his leadership challenged by several members of his own caucus and he had aroused some criticism for meddling with the provincial Quebec Social Credit Party.[45] There had also been some administrative gaffes such as nominating two candidates in one riding and no candidate in some ridings that had traditionally been strong in their previous support for Social Credit. Perhaps one of the most controversial positions taken by the leader was stating that he would accept Leonard Jones into Social Credit if he endorsed Social Credit economic ideology. But despite all of these difficulties and controversies, to the surprise of many, Social Credit took 11 Quebec seats. Given the predictions of the collapse of the party, this was an excellent result for both the party and its leader. However, the party ended up being one seat shy of retaining its parliamentary status as an "official" party.[46]

The Liberals recaptured 19 seats that they had lost to the PCs and the NDP in 1972 and strengthened their hold in Quebec, largely at the expense of Social Credit (see Table 7.1). It was not the majority that they had won in 1968 with 155 seats, but it was a majority nonetheless. The Liberals rebounded in almost every province, but the Ontario result was the key; there, they gained 8 percent of the popular vote and 19 additional seats.

Many Conservatives blamed the press for the failed Conservative campaign. While there was certainly some negative press coverage of Stanfield, the truth of the matter was that the PC campaign was poorly managed. In making wage and price controls the centrepiece of his campaign, Stanfield was vulnerable to challenges about the nuts and bolts of the policy. Indeed, the substantive details of this policy had never been worked out. He had been purposely vague about the scheme in order to reaffirm his personal approach to leadership, which was one of forging consensus. As George Perlin suggested:

> He has always tried to formulate policy statements in general terms that permit the adherence of the largest number of interests. The difficulty was that, in this case, general language provoked maximum concern. The benefits of an incomes policy were cast in doubt by the Liberal argument that inflation is an international problem for which there is no domestic solution; meanwhile, all groups with any leverage to adjust their incomes feared that controls would deprive them of their only defence against inflation.[47]

Perlin hypothesized that the Progressive Conservative Party suffered from a "minority party syndrome." It had always suffered from an endemic condition of internal conflicts, weak constituency organization, problematic communication between the national organization and constituencies and *ad hoc* campaigns. The minority party syndrome refers to the idea that the party's minority status is constantly self-generating.[48]

When applied specifically to the Conservatives, the result of this "syndrome" is that the party never seems to be happy with its leadership. This is important for a whole host of reasons. Given the organizational disunity of Canadian parties, the role of leaders both within these organizations, as well as a spokesperson for them, has become critical for electoral success, particularly in the television age. In both the 1972 and the 1974 elections, the Conservative leader did not present an appealing image that was capable of attracting new and undecided voters. A slight flirtation with the Stanfield Conservatives had occurred in 1972, but two years later the Trudeau Liberals were swept back into power with a majority.

Research conducted for the elections in the 1965, 1968, and 1974 National Election Studies indicates that, when confronted with a question of which factor — party leader, party as a whole, or local candidate

FIGURE 7.5

Federal Party Identification in 1974

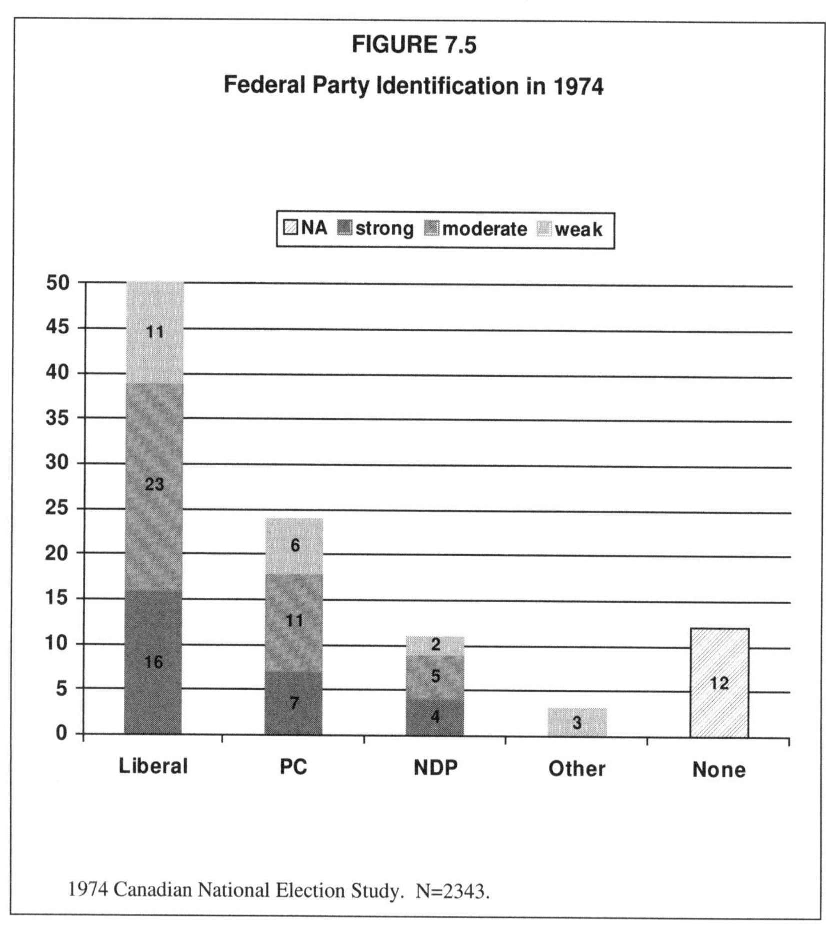

1974 Canadian National Election Study. N=2343.

— was most important to their voting choice, 30 percent, 42 percent, and 33 percent, respectively, of the respondents in these studies selected party leaders.[49] In 1974, Trudeau was the only leader to have a mean thermometer score (62) above the neutral point (50). Trudeau's average thermometer rating was positive in all provinces except Manitoba, while Stanfield's was only positive in the three Maritime provinces. Given that the Canadian National Election Studies since 1965 have found that, for a sizable proportion of the electorate, partisanship is either weak, unstable over time, or inconsistent across levels of the federal system, the importance of leadership can be a critical factor.[50]

Conclusion

In the final analysis, the 1974 election was a confirming election for the Trudeau dynasty, despite its electoral stumble two years earlier. After the election, a measure of party identification showed that nearly half of the electorate thought of themselves as Liberals, about twice as many as those who considered themselves Conservatives (see Figure 7.4). Despite coming so close to capturing power in the 1972 election, Stanfield made the decision shortly after the election that 1974 would be the last he would fight as the leader of the federal Conservative Party. Although he had managed to heal some of the wounds of the party left over from the Diefenbaker era, the Tories continued to be mired in party disunity and regional factionalism. And until such time that they could make significant breakthroughs in Quebec and Ontario, it was likely that the quest for power would be elusive.

The 1974 election also marked the end of David Lewis's political career as he failed to win his own seat. Perhaps this was the price that he and the NDP had to pay for holding the balance of power. Criticized as being too cozy with the Liberals by their own supporters and seen by the public as the villains that made the government fall early in its mandate, the NDP suffered at the polls. For their part, Réal Caouette and his Social Crediters survived, but lost official party status in the House. The 1974 election results represented the beginning of the end for Social Credit. Its appeal to younger and urban voters was minimal, and its long-time supporters and party workers were aging. Michael

Stein interpreted the result as suggesting that sooner or later a right-of-centre alliance of Conservatives and Social Crediters would bring about the end of the Social Credit phenomenon in Canada.[51]

As for Trudeau and the Liberals, their dynasty was consolidated in 1974. Three fundamental building blocks were established. Despite Trudeau's controversial image in Quebec itself, he was perceived as the one leader who could maintain national unity in the face of threats to the country. Second, the series of social welfare measures that his government enacted in the 1972–74 period, under the prodding of the NDP, allowed Trudeau to recapture the mantle of custodian of the welfare state, established for the Liberal Party by King, St. Laurent, and Pearson. Finally, the Liberal victory in the 1974 election, fought as it was over economic issues, put this essential issue-area in the Trudeau camp, as well. The next five years would see the entry of two new party leaders as the opposition parties jockeyed to test the Trudeau dynasty. And the majority they achieved in 1974 would give the Liberals the time they needed to demonstrate to Canadians, once and for all, whether they could manage the economy.

Jean-Marc Carisse, photographer.

Pierre Trudeau campaigning in Mount Royal, 1981.

Notes

1. Geoffrey Stevens, *Stanfield* (Toronto: McClelland & Stewart, 1973), 252.
2. Stevens, *op. cit.*, 196–97.
3. *Globe and Mail*, October 11, 1972: 1.
4. For an account of the changing nature of the post-war settlement, see Janine Brodie and Jane Jenson, *Crisis, Challenge, and Change: Party and Class in Canada Revisited*, 262–72.
5. Joseph Wearing, *The L-Shaped Party: The Liberal Party of Canada, 1958–1980* (Toronto: McGraw-Hill Ryerson Limited, 1981), 197.
6. John Rolfe, *Globe and Mail*, September 2, 1972: 1.
7. Pierre Elliott Trudeau, *Memoirs* (Toronto: McClelland & Stewart, 1993), 57.
8. Wearing, *The L-Shaped Party*, 171.
9. See note 6.
10. Stevens, *Stanfield*, 184.
11. David Lewis, *Louder Voices: The Corporate Welfare Bums* (Toronto: James Lewis and Samuel, 1972), quote taken from back cover.
12. Desmond Morton, *The New Democrats 1961–1986: The Politics of Change* (Toronto: Copp Clark Pitman,1986), 139.
13. Jon H Pammett and John Myles, "Lowering the Voting Age to 16," in Kathy Megyery, ed., *Youth in Canadian Politics* (Toronto: Dundurn Press, 1991), 95.
14. Elections Canada, *A History of the Vote in Canada* (Ottawa: Queen's Printer, 1997), 102.
15. Data from CIPO #355 (September 1972).
16. As quoted in James Stewart, the *Montreal Star*, October 12, 1972.
17. William Johnson, "Stanfield-Wagner Coalition Eclipses Party in Quebec," *Globe and Mail*, Friday September 29, 1972: 1.
18. Richard Cleroux, "How Wagner Was Chosen As PC Lieutenant in Quebec," *Globe and Mail*, September 25, 1972: 1–2.
19. George C Perlin, *The Tory Syndrome: Leadership Politics in the Progressive Conservative Party* (Montreal: McGill-Queen's University Press, 1980), 119.
20. Wearing, 200.
21. Geoffrey Stevens, "Return of the Rainmaker," *Globe and Mail*, May 11, 1973.
22. The Toronto group as they were called included Keith Davey, Jim Coutts, Dorothy Petrie, Kathy Robinson, Chris Yankou, Martin O'Connell, John Roberts, Boyd Upper, Tony Abbott, Bob Kaplan, Gordon Floyd, Gordon Dryden, and Jerry Grafstein. See Christina McCall-Newman's article in Dan Azoulay (ed.) *Canadian Political Parties* (Toronto: Irwin Publishing, 1999), 452.
23. Geoffrey Stevens, "Return of the Rainmaker," *Globe and Mail*, May 11, 1973.
24. Jack Cahill, "Trudeau Chooses Pragmatism Over Philosophy," *Toronto Star*, November 28, 1972.

25. Desmond Morton, "NDP Can Get More Done By Avoiding Another Election," *Toronto Star*, February 2, 1973.
26. Geoffrey Stevens, "What a Difference, Indeed," *Globe and Mail*, April 19, 1973.
27. Morton, 163–64.
28. George Perlin, "The Progressive Conservative Party in the Election of 1974," *Canada at the Polls: The General Election of 1974*, 105.
29. Keith Davey, *The Rainmaker* (Toronto: Stoddart, 1986), 165.
30. Davey, *The Rainmaker*, 182.
31. Norman Webster, "Trudeau Promises Whole New Election Platform Next Week," *Globe and Mail*, May 30, 1974: 8.
32. Norman Webster, "Trudeau's Political Kung Fu," *Globe and Mail*, May 27, 1974: 1.
33. George Radwanski, *Trudeau* (Toronto: Macmillan, 1978), 269.
34. William Irvine, "An Overview of the 1974 Federal Election in Canada," in Howard Penniman, *Canada at the Polls: The General Election of 1974*, 46.
35. Lawrence LeDuc, "The Measurement of Public Opinion," in Penniman, *Canada at the Polls: The General Election of 1974*, 211.
36. Stephen Clarkson, "Pierre Trudeau and the Liberal Party: The Jockey and the Horse," in Penniman, *Canada at the Polls: The General Election of 1974*, 90.
37. William Johnson, "Stanfield Promises a Balanced Budget," *Globe and Mail*, June 7, 1974: 1.
38. *Globe and Mail*, May 31, June 3, and June 12, 1974.
39. As quoted in Michel Vastel, *The Outsider: The Life of Pierre Elliott Trudeau* (Toronto: Macmillan, 1990), 190.
40. Clarkson, "Pierre Trudeau and the Liberal Party: The Jockey and the Horse," 80–81.
41. LeDuc, "The Measurement of Public Opinion," 240.
42. Harold D. Clarke, Jane Jenson, Lawrence LeDuc, and Jon H. Pammett, *Political Choice in Canada* (Toronto: McGraw-Hill Ryerson Limited, 1979), 279.
43. Clarke et al., *op. cit.*, 280.
44. Jon H. Pammett, Lawrence LeDuc, Jane Jenson, and Harold D. Clarke, "The 1974 Federal Election: A Preliminary Report." Paper presented at the 1975 Annual Meeting of the Canadian Political Science Association, 10, 12.
45. Caouette backed a candidate (Yvon Dupuis) for the leadership of the Quebec Social Credit Party who led it to a disastrous defeat in the 1973 provincial election. Caouette's intervention in provincial politics was opposed by a number of provincial members of Social Credit.
46. In 1974, the perks of being an official party included paying for the leader's salary and a research budget of $42,000, which would allow for the hiring of a secretary and other office workers.
47. Perlin, *The Tory Syndrome*, 112.
48. See Perlin, *op. cit.*, 118–19, for a more detailed discussion of this syndrome.

49. Clarke et al., *Political Choice in Canada* (Toronto: McGraw-Hill Ryerson), 208.
50. Clarke et al., *Political Choice in Canada*, 214.
51. Michael Stein, "Social Credit in the General Election of 1974," in Penniman, *Canada at the Polls: The General Election of 1974*, 180.

Selected Reading

Clarke, Harold D., Jane Jenson, Lawrence LeDuc, and Jon H. Pammett. *Political Choice in Canada* (Toronto: McGraw-Hill Ryerson, 1979).

Clarkson, Stephen. *The Big Red Machine* (Vancouver: UBC Press, 2005).

Davey, Keith. *The Rainmaker: A Passion for Politics* (Toronto: Stoddart, 1986).

McCall, Christina, and Stephen Clarkson. *Trudeau and Our Times, Volume 2: The Heroic Delusion* (Toronto: McClelland & Stewart, 1994).

Morton, Desmond. *The New Democrats 1961–1986: The Politics of Change* (Toronto: Copp Clark Pitman, 1986).

Penniman, Howard, ed. *Canada at the Polls: The General Election of 1974* (Washington, D.C.: American Enterprise Institute for Public Policy Research, 1975).

Perlin, George C. *The Tory Syndrome: Leadership Politics in the Progressive Conservative Party* (Montreal: McGill-Queen's Press, 1980).

Stevens, Geoffrey. *Stanfield* (Toronto: McClelland & Stewart, 1973).

Wearing, Joseph. *The L-Shaped Party: The Liberal Party of Canada 1958–1980* (Toronto: McGraw-Hill Ryerson, 1981).

CHAPTER 8

THE CLARK INTERLUDE AND THE RETURN OF THE LIBERALS

The economy in the late 1970s looked much as it had for most of the decade; external and domestic problems were taking their toll. The inflation rate remained high for the year after the Liberal victory of 1974, until public concern about the inflation problem reached a peak in October of that year, when fully 84 percent of the public told the Gallup Organization that inflation was the most important problem facing Canada.[1] When this situation continued on into 1975, the Trudeau government decided it needed to take some action as its popularity began to drop (see Figure 8.1).

Despite his previous disdain for a wage and price control program during the 1974 election, Trudeau decided that such a policy was the only option. At first, the policy was to be a "voluntary" program of wage and price restraint, and Finance Minister John Turner toured the country to persuade business and labour to temper their actions and demands. When this did not produce results, and shortly after Turner's resignation (more fully described when he is profiled in Chapter 9), Trudeau announced a program of wage and price controls, complete with an Anti-Inflation Board and Secretariat to oversee compliance. This decision angered the Conservative opposition. During the election campaign of 1974, Trudeau and the Liberals had ridiculed the Conservative proposal on wage and price controls on the grounds that it was impractical (see Chapter 7).

The anti-inflation program also met a chorus of criticism from both labour and industry. For workers and their unions, the program was basically a system for limiting wage settlements, since that was the only part of the program that was relatively simple to implement. For business, any attempt to control prices was seen as interference in the marketplace by a government which was already suspect because of Trudeau's past history of leftist writings and occasional musings that the capitalist system wasn't working well anymore.[2] The result over the next year was a modest drop in the inflation rate, but the main factor in accomplishing this was a restrictive monetary policy imposed by the Bank of Canada, which in turn brought about a rise in unemployment as businesses scaled back their operations.

By 1978, when the controls program ended, the unemployment problem was of equal public concern with inflation. The term "stagflation" was widely used to describe a condition where inflation and unemployment were both high, growth was low, and government debt was increasing. Turner's successor as finance minister, Donald

FIGURE 8.1
Federal Vote Intention, 1974–1980

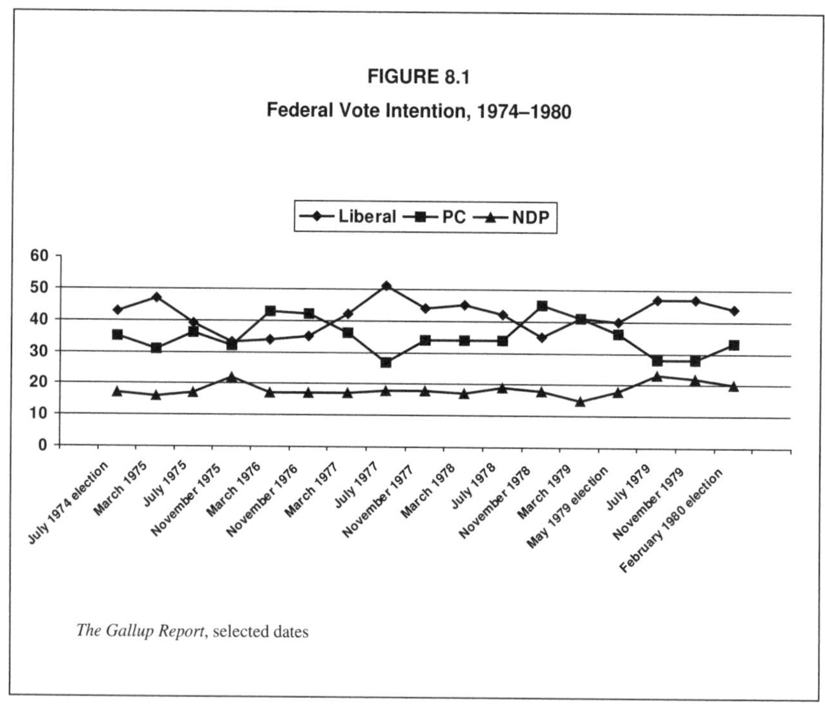

The Gallup Report, selected dates

Macdonald, lasted only two years in the job before he, too, decamped to Bay Street. His replacement, Jean Chrétien, had little experience with finance, and Trudeau himself seemed to be running economic policy. His sudden announcement in 1978 that two billion dollars would be cut from expenditures caught Chrétien by surprise. Some years later, Chrétien would express the view that this action "almost destroyed my career in the process."[3]

The economic quagmire faced by Canada during the decade of the 1970s played a major part in the erosion of public confidence in the Liberal government. A major new challenge arose with the surprise election of a Parti Québécois government in Quebec in November 1976. As the focus of national politics shifted to questions of national unity, the federal government's bilingualism program, never popular in the West, appeared costly and ineffective in the wake of the PQ victory. As soon as they achieved power in Quebec, the Parti Québécois government introduced Bill 1 (later Bill 101), which required that French be designated the official language of the province and therefore also the language of education of children in most circumstances, as well as the predominant language in commerce. In addition, demands by air traffic controllers in Quebec that they use French in communication with aircraft threatened a national air strike just before the opening of the Olympic Games in Montreal. Resignations of prominent cabinet ministers Jean Marchand and James Richardson followed the language disputes, and tarnished Trudeau's reputation as the person who could bring the linguistic solitudes together. Trudeau put his efforts into a series of constitutional initiatives, including (re)patriation of

TABLE 8.1

Party Leadership Conventions, 1975–1976

DATE	PARTY	LOCATION	WINNER	# CANDIDATES*	# BALLOTS	RUNNER-UP**
1975 07 04	NDP	Winnipeg	Ed Broadbent	5	4	Rosemary Brown
1976 02 19	PC	Ottawa	Joe Clark	12	4	Claude Wagner

* On first ballot

** On final ballot

the Constitution from Britain with a charter of rights and reforms to the Senate, but opposition from provincial governments caused the Liberals to temporarily abandon these initiatives.[4] The government seemed to be reeling from crisis to crisis, although its standing in the polls actually improved following the PQ victory in Quebec.

An Unexpected Conservative Leader

After the 1974 election, there was a growing sense within the Conservative camp that the party needed a new leader. When Robert Stanfield announced that he was stepping down after three unsuccessful election campaigns, the Conservative leadership appeared to be a prize worth having. Trudeau's personal popularity had waned, particularly in Quebec. It was no accident that two Conservative leadership candidates emerged from that province, with strong arguments that they were the ones to lead the party to a Quebec breakthrough, and hence to national power. Both of these men had appeal, but both had significant handicaps in their quest for the leadership.

Claude Wagner had been a prominent cabinet member in the former Liberal government in Quebec, and subsequently a provincial court judge. He had a high profile, but an aloof manner, and in addition engendered the suspicion that his conversion to the Conservatives might have been opportunistic (see Chapter 7). Brian Mulroney, a longtime backroom political operator for the Conservatives, had been instrumental in recruiting Wagner, and had a province-wide reputation as a labour conciliator. However, Mulroney had never sought public office of any kind, and seemed to be seeking the top job without serving any meaningful apprenticeship. (Mulroney will be more fully profiled in Chapter 9.)

Other leadership candidates were plentiful. No fewer than nine of the party's prominent MPs threw their hats into the ring. The main reason for this interest was the perception that the two leading candidates, Wagner and Mulroney, would have difficulty winning over many of the delegates who arrived at the convention supporting other candidates — therefore, the candidate who could emerge after the first ballots as a "third force" would have a good chance to win. The candidates came from all regions of the country, demonstrating that the Progressive Conservative Party was a viable national organization that had a chance to appeal across many of the divisions of Canadian society.

Library and Archives Canada. Duncan Cameron, photographer.

Joe Clark at 1976 Progressive Conservative convention, Ottawa.

The eventual winner of the leadership, Joe Clark, was not initially the leading contender to emerge as the "third force." For one thing, at 37 years of age, he was the youngest of all those seeking the leadership; he had been elected for the first time in the election of 1972. For another, he had no substantial career in any other profession than politics, having worked on a variety of campaigns throughout his student days and beyond. Clark had long been involved with the Conservative Party as a student while attending the University of Alberta between 1957 and 1961, and subsequently became president of the national PC student federation. [5] He was from the small town of High River, Alberta, not a part of the country where the Conservatives needed to augment their support through the choice of a leader. Finally, Clark was virtually unknown outside the party, a fact that caused him to be nicknamed "Joe Who?" by the press, once he was chosen as leader on the fourth ballot.

The key to the Clark victory was the series of ballots necessitated by the large number of candidates, and the desire of many of the delegates to find a candidate who would be moderate and electable, much the same dynamic that permeated the 1967 convention that had chosen Robert Stanfield. One candidate, Flora Macdonald, was able to transfer virtually all of her delegate support to Clark once it became clear that he had a better chance to advance to subsequent ballots. In Macdonald's case, the initial support pledged to her was greater than the number of votes she received. The fact that Flora was a woman, that she did not have a university or other professional education, and that delegates felt she could not win an election were all factors that affected her vote totals. In addition, she had worked for the ousting of John Diefenbaker during the 1960s (after Diefenbaker fired her as party secretary), a factor which meant that some in the party were determined not to see her as leader.[6] In addition to Macdonald, who was on the left of the party, Sinclair Stevens, aligned with the party's right wing, also supported Clark, thereby broadening his middle-of-the-road appeal.[7] On the final ballot, the Mulroney support split in Clark's favour, giving him the leadership ahead of Wagner by a mere 65 votes.[8]

Despite the bruising battles at the convention, things started well for Clark. For twelve months after the leadership convention, the Conservatives enjoyed a consistent lead in the Gallup poll (see Figure 8.1). In addition, in October 1976, 36 percent of Canadians believed Clark would be a better prime minister than Trudeau, who was favoured by only 28 percent.[9] This was the first time that Trudeau had trailed an opponent on a preferred leader scale since he became prime minister in 1968. However, the honeymoon that Clark enjoyed with the voters would not last long. In his first two years as leader, Clark had great difficulty generating a positive image among the public at large. When asked in election surveys at the time of the 1979 election, many Canadians could not think of much to say about Clark one way or the other, and those that could emphasized his youth, his enthusiasm, or his determination. As often happens with leader images, however, the flipside of such descriptions emerged as negative images for Clark. "Youth was transformed into immaturity and inexperience, and determination into a penchant for making hasty, ill-considered decisions and sticking to them."[10] In a sense, even after he became prime minister, Canadians in general never felt they learned very much about Joe Clark, or warmed to him. Conservative fortunes took a nosedive in 1977, exemplified by the party's failure to win any of the six by-elections that were held in May of that year. Rumblings began to be heard within the Tory ranks that perhaps Clark should be replaced.

An NDP Renewal

David Lewis had been defeated in the 1974 election, and given his age and the paucity of safe NDP seats that might provide a by-election opportunity, he decided to retire. Lewis had been the first Ontario-based leader of a party that originated in the West as the CCF, and had heretofore been led by westerners. The party in 1975 was at a low point; after its success in the 1972 election and its prominent role in supporting the Liberal minority government and exacting some policy concessions from it. However, the party's vote in 1974 had dropped sharply, and it lost nearly half its seats (see Chapter 7). What many in the party felt it needed was a leader from a new generation of socialists, not associated with those who wrote the *Regina Manifesto* but rather someone who could take advantage of the potential votes for the party in urban Canada, particularly Ontario and British Columbia. Someone was also needed who could mobilize support from the Canadian Labour Congress and its affiliated unions, which had been so important in the founding of the new party in 1962, but which had been muted on the campaign trail since that time.[11]

Unlike the Conservative leadership race, where the two leading candidates were relative newcomers to federal politics, the front-runner from the beginning in the NDP contest was Ed Broadbent. Abandoning a career as a university professor, he had been first elected to Parliament in 1968, and had been leader of the NDP caucus during the 1972–74 period.[12] Despite this experience, he was only 39 when he sought and won the leadership in 1975.[13] The parliamentary spectacle from 1976 to 1979 of two much younger opposition leaders attacking the aging Trudeau was a distinct change in scenario from the days when he faced older men across the House of Commons aisle.

The 1979 Election

When, at the end of March, the 1979 election was called for May 22, it was referred to as "long-awaited," and as having "ended more than 18 months of speculation."[14] In 1977, the Liberals were riding a crest of popularity produced in equal parts by support for Trudeau, and growing disenchantment with the new Conservative leader. Trudeau's high ratings, however, had more to do with sympathy for him as a result of the actions of his wife Margaret and their subsequent separation, and a belief that he was needed as a bulwark against the separatist government of Quebec.[15]

There had been a general expectation that an election would be called in 1978. As that time came, Trudeau, perhaps for a combination of personal and political reasons, hesitated and delayed. The inflation and unemployment numbers were both edging upward, and GDP growth was down (see Figure 7.1). Some political moves, such as the luring of western Conservative stalwart Jack Horner to cross the floor of the House of Commons to take up a Liberal cabinet post, had detrimental effects on party morale. This, and a series of scandals, raised the level of public cynicism about a government that had been accused by the auditor general in 1976 of "having lost, or [been] close to losing, effective control of the public purse."[16] Several cabinet ministers resigned after having been implicated in scandals. All of these events culminated in a sudden dip in the polls for the Liberals, and the decision was made to put off the election.

Fifteen by-elections were called instead, in October 1978. Canadian voters voiced their disenchantment with the Trudeau government when the Liberals suffered the worst by-election defeats that any government had endured since Confederation.[17] The biggest loss was in Toronto, where the Liberals lost all four ridings they had held, despite having two star candidates — Doris Anderson, the former editor of *Chatelaine*, and John Evans, the former president of the University of Toronto. In the aftermath of the by-election defeats, others who had been approached as potential Liberal candidates began to back away.

Delaying an election until the legal time limit is running out puts a government on the defensive and limits its strategic options. Despite this, Trudeau bravely stated his issues in order of priority. One after the other, these were the three issue areas identified in this book as key to the maintenance of a dynasty in Canadian federal politics: "The challenge to national unity; new economic policies to guarantee employment and prosperity; new social policies to improve the quality of life."[18] There were other topics, like restraint of spending, security of energy supply and redistribution of resource revenues, but Trudeau clearly understood that he would succeed or fail on his ability to persuade the country that he remained the best leader to deal with the economy, Confederation issues, and the social welfare of Canadians. He also knew that he was extremely vulnerable on the first two. In 1978, economic indicators showed inflation and unemployment both over 8 percent. The federal budget deficit had also risen sharply — from $676 million in 1974 to $11.8 billion by 1978. Economic problems appeared to be spiralling out of control. And on the national unity front, the Parti Québécois under René Lévesque enjoyed substantial popularity and was preparing for a referendum which could break up the country.

The Liberals fought the 1979 election with a highly centralized operation centred in the Prime Minister's Office (PMO). Principal Secretary Jim Coutts and campaign co-chairs Keith Davey and Marc Lalonde determined the strategy, which gave the impression of isolating the leader from the rest of the party.[19] Running under the slogan "A Leader Must Be a Leader," Trudeau ridiculed Tory leader Clark constantly as someone with ideas that were either wrong or downright silly. In a speech in Hamilton, Trudeau picked on a discussion paper Clark had used during his leadership campaign that suggested that those who courted ill health through smoking or poor diets might pay higher health insurance premiums:

> How is he going to [police] it? Is he going to send his Fat Squad or his Smoke Squad around to your house to check your ashtrays and see 12 butts and say "Oh, your OHIP premiums are going up five bucks a month"? Or is he going to send some inspector to your door and if he finds you watching television or drinking beer or eating some of those greasy chips, up another $10 a month?[20]

With these comments, Trudeau was demonstrating the same contempt for his opponents that had been in evidence in 1974, when he ridiculed the PC wage and price control proposal by pointing to his audience and saying, "Zap! You're frozen." The fact that he had later picked up and implemented the same policy he had denigrated during the campaign seemed lost on him.

This was a far different Trudeau than the one who got elected having "Conversations with Canadians" in 1968. The Liberal leader combined these withering and sarcastic attacks on his opponents with some efforts to delineate the elements of his own issue agenda. Having identified national unity as the top issue, Trudeau criticized anyone who maintained it wasn't — who cared, he said, whether unemployment was reduced by a point if the country went up in smoke.[21] The problem for this position was that approximately twice as many people identified economic problems as the most important issue in the campaign than pointed to those involving Confederation (see Table 8.2). Nevertheless, Trudeau pledged to repatriate the Constitution, without agreement with the provinces if necessary, and to put the question to a referendum if he had to. The "Magnificent Obsession"[22] with a unified and independent Canada was on full display in his campaign rhetoric. And, as it turned out, people in Quebec were listening.

The economy was another matter, particularly in English Canada. We noted in the previous chapter the overwhelming public concern with inflation in 1974. Table 8.2 shows that inflation continued to be the number one economic problem identified by the public in 1979, an understandable situation since the inflation rate had crept back up (see Figure 7.1). The difference from the 1974 campaign was that few people were talking about the specific solution of wage and price controls, after these had been tried with limited success in the intervening period. Rather, the Liberal solution was an austerity program, propounded by a Trudeau who was now a convert to neo-conservative economics, and who had made unilateral declarations of spending cuts in 1978. This position was designed to show that the government was prepared to get serious about its potential contribution to inflation, but a program of cutbacks and public service payroll reductions left no room for innovation in new spending programs to try to prime the economy or to stimulate regional economic growth. Local constituency candidates were left with little room to manoeuvre when the campaign discussion focused on benefits close to home.

Neither did they have much to promise when it came to alleviating unemployment, another serious economic problem. The unemployment rate had also moved up — from just above 5 percent in 1974 to more than 8 percent in 1978. Given the growth of the deficit, new spending programs to create jobs were out of the question for the Liberals. Their strategy was to downplay the importance of economic issues and emphasize, as they had in 1974, that there was a limited amount that any national government could do to affect these worldwide economic trends. More important was national unity, which could be promoted by constitutional repatriation. To supplement this position, the Liberals made a foray into the third important issue area, that of social welfare. Changes to the Canada Pension Plan were suggested, so that housewives would be eligible to contribute to it and receive benefits. In addition, private pensions would be made more "portable" by reducing the number of years required to work before transferring to another job was allowed with pension benefits accompanying the worker.[23] Costs, however, were carefully not attached to these proposals.

The Conservative campaign strategy was precisely the opposite of the Liberals. They had no interest in debating the national unity question, particularly given their residual weakness in Quebec, and social policy proposals were not going to win the Conservatives many votes. Rather, campaign director Lowell Murray and pollster Allan Gregg determined on a "Let's Get Canada Moving Again" appeal. This put the focus directly on the economy, where the public would be constantly reminded of the inadequacies of the Liberals' performance over more than a decade. In an effort to create their own attractive alternative policies, but wary of their 1974 experience, the Conservatives settled on a proposal to cut taxes, headlined by a promise to allow the interest paid on mortgages to be deducted on income tax returns.[24] "Mortgage deductibility" ended up being hotly debated during the campaign, but was cited by relatively few people as a specific reason for voting in the election. Nevertheless, it did demonstrate that the Conservatives had some different ideas of how to stimulate the economy that were in contrast to the Liberal austerity program.

TABLE 8.2

Most Important Issues in the 1979 and 1980 Elections

Percent (multiple response)*

	1979	1980
Economic Issues		
Inflation / Cost of Living	14	14
The Economy (general)	11	9
Unemployment / Jobs	10	4
Taxes (including mortgage deductibility)	8	3
Oil prices / Development / Energy policy	4	31
Government spending / The Budget	4	17
Other economic issues	1	1
National Unity		
Quebec separation / The Referendum	15	6
National unity (general)	8	4
Control of natural resources	5	1
Bilingualism / Language issues	3	-
Federal-provincial relations	2	3
Foreign policy / Defence	2	3
Social Welfare		
Social issues / Health / Housing / Pensions	5	2
Environmental issues	5	1
Other Issues		
Leaders / Leadership	14	15
Need for change / The parties	8	8
The election / Majority government	1	4
Other issues	2	2
No Important Issues / Don't Know	**28**	**22**
	N=2,668	N=1,786

* National Election Studies, 1979, 1980

TABLE 8.3

Party Seen as Closest on Most Important Issues, 1979

(row percentages)*

	Liberals	PCs	NDP	None
Issues				
Economic issues (all)	22%	36	21	20
National unity (all)	58%	18	5	16
Energy and resources	32%	35	14	16
Social welfare (all)	31%	28	23	15
Other issues	24%	48	8	18

*1979 National Election Study. N = 1,896. Respondents mentioning other parties included in percentages but not shown in table.

The Conservative strategy of "damage avoidance" carried over to the televised leaders' debate held during the campaign. This was only the second such debate held in Canada — the 1968 debate (see Chapter 6) having been followed by two elections where one party or the other decided that it was not in its interest to hold one. The same reasoning was initially present in 1979, as well, as the Liberals were anxious for an encounter that would allow Trudeau to demonstrate his intellectual mastery over his opponents. The Conservatives eventually decided that the appearance of "ducking" the debate would be worse than what might happen during it, and agreed to participate. The debate format was one where journalists posed questions, and the three leaders took turns debating in pairs. The questions, however, differed in the three pairings, making it difficult for viewers to directly compare the leaders' ability to deal with all the issues.[25]

The debates attracted a large television audience, and appeared to create a generally favourable impression on viewers. Joe Clark, however, received more negative than positive mentions in a post-debate questionnaire, with a number of people considering him "weak" in comparison to the other leaders.[26] However, the "negatives" associated with Clark's debate performance were not so serious as to deter people from voting Conservative if they were otherwise inclined to do so.

For Ed Broadbent, the leadership debates were a heaven-sent opportunity to place the NDP on an equal footing with the other two parties, and to establish his image with the public. An experienced speaker, thoughtful and measured, Broadbent made the most of his opportunity, particularly in the lead-off pairing with Clark. Positioning the NDP as a viable opposition to the Liberals was particularly important to Broadbent because the party was fearful that voters might feel it necessary to vote Conservative in order to defeat the Liberals. The

FIGURE 8.2

Party and Leader Thermometer Scale Ratings, 1979–1980

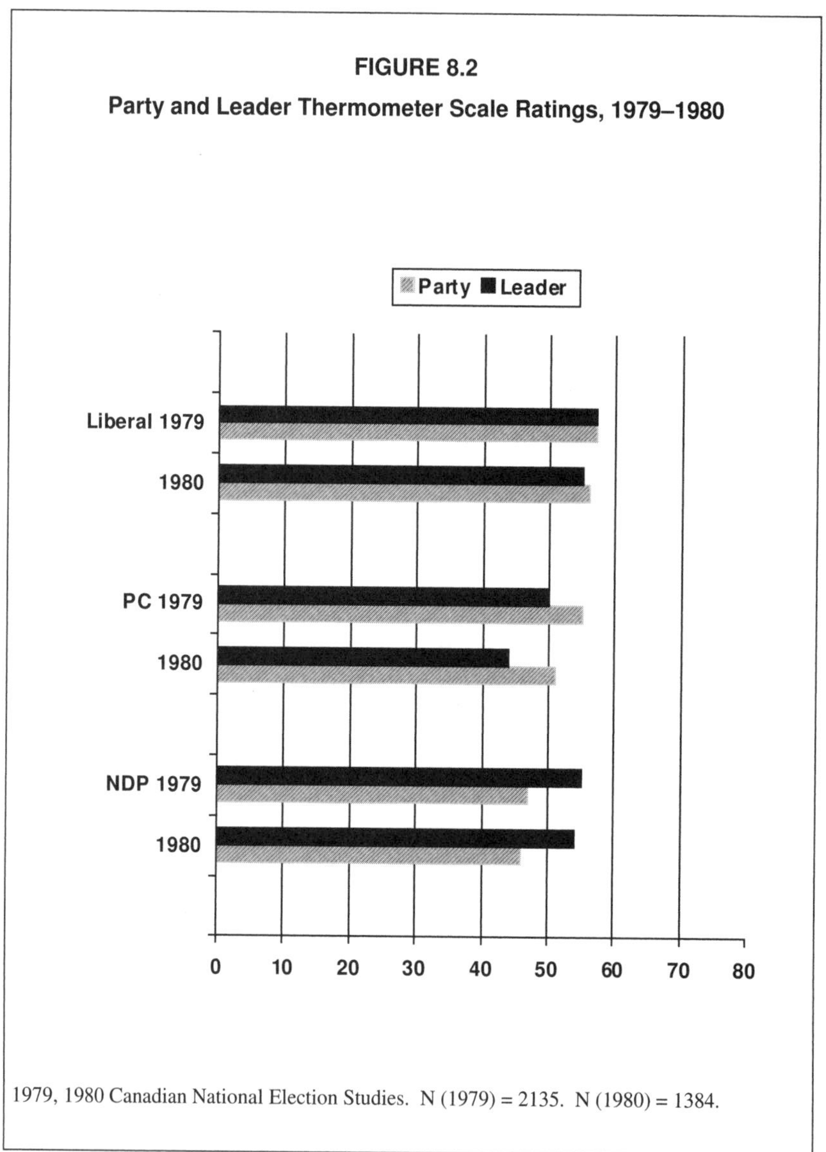

1979, 1980 Canadian National Election Studies. N (1979) = 2135. N (1980) = 1384.

positive impression made by Broadbent in the debates, together with the decision of the party to centre its campaign on a series of television appearances by its leader, was bolstered by the party's advertising, which made overt comparisons between Broadbent and the other leaders.[27] But Broadbent spent much time during the campaign trying to avoid the question of which party the NDP would support in the event of a minority outcome.[28] A series of policy proposals to deal with inflation (curbs on price increases), unemployment (a national industrial strategy), energy security (expanding Petro Canada), and tax reform (raising corporate taxes) tended to be overlooked in the battle between the two major parties.

The variety of issues cited by respondents to the 1979 National Election Study (see Table 8.2) indicates that all parties could claim some success in setting the agenda during the campaign. This differential pattern of success is reinforced by Table 8.3, where it can be seen that those citing issues related to the state of Confederation and national unity were much more likely to see the Liberals as closest to them. Similarly, the Liberals were successful in attracting voters concerned with social welfare issues. The Conservatives scored well with voters citing the party's mortgage deductibility proposal as the top election issue, and also with those who felt the main issue in the election was simply the need for a change of government. Economic issues were more dispersed in their appeal, but for the most part favoured the opposition. Pluralities citing general economic problems favoured the Conservatives, and those concerned specifically with unemployment were more likely to choose the NDP.[29] The issue effects in 1979 did not work decisively in any one direction.

Despite this, the switching patterns between 1974 and 1979 heavily favoured the Conservatives, and to a more limited extent the NDP (see Figure 8.3). In looking at the total electorate, over five times as many people switched to the PCs from a 1974 Liberal vote as did the reverse, and three times as many 1974 Liberals went in the NDP direction. It is likely that if these trends had been reinforced by the behaviour of newly eligible voters and previous non-voters, the Conservatives might well have won a majority of the seats. However, as these data indicate, there was only a small preference for the Conservatives in the group that did not vote in 1974, and a substantial preference for the Liberals in that group of newly eligible (mostly young) voters who cast their first vote in

1979. This group was particularly numerous because of the long five-year time period which had passed since the previous election.

The weakness of the Conservatives in attracting this group did not begin with the 1979 election, and did not end there either. Throughout the Trudeau years, the Liberals maintained a consistent advantage among younger voters, with new and younger cohorts comprising an increasing share of the total electorate.[30] The magnetism of Trudeau himself, combined with the stability of the Liberal dynasty that began with Pearson and continued with Trudeau, contributed to the inclination of newly entering cohorts of the voters to choose the Liberals and to continue to vote for them.

The limited nature of the Conservative victory in 1979 was reinforced by the regional patterns of the voting (see Table 8.4). The Conservatives did very well in Ontario (57 of 95 seats), in Alberta (all 21 seats), and in British Columbia (20 of 29 seats). They also did reasonably well in the

FIGURE 8.3
Electoral Turnover, 1974–1979 and 1979–1980

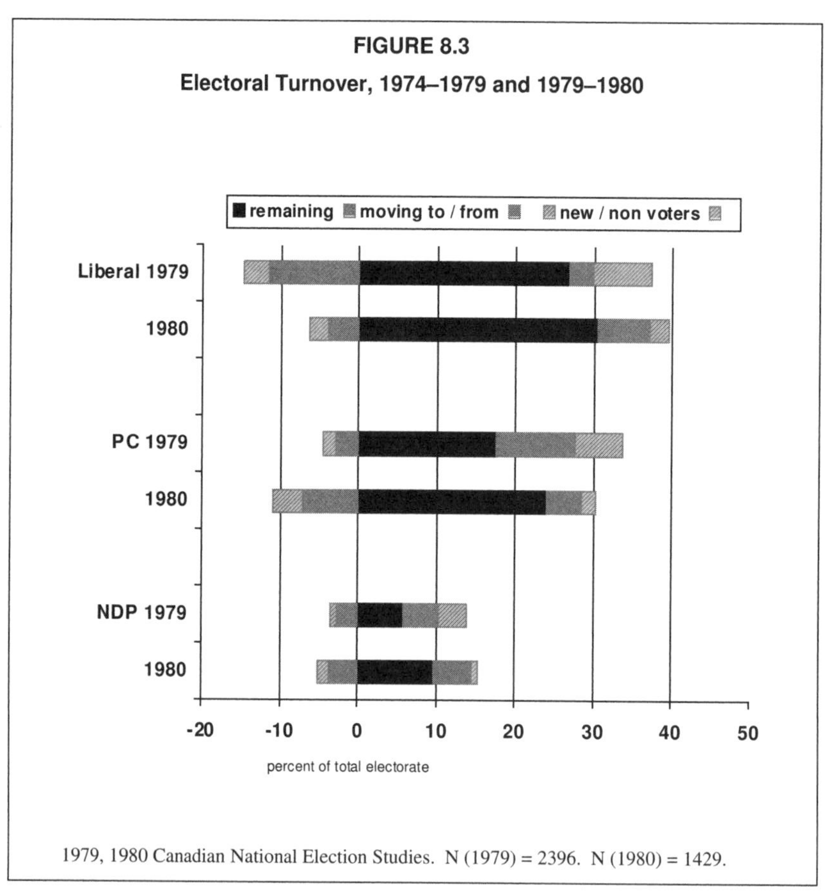

1979, 1980 Canadian National Election Studies. N (1979) = 2396. N (1980) = 1429.

other western provinces, and in the East. However, the Liberals swept Quebec (67 of 75 seats), leaving six for the declining Créditiste Party, and only two for the Conservatives. The fact that the Liberals piled up 62 percent of the vote in Quebec contributed to an overall result whereby the Liberals actually received four more percentage points of the national vote than the victorious Conservatives. The NDP benefited from many voters who did not feel comfortable supporting either of the two major parties, and/or were attracted to their new leader, who consistently ran well ahead of his party in popular appeal (see Figure 8.2). They won a total of 26 seats — a net gain of 10 over 1974 (see Table 8.4).

The Conservatives Form a Government

With only 36 percent of the vote and two seats in Quebec, the Conservatives could not have hoped to form a majority government. Their mandate was limited by the regional patterns of the voting, by the splits in public opinion on their policy positions, and by the choices of newly entering voters to support other parties. Nevertheless, the party felt that its best strategy was to act as if it had received majority support. Visions of the way in which John Diefenbaker had parlayed a minority in 1957 into a massive majority in 1958 (see Chapter 4) danced in their minds. Thrown suddenly into opposition in 1957, the Liberals were unprepared and performed poorly — the natural result of a dynasty. Expectations were widespread in 1979 that Pierre Trudeau would not adjust to the role of Opposition leader, and that the Liberals would be unable to cope with the new situation in which they found themselves.

Mindful of potential public skepticism of their ability to govern, Clark and his colleagues did not meet Parliament immediately, but spent four months following the election preparing their approach. Appointing a cabinet proved to be a challenge, given the paucity of Conservative members from Quebec. Clark addressed this problem by appointing several unelected senators to his cabinet, and by appointing a defeated Conservative candidate, Robert de Cotret, to the Senate and naming him Minister of Industry, Trade and Commerce. The strategy was to get through this initial period of transition, govern effectively for two years, and then seek a majority.

Unfortunately for them, this preparatory period was not successful in establishing an image of competence. Rather, the new government was forced to backtrack on some of its election promises, such as moving the Canadian embassy in Israel from Tel Aviv to Jerusalem. Already the subject of sarcastic commentary that the proposal was simply designed to lure Jewish votes, the initial post-election decision to carry through with it drew fire, not only from Arab governments in the Middle East, but also from domestic Canadian companies like Bell Canada, which felt that their economic contracts with these Arab governments could be jeopardized.[31]

Another problem area involved the government-owned oil company Petro Canada. Always a sore point in Western Canada, Petro Canada had been established by the Liberals as a condition of NDP support during the minority period in 1973. It was designed to provide a measure of domestic energy security in the face of rising oil prices. During the 1979 campaign, the Conservatives had promised to "privatize" it, both on the grounds of ideological opposition to state industry and on pragmatic grounds that it was not needed. In the latter months of 1979, however, the revolution in Iran led to a $10 a barrel jump in the price of oil, a situation which made it much less clear that getting rid of Petro Canada was good public policy. The Alberta government, representing an oil-producing province, was still keen on privatization, but Ontario, representing consumers, was not.

With Conservatives in power in both of these provinces, the spectacle of quarrelling among Tory provincial and federal politicians was not helpful to the party's image. Hesitantly, the Clark government decided that it wanted things both ways, and announced that it would privatize part of Petro Canada and keep another part in state hands. Finally, the government signalled that the tax-relief promises made during the campaign were going to be forthcoming much more slowly than originally indicated. In particular, the much-heralded mortgage deductibility provision was announced as having much lower limits than expected, and other tax breaks were to be postponed. The government's explanation was that they needed to get the country's financial house in order in order to fulfil their policy proposals, but the sudden drop in popularity of the Conservatives (see Figure 8.2) indicated that much of the public regarded these actions as further indications of ineptitude.

Despite these early signs of Conservative vulnerability, Pierre Trudeau decided in November of 1979 to resign as Liberal leader. Beset by his marital difficulties, and discouraged by his political prospects, Trudeau felt he did not have the energy to continue.[32] He also realized that the Liberal defeat was in part a personal rejection of his leadership. Supporters of two former finance ministers, Donald Macdonald and John Turner, were positioning their men to compete for the leadership (until Turner abruptly announced that he would not run). These two candidates with strong economic backgrounds aimed to improve the party's credibility in dealing with the country's finances — a policy area where the Liberals in general and Trudeau in particular were especially vulnerable. Support for the Liberals remained in the national unity issue area; the Conservatives' poor showing in Quebec reinforced the party's image as anathema to Quebecers. Quebec was also a major "consumer" province in terms of energy, where policies designed to please the West would not be well received. The social policy area was also one where the Liberals retained much of their traditional strength. It would be on issues relating to the economy that the Conservative government had their best hope to demonstrate their competence and expand their electoral support.

In order to seize the initiative on economic matters, and to stake a claim to solving problems with energy supply, the Conservatives delivered a budget in December. It was comprised of a series of fiscal changes and a combination of tax increases and tax credits, but the one proposal which caught everyone's attention dealt with energy taxation. Citing the need for "short term pain for long term gain," Finance Minister John Crosbie proposed to introduce an excise tax of 18 cents per gallon on fuel for transportation. Its impact was dramatic, because an energy price increase of this magnitude was totally unexpected, and because it seemed to hit energy consumers of all income levels (though a tax credit for low-income earners was also proposed).

Opinion was divided on the merits of the budget, with some applauding the conservation efforts that were expected to follow such a price increase, and others decrying the lack of specificity about what the increased tax revenue would be spent on (some suggesting that it would go to offset the mortgage interest deductibility proposal). It certainly caused many observers to contrast the gasoline tax increases with the 1979 Tory campaign promises of tax reduction. But the most important impact of the Crosbie budget was to galvanize the opposition parties into action. Unanimously, they decided to vote against it, and this they did in short order, bringing the Conservative government down after only 259 days in office.

Opinions differ as to whether the Conservatives deliberately entertained, or even courted, defeat because they thought that Liberal "arrogance" in voting them out of office would backfire, or whether the defeat was the result of parliamentary miscalculation. In either case, there is no doubt they felt that right was on their side.[33] In his memoirs, Crosbie explains why the PCs were confident that the government would not fall:

> I shared the cabinet's conviction that, if the Opposition parties were so foolhardy as to bring down our new administration in Parliament, the Canadian people would punish them at the polls.[34]

Strategically, the Conservatives were emboldened because the Liberals were officially leaderless, and seemingly in no position to fight an election. If Pierre Trudeau was dragooned into leading them one last time, the Conservatives felt that the country would confirm its repudiation of his leadership. If they tried to quickly choose a new leader, that person would not have time to mount an effective campaign. Indeed, apparently a number of Liberals felt the same way, and were themselves uneasy about seizing the opportunity to defeat the Conservatives over the budget.[35] In the end, the governing Conservatives fell by a vote of 139 to 133.[36] The election date was set for 18 February 1980. In his memoirs, Crosbie noted: "To our later regret, we paid little attention to the November Gallup poll, which was published on December 3, just eight days before Budget Day. It showed a steep drop in Conservative popularity from 36 percent in summer/fall to 28 percent in November, 19 points behind the Liberals."[37]

Pierre Trudeau, while he voted against the budget with the other Liberals, was genuinely ambivalent about his future role as leader.[38] Despite the fact that he was asked to return by the party caucus, and by the Liberal national executive, he took some time to decide. Once again, personal factors were foremost; he had bought a new house in Montreal, and planned his retirement. Press Secretary Patrick Gossage remembers that "he was distracted in a way I had never seen him before."[39] The factor which seems

TABLE 8.4

Results of the 1979 and 1980 Federal Elections, by Province

		— Liberal —		— PC —		— NDP —		— Other —	
		1979	1980	1979	1980	1979	1980	1979	1980
Newfoundland	votes (%)	38	47	31	36	31	17	-	-
	seats (#)	4	5	2	2	1	0	-	-
Prince Edward Island	votes (%)	40	47	53	46	7	7	-	-
	seats (#)	0	2	4	2	0	0	-	-
Nova Scotia	votes (%)	36	40	45	39	19	21	-	-
	seats (#)	2	5	8	6	1	0	-	-
New Brunswick	votes (%)	45	50	40	33	15	16	-	1
	seats (#)	6	7	4	3	0	0	-	-
Quebec	votes (%)	62	68	13	13	5	9	20	10
	seats (#)	67	74	2	1	0	0	*6	0
Ontario	votes (%)	37	42	42	36	21	22	1	-
	seats (#)	32	52	57	38	6	5	-	-
Manitoba	votes (%)	24	28	44	38	33	34	-	-
	seats (#)	2	2	7	5	5	7	-	-
Saskatchewan	votes (%)	20	24	42	39	37	36	1	1
	seats (#)	0	0	10	7	4	7	-	-
Alberta	votes (%)	21	21	67	66	10	10	3	3
	seats (#)	0	0	21	21	0	0	-	-
British Columbia	votes (%)	23	22	45	41	32	35	1	2
	seats (#)	1	0	20	16	8	12	-	-
Yukon / NWT	votes (%)	33	37	37	32	29	31	1	-
	seats (#)	0	0	2	2	1	1	-	-
TOTAL CANADA	votes (%)	40	44	36	33	18	20	6	3
	seats (#)	114	147	136	103	26	32	*6	0

* Social Credit

to have weighed most heavily in his decision to return was the upcoming referendum in Quebec on sovereignty association for the province; he felt he could better participate in the defeat of that initiative from the position of prime minister. The unfinished constitutional agenda also attracted him. A renewed Trudeau government would be able to make another attempt to repatriate the Constitution and implement his long-cherished Charter of Rights. A "national unity" agenda would be the primary purpose of a new Trudeau government.

The 1980 Election

The 1980 election was fought over a different set of issues than that of 1979. The first glaring difference was that while national unity was the lead item in the previous Liberal platform, the subject would be barely mentioned this time. In large part, this was a result of the Clark government's defeat over its budget, and in particular the gasoline tax proposal. Unprepared for an election, the Conservatives were forced to rely on the same set of issue priorities they had campaigned on nine months earlier, minus those which had been abandoned, such as moving the embassy in Israel and immediate tax cuts. They were also forced to add those policies which had been crystallized by the budget. The Conservative campaign got off to a slow start. In the first week, Clark took some heat for being unable to estimate the price of Conservative campaign promises, complaining that he did not have a "magic accountant." According to some observers, this was his worst moment of the campaign.[40] There was no question that his government had made some mistakes and that a number of them were caused by the inexperience of his cabinet. Campaigning on the slogan "Real Change Deserves a Fair Chance," Clark argued that his government had had only a short time to work on its agenda, that it had made some mistakes but had signalled its intention to fulfil many of its previous promises, and that it deserved an opportunity to govern for a reasonable period of time before being judged.[41] For many people, however, that judgment had already been made.

Despite the fact that opinion was divided about the wisdom of the specific large rise in energy taxation provided by the budget, this proposal proved to be an albatross for the Conservatives in a number of ways. In the first place, it was not clear how this large tax increase would improve the overall supply of energy, since the extra revenue would accrue to the government and not to private energy suppliers. The Conservative government was not proposing, for example, to channel extra tax revenues to Petro Canada, the state-owned oil company, for exploration and development — rather, they were committed to dismantling that Crown corporation or selling it to private interests.

The tax increase might encourage energy conservation, but what exactly was the government going to use the extra money for? There were implications it might be used to pay down the national debt, but such a move, fiscally responsible though it might be, was not the substance of dramatic election oratory. More damaging for the Conservatives were the hints that it might be used to extend the tax credits for mortgage interest. There was an announcement early in the campaign that if the government was re-elected they would double the amount originally announced for the limits of such deductions.[42] The mortgage deductibility plan, however, continued to be controversial, since it would benefit primarily middle-class homeowners rather than the less well-off sections of society. The fact that the large "tax grab" was not specifically targeted to some generally approved spending target handicapped the Conservatives when they argued that it was necessary, and perpetuated the feeling that the government did not really know what it was doing.

The Liberal strategy was to run a low-key campaign, counting on public anger with the Conservatives to defeat them, and endeavouring not to do or say anything which might dissipate the lead they had in the polls. This involved "hiding" their two key electoral assets, proven leadership in the person of Pierre Trudeau and the public belief that the Liberals were the party most likely to be able to organize a defence of federalism against the upcoming Quebec referendum. The last thing the Liberals felt they needed on the hustings was a freewheeling Trudeau, promoting his plans for constitutional repatriation with a Charter of Rights and delivering biting criticisms of Quebec nationalism. After all, many "soft nationalist" voters in that province also supported the federal Liberals. Furthermore, there was always a chance that the "arrogant Trudeau" would emerge, perhaps in the process creating some sympathy for Joe Clark and the Tories. As Clarkson puts it, the 1980 strategy was "Hiding the Charisma: Low-Bridging the Saviour."[43] For those who loved

Trudeau, he was still there; for those who hated him, at least he was out of sight. Unlike 1979, no leader debates took place in 1980.

The Liberals announced a five-point election program, but these were quite different from the key points of the 1979 campaign. Gone altogether was the need to respond to the challenge to national unity. Liberal strategists felt there was little benefit in reasserting Trudeau's established advantage in dealing with this issue. The Liberal platform drastically toned down the previous economic policies to guarantee employment and the new social policies to improve the quality of life. Replacing these in the economic issue area were the commitment to be vigilant in managing federal finances, to support industry in creating more jobs, and to strengthen regional economies. Although these were generalities, they placed the emphasis firmly on elements of the material standard of living of Canadians, rather than the finer points of the Constitution. Furthermore, they implied the importance of government action, something which subtly differentiated the party from the free enterprise rhetoric of the Tories.

Given the uncertain pricing situation of imported oil, and the emphasis of the Conservative budget, the Liberals stated a priority for "achieving energy security at a fair price for all Canadians." In concrete terms, the party proposed to counter the price differential between domestic and more expensive foreign prices for imported oil by creating an overall "blended price," which would charge everyone a similar amount for their fuel.[44] There were several implications here. The government was going to maintain a major role in setting and regulating oil prices. Given that a referendum in Quebec was expected sometime in 1980, an oil and gas policy that would assure Quebecers a guaranteed supply of oil and gas could be used as an argument to support the federal cause. A separate Quebec would receive no such guarantees. Trudeau committed to a "made-in-Canada blended price, energy security, an expanded Petro Canada and stepped-up Canadianization" of the energy sector.[45] Eastern Canadian consumers were not to be subjected to the full brunt of rising oil prices from imported oil, while westerners maintained the benefits of cheaper domestic production. Western producers were not going to be allowed the option of raising their prices to meet the world price and reap the profits. And finally, taxpayers would be spared the whopping 18-cent-per-gallon tax on gasoline contained in the Conservatives' ill-fated budget.

To firm up their appeal on the third issue, that of social welfare, the Liberals put aside their austerity pledge to announce that they would raise that part of the Canada Pension Plan based on need, known as the Guaranteed Income Supplement, by $35 a month for each household that qualified.[46] The money to finance this, it was implied, would come from corporate taxes rather than individuals. Very shortly after this announcement, the NDP unveiled their own social program, which promised to raise the full old-age pension (not just the portion for low-income earners) by $40 a month. The party announced plans for additional "shelter grants" for those elderly persons in need.[47] Placed immediately on the defensive over the pension rise proposals, Clark reacted the next day by saying he would not enter into "any election bidding" on pensions, and would resist the suggestion he "up the ante" to $45. The headline for Clark was "Can't Promise Pension Rise, PM Says."[48] It was hardly the news beleaguered Tory candidates wanted to hear when planning their speeches for local rallies.

Once again, the NDP sensed enhanced opportunities. They had done well in 1979 in a situation where the public was displeased with the government and hesitant about the main challenger. Now the situation appeared very similar, with the apparent fortunes of the other parties simply reversed. All the public opinion polls indicated that the electorate

Library and Archives Canada. Robert Cooper, photographer.

Pierre Trudeau with Queen Elizabeth II, signing the Constitution, Ottawa, 1982.

was looking for an alternative to the current government, and was less than enthusiastic about bringing back the previous one. Ed Broadbent appeared to be increasing his personal popularity, and was once again the centrepiece of the NDP campaign. Although handicapped by the lack of a leaders' debate, since the Liberals were determined to avoid one, the party's economic and social policy agenda resonated well with its natural constituencies in the West and in urban Ontario. However, many Canadians had deeply felt suspicions regarding the NDP's ability to manage the economy, while Broadbent and his colleagues had little to say about how they would deal with a sovereign Quebec.

TABLE 8.5

Turnover in Partisanship and Vote, 1974, 1979, and 1980 Elections

		PARTY IDENTIFICATION		
		Maintaining the same party identification in three elections	**Changing party identification at least once**	**Moving to or from non-identification**
VOTE	**Voting three times for the same party**	41	3	7
	Switching at least once	11	16	9
	Not voting at least once	13	6	6

Canadian National Election Study Panel. Percentages are of total sample. Number of cases for this analysis is 791. Excludes non-voters in all three elections.

Rows and columns do not total, and do not total to 100 percent, because not all categories are mutually exclusive. For example, someone who switched in one pair of elections and did not vote in the third is counted in both relevant cells.

Table adapted from Harold D. Clarke, Jane Jenson, Lawrence LeDuc, and Jon H. Pammett, ***Absent Mandate: Interpreting Change in Canadian Elections*** (Toronto: Gage, 1991), 58.

A Volatile Electorate

All political parties were cognizant of the volatility of the Canadian electorate, which could produce quite different results over relatively short spans of elections. A Trudeau landslide in 1968 had been followed by near defeat in 1972 and restoration of the Liberal majority in 1974. Now, less than a year following their defeat, the Liberals appeared poised to return to power. The extent and nature of this volatility was revealed by the Canadian Election Studies, which were designed in this period to incorporate a "panel" whereby the same respondents were interviewed in the three elections (1974, 1979, and 1980), thus allowing us to draw a picture of the amount of stability and change in behaviour of the same people on these three voting opportunities. Table 8.5 looks at the voting behaviour in three elections of those who had various degrees of feeling for the parties. It shows several different kinds of change.[49] Only 41 percent of this group of eligible voters voted in the three elections for the same party, and also maintained an "identification" with that party — that is, felt closer to it than any other party. The rest changed in a variety of ways. Some maintained an identification with the same party but cast at least one of their votes for some other party, indicating that "their" party had disappointed them in some way. A somewhat larger group, 16 percent, changed both their vote and the party they felt closest to at least once during that period. In addition, the table shows two other forms of electoral change. Some people, both those who were consistent in their votes and those who were not, moved to or from a feeling of partisan closeness to *any* political party. And finally, a substantial number of people moved in and out of the active electorate, choosing not to cast a vote at all.

Conclusion

The 1980 election restored the Trudeau dynasty. The Conservative defeat was decisive, as the party lost seats in every part of the country (see Table 8.4). Despite its difficulties in making its case, however, the primary reasons for the defeat had little to do with the election issues. For those citing various specific issues as important to them, and counting those who stayed with the same party they had supported last time, there were no major patterns favouring one party over the other. Rather, the Conservatives' problems stemmed from two other sources. The first was the lower turnout of voters (69 percent in 1980 versus 75 percent in 1979), a factor which worked strongly against the PCs. Almost as large a proportion of the electorate moved from a 1979 Conservative vote to non-voting in 1980 as switched to the Liberals. In contrast, the Liberals and the NDP were both able to hold on to a higher proportion of their previous voters (see Figure 8.3).

The second factor was leadership. Despite the "low bridging" of Trudeau, he was far and away the most popular leader in 1980, and was a major factor allowing the party to hold on to such a high proportion of its previous support.[50] Figure 8.2 shows that the average rating of Clark on a scale of 0–100 declined to 44 in 1980 from an already low mark of 50 — the lowest score for a major party leader since National Election Studies began. By this time, the Canadian public was well aware of Pierre Trudeau's faults and failings. He was arrogant and disdainful of others; he was autocratic and consolidated power within his own office; he was highly erratic as a public speaker; he had a bad record on the economy and didn't actually seem very concerned with it; he had an obsession with the Constitution that was not shared by most of the country. But even at its lowest ebb, in 1980, Trudeau's average rating on the 100 point scale only declined to 55, on the warm side of the neutral mark. He was respected for his intellect, loved for his charisma, and the subject of pride when compared internationally to other leaders. He was firmly in power again, and the Liberal dynasty, shaky as it had proven to be under Trudeau's leadership, was again restored. The brief and relatively uneventful Clark interlude was over.

Notes

1. Data on the economic problems of the 1970s, and the public reaction to them, may be found in Jon H. Pammett, "Inflation, Unemployment and Integration," in Jon H. Pammett and Brian W. Tomlin, eds., *The Integration Question: Political Economy and Public Policy in Canada and North America* (Toronto: Addison-Wesley, 1984), 95–111.
2. Trudeau consulted with John Kenneth Galbraith about the implementation of wage and price controls. See Christina McCall and Stephen Clarkson, *Trudeau and Our Times, Volume 2: The Heroic Delusion* (Toronto: McClelland & Stewart, 1994), 125.

3. Jean Chrétien, *Straight From the Heart* (Toronto: Key Porter, 1985), 117.
4. John Meisel, "The Larger Context: The Period Preceding the 1979 Election." In Howard Penniman, ed., *Canada At the Polls, 1979 and 1980* (Washington, American Enterprise Institute, 1981), 27.
5. David L. Humphreys, *Joe Clark: a Portrait* (Toronto: Totem, 1978).
6. Alvin Armstrong, *Flora Macdonald* (Toronto: Dent, 1976), 202–03.
7. Michael Nolan, *Joe Clark: The Emerging Leader* (Toronto: Fitzhenry and Whiteside, 1978), 19.
8. Robert Krause and Lawrence LeDuc, "Voting Behaviour and Electoral Strategies in the 1976 Progressive-Conservative Leadership Convention," *Canadian Journal of Political Science* 12 (1979), 97–136.
9. Canadian Institute of Public Opinion (CIPO), *Gallup Report*, October 16, 1976.
10. Harold D. Clarke, Jane Jenson, Lawrence LeDuc, and Jon H. Pammett, *Absent Mandate: The Politics of Discontent in Canada* (Toronto: Gage, 1984), 113.
11. Walter D. Young, "The New Democratic Party in the 1979 Federal General Election," in Howard R. Penniman, ed., *Canada at the Polls, 1979 and 1980: A Study of the General Elections* (Washington, American Enterprise Institute, 1981), 191–92.
12. A good biographical sketch of Broadbent is to be found in Alan Whitehorn, *Canadian Socialism: Essays on the CCF-NDP* (Toronto: Oxford, 1992), Chapter 7.
13. Broadbent was elected on the fourth ballot, although he led on each. Other candidates were John Harney (a university professor from Toronto and former MP), Lorne Nystrom (an MP from Saskatchewan), and Rosemary Brown (a member of the British Columbia legislature).
14. Jeffrey Simpson, "PM Calls the Election: It's May 22nd," *Globe and Mail*, March 27, 1979: 1.
15. Stephen Clarkson and Christina McCall, *Trudeau and Our Times: Volume 1, The Magnificent Obsession* (Toronto: McClelland & Stewart, 1990), 139–43.
16. John Saywell, *Canadian Annual Review of Politics and Public Affairs* (Toronto: University of Toronto Press, 1976), 27.
17. Gossage, Patrick, *Close to Charisma: My Years Between the Press and Pierre Elliot Trudeau* (Toronto: McClelland & Stewart Limited, 1986), 149.
18. Pierre Trudeau, text of election announcement, as reported in the *Globe and Mail*, March 27, 1979: 9.
19. Stephen Clarkson, *The Big Red Machine: How the Liberal Party Dominates Canadian Politics* (Vancouver, UBC Press, 2005), 64–66.
20. Jeffrey Simpson, "PM's Attack on Clark Is Turned Up to Full Blast," *Globe and Mail*, April 23, 1979: 1.
21. *Ibid.*
22. See note 15.

23. Jeffrey Simpson, "Housewives Should Be Eligible for Pension Plan, Trudeau Says," *Globe and Mail*, April 28, 1979: 1.
24. John Courtney, "Campaign Strategy and Electoral Victory: The Progressive Conservatives and the 1979 Election," in Howard R. Penniman, ed., *Canada at the Polls, 1979 and 1980: A Study of the General Elections* (Washington, American Enterprise Institute, 1981), 148.
25. Lawrence LeDuc and Richard Price, "Great Debates: The Televised Leadership Debates of 1979," *Canadian Journal of Political Science*, Vol. 18 (March 1983), 135–54.
26. *Ibid.*, 146.
27. Whitehorn, *op. cit.*, 94.
28. Jeffrey Simpson, "Broadbent's Campaign Staged to Fit Television Screen," *Globe and Mail*, May 14, 1979: 8–9.
29. A more detailed analysis of the voting patterns for 1979 may be found in Harold D. Clarke, Jane Jenson, Lawrence LeDuc, and Jon H. Pammett, "Voting Behaviour and the Outcome of the 1979 Election: The Impact of Leaders and Issues," *Canadian Journal of Political Science 15* (1982), 517–52.
30. *Ibid.*, 545.
31. William Irvine, "Epilogue," in Penniman, *op. cit.*, 341–42.
32. McCall and Clarkson, *op. cit.*, 145–46.
33. Jeffrey Simpson, *Discipline of Power: The Conservative Interlude and the Liberal Restoration* (Toronto: Personal Library, 1980), 18.
34. John Crosbie and Geofffrey Stevens, *No Holds Barred*, 165.
35. Simpson, *Discipline of Power*, 32.
36. Two Créditises attended the vote but abstained, one Liberal was absent, and three Conservatives were absent for the vote.
37. Crosbie, 176–77.
38. Clarkson and McCall, *op. cit.*, Chapter 8.
39. Patrick Gossage, *Close to the Charisma* (Halifax, Goodread, 1986), 189.
40. Stevens, Geoffrey, "Leadership Still Issue As Campaign Closes," *Globe and Mail*, May 19, 1980: A1.
41. Mary Trueman, "Students Rough on Clark Over Broken Promises," *Globe and Mail*, January 11, 1980: 1–2.
42. "Mortgage Tax Credit Value Would Double if PCs Return," *Globe and Mail*, January 16, 1980: 1.
43. Clarkson, *The Big Red Machine*, 87.
44. Mary Trueman, "Liberals Promise Two Prices for Oil," *Globe and Mail*, January 26, 1980: 1.
45. McCall and Clarkson, *op. cit.*, 154.
46. Mary Trueman, "Would Boost Monthly Pension Aid by $35 a Household, Trudeau Says," *Globe and Mail*, January 16, 1980: 1.
47. James Rusk, " NDP Promises $40 Pension Increase," *Globe and Mail*, January 24, 1.

48. Robert Sheppard, "Can't Promise Pension Rise, PM Says," *Globe and Mail*, January 25, 1.
49. For a more extensive analysis of the voting patterns in the 1980 election, see Harold D. Clarke, Jane Jenson, Lawrence LeDuc, and Jon H. Pammett, *Absent Mandate: Interpreting Change in Canadian Elections* (Toronto: Gage, 1991), 140–43.
50. See the table of leader effects in *Absent Mandate*, second edition, 137.

Selected Reading

Clarke, Harold D., Jane Jenson, Lawrence LeDuc, and Jon H. Pammett. *Absent Mandate: The Politics of Discontent in Canada* (Toronto: Gage, 1984).

Clarkson, Stephen, and Christina McCall. *Trudeau and Our Times, Volume 1: The Magnificent Obsession* (Toronto: McClelland & Stewart, 1990).

Davey, Keith. *The Rainmaker: A Passion for Politics* (Toronto: Stoddart, 1986).

Humphreys, David L. *Joe Clark: A Portrait* (Ottawa: Deneau and Greenberg, 1978).

McCall-Newman, Christina. *Grits: An Intimate Portrait of the Liberal Party* (Toronto: Macmillan, 1982).

Morton, Desmond. *The New Democrats 1961–1986: The Politics of Change* (Toronto: Copp Clark Pitman, 1986).

Penniman, Howard, ed. *Canada at the Polls 1979 and 1980: A Study of the General Election* (Washington, D.C.: American Enterprise Institute for Public Policy Research, 1981).

Simpson, Jeffrey. *Discipline of Power: The Conservative Interlude and the Liberal Restoration* (Toronto: Personal Library Publishers, 1980).

Troyer, Warner. *200 Days: Joe Clark in Power* (Toronto: Personal Library Publishers, 1980).

CHAPTER 9

THE END OF THE TRUDEAU DYNASTY AND THE MULRONEY LANDSLIDE

Almost as soon as Pierre Trudeau had welcomed Canada to the 1980s, it became clear that the 1980s would provide even worse economic times than the inflation-rocked 1970s. The unemployment rate, which had been working its way gradually upward, moved in 1982 into double figures (11 percent) for the first time since the Great Depression of the 1930s, and inflation remained above 10 percent (see Figure 9.1). As recession (some called it a depression) hit, the gross national product dove into negative territory. The value of the Canadian dollar slipped 10 cents against the American dollar, and interest rates rose to record heights of over 20 percent in an effort by the Bank of Canada to support the dollar and restrain inflation. The result of this crunch was a rise in business, farm, and personal bankruptcies. The Trudeau government found itself beleaguered on all economic fronts.

The economic crisis was exacerbated by Trudeau's decision to bring in the National Energy Program in 1980, a move which has been characterized as "no[t] primarily intended to produce good economics."[1] The National Energy Program (NEP) was the culmination of a number of interventions of the Trudeau government into the energy sector. Petro Canada, a government-owned oil company, had been incorporated during the minority government of 1972–74 as one of the concessions to the NDP for its support.[2] The Foreign Investment Review Agency had been used to prevent foreign takeovers in the energy sector, and domestic oil prices had been held below world levels in order to aid Canadian industry, homeowners, and drivers. As outlined in Chapter 8, the Conservative attempt to reverse some of these policies had been instrumental to its defeat in the House of Commons and the election of 1980. On the Liberals' return to power, the energy portfolio was given to Marc Lalonde, who proposed to fix the energy situation once and for all.[3] He and his officials constructed a comprehensive program, which was introduced in the 1980 budget.[4] It presented the NEP as a response, not only to the increased oil prices of the late 1970s, but also to Canada's reliance on foreign oil, as well as foreign domination of the oil industry. Its stated goal was to stimulate new investment and oil production by using incentives, and by providing Petro Canada with an automatic quarter interest in new oil production on the Canada Lands in the West and North.

The National Energy Program was met by a predictably hostile reaction from Alberta, and implemented only after a series of negotiations and

FIGURE 9.1
Main Economic Indicators, 1978–1990

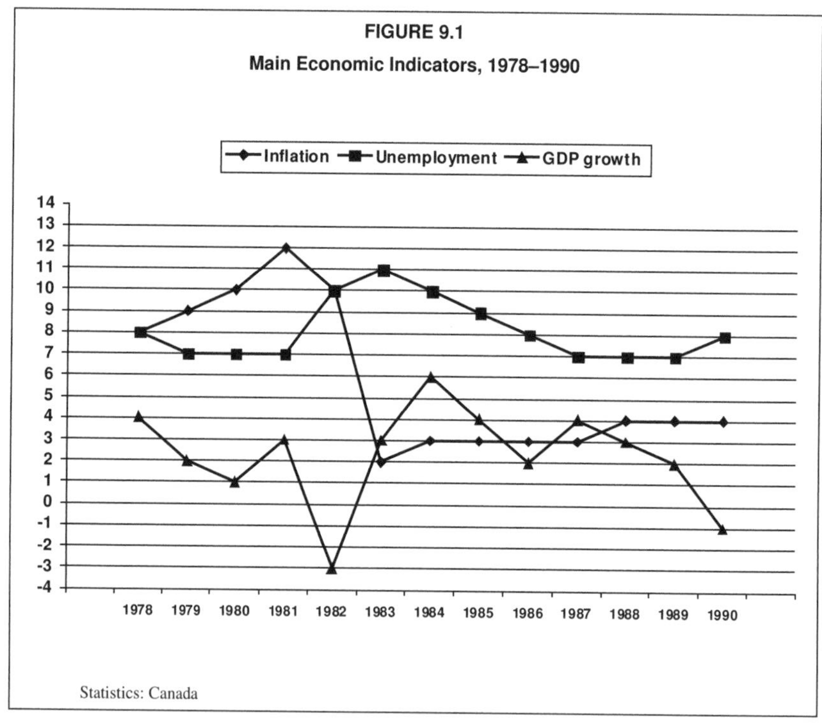

Statistics: Canada

compromises. The Liberals eventually agreed to an increase in oil prices to world levels, benefiting both the federal government and Alberta through tax revenues. Such price increases, however, also fuelled inflation, which remained high until 1983, putting the Bank of Canada in a position where lowering interest rates in an attempt to stimulate economic growth might also risk adding to inflationary pressures.[5] This combination of events fostered an atmosphere of pessimism and gloom among Canadians with respect to both their personal economic prospects and those of the country,[6] a mood which was only exacerbated by the federal–provincial confrontation on the energy issue. Not surprisingly, Liberal Party popularity began to slide (see Figure 9.2), particularly in the West.

At the same time, Pierre Trudeau decided to use his unexpected return to power to reintroduce his longtime agenda of constitutional reform. He had personally played a major role in the defeat of the 1980 referendum in Quebec, which asked the people of the province to give the government of Quebec a mandate to negotiate sovereignty in association with Canada[7]. The result of the referendum, a rejection of the proposal by a margin of 60 percent to 40 percent, gave Trudeau an

FIGURE 9.2

Federal Vote Intention, 1980–1984

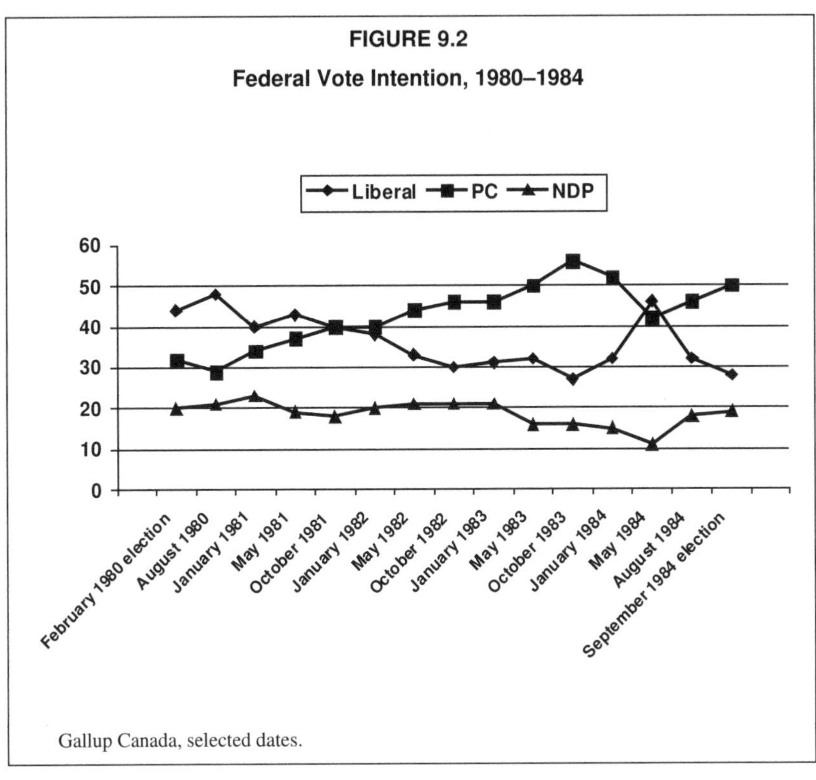

Gallup Canada, selected dates.

opening to move in the direction of constitutional change, since he had insisted during the referendum campaign, in a series of speeches given in Quebec, that a NO vote would not be interpreted as a vote for the status quo but rather for a "renewed federalism."

The day after the referendum defeat, Trudeau initiated a series of negotiations with the provinces to develop a formula for constitutional amendment which would allow "repatriation" of the document from its nominal control by the British Parliament. At this stage of his career, this was a Trudeau who was determined to accomplish his goal using whatever means were necessary. According to Stephen Clarkson and Christina McCall, "what set the Trudeau of 1980 apart from the Trudeau of the 1970s was the integration of various facets of himself into a fully mature, versatile, political actor."[8] He also knew that this was his last chance to achieve his lifelong ambition of giving Canada its own constitution.

At the beginning of the process, Trudeau made it clear that he was determined to accomplish the constitutional changes, with or without the agreement of the provinces. If they did not want to sign a new constitution, he would take it to the people in a referendum for approval, and would demand that the British government approve it. In this atmosphere, negotiations broke down a number of times. One of the main sticking points was Trudeau's insistence that the constitution include a Charter of Rights and Freedoms, outlining a set of basic entitlements and civil liberties for individuals and groups.

The Charter was popular with the public, but not with the majority of the provincial governments, which foresaw a diminution of their legislative powers. The federal government, led by Justice Minister Jean Chrétien, asked the Supreme Court to rule on the legality of unilateral federal action instructing Britain to amend the constitution by adding the Charter and turning the document over to Canada. The Court ruled that taking such action was legal, but that convention required "a substantial degree of provincial consent".[9]

In the meantime, eight of the 10 provinces (excluding Ontario and New Brunswick) agreed on a common constitutional plan — one that was quite different than the prime minister's. In a last ditch federal–provincial conference, a deal was brokered by Chrétien and several of his provincial justice minister colleagues, which accepted the Charter but added a "notwithstanding clause" that would allow governments to override some of the rights contained in it should they wish to do so.[10]

René Lévesque was left out of these last-minute bargaining proceedings and refused to endorse the agreement because it failed to protect French rights and interests. The repercussions of leaving Quebec out of the negotiations would be felt for years to come. Apprehension about the lack of agreement from the government of Quebec, as well as a general national fatigue with endless discussions of such abstract matters clouded the feeling of accomplishment which might have been expected to surround Trudeau and the Liberals as they "brought home the constitution." His role in the constitutional negotiations made Jean Chrétien popular in the rest of Canada, but turned him into a pariah in parts of his home province. For the rest of his career, even after he became prime minister, Chrétien would be attacked for his "betrayal of Quebec." These attacks came not only from Quebec separatists but also from some fellow Quebec Liberals (see Chapter 11).

The number of important events which packed the period preceding the 1984 election mark it as one of the "most extraordinary in the political history of Canada."[11] Not the least of the developments was a dramatic shift in the popularity of the country's two major political parties (see Figure 9.2). Almost as soon as 1980, with its federal election and Quebec referendum, had come to a close, the popularity of Trudeau and the Liberals began to slide, until it reached 30 percent in the October 1982 Gallup poll. The NDP maintained its share of about 20 percent of likely vote support in the same polls. And the stock of the Progressive Conservatives, under the leadership of Joe Clark, rose until 46 percent of Canadians told Gallup they would vote Conservative if an election were held in late 1982. Faced with this situation of almost unprecedented popularity, the Conservatives, who might have been expected to start preparing for government, turned inward and attacked their leader.

The Conservatives Choose a New Leader

Joe Clark's problems in establishing the confidence of his fellow Conservatives stemmed ultimately from the nature of his 1976 leadership victory, and were reinforced by his inability to sustain the hard-won Conservative government of 1979 (see Chapter 8). Clark had been a solid leadership candidate in 1976, but few people saw him as the best hope for the party from the outset. Rather, he became the compromise choice when the front-runners, Claude Wagner and Brian Mulroney, proved to be too divisive within the ranks of party delegates. But even in the top job, Clark never seemed to be able to measure up to the standards of leadership established by Trudeau. And the fact that he let power slip out of Conservative hands so quickly after the 1979 election victory was never forgotten by many in the party, even by those who wanted to give him the benefit of the doubt.

Clark also suffered from a weak image in Quebec and Ontario — vital provinces to the party should it ever wish to form a majority government. His decision to oppose Trudeau on the question of repatriating the constitution with the Charter of Rights failed to increase his support in Quebec and put him at odds with the Ontario Conservative provincial government, as well as much of that province's population.[12] It also put him at odds with Brian Mulroney, his main challenger for the leadership. Mulroney, unlike Clark, offered the possibility of a Conservative revival in Quebec. He also opposed Clark's view of Canada as a "community of communities," in which more power would be devolved to the provincial governments.[13] Clark had a major "Quebec problem" within the Party, and an "Ontario problem" within the electorate. On both grounds, many members of the PC parliamentary caucus were lukewarm at best about their leader.

The Conservatives' lack of confidence in Clark was accentuated by the fact that the Liberals seemed to have two aces in the hole should they conclude that Pierre Trudeau could not win another election for them. Former cabinet ministers Donald Macdonald and John Turner had retired from politics to private business in Toronto, but were widely seen as having retained their previous popularity, and as being ready to take over the party leadership if or when the opportunity arose. Had Trudeau's abortive resignation after his 1979 election loss been carried through, Macdonald was poised to run in a leadership convention with good chances of winning. However, once Macdonald was appointed to head a Royal Commission on the Economic Union and Development Prospects for Canada in 1981, the mantle of "leader in waiting" was assumed by another former finance minister, John Turner. Turner was widely seen as having a more favourable national image than Clark, particularly in Ontario and Quebec.

There were a number of opportunities for the Tories to express a lack of confidence in the leader. Ever since the bitter experience of the

Diefenbaker years, the party's constitution had called for a biennial party policy convention, at which a vote would be taken on the possibility of holding a leadership convention. The first of these "leadership reviews" after the 1980 defeat came in 1981, when two-thirds of the delegates to the policy convention voted against holding a new leadership convention. In January 1983, another policy convention was held. In the interim, much debate occurred within the party as to how much support would be "enough" to indicate support for the leader. In this case, it was essentially up to Clark to interpret the meaning of the vote. He is thought to have made an undertaking to the caucus that he would secure an increase

Jean-Marc Carisse, photographer.

John Turner at press conference, Ottawa, 1984.

on his 1981 support (that is, fewer delegates voting for a convention) in order to proclaim his position as leader secure.[14] When the 1983 vote was virtually identical (one-third of the delegates supported a leadership convention) Clark felt he had no option but to call one. One reason for this was that "fully 50 percent of Clark's parliamentary colleagues had voted for a leadership convention."[15] Without the caucus behind him it would have been difficult to function in opposition. Delegate surveys showed that a perceived lack of competence was the major reason for the lack of confidence in Clark.

Despite what some perceived as the humiliation of not being able to raise his support among delegates even though the party was enjoying a massive lead in the polls, Clark felt he could win a leadership contest. If he could do that, the margin of victory would not matter, since there would be many candidates and probably many ballots. He would have thereby re-established his leadership authority, and the caucus would have to fall into line and support him, at least through the next election. Furthermore, a convention would provide an additional boost of publicity for the party, remove the perception of "wimpyness" which often surrounded Clark, and put the ball back in the Liberal court, where *they* might be expected to engage in a bout of internal discord about leadership. If Trudeau had to give way to Turner, the distaste those two men felt for each other might produce some negatives for the government.

Seven challengers contested the PC leadership in 1983, indicative not only of the amount of discontent with Clark but also of the amount of unsatisfied ambition in Tory ranks. A number of successful businessmen (Brian Mulroney, John Crosbie, Michael Wilson, Peter Pocklington), who were used to taking leadership positions in industry, felt confident that they could handle political leadership, as well. Only two of these men, however, had the political strength to pose a real threat to Clark. One was John Crosbie, who had been finance minister in Clark's ill-fated 1979 government, and was the author of the infamous budget containing an 18-cent-per-gallon gasoline tax ("short term pain for long term gain.").[16]

Crosbie was primarily a Maritime regional candidate, but he emerged as a possible compromise choice for those who wanted to replace Clark but were not prepared for any of a number of reasons to opt for Brian Mulroney. Ultimately, despite the affection the convention held for Crosbie, he came to grief from "his proposal to consider free trade with the United States and his inability to speak French."[17] The first of these issues might not have been so devastating for him, especially considering the subsequent adoption of a free trade platform by the Tories. The second, however, was a major problem, considering the party's attempts to create a viable organization in Quebec, and also considering the presence in the race of an attractive Quebec candidate. More important, perhaps, than the fact that Crosbie had difficulty in French was the fact that he felt it was not necessary to make the attempt.

Brian Mulroney was the son of an electrician from Baie-Comeau, Quebec. His upbringing gave him two qualities not normally associated with leaders of the Progressive Conservative Party of Canada; he was working-class, and he had a background of immersion in French-Canadian culture.[18] Mulroney identified himself as a Quebecer, making a conscious choice to attend law school at Laval rather than an anglophone university, and working at his French until he became completely fluent.[19] Naturally gregarious, Mulroney created vast networks of friends he could call on for support and advice. His undergraduate circle at St. Francis Xavier, where he joined the Conservative Party, included Lowell Murray and Pat MacAdam. His Laval classmates included Michael Meighen, Peter White, and Lucien Bouchard. All of these men were to play an important part in Mulroney's rise to the leadership of the Tories,

Library and Archives Canada. Ed McGibbon, photographer.

Brian Mulroney and Mila Mulroney, Progressive Conservative convention, 1983, Ottawa.

and in the subsequent governments that he formed. His contacts with politicians included Union Nationale stalwarts like Daniel Johnson, Tory cabinet ministers like Davie Fulton, and even John Diefenbaker, who supposedly called him in 1960 "the future Prime Minister of Canada."

Brian Mulroney was not unique in being selected leader of an important Canadian political party without having a seat in Parliament, but he was unique in reaching that position without ever having sought public office. All of his activity within the Conservative Party took place behind the scenes. He supported Dalton Camp's efforts to replace John Diefenbaker as leader in 1966, working initially for Davie Fulton but switching his support to Robert Stanfield at the convention. He worked as counsel to the Cliche Commission, investigating crime on the Montreal waterfront, a position that made him a household name in Quebec. He played a major part in the recruitment of Claude Wagner, former provincial Liberal cabinet minister and later a judge, to Conservative ranks in 1972. This development was not only to prove unsuccessful in improving the party's overall showing in Quebec in the 1972 and 1974 elections (producing resentment of Mulroney within the party in the process), but also produced a formidable Quebec opponent (Wagner) in the 1976 Conservative leadership convention where Mulroney also sought the leadership. Mulroney's loss to Joe Clark at that convention (see Chapter 8) embittered him for a period, and caused him to withdraw from some of his political activity into positions in industry, later becoming president of the Iron Ore Company of Canada.[20]

But Mulroney was too ambitious to pass up a second opportunity to become PC leader and prime minister of Canada. As the Clark government stumbled its way back into opposition in 1980, and as the problems for the party grew in Quebec, Mulroney built networks promoting himself as the future leader, all the while maintaining a public pose of support for Clark. In 1982, Mulroney supporters took over the Quebec Conservative party, incorporating in the process much of the previous Wagner organization. When the 1983 leadership convention was called, Mulroney was ready. He had learned a lesson from his unsuccessful run for the leadership in 1976. At that time, he was seen to run a "Cadillac campaign," spending freely and engendering resentment at his seeming arrogance. This time his campaign was going to be low-key and low-budget when it came to such things as entertainment of delegates and models of cars used for transportation, but thorough and modern when it came to tracking delegates and

TABLE 9.1

Party Leadership Conventions, 1983–1984

DATE	PARTY	LOCATION	WINNER	# CANDIDATES*	# BALLOTS	RUNNER-UP**
1983 06 08	PC	Ottawa	Brian Mulroney	8	4	Joe Clark
1984 06 14	Liberal	Ottawa	John Turner	7	2	Jean Chrétien

* On first ballot

** On final ballot

working to persuade them that Brian Mulroney could provide the winning touch that would capitalize on the unpopularity of the Liberals.

The Conservative leadership convention of 1983 came down to a fourth ballot, as the other candidates dropped away, leaving Mulroney and Clark alone. Mulroney had been gradually increasing his vote totals as the ballots went along, whereas it appeared that Clark was nobody's second choice. Clark's vote on the second ballot was less than on the first, and his vote on the third was lower still. The mood for change in the leadership seemed irresistible. Analysis of the convention voting concluded that "Brian Mulroney put together a more broadly based coalition than either of his predecessors, Robert Stanfield or Joe Clark."[21]

Mulroney the pragmatist, untied to ideology, with a background running a big business and yet a reputation of dealing fairly with labour, devoted to consensus-building and friendship, bilingual, and bicultural like the country, but a proponent of "One Canada," seemed to be the man of the hour. A short time after Mulroney's election as leader, the Gallup poll showed the Conservatives with 56 percent of public support (see Figure 9.2).

The Liberals Choose a New Leader

As was widely anticipated, Pierre Trudeau decided to bow out once again, this time while he was on top, satisfied by the constitutional success he had achieved in 1982. Popularity ratings, for both himself and his party, remained too low to have any confidence that another election victory was possible. He was not cut out to be Leader of the Opposition, as he had learned in 1979. In February of 1984 he announced, after some meditation, that he would be leaving in June. The Liberals, too, were heading for a leadership convention, and they also needed to decide between two different kinds of candidate, one of them an outsider. The outsider in this case, John Turner, had been an insider until 1975: first as a candidate for the Liberal leadership against Pierre Trudeau in 1968, then as finance minister in Trudeau's government between 1972 and 1975. As with Brian Mulroney, the ambitious Turner did not take defeat lightly; by 1975 he had decided to withdraw from politics.

Interpretations of the reasons for Turner's resignation differ. As far as Jean Chrétien, a cabinet colleague at the time, was concerned, the reasons were personal:

> Turner had been making a personal sacrifice for many years in terms of what he could have been earning in the private sector. He and his wife had grown up accustomed to a certain lifestyle; they had four children to be educated; and it was obvious that Trudeau intended to stay as Prime Minister for a while longer. There were no mysteries or complications about why he quit. [22]

Pierre Trudeau wrote that "since he had given me no prior warning of his unhappiness, I was surprised and disappointed," but that Turner told him, "I've got my family to look after. It's that time in life."[23]

Turner, however, amplified this personal explanation in later years with the position that his resignation expressed unhappiness with the Trudeau government's economic policy, which he was being asked to implement as finance minister. Turner was convinced that the way to deal with inflation (or "stagflation" as it was becoming known) was to curtail government spending and promote a voluntary system of wage and price restraint. "Turner was a free-enterpriser" his biographer maintains, whereas "Trudeau was convinced that the free-market system wasn't working." [24] Trudeau had been reading the recent work of economist John Kenneth Galbraith, and became convinced that direct control of wages and prices would be necessary, despite what he had argued in the 1974 election campaign (see Chapter 7).[25]

As the years went on, the image that Turner had quit because of policy differences grew and was nurtured. At the time, the impression was left with a number of people that Turner just wanted to be reassured he was needed and that the prime ministership might be in the future for him.[26] Trudeau, however, did not do things that way. According to Keith Davey, the two men were completely different: "Turner wanted to be loved. Trudeau just wanted to be left alone."[27] Much later, Trudeau wrote, "You can tell me I handled it badly, tell me I should have got down on my knees and begged him to stay. But that's not how I saw politics, then or now. Politics is a difficult game and you have to have your heart in it."[28] Trudeau simply wished Turner good luck with the rest of his life.

So, as Mulroney had done, John Turner went into the world of business (in his case as a lawyer) to bide his time, cultivate his networks, and wait for the next opportunity for leadership. There were a number of similarities between Mulroney and Turner. Both were avid networkers, prizing loyalty to themselves above all else and fiercely loyal to those who supported them; both also were outgoing and gregarious, impatient with those they saw as "technocrats."

"My skills are people skills," Turner told a journalist, "and these are the skills required to put a human face on technology and government."[29] Both Mulroney and Turner disliked the leaders they replaced and consciously felt they could bring a different, more human style to government. Both men, though not right-wing in any extreme sense, wanted to make their parties more business-oriented and supportive of economic policies favoured by industry.

Not all Liberals thought Turner would be the right choice, despite the "winnability factor" that surrounded him, and the repeated references to the Liberal Party's tradition of alternating French- and English-speaking leaders since the time of Laurier. Jean Chrétien, who had held a number of cabinet portfolios dating back to the Pearson years, felt he had a chance to win. Originally, his plan was to portray himself as the compromise choice if the convention became deadlocked between Macdonald and Turner. Once he realized that Turner alone would be the opposition, he suggested that Turner had become "out of touch … about politics since his resignation," and that "his right-wing image bothered a lot of Liberal MPs."[30] Besides a lot of caucus support, Chrétien felt he had Trudeau's encouragement. Be that as it may, Turner was the clear winner of the convention. Although elected constituency delegates were split between the two men, the ex-officio delegates representing party elites and officials heavily favoured Turner.[31]

John Turner's decision to dissolve Parliament and call an election very shortly after he won the leadership was a risky and ultimately disastrous strategy. It must have been at least partly motivated by the sudden boost of popularity his selection as Liberal leader gave the party, and perhaps partly by the fact that Pierre Trudeau had successfully followed a similar strategy in 1968. The Gallup polls, after showing the Conservatives ahead for over two years, with both Joe Clark and Brian Mulroney at the helm, suddenly vaulted the Liberals into a narrow lead (see Figure 9.2). Without pausing to consider whether this was a solid expression of likely voting intentions or just a temporary blip in volatile public opinion, Turner interpreted it as the former. Most Trudeau advisers were immediately replaced, but, according to accounts of meetings at the time, almost all the replacements, loyal as they were to Turner, advised against an immediate election:[32]

> For simple public relations reasons, taking a few months to act as head of government — welcoming the Queen on her scheduled visit to the Maritimes and Ontario, greeting the Pope on the first papal visit to the country, congratulating Canadian medalists at the Olympics, cutting ribbons, announcing projects — would have given the public a chance to firm up its image of John Turner as Prime Minister.[33]

Turner rejected this reasoning and decided to seize the opportunity to win an election on his own.

Thus, by 1984, the question was whether the Liberal dynasty would continue, or perhaps be replaced by a new one. The leadership of both of the major parties had been swept away, to be replaced by two extremely ambitious men, popular (at least initially) with the public, who seemed likely to dominate the Canadian political stage for a generation. At the outset it was unclear whether John Turner or Brian Mulroney would be better positioned to win the public trust over the long term, but there was a general assumption that the competition would be intense. As it transpired, the battle was more lopsided than anyone expected.

The 1984 Campaign

The Liberal Party had made few concrete preparations for an election; what plans there were had been undertaken by the staff of the former prime minister on the assumption that Trudeau would be running another campaign and would require a platform suited to his philosophy. Upon taking office, Turner summarily dismissed most of these people. Few candidates had been nominated, in contrast to the other parties. Turner, again against the advice of all, decided to manage his own campaign, with the reluctant assistance of Bill Lee, one of the few people around Turner with campaign experience. Policy was not developed, and could not be intuited from Turner's pronouncements during the leadership campaign except in the most general terms. The campaign was to be centred around the leader.

This election campaign was the first since 1968 (and only the fourth time in Canadian history) in which both the Liberals and Conservatives were fighting an election with leaders newly chosen since the previous contest.[34] Not only were they inexperienced, but 1984 shaped up to be an election campaign between two of the most egotistical, ambitious men to ever lead Canadian political parties.

FIGURE 9.3

Party Leader Thermometer Scale Ratings and Debate Performance Scores, 1984

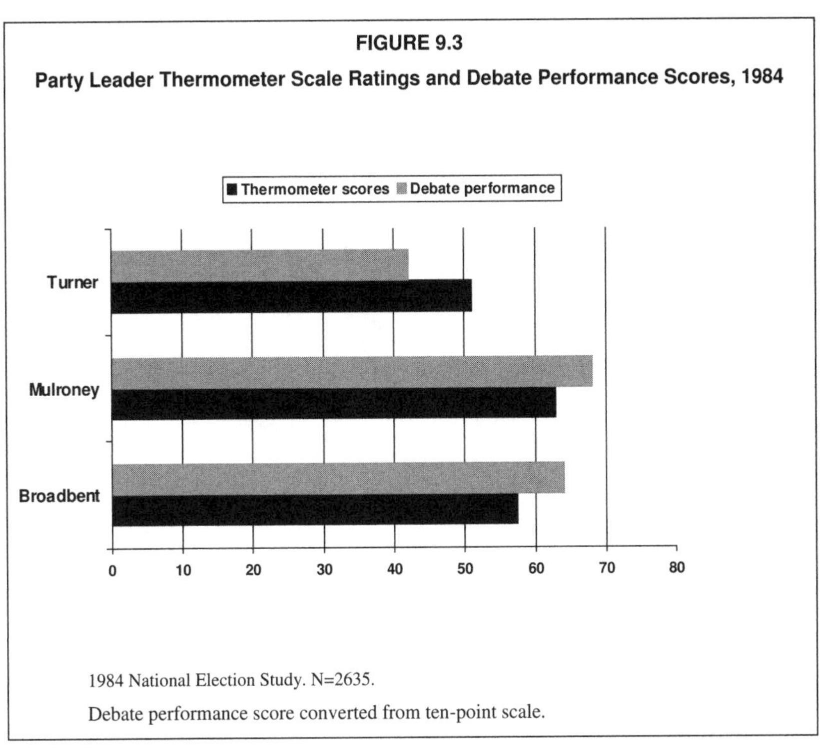

1984 National Election Study. N=2635.

Debate performance score converted from ten-point scale.

As John Turner prepared to create a campaign around himself on short notice, Brian Mulroney had been giving his eventual legacy a lot of thought. "Brian just doesn't want to be Prime Minister," his friend Lucien Bouchard once observed, "He wants to live in history."[35]

Mulroney's sympathetic biographer, Ian Macdonald, reports that,

> Mulroney had confided to his top policy advisor that he would like to be remembered in history for four points: first, for eventually achieving a constitutional settlement that included Quebec; then, for a restructuring of the Canadian economy; third, for consolidating a distinctive role for middle powers in the world; and finally, as an extension of his interest in the minority rights question, improved economic and social conditions for the country's native peoples.[36]

Mulroney's subsequent evaluation was that he had succeeded: "You cannot name a Canadian Prime Minister who has done as many significant things as I did, because there are none."[37]

Brian Mulroney knew that he needed to give substance to an image heretofore remarkably devoid of substantive policy positions. At heart a total pragmatist, he had presented himself to the Conservative convention of 1976 as somewhat left of centre, as a contrast to Claude Wagner in the contest to represent Quebec. At the 1983 convention, he recast himself as right of centre, an experienced businessman who knew how to run a country, in contrast to Joe Clark, who did not. His choice of areas of emphasis mentioned above is interesting, however. Achieving a constitutional settlement would make Mulroney the champion of national unity. Recasting the economy would lay claim to the issue area of economic growth and development. Improving the lot of Native peoples would add a new dimension to the whole area of social policy, rather than fight battles over traditional grounds like health and welfare, where the other parties held established reputations. If the Conservative Party could establish its credentials in these three areas they would capture the entire important issue agenda of Canadian politics and lay the basis for a new dynasty. Mulroney's place in history would indeed be assured.

It has gone down on the record that John Turner's decision to call an "early" election was a mistake, but in his defence, a number of indicators appeared to him to be favourable in early July. While he was in England seeking the Queen's agreement to postpone her scheduled August visit, the *Globe and Mail* published a front-page story that reported a drop in the unemployment rate and a rise in the value of the dollar.[38] At the same time, the Gallup poll was showing the Liberals with an 11-point lead in popularity, findings no doubt mirrored by the party's internal polling. And, in the "Who would make the best Prime Minister?" question asked by Gallup, the results published during the campaign continued to show Turner ahead. In a survey taken at the end of June and published in early August, Turner led Mulroney by 39 percent to 22 percent, and in one taken in late July and published in mid-August, he still led by a margin of 33 percent to 29 percent.[39] The time lag in the publication of these findings led to the incongruous situation in the newspapers in which stories about the leader's gaffes and the party's organizational turmoil were followed by stories of John Turner's popularity, seemingly in spite of it all.

In reality, John Turner's popularity was severely affected by several developments that occurred early in the campaign. One of these was the revelation of his habit of patting the bottoms of attractive Liberal women in public; his reply that he was "a tactile politician"[40] only served to make things worse. More important was the position he took over the deal he had reached with his predecessor, Pierre Trudeau, to make a large number of "patronage appointments" of Trudeau loyalists as one of his first acts as the new prime minister. Although heavily criticized for this when it happened, he appeared to have weathered the storm. However, Turner unwisely decided to pursue the subject himself in the televised leaders' debates held early in the campaign, on the grounds of some joking remarks Mulroney had made (and apologized for) about providing some Tory patronage if he got the chance. Mulroney's riposte ("you had an option, sir …") was considered by some to be the "knockout punch" of the debates, and it put Turner on the defensive for the rest of the campaign. Mulroney later, and perhaps disingenuously, remarked, "At this point, I know there's been a dramatic, historic exchange, but I wasn't sure whether I had helped or hurt my case."[41]

Data from the 1984 National Election Study confirms the impression that the debates were costly to Turner. The public rated Turner's debate performance only at 4.2 out of 10, while Mulroney was given 6.8, and NDP leader Ed Broadbent scored 6.4 (see Figure 9.3). While the overall thermometer score for Turner was a little better than his debate score (just over 50 out of 100) it was still much lower than the other two leaders. It appears that many voters previously favourable to him soured on Turner during the election campaign and were joined in their negative views by those who had not made up their minds about him.

The positive opinion the public had about Brian Mulroney should not mask the fact that he had a credibility problem to overcome. The precociousness of his early political career behind the scenes was general public knowledge, particularly given his unsuccessful run for the Conservative leadership in 1976 without ever having sought elective office. Similarly, his reputation for disloyalty and backstabbing related to ousting Joe Clark from the leadership prior to and during 1983 was both more recent and more negative. As president of the Iron Ore Company, he had presided over the closing of the company town of Shefferville in northern Quebec, close to the place he was brought up and claimed to love so much. And his deep voice and hearty manner made him appear insincere at times, even as he was frequently the centre of attention; as one commentator said, he "used lots of oxygen every time he entered a room."[42]

The sincerity and trust problem was one the Conservative campaign manager, Norman Atkins, and the party's pollster, Allan Gregg, knew they had to address. This was especially true since the Liberals were running television advertisements attacking Mulroney as the man who had closed Shefferville (implication: he would close the whole country if he were put in power) and the "20-billion dollar man" who made promises purely for the sake of getting into power. The Conservative campaign managers decided to forego thoughts of attacking the Liberals in the same vein, and ran a positive campaign based on Mulroney asking Canadians to help him improve the country; the slogan was "We can do better together." The Tory television advertisements showed Mulroney talking directly to people, "suppressing his usual highly partisan, highly exaggerated, highly facile style … [and] project[ing] himself as earnest, informed, caring and very sincere."[43]

The comparison of party leader images shown in Table 9.2 clearly favoured Mulroney on many dimensions, though the rating on "sincere" was stronger for NDP leader Ed Broadbent than either of the other two leaders. Broadbent was also very positively perceived on the dimensions of "decent," "sure of himself," and was not considered "arrogant," "nervous," or "shallow."

TABLE 9.2

Leader and Party Image Dimensions, 1984

	Brian Mulroney	**John Turner**	**Ed Broadbent**
Arrogant	3.84	3.88	2.99
Competent	5.28	4.20	4.66
Ruthless	3.81	3.52	3.09
Commands respect	5.25	4.27	4.78
Nervous	2.89	4.47	2.97
Decent	5.30	5.06	5.41
Slick	5.00	4.07	3.61
Sincere	4.79	4.47	5.21
Shallow	3.38	3.73	2.91
Sure of himself	5.90	4.14	5.20
Dull	3.13	4.05	3.50
Warm	4.85	3.87	4.81
Represents change	5.50	3.57	4.91
Listens to the views of your province	4.77	3.88	4.59
	Conservative Party	**Liberal Party**	**NDP**
Competent	4.96	3.80	3.95
Listens to Atlantic	4.75	3.85	4.24
Listens to Quebec	5.26	4.99	4.09
Listens to Ontario	5.48	5.24	4.91
Listens to West	5.07	3.67	4.86
Concerned with ethnic minorities	4.42	4.46	4.85
Committed to women's issues	4.49	4.14	5.11

1984 Canadian National Election Study. N = 3,380. Table entries are mean scores on 7 point scale with "Fits not at all" and "Fits very well" as the 1 and 7 points.

Mulroney scored highly on "competent," "commands respect," "decent," "sure of himself," and "represents change," among other things.

For John Turner, "decent" was about the only characteristic that survey respondents thought "fit him very well." It is worth noting that decency, honesty, and sincerity were also the main components of another unsuccessful Canadian political party leader, Robert Stanfield.[44] We can also note from Table 9.2 that Mulroney's score was ominously high on one dubious characteristic, "slick," which would grow and come to dominate his image in a few short years. The "negatives" in party leader images are often there from the beginning.[45]

The New Democratic Party entered the 1984 election campaign in an apprehensive mood. After remaining steady in most polls in the inter-election period (see Figure 9.2), they suffered a drastic diminution in their projected support between mid-1983 and the spring of 1984, as the major parties chose new leaders. Internally, the party was undergoing a difficult time, with recriminations about the reasons for the party's fall in the polls. Leader Ed Broadbent had supported Pierre Trudeau's constitutional repatriation, and had also made a number of speeches indicating a potential shift away from traditional NDP policies of economic stimulation and spending; neither of these moves was universally supported within the party.[46]

As the debate performance rating and the overall leader thermometer indicate (see Figure 9.3), Ed Broadbent was an important part of the NDP campaign and a major reason why the party managed to turn their fortunes around, to the point that they achieved a result similar to that of 1980, itself a high-water mark of NDP success. The similarity between the right of centre stances of both the Liberals and the Conservatives made the NDP stand out more clearly than it had during the Trudeau years. They made a point of emphasizing that they were fighting for "ordinary people" against the other parties led by the "Bobbsey Twins of Bay Street."[47] Once the Liberal slide in popularity began, the NDP competed for disenchanted Liberal voters who were nervous about switching to the Mulroney-led Conservatives. The NDP could be seen as "welfare liberals," a safe haven for those concerned with the dominance of "business liberals" in the Liberal Party itself.[48] Then, when it became apparent that the Conservatives were heading for a sweeping majority, the NDP asked for votes so that a real opposition would exist in the House of Commons.

The Conservatives' choice of the Quebecer Brian Mulroney as their new leader, and their rejection of the candidacy of John Crosbie, who found it impossible to learn French, were important signals that the party was serious about becoming a national party. More than that, Conservatives saw in Mulroney the chance to remake the party into the champion of national unity, a position it had not held since the John A. Macdonald years. The Conservatives were helped along immeasurably in this regard by the Liberals' choice of John Turner as leader, not so much because he was not a Quebecer (though he had lived and practiced law in Montreal), but because, in his efforts to distance himself from Trudeau, he also distanced himself from Trudeau's commitment to bilingualism.

In his initial press conference, when he announced his candidacy for the leadership in 1984, Turner took the opportunity of a question asking about French-language rights in Manitoba to stake out his position. The House of Commons had just passed a unanimous resolution urging the provincial government to make French an official language of the province and to provide some French-language services. Turner, however, was at pains to state that, while he supported the resolution, the question of language rights was one under provincial jurisdiction. By implication, therefore, the federal government should keep its hands off the bilingualism issue.[49] This barely-coded attempt to win western support had repercussions. An immediate one was that Jean Chrétien moved to challenge him for the leadership, because he perceived Turner was vulnerable in that "he wanted to woo the West by being soft on bilingualism."[50]

The election saw further important signals of Brian Mulroney's decision to emphasize his connection to Quebec. In deciding which riding to contest in the election, Mulroney had several choices. He could continue to represent Central Nova, where the incumbent member had given up his seat in 1983 in order to allow Mulroney to enter the House of Commons as Leader of the Opposition. He was being urged to run in Brome-Missisquoi, a seat in the Eastern Townships of Quebec with a Conservative past and a large English population. Instead of taking these "easy options" he decided to run for election from Manicouagan, "a remote riding with no Conservative history and a reputation for militant trade unionism and strikes."[51] This constituency, which included his hometown of Baie-Comeau, was currently represented by a popular young Liberal MP, and would be by far the most difficult option for victory. But the symbolic choice of a rural Quebec riding was a fortuitous one. It was not the first or last time Mulroney would "roll the dice,"[52] but this time it was successful.

A third symbol came with the leaders' debates. The 1984 campaign was the first campaign in which the leaders debated extensively in French. Previous debates had seen some leaders speak in French (Trudeau at times in 1968 and 1979, Réal Caouette in 1968, Joe Clark in 1979), but 1984 was the first time in which all leaders agreed to a separate encounter exclusively conducted in that language. For Ed Broadbent, the French debate was a struggle. For Turner and Mulroney, it was a chance for two anglophones to show how well they could speak the language; this test of credibility was won by Mulroney, whose colloquial and fluent French far outshone Turner.

About a month before election day, Mulroney made an important speech to a group of Conservative election organizers, which established the nature of his appeal in Quebec, and the one he wanted transmitted in local campaigns. Significantly, in Sept-Îles (not in a big city) he gave an address, written by his close friend and sovereignty-proponent Lucien Bouchard, in which he pledged the federal government to reconcile with the provincial government of Quebec over the constitution and to bring Quebec back into the Canadian family with "honour and enthusiasm." The provincial government, run by the sovereigntist Parti Québécois, was the "duly and legitimately elected Quebec government,"[53] according to Mulroney. The Conservative Party wants a strong Quebec, not a weak Quebec, he said.

A government Mulroney would lead would give the provinces a voice in federal policy, including economic policy: "We will set up a federal–provincial advisory and coordinating body. It will operate at the highest level, namely with the 11 leaders themselves working together."[54]

All of these statements were carefully designed to win support among Quebec nationalists, who would be pleased with the promises of more power to the province. Later, in other provinces, Mulroney returned to the same message. In Ontario, he defended the presence of former separatists as Conservative candidates in Quebec by saying that his party stands for "national reconciliation and national renewal."[55] In Nova Scotia, Mulroney accused the Liberal Party of having "a well articulated and well-defined" policy to "brutalize the government of Quebec."[56] He went on to add that this Liberal policy could be expected to continue, even if the provincial Liberals were to win the next Quebec election; it was widely known that many provincial Liberals, led by former premier Robert Bourassa, were covertly and sometimes openly supporting the Tories. A number of old scores were being settled.

Although the Conservatives' national unity appeal was primarily based on their claim to be able to represent Quebec to the rest of the country and vice versa, Mulroney did not neglect the West. Early in the campaign, while the Liberals were still trying to get organized, he made a symbolic visit to Prince Albert, the riding in Saskatchewan represented for many years by John Diefenbaker. With Conservative provincial premiers and other leaders on hand, he promised "a return to the days of John Diefenbaker's 'One Canada,'" [and] pledged that a Tory government would make the West "a powerful instrument of national growth."[57] Although relatively few Canadians identified national unity issues as the most important in the election, the image Mulroney created of a man who could bring the country together lay behind some of the public perceptions that leadership was the issue, or that there was a need for change.

As Table 9.3 indicates, the most important issues in the 1984 election were generally economic ones. The dire economic situation, particularly with regard to unemployment, was on the minds of most voters. No comprehensive economic programs were offered by the Liberals and Conservatives, however, and surprisingly few specific "quick fix" ideas emerged either. For Turner, who was portraying himself as a change from the previous Liberal government, which had not fared well in dealing with economic problems, the main policy proposal was a training program for jobless youth who had left school and were under 21.[58]

The Conservatives preferred to propose a tax credit scheme for employers hiring young people. A more comprehensive plan might have been expected from the NDP, but that party focused on a jobs plan for youth, as well. In addition, Ed Broadbent proposed to direct "the Bank of Canada to gradually reduce its lending rate to a level just 2 percentage points above the rate of inflation."[59] This move would result in a lowering of interest rates overall, and a boost to economic growth and job creation. Mulroney, declaring "jobs, jobs, jobs" to be his top three priorities, stated that a change in government, to one more friendly to business, would bring about an impetus toward economic growth.

TABLE 9.3

Most Important Issues in the 1984 Election

Economic Issues	
Unemployment / Jobs	36
The economy in general	17
Government spending / The deficit / The Budget	12
Taxes	3
Inflation / Cost of living / Wage and Price Controls	2
Oil prices / Energy policy	1
Other economic issues	3
National Unity	
Foreign policy / Defence	3
National unity / The Constitution / Intergovernmental relations	2
Quebec separatism / The referendum	2
Bilingualism / Language issues	1
Social Welfare	
Housing / Health / Pensions / Women's issues	11
Environmental issues	1
Other Issues	
Change / The parties / Retrospective evaluations	14
Leaders / Leadership	8
Trust, patronage, majority government, the polls	4
All other issues	4
None / No Important Issues / Don't Know	25

* 1984 Canadian National Election Study. N = 3,377.

TABLE 9.4

Results of the 1984 Federal Election, by Province

		Liberal	PC	NDP	Other	PC Net Gain / Loss from 1980
Newfoundland	votes (%)	36	58	6	0	
	seats (#)	3	4	0	0	+2
Prince Edward Island	votes (%)	41	52	7	1	
	seats (#)	1	3	0	0	+1
Nova Scotia	votes (%)	34	51	7	15	
	seats (#)	2	9	0	0	+3
New Brunswick	votes (%)	32	54	14	0	
	seats (#)	1	9	0	0	+6
Quebec	votes (%)	36	50	9	6	
	seats (#)	17	58	0	0	+57
Ontario	votes (%)	30	48	21	2	
	seats (#)	14	67	13	1	+29
Manitoba	votes (%)	22	43	27	8	
	seats (#)	1	9	4	0	+4
Saskatchewan	votes (%)	18	42	38	2	
	seats (#)	0	9	5	0	+2
Alberta	votes (%)	13	69	14	4	
	seats (#)	0	21	0	0	
British Columbia	votes (%)	16	47	35	2	
	seats (#)	1	19	8	0	+3
Yukon / NWT	votes (%)	25	47	24	4	
	seats (#)	0	3	0	0	+1
TOTAL CANADA	votes (%)	28	50	19	3	
	seats (#)	40	211	30	1	+108

The lack of comprehensive economic policy discussion during the 1984 election campaign was the product of several factors. As already mentioned, the decision by Turner to call an election immediately after winning the leadership meant that such plans were not developed, and initial indications of his personal popularity persuaded him and his advisers that they might not be needed. As for the Conservatives, interim party leader Erik Nielsen claims that he oversaw the production of a comprehensive election program during the leadership convention that chose Mulroney. However, Nielsen admits, "I had never really met Mulroney," and much of his subsequent advice to the new leader consisted of a candid briefing on the strengths and weaknesses of the members of the Conservative caucus.[60] Certainly, there was nothing in the Conservative campaign that would presage the adoption of a Free Trade Agreement with the United States, a proposal that would in government become the core of the Conservatives' economic plan.

On the economic issues of the 1984 campaign, the Conservatives enjoyed an enormous advantage in public opinion. Whether the issue

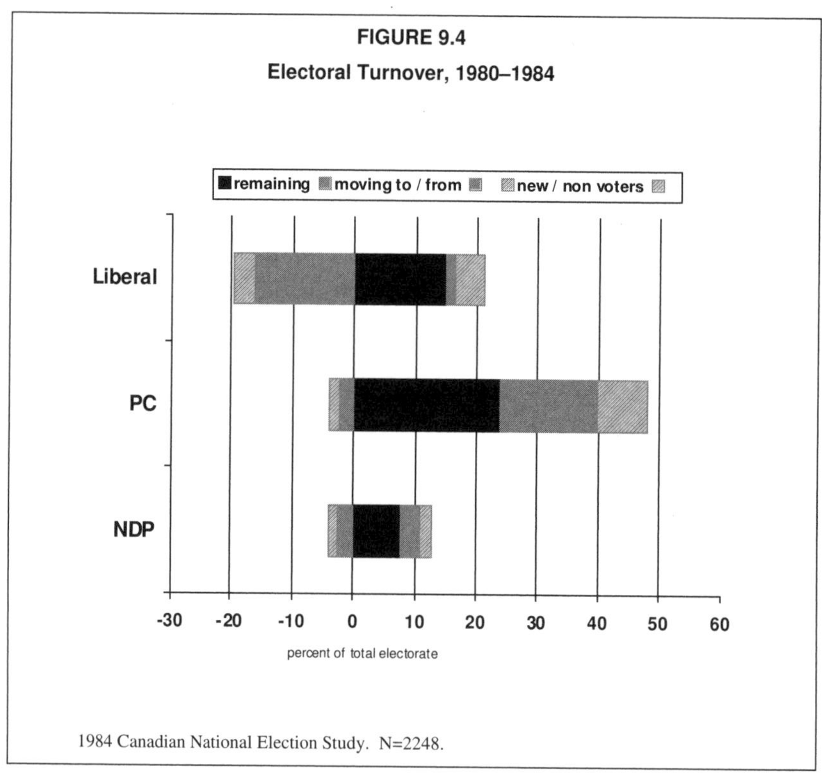

was defined generally as "the state of the economy," or somewhat more specifically as "unemployment" or "job creation," both those switching their votes and those remaining with the same party they had supported in 1980 heavily favoured the Conservatives.[61]

Figure 9.4 shows that a very large number of voters switched from other parties in 1980 to a 1984 Conservative vote.[62] A high proportion of these voters (over two-thirds) felt that economic issues were the most important ones in the election. For the most part, however, this was tantamount to identifying the economy as the top priority for a new government, and an expression of hope that the PCs could do a better job at it than the Liberals had recently been doing.

The third important issue area — that of social welfare issues — also worked in favour of Mulroney and the Conservatives in 1984. Using an inflated rhetoric that would return to haunt him later, Mulroney attacked the Liberals for having "gravely jeopardized the notion of universality in social programs in Canada"; for the Conservatives, on the other hand, universality was a "sacred trust not to be tampered with."[63]

For the first and last time, the 1984 election campaign featured a third leaders' debate, this one specifically on women's issues. Not coincidentally, just prior to this mid-August event, all of the parties issued social policy platforms. The Conservatives' was the most extensive:

> Mulroney promised to improve income support for the elderly and to provide new funds for medical care as well as additional funding for day-care programs … the Tory leader said the party would extend the federal spouses' allowance to all eligible widows between the ages of 60 and 65 … would restore the full indexing of the old-age pension to the cost of living … also increase the guaranteed income supplement … [and] start negotiations with the provinces for pension reform.[64]

On each of these subjects, Mulroney waxed eloquent: "It is a national disgrace that we have betrayed a generation of Canadians … it is insensitive and wrong to expect a widow at age 61 or 62 to return to the workplace … we are determined that growing old in Canada will not mean growing poor … no longer can child care be considered a luxury of the rich or a support program for the poor."[65] The self-righteousness which surrounded Mulroney's rhetoric on these and other subjects led directly to charges of hypocrisy when the promises were not fulfilled later on.

As if their deficiencies on the issues were not enough, the Liberals suffered from a very public reorganization dispute right in the middle of the campaign. Turner's campaign manager, Bill Lee, resigned on August 5, charging ineptitude on the part of those around Turner, and by implication, Turner himself. Lee, who had worked for Turner in the leadership campaign but had only reluctantly agreed to run the election campaign, was quoted as saying, "I can't believe that they had such an inadequate organization," and that he "could not put up with the inefficiency" in the Prime Minister's Office.[66]

Far from being the "tempest in a teapot" that the Liberals hoped it would be, these remarks were followed by a whole week of media headlines

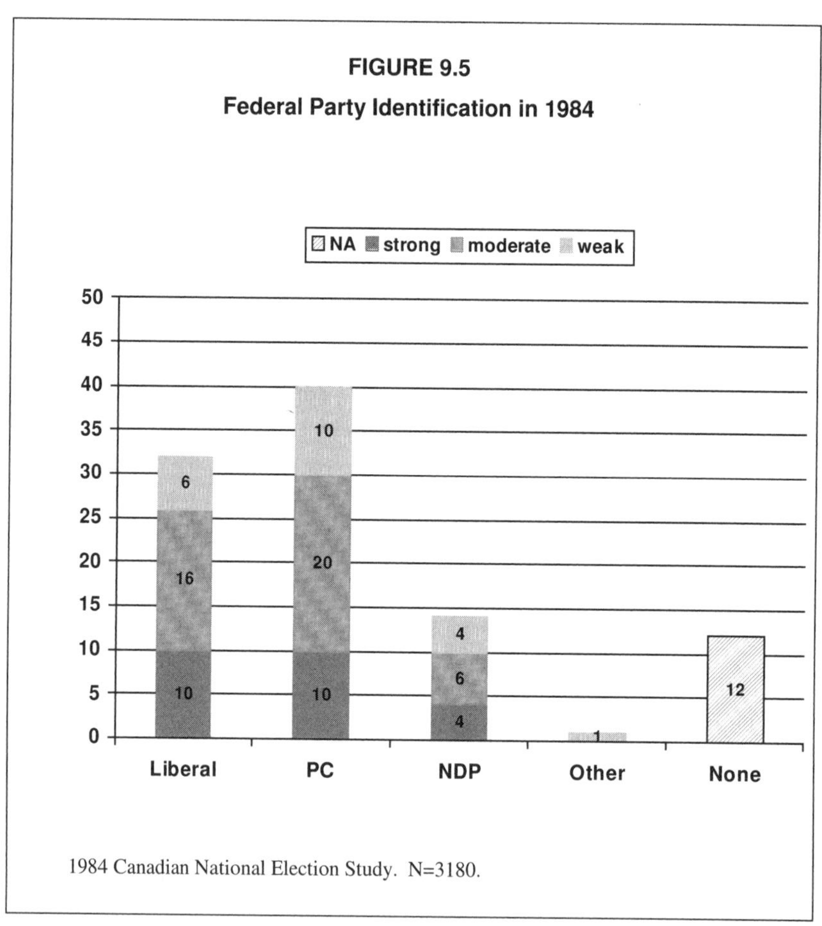

FIGURE 9.5
Federal Party Identification in 1984

1984 Canadian National Election Study. N=3180.

when Lee was replaced by Liberal "Rainmaker" Keith Davey in an effort to salvage the campaign. In order to claim that he was in charge, Turner asserted that he had fired Lee, while the latter insisted that he had resigned. These disputes were extremely damaging to the image of the Liberal leader and his campaign, already faltering and falling behind in the public opinion polls. According to McCall and Clarkson, "under John Turner, the Liberal Party fell apart. Without Pierre Trudeau, its centre could not hold."[67] The public post-mortems began before the election was even held, with damaging internal party documents leaked to the press.[68] On election eve, John Turner was quoted as exhorting his troops, "I urge you not to give up.... Fight right to the end."[69]

The 1984 election produced a massive electoral change. Much of the change appears to have occurred during the campaign itself, in response to the changing issue and leader dynamics.[70] It is also likely that the electorate was hungry for change. At the same time, Mulroney had taken many of the same positions as Trudeau had, on the constitution and on bilingualism. On the economic issues of the election, the Turner Liberals had little to offer, and a poor short-term legacy to refer to. The vote-switching displayed in Figure 9.4 was not only extremely high, but it was almost unidirectional. Almost as high a proportion of the electorate switched from a 1980 Liberal vote to a 1984 PC vote as stayed with the Liberals in the two elections. And very few people went in the other direction.

In the 1984 election, more government members were elected than for any other in Canadian history, even more than for John Diefenbaker when his Tories swept the country in 1958. With 50 percent of the total vote, Mulroney got almost as high a percentage as Diefenbaker and John A. Macdonald. Too many members to keep happy, as Mulroney himself recognized, but a real national Conservative government, with substantial membership from all provinces. Quebec had suddenly given Mulroney 50 percent of its vote, and 58 of its 75 seats, beyond anyone's wildest dreams. For the Liberals, on the other hand, the election was a total disaster, unmitigated by Turner's own personal victory in Vancouver, since that meant he would continue to lead the party for six more years. It would take another election defeat before Jean Chrétien gave the party the chance to win back power.

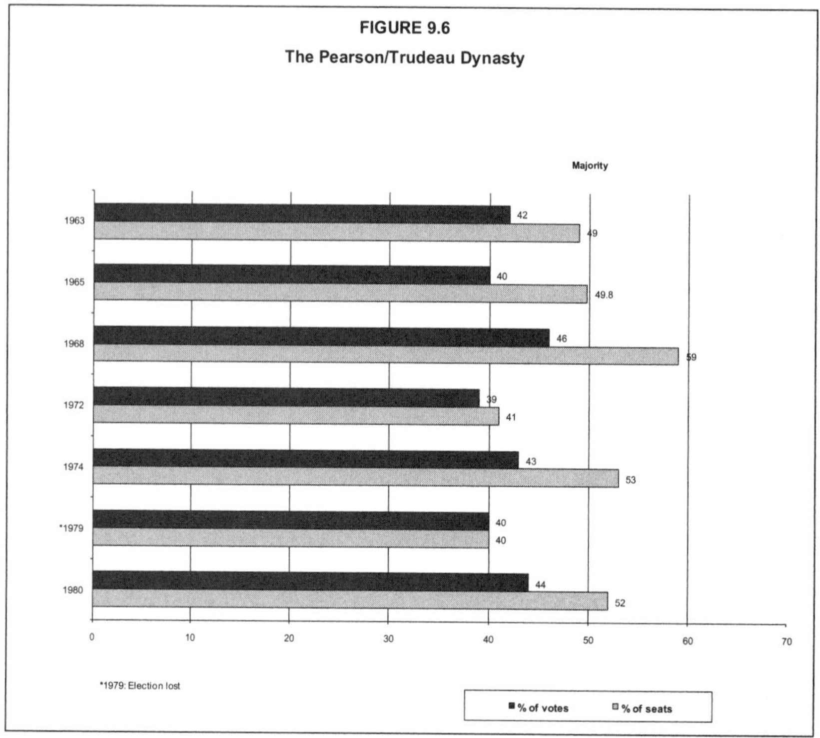

FIGURE 9.6
The Pearson/Trudeau Dynasty

The Trudeau Dynasty

Pierre Trudeau was in power for more than 15 years, with only a nine-month interlude following the 1979 election. While he was in charge of the Canadian government, five American presidents occupied the Oval Office in Washington. The Thatcher Era in Great Britain came and went. Three very different men served as secretary general of the United Nations, and 30 new countries were admitted to membership in the world organization. Only King and Macdonald served as prime minister longer than Trudeau.

Longevity in office is of course only one qualification for the existence of a dynasty. But Pierre Trudeau established his mastery of the Canadian political agenda by virtue of his intellect and his personal appeal. Although he was a conflictual figure, he was able to position his government on the side of national unity by leading the forces that defeated the Quebec Referendum of 1980, by enhancing bilingualism, and most of all by personifying French power in Ottawa. That he alienated the West (and parts of Quebec, as well, in the process) was also part of his legacy. His chosen method to promote Canadian nationhood was constitutional reform, an agenda he was only able to successfully pursue after he unexpectedly returned to power in 1980. Trudeau's Charter of Rights and Freedoms is likely to be cited as his single most significant achievement in terms of lasting impact on Canadian government. However, he also defined what it meant to be a Liberal — someone who aims to build a "Just Society."

Trudeau was less successful in achieving mastery over the economic policy agenda. The decade of the 1970s was beset with economic problems, inflation, unemployment, low growth, high interest rates, a currency of declining value, and scarcity of energy supply. Through it all, Trudeau managed to persuade Canadians that the problems were not of his government's making. Rather, they were part of a worldwide phenomenon. His solutions were not part of a grand economic plan. They were short-term policies like wage and price controls, and subsequent voluntary guidelines. The main stroke of economic policymaking after the return of the Trudeau regime was the creation of the National Energy Program, which led to further economic difficulties. However, Trudeau gave the impression of action rather than inaction in the economic realm, and he was aided in the period by the similar lack of comprehensive economic policy agendas put forward by the other parties. Relatively speaking, Trudeau engendered public confidence. The circumstances of his initial election as leader in 1968, the outpouring of public affection, seemed to remain in the background even when disillusionment later set in.

And what of a Mulroney dynasty, which might have followed Trudeau? All of the potential building blocks were there in 1984. The Conservatives had captured the public's imagination, and had mastered all three of the important policy/issue areas needed for success — economic issues, national unity, and the social agenda. But could that success be established for the long term? The nature of the Mulroney victory in 1984 engendered some doubts. His image, though extremely positive during the campaign, still had not completely overcome a public feeling that he was a master of blarney, not substance, that he would say anything to get elected, or that he would propose to do things differently and then do them the same old way.

The issue advantage enjoyed by the Conservatives was not based so much on substantial proposals about what the party would do in power, but on dislike of the alternative — an unwillingness to once again entrust the government to a Liberal Party which seemed so disorganized that it did not even know how to conduct an election campaign. In the post-election 1984 National Election Study, only 40 percent of Canadians declared that they thought of themselves as Progressive Conservatives, 10 percent fewer than had voted for the party (see Figure 9.4). In addition, only 10 percent of Canadians felt "very strongly" attached to the Conservative Party. Despite this, however, Mulroney and the Conservatives in late 1984 were firmly in control, facing a disorganized and dispirited opposition. Their own actions in the next four years would go a long way to determining the fate of the Progressive Conservative Party of Canada.

Notes

1. G. Bruce Doern and Glen Toner, *The Politics of Energy: The Development and Implementation of the NEP* (Toronto: Methuen, 1985), 2.
2. Christina McCall and Stephen Clarkson, *Trudeau and Our Times, Vol. 2: The Heroic Delusion* (Toronto: McClelland & Stewart, 1994), 110.
3. *Ibid.*, Chapter 5.
4. Energy Mines and Resources Canada, *The National Energy Program 1980* (Ottawa: Supply and Services, 1980).
5. For a detailed description of the situation between 1980 and 1984, see John Meisel, "Introduction," in Howard Penniman, ed., *Canada at the Polls, 1984* (Washington, American Enterprise Institute, 1988), 1–36.
6. Jon H. Pammett, "Inflation, Unemployment and Integration," in Jon H. Pammett and Brian W. Tomlin, eds., *The Integration Question: Political Economy and Public Policy in Canada and North America* (Don Mills: Addison Wesley, 1984), 93–104.
7. The English version of the referendum question reads: "The government of Quebec has made public its proposal to negotiate a new agreement with the rest of Canada, based on the equality of nations; this agreement would enable Quebec to acquire the exclusive power to make its laws, levy its taxes and establish relations abroad — in other words, sovereignty — and at the same time to maintain with Canada an economic association including a common currency; any change in political status resulting from these negotiations will only be implemented with popular approval through another referendum; on these terms, do you give the government of Quebec the mandate to negotiate the proposed agreement between Quebec and Canada?"
8. Stephen Clarkson and Christina McCall, *Trudeau and Our Times, Vol. 1: The Magnificent Obsession* (Toronto: McClelland & Stewart, 1990), 277.

9. Peter Russell, *Constitutional Odyssey*, second edition (University of Toronto Press, 1993), 118–19.
10. The "notwithstanding clause" is discussed in several of the articles in Keith Banting and Richard Simeon, eds., *And No One Cheered: Federalism, Democracy and the Constititon Act* (Toronto: Methuen, 1983). See also Row Romanow, John White and Howard Leeson, *Canada ... Notwithstanding: The Making of the Constitution, 1976–1982* (Toronto: Carswell Methuen, 1984), David Milne *The Canadian Constitution* (Toronto: Lorimer, 1991), and Clarkson and McCall, Vol. 1., *op. cit.*
11. Alan Frizzell and Anthony Westell, *The Canadian General Election of 1984* (Ottawa: Carleton University Press, 1985), 1.
12. Rae Murphy, Robert Chodos, and Nick Auf der Maur, *Brian Mulroney: The Boy from Baie-Comeau* (Toronto: Lormier, 1984), 148.
13. *Ibid.*, 148–52. It didn't help Clark that Trudeau derided his position as being "a confederation of shopping centres."
14. John C. Courtney, *Do Conventions Matter? Choosing National Party Leaders in Canada* (Montreal, McGill-Queen's University Press, 1995), 42.
15. Patrick Martin, Allan Gregg, and George Perlin, *Contenders: The Tory Quest for Power* (Scarborough, Prentice-Hall, 1983), 28.
16. For a discussion of this budget as an election issue in 1980, see Harold D. Clarke, Jane Jenson, Lawrence LeDuc, and Jon H. Pammett, *Absent Mandate: Interpreting Change in Canadian Elections* (Toronto: Gage, 1991), 141.
17. Martin, et al, *Contenders*, 115.
18. Murphy, et al, *Brian Mulroney*, 1–3.
19. John Sawatsky, *Mulroney: The Politics of Ambition* (Toronto: Macfarlane Walter & Ross, 1991), 111–12. Other details in this paragraph are contained in this book, Chapters 4–7.
20. In addition to the biographies of Mulroney by Sawatsky and Murphy et al already referenced, see L. Ian MacDonald, *Mulroney: The Making of the Prime Minister* (Toronto: McClelland & Stewart, 1984), and Michael Bliss, *Right Honourable Men* (Toronto: Harpercollins, 1994), Chapter 10.
21. Martin, et al, *Contenders*, 205.
22. Jean Chrétien, *Straight from the Heart* (Toronto: Key Porter, 1985), 77–78.
23. Pierre Trudeau, *Memoirs* (Toronto: McClelland & Stewart, 1993), 193.
24. Jack Cahill, *John Turner: The Long Run* (Toronto: McClelland & Stewart, 1984), 80.
25. Christina McCall and Stephen Clarkson, *Trudeau and Our Times, Volume 2: The Heroic Delusion* (Toronto: McClelland & Stewart, 1994), 125. See also Cahill, 180.
26. Christina McCall-Newman, *Grits: An Intimate Portrait of the Liberal Party* (Toronto: Macmillan, 1982), 229.
27. Keith Davey, *The Rainmaker: A Passion for Politics* (Toronto: Stoddart, 1986), 200.
28. Trudeau, *Memoirs*, 194.

29. Ron Graham, *One-Eyed Kings: Promise and Illusion in Canadian Politics* (Toronto: Collins, 1986), 213.
30. Chrétien, *Straight from the Heart*, 197.
31. Graham, *One-Eyed Kings*, 245.
32. Greg Weston, *Reign of Error: The Inside Story of John Turner's Troubled Leadership* (Toronto: McGraw-Hill Ryerson, 1988), 63–65.
33. Stephen Clarkson, "The Dauphin and the Doomed: John Turner and the Liberal Party's Debacle," in Howard Penniman, ed., *Canada at the Polls, 1984* (Washington: American Enterprise Institute, 1988), 105.
34. In 1968 Pierre Trudeau and Robert Stanfield were fighting their first election. The other two instances were Louis St. Laurent and George Drew in 1949 and Mackenzie King and Arthur Meighen in 1921.
35. Macdonald, *Mulroney*, 299.
36. *Ibid.*, 298.
37. Mulroney, quoted in Peter C. Newman, *The Secret Mulroney Tapes* (Toronto: Random House, 2005), 395.
38. Thomas Walkom, "Sweet Dreams: Polls, Jobs Boost PM's Fortunes," *Globe and Mail*, July 7, 1984: A1.
39. *Toronto Star*, August 6, 1984: 1, 6, and August 16, 1984: 1, 4.
40. *Globe and Mail*, July 21, 1984: 1.
41. Mulroney quoted in Newman, *op. cit.*, 81.
42. Jeffrey Simpson, *Faultlines: Struggling for a Canadian Vision* (Toronto: HarperCollins, 1993), 271.
43. Graham, *One-Eyed Kings*, op. cit., 304.
44. Harold D. Clarke, Jane Jenson, Lawrence LeDuc, and Jon H. Pammett, *Political Choice in Canada* (Toronto: McGraw-Hill Ryerson, 1979), 226.
45. Harold D. Clarke, Jane Jenson, Lawrence LeDuc, and Jon H. Pammett, *Absent Mandate: Interpreting Change in Canadian Politics* (Toronto: Gage, 1991), 99.
46. Nick Hills, "The NDP Survivors," in Alan Frizzell and Anthony Westell, *The Canadian General Election of 1984* (Ottawa: Carleton University Press, 1985), 38–53.
47. Terence Morley, "Anniliation Avoided: The New Democratic Party in the 1984 Election Campaign," in Penniman, ed., *Canada at the Polls, 1984*, 121.
48. William Christian and Colin Campbell, *Parties, Leaders and Ideologies in Canada* (Toronto: McGraw-Hill Ryerson, 1996), 141.
49. For descriptions of this incident, see Weston, *Reign of Error*, op. cit., 47, and Simpson, "The Vincible Liberals," 19–20.
50. Chrétien, *Straight from the Heart*, 202.
51. Macdonald, *Mulroney*, op. cit., 279.
52. *Ibid.* The most famous use of that expression was when Mulroney described the construction of the Charlottetown Constitutional Accord. See Chapter 11.
53. Graham Fraser, "Mulroney Willing to Reopen Constitution Talks with PQ," *Globe and Mail*, August 7, 1984: 5.

54. Robert McKenzie, "Mulroney Vows Greater Voice for 10 Premiers," *Toronto Star*, August 7, 1984: A1, 4.
55. Joe O'Donnell, "Time to Heal Damage Done by Separatism, Mulroney Says," *Toronto Star*, August 9, 1984: A1.
56. Lawrence Martin, "Mulroney Says Liberals Have Quebec Bias," *Globe and Mail*, August 20, 1984: A1.
57. "Mulroney Pledges Revival for West," *Globe and Mail*, July 5, 1984: A8.
58. Hugh Winsor, "Turner Unveils Plan to Aid Jobless Youth," *Globe and Mail*, August 3, 1984: A1.
59. Thomas Walkom, "Would Cut Bank Rate, Broadbent Says," *Globe and Mail*, August 10, 1984: A3.
60. Erik Neilsen, *The House Is Not a Home* (Toronto: Macmillan, 1989), 219. An Appendix to this book gives Nielsen's candid, and sometimes damning, opinions of his colleagues, many of whom went on to feature in the Mulroney cabinets.
61. Clarke, Jenson, LeDuc, and Pammett, *Absent Mandate*, second edition, 145.
62. Of these, 13.4 percent being Liberal to Conservative switches. 1984 National Election Study.
63. *Globe and Mail*, August 18, 1984: A2.
64. Robert Sheppard and James Rusk, "PCs, Liberals Plan Reforms in Social Aid," *Globe and Mail*, August 11, 1984: A1, 2.
65. *Ibid.*
66. Paula Todd, "'Inefficiency' Led to Resignation Turner's Campaign Chief Says," *Toronto Star*, August 6, 1984: A1, 4.
67. McCall and Clarkson, *Trudeau and Our Times*, 415.
68. Hugh Winsor, "Decline Began Before Campaign, Liberal Party Documents Disclose," *Globe and Mail*, August 31, 1984: A1.
69. Bob Hepburn, "Turner Implores Liberals to 'Fight Right to the End,'" *Toronto Star*, September 2, 1984: A14.
70. Barry J. Kay, Steven D. Brown, James E. Curtis, Ronald D. Lambert, and John M. Wilson, "The Character of Electoral Change: A Preliminary Report from the 1984 National Election Study," in Joseph Wearing, ed., *The Ballot and its Message: Voting in Canada* (Toronto: Copp Clark Pitman, 1991), 285.

Suggested Reading

Cahill, Jack. *John Turner: The Long Run* (Toronto: McClelland & Stewart, 1984).

Clarke, Harold D., Jane Jenson, Lawrence LeDuc, and Jon H. Pammett. *Absent Mandate: Interpreting Change in Canadian Politics* (Toronto: Gage, 1991).

Frizzell, Alan, and Anthony Westell. *The Canadian General Election of 1984* (Ottawa: Carleton University Press, 1985).

Kay, Barry J., Steven D. Brown, James E. Curtis, Ronald D. Lambert, and John M. Wilson, "The Character of Electoral Change: A Preliminary Report from the 1984 Election Study," in Joseph Wearing, ed, *The Ballot and Its Message: Voting in Canada* (Toronto: Copp Clark Pitman, 1991).

MacDonald, L. Ian. *Mulroney: The Making of the Prime Minister* (Toronto: McClelland & Stewart, 1984).

Martin, Patrick, Allan Gregg, and George Perlin. *Contenders: The Tory Quest for Power* (Scarborough, ON: Prentice-Hall, 1983).

Murphy, Rae, Robert Chodos, and Nick Auf der Maur. *Brian Mulroney, The Boy from Baie Comeau* (Toronto: Lorimer, 1984).

Penniman, Howard, ed., *Canada at the Polls, 1984* (Washington: American Enterprise Institute, 1988).

Sawatsky, John. *Mulroney, the Politics of Ambition* (Toronto: Macfarlane Walter & Ross, 1991).

Weston, Gregg. *Reign of Error: The Inside Story of John Turner's Troubled Leadership* (Toronto: McGraw-Hill Ryerson, 1988).

CHAPTER 10

THE FREE TRADE ELECTION OF 1988

The election that took place on November 21, 1988, was one of the most important and dramatic political events in modern Canadian history. Like the "reciprocity" election of 1911 (see Chapter 2), the 1988 contest involved the fundamental issue of Canada's economic relationship with the United States. Its centrepiece was the controversial Canada–U.S. Free Trade Agreement (hereafter FTA), which had been signed in Washington in October 1987 and debated in Parliament in the months preceding the call of the election. Although the large Conservative majority in the House of Commons assured passage of the FTA, it quickly became clear that the agreement would face a more difficult hurdle in the Senate, which still contained a majority of Liberal appointees. When Liberal leader John Turner, who had staunchly opposed what he repeatedly referred to as the "Mulroney Trade Deal," asked Liberal Senators to delay voting on the FTA until after the election had taken place, the stage was set for a campaign in which this single issue would play a dominant role. In a press conference following the announcement of his strategy, Turner invoked a populist theme — "Let the people decide." The implication was that the election to follow would be a kind of referendum on the FTA.[1]

An election, however, is not a referendum.[2] Had it been so, it is probable that the FTA would have been defeated, a point that will become clearer as we examine both the levels of public support for the agreement and the patterns of voting behaviour in the election. Polls in the months prior to the election consistently found a plurality of Canadians opposed to the agreement, albeit with large and growing numbers of "undecided" respondents (see Figure 10.5). While the Conservatives ultimately won a second majority government, they did so with a mere 43 percent of the total vote. More Canadians voted for the two parties that opposed the FTA — the Liberals and NDP — than for the Tories. Many interpretations of the 1988 election stress the idea that it provided a venue for the resolution of an important and divisive issue of public policy, but the evidence suggests that it was much more complex than that.[3] The reality was that this election, like most of the others discussed in this book, was a struggle for political power that involved multiple issues, partisan strategies, images and perceptions of party leaders, and several significant campaign events, including the dramatic televised debates between the leaders that took place midway through the campaign. The 1988 election differed from some others only in the singularity of focus on the FTA found in the

Library and Archives Canada. Peter Bregg, photographer.

President Reagan and Prime Minister Mulroney, Quebec City, 1985.

media and in much of the campaign rhetoric. Given the volatility of the Canadian electorate throughout much of this period, its outcome was never a certainty, no matter what the public may have felt about the controversies surrounding Mulroney's historic trade agreement with the United States.

The first two years of the Mulroney government proved particularly difficult. Despite using charges of patronage as an effective weapon against Turner in the 1984 election, accusations of patronage and scandal dogged the Mulroney government in much the same way. As it transpired, Mulroney was even *more* vulnerable on these issues because of his high-profile criticism of Turner's handling of the patronage issue when he had succeeded Trudeau as prime minister in 1984. The clash between Mulroney's public, often sanctimonious, posturing on the patronage issue and his well-known private disregard for such positions grated on the public consciousness, as he made many aggressively partisan appointments almost from the very inception of his tenure.[4] A number of scandals involving individual cabinet ministers added to the government's growing reputation for loose ethics.[5] Some of Mulroney's cabinet difficulties were no doubt the result of inexperience among his ministers, since there were few with previous experience in government (including Mulroney himself).

But the steady drumbeat of scandals and ministerial resignations gradually took its toll. The low point for the government in this area came in May 1986, when Michel Gravel, a Quebec Tory MP, was charged with 10 counts of bribery, 32 counts of defrauding the government, and 8 counts of breach of trust. The ensuing scandal spread widely through the Mulroney administration, exposing a pattern of corruption in Quebec land deals, and claiming two more cabinet ministers among its victims.[6] The Tories' decline in the polls was dramatic (see Figure 10.2). From its high point following the 1984 election, the governing party dropped to a position barely even with the Liberals within little more than a year. By early 1987, it stood at a low point of 22 percent, well behind both the Liberals and NDP. At that point, the government's prospects for re-election looked bleak. Many backbench Tory MPs feared that Mulroney was leading the party to the brink of electoral disaster, but Mulroney was not about to give up without a fight.

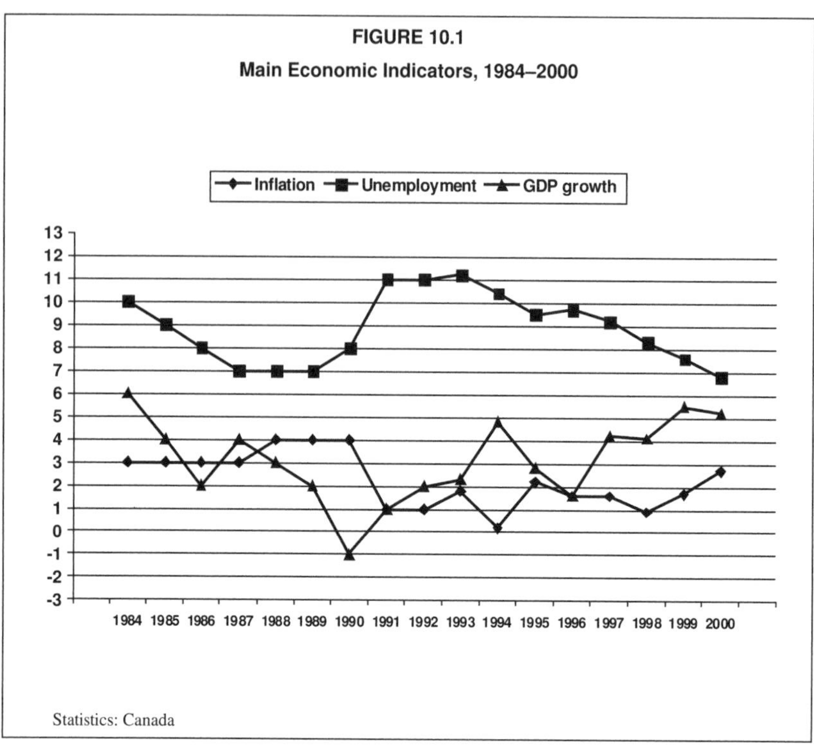

FIGURE 10.1
Main Economic Indicators, 1984–2000

Statistics: Canada

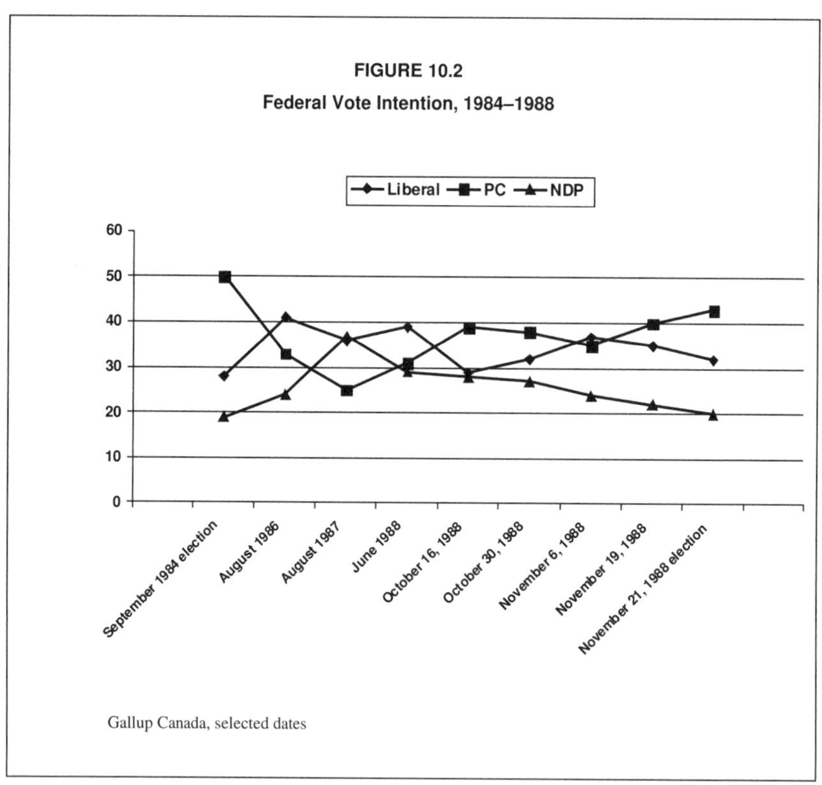

FIGURE 10.2
Federal Vote Intention, 1984–1988

Gallup Canada, selected dates

"Managing Change"

The Conservatives organized their 1988 campaign for re-election around the theme of "Managing Change." While somewhat vacuous as a campaign slogan, this theme had several advantages for a party in power. First, it drew attention to the government's accomplishments, particularly in the economic sphere. Mulroney had the good fortune to preside over a strengthening economy during virtually all of his first term in office, and the Conservatives did not hesitate to take credit for the improved economic climate. They had come to office just as the economy was beginning to emerge from the deep recession of the early 1980s, and had campaigned in 1984 on the theme of "jobs, jobs, jobs" (see Chapter 9). Unemployment and inflation, the twin curses of the Canadian economy during most of the previous decade, had both peaked just prior to the Conservatives' coming to power (see Figure 10.1). Afterward, inflation had fallen dramatically with the onset of the recession and the draconian application of tight monetary policy by the Bank of Canada. Spurred in part by a booming American economy in the mid 1980s, unemployment came down steadily during each year that the Tories had been in office. Calling attention to these accomplishments was certainly as important to the Conservative campaign as justifying the FTA. However the "change" theme, being general in nature, did not exclude the FTA either. Within this context, Mulroney could point to past economic achievements and imply that even better times lay ahead.

Neither was the "managing change" theme confined only to economic issues such as inflation, unemployment, or trade. It also had the advantage of incorporating the "national unity" portfolio, which had likewise seemed to improve substantially during Mulroney's tenure in office. Trudeau's confrontational relations with the western provinces over the National Energy Program, and his relentless battles with the PQ government in Quebec, had left federal–provincial relations in a dismal state by the end of his fourth and final term in office. Shortly after coming to power, Mulroney convened a First Ministers' Conference, which he heralded as the beginning of a new era in federal–provincial relations.

The controversial National Energy Program was quickly scrapped. Relations between the federal government and the provincial governments in the West were generally good, and westerners held important portfolios in Mulroney's government.[7] Then, in December

1985, Robert Bourassa led the Liberal Party back to power in Quebec. Thus, barely more than a year after the Mulroney Conservatives had come to office in Ottawa, the entire landscape of federal–provincial politics seemed to have changed. In April 1987, Mulroney and the 10 provincial premiers negotiated the Meech Lake Accord, which held out the promise of ending Quebec's constitutional isolation and constructing a new framework for federal–provincial co-operation.

The Meech Lake Accord, named for the government conference centre where the negotiations took place, represented the accommodations necessary to meet five conditions that Quebec had set out in order to secure its accession to the 1982 Constitution. These conditions, which had been a part of Bourassa's 1985 election platform, were (1) recognition of Quebec as a "distinct society," (2) a role in setting immigration policy, (3) a voice in the appointment of the three Quebec judges on the Supreme Court, (4) the right to opt out of federal spending programs in areas of provincial jurisdiction without financial penalty, and (5) the restoration of a Quebec veto on constitutional amendments.[8]

Through several rounds of quiet federal–provincial diplomacy leading up to the Meech Lake sessions, these five principles had been gradually crafted into general statements capable of securing support from all 10 provinces. Bourassa, who in his first term as Quebec premier (1970–76) had been involved in earlier constitutional negotiations, understood this process well. But reconciling a set of conditions to satisfy Quebec with the political and constitutional interests of 10 other governments had not been easy to accomplish. Despite the controversies that would later surround it, Mulroney could point to the signing of such an agreement as a further positive accomplishment of his first four years in office. The fact that Meech Lake would ultimately fail to secure ratification within the three-year timetable set for it to come into effect lay well in the future (see Chapter 11).

The focus of attention on the issues of free trade and the Meech Lake Accord was not unwelcome from the point of view of the Conservatives. While it posed some risks for the government, it also held advantages, the most obvious of which was the diversion of attention away from issues of patronage, scandal, and corruption. But there were other advantages as well.

Free trade had always been a difficult issue for the Liberals, since historically that party had generally supported the principle of freer

North American trade. A free trade agreement with the United States had, in fact, been proposed by the Macdonald Commission, which was chaired by Pierre Trudeau's former minister of finance.[9] But the Liberal Party also contained economic nationalists, who believed that closer economic ties with the United States posed serious dangers to Canada's political sovereignty.[10] In his pronouncements, Turner often seemed to straddle these two wings of the party, at times uncomfortably. A "business Liberal" who, like many others in his party, supported free trade with the United States "in principle," Turner had to develop a more specific argument against the FTA that was credible, both to members of his own party and to the electorate at large. Further, the FTA was also opposed by the NDP, thus allowing the Conservatives to exploit divisions among their opponents. So long as the NDP commanded a share of the vote nearly equivalent to that of the other parties, a second Conservative majority could conceivably be won with a much smaller percentage of the vote than the party had obtained in 1984. Under these assumptions, the prospects for a second Mulroney government, and perhaps a Mulroney dynasty, seemed somewhat brighter.

Formal negotiations with Washington began in early 1986 and continued in fits and starts until an agreement was finally struck in October 1987. The negotiations were never easy and had, in fact, been broken off by Mulroney's chief negotiator, Simon Reisman, only a month before an agreement was finally reached. In December 1987, the final text of the FTA was tabled in the House of Commons. It was a thick and complex document, with its provisions open to various interpretations. The timing of this shift of attention to the FTA that began with the commencement of debate in Parliament was not entirely accidental. Mulroney's political aides had always assumed that the election would take place sometime in the fall of 1988, exactly four years after the Tories' 1984 landslide. Thus, as 1988 dawned, the move to an election footing was all but preordained. The two major projects of the Mulroney regime — the FTA and the Meech Lake Accord — were now completed. A series of high-profile international events was planned or already in place, ranging from the Calgary Winter Olympics to a G-7 economic summit, scheduled to be held in Toronto in June. Despite the poor poll numbers, the prime minister remained convinced that his prospects for re-election were good. His government would run on its two cornerstones of policy achievement — the FTA and Meech Lake — together with a climate of continued economic growth and prosperity.[11] Against the backdrop of a successful Calgary Olympics and a celebratory Toronto summit, his upbeat outlook almost seemed justified. Also fuelling his optimism were John Turner's well-known vulnerabilities. An election, as Mulroney well knew, was a contest not only of parties and issues, but also of leaders.

The 1988 Campaign

While the polls showed the risks, patterns of partisanship were not unfavourable to the Conservatives in 1988, although it was by then a well-established fact of Canadian politics that elections cannot be won on the basis of partisan appeals alone. While more Canadians at that time identified with the Progressive Conservative Party than with the

FIGURE 10.3
Federal Party Identification in 1988

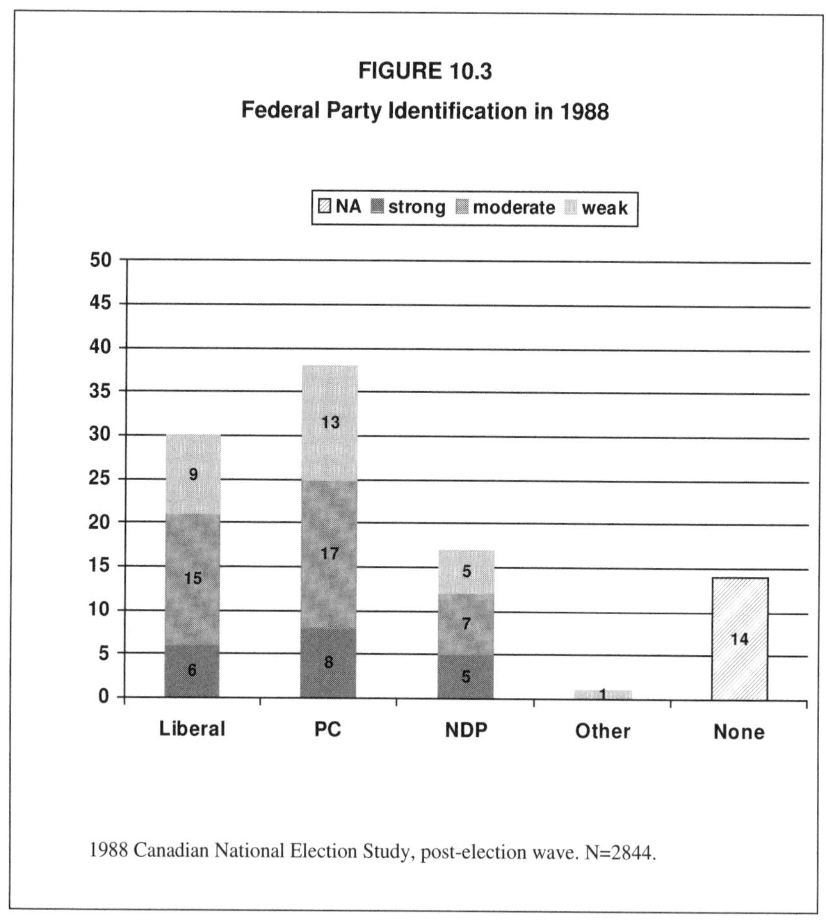

1988 Canadian National Election Study, post-election wave. N=2844.

Liberals, only 13 percent of the total electorate in 1988 could be classified as "very strong" Conservatives (see Figure 10.3). Almost as many voters still identified with the Liberals, but identification with both of the major parties continued to be generally weak. Panel studies had also tracked a considerable degree of movement in the partisan attachments of many Canadian voters from one election to another.[12] Voters whose allegiance Mulroney had won in 1984 could not necessarily be counted upon to support him a second time, but at least most of them were not committed elsewhere.

Leadership was potentially an area of greater strength for the Conservatives in 1988, even though Mulroney's image had declined sharply from the heady days of 1984. After four years as prime minister, the number of Canadians who had begun to see Brian Mulroney as a man who could not be trusted had gone up sharply.[13] But other negative elements in his personal image as a party leader were more muted. He was still slightly more popular than his party, and far ahead of John Turner (see Figure 10.4).

FIGURE 10.4

Party and Leader Thermometer Scale Ratings, 1988

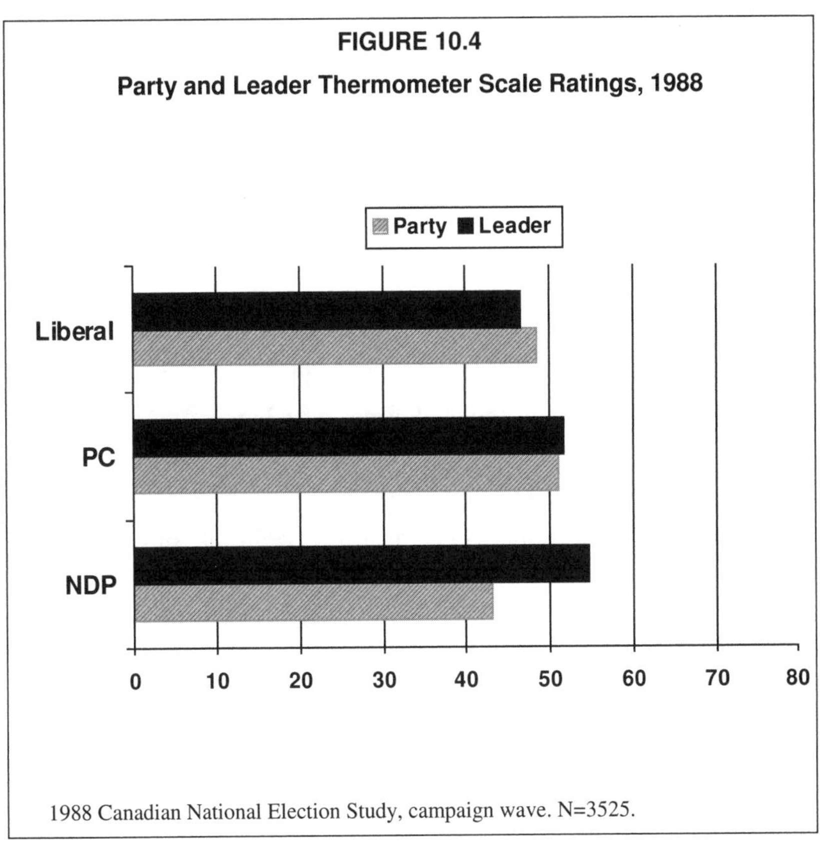

1988 Canadian National Election Study, campaign wave. N=3525.

Aware of the role that the debates had played in the 1984 election, Mulroney remained confident that he could beat Turner, both in the debates that would take place during the campaign and in the election itself. The years following his massive defeat in 1984 had not been kind to Turner. Once the "golden boy" of Canadian politics, his thermometer scale rating of personal popularity had by 1988 fallen to an extremely low level. Although Turner survived a leadership review vote in November 1986, doubts about his leadership abilities were widespread throughout the Liberal Party. He seemed increasingly to project the image of a political figure whose time had passed, and the party had grown restless under his uncertain stewardship.[14] But, as attention shifted toward the free trade issue, Turner seemed to become invigorated. He became convinced almost as soon as the text of the FTA was published that Mulroney's negotiators had given away too much and gotten too little in return. When he asked the Liberal majority in the Senate to "let the people decide" in July 1988, it was Turner, and not the prime minister, who seemed to be setting the agenda for the election that would shortly follow.

But the man that Mulroney had more reason to fear than John Turner was Ed Broadbent. Fighting his fourth election as NDP leader, Broadbent had the reputation for honesty and sincerity that Mulroney lacked.[15] Broadbent's reputation as an intelligent and principled political leader had remained intact throughout his tenure, and he was generally rated above both his own party and the other leaders in the polls (see Figure 10.4). The public genuinely liked him, and any doubts that they had were more about his party than about the man himself. There had been a brief period in the summer of 1987 when the NDP surged ahead of the other two parties in the Gallup poll (see Figure 10.2). In a hard-fought campaign against Mulroney and Turner, Broadbent would almost certainly be a force to be reckoned with.

By the time the election call came at the beginning of October, the Conservatives at last appeared to be well positioned. The first Gallup poll published following the election call gave them a 10-point lead over the Liberals. But the polls at this time were difficult to interpret. The Tory revival had been so rapid that one could see either a strong resurgence that would carry them through to victory or an unusually high level of volatility that could render any forecasts uncertain. The potential impact of the free trade issue was also difficult to gauge. Indeed, all three parties were, each for its own reasons, wary of making the FTA the centrepiece of their electoral strategy going into the election.

Mulroney himself knew that the agreement would generate controversy, and that his own image as prime minister and the record of his government would also inevitably be a part of any campaign. Turner, whose image as a party leader had declined sharply after his disastrous losing campaign in 1984, also had a serious problem of credibility with a large part of the electorate.[16] His vow to "tear up" the agreement if the Liberals returned to power appeared rash, and further exacerbated the divisions that already existed within his own party over the free trade issue. Ed Broadbent, whose image in opposition had held up much better than Turner's over the preceding four years, realized that sharing opposition to the FTA with the Liberals placed the NDP in a poor strategic position and ran the risk of marginalizing his party in a campaign focused solely around this one issue. Further, the agreement was more popular in the West, where the NDP had hopes of making electoral gains. Thus, at the beginning of the campaign, all three party leaders, each for his own strategic reasons, sought to emphasize other issues and themes.

The Liberals opened the campaign by announcing a 40-point program, designed in part to take the emphasis off the free trade issue and to make them appear as a party well prepared to return to government. But it did little to quiet continued rumblings, especially when Turner seemed unable to explain some of the details of his own policies. The Liberal campaign had gotten off to a highly uncertain start, while the smoothly running Conservative machine appeared to be coasting to victory. A widely cited Environics poll, published at the end of the second week of the campaign, had the Liberals placing third with only 25 percent of the vote, and the Tories leading the NDP 42 percent to 29 percent. Graham Fraser described the state of mind of Liberal Party strategists two weeks into the campaign as "frenzied panic."[17] Now well behind in the polls and dragging a seemingly unshakeable reputation for inept leadership, there were few who believed that Turner could revive sagging Liberal hopes. There were even rumours in some circles that Turner might be dumped as leader in mid-campaign. Jean Chrétien, who had left politics in mid-1986 to enter private law practice in Montreal, was seen by some as a credible replacement for Turner — someone who might at least avert the electoral disaster that appeared to be looming. Heading into the leaders' debates, scheduled to take place in the last week of October, there was little reason to expect a Liberal turnaround.

The Debates

The first of the two debates between the three party leaders that took place midway through the campaign was in French. Given his poor performance in the 1984 debates, and the generally negative state of his public image, expectations for Turner were low. But low expectations can sometimes serve a candidate well in televised debates.[18] More comfortable in French against the fluently bilingual Mulroney than he had been in 1984, and displaying a strong command of the issues, Turner gave a solid performance in this first of the two direct televised encounters between the leaders. Surprisingly, most Quebec news media declared Turner the winner of the French debate, in part because he more than exceeded the low expectations that had been set by his 1984 debate performance.[19] The stage was thus set for the English debate on the following night, which was to have a dramatic effect on the evolution of the campaign.[20]

Turner's overall performance in the English debate was equally strong, but the encounter was remembered especially for the dramatic moment in the middle of the debate when Turner, facing Mulroney directly, gave his assessment of the FTA. With Mulroney continually interrupting, Turner laid out his indictment in passionate and highly personal terms:

Canadian Press. Fred Chartrand, photographer.

John Turner and Brian Mulroney, 1988 televised leaders' debate.

> **JT:** "I happen to believe that you've sold us out …"
> **BM:** "You don't have a monopoly on patriotism …"
> **JT:** "Once a country yields its investment, once a country yields its energy …"
> **BM:** "Wrong again …"
> **JT:** "With one stroke of a pen … you have thrown us into the North–South influence of the United States, and will reduce us, I am sure, to a colony of the United States because, when the economic levers go, political independence is sure to follow."
> **BM:** "Mr. Turner, it is a document that is cancellable on six months notice."
> **JT:** "Cancellable? You're talking about our relationship with the United States."
> **BM:** "Mr. Turner, be serious …"
> **JT:** "Well, I am serious. I have never been more serious in my life."

The atmosphere in the days immediately following the debate was electric. Turner was widely proclaimed the winner of the two debates in the media, an outcome readily confirmed by survey evidence.[21] Clips of the debates were widely used in Liberal campaign spots in the weeks following, and polls published in the two weeks following the debates showed substantial Liberal gains. Almost as much of a shock to the Conservatives as the debate itself was the Gallup poll published on November 7, which placed the Liberals in the lead at 43 percent, followed by the Conservatives at 31 percent, and the NDP at 22 percent. While this poll was later somewhat discounted, it fuelled new speculation in the media about the possibility of a Liberal majority government.[22] Suddenly, the outcome of the election, as well as the future of the FTA, was thrown into doubt.

The NDP campaign, which had loomed so large as a potential factor at the beginning of the contest, seemed to lapse into irrelevance after the debates. The two "heavyweights" — Turner and Mulroney — from that point onward, turned the remaining weeks of the election campaign largely into a two-person, one-issue affair.

Evidence from studies of campaign debates, both in Canada and the United States, suggests that their effects on public opinion, no matter how dramatic, often begin to dissipate fairly quickly after the event.[23] In part, this is why party strategists often press to schedule such events earlier in the campaign rather than in the final week, thereby minimizing the risks.

In addition to their effect on the polls, the 1988 debates also had an immediate impact on the focus of the Conservative campaign. Party strategists quickly abandoned their bland "managing change" theme in favour of hard-hitting negative advertising aimed directly at destroying John Turner's credibility. One well-known ad, showing a map with the border being removed, contained the voice-over "John Turner says there is something in the Free Trade Agreement that threatens Canada's sovereignty. That's a lie …"; then a firm hand drew the line back in. Another, carefully tested in focus groups before airing, showed men and women in simulated "on the street" interviews, saying things like "I think Turner is more interested in saving his job than he is in saving mine."[24] These new ads, explicitly crafted to exploit Turner's most obvious weaknesses, were highly effective. This "Bomb the Bridge" strategy, as it would come to be called, would set a new standard of negative campaigning in Canadian elections and, because of its apparent success, would also influence strategic choices in subsequent campaigns.[25]

At about the same time, the Conservatives' many corporate allies took advantage of the then lax regulations regarding third-party election advertising by pouring millions of dollars into a parallel campaign to defend free trade.[26] With three weeks remaining in the campaign, these twin onslaughts began to have their intended effect. Combined with the official Conservative advertising attacking Turner, the free trade advocacy ads saturated both television and newspapers in the final days of the campaign. A Gallup poll published on November 14 had the two parties dead even, as did polls done at around the same time for the CBC and CTV.[27] But subsequent polls published in the week before the election all had the Tories back above 40 percent, with a lead over the Liberals ranging between 5 (Gallup) and 11 (CTV) percentage points. There seemed little doubt that the late advertising blitz had done its work. Nevertheless, few were willing to venture firm predictions in an atmosphere that had proven so volatile.

Surveys of the electorate before and after the 1988 election broadly confirm that it had become essentially a one-issue affair. As Table 10.1 indicates, when asked to name the "most important issue," respondents overwhelmingly mentioned free trade, and many also indicated that the FTA was an "important" factor in their voting decision.[28] But this

TABLE 10.1

Most Important Issue in the 1988 Election

Percent (multiple response)	
Economic Issues	
Free trade	63
Taxes / The Budget / Deficits	4
Unemployment / Jobs	4
Other economic	2
National Unity	
Sovereignty / Meech Lake	2
Social Welfare	
Environment	6
Abortion	3
Seniors' issues	2
Day care	1
Social services	1
Health care	1
Other social	1
Other Issues	
Leadership	1
Corruption, scandals	1
Other issues	3
None, Don't Know	15

1988 Canadian National Election Study, campaign wave. N = 3,445.

does not necessarily mean that the free trade issue was the only element affecting the behaviour of voters in 1988. For many, the overall record of the party — particularly the governing party — or the perceived personal qualities of the leaders are equally or more important.[29] For those voters who supported the FTA *and* believed that Brian Mulroney was the best choice as prime minister, the voting decision was relatively easy. But for those who had doubts about free trade, or who preferred Turner or Broadbent, the choice was more complex. In the outcome of the 1988 election, the division of anti-FTA votes between the Liberals and NDP undoubtedly contributed more to the Tory victory than did any shift of opinion regarding the agreement itself.

In the end, enough Canadians (43 percent) voted Conservative to deliver a second Mulroney majority government, thus assuring ratification of the FTA.[30] But it would be wrong to conclude that, in doing so, the Canadian electorate necessarily endorsed the agreement. The same Gallup poll that forecast a second Conservative majority

FIGURE 10.5

Public Opinion on the Free Trade Agreement, October–November 1988

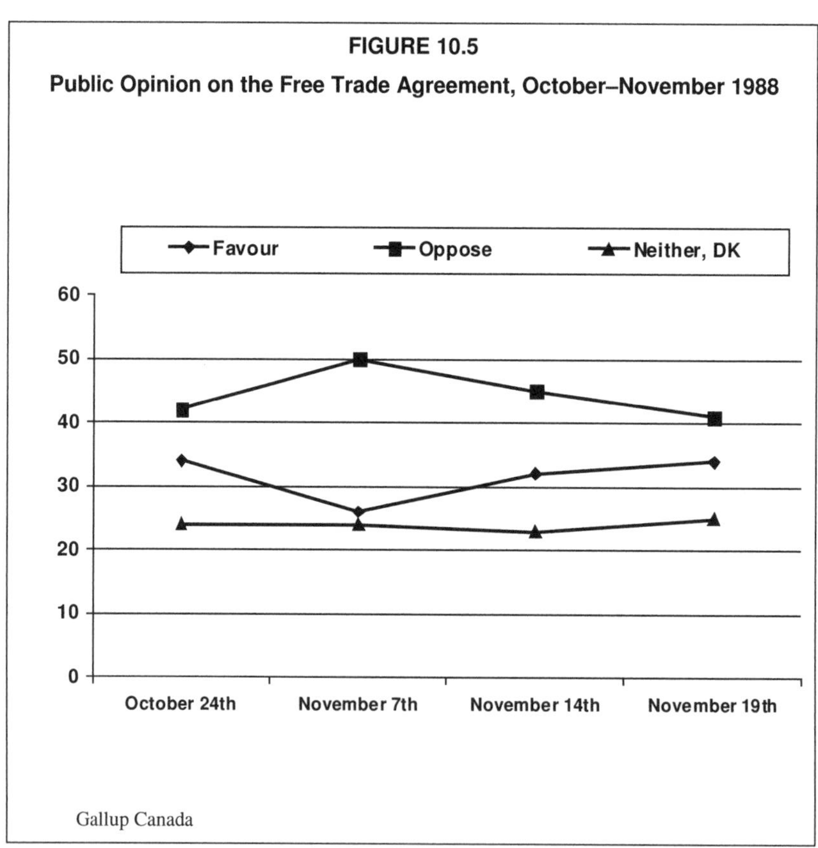

Gallup Canada

government in the final days of the campaign continued to find a plurality of Canadians opposed to the FTA, with large numbers remaining undecided about the merits of free trade (see Figure 10.5). The percentage of the electorate opposed to the FTA rose by 8 percent following the debate, according to the Gallup survey done at that time, and it came down only slowly afterward. An exit poll, conducted on the day of the election by the Carleton University Survey Centre, shows the complexity of the fit between attitudes toward the FTA and voting behaviour in the election (see Figure 10.6). Those who favoured the FTA were far more likely to vote Conservative, while those who opposed it divided their votes between the Liberals and NDP. Among those who remained undecided about the agreement, even as they were casting their vote, support tilted slightly in favour of the Tories. Opinion remained sharply divided regarding the merits of the agreement itself, and a substantial number of voters remained undecided about it even as they were casting their votes.

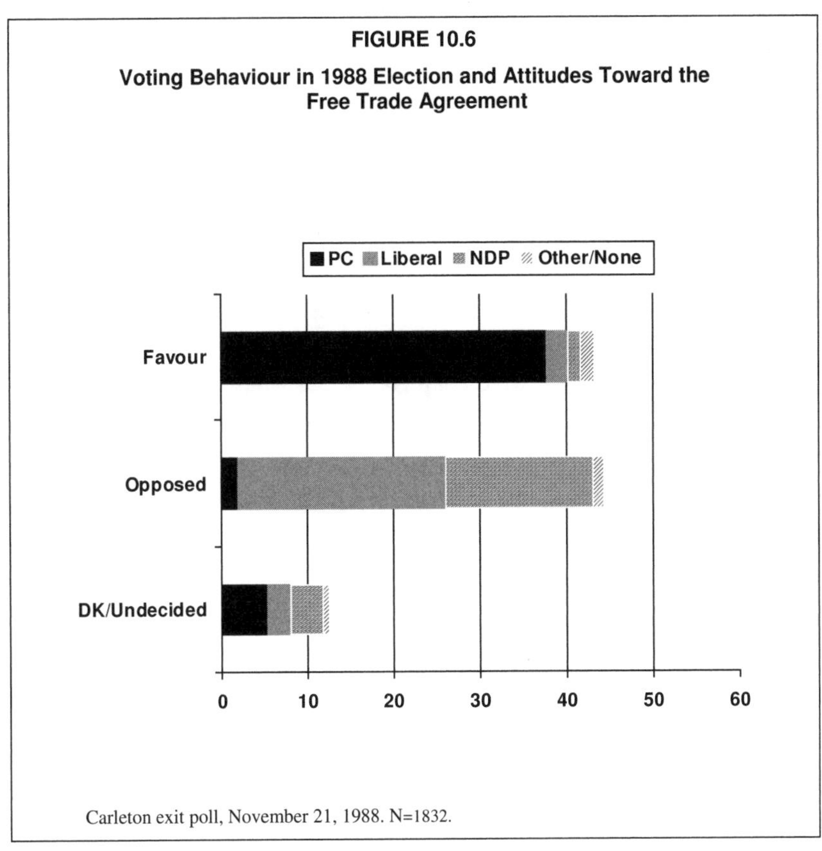

Interpreting the result of the 1988 election is therefore not without complications, in spite of the seemingly dominant role played by the FTA throughout the campaign. A government that has been re-elected will generally claim endorsement of its record in office. But this does not necessarily imply a mandate for all of its policies. And, of course, in re-electing Mulroney the voters were also rejecting Turner. In spite of his brief moment of triumph during the middle part of the campaign, Turner was one of the least successful Liberal leaders in Canadian history. Having waited so long to attain the party leadership, Turner led his party to two consecutive defeats. He would resign the leadership shortly after the election, to be replaced by the man that he had defeated in the 1984 leadership contest — Jean Chrétien. Although briefly out of political life during the Mulroney years, Chrétien would ultimately be well positioned to capitalize on the events of the second Mulroney government, and to lead the Liberals back to power in 1993 (see Chapter 11).

As is so often true in Canadian elections, the 1988 results also displayed a number of distinctive regional patterns. The Liberals, in fact, outpolled the Tories in all four Atlantic provinces, and fought them to a virtual tie in Ontario (see Table 10.2). Only in Quebec and Alberta did the Conservatives manage to register gains over their 1984 performance, although the large majority that they held going into the election meant that even their overall loss of 42 seats did not place them in any real danger. Looking at the 1988 results, there could have been good reason to believe that the establishment of a new dynasty might be in the making, despite the turbulence of the early Mulroney years. Unlike Diefenbaker before him, Mulroney had managed to attain a second Conservative majority government. With the Meech Lake Accord, he had restored (at least temporarily), a sense of national unity, and he continued to benefit from the solid performance of the economy. While his vow to protect social programs was not entirely believed by many observers, it indicated that Mulroney had at least a keen *political* understanding of this third key issue area.

In his first term in office and in his successful campaign for re-election, Mulroney had proven adept, although not always sure handed, at the practice of brokerage politics.[31] The tenuous alliance between western and Quebec interests that Mulroney cobbled together had held up well in the face of the unexpectedly strong challenges from both the Liberals and NDP. But the seeds of its dissolution were already being planted.

TABLE 10.2

Results of the 1988 Federal Election, by Province

		PC	Liberal	NDP	Other	PC Net Gain/ Loss from 1984
Newfoundland	votes (%)	42	45	12	1	
	seats (#)	2	5	0	0	-2
Prince Edward Island	votes (%)	41	50	7	1	
	seats (#)	0	4	0	0	-3
Nova Scotia	votes (%)	41	47	11	1	
	seats (#)	5	6	0	0	-4
New Brunswick	votes (%)	40	45	9	5	
	seats (#)	5	5	0	0	-4
Quebec	votes (%)	53	30	14	3	
	seats (#)	63	12	0	0	+5
Ontario	votes (%)	38	39	20	3	
	seats (#)	46	43	10	0	-21
Manitoba	votes (%)	37	36	21	5	
	seats (#)	7	5	2	0	-2
Saskatchewan	votes (%)	36	18	44	1	
	seats (#)	4	0	10	0	-5
Alberta	votes (%)	52	14	17	17	
	seats (#)	25	0	1	0	+4
British Columbia	votes (%)	34	21	37	7	
	seats (#)	12	1	19	0	-7
Yukon / NWT	votes (%)	30	30	37	3	
	seats (#)	0	2	1	0	-3
TOTAL CANADA	votes (%)	43	32	20	5	
	seats (#)	169	83	43	0	-42

Almost unnoticed in the 1988 result was the performance of the newly founded Reform Party, which had run candidates in many western constituencies, including all 26 Alberta ridings and many in British Columbia. Its new leader, Preston Manning, received over 11,000 votes (28 percent), placing second to Joe Clark in his Yellowhead constituency. Highly critical of the Conservatives' strong Quebec focus, and arguing that Mulroney had paid little attention to the grievances of the West, Reform would ultimately destroy much of the western political base built up by Diefenbaker and retained successfully by Mulroney in both 1984 and 1988. His Quebec base would slowly slip away with the demise of the Meech Lake Accord in 1990, and the defection of many of the Quebec nationalists in the Conservative caucus to the Bloc Québécois. But, in the 1988 outcome,

FIGURE 10.7

Electoral Turnover, 1984–1988

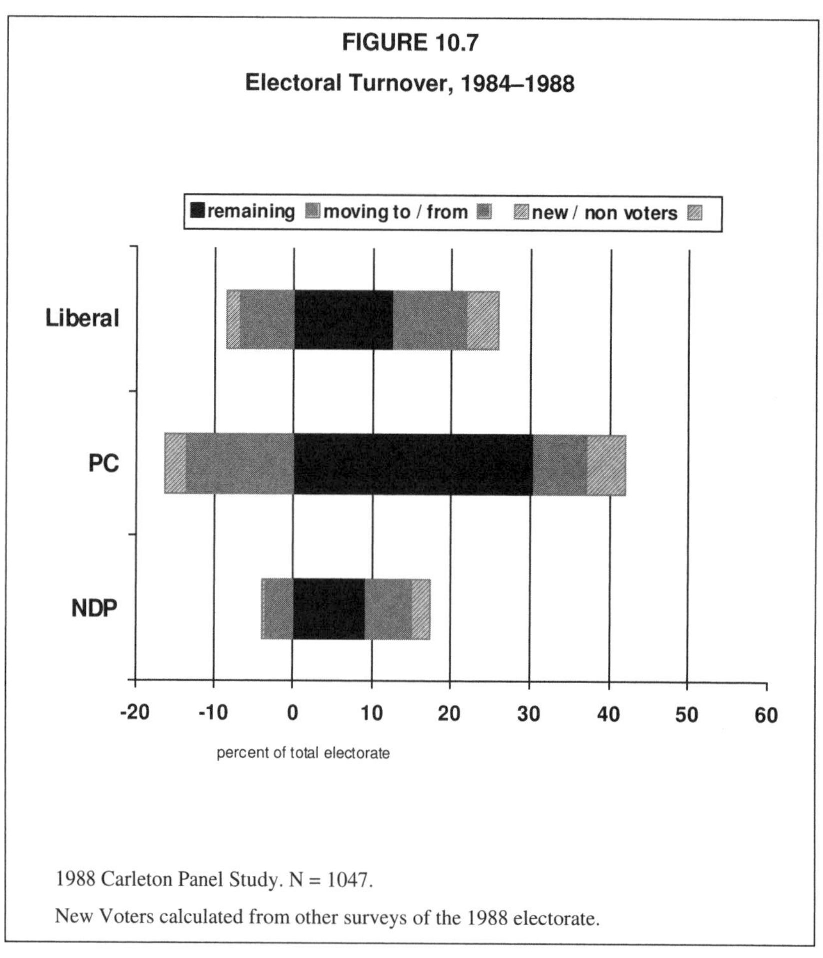

1988 Carleton Panel Study. N = 1047.

New Voters calculated from other surveys of the 1988 electorate.

only a few glimpses of these future difficulties that would later destroy the Conservative coalition were visible.

The federal election of 1988 would also prove to be the high point for the NDP, in spite of its failure to surpass the Liberals or to make its long sought after breakthrough in Quebec. The NDP total of 43 seats, obtained with just over 20 percent of the popular vote represented the party's best performance, although it fell well short of the lofty expectations that might have been generated by the surge in the polls in 1986–87. Broadbent would also retire from the political arena shortly after the 1988 election, having led his party in four consecutive election campaigns, and could rightly claim a solid political achievement for his long tenure in the leadership. Having steered the NDP steadily toward the political centre, he would pass on to his successors a party seemingly well positioned to compete on an equal footing with both the Liberals and Conservatives. During much of the late 1980s, political pundits speculated routinely on the transition of the Canadian party system to a genuinely three-party configuration, or on the possibility that the NDP might eventually displace the Liberals, just as Labour had done in Britain in the earlier part of the twentieth century. Even in the aftermath of the 1988 election, such possibilities did not look entirely unrealistic. There was little indication then of the sea change that was to come in 1993 (see Chapter 11).

The controversy over third-party advertising in the 1988 election led to the appointment of a Royal Commission on Electoral Reform and Party Financing (the Lortie Commission). Its inquiry also generated a raft of new academic studies of election campaigns and related issues. While its mandate was to consider reforms of the electoral process (not the electoral system), and particularly the financing of campaigns, the RCERPF inquiries produced 23 volumes of research studies in support of its work, many of them authored by political scientists. Among these volumes were *Interest Groups and Elections in Canada* (ed. F. Leslie Seidle), *Women in Canadian Politics: Toward Equity in Representation* (ed. Kathy Megyery), *Representation, Integration and Political Parties in Canada* (ed. Herman Bakvis), *Media, Elections and Democracy* (ed. Frederick Fletcher), and *Making Representative Democracy Work: The Views of Canadians* (André Blais and Elisabeth Gidengil). This surge of academic activity not only enhanced existing knowledge of the electoral process and related topics, but it also influenced the recommendations of the commission, whose final report, published in 1991, recommended a wide variety of reforms intended to strengthen political parties and assert their independence from interest groups.[32]

What the 1988 election result, together with the events of the campaign, did clearly disclose was the continued volatility of the Canadian electorate. One of the major studies of the 1988 election was that conducted by Richard Johnston, André Blais, Henry Brady, and Jean Crête for their book *Letting the People Decide*. Designed specifically to track the movement of voters across the length of the formal campaign, this study employed a rolling cross-section survey design, interviewing a total of 3,609 respondents over the duration of the campaign at a rate of approximately 77 interviews per day. Some of these respondents were also re-interviewed after the election, thus creating a pre/post-election panel in addition to the rolling cross-section survey with which they had tracked the campaign. This design proved quite powerful for measuring the impact of certain campaign events, such as the leadership debates or the Conservatives' late campaign advertising blitz.[33] Together with earlier studies of the Canadian electorate, the 1988 study also confirmed the relative weakness of partisan attachment of many Canadian voters, and highlighted their vulnerability to short-term appeals based on issues or leaders. Even across a period as short as a five- or six-week campaign, it was clearly possible for a party to win or lose a sufficient amount of support to make a critical difference in the outcome of an election.

A smaller panel study of 1984 voters conducted by the authors of *Absent Mandate* likewise disclosed considerable volatility in the 1988 electorate. That study found that nearly one in three voters changed parties between the 1984 and 1988 elections, a somewhat higher rate than had been found in previous panel studies of similar design.[34] As is seen in Figure 10.7, just over 30 percent of the electorate in 1988 consisted of voters who had supported the Conservatives in two consecutive elections. Although this figure is roughly comparable to that found in earlier elections, it nevertheless discloses considerable shifting from one election to another in the bases of party support. When combined with the more predictable changes in the electorate that occur between elections — the entry of newly eligible voters, for example, or the circulation of non-voters — it is clear that even successful parties such as the Conservatives in 1988 cannot count on a broad base of loyal supporters who will stick with them from one election to the next. Just how fragile is the coalition of support put together by a party in an election would become evident in the rapid disintegration of the Conservative vote that took place over the next few years, culminating in their electoral disaster of 1993.

Conclusion

The re-elected Mulroney government learned little from its brush with possible defeat in the 1988 contest. With the free trade agreement quickly ratified by the new Parliament, the government pressed ahead with its controversial plan to introduce a Goods and Services Tax (GST) almost immediately after the election. Because the proposed GST had received virtually no attention during the election campaign, its introduction so soon afterward seemed like duplicity. It reminded many Canadians of an earlier incident, which had occurred shortly after the 1984 election, in which Mulroney appeared to be violating his vow to treat social programs as a "sacred trust" when he quickly, and with little discussion, introduced legislation to de-index old-age pensions. The GST would later prove to be a "hot button" for all of the resentment that had built up regarding Mulroney's leadership style, as well as a controversial issue in its own right.

During his second term, Mulroney would also expend much of his remaining political capital on attempting to bring to fruition his much sought after constitutional settlement — first in a last ditch attempt to salvage the Meech Lake Accord and, after its failure, in a new initiative with the provinces. Within nine months of their dramatic 1988 election victory, the Conservatives had once again slumped to 27 percent in the opinion polls, well behind the Liberals at 43 percent.[35] Mulroney's personal standing with much of the electorate, already eroding at the time of the election, sagged farther, eventually eclipsing even the lows recorded by John Turner.[36] By 1990, the Canadian economy was sliding into recession. This time, Conservative fortunes would not revive. The next election would bring not merely the loss of power, but the destruction of a party.

Notes

1. On this theme, see Richard Johnston, André Blais, Henry Brady, and Jean Crête, *Letting the People Decide* (Montreal: McGill-Queen's University Press, 1992), especially 3–15.
2. But the idea of a referendum on free trade was certainly considered and discussed, and played into the strategies chosen by the parties, both before and during the election campaign. See Gerald Caplan, Michael Kirby, and Hugh Segal, *Election* (Toronto: Prentice Hall, 1989).
3. Johnston et al., *Letting the People Decide*, 141–67.
4. See, for example, Claire Hoy, *Friends in High Places: Politics and Patronage in the Mulroney Government* (Toronto: Key Porter, 1987), and Jeffrey Simpson, *Spoils of Power: the Politics of Patronage* (Toronto: HarperCollins, 1988). See also Michel Gratton, *So What Are the Boys Saying?: An Inside Look at Brian Mulroney in Power* (Toronto: McGraw-Hill Ryerson, 1987).
5. The first casualty was Robert Coates, who resigned as minister of national defence in February 1985, only five months after taking office. He was followed by John Fraser (Fisheries), Marcel Masse (Communications), Suzanne Blais-Grenier (Environment), Andrée Champagne (Youth), and Sinclair Stevens (Regional Economic Expansion) during the period from September 1985 to May 1986. Masse was later reinstated.
6. André Bissonette (Minister of State for Small Business) was dismissed from the cabinet by Mulroney in January 1987, and Roch Lasalle (Public Works) resigned a month later.
7. Among them, Joe Clark (Alberta) — Minister of External Affairs; Pat Carney (British Columbia) — Minister of Energy, Mines and Resources; Jake Epp (Saskatchewan) — Minister of Health and Welfare; Harvie Andre (Alberta) — Minister of Supply and Services, John Fraser (British Columbia) — Minister of Fisheries and Oceans; and Don Mazankowski (Alberta) — Minister of Transport. The former premier of Manitoba, Duff Roblin, became government leader in the Senate. Following a cabinet shuffle in June 1986, Mazankowski was named deputy prime minister.
8. For more information on the Meech Lake negotiations, see Peter H. Russell, *Constitutional Odyssey*, second edition (Toronto: University of Toronto Press, 1993), 127–53.
9. See the *Report of the Royal Commission on the Economic Union and Developments Prospects for Canada* (Toronto: University of Toronto Press, 1985).
10. Walter Gordon, for example, who served as Lester Pearson's minister of finance, represented one such prominent figure. See Chapter 5.
11. Graham Fraser, *Playing for Keeps* (Toronto: McClelland & Stewart, 1989), 40–42.

12. See Harold D. Clarke, Jane Jenson, Lawrence LeDuc, and Jon H. Pammett, *Absent Mandate: Interpreting Change in Canadian Elections*, second edition, 54–60. See also Johnston et al., *Letting the People Decide*, 168–96.
13. Clarke et al., *Absent Mandate*, second edition, 97–99. For a more detailed exploration of the images of the party leaders, see Lawrence LeDuc, "Leaders and Voters: The Public Images of Canadian Political Leaders," in Maureen Mancuso et al., eds., *Leaders and Leadership in Canada* (Toronto: Oxford University Press, 1994), 53–74.
14. For a more detailed exploration of some of Turner's difficulties during this period, see Greg Weston, *Reign of Error* (Toronto: McGraw Hill Ryerson, 1988).
15. Clarke et al., *Absent Mandate*, second edition, 96–97.
16. Clarke et al., *Absent Mandate*, second edition, 99–101. See also Weston, *Reign of Error*.
17. Graham Fraser, *Playing for Keeps*, 228.
18. Lawrence LeDuc, "Party Strategies and the Use of Televised Campaign Debates," *European Journal of Political Research*, Vol. 18 (1990), 121–41.
19. See Alan Frizzell and Anthony Westell, "The Media and the Campaign," in Allan Frizzell, Jon H. Pammett, and Anthony Westell, eds., *The Canadian General Election of 1988* (Ottawa: Carleton University Press, 1989), 78–79. See also Johnston et al., *Letting the People Decide*, 27–28, 132–38.
20. *Le Devoir*, October 25, 1988. See also Johnston et al., *Letting the People Decide*, 180–92 for evidence on the dynamics of public opinion regarding the leaders following the debates.
21. On a ten-point performance scale, Turner scored 6.7 compared with Mulroney (5.8) and Broadbent (4.9). Clarke et al., *Absent Mandate*, second edition, 102–04. See also Johnston et al., *Letting the People Decide*, 132–40.
22. Other polls at about the same time also showed substantial Liberal gains, but none of them placed the Liberals as far ahead as did Gallup. On the movement of the polls during this period, see Allan Frizzell, "The Perils of Polling," in Frizzell et al., *The Canadian General Election of 1988*, 95–97. See also Lawrence LeDuc, "Voting For Free Trade? The Canadian Voter and the 1988 Federal Election," in Paul Fox and Graham White, eds., *Politics: Canada*, seventh edition (Toronto: McGraw Hill Ryerson, 1991), 351–66.
23. LeDuc, "Party Strategies and the Use of Televised Campaign Debates," *op. cit.*
24. Graham Fraser, *Playing for Keeps*, 421–23.
25. Graham Fraser, *Playing for Keeps*, 308–27. See also Gerald Caplan, Michael Kirby, and Hugh Segal, *Election*, 173–97.
26. The controversy over the role of third-party advertising during the 1988 election campaign led afterward to the appointment of a Royal Commission on Electoral Reform and Party Financing (the Lortie Commission) and subsequently to the enactment of new legislation requiring registration and financial reporting of third-party activity in election campaigns. Some of these new regulations were later challenged under the Charter of Rights,

but were upheld by the Supreme Court (Harper v. Canada). Elections Canada (*www.elections.ca*).

27. Frizzell, "The Perils of Polling," 94–95.
28. Clarke et al., *Absent Mandate*, second edition, 145–48.
29. Clarke et al., *Absent Mandate*, second edition, 113–17.
30. The FTA was formally ratified by Parliament following the election, and came into effect on January 1, 1989.
31. For a comparison of Trudeau and Mulroney in this regard, see Peter Aucoin, "Organizational Change in the Machinery of Canadian Government: From Rational Management to Brokerage Politics," *Canadian Journal of Political Science*, Vol. 19 (1986), 3–27.
32. Royal Commission on Electoral Reform and Party Financing, *Reforming Electoral Democracy* (Ottawa: Government Publications, 1991).
33. Johnston et al., *Letting the People Decide*, 118–38, 168–96.
34. In the 1988 study, 30 percent of the panel respondents were found to have switched parties, while another 6 percent moved to non-voting. In a 1984 study, the comparable figures were 28 percent and 9 percent respectively. Clarke et al., *Absent Mandate*, second edition, 117–21.
35. *The Gallup Report*, August 17, 1989.
36. Clarke et al., *Absent Mandate*, third edition, 75–78.

Selected Reading

Bercuson, David, Jack Granatstein, and W.R. Young. *Sacred Trust?: Brian Mulroney and the Conservatives in Power* (Toronto: Doubleday, 1986).

Cameron, Duncan, ed. *The Free Trade Deal* (Toronto: Lorimer, 1988).

Caplan, Gerald, Michael Kirby, and Hugh Segal. *Election: The Issues, the Strategies, the Aftermath* (Toronto: Prentice-Hall, 1989).

Clarke, Harold D., Jane Jenson, Lawrence LeDuc, and Jon H. Pammett. *Absent Mandate: Interpreting Change in Canadian Politics* (Toronto: Gage, 1991).

Fraser, Graham. *Playing for Keeps: the Making of the Prime Minister, 1988* (Toronto: McClelland & Stewart, 1989).

Frizzell, Allan, Jon H. Pammett, and Anthony Westell, eds. *The Canadian General Election of 1988* (Ottawa: Carleton University Press, 1989).

Gollner, Andrew, and Daniel Salee, eds. *Canada under Mulroney: An End of Term Report* (Montreal: Vehicule Press, 1988).

Hogg, Peter. *The Meech Lake Constitutional Accord: Annotated* (Toronto: Carswell, 1988).

Johnston, Richard, André Blais, Henry Brady, and Jean Crête. "Free Trade and the Dynamics of the 1988 Election," in Joseph Wearing, ed. *The Ballot and Its Message* (Toronto: Copp Clark, 1991).

Johnston, Richard, André Blais, Henry Brady and Jean Crête. *Letting the People Decide: Dynamics of a Canadian Election.* (Montreal: McGill-Queen's University Press, 1992).

LeDuc, Lawrence. "Voting for Free Trade?: The Canadian Voter and the 1988 Federal Election," in Paul Fox and Graham White, eds. *Politics: Canada*, seventh edition. (Toronto: McGraw-Hill Ryerson, 1991).

Lee, Robert Mason. *One Hundred Monkeys.* (Toronto: Macfarlane and Ross, 1989).

CHAPTER 11

THE PROGRESSIVE CONSERVATIVE CATACLYSM OF 1993

It has now become a political cliché to describe the 1993 federal election as an "electoral earthquake"[1] with results of "cataclysmic" consequences,[2] but in this case the metaphor is fitting. While the volatile Canadian electorate has rejected incumbent governments in the past, the virulence of its rebuke to the PCs in 1993 was unprecedented, both in terms of the number of seats lost and the decline in popular vote.

The Mulroney landslide in 1984 held the promise of positioning the PC Party for long-term electoral success; they won a majority of seats in every province and territory — something no party had ever done before (see Chapter 9). From the moment he became party leader in 1983, Brian Mulroney demonstrated an understanding of the necessity to favourably position his party along the building blocks of electoral success in Canada. He had done so by stressing economic prosperity, constitutional harmony, and the protection of the "sacred trusts" of Canada's social safety net, and had been rewarded with two consecutive electoral majorities.

Despite these early successes, in the span of nine years the vote for the Progressive Conservative Party dropped from 50 percent in 1984 to 16 percent, and the number of seats from 211 to 2. Despite a legacy pre-dating Confederation, the Progressive Conservative Party was not merely thrown out of office in 1993, but almost out of the House of Commons. For the only time in its history, the party of John A. Macdonald lost "official status" in the House of Commons[3] and, as we will see in subsequent chapters, never fully recovered.

Certain continuities can be found in the 1993 debacle despite the unprecedented scope of the PC defeat.[4] First, the Liberals were back in power with a majority government, as they had been for much of the twentieth century.[5] Second, in 1993, Canadians elected their fourth consecutive majority government, extending a period of parliamentary stability that stood in contrast with the years between 1957 and 1980. Third, the two new parties — the Reform Party of Canada and the Bloc Québécois — represented the perennial Canadian realities of western protest and Quebec nationalism. Fourth, post-mortems of the campaign suggested that the unparalleled Conservative defeat was largely due to the lacklustre campaign waged by the party in 1993.[6]

Bad election campaigns run by governing parties are not unknown in Canada. In some ways the Conservative campaign of 1993 resembled the Liberal campaign of 1984. In both cases, the party had changed their leader shortly before calling the election, in an attempt to put a new face on the party. Both went into campaigns based on images of novelty without substantive policy programs. Both ran into organizational difficulties through the lack of experience of their headstrong leaders. Both lost badly. While poor campaign strategy contributed to the downfall of the PCs, it is not a total explanation of the scope of their defeat. The interplay of several other factors, such as poor economic conditions, the concurrent re-emergence of western discontent and revival of the Quebec *indépendentiste* movement despite the 1980 referendum defeat, and failed leadership, played a part.

The election was preceded by a series of constitutional negotiations, featuring the collapse of the Meech Lake Accord and the referendum on its successor constitutional agreement, the Charlottetown Accord, which took place in 1992. Following his victory in the "free trade" election of 1988, Brian Mulroney spent the ensuing years embroiled in constitutional matters, in the process depleting what he had left of political capital. As discussed in the previous chapter, Mulroney had hoped that the Meech Lake Accord, negotiated in 1987, would finally free Canada from its constitutional quagmire.

Broad public and political support had initially greeted the signing of the Meech Lake Accord. A Gallup poll conducted in May 1987 showed that 56 percent of Canadians approved of the agreement that would lead to Quebec signing the Constitution, while only 15 percent disapproved. Another 28 percent of Canadians were unsure.[7] The Quebec government moved quickly to ratify the constitutional resolution on June 23, 1987, starting the clock on the three-year ratification process. The House of Commons approved the Accord on June 22, 1988,[8] and seven other provinces followed in short order. Everything appeared in place for a successful conclusion of the Quebec issue and the province's reintegration into the constitutional family. But it was not to be. One important obstacle to the accord emerged as a result of a change in the Liberal leadership.

The 1990 Liberal Leadership Convention

Despite a valiant effort in the 1988 campaign, John Turner knew that his time as Liberal leader had passed. He resigned in early 1990 and the stage was set for a Liberal leadership convention to be held on June 23. A total of five candidates sought the leadership (see Table 11.1) but two candidates mattered most — Jean Chrétien and Paul Martin. Before entering public life, Paul Martin had been an extremely successful businessman, running Canada Steamship Lines, as well as other interests. In the 1988 election, he ran for Parliament with the clear intention of ultimately challenging for his party's leadership. Martin's first involvement in party politics occurred during his father's 1968 leadership bid when he witnessed, first-hand, the agony of defeat. An old friend of his once remarked, "The motivation that drives him is that he would never want to repeat the experience of his father; he would never want to be the person who ran and lost. That is absolutely his worst nightmare."[9]

But in 1990, the party membership agreed that it was Jean Chrétien's time. After losing the leadership contest to Turner in 1984, Chrétien ran in the election and was one of only 17 Quebec Liberal MPs to survive the Mulroney landslide. Then, faced with a large PC majority and Turner continuing in the leadership, he resigned in 1986 and returned to private life. When Turner stepped down in 1990, Chrétien thought it was his turn, and resented the fact that Martin had undertaken to challenge him for the leadership. But it was necessary for Martin to run in 1990. First, it gave him the opportunity to showcase his credentials and position himself as "heir apparent." Second, Martin used the race to recruit bright and energetic people who would become the next generation of Liberal insiders. They moved up the party ranks to eventually control most of the party apparatus, and played important roles in Martin's future political success. Right from the start, they were very loyal to Martin, showed little respect for Chrétien, and generally considered themselves superior to those surrounding their opponents. This air of superiority became increasingly prominent over the years and had a significant impact on the subsequent internal feud which beset the Liberal Party (see Chapter 13). But in 1990, nothing could stop Chrétien, who would go on to win the leadership and (three years later) become prime minister.

Jean Chrétien was well known to Canadians as "the little guy from Shawinigan." Someone who had grown up with Chrétien in the working-class village of La Baie Shawinigan would have been hard-pressed to predict his illustrious accomplishments. The simple fact that he survived infancy as the 18th of 19 children defied the odds, since 10 of his siblings died before they reached the age of 2. Right from the start, Chrétien was the underdog and seemed to relish the role. He was small, rail thin, awkward-looking, and, in addition, he was born with a hearing defect. But he was also a fighter, never one to run away from a battle either in the streets or in the schoolyard. When he was 12, he suffered an injury, leaving him with a permanent

TABLE 11.1

Party Leadership Conventions

1988–1993

DATE	PARTY	LOCATION	WINNER	# CANDIDATES*	# BALLOTS	RUNNER-UP**
1989 30 11	NDP	Winnipeg	Audrey McLaughlin	7	4	David Barrett
1990 20 06	Liberal	Calgary	Jean Chrétien	5	1	Paul Martin, Jr.
1993 11 06	PC	Ottawa	Kim Campbell	5	2	Jean Charest

* On first ballot

** On final ballot

facial deformity. As a young teenager, Chrétien was more interested in sports than in studying, until he discovered politics. After attending his first political meeting, he was addicted. Like most young activists at the time, he opposed the unbridled patronage of the Duplessis machine and the political meddling of the clergy in Quebec. However, unlike many in his generation, he espoused a strong pro-Canada stance rather than the nationalistic position promoted by a great number of his contemporaries.[10] Throughout his political career, Chrétien would never waver in his support for Canadian unity even when clashing against the charismatic Quebec nationalists of his time — Quebec premier René Lévesque, and subsequently Jacques Parizeau and Lucien Bouchard.

Chrétien's first significant role in federal politics came during the reorganization of the Liberal Party following the Diefenbaker victory of 1958. As a delegate to the leadership convention, Chrétien had intended to support the front-runner, Lester B. Pearson. But after meeting the other major candidate, Paul Martin Sr., he changed his mind. Characteristically, Chrétien saw that Martin was the underdog, and he switched his support accordingly.[11] Five years later, Chrétien won his first election and never looked back.

In the course of the 1990 leadership race, and long after he had built an overwhelming lead, Chrétien found himself being criticized because he opposed the Meech Lake Accord. On one occasion, however, he appeared to contradict this position and argue for its passage.[12] Taken aback by the growing anxiety over the impending consequences of the collapse of the constitutional accord, Chrétien and his team realized that whoever succeeded Mulroney would inherit a difficult set of circumstances.[13] He also understood the dangers of being positioned on the wrong side of one of the three building blocks of Canadian electoral politics, and therefore changed his mind. Martin and his organization could not believe Chrétien was not challenged about a flip-flop on such an important issue. As Susan Delacourt noted in *Juggernaut* (2003):

> After having denigrated Martin and others for the better part of six months for their support for the Meech Lake Accord, Chrétien suddenly seemed to be coming over to their side with apparent political impunity.... At that point, there was no hope for Martin to win the

> Liberal leadership, but his team was determined to show Chrétien for the unprincipled opportunist they believed him to be.[14]

Despite the aggressive tactics from the Martin camp, the convention was a one-sided affair, with Chrétien winning on the first ballot. While the results forced Martin to find a peaceful accommodation with the party leader, the antagonism between the two men never subsided (see Chapter 13).

"Rolling the Dice"

The deadline for passage of the Meech Lake Accord came and went within a few hours after Chrétien's victory on June 23, 1990, the eve of St-Jean-Baptiste Day, the national holiday of French-speaking Quebecers. Its demise was interpreted in Quebec as an "affront." The next day the streets of Montreal turned blue and white with fleurs-de-lys, in an unequivocal display of nationalist solidarity. Sovereigntists called for an immediate referendum, and polls suggested that close to 60 percent of Quebecers would have favoured sovereignty if a referendum were held at that time.[15] Throughout the rest of Canada, feelings were also boiling over. In some quarters, people clamoured for Quebec to become a province like the others or to leave the country — and not necessarily on the most magnanimous terms. There was anger also among those groups that had felt excluded from the Meech Lake negotiations and wanted to see their own constitutional goals realized.

There were several reasons for the failure of the constitutional amendment. For one, the three-year ratification process made it difficult to keep momentum going. Moreover, political and partisan realities stalled the process in three provinces. New Brunswick PC premier Richard Hatfield was soundly defeated at the polls, and the new Liberal premier, Frank McKenna, expressed doubts about the Accord. In Manitoba, the NDP government fell and a new minority Conservative government was restrained in its ability to ratify the deal by the Liberals, who held the balance of power. But of greater consequence was the election of a new Liberal government in Newfoundland headed by Clyde Wells. Wells had been a legal adviser to the federal government during the 1980–81 constitutional negotiations and was a strong advocate of centralized federalism. The day after his party was elected in Newfoundland, he declared that he had a mandate to renegotiate the Accord, and the Newfoundland legislature rescinded its previous ratification.

Prime Minister Mulroney had been adamant that the Accord could not be reopened, but when it appeared that the ratification process was in a deadlock, he appointed a parliamentary committee to try to find a compromise. The committee proposed to adopt a follow-up resolution to the Meech Lake Accord, delineating and clarifying the limits of Quebec's status as a "distinct society." This prompted Lucien Bouchard to leave the Progressive Conservatives after accusing his colleagues of trying to weaken the Meech Lake Accord. The resignation of Bouchard, who had been a high-profile and influential member of the Mulroney government, was a personal blow to Mulroney.[16] Having flirted with the notion of Quebec sovereignty in the late 1970s and early '80s, Bouchard added credibility to Mulroney's commitment "to bring Quebec back within Canada's constitutional family," and his sudden departure seriously compromised those efforts.

With hope of ratification of the Meech Lake Accord rapidly fading, Mulroney and the premiers met to devise a last-minute compromise to save the Accord. Mulroney succeeded in putting the ratification process back on track, only to reignite the atmosphere of acrimony only days later when he declared in a *Globe and Mail* interview that the last-minute ploy with the premiers had worked because he knew when to "roll all the dice."[17] It soon became apparent that there was growing public antipathy toward the Accord, either because of the secrecy surrounding the negotiation process or because of its substance.

The "Rest of Canada" or "ROC" — as it became customary to describe the English-speaking provinces — grew increasingly restless with the fact that the new constitutional agreement only addressed Quebec's concerns, and they rejected the prime minister's argument that this was to be the "Quebec Round" of constitutional negotiations.[18] The uproar over the Mulroney interview was as much a reaction to the distasteful smugness of the comments as to the public disapproval of having "eleven men in suits"[19] determining the future of the country in closed-door meetings. In the end, nothing could save the constitutional deal.

After the death of the Meech Lake Accord, Mulroney had pressing political reasons to try once again to bring an end to Canada's constitutional saga. By 1990, he was already halfway through his second mandate, and his low personal popularity made his chances of a third consecutive electoral majority appear dismal. PC support had dropped below 30 percent in June 1989 and continued its downward spiral until December 1992, when it stood at a mere 19 percent.[20] Adding to the party's troubles were Mulroney's own approval ratings. Only 28 percent of Canadians approved of the way Brian Mulroney was handling his prime ministerial responsibilities less than a year after his re-election in November 1988. Throughout his second term, the prime minister's approval ratings dropped steadily, reaching a low of 11 percent in February 1992. By that time, more than four in five Canadians (81 percent) disapproved of his performance. In such an environment, the prime minister was in need of a policy success story.

Always the gambler and drawn to political high-stakes,[21] Mulroney calculated that with a new constitutional deal he would be in a position

FIGURE 11.1

Federal Vote Intention, 1988–1993

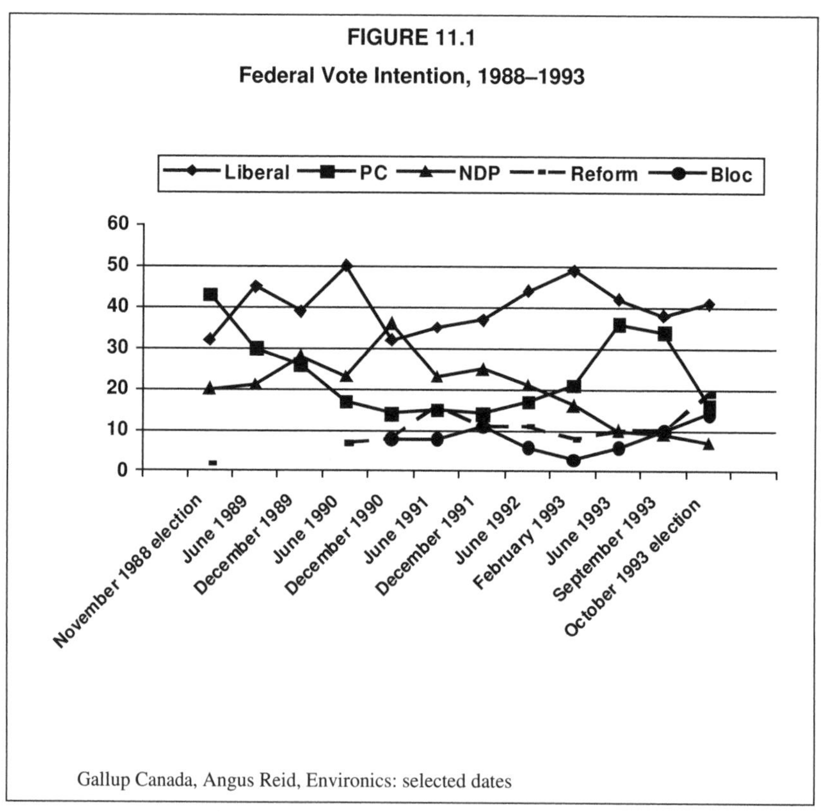

Gallup Canada, Angus Reid, Environics: selected dates

to risk going to the electorate for a third time, despite Canadians' misgivings about his leadership. With such electoral motivations in mind, Mulroney embarked on a new "Canada Round" of constitutional negotiations, determined not to repeat past mistakes. The aim was to convey a sense of openness, inclusion, and moderation that would lead to a successful resolution of the constitutional issue. Accordingly, a process driven by consultation was established to ensure that every Canadian who wanted to express his or her opinion on the Constitution could do so. Between the death of the Meech Lake Accord and the Charlottetown referendum, Canadians were asked, prodded, and encouraged to participate in a throng of commissions, meetings, and inquiries.

The first commission, under the chairmanship of Keith Spicer, was set up specifically to promote dialogue among all Canadians, and to encourage the development of a new consensus about the country's future. The Spicer Commission tabled a report on June 27, 1991, concluding that there was "a fury in the land against the Prime Minister,"[22] — not exactly the message Mulroney had in mind when he appointed

FIGURE 11.2

Mulroney Approval Ratings, 1985–1992

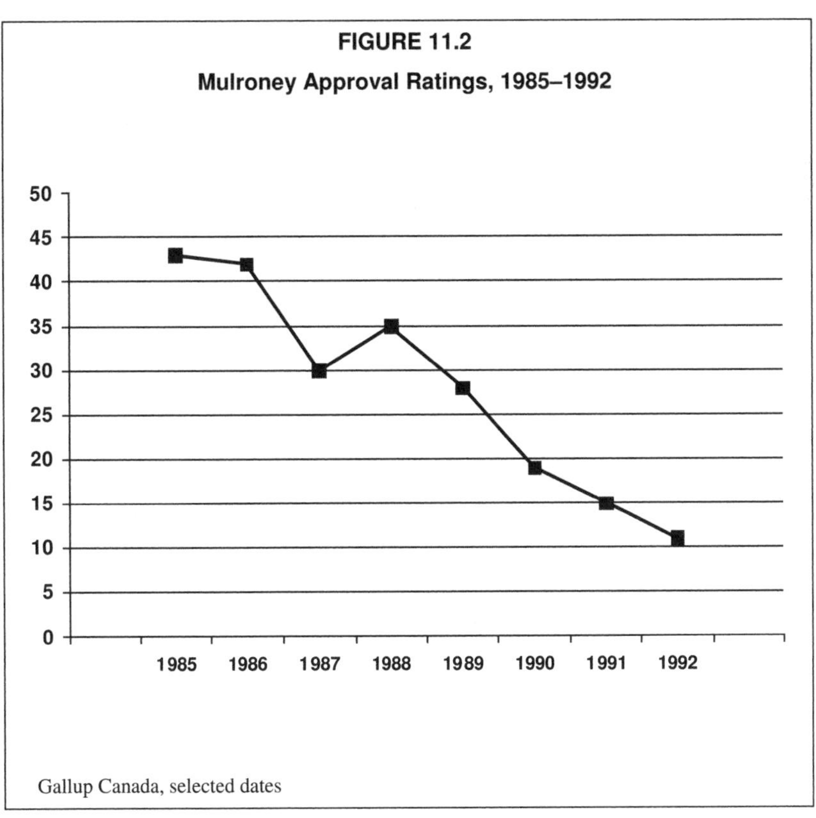

Gallup Canada, selected dates

that commission. Also, a special joint committee of the Senate and the House of Commons — the Beaudoin-Edwards Committee — was established to examine the amending formula and the process for achieving constitutional change.[23]

The Beaudoin–Edwards Report proposed that federal legislation be adopted to allow the federal government, if it so desired, to hold a consultative referendum on a constitutional proposal. This recommendation would ultimately influence the government's decision to hold a referendum on the Charlottetown Accord.[24] In addition, all provinces and territories took initiatives of their own to examine the constitutional question. Despite differences in structure and scope, one thing was common to them all: they sought to obtain a clearer understanding of the views of their respective populations on the Constitution and to project at least the perception of openness and inclusion.

In Quebec, Premier Bourassa had decided, after the failure of the Meech Lake Accord, to stay away from any negotiation involving the other provinces and the federal government. Bourassa's position was that Quebec would decide its own future, but would be willing to consider an offer from the rest of Canada if it was made available in time to meet Quebec's own timetable. The loss of Bourassa as an active participant in the constitutional negotiations was another severe strategic and personal blow to Mulroney. Without Bourassa, Mulroney could no longer depend on a team of Quebec Liberal strategists and organizers to develop and implement a post-Meech constitutional strategy, and he also had to contend with a much more stringent set of constitutional demands than those contained in the Meech Lake Accord.[25] Quebec's "Allaire Report" rejected what it considered the largely symbolic approach of the Meech Lake round of negotiations and focused squarely on a substantive new distribution of powers that would expand the jurisdiction of Quebec considerably at the expense of the federal Parliament.[26] The report also recommended that a Quebec referendum be held before the end of the fall of 1992, either on a Quebec–Canada proposal for reform or on the accession of Quebec to sovereignty.[27] In addition, another commission, co-chaired by two highly respected Quebecers, Michel Bélanger and Jean Campeau, concluded in its report that there were only two possible solutions to end the impasse between Quebec and the rest of Canada: a profoundly altered federal system or Quebec sovereignty.[28]

It was in this frenzied and polarized atmosphere that Brian Mulroney made the politically surprising move of appointing his long-time rival Joe Clark to head the final round of negotiations.[29] As David McLaughlin pointed out in *Poisoned Chalice*:

> One of the most curious ironies of the 1991–92 constitutional debate was that the politician who had secured unanimity amongst First Ministers to amend the Constitution on two separate occasions — Brian Mulroney — was deemed irretrievably sullied as a negotiator, while the politician whose "community of communities" view of the country had been derided for years as lacking in vision — Joe Clark — was now looked upon as the most trusted man to save the nation.[30]

This was the latest twist in one of the most interesting political relationships in Canadian history. As we discussed in Chapters 7 and 9, Clark had defeated Mulroney for the leadership of the PC Party in 1976 only to lose the leadership to Mulroney seven years later. Unlike the lingering animosity between Chrétien and Martin following their leadership battle, Mulroney and Clark learned to live with each other after the 1983 leadership race. Despite the strains, Clark served in Mulroney's government as external affairs minister between 1984 and 1991, and became a highly respected cabinet minister. By appointing Clark to handle the national unity portfolio, Mulroney resigned himself to the reality that his public reputation was tarnished to such an extent that he had become a hindrance to any successful resolution of Canada's constitutional impasse. His decision to step aside demonstrated a willingness to put the future of the country ahead of his own personal ambitions.

Clark succeeded in negotiating an agreement with the First Ministers. The Charlottetown Accord, as it became known, built on the Meech Lake Accord but was more far-reaching than previous constitutional proposals. It included the recognition of Quebec as a "distinct society" and proposed to establish an elected senate with equal representation for all provinces. To appease Quebec over its decline in influence in the upper chamber, the province was guaranteed in perpetuity a minimum of 25 percent of elected representatives in an enlarged House of Commons. The Charlottetown Accord also put forth new divisions of federal and provincial powers through the granting of greater autonomy to provincial governments in the areas of culture, fisheries, labour, and resource policy. A social charter was included to protect health care, education, social services, the environment, and workers' rights. It also proposed closer collaboration between Ottawa and Aboriginals with the recognition of Aboriginal self-government as an inherent right. Finally, it granted all provinces a veto over fundamental constitutional changes with regard to matters of representation or federal institutions.[31]

In order to reflect the spirit of openness of this round of constitutional negotiations, Canadians would be asked to ratify the agreement through a referendum. Referenda have been rarely used in Canada to seek popular approval for a policy,[32] but this time there was a general consensus that after the failure of the Meech Lake Accord, some sort of public ratification was needed. Thus, for the first time in the country's history, Canada's political leaders decided to ask the voters to endorse a package of constitutional amendments — the Charlottetown Accord. In fact, two referendums were to be held on October 26, 1992; one in all of Canada, except Quebec, under the jurisdiction of the federal government, and one in Quebec under that province's jurisdiction. The following question would be put to the people in both referendums: "Do you agree that the Constitution of Canada should be renewed on the basis of the agreement reached on August 28, 1992?"[33] It was assumed that the Canadian public was as willing as their politicians to put an end to more than 30 years of constitutional squabbling. This was to be Mulroney's last miscalculation.

The 1992 Referendum

The referendum campaign for the public ratification of the Charlottetown Accord should have succeeded. The Accord had virtually unanimous support from the political elites and third-party organizations that commanded media attention and credibility and it had all-party parliamentary support. The YES side recruited the best organizers, had unlimited financial resources, and, initially, broad public support. [34] What it lacked was a simple and compelling message. Supporters emphasized that a YES result would end the constitutional bickering, would create economic growth and unite the country. In contrast, they said, a NO result would stall if not destroy the economy, create disunity, and possibly lead to the breakup of the country. The Accord was sold largely as an acceptable and honourable compromise that would avoid the unhappy consequences of failure, but fell short in proposing any rousing vision of the future.

Despite public support and apparent strength, the fact was that the YES committees were poorly organized at the outset. In contrast, the NO committees were focused and attacked specific controversial elements of the agreement, making the case that the whole deal should be rejected if voters believed that even just one element was deemed unacceptable. Preston Manning and the Reform Party deftly articulated the public mood by urging Canadians to "know more."[35] Pierre Elliott Trudeau was reported to have opposed the Accord on principle, because it would

> institutionalize constitutional bickering … create a hierarchy of classes of citizens … that its distinct society clause and recognition of aboriginal self-government would make collective rights trump individual ones, and that it would spell the end of social programs in poor provinces.… A YES vote would also ensure that the blackmail from Quebec would continue.[36]

In the final analysis, Canadians were in no mood to be lectured by the political establishment. As Allan Gregg commented in the fall of 1992, "Canadians are not only angry at themselves for having been too deferential for too many years, they want to punish those people in power who stole their dreams."[37]

And punish them they did. Four provinces voted YES: Newfoundland, Prince Edward Island, and New Brunswick by solid margins, and Ontario, barely. Quebec and the western provinces rejected the Accord decisively. In fact, British Columbia (68.6 percent), Manitoba (61.6 percent), and Alberta (60.2 percent) rejected the Accord even more decisively than Quebec (56.6 percent), ensuring that no one could suggest that one part of the country had rejected another part or that there was any point in trying to keep the constitutional issue alive.

Several factors were suggested to explain the defeat of the Accord, which can be categorized into four groups:

- The substance of the agreement, in particular specific provisions such as the "distinct society" clause, Senate reform, and Aboriginal self-government;
- Groups and benefits including perceived gains or losses by particular provinces, regions or groups;
- Dissatisfaction with politics namely the lack of trust in parties and leaders; and
- Reinforcing cleavages.[38]

Early on, while Canadians generally supported the constitutional package as a whole, it became apparent that most objected to specific parts of the deal — especially the recognition of Quebec as a distinct society and Quebec's guarantee of 25 percent of seats in the House of Commons.[39] In Quebec, the perception that the province was relegated to "a mere province-like-the-others" status was an important determinant

TABLE 11.2

Charlottetown Referendum Results, by Province

Province	YES	NO	Turnout
Newfoundland	63.2	36.8	53.3
Prince Edward Island	73.9	26.1	70.5
Nova Scotia	48.8	51.2	67.8
New Brunswick	61.8	38.2	72.2
Ontario	50.1	49.9	71.9
Manitoba	38.4	61.6	70.6
Saskatchewan	44.7	55.3	68.7
Alberta	39.8	60.2	72.6
British Columbia	31.7	68.3	76.7
Northwest Territories	61.3	38.7	70.4
Yukon Territory	43.7	56.3	70.0
TOTAL CANADA	45.7	54.3	71.8

of the final referendum results.[40] Consequently, Mulroney's stratagem to offer something to everyone to placate dissension backfired. More importantly, the referendum provided Canadians with a rare opportunity to pass judgment on the nation's political establishment,[41] and, as Richard Johnston and his colleagues put it, "Canadians could not resist using the referendum to chasten their leaders."[42] In the final analysis, all of those factors combined to lead to the rejection of the Accord, but each region of the country reacted differently and used a specific combination of these factors to arrive at the same conclusion.

What was clear to most was that a third successive election victory for the Progressive Conservatives under Brian Mulroney's leadership was impossible. The unpopularity of its leader, the two constitutional defeats, and the onset of a severe economic recession had turned the public against the Tories (see Figure 11.1).

As mentioned at the beginning of this chapter, Mulroney had understood that the recipe for political success rested on a positive economic record, a commitment to protect social programs, and some success on the national unity front. However, the deficit had risen to about 30 billion dollars by 1991 and was now threatening the government's ability to continue to fund social programs. Such poor economic performance, combined with the collapse of two constitutional initiatives, meant that Mulroney's winning coalition of the last two elections, anchored by Alberta and Quebec, had come unglued. Unlike other times when PC supporters became disenchanted with their party, this time disillusioned Conservative supporters were able to find homes in not one but two newly emerging political parties. This was to have devastating electoral consequences.

Two New Political Parties and a New PC Leader

Moderate nationalists in Quebec, who had once gravitated to Mulroney as a native son, became either radicalized or marginalized politically following the demise of the Meech Lake Accord and the failure of the Charlottetown referendum. After leaving the cabinet and the Conservative caucus in protest, Lucien Bouchard originally believed that his career in politics was over, and he had planned to return to his law practice. But events in Ottawa and in the province of Quebec precipitated his return to centre stage. Two Liberal MPs left the party, declaring that they were unable to serve under their new leader, Jean Chrétien, whom they considered a key architect of both the repatriation of the Constitution against Quebec's interests back in 1981 and the defeat of the Meech Lake Accord.[43] On July 25, 1990, Bouchard announced the name and mission of a new political movement. The Bloc Québécois was originally meant to be a group of independent MPs, rather than a political party. It was established to represent the interests of Quebec in the federal arena, and present Quebec's demands.[44] Shortly after its inception, the group ran a candidate in a Montreal by-election. In August 1990, Gilles Duceppe became the first openly sovereignist Quebec MP to be elected to the House of Commons. Within a year, the informal group had evolved into a federal political party. The failure of the Charlottetown Accord legitimized its existence, and confirmed that this newly formed Bloc Québécois, under the leadership of Bouchard, would present candidates in the next federal election and lead the battle for Quebec sovereignty.

Meanwhile, traditional conservatives in the West, as well as many in Ontario, were gravitating toward the Reform Party. Motivated primarily by a populist agenda that rejected the practice of modern brokerage politics, Reform advocated fundamental institutional changes to Parliament and improvements to the democratic process. It also promoted traditional values with a focus on fiscal discipline and small government. Leader Preston Manning had formed the party to work within the system as an alternative to the Liberals and Conservatives.[45] In the 1988 election, the new party ran candidates in 72 ridings west of Ontario, garnering 275,000 votes. In 1989, Reformer Deborah Grey was elected in an Alberta by-election and became the party's first MP.[46] Manning astutely used the 1992 referendum as a national springboard for the new party, and the defeat of the Charlottetown Accord made him a national political figure. He then indefatigably travelled across the country to promote his vision of a "New Canada"[47] and improve his party's electoral readiness. The most important convert during that time was Rick Anderson, a highly regarded Ottawa-based Liberal strategist, who became one of Manning's most influential confidantes. Reform could now rely on a moderate, talented, and experienced campaign strategist who knew how to run a national campaign. As the election neared, the party nominated 207 candidates outside Quebec and was poised to run its first campaign on the national stage.

Brian Mulroney announced his intention to resign on February 24, 1993, precipitating a Conservative leadership race. With the office of prime minister in the balance, one would have expected a crowded field of candidates and a dramatic race. However, Kim Campbell had emerged as the front-runner even before Mulroney's resignation.

Campbell had run for public office twice unsuccessfully: in 1983 as a Social Credit Party candidate for a seat in the British Columbia legislative assembly and for the leadership of that party in 1986. She was elected in 1986 to the B.C. legislative assembly as a Socred member, and from there began her meteoric rise. She resigned from the legislature to run in the 1988 federal election as a Progressive Conservative, won her seat, and immediately joined the cabinet as minister of state for Indian affairs and northern development. Two years later, Campbell became Canada's first female minister of justice and attorney general. In a 1993 cabinet shuffle, she was appointed as the first female minister of national defence.[48]

Kim Campbell's appeal derived partly from the fact that she was the opposite in so many ways of what Canadians had come to dislike about Brian Mulroney. By the time Mulroney resigned, a consensus had already emerged among Ottawa insiders, key provincial Tories, riding association presidents, and the party establishment that Kim Campbell was the best candidate to beat the Liberals. Therefore, the most experienced cabinet ministers — Michael Wilson, Barbara MacDougall, Perrin Beatty, and Bernard Valcourt — announced that they would not run for the leadership. There seemed to be such a coalescing of support behind Campbell that even Environment Minister Jean Charest initially balked at the futility of joining the race, only to be persuaded by Mulroney himself that he should run for the good of the party.

The failure to present a broad and vibrant slate of leadership candidates and a vigorous debate of ideas that would truly rejuvenate the party was a risky move. As if to signal what was to come, Campbell ran a poor leadership campaign and frittered away her early lead. It became evident that she was not fully informed about the way the party operated, and that she had not developed a vision of what her prime ministership might achieve. Her own personality and lack of political experience also worked against her. Campbell did not seem to grasp or to be able to adjust to the dynamics of a leadership race. Thus, instead of a coronation, Kim Campbell won the leadership on a close second ballot. There were immediate hints of trouble ahead. Campbell's acceptance speech contained only a dutiful reference to

Charest's strong campaign, and ignored the basis of success of her predecessor in unifying the party.[49] It was also clear that little thought had been given to the post-convention period, and to the election campaign that would shortly follow.[50]

The Campbell Government

On June 25, 1993, Kim Campbell was sworn in as Canada's 19th prime minister and became the first woman to hold that position. With her government in the fifth year of its mandate and an election looming, she needed to adjust quickly to her new role. In her first two weeks as prime minister, Campbell restructured the cabinet, downsizing it from 35 to 24, and reduced the number of government departments, reorganizing them into new thematic areas. She kicked off a pre-election summer tour by celebrating Canada Day on both the east and west coasts; and convened a meeting with the premiers to discuss the economy. She then flew off to Tokyo to attend the G-7 Summit. The strategic objective was to show Canadians that a new prime minister was effectively putting a new face on the PC government. Campbell had stated her intention of "doing politics differently," and the initial public response was positive. In August 1993, 51 percent of Canadians approved of the way Kim Campbell was performing as prime minister, ahead of Jean Chrétien's approval rating (37 percent).[51] She hoped to carry that momentum into the election campaign.

In the fall of 1993, there was only one topic on the minds of voters — the state of the economy. Economic growth had begun to slow in 1989, and the economy shrank for four consecutive quarters in 1990–91 (see Figure 10.1, page 374). Unemployment rose, as corporations went bankrupt, "downsized" to cut costs, or moved production to the United States. The recovery in 1991–92 was not widely felt and was a fleeting memory by the time the 1993 election was called. The public was running out of patience and had a long list of potential culprits for the dire economic situation. Some blamed free trade with the United States, others focused on the replacement of a hidden tax at the manufacturing level with a highly visible and irksome tax on goods and services (the GST), while others concentrated on the Bank of Canada's relentless pursuit of zero inflation for plunging the country into a recession. But above all, the main villain was

TABLE 11.3

Most Important Issues in the 1993 Election

	Percent (multiple response)
Economic Issues	
Unemployment	43
Debt / Deficit	14
Taxes	6
General financial concerns	4
General economic concerns	4
Other economic	2
National Unity	9
National unity	3
Ethnic relations / Separatism	3
The flag	2
U.S. influence	1
Social Welfare	
Health care	5
Pensions	2
Other social	3
Other issues	
Integrity / trust	3
Concern about next government	2
Need for stable government	2
Need for change	2

1993 Canadian National Election Study. N = 3,775.

the Tory government, and the solution to the current economic problems was to remove it from power as soon as possible.[52]

As Table 11.3 indicates, more than two-thirds of Canadians mentioned matters related to the economy as the most important election issue. Unemployment (43 percent) topped the list of concerns, well ahead of any other issues, economic or otherwise. Only 10 percent of Canadians mentioned social issues as their top election concern. Canadians were also unequivocally tired of constitutional matters with a mere 9 percent citing Confederation issues — including 3 percent

Jean-Marc Carisse, photographer.

Kim Campbell speaking at press conference, Ottawa, 1993.

concerned specifically about national unity — despite the unfinished business of the failed constitutional episodes.

In this adverse climate of public opinion, the new prime minister decided to concentrate on *leadership* in her opening campaign statement. She stated that she believed it was "time for new leadership that listens, leadership that learns, and leadership that takes action, new leadership that is able to leave the '70s behind, leadership attuned to the needs of the '90s."[53] It thus became clear that the 1993 PC campaign would be about Kim Campbell. It was also clear that Tory strategists perceived Jean Chrétien as a liability for the Liberals, and that they liked the contrast between Campbell's youth and Chrétien's long political past. The PC campaign intended to portray the Liberal leader as "yesterday's man" in the hope that the electorate would prefer youth over experience.

Guided by the polling data from party pollster Michael Marzolini, the Chrétien Liberals presented an effective contrast to the issueless PC campaign. One week into the election campaign, the Liberals released a 100-page "Red Book," the party's formal election platform. This was a departure from previous election campaigns in Canada. While British and American parties routinely issue platforms or manifestoes, such comprehensive formal documents have been generally absent in Canadian elections. The 1993 document, *Creating Opportunity: The Liberal Plan for Canada*, was more than just a detailed presentation of the party's issue positions. It was an effective campaign tool that was in sync with Canadians' main issue concerns. Chrétien stressed throughout the campaign that he had a plan for economic renewal, and the Red Book could be cited as evidence to support his claim.[54]

For the NDP, the low level of public concern over social issues put the party at a disadvantage. The Canadian public has always viewed the NDP as weak on economic issues, and the disastrous economic performance of Bob Rae as premier of Ontario did nothing to alter that perception. However, the NDP felt it had learned from its mistakes and hoped that with a new leader, it could overcome its perceived weaknesses. After the disappointing 1988 election, Ed Broadbent stepped down as leader and was replaced by Audrey McLaughlin. Her fourth-ballot victory on December 2, 1989, was an historic moment as McLaughlin became the first woman to lead a national political party in Canada. Early on, the new leader had to decide what to do with the party's constitutional position. Over the years, the NDP had often opposed the two mainstream federal parties. But in

1992, the NDP decided to support the Charlottetown Accord. With that decision, the NDP joined with the Liberal and Conservative parties and this proved damaging to its support in Western Canada, where the Accord had been overwhelmingly defeated in the 1992 referendum. However, the NDP in the 1993 election was more concerned with establishing its relevance in addressing economic issues. It had been crowded out of the free trade debate in the 1988 election and had been repeatedly chastened for its inability to articulate a coherent economic message. Determined not to repeat that strategic error, McLaughlin focused on NAFTA as one of her priorities in 1993. Unfortunately, NAFTA did not emerge as a prominent issue in the campaign. As a result, the NDP looked like it was fighting the battles of the previous election and appeared, once again, out of step with the priorities of the electorate.

A Five-Party Campaign

The precariousness of the PC strategy became evident during the first press conference of the campaign. On the two main issues of the campaign — jobs and the deficit — Campbell was unable to present compelling answers. As David McLaughlin wrote in *Poisoned Chalice*,

> On unemployment, the Prime Minister was asked how long Canadians would realistically have to wait before unemployment dropped below ten percent. Her answer was indeed "realistic," saying that structural unemployment was an international problem plaguing all industrialized countries and that Canada would suffer with them for the next few years. Left at that, she might have emerged unscathed. Campbell went on, however, to sum up her vision of Canada: "by the turn of the century, [Canada will be] a country where unemployment is way down." [55]

The Liberal campaign reacted immediately. Jean Chrétien criticized Campbell's assertion that unemployment would remain high for the foreseeable future. He countered by stating that Canadians wanted a government that would work to create jobs now, not in the next century. With this statement, the Liberals effectively focused their message on jobs rather than on leadership. In contrast, the Tories' inability or unwillingness to respond to Chrétien about the issue of greatest importance to the electorate — and a pillar of success in Canadian elections — meant that by the end of the first day of the campaign, the early signs of the upcoming political cataclysm were emerging.

Jean-Marc Carisse, photographer.

Jean Chrétien holding the "Red Book," 1993 election campaign.

If the first day was difficult for Kim Campbell and the PC campaign on the economic front, things would only get worse two weeks later. On September 23 — Day 16 of the campaign — when answering a question from Leslie Jones of CTV News, Campbell said, "I think that the election campaign is the worst possible time to have such a dialogue on social programs."[56] Later, Jones remembered, "I could not believe what she said."[57] Campbell did not appear to realize her blunder and the hole that she was digging for herself. She went on to say: "Because I think it takes longer than 47 days to tackle an issue that's that serious.... The issues are too complex to try to generate some kind of blueprint in the 47 days available in an election campaign."[58]

"Election Not Time to Debate Cuts: PM,"[59] headlined the *Toronto Star*; "PM Won't Touch Key Issues,"[60] said the *Globe and Mail*. Meanwhile, Jean Chrétien was able to show his experience by sticking to the campaign script calling for continuous attacks on a "heartless" Campbell for not caring about jobs, together with frequent references to his Red Book and the specific promises it contained. His personal style was also well suited as a contrast to his opponents' campaigns. As Stephen Clarkson observed:

> *"Le p'tit gars de Shawinigan"* was not too aggressive, compared to Campbell whose style was belligerently partisan, not too scary, compared to Manning's fierce commitment to a zero deficit, and not too charismatic, compared to Bouchard's unabashed determination to lead francophones to his promised land.[61]

The strategy was working. In a CBC/Environics poll,[62] the Liberals were solidly in the lead with the support of 36 percent of decided voters, ahead of the Conservatives at 31 percent. With the campaign in its fourth week, the PC campaign team hoped that the televised leaders' debates could turn the tide in their favour.

For the first time, there were five party leaders invited to participate in the debates, and the format therefore needed to be modified. The French debate was held first on October 3 and lasted two hours, with the final 30 minutes devoted to questions from the audience. Preston Manning, who did not speak French, read a prepared statement in English with simultaneous translation at the beginning of the debate and a closing statement, but did not participate in the actual debate. With four leaders crowding the stage, there was no formal one-on-one debating, but this did not preclude lively exchanges.

Campbell pointed out to Bouchard the seeming contradiction of having separatist candidates running for the federal Parliament, citing René Lévesque's belief that the place for separatists was in Quebec City, not Ottawa. Bouchard went on the attack: "You have no business raking over the ashes of René Lévesque.... What happens if Quebecers send a large number of Bloc members to Ottawa? Will you refuse to receive them?" Bouchard went on to portray the Tory leader as both anti-democratic and a non-Quebecer.[63] The English debate was held the following night. Bouchard attacked Campbell again, this time over the size of the federal deficit. In a memorable exchange, a fiery, finger-pointing Bouchard accused Campbell of "hiding the truth."[64] As with most leaders' debates, it was difficult to pick winners and losers; however, it was generally agreed that Campbell did not perform well enough to turn around the floundering PC campaign. In this sense, the debates were a lost opportunity for the Conservatives.[65]

They were also a lost opportunity for Audrey McLaughlin, who was fighting her first election as leader. The first female leader of a major party, and first party leader from the North (she represented the Yukon), McLaughlin presented herself as a contrast in style from her combative predecessor, Ed Broadbent, by avoiding abrasive criticism of the opposing parties.[66] Though initially popular, McLaughlin was marginalized during the leaders' debates, by her positioning on the edge of the stage, her difficulties in French, and by the aggressive exchanges between the other party leaders.[67]

The five-party dynamics of the 1993 campaign were causing trouble for the Conservatives. While Campbell was busy attacking the Chrétien Liberals, PC support was eroding on two regional fronts — in Quebec and in the West. Lucien Bouchard and the Bloc Québécois were in the most enviable situation, relying on the organizational support of the provincial PQ machine and not having to run a national campaign. The Bloc could therefore concentrate its efforts and message toward one audience — Quebecers.[68] Bouchard was very effective in delivering the campaign's main message — the need to defend Quebec's interests in Ottawa. His campaign slogan, *"On se donne le vrai pouvoir,"* tapped into Quebecers' search for self-determination in the aftermath of the failures of both the Meech Lake Accord and the Charlottetown referendum. It also aimed at those Quebecers who had embraced Lévesque's *beau risque* strategy, on which Mulroney's Quebec strategy had been built in 1984.

Preston Manning and the Reform Party clearly exceeded expectations in the 1993 election, even their own.[69] Reform's campaign strategy was built around a clear focus on the party leader backed by an army of volunteers at the local level canvassing door-to-door and dropping campaign literature. These volunteers allowed Reform to run a very professional and effective campaign on a shoestring budget.[70] Reform's position as the only national party to have campaigned on the winning NO side in the Charlottetown referendum cemented the party's populist credentials. However, that success did not immediately translate into broad popular appeal. For over a year after Charlottetown, public opinion polls had been measuring a steady decline in Reform support (see Figure 11.1). The 1993 election was a critical test for the viability of this new party. As Manning put it, "This election is not just about what the politicians have to say to the people. This election must be about what the people want to say to the politicians."[71]

While similar to Campbell's opening statement, Manning was the one "doing politics differently." Buoyed by having positioned himself favourably on the national unity issue during the 1992 referendum, Manning presented a clear economic plan with his "zero-in-three" timeframe to eliminate the federal deficit. Manning's deficit message was particularly troublesome for the Campbell campaign, since it undermined PC credibility among those voters who believed the deficit to be the most important election issue. But unlike the Bloc, the Reform campaign team could not tap into existing provincial party organizations. As a result, the increased national scrutiny caused some problems. Gaffes by inexperienced or unsuitable local candidates may have cost Reform a real breakthrough in Ontario as well as the coveted Official Opposition status in the House of Commons.[72]

The NDP played only a minor role in the PC debacle. Despite the high expectations created by their new leader, and a more direct economic message, the NDP was forced into a fight for survival.[73] Part of the image-making of the Reform Party and the BQ was to contrast themselves with the three older parties. In so doing, both undermined the NDP as a vehicle for protest voters, but the Reform Party was clearly doing most of the damage. Manning reminded voters that the NDP had sided with the elites in the Charlottetown referendum, and in doing so established Reform as the voice of protest in the West.[74]

FIGURE 11.3

Party and Leader Thermometer Scale Ratings, 1993

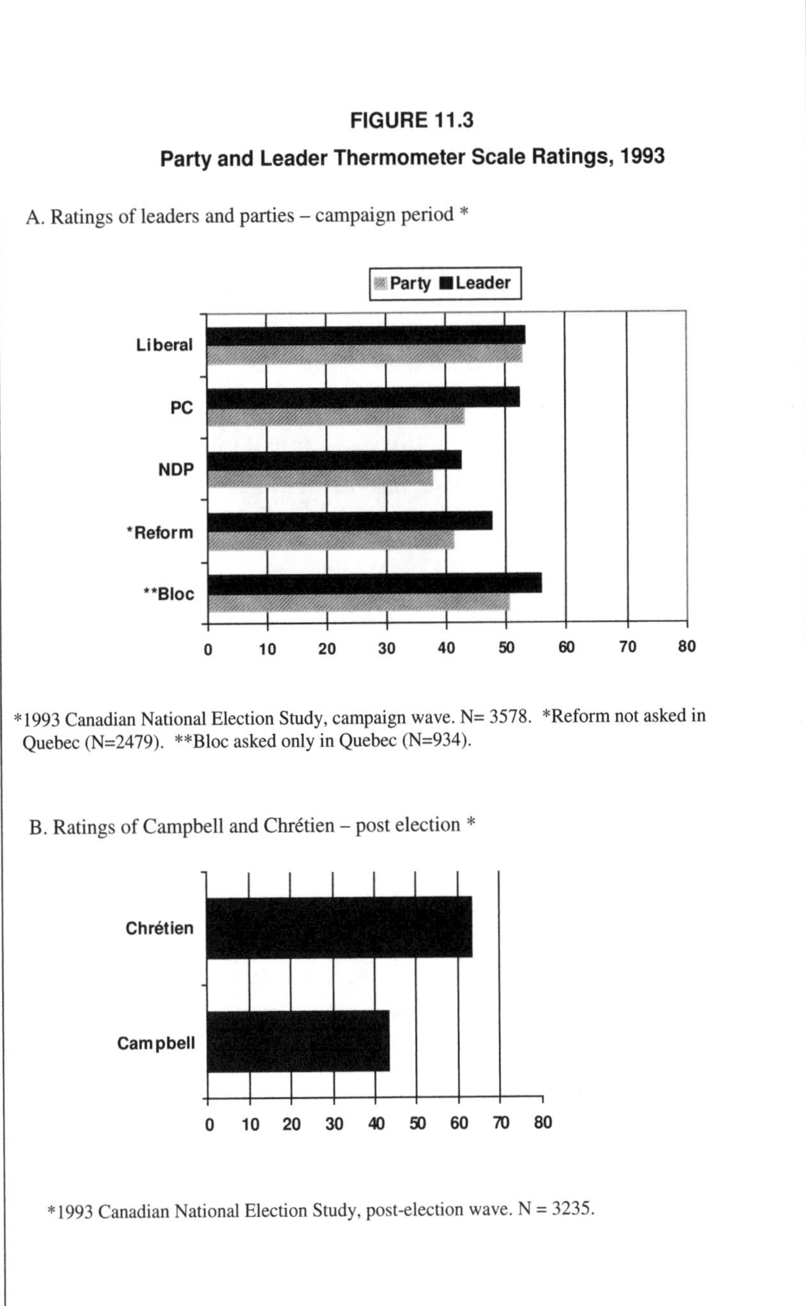

*1993 Canadian National Election Study, campaign wave. N= 3578. *Reform not asked in Quebec (N=2479). **Bloc asked only in Quebec (N=934).

*1993 Canadian National Election Study, post-election wave. N = 3235.

The PC campaign started the last two weeks of the campaign behind both the Liberals and the Reform Party in popular support. In a desperate move, the PC campaign team decided to launch an all-out personal attack on Jean Chrétien in a series of television advertisements. The logic behind the "Chrétien Attack Ads" — as they became known — was based on the belief that Campbell's impression ratings were higher than those of her opponent. However, as Figure 11.3 indicates, whatever leadership advantage Kim Campbell may once have enjoyed was gone by the end of the campaign. The negative ads used distorted images of Chrétien's face, designed to make voters feel embarrassed about him as a potential prime minister. But whatever effect they may have had worked in the opposite direction, as Campbell's rating dropped precipitously over the course of the campaign, while Chrétien's rose (see Figure 11.3B). Campbell was allegedly caught completely off-guard by the ads.[75] She contended that the decision to produce and run the ads was made by Allan Gregg as pollster and chief strategist, John Tory as campaign manager, and Tom Scott, the party's advertising agent. The furor created by the ads was the final nail in the coffin of the PCs' electoral hopes.

A Political Cataclysm

On election day, Canadians elected 177 Liberals, 54 Bloc members, 52 Reformers, 9 NDP, and only 2 PC candidates — Jean Charest and the popular mayor of Saint John, New Brunswick, Elsie Wayne. The scope of the PC defeat was unprecedented. All of the members of the cabinet lost their seats[76] — with the exception of Charest. Campbell herself was defeated in her Vancouver riding — only the third time in Canadian history that a sitting prime minister lost an election and was unseated at the same time.[77] The Conservatives were shut out of Ontario for the first time in Canadian history. Of those who had voted in the 1988 election, over half switched to a different party in 1993, a massive swing even by the standards of the often volatile Canadian electorate.

The altered political landscape was the result of the fact that, unlike previous elections, when disgruntled voters turned to one of the traditional parties to punish the incumbent party, the 1993 election offered *two* simultaneous vehicles of regional protest. As Figure 11.4 clearly shows, the majority of both Reform and Bloc voters had supported the PCs in 1988. The PCs also suffered important erosion of their support to the Liberals. In contrast, the Liberals were effective in keeping their previous voters, as well as in attracting voters entering or re-entering the electorate. Thus, the simultaneous successful attacks by Reform and the Bloc on the Mulroney coalition were largely responsible for the collapse of the PC Party in 1993.

Reform made a major breakthrough in British Columbia and Alberta. Manning's success depended largely in his party's ability to present itself as the voice of discontent with the federal government, a role usually filled by the NDP and in an earlier time by Social Credit and the Progressives. As the only party leader opposing the Charlottetown Accord, Manning was able to position the Reform Party as the only real vehicle for registering protest in B.C. and it was rewarded with 36 percent of the vote and 24 seats in that province. Similarly in Alberta, the Reform Party became the latest incarnation of right-wing populist protest, with Manning being able to capitalize on his insistent message that "the West wants in."

FIGURE 11.4

Electoral Turnover, 1988–1993

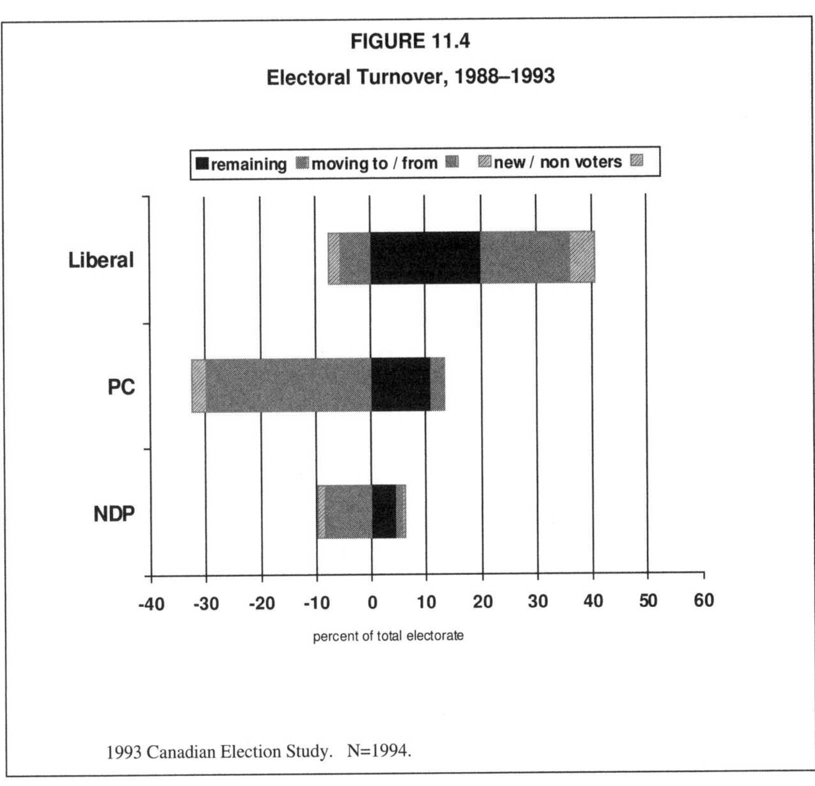

1993 Canadian Election Study. N=1994.

In Quebec, the 1993 election was in line with the traditional tendency to vote *en bloc* noted in previous chapters. Lucien Bouchard and the Bloc displaced the PC Party as the most convincing defenders and representatives of Quebec's interests in Ottawa in the same way that Brian Mulroney eclipsed the Liberals in 1984. More specifically, with Mulroney's resignation and his succession by Kim Campbell, the PCs could no longer rely on a "native son" to promote their commitment to the protection of Quebec francophones at the federal level. That mantle was now assumed by Bouchard, whose credentials rested on his resignation from government rather than accepting any dilution of the Meech Lake Accord. Given the widespread appeal that he enjoyed as a leader, the Bloc captured 54 seats in the province with close to half of the popular vote (49.3 percent).

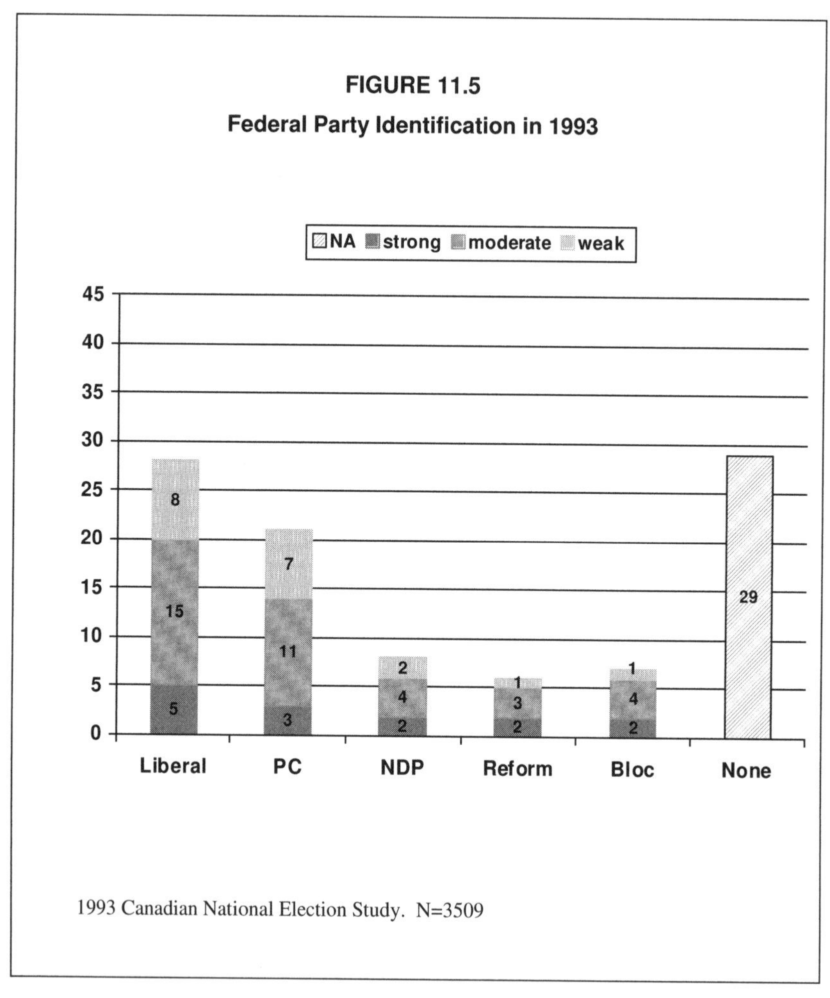

TABLE 11.4

Results of the 1993 Federal Election, by Province

		PC	Liberal	NDP	Reform	Bloc	PC Net Gain / Loss from 1988
Newfoundland	votes (%)	27	67	4	1	-	
	seats (#)	-	7	-	-	-	-2
Prince Edward Is.	votes (%)	32	60	5	1	-	
	seats (#)	-	4	-	-	-	-
Nova Scotia	votes (%)	24	52	7	13	-	
	seats (#)	-	11	-	-	-	-5
New Brunswick	votes (%)	28	56	5	9	-	
	seats (#)	1	9	-	-	-	-4
Quebec	votes (%)	14	33	2	-	49	
	seats (#)	1	19	-	-	54	-62
Ontario	votes (%)	18	53	6	20	-	
	seats (#)	-	98	-	1	-	-46
Manitoba	votes (%)	12	45	17	22	-	
	seats (#)	-	12	1	1	-	-7
Saskatchewan	votes (%)	11	32	27	27	-	
	seats (#)	-	5	5	4	-	-4
Alberta	votes (%)	15	25	4	52	-	
	seats (#)	-	4	-	22	-	-25
British Columbia	votes (%)	14	28	16	36	-	
	seats (#)	-	6	2	24	-	-12
Yukon / NWT	votes (%)	17	44	25	10	-	
	seats (#)	-	2	-	-	-	-
TOTAL CANADA	votes (%)	16	41	7	19	14	
	seats (#)	2	177	9	52	54	-167

One independent candidate was elected in Quebec.

As a result of developments in the West and Quebec, the political landscape was altered to such an extent that some have suggested that the 1993 election marked the beginning of a fourth party system in Canada,[78] with the emergence of two strong political parties devoted to the articulation of alienation, discontent, and regional interests. Looking at party identification, there was certainly some evidence that the political landscape had changed. However, while the two new parties had reasons to celebrate their electoral breakthrough, Figure 11.5 shows that both the Bloc (7 percent) and Reform (6 percent) would not be in a position to count on a significant proportion of Canadian voters forming a longer lasting identify with those parties. At that point in time their success depended more on a rejection of the traditional parties — mainly the PCs and NDP — than a genuine embrace of these new actors. By the same token, the Liberals did not attract a significant number of new voters identifying themselves as "Liberals," and while both the PCs and NDP saw erosion in party identifiers, the erosion was not as dramatic as the election results suggested. The most important development was the significant increase in the number of Canadians who claimed to have no party identification (29 percent — up from 14 percent in 1988, see previous chapter). Those voters moved away from the PCs and to a lesser extent the NDP, but had been left stranded by the other political parties.

Conclusion

An historically unique feature of the 1993 PC debacle is that, unlike 1896, 1962, and 1980, the three pillars of the archetypal formula discussed in this book came unravelled for the PCs at the same time. It was the concurrent resurgence of western alienation and Quebec constitutional discontent that led to the end of the Mulroney interlude. The PCs inability to win a single seat in Ontario added to the magnitude of their defeat. Throughout the years, the party had repeatedly cobbled together a coalition of western conservatives and decentralists, nationalistic Quebecers, and a solid base of Ontario support, to defeat the Liberals. Once elected, the exercise of power involved trying to satisfy all sides of that coalition. But inevitable differences pushed the sides apart, and electoral defeat ensued, highlighting the fragility of every Conservative government and the long-term challenge that they have faced in attempting to build an enduring electoral dynasty since the time of Macdonald.

While Brian Mulroney had initially been successful in repositioning his party on the key issue dimensions, all of the remnants of these efforts had dissipated by 1993. Failed constitutional deals, inability to meet Quebec's demands, the recession, deficits, and rising unemployment were the immediate legacies of the Mulroney years that lingered in voters' minds as they entered the polling booths. Failures in these key issue areas resulted in Canadians' determination to punish Brian Mulroney despite the change in party leadership. For her part, there was little that Kim Campbell could ultimately have done to prevent the PC defeat, but her poor campaign performance also contributed to its scope. A better campaign might have blunted the PC collapse in Ontario, which was largely the result of PC voters turning to Reform. Reform outpolled the PCs 20 percent to 18 percent in Ontario (see Table 11.4), in the process contributing to the election of 98 Liberal MPs and one Reform member in that province.

In the end, too many voters just did not see any good reasons to continue to support the Conservatives. As a senior PC adviser lamented, "It is absolutely amazing that over two million Canadians resisted the very strong reasons not to vote for us."[79] As they had done in 1921, 1926, 1935, 1963, and 1980, the Liberals managed once more to recover from electoral defeat to prevent the establishment of a lasting Conservative dynasty. They were back in power, and looking ahead to another long period of electoral dominance with Jean Chrétien at the helm.

Notes

1. See Munroe Eagles et al., *The Almanac of Canadian Politics*, second edition (Toronto: Oxford University Press, 1995).
2. See Richard Johnston et al., *The Challenge of Direct Democracy*: The 1992 Canadian Referendum (Montréal and Kingston: McGill-Queen's University Press, 1996).
3. To have official status in the House of Commons, a political party must have a minimum of 12 elected members.
4. For instance, see Harold D. Clarke et al., *Absent Mandate: Canadian Electoral Politics in an Era of Restructuring*, third edition (Toronto: Gage Educational Publishing Company, 1996), and Jon H. Pammett, "Tracking

the Votes," in Alan Frizzell et al., eds., *The Canadian General Election of 1993.*

5. See, for example, André Blais et al., *Anatomy of a Liberal Victory: Making Sense of the Vote in the 2000 Canadian Election* (Peterborough: Broadview Press, Ltd., 2002), and Clarkson, Stephen, *The Big Red Machine: How the Liberal Party Dominates Canadian Politics* (Vancouver: UBC Press, 2005).
6. For a detailed account of the internal PC campaign, see David McLaughlin, *Poisoned Chalice: The Last Campaign of the Progressive Conservative Party?* (Toronto: Dundurn Press, 1994).
7. Gallup poll, June 1987.
8. Peter C. Newman, *The Secret Mulroney Tapes: Unguarded Confessions of a Prime Minister* (Toronto: Random House Canada, 2005), 7.
9. As quoted in John Gray, *Paul Martin: The Power of Ambition* (Toronto: Key Porter Books, 2003), 239.
10. More details about Chrétien's childhood and its impact on his political career can be found in Lawrence Martin, *Chrétien: The Will to Win* (Toronto: Lester Publishing Limited, 1995), as well as in Chrétien's autobiography, *Straight from the Heart* (Toronto: Key Porter Books, 1985).
11. John Gray, *Paul Martin*, 93.
12. Susan Delacourt, *Juggernaut: Paul Martin's Campaign for Chrétien's Crown* (Toronto: McClelland & Stewart Ltd., 2003), 61.
13. *Ibid.*
14. *Ibid.*, 62.
15. Canadian Opinion Research Archives, Queen's University. Support for sovereignty hovered around 60 percent for more than a year after the demise of the Meech Lake Accord.
16. For more on this, see Brian Mulroney, *Memoirs: 1939–1993* (Toronto: McClelland & Stewart, 2007), 869–93.
17. See Susan Delacourt and Graham Fraser, "Marathon Talks Were All Part of Plan, PM Says," *Globe and Mail*, June 12, 1990: A1.
18. Richard Johnston et al., *The Challenge of Direct Democracy*, 44–46.
19. David McLaughlin, *Poisoned Chalice*, 7.
20. See *The Gallup Report*, November 1988 and February 1992.
21. For an understanding of Mulroney's character and motivations, see John Sawatsky, *Mulroney: The Politics of Ambition* (Toronto: McFarlane Walter & Ross, 1991), and Peter C. Newman, *The Secret Mulroney Tapes.*
22. See Keith Spicer, *Citizens' Forum on Canada's Future* (Ottawa: Supply and Services Canada, 1991).
23. As evidence of the scope of the consultative approach taken by the Mulroney government, the committee received over 500 briefs, heard 209 groups or individuals, and travelled to every province and territory before delivering its report in mid-1991.
24. For more details, see Peter H. Russell, *Constitutional Odyssey: Can Canadians Become a Sovereign People?* (Toronto: University of Toronto Press, 2004).

25. For more details on Robert Bourassa's handling of the Charlottetown negotiations, see Jean-François Lisée, *Le Naufrageur* (Montréal: Boréal, 1994).
26. Jean Allaire was a well-known Liberal who went on to establish a new political party in Quebec — L'Action Démocratique du Québec (ADQ) — after the failures of both Meech Lake and the Charlottetown Accord. Allaire was the ADQ's first leader.
27. For an in-depth look at the work of this commission, as well as the Bélanger-Campeau Commission, see Alain-G. Gagnon and Daniel Latouche, *Allaire, Bélanger, Campeau et les autres: Les Québécois s'interrogent sur leur avenir* (Montréal: Editions Québec/Amérique, 1991).
28. See Alain-G. Gagnon and Daniel Latouche, *Allaire, Bélanger, Campeau et les autres: Les Québécois s'interrogent sur leur avenir* for more details.
29. For more on this, see Brian Mulroney, *Memoirs: 1939–1993*, 1,000–003 and 1,023–101.
30. David McLaughlin, *Poisoned Chalice*, 23.
31. "Premiers Begin Sales Campaign," *Globe and Mail*, July 9, 1992: A4.
32. Previous federal referendum were on Prohibition in 1898 (Chapter 2) and on Conscription in 1942 (Chapter 3).
33. *Referendum Act*, S.C. 1992, c. 30.
34. See the evolution of public opinion about the accord in Richard Johnston et al., *The Challenge of Direct Democracy*, 72.
35. See Preston Manning, *Think Big: My Adventures in Life and Democracy* (Toronto: McClelland & Stewart Ltd, 2002), Chapter 6.
36. André Picard, "Trudeau Denounces Accord," *Globe and Mail*, October 2, 1992: A1–2.
37. Peter C. Newman, *The Canadian Revolution 1985–1995: From Deference to Defiance* (Toronto: Viking, 1995), xviii.
38. Lawrence LeDuc and Jon H. Pammett, "Referendum Voting: Attitudes and Behaviour in the October 1992 Referendum," *Canadian Journal of Political Science*, Vol. 28 (1995), 1–31.
39. Richard Johnston et al., *The Challenge of Direct Democracy*, 274–75; see also Neil Nevitte, Richard Johnston, André Blais, and Elisabeth Gidengil, "The People and the Charlottetown Accord," in Ronald L. Watts and Douglas M. Brown eds., *Canada: The State of the Federation* (Kingston: Institute of Intergovernmental Relations, 1993), 19–43.
40. *Ibid.*, 218.
41. Harold D. Clarke et al., *Absent Mandate*, 169.
42. Richard Johnston et al., *The Challenge of Direct Democracy*, 3.
43. Manon Cornellier, *The Bloc* (Toronto: James Lorimer & Company, 1995), 5–12.
44. *Ibid.*, 31.
45. Frank Dabbs, *Preston Manning: The Roots of Reform* (Vancouver: Greystone Books, 1997), 106.
46. For more details, see Preston Manning, *Think Big*, Chapter 2.

47. See Preston Manning, *New Canada* (Toronto: Macmillan of Canada, 1991).
48. For more details on Kim Campbell's life and political career, see Murray Dobbin, *The Politics of Kim Campbell: From School Trustee to Prime Minister* (Toronto: Lorimer, 1993).
49. In several instances in his memoirs, Brian Mulroney mentioned the lessons he learned from John Diefenbaker and Joe Clark on how not to treat a caucus and leadership opponents. See Brian Mulroney, *Memoirs: 1939–1993.*
50. Peter Woolstencroft, "'Doing Politics Differently': The Conservative Party and the Campaign of 1993," in Alan Frizzell et al., *The Canadian General Election of 1993*, 12.
51. *The Gallup Report*, August 16, 1993.
52. Alan Frizzell et al., *The Canadian General Election of 1993*, 2–3.
53. As quoted in David McLaughlin, *Poisoned Chalice*, 178.
54. Stephen Clarkson, "Yesterday's Man and His Blue Grits: Backward Into the Future," in Alan Frizzell et al., *The Canadian General Election of 1993*, 33–34.
55. David McLaughlin, *Poisoned Chalice*, 179.
56. *Ibid.*, 207.
57. *Ibid.*
58. *Ibid.*, 208.
59. Rosemary Speirs, "Election Not Time To Debate Cuts: PM," *Toronto Star*, September 24, 1993: A1.
60. Jeff Sallot and Hugh Windsor, "PM Won't Touch Key Issue," *Globe and Mail*, September 24, 1993: A1.
61. Stephen Clarkson, "Yesterday's Man and His Blue Grits: Backward Into the Future," in Alan Frizzell et al., *The Canadian General Election of 1993*, 37.
62. Geoffrey York and Susan Delacourt, "Liberals Outstrip Tories in Polls," *Globe and Mail*, September 27, 1993: A1.
63. *Ibid.*
64. Susan Delacourt and Jeff Sallot, "BQ, Reform Grill Campbell Over Deficit," *Globe and Mail*, October 5, 1993: A4.
65. Lawrence LeDuc, "The Leaders' Debates," in Alan Frizzell et al., *The Canadian General Election of 1993*, 138.
66. Alan Whitehorn, *Canadian Socialism* (Toronto: Oxford University Press, 1992), 245.
67. Alan Whitehorn, "The NDP's Quest for Survival," in Alan Frizzell, Jon H. Pammett, and Anthony Westell, eds., *The Canadian General Election of 1993* (Ottawa: Carleton University Press), 48–52.
68. André Bernard, "The Bloc Québécois," in Alan Frizzell et al., *The Canadian General Election of 1993*, 80.
69. See Preston Manning, *Think Big*, Chapter 4.
70. Faron Ellis and Keith Archer, "Reform: Electoral Breakthrough," in Alan Frizzell et al., *The Canadian General Election of 1993*, 67.
71. *Ibid.*, 69.

72. One such incident was that of John Beck, the Reform candidate in York Centre, whom Manning was forced to remove because of racist and anti-immigrant remarks made during the campaign. See Lionel Lumb, "The Television of Inclusion," in Alan Frizzell et al., *The Canadian General Election of 1993*, 119–20, and Manning's reactions to the incident in Preston Manning, *Think Big: My Adventures in Life and Democracy*, 86–87.
73. See Alan Whitehorn, "The NDP's Quest for Survival," in Alan Frizzell et al., *The Canadian General Election of 1993*, Chapter 4.
74. *Ibid.*
75. David McLaughlin, *Poisoned Chalice*, 253.
76. It should be noted that prominent ministers Michael Wilson, Don Mazankowski, Joe Clark, and John Crosbie did not seek re-election.
77. It previously happened to Arthur Meighen twice — in 1921 and 1926.
78. R. Kenneth Carty, William Cross, and Lisa Young, *Rebuilding Canadian Party Politics* (Vancouver: UBC Press, 2000).
79. As quoted in Peter Woolstencroft, "'Doing Politics Differently': The Conservative Party and the Campaign of 1993," in Alan Frizzell et al., *The Canadian General Election of 1993*, 23.

Selected Reading

Carty, R. Kenneth, William Cross, and Lisa Young. *Rebuilding Canadian Party Politics* (Vancouver: UBC Press, 2000).

Clarke, Harold D., Jane Jenson, Lawrence LeDuc, and Jon H. Pammett. *Absent Mandate: Canadian Electoral Politics in an Era of Restructuring*, 3rd edition (Toronto: Gage, 1996).

Clarke, Harold D., Allan Kornberg, and Peter Wearing. *A Polity on the Edge: Canada and the Politics of Fragmentation* (Peterborough, ON: Broadview, 2000).

Cornellier, Manon. *The Bloc* (Toronto: Lorimer, 1995).

Dabbs, Frank. *Preston Manning: The Roots of Reform* (Vancouver: Greystone, 1997).

Frizzell, Alan, Jon H. Pammett, and Anthony Westell, eds. *The Canadian General Election of 1993* (Ottawa: Carleton University Press, 1994).

Johnston, Richard, André Blais, Elisabeth Gidengil, and Neil Nevitte. *The Challenge of Direct Democracy: The 1992 Canadian Referendum* (Montreal: McGill-Queen's University Press, 1996).

Lisée, Jean-François. *Le Tricheur: Robert Bourassa et les Québécois 1990–1991* (Montréal: Boréal, 1994).

Lisée, Jean-François. *Le Naufrageur: Robert Bourassa et les Québécois 1991–1992* (Montréal: Boréal, 1994).

Martin, Lawrence. *The Antagonist: Lucien Bouchard and the Politics of Delusion* (Toronto: Viking, 1997).

Martin, Lawrence. *Chretien: The Will to Win* (Toronto: Lester, 1995).

McLaughlin, David. *Poisoned Chalice: The Last Campaign of the Progressive Conservative Party?* (Toronto: Dundurn Press, 1994).

Mulroney, Brian. *Memoirs: 1939–1993* (Toronto: McClelland & Stewart, 2007).

Russell, Peter. *Constitutional Odyssey: Can Canadians Become a Sovereign People?* (Toronto: University of Toronto Press, 1992).

CHAPTER 12

THE CHRÉTIEN/MARTIN DYNASTY

The 1993 election was a decisive defeat for the Progressive Conservatives, but was not necessarily a decisive mandate from the public for the Liberals. Its outcome left the party firmly in power, with a 59-seat majority in the House of Commons. But it was unclear if this was the result of genuine voter enthusiasm for the Liberals, or simply an indication that the party was a safe choice in an unstable situation. Jean Chrétien enjoyed high personal popularity ratings, but did people really like him, or were they just making invidious comparisons with the other leaders? Certainly, the situation was fraught with uncertainty. The Liberal majority was predominantly the result of winning 98 of the 99 Ontario seats. With the rise of Reform in the West, the Liberals won only four seats in Alberta (out of 24) and six in British Columbia (out of 32). Reform, with its blend of western populism and social conservatism, held only two seats east of Saskatchewan.

The Official Opposition was formed by the Bloc Québécois, a new party dedicated to independence for Quebec. Disastrous election results had placed not only the Progressive Conservatives, but also the New Democratic Party firmly in survival mode. Amidst this unusual configuration of parties, there was a major opportunity for the creation of a new dynasty if the building blocks were carefully put in place.

The economy was preeminently important, as Chrétien had emphasized economic issues during the election campaign. The Red Book promised a short-term job-creation program, and the new finance minister, Paul Martin, was under instructions to implement this in his initial budget. But first, Chrétien had to decide what to do with the North American Free Trade Agreement (NAFTA). This treaty was a continent-wide version of the Free Trade Agreement around which the 1988 election had been fought (see Chapter 10). During the election campaign, Chrétien had promised to renegotiate the new trade agreement before signing it. He stopped short of promising to rescind the agreement but he had raised expectations that he would take a hard stance and extract some concessions from Washington before approving it. Chrétien was quickly re-acquainted with the political reality that a promise made as a campaigning politician — especially when in opposition — is a far cry from action. Despite last-minute efforts, Chrétien failed to convince the Clinton administration, who were themselves under pressure from Congress to get the treaty ratified. The text of the treaty was not changed, and Chrétien had to make do with "side agreements," and non-binding declarations on such things as energy security, subsidies, and dumping.[1]

While Chrétien had expected to deal with NAFTA, he was unprepared for his second early economic challenge. In the months preceding the 1993 election campaign, Chrétien had mused about forcing John Crow, then governor of the Bank of Canada, to relax his strict monetary policy. During the 1990 Liberal leadership race, Chrétien's main opponent, Paul Martin, had voiced similar concerns, but both men had ignored the issue during the election campaign. When, after the election, disagreements continued with Crow and compromises failed, Martin, now finance minister, notified Chrétien of his intention to replace the governor. After the initial surprise, Chrétien backed his finance minister and Crow was replaced.[2] This episode is important for two reasons. First, it shows that early on, Chrétien and Martin were ready to work together, a fact that was lost when the two later became embroiled in a divisive succession battle. Second, nothing Chrétien did appeared to have had a negative impact on the Liberals' commanding lead in the polls over their opponents (see Figure 12.1). Chrétien was becoming known as the "Teflon man." Within just a few months, Chrétien was at ease in his role as prime minister, relying on his years of experience in government to make a smooth transition to power. His folksy, no-nonsense style was a welcome departure from that of his predecessors and seemed to charm the Canadian electorate. Moreover, he had silenced those who, during the past campaign, had dismissed him as "yesterday's man."

In 1995, Chrétien faced the two defining crises of his tenure as prime minister. Together, that year's budget and the Québec referendum impacted the subsequent four federal elections and reshaped Canada. For Chrétien, they were important challenges because they gave him the opportunity to position his government to consolidate its appeal on the three pillars of Canadian electoral politics — the economy, continued commitment to Canada's social safety net despite fiscal restraints, and national unity. His ability to deal with the first two but not the last defined his political legacy, and limited the length of the latest Liberal dynasty.

The focus in the 1993 election had been on the issue of unemployment and job creation, a reflection of the recession which had taken hold in the latter years of the Mulroney administration. Indeed, when the Liberals took office in 1993, unemployment had reached 11.4 percent, a level reminiscent of the early 1980s when discontent with the Trudeau administration helped to bring about the end of that dynasty. These economic

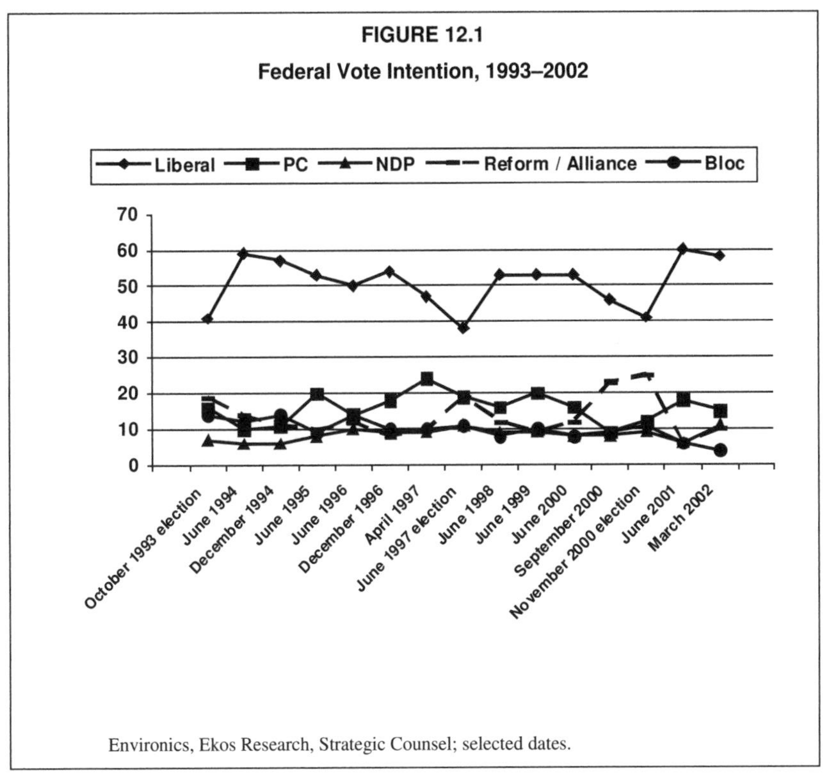

FIGURE 12.1
Federal Vote Intention, 1993–2002

Environics, Ekos Research, Strategic Counsel; selected dates.

conditions motivated the implementation of a job-creation program in the first Martin budget but fiscal realities and continued pressure from the Reform Party kept the deficit issue at the forefront.

As the 1993–94 federal deficit reached $45 billion with no signs of subsiding, Paul Martin found himself in the exact position that had made him so reluctant to accept Chrétien's offer to become finance minister in the first place. Martin did not want to be perceived as a heartless and dour fiscal conservative. He was excited by growth and innovation, not deficit reduction. When he tabled his first budget in 1994, he attempted to juggle his personal predilection for innovation, the need for fiscal restraint, and preserving the Liberal tradition of social activism. The verdict from the economic and fiscal elite was harsh and unequivocal. The next day, the *Globe and Mail* entitled its coverage "Martin Cowers Before Debt Mountain."[3] The financial markets also reacted negatively. By May, higher than predicted interest rates had derailed the budget predictions and Martin was forced to go back to the drawing board to contemplate introducing major spending cuts.

The measures introduced in the 1995 federal budget were of historic severity. They involved dramatic cuts in government spending, reduction in the size of several departments, and, most controversially, a drastic reduction in transfer payments to provincial governments for health, welfare, and education.[4] The 1995 budget was the result of months of deeply divisive internal discussions, with Martin and his cabinet colleagues quarrelling over the size of each department's cuts. Because of its draconian nature, the 1995 budget was judged a success. It re-established Canada's fiscal credibility on the world stage and was the first step toward the elimination of the deficit and subsequent budget surpluses. As Martin explained:

> If I didn't demonstrate unequivocally how we were taking hold, that budget would have failed. And that budget, in my opinion, was the last chance Canada had, or we would have become Argentina Light — meaning not as bad as Argentina but damned near. Our credibility in the world was so low that the markets were ready to absolutely kill us and drive interest rates through the roof ... so we had to do it. But I've got to tell you, that was not an easy decision.[5]

The fiscal decisions Jean Chrétien and Paul Martin took in the 1995 federal budget radically changed the nature and dynamic of the relationships between Ottawa, Canadians, and the provincial governments. That budget demonstrated that the Chrétien government was serious about fiscal responsibility and showed the international community that Liberals were ready to take hard spending decisions to restore financial order in Canada. But it strained federal–provincial relations as Ottawa downloaded the financing of the social safety net and local services onto the provinces. At the same time, it reduced Ottawa's capacity to dictate how provincial governments delivered some of those social services — a new leverage that both Alberta and Quebec would use in later years to pursue their own directions in the area of social policy. Politically, it undercut the electoral strategy of Reform, which had continued to charge that the Liberals were unwilling to make hard economic decisions.

The other crucial event of 1995 almost broke up the country. On September 11, 1995, Quebec premier Jacques Parizeau announced that, in a referendum to be held on October 30, Quebecers would be asked the following question:

> Do you agree that Quebec should become sovereign, after having made a formal offer to Canada for a new Economic and Political Partnership, within the scope of the Bill respecting the Future of Quebec and of the agreement signed on June 12, 1995?

Full of ambiguity, and reminiscent of the 1980 question asking for a mandate to negotiate sovereignty association (see Chapter 9, note 7), the move by the sovereignist Parti Québécois government initially appeared quixotic, in that few observers gave the referendum much chance of passing. Federalists were emboldened by the apparent disarray of the YES side. Parizeau, as Quebec premier, and Lucien Bouchard, as Leader of the Official Opposition in Ottawa, feuded over referendum strategy and control of the sovereigntist movement, epitomizing the great divide in the movement going back to the 1960s. Parizeau favoured a hard line, in the tradition of Pierre Bourgault,[6] while Bouchard preferred the more pragmatic approach followed by René Lévesque. This lack of cohesion on the YES side allowed federalists to gain early momentum.

Reluctantly accepting that he was seen as a liability for those opposing the referendum in Quebec, Chrétien refused to comment on the question or the campaign, and abdicated the leadership of the NO campaign to Quebec Liberal leader Daniel Johnson. While Chrétien refused to make predictions, his chief of staff and long-time friend and adviser Eddie Goldenberg expected to match if not surpass the 1980 results.[7] But with three weeks left in the referendum campaign, the sovereigntists gained momentum by naming Lucien Bouchard as negotiator-in-chief. This meant that if the YES side won the referendum, it would be Bouchard, not the abrasive and unpopular Parizeau, who would negotiate with the federal government. Now, instead of squaring off with Chrétien in the House of Commons, Bouchard was on the campaign trail, where his effective rhetoric and personal charisma reignited the sovereigntist message. Bouchard was also effective at mocking Ottawa and demonizing Chrétien. Despite his street-fighter reputation, Chrétien did not answer in kind. As days passed, the NO side seemed unable to agree on a common strategy to respond to the newly reenergized YES campaign.

By October 15, with only 15 days left until the vote, the NO side realized it had to act. Plans were made to hold a massive pro-Canada rally in Montreal; the idea was to respond to the growing sense that the NO side had to start injecting some emotion into their defence of Canada and move away from the purely economic rhetoric they had been using. As in 1980, federalists initially believed they could convince Quebecers to stay in Canada by pointing out the dire economic consequences of separation. But in 1995, in the aftermath of Martin's large federal budget cuts and drastically reduced government spending, the economic argument sounded less convincing, and was no match for Bouchard's more emotional rhetoric. Bouchard crisscrossed the province and encouraged Quebecers to come together; he told them that "a YES vote will lead to unity of all Quebecers. We will all be sovereigntists, so much so that people will no longer refer to us as sovereigntists but simply as Quebecers."[8]

The pro-Canada rally also addressed the growing unease of Liberal MPs and cabinet ministers from outside Quebec who were frustrated by the fact that they were forced to the sidelines as their country was moving closer to breaking up. The rally was a massive organizational success for the NO side. Over 100,000 people from all over the country flocked to Montreal to "save Canada." While the impact of the rally on the final results remains uncertain, it finally galvanized Chrétien to fight back. He took control of the campaign strategy, alongside his trusted advisers Jean Pelletier, John Rae, and Eddie Goldenberg.[9] They came to the conclusion that the prime minister would have to convey a message of change to Quebecers.

For several years, former premier Johnson had tried to convince Chrétien to open the door to a significant transfer of powers to Quebec and even to a constitutional amendment recognizing Quebec as a distinct society. The man responsible — or blamed — for the repatriation of the Canadian Constitution, the man who despised and dismissed Quebec sovereigntists and their never-ending demands, the man who acted as Trudeau's constitutional "hatchet man," went on the air on October 25 and promised to recognize Quebec as a distinct society if Quebecers decided to stay in Canada. In his television address, he stressed the consequences of breaking up the country and promised change. Then he retreated to Sussex Drive and awaited the verdict of his fellow Quebecers.

An astonishing 93.5 percent of eligible voters participated in the 1995 Quebec Referendum. The result was extremely close — 50.6 percent opposed and 49.4 in favour — with only about 54,000 votes separating the two sides.[10] Chrétien's inconsistent handling of the NO campaign reaffirmed the perception that he was a spent force in his native province. But the always defiant and proud Chrétien was unwilling to accept this judgment about himself. Some of his subsequent actions in Québec would later lead to the biggest scandal of his administration, a scandal that plagued his beleaguered successor, eventually led to the defeat of his government, and jeopardized future Liberal electoral support. But, in the aftermath of the referendum, Chrétien moved quickly. As Jean Pelletier said later, "Chrétien is a practical man, not an ideologue. If a formula no longer answers the need of the day, he looks for something else."[11]

Chrétien announced federal recognition of Quebec as a distinct society and a proposal for Ottawa to shift control of labour-market training to the provinces. He then recruited two new "star" candidates — Stéphane Dion and Pierre Pettigrew — to run in forthcoming by-elections in Quebec, appointing both to his cabinet — Dion as minister of intergovernmental affairs and Pettigrew as minister for international co-operation. Justice Minister Allan Rock was commissioned to ask the Supreme Court of Canada to rule on the legality of a province's right to secede from Canada. Following this flurry of activity, Chrétien gradually turned his attention to the arena where he felt more comfortable. Thus repositioned, he began to prepare for the next federal election, which took place a few months ahead of schedule, in June 1997.

The 1997 Election

The regional arithmetic appeared to favour the Liberals. They retained a strong lead in Ontario, which had provided the basis of their majority in 1993. Since then, the Reform Party had failed to make any significant inroads in that province and the Progressive Conservatives continued to languish.[12] Unlike the other parties, whose support was regionally concentrated, the Liberals had reasonable expectations of picking up seats in all regions. In Quebec, the Bloc would win a large number of seats, perhaps even the majority in the province. However, their appeal was limited to the sovereigntist forces, leaving Quebec federalists with the Liberals as the only option to safeguard their interests. In Western Canada, Reform had become the predominant party, even in British Columbia, but once again the Liberals could count on some bastions of support, particularly in the major cities. The NDP, with its new leader, Alexa McDonough, had established a foothold in the Atlantic provinces. In each of these areas, however, the Liberals successfully positioned themselves as the only party that had a real chance of articulating and meeting national interests.[13]

Because the election had been called early, the timing was the first issue that Chrétien would have to face when addressing the media. However, the simple question of why it was being held ahead of schedule seemed to surprise him when he faced journalists outside Rideau Hall. Moreover, he was unable to articulate a substantive vision or specific policies as reasons for needing a mandate from the electorate. To add to Chrétien's difficulties, he had inadvertently picked a time when flooding from the Red River in Manitoba raised additional questions about timing.[14] Critics painted him as an insensitive prime minister, smugly forcing the country to go to the polls simply because he thought he could win.

But there were good reasons why Chrétien thought he could win. His reasoning related to the Liberal record on the mix of issues that was likely to dominate the election campaign. As Table 12.1 indicates, a strong plurality of Canadian voters (47.7 percent) was mainly concerned with economic issues, including unemployment and the deficit. Unemployment, while still high, was finally down to single digits again (see Figure 12.5). Budget-cutting had pre-empted the opposition attacks on the deficit situation. The Liberals were also convinced that they were more credible than their opponents on social issues such as health care — the most important issue for 9.7 percent of Canadians (see Table 12.1). Finally, despite his shaky performance in the 1995 referendum, Chrétien thought that Canadians, even if by default, would still be more likely to trust him to deal with national unity (chosen by 9.5 percent as the most important issue facing the country). All of the building blocks of electoral supremacy appeared to be in place.

Jean-Marc Carisse, photographer.

Jean Chrétien campaigning in Peterborough, Ontario, 1997 election.

TABLE 12.1

Most Important Issues in the 1997 and 2000 Elections

	1997	2000
Economic Issues		
Unemployment	29	6
Debt / deficit	7	5
Taxes	6	12
General economic concerns	4	4
Other economic	2	1
National Unity		
National unity (all)	10	2
Social Welfare		
Social programs	15	2
Health care	10	45
Education	3	9
Pensions	1	1
Other social	2	3
Other Issues		
Integrity / trust	3	5
Need for change	1	3
All other	8	4
	N=3949	N=3651

Canadian Election Studies, 1997, 2000

Furthermore, the campaign ability of the opposition parties appeared to pose little threat to Liberal dominance. The Bloc Québécois endured a disastrous campaign kick-off, involving a number of mishaps by newly chosen Bloc leader Gilles Duceppe. The Bloc appeared to be suffering from a post-referendum letdown, with a campaign platform less focused than usual on sovereignty, and the decampment of their popular leader Lucien Bouchard to provincial politics.[15] The NDP and PC campaigns began more hopefully. The NDP attacked Chrétien for his cutbacks on unemployment insurance payments, and in so doing, appealed to a newly emerging base in Atlantic Canada, which had been reinforced by the choice of its new leader, Alexa McDonough, from Nova Scotia. Progressive Conservatives, now led by Jean Charest, used the title of the new Liberal Red Book's *Securing **O**ur **F**uture **T**ogether* to criticize the Liberals as being **SOFT** on crime, jobs, and on leadership. However, with little chance of winning, these latter two campaigns had difficulty securing adequate media coverage.

Preston Manning and the Reform Party had, by far, the most dynamic and best-orchestrated start of the campaign. In fact, the Reform campaign had effectively begun a year earlier with the release of their *Fresh*

FIGURE 12.2

Party and Leader Thermometer Scale Ratings, 1997

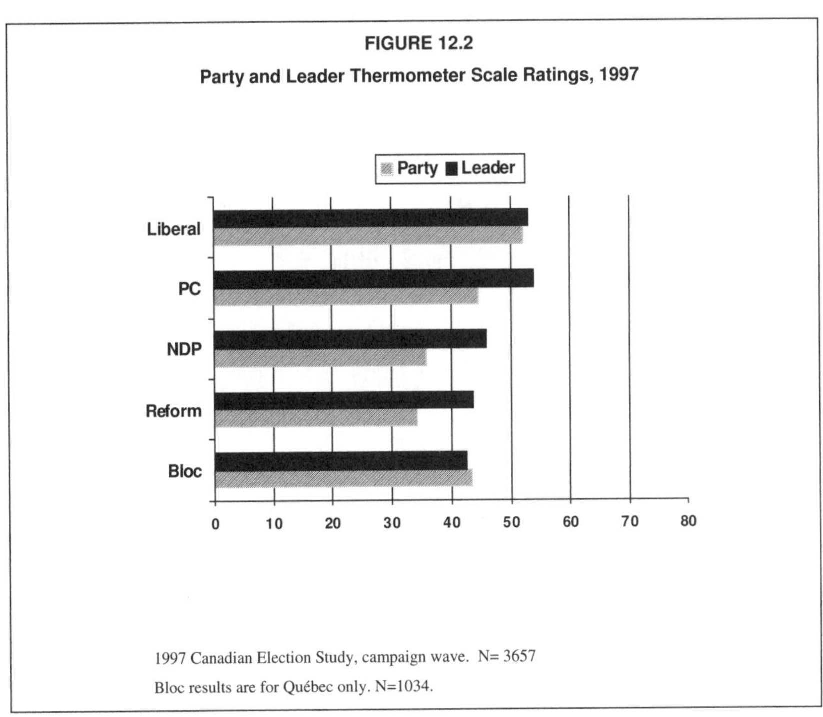

1997 Canadian Election Study, campaign wave. N= 3657

Bloc results are for Québec only. N=1034.

Start election platform. The main sub themes of *Fresh Start for Canadians* related to the economy through tax cuts; social policies that reoriented spending on health, education, and pensions; criminal justice reforms; and a rebalancing of federal and provincial powers. Reform was trying to move away from being a western protest party and thus sought to address a more complete mix of national issues. Manning understood the necessity to break away from his party's focus on western alienation and to position Reform as the party best able to deal with the economic, national unity, and social welfare building blocks of Canadian electoral success.

This more comprehensive platform would be the first of many steps taken by Manning to remake his party into a lasting alternative to Liberal dominance. The decision to release the platform almost a year before the election was inspired by Ontario Conservative leader Mike Harris' similar gambit with his *Common Sense Revolution*. It was also a strategic decision to give as much time as possible to Canadians to realize that Reform policies were not as "scary" as they were often portrayed by the other parties, or by the "Eastern" media. As a result, Reform was well prepared when the early election call came and the party was ready to hit the campaign trail the day Chrétien visited the governor general. The leak of an advance copy of the Liberal platform allowed Preston Manning to stand in the Château Frontenac in Quebec City and release it, branding the Liberal platform as "Goodbye Red Book, Hello Cheque Book."[16]

The televised leaders' debates were held in Ottawa in the second week of May. With three new leaders, this was seen by the opposition parties as a real opportunity to make an impression. This was particularly true for the two parties that had done so badly in 1993. New Progressive Conservative leader Jean Charest was hoping to give credibility to his claim that the PCs still represented the only viable national alternative to the Liberals. NDP leader Alexa McDonough saw an opportunity to return the party to something closer to its 1988 strength. Unfortunately, the debate format was not conducive to any meaningful discussion, since the "free for all" format encouraged constant interruption, with the five leaders forced to talk on top of one another. Charest was seen as doing well in the debates, however.[17] In the French debate, it was the moderator rather than the debating party leaders who provided most of the drama, as she fainted at the opening of a crucial segment where Jean Chrétien was being asked whether he would accept a narrow referendum result in favour of sovereignty. The incident put an early end to the French debate and let Chrétien off the hook. It also deprived Charest of an opportunity to further capitalize on his strong performance the night before.

After the debates, the Liberal campaign went into cruise control, trying to make it to election day without major mistakes, to obtain a second consecutive majority. It was at this point that Reform strategists decided that they needed to make a move to try to attract more support and they chose to do so on the national unity issue. The infamous "Quebec ad" showed pictures of a variety of Quebec federal and provincial party leaders, federalist and separatist, accusing them of juggling with the fate of the country, and arguing that all Canadians should have a say in deciding the fate of the country and not just Quebec politicians. It provoked the intended reaction, and had an immediate and positive impact on Reform voting support. As the Canadian National Election Study demonstrates, Reform gained about seven points in the five days immediately following the ad.[18] The ad shored up support for Reform in British Columbia and led to some gains in Ontario. However, as with the post-debate gains for the Conservatives, the effect of this initiative had vanished almost entirely by election day.[19]

There are three reasons explaining Reform's inability to reap electoral gains from its late-campaign advertising surge. The media coverage attacked the ad as "anti-Quebec" and misreported the content of the ad as Preston Manning calling for an end to prime ministers only from Quebec. For instance, the day after the ad first aired, the *Globe and Mail* ran the headline "Manning Calls Rivals Unity Threat" and suggested that the ad argued that both Chrétien and Charest were described by Manning as "posing as great a threat to national unity as Quebec separatists."[20] Then, Chrétien accused Manning of attempting to divide the country rather than unify it. The NDP leader raised the alarm of a potential civil war, while Charest called Manning a bigot.[21] Manning's unwillingness to respond to those personal attacks reinforced the perception that Manning, although well-versed on the issue, was cold and "lacking in heart."[22] Third, although they had been warned about the storm the ad was likely to create, some Reformers became nervous and were put on the defensive rather than pushing through with their own version of the national unity message. Despite all the criticism, the fact that the party appeared to get improved media coverage in the aftermath of the event, and the fact that it did not appear to adversely affect their vote totals, led all of the parties to re-evaluate the effectiveness of negative advertising.[23]

On June 2, 1997, only 67 percent of Canadians who were registered to vote went to the polls, a continuation of the turnout decline that began in 1993. The Liberals managed to win a reduced majority of the seats (155) with only 38 percent of the vote. While both Reform and the PCs garnered identical vote share at 19 percent, the seat result for these two bitter rivals was quite different. Reform elected 60 members and formed the Official Opposition, while the Progressive Conservatives barely managed to win one-third that many seats. Little else appeared to have changed. However, the election had exposed cracks in the façade of Liberal dominance. Looking at Table 12.2, we can see that while Liberal support dropped only modestly (down by 3 percentage points), the party lost seats in 6 provinces (notably 11 seats in Nova Scotia and 6 seats in flooded Manitoba) while making gains only in Ontario (+3) and Quebec (+7). Despite their claims to be the only party able to represent national interests, the Chrétien Liberals increasingly looked like the party of Central Canada, managing to remain in power only because of a divided opposition.

In 1997, Reform and the PCs both saw their electoral support increase by an identical three percentage points, but they remained engaged in a war of attrition to the Liberals' electoral benefit. A look at the composition of the electorate gives further evidence to the pattern of support emerging

University of Calgary Archives.

Preston Manning campaigning in London, Ontario, 1997 election.

in the post-1993 era. The Liberals managed to retain a strong contingent of supporters who appeared to have very little interest in switching to other parties. The Bloc was in a similar situation but was susceptible to some erosion in support favouring the PCs: Conservative strategists would subsequently understand and try to exploit this weakness. The NDP made a comeback, more than doubling their seat total, finishing particularly strongly in Atlantic Canada. The Reform Party continued to pick up support from both former Liberal and PC voters, but not in sufficient numbers to make the breakthrough they hoped for in Central Canada. As a result, the Liberals, although having slipped to a position perilously close to minority, survived the requisite "test" of their 1993 victory.

Another factor explaining the Liberals' re-election was the resilient popularity of Jean Chrétien. Despite shortcomings such as his mishandling of the 1995 Quebec referendum and his blatantly opportunistic election call, the prime minister was a generally popular figure, more popular than McDonough, Manning, and Duceppe, and almost as popular as the charismatic Jean Charest. As Figure 12.2 indicates, Chrétien continued to register comparatively high ratings, although he had declined somewhat from the levels registered in 1993. Canadians felt comfortable with his low-key style of government and his folksy charm. Both Alexa McDonough and Preston Manning were more popular than their respective parties. Bloc leader Gilles Duceppe, despite a difficult election campaign, was as popular as his party in his home province. More importantly, the Bloc with its new leader had survived a crucial test of its 1993 performance and had demonstrated that it would remain a potent electoral force in Quebec.

The vote dynamics in the 1997 election also shed some light on the lasting impact of the electoral cataclysm of 1993 and what the future held for the respective political parties. Looking at party identification (see Figure 12.4), we see that voters remained ambivalent about the state of party politics at the federal level. Despite being re-elected, the Liberals saw a slight decline in party identifiers from the 1993 election (–3 percent). While managing to increase their vote share, the PCs actually lost voters identifying with their party (down 6 percent from their disastrous 1993 showing), and in so doing, raised doubts about their ability to rebuild their electoral competitiveness. Both the NDP (down 1 percent) and the Bloc (up 2 percent) remained stagnant, while a substantial proportion of Canadian voters continued to simply not identify with any party (28 percent). For its part, the Reform Party (up 2 percent)

TABLE 12.2

Results of the 1997 and 2000 Federal Elections, by Province

		Liberal		Reform / Alliance		NDP		PC		Bloc	
		1997	2000	1997	2000	1997	2000	1997	2000	1997	2000
Newfoundland	votes (%)	38	45	3	4	22	13	37	35	-	-
	seats (#)	4	5	-	-	-	-	3	2	-	-
Prince Edward Island	votes (%)	45	47	1	5	15	9	38	38	-	-
	seats (#)	4	4	-	-	-	-	-	-	-	-
Nova Scotia	votes (%)	28	37	10	10	30	24	31	29	-	-
	seats (#)	-	4	-	-	6	3	5	4	-	-
New Brunswick	votes (%)	33	42	13	16	18	12	35	31	-	-
	seats (#)	3	6	-	-	2	1	5	3	-	-
Quebec	votes (%)	37	44	-	6	2	2	22	6	38	40
	seats (#)	26	36	-	-	-	-	5	1	44	38

Ontario	votes (%)	50	52	19	24	11	.8	19	14	-	-
	seats (#)	101	100	-	2	-	1	1	-	-	-
Manitoba	votes (%)	34	33	24	30	23	21	18	15	-	-
	seats (#)	6	5	3	4	4	4	1	1	-	-
Saskatchewan	votes (%)	25	21	36	48	31	26	8	5	-	-
	seats (#)	1	2	8	10	5	2	-	-	-	-
Alberta	votes (%)	24	21	55	59	6	5	14	14	-	-
	seats (#)	2	2	24	23	-	0	-	1	-	-
British Columbia	votes (%)	29	28	43	49	18	11	6	7	-	-
	seats (#)	6	5	25	27	3	2	-	-	-	-
Yukon / NWT / Nunuvut	votes (%)	35	46	17	18	16	27	24	9	-	-
	seats (#)	2	3	-	-	1	-	-	-	-	-
TOTAL CANADA	votes (%)	38	41	19	26	11	9	19	12	11	11
	seats (#)	155	172	60	66	21	13	20	12	44	38

One Independent candidate was elected in Ontario in 1997.

was unable to reap the benefits of the PC decline in terms of winning new adherents. Preston Manning understood that his party's inability to attract converts to the Reform Party would limit his chances to ever form a government. Although now ensconced in the role of Leader of the Official Opposition, the results left him pondering his next move.

Thus, every party had reasons to celebrate in 1997, but each also had to confront major problems. The Liberals were returned to power, but for optimistic Liberal strategists and supporters the election outcome fell far short of expectations on two fronts. First, the total Liberal vote was just 38 percent — 3 percentage points below its 1993 performance. In the 16 Canadian federal elections since 1949, the party in power lost votes 11 times and the median loss was 3 percentage points, which is exactly what the Liberals lost in 1997. However, the seats they did win were concentrated to an uncomfortable extent in the province of Ontario.[24] The Liberals won because they could count on a larger core of supporters and because their leader remained relatively popular. But as Canadian

FIGURE 12.3

Electoral Turnover, 1993–1997

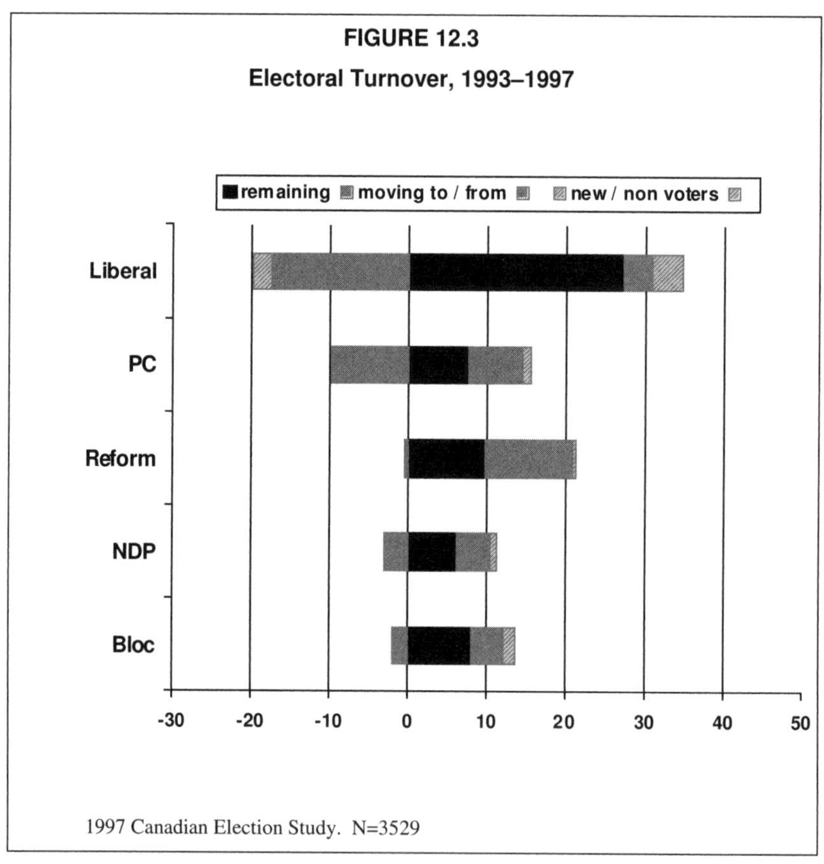

1997 Canadian Election Study. N=3529

history has repeatedly shown, voter loyalty and leader popularity can be ephemeral factors that do not always equate to electoral longevity.

While all the opposition parties recognized that there were problems ahead for them in mounting a future challenge to the Chrétien dynasty, disappointment in the Reform Party was felt most keenly. They had hoped that this would be the occasion where they could transform themselves into a real national alternative government. Within a decade, Manning and his group of Reformers had managed to form the Official Opposition in Ottawa. Despite that achievement, it was Reform's inability to establish a vital Ontario foothold that was the lesson of 1997, leading analysts to speculate about a period of Liberal dominance for years to come.[25] It was also this failure that would dominate the aftermath of the 1997 election.

Building a United Alternative to the Liberals

Preston Manning did not spend any time rejoicing in his becoming Leader of the Opposition. As he interpreted the situation, the 1997 election and his party's inability to make a breakthrough in Ontario was a major setback. More than ever, the possibility of him or any Reformer becoming prime minister was contingent upon fighting with a united front against the Liberals in the next election. The idea of forming a "United Alternative" involved broadening the appeal of Reform to include other conservative forces, and eventually the Progressive Conservative Party as a whole. Reform as a "political brand" had too many negative connotations and was too identified with the West to be generally accepted in other regions. Preston Manning was not interested in remaining the voice of western dissent; he wanted to establish a political entity that could stand as a credible alternative for those Canadians who did not feel represented by the Liberal Party.

When Manning first proposed to create a "united alternative," he was rebuffed by federal PCs and dismissed by much of the national media. For the Tories, it was Manning's Reformers who had split the political right in the first place.[26] By the fall of 1998, the PCs had embarked on their internal process of choosing another new leader to replace Jean Charest, who had left to lead the Quebec provincial Liberals. As a high-profile francophone federalist politician, Charest had been under enormous pressure to move to Quebec politics. The irony of Charest suddenly calling himself a Liberal when he had just fought a federal election against the Liberals was not lost on many. For proponents of the United Alternative (UA), this was a clear signal that a real alternative to the Liberals and PCs needed to be formed.

The Tory solution to fighting the Liberals and fending off Manning and the UA was to hold a leadership contest with a vote of all PC members directly for the leader. Former PC prime minister Joe Clark was persuaded to seek the leadership of his party once again. The voting procedure provided an opportunity for "outsiders" who had an ability to enroll supporters as party members to mount a serious leadership bid.[27] Such an outsider was David Orchard, who had come to some prominence in the mid-1980s when he founded the Citizens Concerned About Free Trade (CCAFT), a non-partisan citizens organization protesting the effects on Canadian sovereignty of the free trade agreements with the United States (FTA and later NAFTA). Orchard was vocal in his opposition to free trade in general and to Brian Mulroney in particular, making him appear to be an unlikely PC leadership candidate. However, he had recruited many new PC members, and on the first ballot, he placed third, less than 1,000 votes behind party stalwart Hugh Segal (see Table 12.3). Subsequently, Segal

TABLE 12.3

Party Leadership Conventions

1995–2000

DATE	PARTY	LOCATION	WINNER	# CANDIDATES*	# BALLOTS	RUNNER-UP**
1995 04 29	PC	Hull	Jean Charest	1	-	-
1995 10 14	NDP	Ottawa	Alexa McDonough	3	1	Svend Robinson[1]
1998 10 24	PC	X	Joe Clark	5	2	David Orchard
2000 07 07	Alliance	Ottawa	Stockwell Day	5	2	Preston Manning

* On first ballot

** On final ballot

X vote of party members conducted at multiple polling stations

[1] Robinson finished first on the first ballot, but withdrew

and other candidates withdrew from the race, and Clark was able to convincingly defeat Orchard on the second ballot.

Preston Manning pressed on with his plans for the United Alternative, gathering support from many provincial PCs, especially from Ontario and Alberta. For the next two years, Reformers were asked to participate in a series of democratic steps in order to build a new political party. The objective was to move beyond the successes of the Reform movement and to create a political vehicle where provincial Conservatives, some provincial Liberals such as those from British Columbia, federal Conservatives, Reformers, "soft" Quebec nationalists, and disenchanted Quebec federalists wanting constitutional change, could unite and stand as a credible alternative to federal Liberals. The first UA convention was held in February 1999. At that convention, the foundational principles for the new political party were introduced and a proposed plan of action was adopted to write a party constitution and platform.

Then Reform Party members had to accept the creation of a new political entity. This was achieved through a party-wide referendum held via a mail-in ballot. On June 10, 1999, 60.5 percent of the participating Reform members (49.5 percent of all card-carrying members) said YES to continue with the UA process. The resulting Founding United Alternative convention completed the task of developing the constitution, principles, and platform for a broader and bigger political vehicle — to be called the Canadian Alliance. A final Reform referendum determined that Reform members agreed to join the Canadian Alliance and the Reform Party then ceased to exist. The final task was to choose a leader for the newly formed Alliance.

On March 27, 2000, Preston Manning resigned as Leader of the Official Opposition to contest the leadership of the Canadian Alliance. However, the calibre of candidates who decided to contest the Canadian Alliance leadership with Manning was disappointing. Party strategists had hoped for the entry of heavyweights such as provincial premiers Ralph Klein of Alberta and Mike Harris of Ontario. The winner of such a high-profile contest would have emerged as a serious candidate to challenge Prime Minister Chrétien. Instead, the new party had to settle for a leadership race between Manning, Alberta finance minister Stockwell Day, and backroom Ontario organizer Tom Long.

Once again a one-member, one-vote leadership selection process had an impact on a party's leadership race. Stockwell Day and his supporters crafted an American-style campaign, recruiting thousands of new members from pro-life, pro-gun lobby, and religious conservative groups. Ignoring the long-term consequences of aligning himself to such politically marginal groups, Day recruited as many people as possible, regardless of what this might mean for the fortunes of the new political party or for the upcoming election campaign.

In contrast, the Manning strategy rested on his desire to use the leadership race as a launch pad for what he considered to be the most important campaign for the Canadian Alliance — the next federal election. Some of his adversaries, however, saw Manning as a liability in national electoral politics, in part because of his strong identity with western populism and his inability to speak French. But looking ahead to a future electoral contest, Manning refrained from criticizing his leadership opponents and concentrated instead on attacking the Liberals. Manning's attempt to balance the short-term needs of his leadership campaign with his perception of the long-term viability of the Canadian Alliance in the end cost him the leadership of the political movement that he had created. To the shock of many, Stockwell Day defeated Preston Manning on the second ballot and became the new leader of the Canadian Alliance. With that outcome, the plan to evolve from a protest party to a mainstream national party had entered a new phase of political uncertainty.

The Liberals Prepare for an Election

When Jean Chrétien approached his closest campaign advisers about calling another "premature" election in 2000, he was met with a mixture of shrugs and looks of disbelief. As Liberal Party pollster and key strategist Michael Marzolini noted, "Courageous decisions are usually avoided in politics. Politicians are by nature risk-averse. They don't tempt fate, and they rarely play fast and loose with public opinion."[28] Hence, conventional wisdom suggested that Chrétien would complete his full term, then maybe step down and hand over the reins of power to Paul Martin, especially if the initial honeymoon enjoyed by Stockwell Day as a new political figure leading a united opposition party did not subside.

Many advised the prime minister that it was better to wait for Day to start making mistakes. But Chrétien's keen political instincts were telling him otherwise, and he became convinced that the new leader and party were vulnerable. He believed he had a good record to present to the electorate. While his conservative adversaries had spent the previous years trying to settle their divisions, Chrétien had made progress on two important policy fronts — national unity and the economy — and he was confident that his achievements would be sufficient to earn him a third consecutive majority.

On the national unity front, Chrétien was determined to reassert federal relevance in Quebec and control over the future of the country. While he had bowed to pressure following the 1995 Quebec referendum and granted Quebec formal recognition as a distinct society, and suggested a veto over constitutional change on matters affecting the province, Chrétien went back to his hardline approach after his re-election in 1997. As with most constitutional issues, the story behind what became known as the *Clarity Act* is detailed, complex, and involved many actors. The wording of the 1995 referendum question, positing as it did the prospect of a unilateral declaration of independence by the province if negotiations with the federal government failed, precipitated a reference to the Supreme Court of Canada. The Supreme Court's decision, as well as some provisions contained in a private member's bill introduced by then Reform MP Stephen Harper in 1996, produced the *Clarity Act*, which was passed by the Commons on March 15, 2000.

The *Clarity Act* built on the constitutional directions outlined in the Supreme Court decision and introduced specific provisions under which Ottawa would regard as legitimate a vote for secession by one of the provinces. Accordingly, the House of Commons was given the right to decide whether a proposed referendum question is clear enough and what constitutes a clear majority. The House of Commons was also given the power to supersede a referendum if it violated any tenets of the *Clarity Act*.[29] Despite the outcry from the Quebec national assembly, the Bloc Québécois, and also some federalists who decried the act as an attack on Quebec's right to self-determination, Chrétien maintained that the act was a necessary federalist show of strength in the aftermath of the 1995 referendum. It also had the political advantage of further dividing conservative opposition forces, with PC leader Joe Clark opposing it, and Manning and subsequently Day supporting it.

Chrétien took other steps to reaffirm Ottawa's presence in his home province. He believed that one of the reasons Quebecers had almost decided to separate from Canada was because Ottawa had abdicated its role in promoting the benefits of federalism in the province. To counter what he believed to be separatist propaganda, Chrétien created the Communications Coordination Service Branch (CCSB) within the Public Works Department, and gave it a mandate to oversee a sponsorship and advertising campaign designed to boost support for federalism. This seemingly innocuous program would eventually lead to the electoral downfall of the federal Liberals and would in the process also tarnish Chrétien's legacy.

Ironically, it was during the same inter-election period that the Liberals escaped from another potential scandal, when the Human Resources Development department was charged with giving away a billion dollars worth of grants with little oversight and auditing.

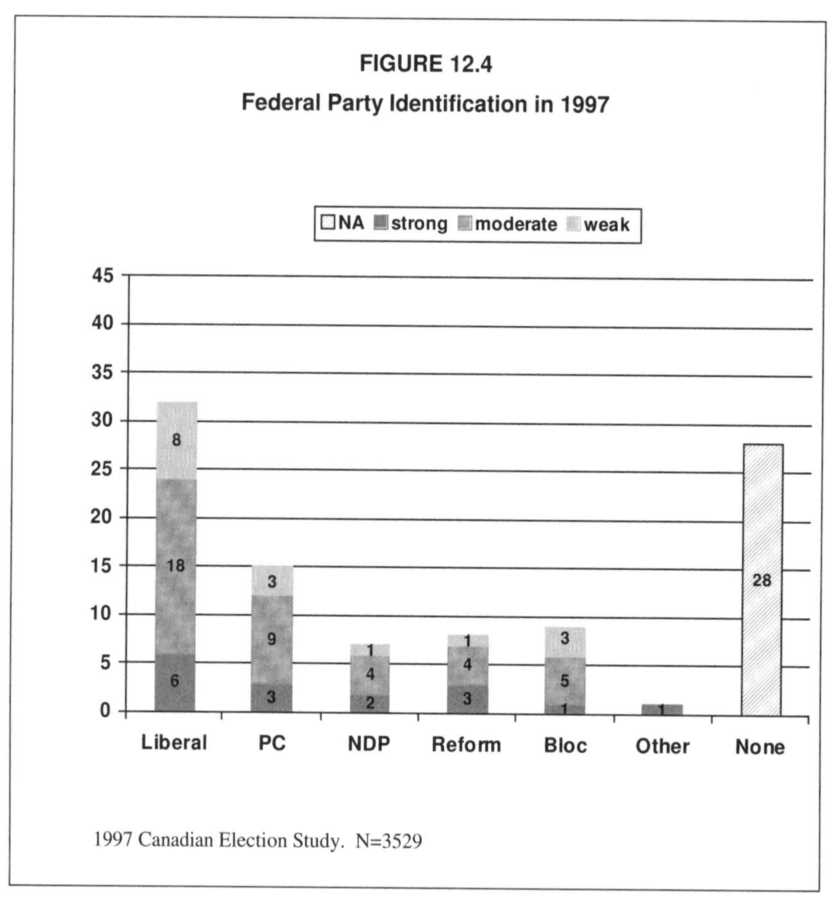

1997 Canadian Election Study. N=3529

Charges by the auditor general of mismanagement were brushed aside by Chrétien but the subject continued in the news for a long period of time. While the HRDC scandal was an example of departmental mismanagement, what later became known as the "Sponsorship Scandal" was different because it also would later tarnish Paul Martin's reputation as a prudent administrator of the country's finances and raise questions about the Liberal record on national unity (see Chapter 13).

The state of the Canadian economy was another reason why Chrétien was eager to go to the polls. The main source of his optimism rested on the steady decline in unemployment from over 11 percent in 1993 to 6.8 percent in 2000. Economic growth was also robust, moving from a sluggish 2.3 percent growth in 1993 to four very strong consecutive years of growth of 4 to 5 percent per year from 1997 to 2000.[30] Inflation remained low at just 2.7 percent.

The healthy economy translated into additional fiscal benefits for the Liberal government. When first elected in 1993, Chrétien had inherited a federal deficit of $42 billion and, as we saw previously, he and Paul Martin were forced to take drastic budget decisions to turn government finances around. Within just four years the federal government recorded

FIGURE 12.5
Main Economic Indicators, 1996–2009

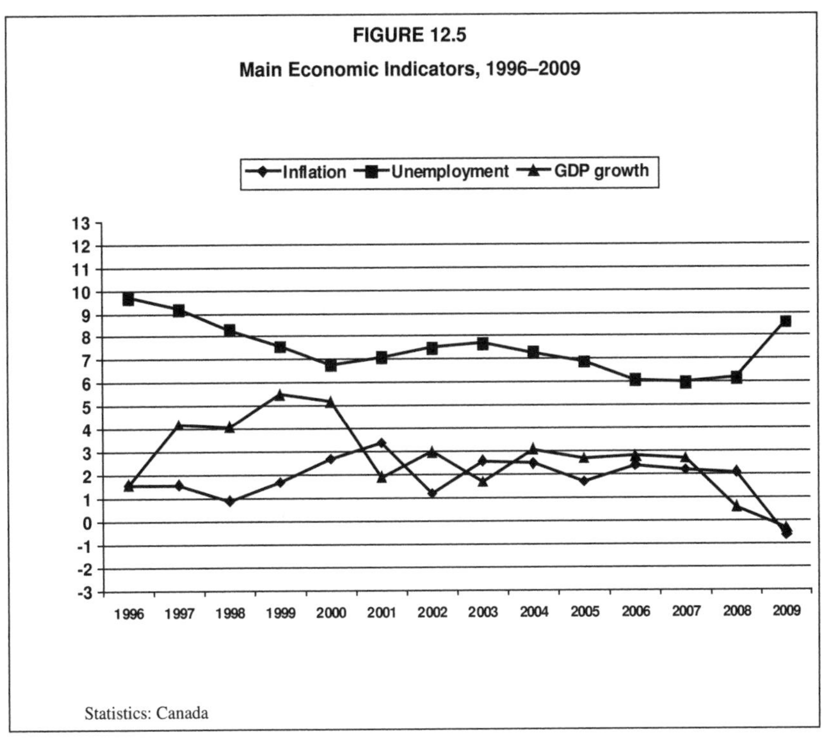

Statistics: Canada

its first budget surplus in 28 years. This allowed Martin to announce positive fiscal news prior to the election. For the first time in decades, the federal government paid down debt by using the $3.5-billion surplus. The budgetary surplus also meant that the net public debt fell in absolute terms for the first time since 1969–70 and the resulting decline in Canada's debt-to-GDP ratio was the largest single-year decline since 1956–57.[31] As economists pointed out, the budget surplus had mainly resulted from the effect of economic growth on revenues. Of the $45.5-billion turnaround — from the $42-billion deficit to the $3.5-billion surplus — only $17 billion[32] were the result of spending cuts, while the growing economy accounted for the remainder. But regardless of how it was achieved, Chrétien and Martin could take credit for balancing the budget and turning the economy around.

Social welfare constitutes the third issue area contributing to the long-term success of any Canadian governmental dynasty. In the contemporary period, this has primarily manifested itself in concern over the state of health care, which increasingly came to dominate the public opinion environment in 2000. In fact, the 2000 election was the first time since public opinion data on this issue is available that health care was the main concern of a plurality of Canadians, displacing the usual economic issues. With 46 percent of Canadians mentioning health care as their most important issue in the federal election, it crowded out other concerns and no other single issue emerged as a close second.

The mixture of economic concerns that had been the main focus of past election campaigns were mentioned by 28 percent of Canadians, with taxes being the dominant economic concern. For the second consecutive election, concerns about national unity and other Confederation issues were negligible (2 percent) and there was no anger about the early election call or other attacks on the integrity of the Liberal government. Hence, if Chrétien was vulnerable at all in 2000 it was on his government's record in cutting transfer payments to the provinces and therefore affecting their ability to deliver social programs in general and health care services in particular. He knew that the other parties would contend that the Liberal government was eliminating the federal deficit on the backs of the provinces. To counter those attacks, Martin allocated $23.4 billion in the 2000 budget as the federal government commitment to health and early childhood development.[33] Then, Chrétien took the strategic decision to cast the debate over health care as a debate about values.

The 2000 Election

When Chrétien stood before Rideau Hall and announced that an election would be held on November 27, 2000, he faced most of the same journalists who had embarrassed him at the start of the 1997 campaign. This time, he had prepared a list of reasons explaining the need for the earliest election call by a majority government since Laurier called an early election in 1911. The reasons ranged from the need for a mandate to deal with the predicted budget surpluses to satisfying the demands of the opposition parties that had been asking for an election.[34] While some pundits found the performance lacking in credibility,[35] it was vintage Chrétien, shrugging off criticism and moving forward regardless of his detractors.

The Liberals did not waste any time attacking the policy proposals of Stockwell Day and the Canadian Alliance. They immediately launched into a forceful appeal to voters to think about their values and beliefs. The election campaign was framed as an opportunity for Canadians to choose between different visions and different values: "This election," Chrétien declared, "offers two very different visions of Canada, two crystal-clear alternatives. The nature of that choice is clear and the right time to choose is now."[36] A week later, Martin claimed that: "Never has there been an election in the history of this country where the line in the sand has been drawn as clearly as it has been between the Liberal vision and the Alliance vision."[37] Liberal strategy was to ensure that Canadians would go to the polls wondering "Does Day think like me?"[38]

The Alliance campaign itself began to unravel even before the election was called. First, there was Day's decision to jet ski to a press conference and answer questions in a wetsuit; this did demonstrate that he was young and vigorous, but it looked too much like a stunt. Then came the decision not to do scrums in the foyer of the House of Commons, but instead to summon the press gallery to a basement room in the Parliament Buildings. The practice was quickly stopped when journalists simply refused to show up to the press conferences. Later on, when Martin introduced his mini-budget in the lead-up to the election campaign, he attacked the Alliance's proposal for a flat tax. Shortly afterward, Day was distancing himself from the tax proposal, despite the fact that he had championed the idea as finance minister in Alberta, had campaigned on the issue during the leadership race, and that it was part of the Alliance's election platform.

These and other minor gaffes might have been overcome, but one that could not related to health care, the number one issue on the public agenda. On October 31, the *Globe and Mail* headlined: "Alliance Supports Two-Tier Health Care."[39] The article was based on comments made by Alliance co-chair Jason Kenney on CTV where he endorsed a European-style parallel health care system. While Kenney and the Alliance insisted that he had simply endorsed more choices for Canadians and not an alternative system, the damage was done. Liberals strategists went into high gear; they started running television commercials about the uncertainty of the Alliance's health care position. Chrétien went on to suggest that his opponents were harbouring a hidden agenda.

The Liberal leader was given more ammunition a few days later when Day was asked about his views on abortion; his decision to rely on anti-abortion activists in order to win the Alliance leadership came back to haunt him. Unable to avoid the issue and risk antagonizing his core supporters, the Alliance leader tried to deflect the query by committing himself to holding a referendum on the issue and to abide by the results. One problem with Day's pledge was that, according to the Alliance's platform, a citizen-initiated referendum could be triggered by collecting the signatures of 3 percent of voters who cast ballots in the preceding election, or about 400,000 names. Cornered, Day made matters worse and simply disavowed his party's referendum policy.[40] Chrétien pounced again, defending a woman's right to choose and raising more questions about Day. The Liberal campaign then received unexpected help from the host of *This Hour Has 22 Minutes*, Rick Mercer. The well-known satirist quickly turned the Alliance's referendum policy into a farce. Through his website, he encouraged Canadians to sign a petition to trigger a referendum to force Stockwell Day to change his name to Doris Day. Within days, more than a million signatures had been collected and Day was becoming a figure of derision.[41]

While the Liberals took the most advantage of Day's self-inflicted wounds, the other parties tried to join the fray. The NDP built its campaign around a platform entitled *Think How Much Better Canada Could Be: The NDP's Commitments to Canadians*. The centrepiece was the NDP's commitment to addressing Canadians' most important concern: health care. The NDP felt comfortable with this issue given its long history as a champion of health care. Hence, the party pledged to increase federal money for health care and to introduce additional home care and pharmacare programs.[42] It challenged Canadians to choose between tax cuts or fixing health care, and while its main attacks were directed toward the Liberals, the Alliance campaign provided unexpected fodder for the NDP and its leader Alexa McDonough. As Day stumbled, the NDP leader began to target the Alliance in the final weeks of the campaign. But as she had done in 1997, McDonough failed to control her often harsh rhetoric, thereby limiting opportunities to widen her support beyond traditional NDP voters.

The Progressive Conservative Party also had a score to settle with the Alliance. Clark's refusal to participate in the United Alternative meant that the two parties were engaged, once more, in a battle for many of the same supporters. Despite Day's campaign problems, the Alliance maintained a large advantage over the PCs in terms of financial resources, incumbent seats, and organization. PC strategists, however, believed that exploiting Canadians' lack of comfort with Day and the Alliance could offset those advantages.

Their first decision was to entitle their party platform *Change You Can Trust: The Progressive Conservative Plan for Canada's Future*. There was no subtlety there: if you wanted change, you could not trust Day and the Alliance and you had to vote for Clark and the PCs. Then the PC campaign turned to a series of highly imaginative negative ads that attacked the Liberals for the unnecessary cost of the election: "Chrétien's 101 Greatest Lies" — especially his 1993 promise to scrap the GST, and the prime minister's unethical behaviour in various government-funded projects.[43] The PC campaign's lack of funds, however, prevented them from capitalizing fully on Day's early troubles. The decision was made to hold back the advertising for the latter stages of the campaign. Accordingly, Clark took on the responsibility to undermine Day, and used the televised leaders' debates to go on the offensive.

The PC leader was the most aggressive of the five leaders, with most of his attacks in the leaders' debates directed at Day.[44] During the health care discussion, Day, against the advice of his strategists, held up a hand-crafted sign declaring NO TWO-TIER HEALTH CARE, a move that violated the debate rules. Clark did not miss a beat and asked Day if he was "trying out for the position of game-show host."[45]

While the debates were inconclusive, a fact benefiting Chrétien, who as the front-runner just hoped to survive, Clark did his best to establish his credentials as a party leader and potential prime minister.

The French debate was more uneventful. Day was largely considered the loser simply because he failed to deliver on expectations about his fluency in French that were created during the leadership campaign and the pre-writ period. The Alliance had boasted about their new leader's bilingual abilities, but Day's French was awkward at best. For his part, Bloc leader Gilles Duceppe attempted to explain the continued significance of voting for the Bloc. But concern about national unity issues was low in 2000, and relevance was the main obstacle to Bloc support. Unlike 1997, Duceppe ran a strong campaign and had grown to become an eloquent performer in debates. Nevertheless, he had difficulty escaping from the general sense that the Bloc message was getting stale.[46]

The final blow to the Day campaign came when the CBC aired a documentary on Stockwell Day's early days in Alberta politics. It recounted an event earlier in his career when Day publicly mentioned that he believed the age of the world was only 6,000 years, meaning that human beings and dinosaurs had been alive at the same time.[47] Liberal strategists could not resist the opportunity. Liberal war-room veteran Warren Kinsella appeared in front of the media with a Barney the dinosaur doll and suggested that Day had mistaken the kid's TV show *The Flintstones* for a documentary.

To the dismay of Alliance members, the man they had selected as leader only five months prior had once more become a subject of ridicule. Day's thermometer scale rating, as measured by the Canadian Election Study, declined over the course of the campaign, registering a low point of just under 40 by the end of the campaign (see Figure 12.7B).

By election day, a Liberal victory was a foregone conclusion. Not only did Chrétien win his gamble and his third consecutive majority, he managed to increase Liberal representation in Parliament. The Liberals won 17 more seats than in 1997, gaining seats in five provinces as well as the Yukon (see Table 12.2). Particularly satisfying for Chrétien was the 10-seat gain in his home province. While still trailing the Bloc in overall representation there, the Liberals' total of 36 seats was their best showing in Quebec since the Trudeau years and appeared to be a vindication for the national unity policies adopted by the prime minister following the 1997 election, including the *Clarity Act*.

The Alliance also managed to make some gains, despite a difficult campaign, picking up a couple of seats in Ontario, as well as in British Columbia and Saskatchewan. While the results could have been worse, it was far from the breakthrough that the new leadership was expecting coming into the 2000 election. The PCs reached their minimum campaign objectives — official party status, electing Clark in his Alberta constituency, and undercutting the Alliance move into Eastern Canada.[48] But with only 12 seats and fifth-party status in the House of Commons, there was little cause for PCs to rejoice.

The NDP also had very little to celebrate. With 13 seats (8 fewer than in 1997), the NDP suffered an important setback, as did the Bloc. Despite a better campaign performance, Duceppe and his party lost seats for the second consecutive election. With 38 seats, the Bloc remained barely ahead of the Liberal contingent in Quebec, and the results would mean renewed internal division about its future.

Several factors explain the Liberal victory. First, the Liberals continued to retain a large contingent of its past supporters and were able to make some gains among prior PC and NDP voters (see Figure 12.6). The Alliance was constrained by its Reform roots and did not attract enough

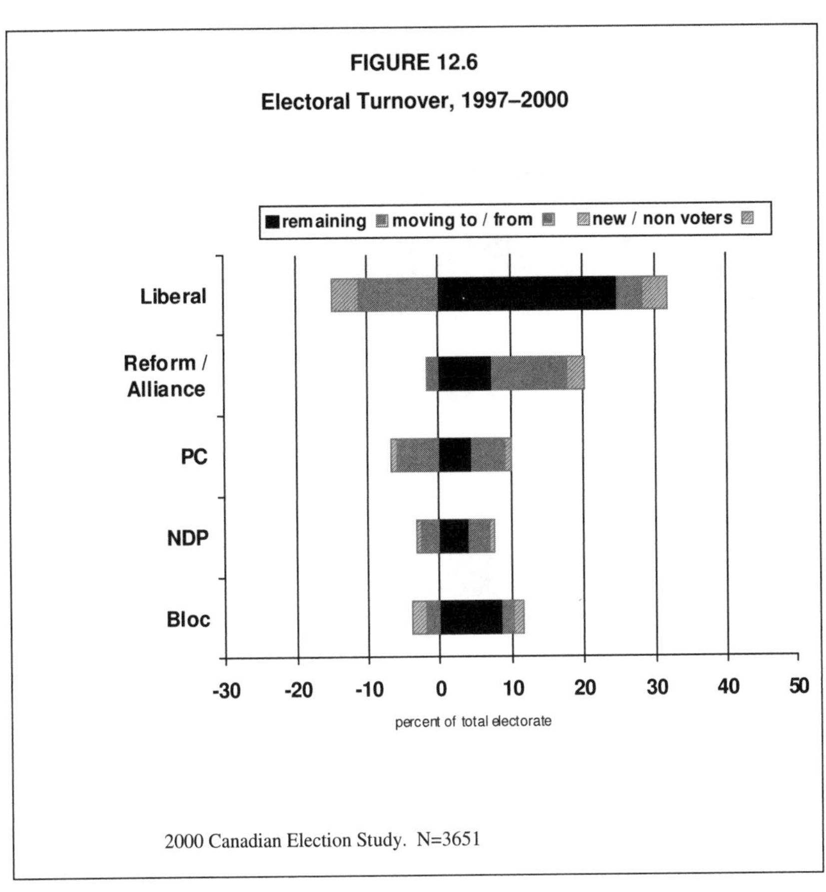

1997 PC voters to finally emerge as the real conservative alternative to the Liberals. The Bloc was also efficient in retaining the support of its loyal supporters, but little else. In contrast, the decline of the NDP was the result of erosion in support benefiting the Liberals.

Leadership also played an important role in the Liberal victory. While Chrétien's overall impression scores decreased between 1997 and 2000 (after having risen slightly in 1997), he remained more popular than his opponents — at least outside of Quebec (see Figure 12.7). A decline in

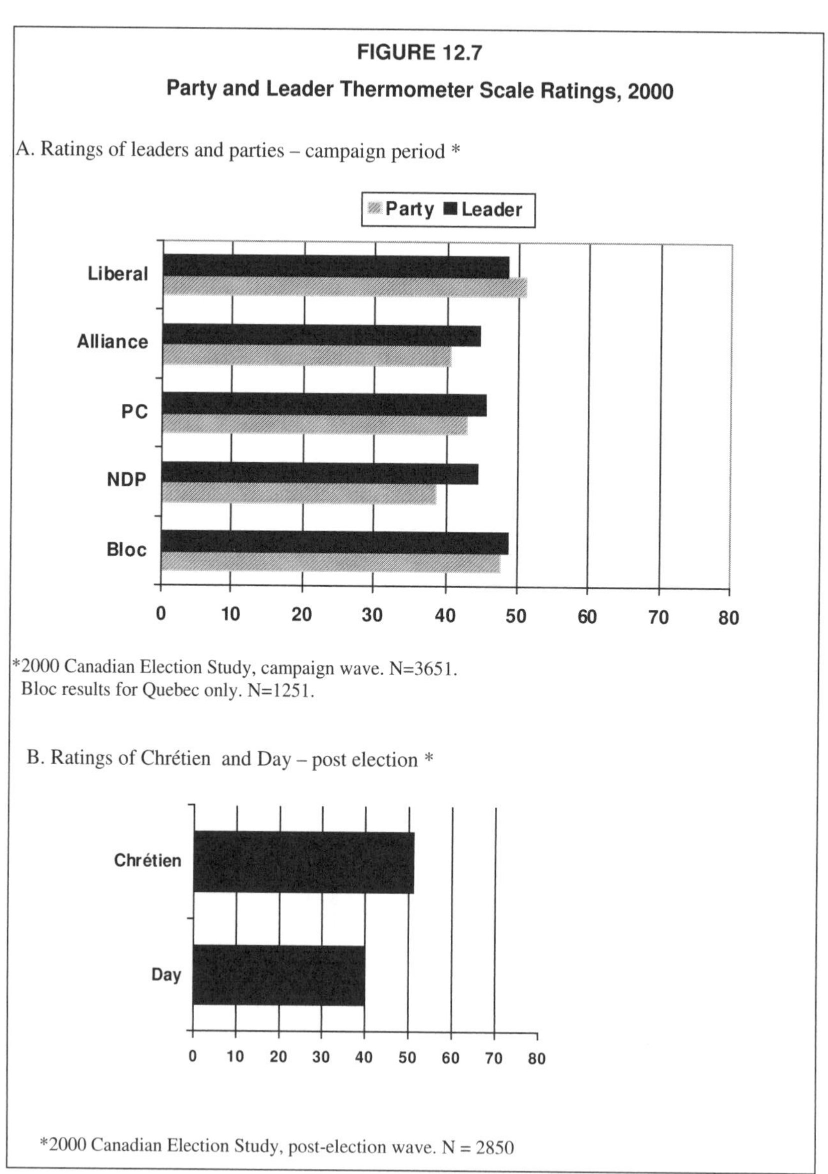

popular images of party leaders fits a common pattern in which party leaders tend to decline in public esteem from the benchmark established in their first election. [49] Likewise, Duceppe and McDonough declined in popularity between 1997 and 2000. Joe Clark fell short of his own benchmark score established in his first incarnation as PC leader back in the 1979 election (51). For his part, Day trailed behind both Chrétien and Clark, and his benchmark rating (45) was considerably lower than Manning's (51) had been. Such a poor showing meant that the Alliance would soon face another leadership crisis, one that the party itself would not survive.

The patterns of party identification in 2000 (see Figure 12.8) showed that, aside from the Liberals, there was not a lot of enthusiasm for any of the other parties. In particular, the PCs saw a further significant decline in the number of Canadians identifying with that political formation (–6 percent), another indication that the party was unlikely to survive in its current state. But the Alliance had been unable to benefit significantly from this erosion and failed to position itself as the party with which

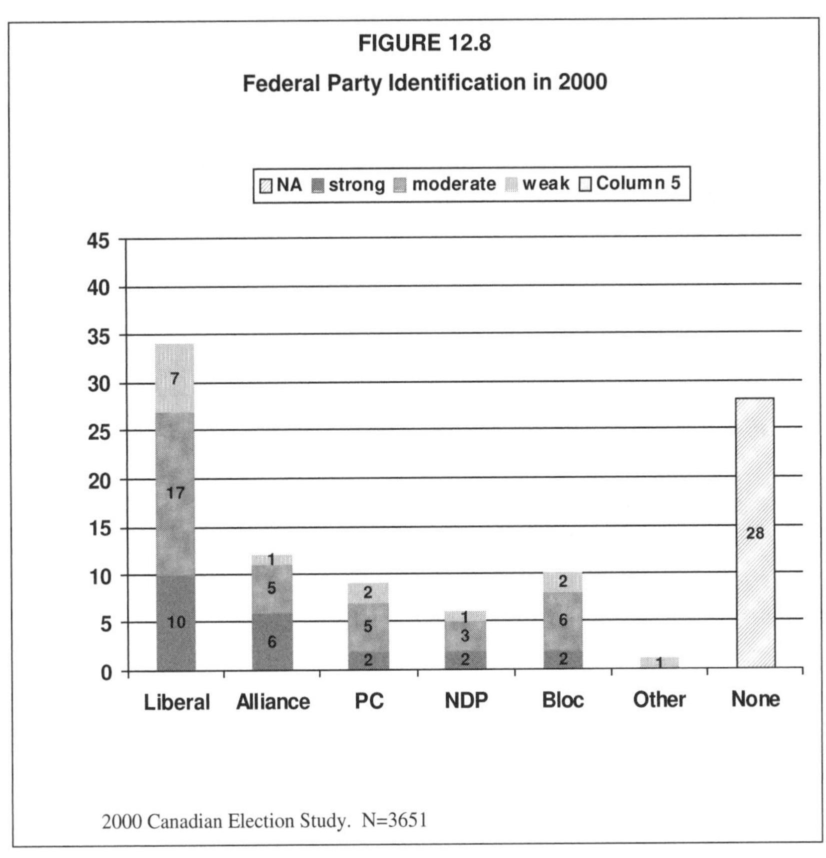

conservatives in Canada could readily identify. Specifically, only 12 percent of the electorate defined themselves as "Alliance identifiers." This was up slightly from the 8 percent garnered by Reform in the previous election but a far cry from the 38 percent of Canadians who had identified with the PCs back in 1988 (see Figure 10.3, page 378). The fact that a significant proportion of voters (28 percent) continued their disinclination to identify with *any* of the federal political parties meant, however, that there were a lot of Canadians who might be available, should a new political party catch their fancy. Such a development was shortly to occur.

The 2000 election will also be remembered for its low turnout. The 61 percent turnout was the lowest (to that date) in Canadian history by a considerable margin, but, in fact, turnout had been declining during the entire Chrétien period.[50] Although the decline in voting likely did not benefit one party over another, there were clear signs that the public was growing more dissatisfied with federal politics. A special study of the reasons for the turnout decline commissioned for Elections Canada after the 2000 election found that there were a variety of reasons for this.[51] For many young people entering the eligible electorate, politics had become a matter of marginal interest, and elections had become events which did not capture their attention. The days when "civic duty" propelled Canadians to

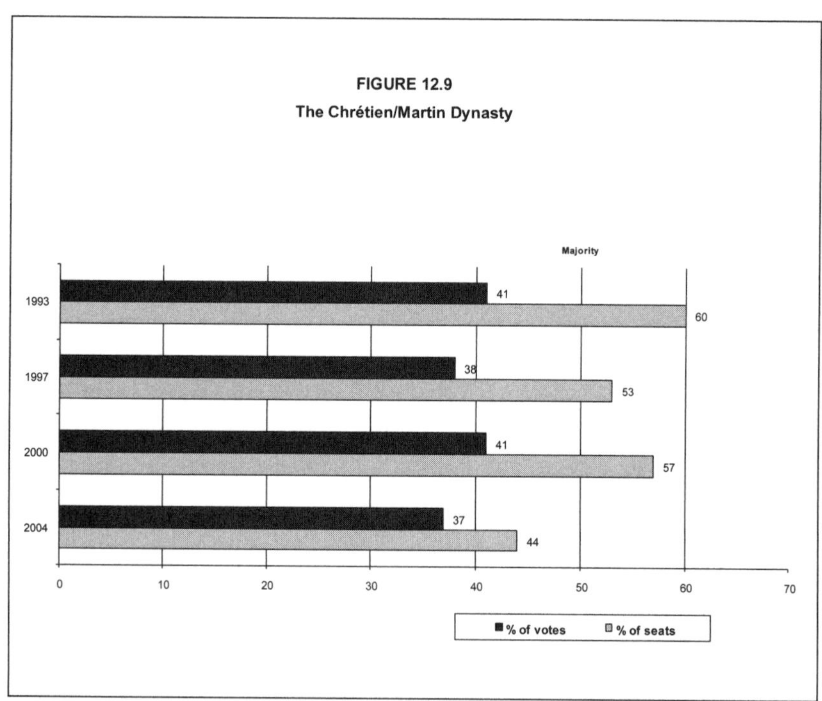

the polls — regardless of the state of party competition or the electoral choices available to them — were fading into the past. A less competitive federal political environment, now so completely dominated by the Chrétien dynasty, together with an increasing generational disengagement from politics, would combine to keep turnout low for some time.

Conclusion

In the aftermath of the election, speculation was rampant about the implications and meaning of Chrétien's apparent dynasty. In *The Anatomy of a Liberal Victory*, Blais et al. argued that under the existing electoral system, the Liberals seemed poised to maintain their dominance of Canadian electoral politics.[52] Their analysis suggested that there was no guarantee that a new party resulting from the merger of the Conservatives and the Alliance would threaten Liberal hegemony through the combined support of those who voted for either party in 2000; rather, many former Progressive Conservatives might instead be tempted to go to the Liberals.[53] Jeffrey Simpson likened the current Liberal dominance to a "Friendly Dictatorship" in the book of the same name and Stephen Clarkson, in *The Big Red Machine*, echoed this sentiment.[54] The Liberals seemed unassailable.

The forecasts of continued Liberal dominance, however, were based on an evaluation of potential external threats to their position. They neglected the looming internal dissension within the dominant party, as well as the hitherto hidden effects of some of the Liberal policies.

First, Chrétien's determination to salvage his image in his native province — and allow him to retire as a beloved figure — led to the misappropriation of public funds and a major public scandal. Then, the Liberals began to think once again that they were the natural governing party in Canada, and more importantly, began to govern as such. A seeming "arrogance of power" had been rebuked by voters in the past elections of 1957, 1979, and 1984, and eventually would be again. Finally, Chrétien seemed unable to gracefully give way to his successor, and lay the groundwork for a continuation of the dynasty beyond his leadership. Thus, the end of the Liberal dynasty would not come from without but from within — and sooner than anyone would have foreseen in the wake of the 2000 election.

Notes

1. For an account of the first Chrétien government, see Edward Greenspon and Anthony Wilson-Smith, *Double Vision: The Inside Story of the Liberals in Power* (Toronto: Doubleday, 1996).
2. Only John Crow (1987–94) and subsequently David Dodge (2001–08) served one term as governor of the Bank of Canada. James Coyne (1955–61) served six years and remained the only governor fired before the end of his term (see Chapter 4).
3. *Globe and Mail*, February 23, 1994: A1.
4. Lawrence Martin, *Iron Man: The Defiant Reign of Jean Chrétien* (Toronto: Viking, 2003), 103.
5. John Gray, *Paul Martin: The Power of Ambition* (Toronto: Key Porter Books, 2003), 155.
6. Pierre Bourgault helped found the pro-Quebec independence political movement *Rassemblement pour l'indépendance nationale* (RIN) in 1960, and became its leader in 1964. He then joined forces with René Lévesque to form the Parti Québécois.
7. See Eddie Goldenberg, *The Way It Works: Inside Ottawa* (Toronto: Douglas Gibson Books, 2006), as well as Edward Greenspon and Anthony Wilson-Smith, *Double Vision*, 305.
8. Rhéal Séguin, "Bouchard Takes Helm of Yes," *Globe and Mail*, October 9, 1995: A4.
9. Lawrence Martin, *Iron Man*, 127.
10. Harold D. Clarke et al., *A Polity on the Edge*, 17.
11. Edward Greenspon and Anthony Wilson-Smith, *Double Vision*, 333.
12. For instance, a Gallup poll release at the end of December 1996 gave the Liberals a 42-point lead over the second place PCs in Ontario.
13. Neil Nevitte, André Blais, Elisabeth Gidengil, and Richard Nadeau, *Unsteady State: The 1997 Canadian Federal Election* (Toronto: Oxford University Press, 2000), 4.
14. Lawrence Martin, *Iron Man*, 173.
15. André Bernard, "The Bloc Québécois," in Alan Frizzell and Jon H. Pammett, eds., *The Canadian General Election of 1997* (Toronto: Dundurn Press, 1997), 135–48.
16. Preston Manning, *Think Big: My Adventures in Life and Democracy* (Toronto: McClelland & Stewart Ltd., 2002), 158–59.
17. Lawrence LeDuc, "The Leaders' Debates: And the Winner Is ...," in Frizzell and Pammett, *The Canadian General Election of 1997*, 218.
18. Neil Nevitte et al., *Unsteady State*, 17.
19. *Ibid.*
20. Jeff Sallott, "Manning Calls Rivals Unity Threat," *Globe and Mail*, May 23, 1997: A1.

21. Preston Manning, *Think Big: My Adventures in Life and Democracy*, 176.
22. Manning, *Think Big*, 179.
23. Nevitte et al., *Unsteady State*, 37.
24. *Ibid.*, 4.
25. See, *Ibid.*, 134–35.
26. For a full discussion, see Hugh Segal, *The Long Road Back* (Toronto: HarperCollins Canada, 2006), and Bob Plamondon, *Full Circle: Death and Resurrection in Canadian Conservative Politics* (Toronto: Key Porter Books, 2006).
27. On the implications of this change in leadership selection processes more generally, see Lawrence LeDuc, "Democratizing Party Leadership Selection," *Party Politics* 7 (2001), 323–41.
28. Michael Marzolini, "The Politics of Values," in Jon H. Pammett and Christopher Dornan, eds., *The Canadian General Election of 2000* (Toronto: Dundurn Press, 2001), 263.
29. For details and analysis of the *Clarity Act*, see Peter H. Russell, *Constitutional Odyssey*, third edition (Toronto: University of Toronto Press, 2004).
30. See *www.statcan.ca*.
31. Department of Finance, *Economic and Fiscal Update, 1998.*
32. *Ibid.*
33. *Ibid.*
34. Shawn McCarthy and Paul Adams, "Chrétien Defends Early Vote," *Globe and Mail*, October 23, 2000: A1.
35. Edward Greenspon, "Covering Campaign 2000," in Jon H Pammett and Christopher Dornan, eds., *The Canadian General Election of 2000* (Toronto: Dundurn Press, 2001), 176.
36. CBC Archives, *The National*, October 22, 2000.
37. CBC Archives, *The National*, October 29, 2000.
38. Michael Marzolini, "The Politics of Values," 266.
39. Shawn McCarthy, "Alliance Support Two-Tier Health Care," *Globe and Mail*, October 31, 2000: A1.
40. Edward Greenspon, "Covering Campaign 2000," 183.
41. See Paul Attallah and Angela Burton, "Television, the Internet, and the Canadian Federal Election of 2000," in Jon H. Pammett and Christopher Dornan, eds., *The Canadian General Election of 2000* (Toronto: Dundurn Press, 2001), 225. As the authors rightfully pointed out, the number of signatures should be treated with some skepticism since it was possible for a single person to vote multiple times.
42. See Alan Whitehorn, "The 2000 NDP Campaign," in Jon H. Pammett and Christopher Dornan, eds., *The Canadian General Election of 2000* (Toronto: Dundurn Press, 2001).
43. See Peter Woolstencroft, "Some Battles Won, War Lost" in Jon H. Pammett and Christopher Dornan, eds., *The Canadian General Election of 2000.* (Toronto: Dundurn Press, 2001).

44. Faron Ellis, "The More Things Change.... The Alliance Campaign," 81.
45. See Peter Woolstencroft, "Some Battles Won, War Lost," 102.
46. See André Bernard, "The Bloc Québécois" in Jon H. Pammett and Christopher Dornan, eds., *The Canadian General Election of 2000* (Toronto: Dundurn Press, 2001).
47. Edward Greenspon, "Covering Campaign 2000," 186.
48. See Peter Woolstencroft, "Some Battles Won, War Lost," 105.
49. See analysis in Harold Clarke et al., *Absent Mandate*, second edition (Toronto: Gage Educational Publishing Company, 1991), especially 90–107. Also see André Turcotte, "Fallen Heroes," in Jon H. Pammett and Christopher Dornan, eds., *The Canadian General Election of 2000* (Toronto: Dundurn Press, 2001).
50. Jon Pammett, "The People's Verdict," in Jon H. Pammett and Christopher Dornan, eds., *The Canadian General Election of 2000* (Toronto: Dundurn Press, 2001), 309.
51. Jon H. Pammett and Lawrence LeDuc, *Explaining the Turnout Decline in Canadian Federal Elections* (Ottawa: Elections Canada, 2003).
52. André Blais, Elisabeth Gidengil, Richard Nadeau, and Neil Nevitte, *Anatomy of a Liberal Victory: Making Sense of the Vote in the 2000 Canadian Election* (Peterborough, ON: Broadview Press, Ltd., 2002), 204.
53. *Ibid.*, 77–78.
54. Jeffrey Simpson, *The Friendly Dictatorship* (Toronto: McClelland & Stewart, 2001), and Stephen Clarkson, *The Big Red Machine* (Vancouver: UBC Press, 2005).

Selected Reading

Blais, André, Elisabeth Gidengil, Richard Nadeau, and Neil Nevitte. *Anatomy of a Liberal Victory: Making Sense of the 2000 Canadian Election*. (Toronto: Broadview, 2002).

Carty, R. Kenneth, William Cross, and Lisa Young. *Rebuilding Canadian Party Politics* (Vancouver: University of British Columbia Press, 2000).

Clarke, Harold D., Allan Kornberg, and Peter Wearing. *A Polity on the Edge: Canada and the Politics of Fragmentation* (Toronto: Broadview, 2000).

Frizzell, Alan, and Jon H. Pammett, eds. *The Canadian General Election of 1997* (Toronto: Dundurn Press, 1998).

Greenspon, Edward, and Anthony Wilson-Smith. *Double Vision: The Inside Story of the Liberals in Power* (Toronto: Doubleday, 1996).

LeDuc, Lawrence. "The Canadian Federal Election of 1997." *Electoral Studies* 17 (1998) 132–37.

LeDuc, Lawrence "The Canadian Federal Election, November 2000." *Electoral Studies* 21 (2002), 655–59.

Manning, Preston. *Think Big: My Adventures in Life and Democracy* (Toronto: McClelland & Stewart, 2002).

Martin, Lawrence. *Iron Man: The Defiant Reign of Jean Chrétien* (Toronto: Viking, 2003).

Nevitte, Neil, André Blais, Elisabeth Gidengil, and Richard Nadeau. *Unsteady State: The 1997 Canadian Federal Election* (Toronto: Oxford University Press, 1999).

Pammett, Jon H., and Christopher Dornan, eds. *The Canadian General Election of 2000* (Toronto: Dundurn Press, 2001).

Pinard, Maurice, Robert Bernier, and Vincent Lemieux. *Un Combat Inachevé* (Quebec City: Presses de l'Université du Québec, 1997).

Simpson, Jeffrey. *The Friendly Dictatorship* (Toronto: McClelland & Stewart, 2001).

Turcotte, André. "*À la prochaine* … Again: The Quebec Referendum of 1995." *Electoral Studies* 15 (1996) 399–403.

Young, Robert A. *The Struggle for Quebec: From Referendum to Referendum?* (Montreal: McGill-Queen's University Press, 1999).

CHAPTER 13

CIVIL WARS, REGIONAL DYNASTIES, AND MINORITY GOVERNMENTS

The 2000 election saw Jean Chrétien become the first leader since Sir Wilfrid Laurier to win a majority of seats in three successive federal elections. Four years later, however, the Chrétien dynasty was over, Chrétien himself was in forced retirement, and a protracted era of minority governments had begun. This situation was the product of the interaction of several factors, including the outbreak of "civil war" within the Liberal Party and the establishment of regional bastions of support within a fragmented party system. Most clearly, however, the Liberals were unable to continue to master the three key issue areas of Canadian electoral success: the economy, national unity and social welfare. The Conservative government, which took power under Stephen Harper in 2006, has similarly been unable to establish the fundamentals of a new dynasty.

Jean Chrétien states in his memoirs that he originally wanted to quit while he was ahead:

> Two terms were enough.... In my mind, I would serve four of the five years for which I had been elected in 1997, lead Canada into the new millennium, announce

> my retirement in the fall of 2000, and leave the country and the party in excellent shape to allow my successor to win another Liberal Majority Government.[1]

But as we have seen in Chapter 12, rather than retire, Chrétien sought and won a third consecutive election victory; this time with an increased majority. Now he had the same decision to make, and began to exhibit signs of the same hesitancy to give up a position he enjoyed, particularly since he saw no roadblocks to the continuation of his dynasty.

The Liberal Civil War Intensifies

Unlike the Conservatives, the transition from one Liberal leader to the next has usually been smooth. For instance, in the 1958 election when John Diefenbaker trounced Lester Pearson within a year of the latter winning the Liberal leadership, Paul Martin, Sr., who had lost the leadership race to Pearson, rallied behind his embattled leader (see Chapter 5). Similarly, no one in the Liberal caucus publicly challenged Pierre Trudeau after his disastrous showing in the 1972 election or after his defeat by Joe Clark in 1979 — in fact, he was brought back as leader to defeat Clark in the 1980 election (see Chapter 8).

But the battle between Jean Chrétien and Paul Martin was different. Their rivalry dated back at least to the time when both men were running for the Liberal leadership in 1990 (see Chapter 11). These two protagonists were more confrontational, vindictive, and aggressive than their predecessors, and both were consumed by personal ambition. On a more substantive level, they differed fundamentally in their approaches to Quebec. Martin had favoured the Meech Lake Accord, whereas Chrétien opposed it until a last-minute conversion. When he became more flexible on the issue prior to the leadership convention, Martin's supporters called him a "*vendu*,"[2] something Chrétien never forgot.

In his memoirs, Martin portrays himself as the one who cared about policy, who asked for and was given the role of assembling the Red Book platform for the 1993 election, and who was given the supremely tough job of minister of finance when deficits were spiralling out of control and hard choices about cuts had to be made. According to Martin, Chrétien "had never fully developed a policy platform,"[3] and he treated Martin's policy initiatives with suspicion.

Despite their antagonism, the two men put aside their differences and focused first on winning the 1993 election and then on running the country. Their relationship was the cornerstone of what became a new dynasty, less than 10 years after the severe Liberal defeat of 1984.

As finance minister, Martin won accolades for his 1995 budget and the subsequent elimination of the national deficit. Such fiscal achievements were possible because Martin and Chrétien found ways to compromise between the need for addressing dire budgetary realities and the Liberal commitment to protecting social programs. But such compromises came with a heavy price, further straining the relationship between the two rivals. For example, Martin wanted to decrease the

Canadian Press. Tom Hanson, photographer.

Jean Chrétien and Paul Martin at 2006 Liberal convention, Ottawa.

financial commitment of the federal government in the Canada Pension Plan as one of the ways to reduce the national deficit, while more left-leaning Liberals were opposed to tackling that issue. With Martin pressing for a resolution, Chrétien equivocated, mindful of the self-inflicted damage done to Brian Mulroney after the 1984 election when his finance minister attempted to de-index old-age pensions (see chapter 10). Martin considered resigning over this issue, and began dealing with Chrétien through an intermediary.[4] The two men also disagreed over Martin's decision to retain the GST in 1996, and over what Martin described as "my deliberate exclusion from the Quebec file."[5]

Chrétien's decision to seek a third mandate in 2000 was too much to bear for the Martin camp. As soon as the election was over, Martin and his supporters in and out of caucus decided to move. By this time, "any personal relationship with the prime minister was … utterly non-existent."[6] Chrétien, however, felt as if "I was damned if I was going to be shoved out the door by a gang of self-serving goons."[7]

The final clash occurred in June 2002. Chrétien decided to put a stop to the behind-the-scenes organizing by Martin and other potential leadership contenders and gave indications that he would stay on as prime minister. Martin was forced out of cabinet, though whether he resigned or was fired is a matter of some dispute between the two men. But Martin's departure did not loosen his hold on the local party organizations in much of the country nor his appeal to the parliamentary caucus. Ultimately, Chrétien announced that he would resign the leadership, but the process of transition inflicted considerable damage to both Martin's image and the Liberal government more generally. In late 2003, Paul Martin became the 14th leader of the Liberal Party of Canada with a first-ballot victory at a leadership convention (see Table 13.1), but he inherited a weakened and divided party.

The Conservative Civil War Ends

Progressive Conservatives and members of the Canadian Alliance might have observed their Liberal adversaries tearing one another apart with some glee, but were hardly in a position to take advantage of the situation immediately after the 2000 election. Their own civil war had been going on since the establishment of the Reform Party in the late 1980s (see Chapters 11 and 12). The cataclysmic defeat of the PCs in 1993 had precipitated a fierce battle for control of the main opposition to the Liberals, and little pointed to a reconciliation of conservative forces.

However, events moved quickly. Less than a year after the 2000 election, a group of Alliance MPs broke away from their party and aligned temporarily with Tory MPs to form a working parliamentary coalition named the Democratic Representative Caucus (DRC). Headed by Joe Clark and Chuck Strahl, the caucus sat as a separate group in the House of Commons.

Meanwhile, the Alliance held a leadership election in March 2002 (see Table 13.1) in which former MP Stephen Harper defeated Stockwell Day for the leadership of that party.[8] Throughout the leadership race, Harper stressed his commitment to strengthen the original ideals of the Reform movement and to move the Canadian Alliance forward. After Harper's victory, former Reform leader Preston Manning retired from politics, making way for Harper to run in Calgary Southwest and easily secure a seat in Parliament. The stage was set for the breakaway Alliance MPs to reintegrate into the Alliance Caucus.

In the meantime, the Progressive Conservatives were preparing to find a new leader to replace Joe Clark. On May 31, 2003, Peter MacKay was elected leader of the Progressive Conservative Party after signing a deal with runner-up David Orchard.[9] The backroom deal was made public and clearly showed that Orchard had agreed to throw his support behind MacKay if the latter promised never to seek to unite the PCs with the Alliance. Despite this pledge, MacKay proceeded to negotiate a merger of his party with the Alliance. As quick and shameless as the deal might have been, at least as seen by some of the outraged supporters of their original parties, Stephen Harper and Peter MacKay actually managed to pull it off. Barely four months after the PC leadership race and about a year and a half after the Alliance's, the two parties announced an agreement to merge and form a new party. On March 20, 2004, Stephen Harper became the first leader of the Conservative Party of Canada.[10]

There are three potential explanations for the success of the merger. First — fatigue. Most Canadian Alliance MPs had been elected as Reformers in 1993, and had lived through three general elections, the arduous years of the United Alternative (see Chapter 12), the DRC episode, and two leadership races. While originally committed to populist

TABLE 13.1

Party Leadership Conventions, 2002–2009

DATE	PARTY	LOCATION	WINNER	CANDIDATES*	BALLOTS	RUNNER-UP**
2002 03 31	Alliance	X	Stephen Harper	4	1	Stockwell Day
2003 01 25	NDP	Toronto	Jack Layton	6	1	Bill Blaikie
2003 05 31	PC	Toronto	Peter MacKay	5	4	Jim Prentice
2003 11 14	Liberal	Toronto	Paul Martin	2	1	Sheila Copps
2004 03 20	CPC	Toronto	Stephen Harper	3	1	Belinda Stronach
2006 12 03	Liberal	Ottawa	Stéphane Dion	8	4	Michael Ignatieff
2009 04 30	Liberal	Vancouver	Michael Ignatieff	1	1	-

* On first ballot X Mail ballot

** On final ballot

ideals, Alliance MPs finally reached a point where they concluded that life in opposition was thankless and difficult: they wanted to get the deal done. Harper came to accept that he needed such a merger if he was ever to become prime minister and MacKay realized he was unlikely to be able to improve his party's dismal parliamentary presence in the near future. Above all, both leaders wanted to prevent the continuation of the civil war of attrition between the two conservative camps.

Second, the fact that the Harper–MacKay deal was negotiated behind closed doors and presented to the respective memberships as a "fait accompli," as well as a necessity, gave a single focal point to the decision and made it relatively simple to pass.

Third, the fear of a Martin "juggernaut" played a significant role in giving impetus to Harper and McKay to negotiate the merger. As long as the two parties remained divided, conservatives would continue to lack credibility as an alternative and were likely to lose badly again. Stephen Harper understood that political reality better than most, having experienced it firsthand.

An economist from Alberta, he had been part of the early group of Reformers, and served as the party's chief policy officer before being elected to Parliament in 1993. In his first term as MP, he was frustrated with the stalemate between Reform and the PCs — which remained virtually tied with Reform in popular support despite having only two MPs — and impatiently looked for a solution. In May 1996, he participated in The Winds of Change Conference organized by conservative activists David Frum and Ezra Levant, whose objective was to "unite the right."[11] When it became clear that those efforts were doomed, Harper decided to quit politics to head the National Citizens' Coalition, an interest group dedicated to the promotion of free enterprise and small government.

Never a strong supporter of Preston Manning's grassroots approach,[12] Harper stayed on the sidelines and did not support the initial attempts to broaden Reform's support into the United Alternative (see Chapter 12). He gambled that the conservative parties were not yet ready to stop fighting each other, but believed that time would eventually come. When the Canadian Alliance failed to make significant advances in the 2000 election and subsequently imploded, the pressure mounted for him to return to politics. However, Harper did not jump back into the fray until he was convinced that the two parties were ready to lay down their arms. By 2004, his gamble of remaining on the sidelines for a time had paid off.[13]

The Changing Issue Balance

Jean Chrétien had built his dynasty by creating a Liberal advantage, clearer at some points in time than others, on the central electoral issues of national unity, the economy, and social welfare. On the economy, the advantage was having Paul Martin as finance minister and being able both to take credit for an improving economy and to claim that his administration had turned budget deficits into surpluses.

On social welfare, the key was planting doubt in voters' minds that the opposition parties would maintain the public health care system and support it with sufficient funding. As outlined in Chapter 12, the 2000 Liberal campaign used statements by prominent members of the Canadian Alliance to portray that party, and its leader Stockwell Day, as being out of touch with Canadian mainstream values when it came to maintaining the social safety net, particularly with regard to health. As social issues became more prominent in elections, the Liberal advantage grew, turning a narrow majority in 1997 to a greater one in 2000.

On national unity issues, Jean Chrétien gave the Liberals the advantage both inside and outside Quebec. In English Canada, Chrétien's "Captain Canada" persona, which he had honed for many years, gave him the image of a Quebecer who loved Canada. In contrast, Reform, Alliance, and Progressive Conservative leaders spoke French with some difficulty and had no Quebec base of support upon which to build.

In Quebec, the Liberal advantage was clear over the other federalist parties and the main battle was with the Bloc Québécois. Even though the strength of the BQ meant that the Liberals did not get a plurality of overall support in the province, the fact that they were likely to form the government meant that a substantial number of Quebec voters still saw advantages to casting a Liberal vote. Chrétien's low-key leadership style allowed him to under-promise and over-perform in the sense of exceeding expectations, in all of the key issue areas.

With the close result of the 1995 Quebec referendum on sovereignty, the Chrétien Liberals began a program of sponsoring a variety of events and projects in Quebec to give visibility to the federal government, and persuade more Quebecers that the Liberals were the right choice. Revelations about this program cast doubt on the Liberals' performance not only on national unity but on the other key issues.

It was Paul Martin's misfortune to finally accede to the leadership of the Liberal Party late in 2003, at a point in time when the Liberal advantage was to come crashing down. The stewardship of the economy was still a Liberal strength, and Martin himself at the head of government was a reassuring figure. But ironically, because of this very success in managing the economy, the issue had shrunk from the forefront of public consciousness. Social welfare issues, predominantly health, were still important for the Liberals, as well, but the advantage for the party was becoming less prominent since the problems plaguing the health care sector seemed to be continuing no matter what amount of money was pumped into it. More fundamental factors — an aging population, longer life expectancies, soaring hospital and medical costs — combined to render most simple fixes ineffective. But the overall image of the party suffered most when the "sponsorship scandal" hit the headlines.

The Sponsorship Scandal Erupts

On February 10, 2004, federal auditor general Sheila Fraser released her report into a government advertising and sponsorship program run by the federal Public Works Department in the province of Quebec. This program had been under suspicion since 2002 when Fraser asked the RCMP to look into alleged misappropriation of funds and suspicious practices in the awarding of contracts. Opposition critics had consistently claimed that the program was a scheme to give lucrative advertising contracts to Liberal Party supporters.

The *Auditor General's Report*[14] used words such as "scandalous" and "appalling" to describe the Liberal government's role in the affair. The program had received $250 million in a four-year period, and more than $100 million of that money went to pay communications consultants with close ties to the Liberal Party. The report revealed that the RCMP, Via Rail, Canada Post, and the Old Port of Montreal were also tied to the misappropriation of funds. More damaging was concern about serious mismanagement — if not misappropriation — of public funds inside the circle of those personally close to Chrétien.

The decisions taken in the aftermath of the release of the *Auditor General's Report* ensured that the scandal would remain in the spotlight for some time. Prime Minister Martin immediately called a public inquiry into the way the sponsorship program had been handled. Public inquiries are called, not only to investigate, but also sometimes to deter questioning and divert attention from a politically difficult issue. Martin, however, wanted to be seen as taking quick action to clean up the situation. He fired Alfonso Gagliano as ambassador to Denmark, since Gagliano had been the minister responsible for the program when the alleged fraud took place.

Martin also felt compelled to deny knowing the particulars of the sponsorship activities, despite the fact that he was finance minister at the time, maintaining he was not informed on Quebec issues because of his deteriorating relationship with Chrétien. Inadvertently, he was starting to raise doubts about his performance as finance minister. To the public it seemed odd that the man they respected for turning around Canada's financial situation would now say he did not know how millions of dollars were spent.

Televised testimony before the inquiry kept the issue in the news even beyond the 2004 election. The "sponsorship scandal" was not the first to hit the Liberals since they came to power in 1993. But unlike previous scandals, such as "Shawinigate"[15] and the "HRDC boondoggle,"[16] it was more damaging because it dealt directly with the party's perceived competence in dealing with both the country's finances and national unity. It also forced Martin to distance himself from the Chrétien record despite his predecessor's three consecutive majorities, and it opened the door for the Conservatives to establish their own credibility in addressing the main issues.

Martin also seemed unprepared for the change in the type of media scrutiny associated with holding the office of prime minister. For years he had enjoyed friendly media coverage. The Ottawa press gallery generally liked the open and accessible Martin and the people around him in contrast to the more distant close-knit group surrounding Chrétien. But on February 17, 2004, in the inside page of the *National Post*, appeared a story suggesting that Paul Martin's shipping company had business ties to a controversial power project partially owned by the son of former Indonesian president Mohamed Suharto.[17]

When journalists began to ask Martin if he was going to sell Canada Steamship Lines, he defiantly told reporters that he would simply remove himself from some government decisions if he were faced with a conflict of interest as prime minister. Two days later, he turned emotional, telling reporters that he would not sell "his beloved Canada Steamship Lines because it would be turning a dream into a nightmare — for himself, for his three sons and for all those who believe that strong Canadian companies should stay in Canada."[18] Shortly after, he turned the company over to his sons.

The evasiveness with which Martin handled the attacks was a first sign of future trouble. Greenspon and Wilson-Smith had previously written about Martin's decision-making process: "how he tended to take a long time to come to decisions, initially resisting advice and then agonizing his way through an internal dialectic process before finally settling, forcefully, on an answer."[19]

This process worked well as finance minister when it made him look as if he was weighing opinions to find the best solutions, but as prime minister it made him look weak and tentative. He came to be perceived as so indecisive that *The Economist* later tagged him "Mr. Dithers."[20] This description resonated with the public and his opponents and in many ways came to characterize his brief prime ministership.

The 2004 Election

Despite slumping poll numbers (see Figure 13.1) and the fact that the 2000 election had been held less than four years previously, Paul Martin decided on an election date in June, neither early enough to use the argument that a new prime minister needed a new mandate nor late enough to allow his electoral prospects to improve.

Martin's opening statement was reflective of the Liberal strategy: he issued a warning that the Harper Conservatives would make Canada look like the United States. He wanted the election to be a choice between the Liberals who would invest billions of dollars a year in health care and social programs and protect Canadian national identity, and a potential Conservative government that would destroy those social programs and introduce American-style policies.[21] Playing on anti-American sentiment is a well-worn Canadian political strategy, but the emphasis on health care reflected the fact that the social policy area was virtually the only issue-related advantage that the Liberals retained.

From the beginning, the Liberals decided that "fixing health care for a generation" was to be their main campaign plank, though as the campaign went on "reducing waiting times" became a more familiar refrain for Paul Martin, in an effort to be more specific about how it would be fixed.

The health care issue did work in the Liberals' favour and appears to have been a major factor in the limited victory they eventually did achieve. However, promises to fix health care had been a staple of Liberal campaigns dating back to the 1993 Red Book, and a decade of federal–provincial infighting over financing had succeeded in persuading Canadians that a "quick fix" was not possible. This was especially true in 2004, since the Liberal plan consisted essentially of allocating sums of money (the most frequently mentioned number at the beginning of the campaign was $9 billion) to existing programs, rather than proposing any reforms to the system.

The Conservatives were well aware that the Liberals had an advantage on the health care issue as the campaign began. The Alliance had suffered in the 2000 election because the Liberals successfully linked them, despite their protestations, with plans to open the system to more private medical care. This time the Stephen Harper Conservatives were determined to fight the Liberals on their own ground, by promising even more money for health care than the Liberals. To a considerable extent,

TABLE 13.2

Most Important Issues in the 2004, 2006, and 2008 Elections

	2004	2006	2008
Economic Issues			
Taxes	8	6	3
General economic concerns	3	3	23
Debt / deficit	3	3	3
Unemployment	2	2	4
Other economic	1	1	1
National Unity			
National unity	1	2	1
U.S. influence	1	1	-
Social Welfare			
Health care	47	36	20
Education	5	4	-
Pensions	2	2	1
Social programs	2	3	2
Environment	-	3	9
Crime / guns	-	-	2
Other social	-	-	5
Other Issues			
Integrity / trust / ethics	16	20	4
Sponsorship scandal	-	5	-
Need for change	2	3	-
Need for stable government	1	-	1
War	-	-	1
Other	5	3	11
2004, 2006, and 2008 Canadian Election Studies.	N = 4,323	N = 4,068	N = 3,247

the health policy area was the centrepiece of Harper's attempt to improve the credibility of the new Conservative Party by moving it to the centre of the political spectrum, and styling it to resemble the Liberals.

The strategy likely worked when health policy alone is considered — the problem was the combination of promises of increased health care spending with substantial proposed tax cuts. The tax cut plan was the centrepiece of the Conservatives' economic platform, a plan that also called for a higher child tax deduction and tax-free withdrawal of money from RRSPs. That combination of policies allowed critics and other parties to ridicule the Conservative's "black hole" in the budget which would result from both raising spending and cutting revenues.[22]

Early in the campaign, the party leaders jostled for position on tax cuts, with Paul Martin pledging not to raise taxes, Stephen Harper promising deep cuts, and new NDP leader Jack Layton promising fiscal responsibility.[23]

Layton, former president of the Federation of Canadian Municipalities and Toronto city councillor, had replaced Alexa McDonough as party leader in 2003 (see Table 13.1). Layton stressed contemporary issues such as environmentalism, feminism, and a commitment to the peace movement.[24] Upon becoming party leader, Layton successfully reversed

FIGURE 13.1
Federal Vote Intention, 2003–2008

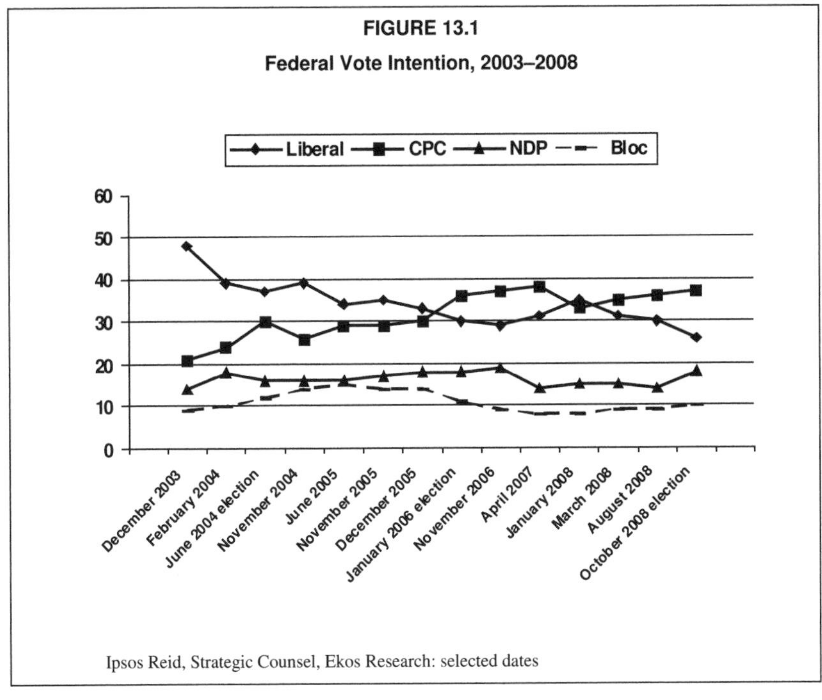

Ipsos Reid, Strategic Counsel, Ekos Research: selected dates

the decline in NDP finances and membership but faced a skeptical press gallery in his attempt to raise his national profile.

Regional appeals were prominent in the 2004 campaign. The Conservatives called for a rebalancing of Confederation through electing senators and advocated changes to equalization payments to appeal to the West.[25] Gilles Duceppe and the Bloc Québécois successfully tapped into similar sentiments by offering a party *"propre aux Québécois,"* a clever slogan translating into a "clean" as well as "genuine" party for Quebecers.[26] Martin targeted several of his pre-election announcements to the West, such as financial support for the cattle industry to recover from an American embargo following a mad-cow scare, and hints that the legislation requiring registration of hunting rifles might be revised.[27] Similar promises were targeted to other regions by all the parties.

The key campaign strategy for the Conservatives and the other opposition parties was to keep the focus firmly on the sponsorship scandal, which had undermined the image of trust and competence that is normally attributed to the Liberal Party. It was not so much the sums of money involved, but rather the revelation that a privileged position had been used to benefit the friends of the party. The fact that those responsible for the sponsorship program had been friends and appointees of Chrétien rather than Paul Martin gave Liberals a false sense of security about being able to deal with the revelations. Although they did not do it, they felt they could say they would clean it up.

The problem with that strategy during the election campaign was that the electorate was not paying much attention to the fine details of who was getting along with whom inside the party. How could Paul Martin, who had been minister of finance when money was being spent in places it should not have been, not have known about it? In the crudest terms, if he did know he was now lying about it, and if he didn't know he was incompetent. In such a "no win" situation, the Martin Liberals suffered a diminution of the public trust.

Neither was Paul Martin the fresh face and appealing leader he might have been had he won the Liberal leadership in 1990. By 2004 he was the oldest of the leaders by a considerable margin. Though he was energetic, the bursts of energy looked at times forced and unconvincing, perhaps not in keeping with a politician of his years, who should project the image of calmness and wisdom that had worked for Macdonald, Laurier, King, St. Laurent, and Trudeau in their later years.

In contrast, Martin often looked frantic, with a hurried speaking style and waving arm movements. If Jack Layton acted much the same way, at least he wasn't so old and he smiled a lot. If Stephen Harper appeared wooden in comparison, at least he wasn't distracting to look at. The persona of the other leaders made Gilles Duceppe look positively presidential, especially during the leadership debates.

With their support trending downward, the Liberals fell back on the only other factor on which they had an advantage — values. "Choose your Canada," said a Liberal fundraising appeal inserted into several of the country's newspapers during the campaign. This negative Liberal advertising took advantage of public doubts about the Conservatives — choose *your* Canada, voters were exhorted, not theirs. The ads also emphasized such things as Harper's past stance favouring taking Canadian troops into Iraq, heavy military spending, and the Conservatives' "hidden agenda" on social issues, especially their supposed plans to limit a woman's right to choose. Surprisingly, since it had negatively affected their support in the past, the Conservative campaign was unprepared to deal with these accusations.[28] In an attempt to quell such attacks, Harper finally denied having any plans to reopen the abortion debate but then added "in the first term." Meanwhile, Conservative campaign ads continued to hammer away at "Liberal corruption."

Canadian Press. Ryan Remiorz, photographer.

Gilles Duceppe campaigning in Huntington, Quebec, 2008 election.

On June 10, the *Globe and Mail* released an IPSOS-Reid poll showing the Liberals and Conservatives in a virtual tie (32 percent for the Liberals and 31 percent for the Conservatives).[29] The Liberal campaign appeared to be unravelling, as Paul Martin's top political adviser, David Herle, was quoted as telling a number of Liberal MPs in a conference call that the Liberals "were in a spiral."[30]

This upturn in Conservative fortunes led Harper to commit his first major mistake of the campaign: he began to talk confidently about his chances of forming a majority government.[31] Harper's comments demonstrated a misjudgment of the public opinion climate. Voters were turning against the Liberals as a way to punish them for the sponsorship scandal and their arrogance in power, despite misgivings toward the Conservatives. Harper gave the Liberal campaign the perfect opening to force the electorate to focus on the consequences of registering their anger toward the Liberals. Their vote would no longer only send a message to the Liberals, it would elect Harper and the Conservatives — a prospect many were not ready to contemplate.

In the closing days of the campaign, the Conservatives made their second major mistake. Responding to the verdict in a murder trial which involved child pornography, the Conservative campaign issued a press release suggesting that Martin was in favour of child pornography because he did not do enough to legislate against it in his years in government. The attack was viewed as unfair and disproportionate and distracted the Harper campaign for several days.[32] The Liberals also received unexpected help from Alberta PC premier Ralph Klein, who publicly mused about the nature of the changes to health care that he would put forward after the election. Former Quebec premier Bernard Landry also helped by suggesting that the Bloc's expected strong showing would reignite the debate over Quebec sovereignty. A campaign that had opened with clashes over supposedly stark choices between two visions of the future stumbled to the finish line.

After initially being in danger of losing power altogether, the Martin Liberals were re-elected in 2004 with 37 percent of the popular vote and 135 seats, 74 of those seats from Ontario. This represented a loss of 37 seats from the 2000 election and a 4 percent drop of popular support (see Table 13.3). The Conservatives elected 99 candidates with 30 percent of the vote, which represented big gains over the Alliance showing in 2000, but still considerably short of the combined Alliance and Progressive Conservative vote total in the 1997 election.

However, academic analysis pointed out that it was always unlikely that the new Conservative Party would be able to count on the combined vote of the two parties which merged to produce it. In particular, Progressive Conservative supporters in previous elections looked much more like Liberal voters than Alliance or Reform voters.[33] The most that realistically could be expected from the merger was to position the Conservatives as a stronger Official Opposition, without the Progressive Conservatives nipping at their heels by maintaining they were the real "national opposition" by virtue of their political history, having some seats outside the West, and having a bit higher vote share in Quebec. The question for the Conservatives in 2004 was whether they had achieved their natural limit in growth and in particular whether they could significantly increase their seat totals in Ontario and make a breakthrough in Quebec in a subsequent election.

Almost all the parties were able to claim they were winners in some way in the 2004 election. Gilles Duceppe ran a smart campaign focused on Quebecers' resentment over the sponsorship scandal and capitalized on the fact that the Liberals simply gave up on making electoral inroads in Quebec. He was rewarded with a strong victory in that province. With 48.8 percent of the Quebec popular vote, Duceppe almost matched the Bloc's best showing in 1993 when they garnered 49.3 percent of the vote under Lucien Bouchard's leadership. The Bloc also succeeded in preventing the Conservatives from rebuilding the Mulroney coalition and, in the process, denied them any chance of forming a government.

For his part, Jack Layton succeeded in reviving the NDP with its best showing since 1988. His most important gains came in British Columbia, where the NDP share in popular vote increased from 11 percent in 2000 to 27 percent. The NDP also made important gains in Ontario (up to 18 percent from 8 in 2000) and in New Brunswick (from 12 percent to 21 percent). And finally, the Liberals could claim a kind of victory in that they had survived the Conservative attacks over the sponsorship scandal and had gone on to win the election, in spite of the fact that they were now a minority government.

Another important factor in explaining the outcome of the 2004 election was the relative positions of the parties and leaders (see Figure 13.2). The Liberals organized the campaign around their new leader and his "Team Martin." But Paul Martin by the time of the election was only slightly more popular than his party and about even with Harper in

TABLE 13.3

Results of the 2004, 2006, and 2008 Federal Elections, by Province

		CPC			LIB			NDP			Bloc		
		2004	2006	2008	2004	2006	2008	2004	2006	2008	2004	2006	2008
Newfoundland	votes (%)	32	43	16	48	43	47	17	14	34	-	-	-
	seats (#)	2	3	-	5	4	6	-	-	1	-	-	-
Prince Edward Island	votes (%)	31	33	36	52	53	48	12	10	10	-	-	-
	seats (#)	-	-	1	4	4	3	-	-	-	-	-	-
Nova Scotia	votes (%)	28	30	26	40	37	30	28	30	29	-	-	-
	seats (#)	3	3	3	6	6	5	2	2	2	-	-	-
New Brunswick	votes (%)	31	36	39	45	39	32	21	22	22	-	-	-
	seats (#)	2	3	6	7	6	3	1	1	1	-	-	-
Quebec	votes (%)	9	25	22	34	21	24	5	7	12	49	42	38
	seats (#)	-	10	10	21	13	14	-	-	1	54	51	49

Ontario	votes (%)	31	35	39	45	40	34	18	19	18	-	-	-
	seats (#)	24	40	51	75	54	38	-	12	17	-	-	-
Manitoba	votes (%)	39	43	49	33	26	19	23	25	24	-	-	-
	seats (#)	7	8	9	3	3	1	4	3	4	-	1	-
Saskatchewan	votes (%)	42	49	54	27	22	15	23	24	26	-	-	-
	seats (#)	13	12	13	1	2	1	-	-	-	-	-	-
Alberta	votes (%)	62	65	65	22	15	11	9	12	13	-	-	-
	seats (#)	26	28	27	2	-	-	-	-	1	-	-	-
British Columbia	votes (%)	36	37	44	29	28	19	27	28	26	-	-	-
	seats (#)	22	17	22	8	9	5	5	10	9	-	-	-
Yukon / NWT / Nunuvut	votes (%)	18	23	35	44	41	30	29	30	25	-	-	-
	seats (#)	-	-	1	3	2	1	-	1	1	-	-	-
TOTAL CANADA	votes (%)	30	36	38	37	30	26	16	17	18	12	10	10
	seats (#)	99	124	143	135	103	77	19	29	37	54	51	49

One Independent was elected in 2004 and 2006, and two in 2008.

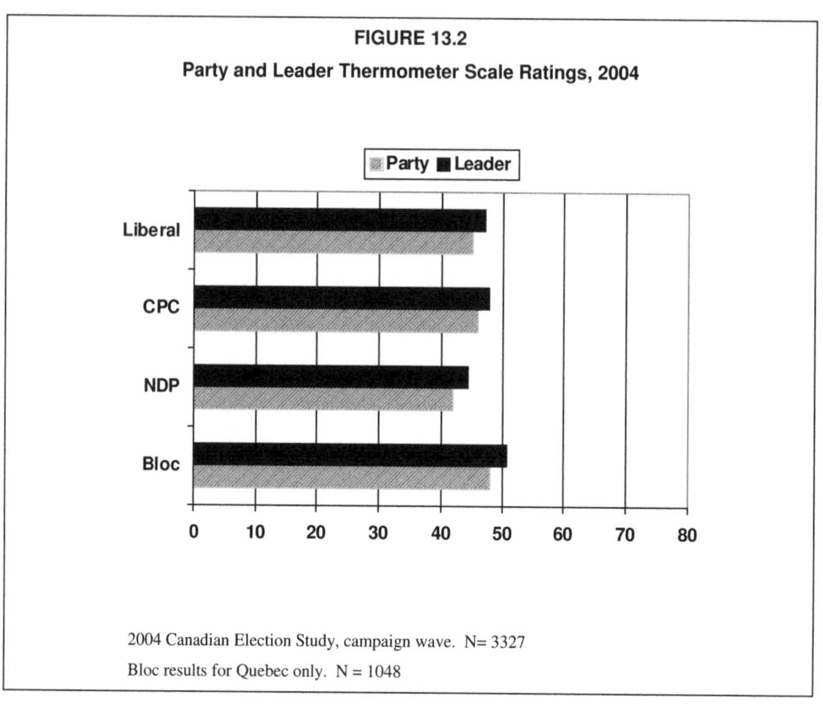

FIGURE 13.2
Party and Leader Thermometer Scale Ratings, 2004

Party
Leader
Liberal
CPC
NDP
Bloc
0
10
20
30
40
50
60
70
80

2004 Canadian Election Study, campaign wave. N= 3327
Bloc results for Quebec only. N = 1048

FIGURE 13.3
Electoral Turnover, 2000–2004

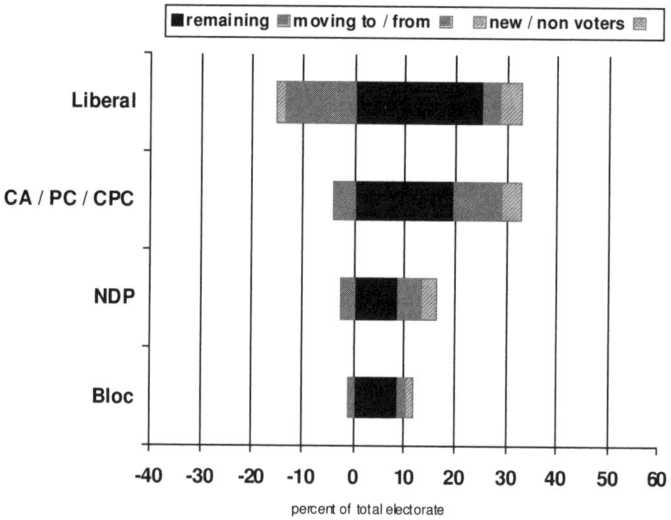

remaining
moving to / from
new / non voters
Liberal
CA / PC / CPC
NDP
Bloc
-40
-30
-20
-10
0
10
20
30
40
50
60
percent of total electorate

2004 Canadian Election Study. N = 2295

terms of personal appeal. Both the Liberals and their leader had slipped considerably in public esteem from the levels of the previous election. The continued erosion of Martin's public image, as well as that of his party, made the eventual Liberal electoral defeat inevitable.

Another contributing factor to the downfall of the Chrétien/Martin dynasty was the ability of the Conservatives to build on their new sources of support, and to make the Conservative brand appear less toxic in the public mind than that of the Alliance had been. As Figure 13.3 shows, the Conservative were finally able to pry significant numbers of voters directly away from the Liberals — a first sign that they were slowly establishing themselves as a national alternative.

The Martin Minority Government

Backed by the strongest Conservative contingent since the Mulroney years, Stephen Harper was determined not to let the minority Liberal government survive for too long and give Paul Martin the chance to rebuild his tarnished image. He planned to keep the Liberals' misappropriation of public funds under the spotlight and bring down the minority government at the earliest opportunity. The Conservative leader moved quickly to fix internal deficiencies that had affected the 2004 campaign — specifically poor media management and a lack of coordination between campaign and communication logistics.[34] He continued to moderate the party platform to make it look more like a Progressive Conservative platform than a Reform or an Alliance one.

To this end, the Conservatives held their inaugural policy convention in Montreal in March 2005. The choice of Montreal as the location was the first sign that Harper wanted to change the image of the party. Both the Reform Party and the Canadian Alliance had been unable to garner even marginal support in the province of Quebec, and Harper wanted to at least attempt to improve that situation. Second, the convention was the occasion to mend the deep divisions dating back to the emergence of the Reform Party in 1987. Public display of unity began during the convention's opening video and the leader's speech portrayed the Conservative Party as one entity rather than a variety of movements. John A. Macdonald, Brian Mulroney,

Preston Manning, and Joe Clark all became Conservative icons of the distant and recent past.

The mood on the convention floor was conciliatory, but Harper and his advisers were committed to get rid of the policies and views that they considered as hindrances to electoral success.[35] Many of the old Reform policies embodying social conservative and populist policies and institutional reforms were abandoned, and the party endorsed official bilingualism. In short, the convention was an exercise in "exorcising the populist ghosts and taming the social conservative agenda."[36]

The Martin Liberals were not as successful in ridding themselves of their past. As is typical in a minority situation, Paul Martin put the best face on the results and asserted that he had been given support to move forward with his Liberal agenda. But within weeks of the election, any attempts at governing were overshadowed by new revelations related to the sponsorship scandal.

For more than a year, Canadians would hear how officials around the prime minister's office oversaw the distribution of sponsorship funds designed in principle to improve the profile of the federal government in Quebec, but in practice enriching a small group of Liberal supporters. The program had been put into place, in the words of Jean Chrétien, "as a necessary part of a strategy in the war against Quebec separatists."[37] Instead, it became "a story of greed, venality and misconduct both in government and in advertising and communication agencies, all of which contributed to the loss and misuse of huge amounts of money at the expense of Canadian taxpayers."[38] Martin did what he could to try to extricate the Liberal Party from the onslaught of revelations and move his policy agenda forward, but to little avail.

Knowing he was on shaky ground and that a new election might come at any time, Martin worked to create a Liberal record that could address the three pillars of success in federal elections. Since social policy was still the key to Liberal support, he concluded a health care deal with the provinces in which Ottawa would spend $18 billion more over six years than it would have spent under previous agreements.[39] The deal also contained a clause exempting Quebec from accountability measures imposed on other provinces. Then, Martin and his provincial counterparts agreed on the core principles of a national child-care program.

Subsequently, in the only budget he had time to table before the government was defeated, Finance Minister Ralph Goodale introduced spending and tax initiatives adding up to $41.8 billion over six years. In total, 82 legislative measures were enacted in 17 months.[40] Despite this frenzy of activity, Martin was unable to remain focused on his agenda. The almost daily stream of stories about envelopes stuffed with cash delivered in Montreal restaurants, contracts awarded without tender and sometimes without any work being done, kickbacks and false invoices, proved to be too much of a distraction.

More importantly for his re-election prospects, a program designed to fight the separatists had ended up reviving the electoral fortunes of the Bloc, to the continued detriment of Liberal prospects in Quebec. The revelations from the Gomery Commission led to an increase in support for Quebec sovereignty, which reached 56 percent in June 2005, its highest level in 10 years.[41] Pre-election polls showed that support for the Bloc Québécois hovered around the 60 percent mark[42] and that the party was poised to better its 1993 electoral performance.

For its part, the NDP reaped tangible legislative benefits from the minority government situation. Eager to survive in the House of Commons, Martin decided not to participate in the controversial U.S. missile-defense shield program, and this decision, while angering the Conservatives, pleased the NDP and won its support. Then Layton and Martin signed an agreement adding $4.6 billion in spending on the environment, social housing, foreign aid, and tuition reduction to the Liberal budget, thus ensuring that the NDP would support it.

The Liberal government tried all it could to stay in office for as long as possible, managing to survive three confidence votes in the House of Commons. The first failed attempt at toppling the government occurred barely three months after the 2004 election. The government had to strike a deal with the three opposition parties two hours before MPs were to vote on a Bloc Québécois motion to amend the Speech from the Throne.[43] Then, faced with mounting corruption allegations surfacing during testimony at the Gomery Commission, Martin went on television to apologize for the sponsorship scandal and pledged to call an election one month after the release of the final Gomery Report.

Two weeks later, as a way to increase his odds of surviving the budget vote, Martin managed to convince high-profile Conservative MP (and former leadership candidate) Belinda Stronach to join his cabinet as minister of human resources and democratic renewal. Her defection, together with last-minute support from Independent MP Chuck Cadman allowed the Liberals to retain power on May 19, 2005, in another confidence vote. But Martin's luck finally ran out. After 17 months, the Conservatives, the NDP, and the Bloc united to defeat the Liberal government on November 28, 2005. Public opinion polls (see Figure 13.1) showed that the outcome of the upcoming election was very much in doubt.

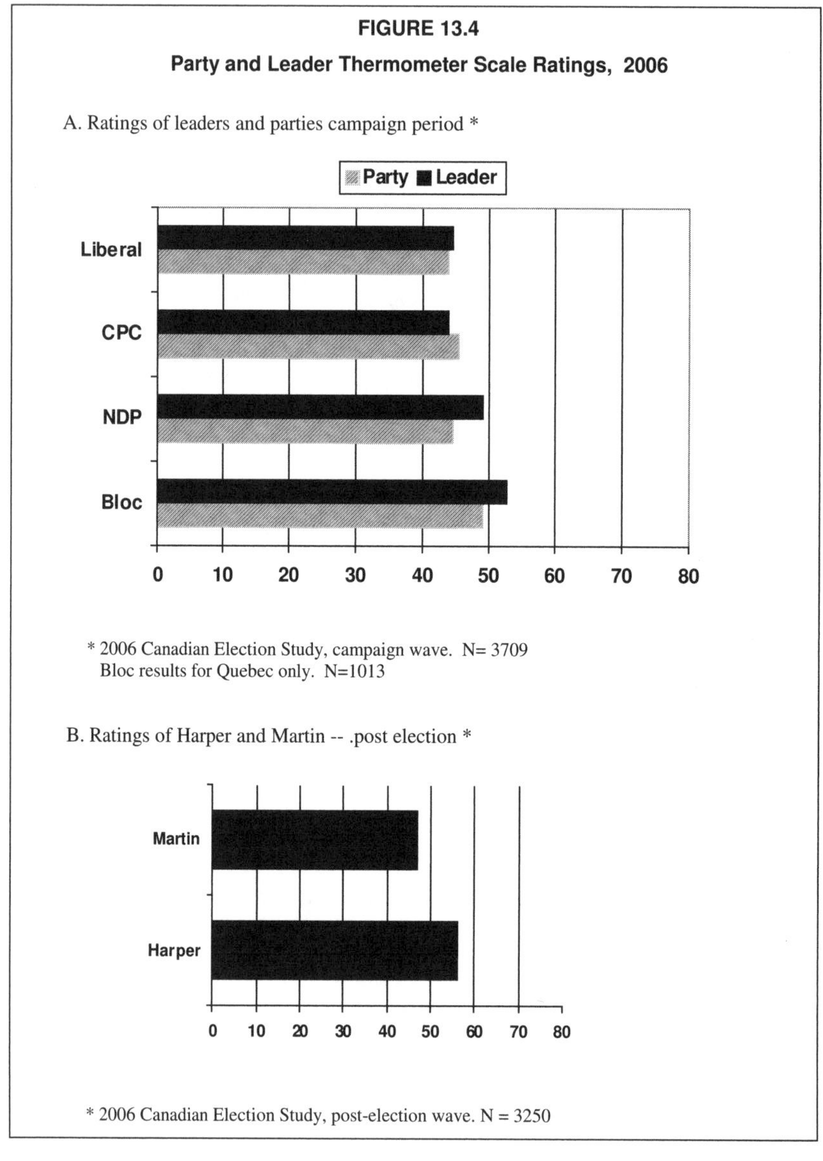

The End of a Dynasty: The 2006 Election

In their campaign, the Conservatives directly took on the two main areas in which the Liberals had an advantage in 2004 — values and social policy. In a controversial move, Stephen Harper chose to announce his party's policy against gay marriage right at the beginning of the campaign, in the context of acknowledging its existence and then assuring people that it would be submitted to a free vote in Parliament to decide the issue. The clear implication of this announcement was that it was a controversial party policy holdover from the Reform Party days which would be disposed of at some point and then forgotten. It was to be the first of many signals from Harper that the Conservatives were to be a centrist party with a broad national and sectoral appeal. Although this announcement generated negative publicity for a few days at the beginning of the campaign, the Conservative attempt to put values questions to the side was ultimately successful. While the Conservatives certainly did not win national advantage on the values question, it became neutralized to the extent that later attempts by the Liberals to raise it did not succeed in the face of other, more important issues.

Another crucial Conservative strategic decision was to develop simple and specific policies in the social and economic policy areas in an effort to overcome the impact of the Liberal budget announcements. The policies were carefully designed to be appealing without being extravagant, given the problems the Liberals faced with their blitz of previous funding announcements. On the social policy front, there were two major promises. Instead of a grandiose pledge such as the Martin promise to "fix health care for a generation" in 2004, Harper proposed a "wait time guarantee" for prompt treatment of a variety of health conditions.

The "wait time" approach was not new — the Liberals and others had promised something similar in 2004. But evidence that waiting times for surgery or treatment were being reduced was not apparent, despite the increased funding put into the health care system. Thus the "guarantee" — although the Conservatives were not specific about the length of time to be guaranteed for different kinds of procedures — was an ambiguous promise, at best. This proposal appeared to be a reasonable approach to improving the health care system, the *public* health care system, and the Conservatives made a point of stressing this message.

The second promise in the social policy campaign agenda came with the daycare issue. A national child care program had been announced, first as a goal, then as the object of an intergovernmental agreement, for a considerable period of time. Perhaps because progress was slow and the actual daycare spaces did not seem to be materializing outside Quebec (where they were created by a provincial government program), the Conservatives believed that they had an opening to advance a different kind of proposal. The Conservative plan was to give every family with a child under six years old $100 a month to help with daycare expenses. Criticism was immediate about the inadequate amount of money this represented, but the Conservative plan had at least two advantages over the Liberal proposal.

First, it was an immediate unilateral federal government solution to what had always been portrayed as an intractable intergovernmental problem. Second, it recognized that parents with small children might need help with child care even if one of the parents was staying at home to look after the child. The Conservative hope was that they might appeal to more traditional families (more likely to be predisposed to the Conservatives in any case because of "values") and offset any support they might lose on the daycare issue to families where both parents were working outside the home. Even if working families had their doubts about the Conservative plan, they could at least feel that the party was taking the issue seriously, and might be worthy of support if other issues were working in their favour.

The same approach of appealing directly to voter self-interest was employed in the economic policy issue area. The Liberals, as mentioned previously, hoped that their proposed income tax cuts would carry the day. The Conservatives, however, chose to compete in the taxation sweepstakes by offering a cut in the Goods and Services Tax (GST). This tax, implemented by the Progressive Conservative government led by Brian Mulroney, had been the subject of intense criticism, particularly by the Liberals in 1993. At that time, Jean Chrétien had promised to get rid of the GST, but the tax stayed in place after the election. With this Conservative promise to lower the GST by a point or two, the Liberals were forced to argue that their income tax reduction plan was actually better for people, even though that reasoning was debatable, and in any event was not clearly explained. As we can see in Table 13.2, health care (36 percent) continued to trump all other issues. Economic issues were mentioned as most important by 15 percent of those surveyed.

Most intriguing in the 2006 election was the situation in Quebec. We have already noted how the sponsorship scandal eroded the Liberal position in the province, but the Bloc was not the only party to gain ground at the expense of the Liberals. The Conservative gain was the most unexpected, as the party had not elected anybody in the province of Quebec in 2004, nor had its predecessors Reform and the Alliance. During the campaign, Stephen Harper gave a number of signals that the Conservatives would be attentive to Quebec's interests.

The Conservative leader spoke of the opportunities a Conservative government would give to Quebec to participate in international affairs, particularly in cultural policy. Going along with these specifics was the Conservative image of being more attuned to provincial rights. Quebec federalists were able to turn to the Conservatives, once that party had established some momentum, in the knowledge that that their votes might be more effective in electing a federalist MP than in sticking with the discredited Liberals. The lacklustre Bloc campaign, which seemed to assume rather arrogantly that everybody in the province would flock to them (*"Ici, c'est le Bloc"*) provided some impetus for a move to the Conservatives.

As the campaign progressed, it became clear that the 2006 election would not be a repeat of the previous two. This time the Liberals would be the ones making the gaffes. In the second week, the Liberal communications director, Scott Reid, dismissed Harper's daycare proposal, suggesting that parents would spend the cash on beer and popcorn, the comment seeming to display Liberal arrogance and a lack of insight about the concerns that many parents had with the issue of affordable child daycare.

Because the long campaign spanned the Christmas period, there was a break between the two halves. This holiday hiatus was described by Stephen Clarkson as "the week that broke the Liberals' back."[44] First, on December 26, a teenage girl was gunned down and six others were injured on Yonge Street in downtown Toronto. This tragic event played into the Conservatives' emphasis on the law-and-order issue. Three days later, the RCMP publicly announced a criminal investigation into whether a tax policy break for income trust investments announced in the November budget had been previously leaked. Once again, questions of ethics and accountability burst onto the front pages, reminding voters of the still lingering sponsorship scandal.[45] By the time politicians returned to the campaign trail, it was too late for the Liberals.

The bifurcated nature of the campaign also saw two sets of leaders' debates, one before and one after Christmas. Viewers who tuned in to the first one saw a Stephen Harper who was quite comfortable in front of the cameras and able to express himself in both official languages. Harper calmly repeated his five key priorities in simple and straightforward language. In contrast, Paul Martin looked nervous and agitated and his syntax was at times incomprehensible.[46] Meanwhile, the NDP concentrated — with some success — on building up the profile of their leader, pointing to the effective and important NDP legislative record in the minority government.[47]

By the time the second round of debates took place in January, the Liberal campaign was in disarray. One important difference between the first and the second set of debates was that Harper emerged as a clearer winner in January. Moreover, Harper became the focus of Duceppe's attacks during the second French debate and his ability to defend himself in French gave him some credibility with the Quebec electorate. The upsurge in Conservative support did not occur until after Christmas, but it picked up momentum after the January debates and into the closing week of the campaign.[48] By the end of the campaign, both Harper and his party had improved their image, while Martin and the Liberals continued to lag (see Figure 13.4B).

Election day 2006 saw the election of the Conservative Party with a minority government, ending the Chrétien/Martin dynasty. That victory can be explained by several factors. Most immediately visible was the ability of the Conservatives to make gains to the detriment of both the Bloc Québécois and the Liberals in Quebec; the Conservatives took 8 of their 10 seats from Bloc incumbents. Harper's ability to communicate in French meant that for the first time in years, Quebecers would hear a decentralist message from someone other than the Bloc. As a result, not only did the Bloc fail to match its 1993 performance, it actually elected a slightly smaller contingent of MPs, despite the fact that it continued to be the dominant party in Quebec federal politics.[49]

These Quebec gains were symbolically important for the Conservatives, strengthening their claim to be a national party and vindicating their decision to pursue a brokerage strategy, much like the old Progressive Conservatives. Equally important was the Conservative ability to gain votes and seats in Ontario — a net gain of 16 seats, all at the expense of the Liberals, who also lost 5 additional seats to the NDP.

The 2006 election continued the erosion of Liberal votes to other parties, while the Conservatives were generally successful in hanging on to votes won in 2004 (see Figure13.5).

Finding new strength in the centre of the country as opposed to the western and eastern regions meant that the Conservative Party now had the base to dream about establishing a new dynasty themselves. As the measure of party identification in the 2006 Canadian Election Study shows (see Figure 13.6), the Conservatives also had begun to pull even with the Liberals in terms of the number of Canadians identifying with the party, although nearly a quarter of all respondents continued to eschew identification with any party. While there were now two national parties that could compete effectively to form a government, the Canadian electorate continued to be volatile.

FIGURE 13.5

Electoral Turnover, 2004–2006

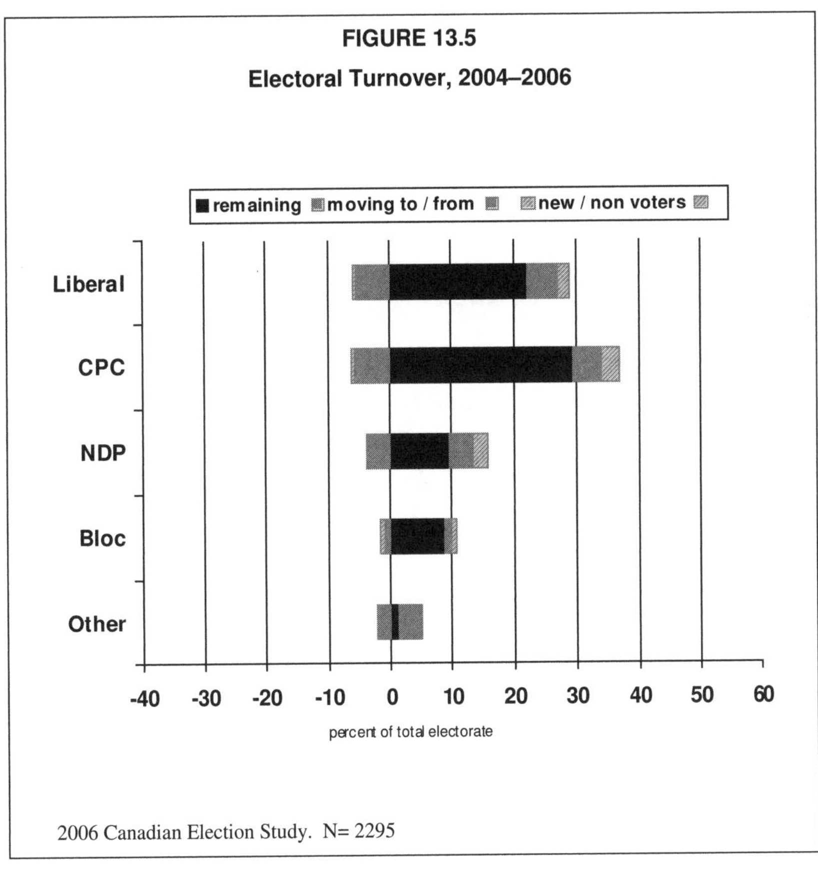

2006 Canadian Election Study. N= 2295

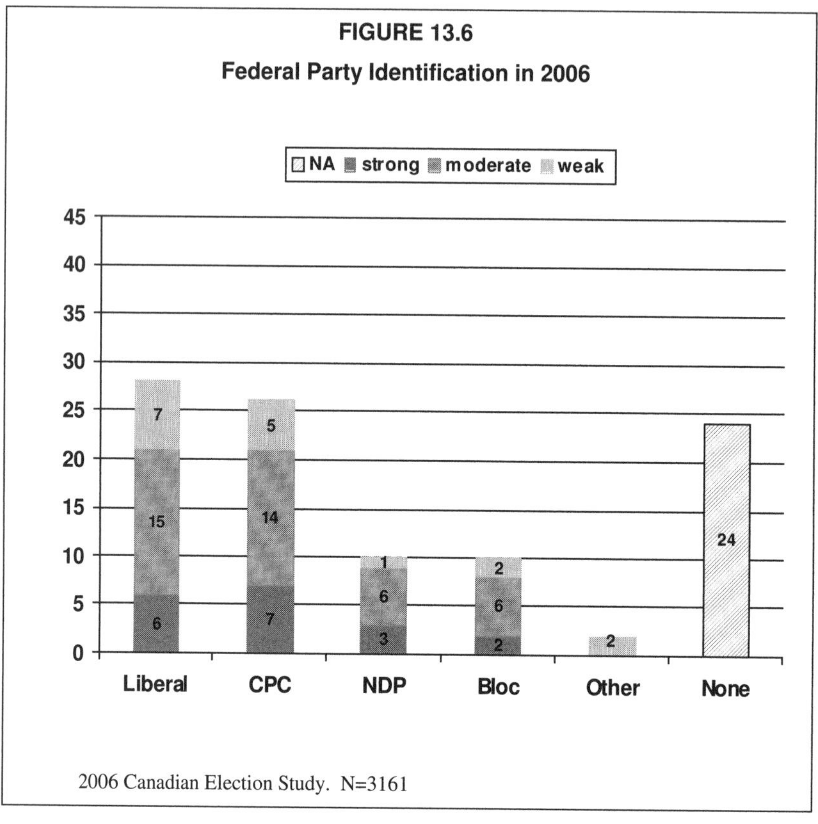

The Conservatives in Power

The new Conservative government needed to move quickly to establish its credibility. Their strategy was to fulfill their pledges from the 2006 election as soon as possible. This would allow them to demonstrate, not only their trustworthiness in keeping their commitments, but also middle-of-the-road positions that would show that they could be trusted to govern. In doing so, they could finally put to rest the perennial accusation that they were harbouring an ultra-conservative hidden agenda. Thus, the Conservative budgets cut the GST and other taxes as promised, and also provided substantial funding for social programs, particularly health care. This money was earmarked to allow the provinces to reduce hospital waiting times as the Conservatives had promised to do, to the limited extent that provincial governments could be encouraged to spend money in their own jurisdictions in ways the federal government wanted.

The inability of the government to determine to what uses its monetary transfers to the provinces were put was also demonstrated by the reaction of the Quebec government to a $9 billion transfer offered as a way to redress the "fiscal imbalance." The provincial Liberal government, locked in a fierce battle for survival after an adverse result in the previous provincial election, promptly used the money to reduce provincial income taxes.[50]

The money, however, took second place to a symbolic measure in the Conservatives' effort to position themselves for further gains in Quebec. During the first session of the new Parliament, the Bloc Québécois put forward a resolution calling for the recognition of Quebec as a nation, and, to considerable surprise, Harper decided to support an amended version of the resolution recognizing the Québécois as a nation within Canada. The Liberals, in the midst of a leadership race to succeed Paul Martin, "were plunged into chaos,"[51] which of course was Harper's intention. Some leadership candidates supported the motion to various degrees (Michael Ignatieff wanted to go further and somehow place the recognition in the Constitution), while others were opposed (Gerrard Kennedy, Ken Dryden, Joe Volpe). To Conservative strategists, the move appeared to bolster the Conservative chances in Quebec, while allowing the party to portray itself as champions of national unity outside the province.

The Conservatives were able to complete the bulk of their legislative agenda despite their precarious minority status because the Liberals, involved in a prolonged race for the party leadership, felt unable or unwilling to defeat the government and bring on yet another election. Moreover, due to the operations of new rules for financing political parties, the party was broke. Those new party financing rules were the results of one of the salvoes fired by Jean Chrétien in the Liberal civil war. The legislation limited financial donations from individuals to $5,000 per year, and from corporations or unions to $1,000, and compensated by instituting a yearly public subsidy for the parties, keyed to vote totals in the preceding election. The target of this draconian change in the law was Paul Martin and his corporate connections, but the peripheral damage hit the Liberal Party worst of all, since the Liberals, unlike the Conservatives, had a poorly developed base of small donations from party members. For much of the period of the first Harper government, the Liberals felt they could simply not afford to run an effective election campaign.

When the Liberal leadership campaign finally came to a conclusion in December, 2006, with no clear front-runner and all the candidates deeply in debt, the party saw an opportunity to renew its organization and membership and create some publicity for itself. The occasion was reminiscent in some ways of the 1976 Progressive Conservative leadership convention, when the two leading vote-getters on early ballots showed little room for growth in support, and a consensus candidate, Joe Clark, came from farther back to win (see Chapter 8).

In this case, there were two other candidates — Michael Ignatieff and Bob Rae, the former premier of Ontario, ahead of the eventual winner, Stéphane Dion. Dion, a surprise choice, had been environment minister in the Martin cabinet, and caught the imagination of many in the party who saw issues around global warming as necessitating some radical shifts in priorities. Dion also appeared to have some credentials in the national unity issue area, as he had led the fight against sovereigntists (without becoming embroiled in the sponsorship scandal) after the 1995 Quebec referendum. It was the first time in Liberal Party history when the eventual winner of a convention did not lead on the first ballot. Dion was not popular in Quebec, and almost immediately became the target of negative Conservative advertising designed to exploit some of his weaknesses.

Despite its precarious minority position in Parliament, the Harper government lasted for thirty months and appeared set to weather another session of Parliament when the prime minister unexpectedly announced his intention to instead seek its dissolution. This came as a surprise, since the government had previously pushed through an amendment to the *Canada Elections Act* providing for fixed-date elections. While the amendment allowed for the possibility that an earlier election could still occur as a result of a parliamentary defeat on a matter of confidence, it did not foresee that it might come about by other means. Thus, the prime minister's sudden decision to seek dissolution of Parliament, which was granted by the governor general, was both controversial and unexpected. It may have been precipitated either by a feeling that the Liberals under Dion were vulnerable or by concern over the risks posed by the looming economic crisis — or both.

The 2008 Election

For the fourth time in less than 10 years, Canadian voters were asked to go to the polls to elect a new government. This represents the busiest decade in Canada's electoral history, rivalled only by the decade prior to Trudeaumania. But unlike the 1968 vote that began the Trudeau dynasty, the outcome of the 2008 election settled very little. It solidified the regional bases of party support that had emerged in 2004 and left the Canadian political system once again in a state of parliamentary paralysis.

The Conservatives decided in 2008 to run a campaign based largely on a strategy of denigrating Stéphane Dion and his Green Shift policy of carbon taxation. While the Liberals intended this policy proposal to be an environmental program coupled with an economic stimulus, the Conservatives' goal was to define it as an ill-conceived economic plan and a "tax on everything."

"Can you afford to pay more?" asked the Conservative campaign advertisements and literature, accompanied by a picture of Stéphane Dion shrugging his shoulders, or a video clip of him declaring that "It is not easy to make policy." The Conservatives, in other words, attempted to secure their advantage in the economic policy area through portraying their main opponents as incompetent on the leadership dimension, as well as having produced a disastrous economic plan in the guise of an environmental one.

Looking at Figure 13.7, it appears that Harper had a good grasp of his leadership advantage over Dion. Harper was much better regarded than Dion — with Harper receiving a 51 mean score compared to 42 for Dion. In fact, Dion trailed all party leaders by a wide margin. He also trailed his party in overall impression. In contrast, Duceppe, Layton, and May were more popular than their respective parties, while the difference in impression between Harper and his party was marginal.

The Liberals were unable to gain ground on their opponents because an emphasis on the environment was a clear misreading of the mood of the country. As Table 13.2 indicates, it was the state of the economy that was on the minds of Canadians. At 31 percent (up from 15 percent in 2006), economic concerns clearly dominated the issue agenda, as the developing economic crisis unfolded during the course of the campaign. This was the highest level of concern over the economy since the 1993 election and it was the first time since the 2000 election that the economy eclipsed health care as the most important issue. Dion's Green Shift barely registered as a top issue, and general concern over the environment stood at just below 9 percent.

The Conservatives were successful in their strategy of ridiculing the carbon tax idea. However, this did not translate for them to equivalent success in the minds of the public as the party that could be trusted over the longer term to guide the economy to further growth and prosperity, and to deal with the looming economic crisis. The first difficulty was that their "Real Plan" for the economy, as outlined in their advertising, was all about generalities. It featured "Balanced Budgets; Lower Taxes; Investing in Jobs; and Controlling Inflation." It did not, however, contain many concrete measures to achieve any of these goals. In 2008, the Conservatives were vulnerable to the charge that they did not have a coherent economic plan of their own at all.

Formulating an appeal to Quebec had been a key element of the Harper Conservative strategy since the 2006 election in their efforts to achieve a majority, as it had been for Brian Mulroney in 1984. As well as the tangible and symbolic policies mentioned above, there were attempts by the federal Conservatives to build on the success of the *Action Démocratique du Québec* in the provincial election of 2007 by implying that the real conservative forces were on the march in the province.

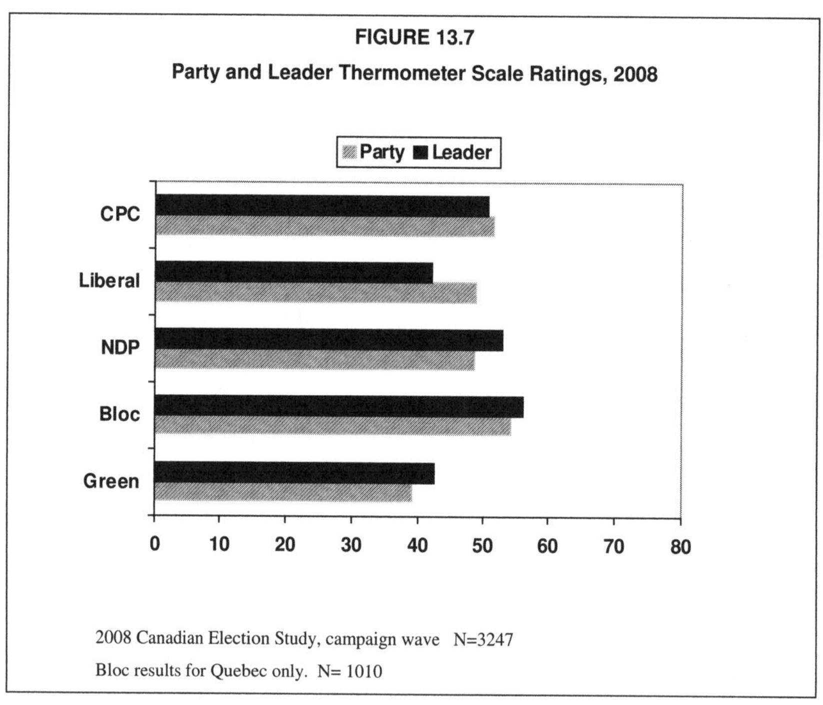

FIGURE 13.7

Party and Leader Thermometer Scale Ratings, 2008

2008 Canadian Election Study, campaign wave N=3247

Bloc results for Quebec only. N= 1010

In appealing to Quebec, the Conservatives also relied heavily on continued criticism of their Liberal predecessors in government. The excesses and corruption of the Sponsorship Scandal were again front and centre. In addition, the fact that Stéphane Dion had been the architect of the *Clarity Act*, a piece of legislation passed under the Chrétien government to allow for the holding of a federal referendum in Quebec if a provincial one was unclearly worded, was used by the Conservatives to attack the Liberals, thereby linking Dion with Chrétien and even Trudeau in opposition to nationalistic Quebec interests. Once again, these tactics harmed the Liberals, but the electoral benefits did not flow to the Conservatives. The Conservatives calculated that Quebec voters would think they might be better off with members on the government side. However, Harper's personal appeal in Quebec was limited; he was, after all, a westerner, whose ideological leanings often appeared out of sync with the Quebec mainstream.

The lack of a positive economic platform with real content in 2008 might not have been a problem for the Conservatives under more stable economic conditions. As it was, this strategy left them vulnerable when the economic crisis escalated during the campaign, with bad economic news from the United States spilling over into Canada. Their initial response was simply to repeat their criticisms of the Liberals: "At a time of global economic uncertainty, we need a responsible plan that protects workers, families, and businesses. Now is not the time for fuzzy theories or risky schemes."[52] Harper's response to Dion's hasty economic recovery plan announced during the leaders' debates was to criticize Dion for creating such a plan, rather than to announce one of his own. Quick action was decried, even as many other countries in the world, especially the United States, began to engage in it. Only after the lack of economic planning in the post-election economic statement almost brought down the government did the Conservatives begin to create a plan for economic stimulus.

The Liberals suffered during the election campaign from the opposite problem to the one faced by the Conservatives. The Green Shift was a highly specific policy that had difficulties similar to other past economic programs of a controversial nature. The Conservatives in the 1974 federal election proposed wage and price controls to deal with double-digit inflation. As documented in Chapter 7, the wage and price control policy was not one that benefited the Progressive Conservatives in that election because as many people opposed it as were in favour. The more details produced about wage and price controls, the more difficulty the PCs of 1974 encountered in trying to explain how the controls would work. Likewise the Progressive Conservative budget in 1979 proposing an 18-cent-per-gallon rise in gasoline prices became a millstone for the party's campaign in the 1980 election, as they were forced to explain how it would be "short term pain for long term gain" (see Chapter 8). For its part, the 2008 Liberal Green Shift likewise had the potential, eminently realized during the campaign, of alienating as many people as it could attract. In addition, it was so complicated that few Liberals, other than Dion, could really explain it.

Stephen Harper's Conservatives, following their minority victory in the 2006 election, might well have believed that the construction of a new political dynasty was possible over the longer term. Their surprising showing in Quebec of 10 seats and 25 percent of the vote undoubtedly suggested to the Conservatives that a breakthrough in the province could be made, particularly if the position of the Bloc in rural Quebec began to weaken.

Yet despite its efforts to woo Quebec voters over the course of its two-and-a-half-year-long minority government, the Conservatives were able to make no such breakthrough in the 2008 election, holding their 10 seats won in 2006 but seeing their share of the Quebec vote decline to 22 percent — 2 percentage points below the Liberals. Efforts by the Conservatives to capture more votes and seats in Quebec were undermined by Harper's decision to announce policies that cut a variety of funding programs in the arts and culture area, including funding for artists displaying their work abroad. In addition, there were announcements that funding would be denied for the production of films that had content the government deemed inappropriate — content such as naughty words in the title. Neither of these policy directions played well in Quebec, and they soon became the subject of savage satirical comment. Trying to justify these decisions during the campaign, Harper appeared to describe federal support for arts and culture as "funding things people don't want,"[53] and ensuing comments about "rich people attending arts galas" only compounded the problem.

"Tough on Crime" legislation proposed during the campaign to jail young offenders, potentially for life, was also seen in Quebec as inhumane and counterproductive. These initiatives, with their overtones of right-wing social conservatism, were designed to appeal to urban dwellers in other provinces, but were perceived negatively in Quebec. And, by failing in their national unity appeal in Quebec, the Conservatives were not able to benefit in the rest of Canada from being perceived as the party which could best "deal with Quebec."

Perhaps more importantly, by concentrating their efforts on such side issues, the Conservatives failed to focus their campaign efforts on positioning themselves favourably along the three pillars of electoral success in Canada. This is illustrated by looking at the electoral turnover between 2006 and 2008 (see Figure 13.8). The Conservatives had made important gains in the previous two elections in their attempts to chip away at Liberal support, with a view to position themselves as a majority alternative to the Liberals. However, these efforts stalled in 2008. As a result, the Harper Conservatives squandered a potential opportunity to turn their minority status into the beginnings of a dynasty.

FIGURE 13.8

Electoral Turnover, 2006–2008

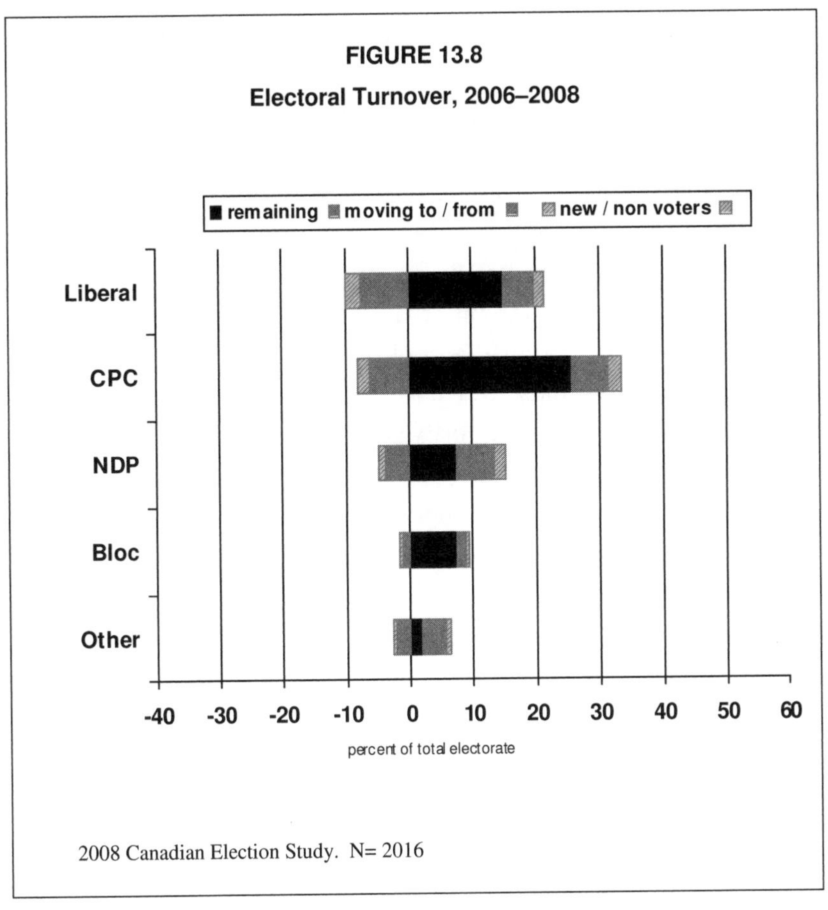

2008 Canadian Election Study. N= 2016

While these campaign missteps were important in their short-term effects, the mere presence of the Bloc has proven to be of greater long-term significance. That party's strength in the Quebec electorate in each of the past three elections has remained remarkably close to its 1993 high of 54 seats and 49 percent of the Quebec vote. In 2004, the Bloc replicated its 1993 totals. Although the Bloc's percentage of the Quebec vote dropped to 38 percent in 2008 — its worst showing since 1997 — the party nevertheless managed to win 49 seats, a decline of only 2 from the 2006 election. Since its sudden arrival on the political scene in 1993, the demise of the Bloc has been regularly predicted. Yet it does not appear to be leaving the stage anytime soon.

The New Democratic Party has also continued to play a major role in restricting governments to minority status since 2000. The NDP's overall vote totals have remained fairly stable during the last three elections, at 16, 17, and 18 percent respectively (see Table 13.3). But the party is competitive in many parts of the country, and small fluctuations in vote totals in key constituencies can substantially affect the number of seats they win in Parliament. For example, the number of seats the NDP has won in Ontario rose from 7 in 2004 to 12 in 2006 to 17 in 2008, even though the party has not increased its share of the popular vote in the province. In Saskatchewan, on the other hand, the party won over a quarter of the overall vote yet did not elect anyone in 2008, whereas in Quebec, its 12 percent gained it one seat. Three-way battles involving the NDP, Conservatives, and Liberals make mastery of the issue agenda of Canadian politics even more important. They also reduce the thresholds needed to win a seat in some instances, and increase the probability of minority government.

Its position as the third most popular party has left the NDP with the tasks during each election campaign, not only of defining its position on the issues of the day, but also of asserting its relevance in the electoral equation.[54] Given the unlikelihood of its forming a government, the NDP has sometimes simply urged voters to elect more New Democrats in order to form a strong opposition. In 2008, however, the party sensed that it was dealing with a situation, because of the relative unpopularity of both the major parties, where substantially more voters might turn their way. They consequently designed a campaign whereby leader Jack Layton declared he was "running for prime minister." The party's reformulation of traditional strong themes of social program protection and enhancement, and addressing economic uncertainty facing ordinary people had substantial appeal, particularly once the economic crisis began to dominate the news. But once again the party's potential voters were faced with strategic decisions whether to support the NDP, or vote Liberal to stop what was potentially a Conservative majority government. In addition, the NDP faced a challenge from the Green Party, gaining in strength and with more credibility in the environmental area than they had, given their criticism of the carbon tax proposal of the Liberals.

Conclusion

The three federal elections of 2004, 2006, and 2008 have all produced minority governments, and these results suggest that the era of electoral dynasties and even majority governments may be over, at least for the time being. The continuing electoral success of five political parties (including the Green Party), each with a relatively strong appeal in some but not all regions of the country, makes it difficult for any of them to achieve a majority government at one point in time, let alone for the three or four elections in succession which would allow us to identify the emergence of a new political dynasty.

To this regionalization of Canadian federal politics we must add in these recent elections the inability of either the Liberals or Conservatives to demonstrate mastery of the three key issue areas of the economy, national unity, and social policy that were critical in maintaining dynasties for King, Trudeau, and Chrétien. The intensity and widespread nature of the current economic crisis, plunging as it has government budgets deep into deficit, will perhaps further erode public confidence in the political sector. Although the Trudeau dynasty was created during the "stagflation" years of the 1970s, neither Stephen Harper nor Michael Ignatieff has established to date the degree of public trust that was vested in Trudeau. Thus, minority governments appear to be the order of the day for now, and the conditions needed to obtain a majority of seats, let alone to establish a new dynasty, may be well into the future. While the partisan "civil wars" that were the dominant force in Canadian federal politics over the past two decades may be coming to an end, their legacy of minority government could conceivably endure for some time.

Notes

1. Jean Chrétien, *My Years as Prime Minister* (Toronto: Alfred A. Knopf, Canada, 2007), 11.
2. Paul Martin, *Hell or High Water: My Life In and Out of Politics* (Toronto: McClelland & Stewart, 2008), 90–91. *Vendu* literally means "sell-out," but in this context "traitor" is a more accurate reflection of the intended meaning.
3. *Ibid.*, 98.
4. Susan Delacourt, *Juggernaut* (Toronto: McClelland & Stewart, 2003), 92.
5. Martin, *op. cit.*, 169.
6. *Ibid.*, 228.
7. Chrétien, *op. cit.*, 259.
8. Tom Flanagan, *Harper's Team* (Montreal and Kingston: McGill-Queen's University Press, 2007), 61.
9. For details of the MacKay-Orchard Deal, see Bob Plamondon, *Full Circle: Death and Resurrection in Canadian Conservative Politics* (Toronto: Key Porter Books, 2006), 263–67.
10. For full details of this series of events, see Flanagan, *Harper's Team*, 90–136.
11. *Ibid.*, 16.
12. Preston Manning, *Think Big* (Toronto: MacMillan & Stewart, 2002), especially 47–49.
13. For more details on those events and about Stephen Harper, see William Johnson, *Stephen Harper and the Future of Canada* (Toronto: MacMillan & Stewart, 2005).
14. See *www.oag-bvg.gc.ca* (accessed November 2003).
15. This refers to allegations that Chrétien intervened in the decision to give a loan to the owner of a hotel in his riding of Shawinigan.
16. This refers to the mismanagement of over one billion dollars in grants by the Ministry of Human Resources.
17. See *National Post*, February 17, 2004: A2.
18. For a full discussion of those events, see John Gray, *Paul Martin*, 204–07.
19. Edward Greenspon and Anthony Wilson-Smith, *Double Vision*, 44.
20. *The Economist*, February 17, 2005.
21. Heather Scoffield and Campbell Clark, "Martin Waves the Flag," *Globe and Mail*, May 24, 2004: A1.
22. Flanagan, *Harper's Team*, 157.
23. Robert Fife, "Martin Pledges Not To Raise Taxes," *National Post*, May 25, 2004: A1.
24. Alan Whitehorn, "Jack Layton and the NDP: Gains but No Breakthrough," in Jon H. Pammett and Christopher Dornan, eds., *The Canadian General Election of 2004* (Toronto: Dundurn Press, 2004), 106.
25. Brian Laghi and Heather Scoffield, "Harper Platform Promises Sweeping Change," *Globe and Mail*, June 12, 2004: A4.

26. Alain-G. Gagnon and Jacques Hérivault, "The Bloc Québécois: The Dynamics of a Distinct Electorate," in Jon H. Pammett and Christopher Dornan, eds., *The Canadian General Election of 2004* (Toronto: Dundurn Press, 2004), 153–55.
27. Stephen Clarkson, "Disaster and Recovery: Paul Martin as Political Lazarus," in Jon H. Pammett and Christopher Dornan, eds., *The Canadian General Election of 2004* (Toronto: Dundurn Press, 2004), 57.
28. Faron Ellis and Peter Woolstencroft, "New Conservatives, Old Realities: The 2004 Election Campaign," in Jon H. Pammett and Christopher Dornan, eds., *The Canadian General Election of 2004* (Toronto: Dundurn Press, 2004), 95.
29. *Globe and Mail*, June 10, 2004: A1.
30. Jane Taber, "The Liberals Are in a Spiral, Top Martin Adviser Says," *Globe and Mail*, June 10, 2004: A1.
31. Jane Taber, "Confident Harper Talks Majority," *Globe and Mail*, June 11, 2004: A1.
32. See a discussion about the impact of the comments in Haroon Siddiqui, "The Best Campaign Since 1988," *Toronto Star*, June 24, 2004: A27.
33. André Blais, Elisabeth Gidengil, Richard Nadeau, and Neil Nevitte, *Anatomy of a Liberal Victory: Making Sense of the Vote in the 2000 Canadian Election* (Peterborough, ON: Broadview, 2002).
34. Faron Ellis and Peter Woolstencroft, "A Change of Government, Not a Change of Country," in Jon H. Pammett and Christopher Dornan, eds., *The Canadian General Election of 2006* (Toronto: Dundurn Press, 2006).
35. See Paul Wells, *Right Side Up* (Toronto: McClelland & Stewart, 2006), 141–46.
36. Faron Ellis and Peter Woolstencroft, "A Change of Government, Not a Change of Country," 65.
37. *Globe and Mail*, November 2, 2005: A11.
38. See *The Gomery Commission Report* — Phase 1 (Ottawa: Supply and Services, 2005). Quote from the *Globe and Mail*, November 2, 2005: A1.
39. See, for example, Don Martin, "Martin's Reign of Error," *National Post*, May 21, 2005: A1, and Paul Wells, *Right Side Up: The Fall of Paul Martin and the Rise of Stephen Harper's New Conservatism* (Toronto: McClelland & Stewart, 2006).
40. Stephen Clarkson, "How the Big Red Machine Became the Little Red Machine," in Jon H. Pammett and Christopher Dornan, eds., *The Canadian Federal Election of 2006* (Toronto: Dundurn Press, 2006), 27.
41. Eric Bélanger and Richard Nadeau, "The Bloc Québécois: A Sour-Tasting Victory," in Jon H. Pammett and Christopher Dornan, eds., *The Canadian Federal Election of 2006* (Toronto: Dundurn Press, 2006), 125.
42. Three polling firms (POLLARA, IPSOS-Reid, and Environics) had Bloc support at 59 percent among decided voters one month before the beginning of the election campaign.
43. See Gloria Galloway, "From Here," *Globe and Mail*, November 29, 2005: A5.

44. Stephen Clarkson, "How the Big Red Machine Became the Little Red Machine," 36.
45. *Ibid.*
46. Stephen Clarkson, "How the Big Red Machine Became the Little Red Machine," 34–35.
47. Alan Whitehorn, "The NDP and the Enigma of Strategic Voting," in Jon H. Pammett and Christopher Dornan, eds., *The Canadian General Election of 2006* (Toronto: Dundurn Press, 2006), 97.
48. See Figure 2 in Eric Bélanger and Richard Nadeau, "The Bloc Québécois: A Sour-Tasting Victory," in Jon H. Pammett and Christopher Dornan, eds., *The Canadian General Election of 2006* (Toronto: Dundurn Press, 2006), 129.
49. See André Turcotte, "After 56 Days … The Verdict."
50. Faron Ellis and Peter Woolstencroft, "The Harper Government Campaigns on Its Record," in Jon H. Pammett and Christopher Dornan, *The Canadian Federal Election of 2008* (Toronto: Dundurn Press, 2009).
51. Brooke Jeffrey, "Missed Opportunity: The Invisible Liberals," in Pammett and Dornan, *op. cit.*
52. Conservative campaign pamphlet delivered during the campaign.
53. *Globe and Mail*, September 12, 2008: A1.
54. Lynda Erickson and David Laycock, "Modernization, Incremental Progress and the Challenge of Relevance: The NDP's Campaign," in Jon H. Pammett and Christopher Dornan, eds., *The Canadian Federal Election of 2008* (Toronto: Dundurn Press, 2009), Chapter 4.

Selected Reading

Chrétien, Jean. *My Years as Prime Minister* (Toronto: Alfred A. Knopf, 2007).

Flanagan, Tom. *Harper's Team* (Montreal: McGill-Queen's University Press, 2007).

Gagnon, Alain, and Brian Tanguay, eds. *Canadian Political Parties in Transition*, third edition (Toronto: Broadview, 2007).

Johnston, William. *Stephen Harper and the Future of Canada* (Toronto: McClelland & Stewart, 2006).

Le Duc, Lawrence, "The Federal Election in Canada: June 2004." *Electoral Studies* 24 (2005), 338–44.

LeDuc, Lawrence. "The Federal Election in Canada: January 2006." *Electoral Studies* 26 (2007), 716–20.

LeDuc, Lawrence. "The Federal Election in Canada: October 2008." *Electoral Studies* 28 (2009), 322–29.

Martin, Paul. *Hell or High Water: My Life In and Out of Politics* (Toronto: McClelland & Stewart, 2008).

Pammett, Jon H., and Christopher Dornan, eds. *The Canadian Federal Election of 2004* (Toronto: Dundurn Press, 2005).

Pammett, Jon H., and Christopher Dornan, eds. *The Canadian Federal Election of 2006* (Toronto: Dundurn Press, 2006).

Pammett, Jon H., and Christopher Dornan, eds. *The Canadian Federal Election of 2008* (Toronto: Dundurn Press, 2009).

Plamondon, Robert E. *Full Circle: Death and Resurrection in Canadian Conservative Politics* (Toronto: Key Porter, 2006).

CHAPTER 14

EXPLAINING DYNASTIES AND INTERLUDES

The normal timing of elections causes us to think of Canadian politics in terms of four- or five-year cycles. A party is elected to form a government and, four or five years later, it is either re-elected or defeated. But we have seen throughout this book that there are other and perhaps more meaningful ways to think about Canadian electoral politics. Canada's most politically successful prime ministers — Macdonald, Laurier, King (followed by St. Laurent), Trudeau (following Pearson), and Chrétien (with Martin) — built electoral dynasties that endured for long periods of time. Mackenzie King served a total of 22 years as prime minister before handing power over to his successor, Louis St. Laurent, who served another nine years. Jean Chrétien served 11 years before handing over the job to Paul Martin who, for most of that time, had been his finance minister. As we have seen over the course of this book, there have been five party/leader combinations that would clearly qualify as "dynasties" over the long sweep of Canadian political history (see Figure 14.1).

These periods of electoral dominance, which in Canada are often identified with the fortunes of individual political leaders, are truly long ones by most comparative standards. In Britain — perhaps the most useful comparison because of institutional similarities — only a few leaders have approached these degrees of political longevity. Churchill, for example, served two terms in office spanning a total of nine years, but these were separated by one stunning electoral defeat (1945). Margaret Thatcher won three consecutive elections, serving a total of 11 years as prime minister. While Gladstone served longer (14 years), his tenure was spread across four interrupted terms in office. American presidents, of course, are now constitutionally limited to two four-year terms, but even before the enactment of the 22nd amendment, only Franklin D. Roosevelt served longer than eight years. The first question we pose therefore is: what explains these patterns of enduring political success enjoyed by Canadian political leaders, and by the parties that they led?

The interludes that we encounter periodically over the course of Canadian political history have been, with a few exceptions, short and sharp. Alexander Mackenzie and R.B. Bennett each served one full term as prime minister, but their administrations ended in electoral defeat, explained to some degree by the economic circumstances of their times. Arthur Meighen's two brief turns as prime minister, first as

Library and Archives Canada.

Mackenzie King at ceremony celebrating the diamond jubilee of Confederation, Ottawa, 1927.

Robert Borden's successor for 18 months prior to the election of 1921, and later for three months in 1926, were brief interludes *within* an electoral cycle, since Meighen failed on both occasions to win the ensuing election. Joe Clark's nine-month interlude began with his minority victory in the 1979 election and ended with his defeat in Parliament and in the 1980 election that followed. The stark contrast between these brief interludes and the successful political dynasties tells much of the story of Canadian federal politics as it has evolved over nearly a century and a half. A second question therefore is: can we explain how and why these brief interludes occurred?

FIGURE 14.1

Dynasties and Interludes in Canadian politics

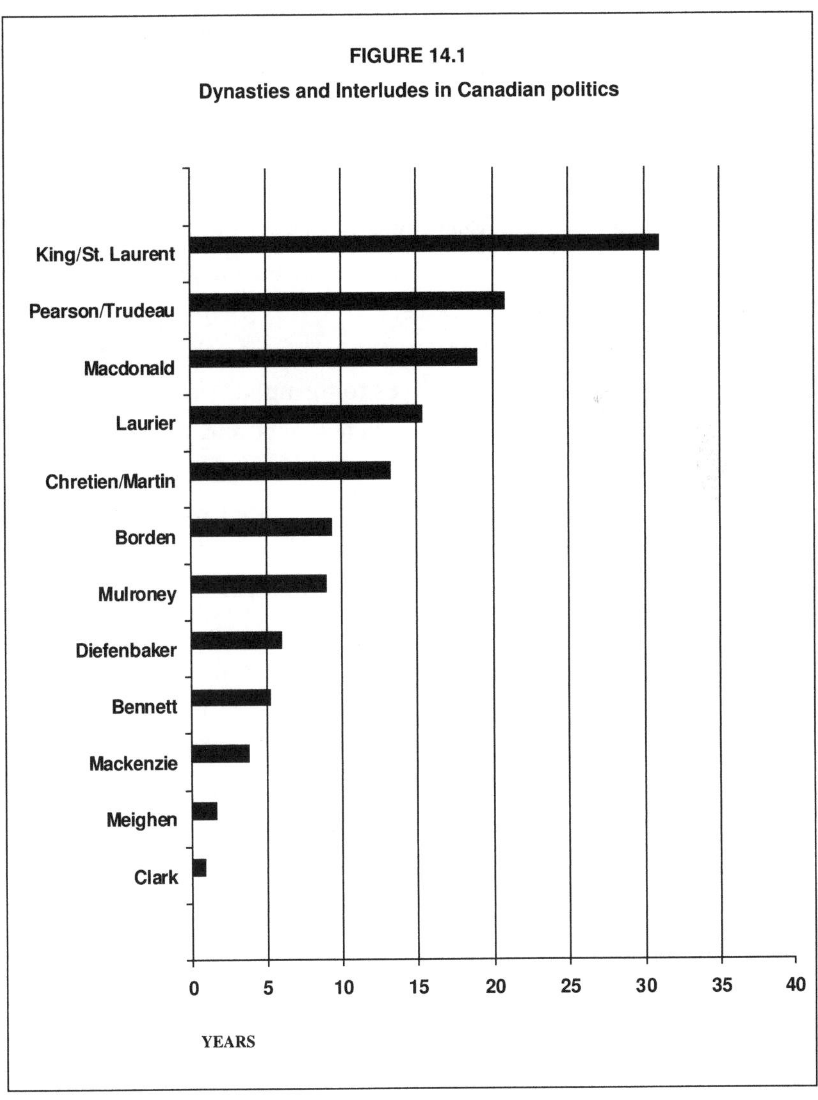

Part of the answer to these complex questions can be found in the cases that do not fit neatly into our typology of "dynasties and interludes." Lester Pearson, for example, served six years as prime minister, and his tenure in the office is highly regarded by historians today, in part because of the significant policy achievements of his administration.[1] But Pearson endured one of the worst electoral defeats in Canadian history at the hands of John Diefenbaker in 1958, and he never succeeded in obtaining a majority of parliamentary seats in the two elections that he won (1963 and 1965). Yet, unlike Borden, he *did* manage to pass the reins of power along to a successor who *did* preside over one of the more enduring political dynasties of recent times. Do we think then of a "Pearson interlude" or a "Pearson/Trudeau dynasty," as is suggested by the configuration employed in Figure 14.1 and as we have argued in Chapters 5 and 6 of this book? Neither term captures with total accuracy the high and low points, the successes and failures, of the Pearson and Trudeau eras of Canadian politics. But, with the benefit of historical hindsight, we can now see that the longevity of the Pearson/Trudeau dynasty rivals those of Macdonald and Laurier, even though neither Pearson nor Trudeau enjoyed unqualified political success over the course of their political careers.

The careers of two other political leaders who fell short of establishing dynasties also can help us to formulate part of the answer to the questions posed above. John Diefenbaker and Brian Mulroney led the Progressive Conservative Party to two of its greatest electoral victories, in 1958 and 1984 respectively, but neither was able to found a political dynasty based on this initial success. Diefenbaker's six-year tenure as prime minister ended ignominiously with his defeat in the 1963 election and his ouster from the party leadership in 1967. Mulroney's two terms culminated in the near destruction of his party in the disastrous 1993 election (see Chapter 11). Both leaders left a political legacy, however, that endured long after their time in office had ended. Diefenbaker bequeathed to his successors a solidly Conservative West and Mulroney a nationalist Quebec. In part, the huge and unwieldy electoral coalitions that these two leaders built explains both their initial success and their ultimate failure. In the longer term, holding these diverse coalitions together proved more difficult than constructing them in the first place.

Parties and Leaders

One remarkable feature of Canadian electoral politics as seen from the perspective of Canadian history is the endurance of our main political parties. In contrast to the fundamental changes that periodically take place in the party systems of many other countries, elections in Canada continue to be fought largely between two parties — Liberal and Conservative — in name the same parties that contested elections in Canada in the nineteenth century. Of course, these parties have undergone many changes over their long history, and they have had to adapt to changing political circumstances on numerous occasions. But they have survived.

True, the Liberal Party of today is not the same as the "Clear Grits" of its formative years, or even the Liberal Party of Pierre Trudeau. And the Conservatives have undergone even more changes over their long history — from John A. Macdonald's "Liberal-Conservatives" to Robert Borden's "Unionists," and John Bracken's "Progressive Conservatives," to mention only a few of the party's many twists and turns. While it appeared after the 1993 calamity that the party might not survive at all, the new Conservative Party of Canada, with its minority victories in the 2006 and 2008 elections, appears to be putting at least some of the old pieces back together. Thus, today's elections continue to be a contest between Liberals and Conservatives for power. Other parties such as the NDP, Bloc Québécois, and perhaps the Greens will continue to be a significant factor in elections, as "third" parties so often have been in the past. And future governments, like the present one, may well command only a minority of the seats in the House of Commons,[2] but are all but certain to be led by either a Liberal or a Conservative prime minister.

One reason for the continued dominance of the two "old" parties can be found in the fact that Canadian elections are conducted using the single-member district, plurality wins, electoral system, which makes it extremely difficult for smaller parties, other than regional ones, to win a large enough number of seats to challenge either of the two main parties. As Alan Cairns argued in an oft-cited essay written in 1968, the structure of the Canadian electoral system has implications not only for the competitiveness of parties, but also for the nature of the parties themselves.[3]

A major change in the shape of Canada's party system could still be precipitated by a change to a more proportional electoral formula

— a proposed reform that continues to be actively debated.[4] Had electoral reform come about during the period after the 1993 election, the new party system which that election produced might well have persisted in some form. But, as parties such as Reform, and its successor, the Canadian Alliance, learned over the course of the next two elections, their prospects of becoming truly competitive with the Liberals remained sharply limited under the existing electoral regime. With the 2003 merger of the Alliance with the remnants of the Progressive Conservatives, the party system began to revert, at first slowly, then more rapidly, toward its former shape. Of the new parties spawned by the collapse of the Mulroney coalition, only the Bloc remains.

The first-past-the-post electoral system has served both to sustain dynasties, and to help create interludes. Both the Trudeau and the Chrétien dynasties were supported by large numbers of Liberal members from Quebec, to a greater extent than the Liberal vote totals in that province might have warranted, had they been translated proportionally into seats. To an even greater extent, Chrétien and his government benefited from a virtual monopoly on parliamentary seats from Ontario, despite the fact that, in 2000 for example, the party won only a bare majority of the votes cast in the province. Conversely, the electoral system in 1984 magnified the scope of the Liberal defeat, and gave the Mulroney PCs so many seats (211) that a new Conservative dynasty appeared imminent. In 1979, the Clark Conservatives won the election despite having a lower share of the popular vote than the Liberals, a fact the party appeared to forget when they allowed themselves to be defeated in Parliament a short time later, thereby creating one of the shortest interludes in Canadian history.

However, the electoral system, important as it is in both shaping and constraining the fortunes of political parties, does not provide a complete explanation for the persistence of the Liberal and Conservative parties in the federal arena. Like their American counterparts, which have also endured for more than a century and a half, Canada's two main political parties have learned to change and adapt in order to survive. Leadership conventions, policy conferences, and (when in power) Royal Commissions are among the institutional devices that the parties have utilized to restructure and reposition themselves in the political arena from time to time.

Both major parties have also proven adept at stealing ideas and policies from the minor parties and from each other. King's Liberals took the steam out of the Progressive movement in the 1920s by adopting many of its policies. Today, elements of the populist rhetoric first associated with Social Credit and later with the Reform Party can be found in the policies embraced by the new Conservative Party. It was a Royal Commission appointed by the Liberal government of Pierre Trudeau (the Macdonald Commission) that proposed a free trade agreement with the United States. But it was the Conservative government of Brian Mulroney that negotiated the agreement and adopted the policy as its own.

Students of the Canadian political process observed long ago that Canadian political parties differ from those in other countries in significant ways. Unlike many European political parties, they are not strongly ideological. Although the terms "left" and "right" are widely used by political commentators and other elites in Canada, they do not resonate with much of the electorate. In the 2000 Canadian Election Study, which asked respondents to categorize their political views as "left" or "right," by far the largest component of the electorate was found in the political centre (39 percent), and another large grouping of respondents (29 percent) rejected the concepts entirely or were unsure how to apply them to their own views (see Figure 14.2). Fewer than a third of the survey respondents (31 percent) chose to describe themselves in ideological terms. Of these, 18 percent placed themselves on the political right, and 13 percent on the left. This observation that Canadian voters are not particularly ideological in their orientation to politics is not new. Lambert et al. reported a similar finding from studies conducted in the 1980s.[5]

Restoring the competitiveness of the party system was always more likely to come about through the emergence of a party and leader that were capable of mounting an appeal to the political centre. This was essentially the key to the success of the Mulroney Conservatives in 1984 and 1988 and, to some extent, of the Diefenbaker Tories in the 1950s. Of course, that has also been the preferred strategy of the Liberals throughout much of their modern history. It was, after all, King whose formula for political success was to campaign from the left, but govern from the right. The 2006 election campaign saw the Conservatives attempt to move away from an emphasis on divisive ideological issues, and to pursue a more traditional centrist electoral strategy, an effort rewarded with a minority victory, thus encouraging the party to continue along this strategic path.

Much the same might be said of other "cleavage" variables based on the many different ethnic, linguistic, and social groups that comprise the Canadian population. While factors such as religion, social class, or ethnicity have been present from time to time in Canadian party politics, such forces have also long been noticeably weaker in Canada than in many other Western countries. In comparing Canada with Britain, the United States, and Australia in the 1960s, Robert Alford noted the comparative weakness of social variables in explaining Canadian voting patterns, and Richard Rose, in a study comparing Canada with a number of European countries, drew similar conclusions 10 years later.[6]

Rather than dividing the electorate along clear and relatively stable lines of social cleavage, Canadian parties often compete for much of the same policy space and many of the same voters. While regional and linguistic divisions are often highly relevant to politics in Canada, the key to national political success has always lain in bridging these differences rather than in exacerbating them. Parties based solely on linguistic or regional grievances can win votes from time to time, as the Progressives demonstrated in 1921 or the Bloc since 1993. But theirs is a strategy of

FIGURE 14.2

Ideological Orientations in the Canadian Electorate

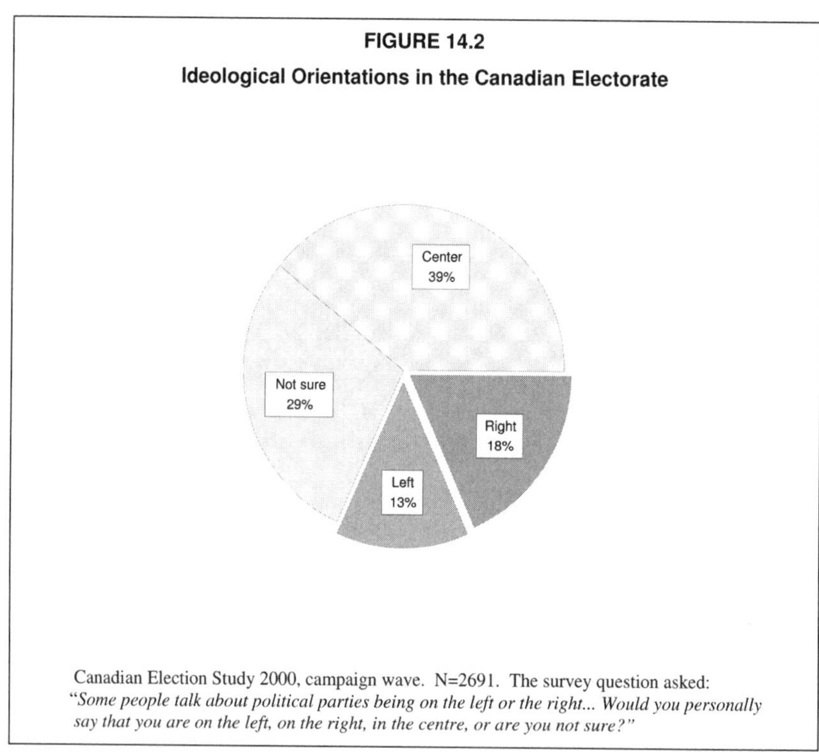

Canadian Election Study 2000, campaign wave. N=2691. The survey question asked: *"Some people talk about political parties being on the left or the right... Would you personally say that you are on the left, on the right, in the centre, or are you not sure?"*

registering political protest or regional identity, not of winning control of a national government.

Office-seeking parties tend to play down social and ideological cleavages, to form electoral alliances across social, regional, and linguistic divides, and to concentrate on framing their electoral appeals around general policy questions of national concern.[7] Their electoral support tends to be based less on the long-term loyalties of particular social groups than on potentially unstable coalitions that can change over time. Such parties only rarely present voters with a clear choice between starkly different policy alternatives. Instead, they search constantly for electorally successful strategies, or repackage variations of established responses to ongoing problems. They organize around leaders rather than around political principles and ideologies, and they expect the leader to work out the various compromises required for the party to compete effectively in elections. Leaders who have been skillful at this style of politics have often enjoyed continued electoral success.

This style of party politics, as it has existed in Canada in various forms over many generations, has been repeatedly referred to by political scientists and other observers as the *brokerage model*. While the term has been employed by many scholars writing about Canadian political parties over the years, it was first stated explicitly by J.A. Corry in his 1946 textbook on Canadian politics.[8] It is now, perhaps more than any other single theoretical understanding of the Canadian party system, the conventional view. The reasons for the persistence of brokerage politics are easy to understand when placed alongside the realities of the Canadian political environment. The risk of ethnic and linguistic conflict and the sensitivity of regional inequalities create a situation in which any national party would be destined to fail if it tried to mobilize the electorate around any single cleavage.

The political reality of such risks has been demonstrated on many occasions over the course of Canadian history and in many different ways — Diefenbaker's weakness in Quebec, for example, or Trudeau's alienation of the West. In more recent years, the failure of Reform, and its successor party the Canadian Alliance, to significantly expand its electoral base beyond the West illustrates the continued existence of these risks.

The brokerage model has many implications for the conduct of electoral politics in Canada, not all of which have been viewed favourably by voters or by scholars. Among the consequences of brokerage politics are the seeming lack of principled differences between the parties, the inconsistencies of many of their policies over relatively short periods of time, and the parochialism of their organizational structures, which frequently emphasize patronage and the settlement of competing claims.

Brokerage politics also places a great deal of emphasis on the role of the leader, whose job it is to act as the "chief broker" among the many different interests and social groups that make up the Canadian mosaic. Parties become identified, not with policies or programs, but with their leaders. A party that cannot win elections often blames the leader, and then transfers its hopes to a new leader who promises to lead it out of the political wilderness.[9]

This interpretation of Canadian party politics helps us to understand the main characteristics of "dynasties" and "interludes" as we have discussed them throughout this book. Leaders such as John A. Macdonald or Mackenzie King, who were particularly adept at the practice of brokerage politics, enjoyed not only electoral success but long tenure in the position of party leader. Others such as John Diefenbaker or Brian Mulroney, who enjoyed initial success in building broad electoral coalitions, failed to hold them together. Leaders such as Trudeau alternately succeeded and failed, but survived nevertheless. And certain other figures such as Arthur Meighen or Joe Clark, either for reasons of personality or circumstance, proved utterly unable to master the brokerage game. As the

Conservative Party of Canada. Herman Cheung, photographer.

Stephen Harper speaking during the 2008 election campaign.

new Conservative Party under Stephen Harper continues its transition to the more traditional ground of brokerage politics, it remains to be seen whether the leader can continue to provide the glue to hold the party together and position it to build on its tenuous electoral successes of 2006 and 2008.

Issues and Policies

The brokerage model of party politics has implications for the ways in which issues are addressed by the parties, and the way in which they are presented and managed in election campaigns. The parties and the leaders who represent them are often wary about dealing with "big" issues in any other way than identifying them as general societal problems — unemployment, inflation, and crime, among others. When deciding which issues to emphasize in a campaign, and how to present them, the modern-day parties employ strategists such as pollsters, consultants, or advertising firms to gauge their electoral appeal. Earlier strategic techniques for vote-getting also allowed political parties to develop their electoral appeals, with political picnics, mainstreeting, or whistle-stopping providing the venues in which to test different campaign themes. Political parties frequently find it in their interest to change the issue focus from one election to the next, lest they become too closely identified with any one side of a particular policy controversy.

Any subject, large or small, discussed during an election campaign can be thought of as an "issue." The ubiquitous use of the word *issue* disguises the fact that subjects of political discussion can take many different forms. Political issues fought over in elections can and sometimes do reflect the major questions of a particular place and time. In some of the earlier elections treated in this book, "the tariff" was a frequent subject of discussion (see Chapter 2). But, although it was often the subject of election oratory, elections in themselves did little to resolve the issue. The parties of the time recognized that farmers, manufacturers, and consumers had quite different interests in the matter, and they therefore tended to discuss the tariff issue in the most general terms. Political parties or candidates often find themselves in agreement in identifying the importance of a particular subject, but stop short of outlining a more detailed policy response. "Jobs,

jobs, jobs" were, according to Brian Mulroney, the "three most important issues" in the 1984 election campaign. A Free Trade Agreement with the United States, which was never mentioned in that campaign, proved to be the path that he ultimately chose to work toward that goal *after* he had assumed office.

This book has examined the issues emphasized in election campaigns over the long sweep of Canadian history. In so doing, we have observed that there is considerable discontinuity in the framing of issues from one election to the next. Sometimes, this is because of the differing social, economic, or political problems which arose at a particular time. It was the high unemployment caused by the economic recession of the early 1980s that led Mulroney to place the main emphasis of his successful 1984 campaign on the creation of jobs. Similarly, the periods of high inflation in the 1970s injected that issue prominently into the 1974 campaign, leading the main contenders to agree on the definition of the problem, but to propose different solutions. We could cite Diefenbaker's use of the pipeline issue in the 1957 campaign, the defence policy issues of 1963, or the "national unity" issue in the 1979 election, which was largely a response to the victory of the PQ in Quebec, as examples of the variability of issues over time.

Table 14.1 displays the "most important issue" cited by respondents to the Canadian Election Studies in four elections spanning four decades. The dominant concern with inflation found in the 1974 study was replaced by an emphasis on unemployment in the elections of the early 1980s and 90s, and that in turn gave way to health care as the most frequently cited issue in 2004.

The prominence of social issues in 2004 can be partly attributed to the general public satisfaction with the state of the economy at that time. Since the economic crisis of 2008, economic issues have returned to a more dominant position (see Chapter 13). The predominant impression here is the variation in specific issues *within* the continuity of the general issue types.

The choice of issue emphasis in a party's campaign is also partly strategic. Parties choose issues on which they or their leaders sense that they have an electoral advantage, or on which they believe their opponents are vulnerable, and inject these into their campaigns. In the 2004 and 2006 elections, the Conservatives, sensing the vulnerability of the Liberals in the wake of the sponsorship scandal, emphasized "corruption" and "accountability" in their campaign rhetoric. The Liberals, in

TABLE 14.1

Most Important Issue in Four Elections, 1974–2004

	1974	1984	1993	2004
Economic Issues				
Inflation, cost of living, prices	33	1	-	-
Wage and price controls	6	-	-	-
Unemployment, jobs	2	28	37	2
Debt, deficits, budget, spending	-	5	14	4
Taxes, GST	-	1	3	6
The economy in general	3	11	9	2
National Unity				
Quebec, language, separatism	1	1	3	-
Free trade, NAFTA	-	-	2	-
Resources, resource policy	-	1	-	1
Foreign policy, U.S. relations	1	-	-	1
Social Welfare				
Social programs	2	-	3	2
Health care	-	-	5	35
Pensions, elderly	4	1	2	2
Women's issues	-	2	-	-
Education, youth	-	1	1	4
Environment	-	-	1	1
Crime	-	-	1	-
Other				
Integrity, trust, patronage, scandals	-	1	2	12
Leaders, leadership	3	6	-	-
"Time for a change", partisanship	2	9	2	3
Majority government, stability	5	-	1	-
N =	2,445	3,377	3,775	4,323

Canadian Election Studies, 1974–2004. The question asked was: "What was the most important issue to you personally in this election?" First response only. Issues included were mentioned by at least 1 percent of respondents in one survey. Respondents mentioning other issues or citing no issues as important are included in percentages but not shown in table.

contrast, emphasized their commitment to social programs, particularly health care, implying that a Conservative government might place these programs at risk.

The 2008 election is a prime example of parties talking past one another in election campaigns. The Conservatives concentrated on portraying themselves as responsible economic managers, while the Liberals promoted the Green Shift program, designed primarily as a plan for environmental sustainability. As we have suggested in Chapter 13, it was partly the Conservatives' ability to impose their definition of the issue agenda which allowed them to achieve a minority victory in 2008.

Canadian political parties are not completely free to pick and choose the issues that they place before the electorate. Quoting Siegfried at the beginning of this book, we noted his observation at the beginning of the twentieth century that electoral success in Canada all but requires a political party to address certain *types* of issues.[10] While we would use slightly different language today to describe these, it is clear that leaders of brokerage parties have had to deal competently with *all* of these issue

FIGURE 14.3

Issue Priorities in Canadian Federal Elections, 1974–2008

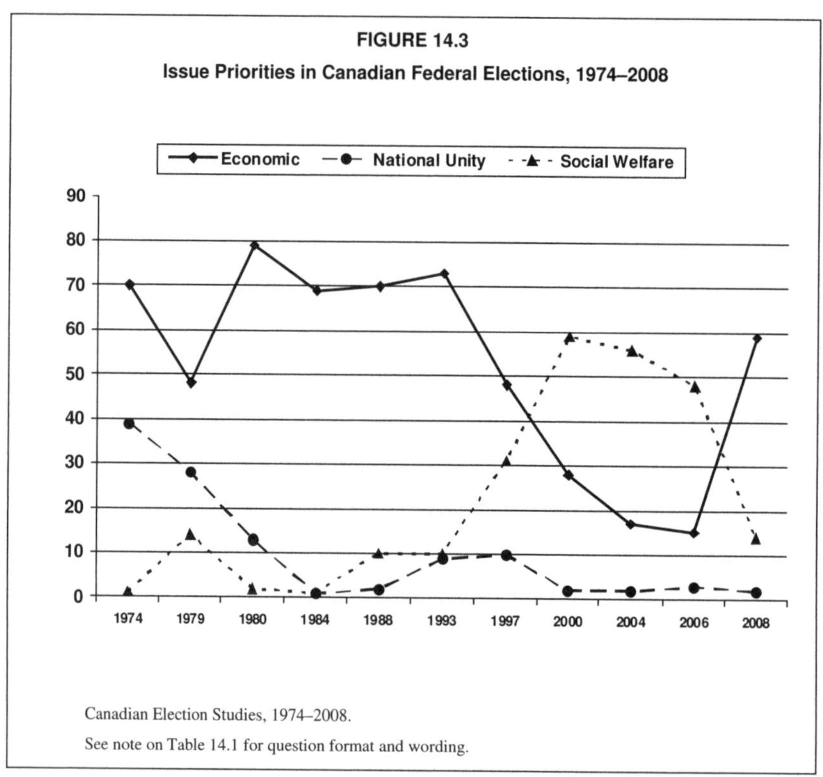

Canadian Election Studies, 1974–2008.

See note on Table 14.1 for question format and wording.

types in order to enjoy continued electoral success. The "prosperity of the country," as Siegfried called it, questions of "national unity," and the management of the public sector are recurring issue themes in many of the election campaigns that we have examined in this book. Siegfried also recognized the importance of leadership as an "issue," a theme which likewise recurs in many modern-day election campaigns, just as it did in the earlier ones. Thus, while a comparison of issue themes across election campaigns shows us that there is considerable variability from one election to another, it also discloses the continuity of certain kinds of issues in national politics. "Inflation," "unemployment," and "budget deficits" appear as different issues in several campaigns. But they are all *economic* issues that address what Siegfried would have called "the prosperity of the country."

Figure 14.3 shows the response to the open-ended question on "what was the most important issue to you personally in the [year of the] election?" in National Election Surveys since 1974. This shows that, until the late 1990s, economic issues dominated the public's agenda. The issues identified as most important were not always the same specific economic problem or policy — they varied from the state of the economy generally, to inflation (in 1974), to unemployment (in 1979), to taxation (in 1980), to jobs (in 1984), to free trade (in 1988). Social welfare issues, primarily related to health care, have tended to predominate in some elections in the last decade, prominently in 2000, 2004, and 2006. And national unity, manifested in issues of bilingualism, federal–provincial relations, and Quebec, has been perennially important, at a lower but fairly constant level.

In elections over the course of Canadian history, parties and leaders that have held power for substantial periods of time were often seen by voters as the ones best able to deal with the economy and national unity, and, in the years since the Great Depression, social welfare issues.

While the specific campaign issues associated with each of these key areas may be short-term in nature, the areas themselves are of longer term importance. It has proven to be all but impossible to construct a foundation for continued political success in Canada without mastery of all three of these core issue areas. Allied with these in solidifying a continuing base of electoral support has been an image of competence in managing government, as well as an advantage in leadership defined more generally. In other words, a competent, trusted leader, who is able to provide voters with reassurance in each issue area, has always been a party's best electoral asset. A combination of public preferences on these factors has allowed some Canadian political leaders to sustain themselves in power for long periods of time, providing the foundations for the five dynasties mentioned earlier.

Leaders who have failed to deal effectively with these three principal types of issues, whether because of their own inability to do so or because of the particular circumstances in which they found themselves, have at times won elections, but have not been able to establish "dynasties." Put in today's terms, a successful leader needs to be able to demonstrate to the electorate that he or she is best to manage the economy, hold the country together, and deal with welfare state issues such as health care, unemployment insurance, and pensions. A leader who can sustain such a favourable positioning has the potential to build a political dynasty as defined in this book. A prime minister who has the misfortune to preside over a period of economic recession, or who is forced to cut funding for essential public programs, will find electoral survival difficult. Likewise, a leader who is unable to appeal across the country's regional and/or linguistic dividing lines is unlikely to be able to win a majority government.

Pierre Trudeau's career as Liberal leader demonstrates many of these risks. At first a unifying figure, Trudeau's Liberals won a solid majority in the 1968 election. But the accumulation of economic problems, and Trudeau's handling of the FLQ crisis in 1970, nearly cost him re-election in 1972. Trudeau, like King after the 1925 election, eventually navigated through these difficulties and returned with a majority government in 1974. Once again, however, the combination of economic adversity and national unity hampered Trudeau's chances of founding a new Liberal dynasty. His defeat in the 1979 election appeared at the time to herald the end of his political career, which would have, at that point, spanned 11 years in office. But Joe Clark's mishandling of the minority government, together with his inability to make a breakthrough for his party in Quebec, combined to allow Trudeau and the Liberals to return to power in 1980. Although he succeeded in realizing his ambition to repatriate the Constitution and establish a charter of rights during that final term, Trudeau's alienation of the West through the National Energy Program, along with the deep economic recession of the early 1980s, doomed the Liberals to defeat. His successor, John Turner, led the party to one of its worst electoral disasters in 1984.

Trudeau's career illustrates many of the pitfalls of brokerage politics in Canada. During his early years in office, Trudeau did not play the brokerage game well, and he often publicly disdained many of its more obvious requisites. "Why should I sell your wheat?" he once told western farmers, before delivering a lecture on the difficulties of international commodity marketing. But Trudeau, who had come into politics from outside the Liberal Party, learned from these early mistakes, and gradually adapted to the political realities that confronted him. Had the economy been kinder, he might even have avoided outright defeat in 1979. Few western governments, including those in the United States, Britain, Germany, and France, were able to survive the economic shocks of the late 1970s. For most national leaders who were defeated at that time — Jimmy Carter, James Callaghan, Helmut Schmidt, Valéry Giscard d'Estaing — it meant the end of their political careers. But Trudeau returned after a short interlude in opposition, thanks to a bit of political good fortune and the mistakes made by Clark. We acknowledge that luck can play a role in politics. Had Mackenzie King *won* the election of 1930 instead of losing it, the Depression would almost certainly have ended his political career.

The Conservative government elected in 2006 and 2008 is not immune to these constraints, in spite of the apparent short-term weakness of their principal opponents. However, the question of "prosperity" may well be beyond its control. Economies have always responded to forces beyond the reach of governments. But in an age of increasing globalization, and with many of the key economic variables being influenced in greater measure by its NAFTA partners, *any* Canadian government is increasingly at risk of being unable to turn the economic issues of the day to its political advantage. Rightly or wrongly, governments of any political stripe are blamed for macroeconomic adversity. The recession of 2008, even though its causes lay predominantly outside Canada, brought with it higher unemployment, budget deficits, and continuing economic uncertainties. Few democratic governments survive these kinds of conditions. While there may no longer be references to "Bennett buggies" in everyday political conversation, the voters know who to blame. And opposition parties, whatever their particular ideological or policy orientation, take full advantage.

The other two issue areas that we have emphasized throughout this book likewise have elements that are difficult for governments to control or influence; however they may be more amenable to the intervention of political leaders than is the state of the Canadian economy. "National unity" has had multiple meanings over the course of Canadian history, but it has consistently been one of the core issue areas with which every prime minister must deal with some success in order to remain in office. Macdonald, Laurier, and King all demonstrated great sensitivity to this concern over the course of their long political careers. Trudeau and Chrétien, in spite of their attentiveness to federal–provincial matters, proved to be more polarizing figures in some parts of the country. Borden and Diefenbaker, for different reasons, failed to broker the key issues of national unity that arose during their times in office (see Chapters 2 and 5).

Since the 1970s, the rise of a more nationalist Quebec has presented a challenge (or an opportunity) to every federal prime minister who has occupied the office. The standoff between Trudeau's and Lévesque's competing visions of the country virtually redefined the politics of the late 1970s and early 1980s, and the aftershocks of Quebec's first referendum in 1980 continued to reverberate throughout the next decade. The events surrounding the second referendum in 1995 constituted the greatest single crisis of Jean Chrétien's stewardship. To some extent, Trudeau's preoccupation with the issue of Quebec separatism, and with constitutional renewal in his later years, may also have led indirectly to his alienation of the West and his inability to manage economic issues effectively. The return of the Bourassa government in Quebec in 1985 opened the door for Brian Mulroney's constitutional initiatives (see Chapters 10 and 11).

In all of these instances, the issue was thrust onto the national agenda by events having relatively little to do with federal politics. But the prime minister of the day was forced to deal with them regardless. In true brokerage fashion, the Harper government has given considerable attention to Quebec, having become convinced, as have many of its predecessors, that the key to electoral success lies in bridging Canada's linguistic and regional divides rather than in exploiting them. Success on that issue front will largely determine whether Harper might be able to turn his current minority government into a lasting political dynasty.

The third critical issue area that we have emphasized throughout this book is social issues, by which we mean the management of the modern welfare state. This has also become a central concern of every prime minister regardless of party. Whether Canadians believed Brian Mulroney's designation of Canada's core social programs as a "sacred trust" is less important than the fact that he felt compelled to make such a declaration in the first place. It was not accidental that Stephen Harper in the 2006 election campaign identified a reduction of hospital waiting times as one of his five issue priorities.[11]

But, as an area of provincial jurisdiction, health care issues are not always responsive to federal policy initiatives, other than through the rather awkward mechanism of federal–provincial fiscal transfers. We might add to this observation the fact that some of the causes of recent pressures on the Canadian health care system derive not from a failure of policy but from more fundamental factors such as an aging population, technological advances in medicine, and rising health care costs. Governing parties are increasingly held accountable, not only for the performance of the economy, but also for their ability or inability to respond to the many pressures that threaten the large public sector programs on which Canadians have come to depend.

Other types of issues that may have little to do with public policy also sometimes intrude on elections. Following the period of minority government in 1972–74, Prime Minister Trudeau managed to persuade a significant number of voters that the "most important issue" in the 1974 election campaign was the restoration of a majority government. Given that the Liberals were the party most likely to be able to obtain such a majority, emphasis on this type of issue was in part strategic. But it also reflected to some degree the political uncertainty of the times. In 2008, the subtext of the Conservatives' decision to call an early election was so that they could appeal to the electorate to give them the majority they had failed to achieve in 2006. This time, however, there was less attention paid to the issue, and some doubt among the electorate that the Conservatives should be trusted with a majority.

In the 2004 and 2006 federal elections, the Conservatives' repeated emphasis on issues such as "corruption" and "accountability" served to deflect the issue agenda onto the question of integrity of those in government. A Liberal government, seriously wounded by scandal, was deemed to be vulnerable on these types of issues, and the opposition took full advantage of that vulnerability over the course of those two campaigns. This was certainly not the first time that scandal had overturned a Canadian government: the first such instance was in 1874 (see Chapter 2) when John A. Macdonald was relegated to the opposition benches. Scandals played an important part in the elections of 1925 and 1963, as well. When they arise, they tend to blunt the ability of a government seeking re-election to appeal on any of the standard issue dimensions, since they undermine the public's trust that they will carry out their promises honestly.

Elections and Voters

A major consequence of brokerage politics is that no party is able to count on a large, stable base of supporters who will remain loyal to it through bad times as well as good. Uncertain about where the parties *really* stand on many fundamental issues, voters are often willing to desert one party or leader and transfer their support to another as circumstances change. Such flexible partisanship helps to account for much of the volatility that we see in federal elections in Canada, and provides fertile ground for the sudden rise of new parties and political actors. A brokerage party system spawns a highly volatile issue agenda and creates the conditions for potentially abrupt changes in party leader images. Since large segments of the electorate are sensitive to these short-term forces, the possibility of substantial swings in party support from one election to the next is always present. Yet despite this volatility, or perhaps because of their ability to cope with it, some leaders have managed to put together a string of victories in elections, and sometimes even to create favourable electoral ground for their successors.

Long-term feelings of partisanship on the part of the electorate have little to do with this process. Studies of Canadian voting behaviour have shown repeatedly that many Canadian voters do not have strong ties to political parties, and that there is a much greater element of volatility in Canadian federal politics than is disclosed by aggregate election results or by data on party preference at any given point in time. Following their solid election victory in 1993, the Liberals came perilously close to being reduced to a minority in the 1997 election (see Chapter 12).

Similarly, the 2000 victory was misread by many as clear evidence of continued Liberal dominance, when in fact the party remained highly vulnerable, as the events of 2004 would subsequently demonstrate (see Chapter 13). This pattern is not an artifact of a sudden patch of political volatility, or an observation that applies only to the recent period. Ever since 1965, when national survey data became available, we have seen an electorate in which there is considerable partisan instability even during periods when there has been little aggregate change in electoral outcomes.[12] Herman Bakvis has similarly observed that the combination of weak party alignments and long periods of relative electoral stability represents a peculiarly Canadian "paradox."[13]

Figure 14.4 shows the continued weakness of partisan ties, and the electoral unreliability even of supporters of the major parties. Even in 2008, perhaps their weakest point for many decades, almost a third of Canadian voters do identify in some way with the Liberal Party. However, only about five percent of all respondents considered themselves "very strong" Liberals. In fact, fewer than 15 percent of recent samples have considered themselves "very strong" party supporters, and at least another fifth of the electorate declare no partisan attachment at all. Added together, there are more weak partisans or non-partisans in the Canadian electorate than there are Liberals, and

FIGURE 14.4

Party Identification in the Canadian Electorate, 1974–2008

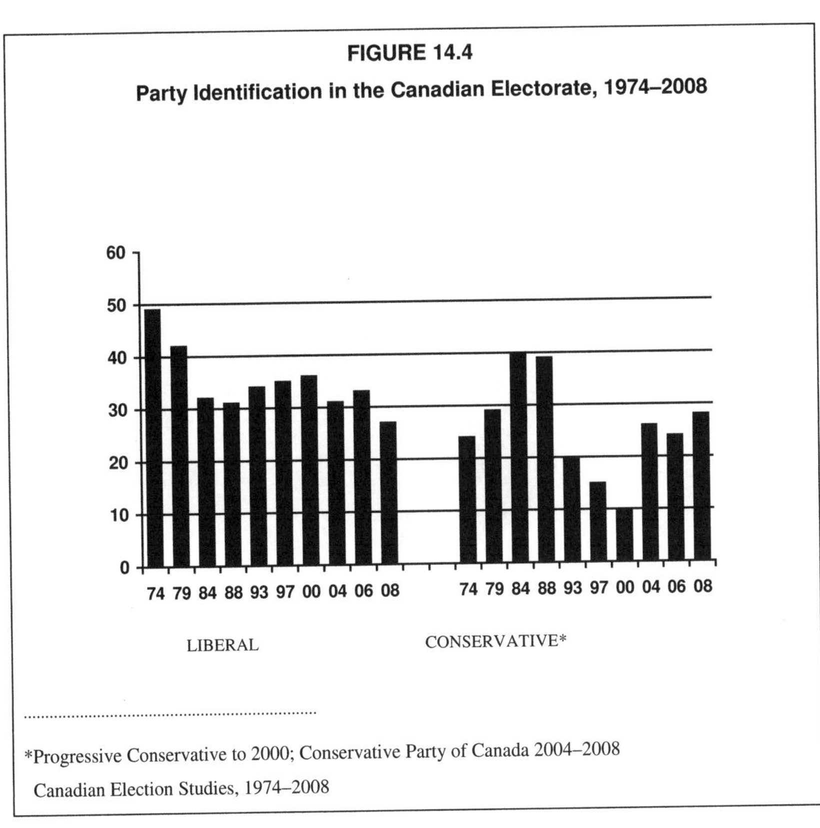

*Progressive Conservative to 2000; Conservative Party of Canada 2004–2008

Canadian Election Studies, 1974–2008

the percentage of Canadians who do not identify with *any* of the federal political parties has risen considerably in recent years.[14] If we are searching for a solid base of partisan support within the Canadian electorate, it is increasingly difficult to find one. The Liberal Party is considerably weaker today in core support within the electorate than it was in the 1960s and 1970s, and cannot win an election through appeals to partisans alone.

Support for the new Conservative Party in turn, while at near parity with the Liberals in 2008, is much lower than the Progressive Conservatives enjoyed during the 1980s under Brian Mulroney, and now rests at about the levels enjoyed by the PCs under Clark in the late 1970s.[15] Core support for the new party is still, even after its two election victories, less than the sum of its former parts — Reform/Alliance and the Progressive Conservatives.

While the Liberals since 1993 seem to have settled at a lower level of support in the electorate than they previously enjoyed, the Conservatives also appear stalled at relatively low levels of core support. This, of course,

FIGURE 14.5

Vote Switching in the Canadian Electorate

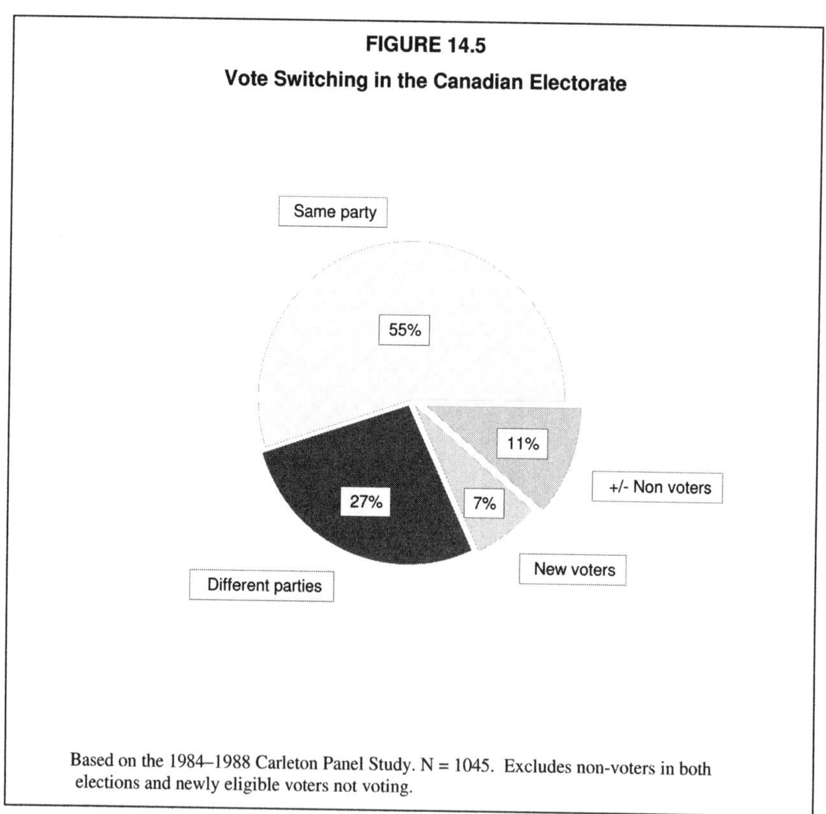

Based on the 1984–1988 Carleton Panel Study. N = 1045. Excludes non-voters in both elections and newly eligible voters not voting.

did not prevent the Conservatives under Stephen Harper from winning the 2006 and 2008 elections, and it does not mean that they cannot win another under these same conditions. It means simply that they, like the Liberals, would have to do so, in typical brokerage fashion, by appealing to at least some voters who identify with other parties, or who claim to be independent of partisan feelings

Evidence from national surveys since 1965 confirms that there is considerable volatility in the electorate from one election to the next. This is precisely what we would expect from voters with weak partisan attachments and political parties that typically frame their electoral appeals around their leaders, or around issues on which they believe they can achieve a short-term advantage.

In many of the chapters in this book dealing with particular elections, we have included a figure showing the turnover of the electorate from one election to another where such data were available based on surveys conducted at the time. Figure 14.5 presents a snapshot of the electorate based on the 1984–88 period. We chose this period to illustrate the pattern of electoral turnover because it is fairly typical of a time in which

FIGURE 14.6

Turnout in Federal Elections, 1958–2008

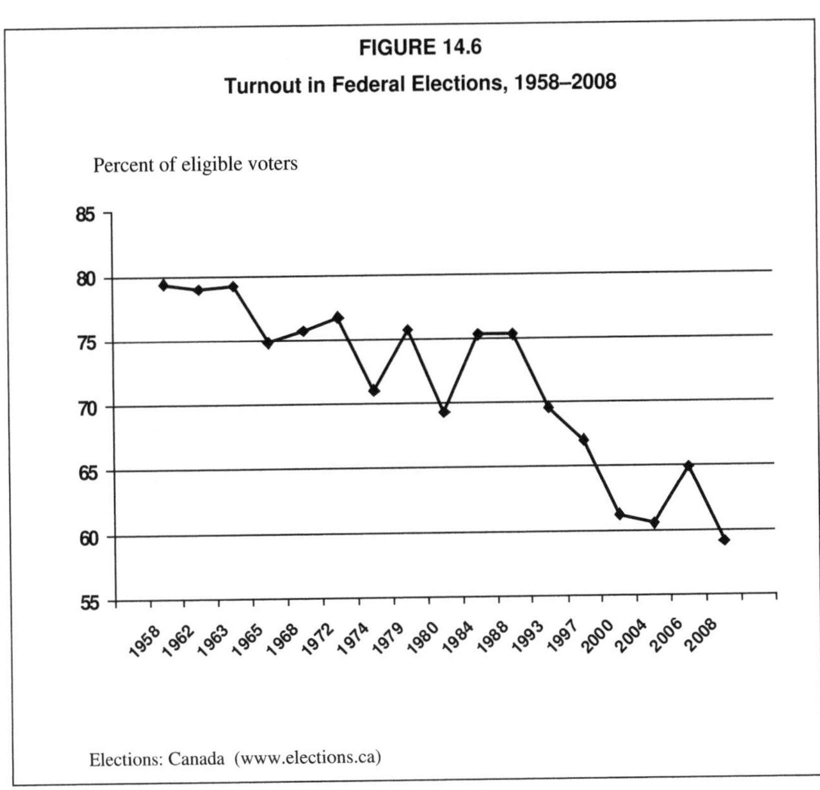

Elections: Canada (www.elections.ca)

a governing party was re-elected and also because panel data covering both elections exist for this period. Other periods might be slightly more volatile — or slightly less — but the model of voting behaviour that they suggest does not differ greatly from one election to another.

Across the two elections shown in Figure 14.5, we find slightly more than a quarter of the electorate moving its support from one party to another.[16] Only half stay put. In any election, much of the electorate is up for grabs for the campaigning parties. The total amount of movement in the electorate is also affected by the participation rates of newly eligible voters, and by the extent of non-voting, both of which will vary somewhat from one election to another and both of which contribute to the overall rate of volatility.

The Voting Turnout Decline

It is particularly important to include voting turnout in our calculations, as turnout has been going down in Canada for a considerable period of time. In fact, turnout in federal elections began a steep decline in 1993 and then moved lower in subsequent elections, reaching a new historic low of just under 59 percent in 2008 (see Figure 14.6). While a considerable part of this decline can be explained by patterns of generational change and other demographic factors, there is little doubt that the lack of competitiveness in the party system after 1993 has also contributed to the withdrawal of potential voters from the electoral process.[17] Citizens with no partisan leanings or weak partisan attachments are more difficult to mobilize in elections. The strong regional patterns which have been evident in recent years may also contribute to the ongoing tendency of many Canadians to withdraw from electoral participation. Thus, people in many parts of the country could readily surmise that their vote would have little influence on the outcome of the election, either nationally or in their own local constituencies.[18]

Turnout rebounded somewhat in the 2006 election, in part because of the context of that election and the fact that it was more competitive, at least at the aggregate level.[19] But despite the change of government in 2006, federal politics in Canada remained highly regionalized, and patterns of competition were weak in many constituencies. When the

2008 election was held, turnout declined once again, to the point where almost a million fewer Canadians voted than in the previous election. Given that one of the most important factors driving turnout down in recent years has been the reluctance of newly eligible young voters to enter the electorate, it is doubtful that turnout in federal elections will recover to pre-1993 levels.

However, variations in turnout contribute to electoral volatility, regardless of the direction. If voters withdraw from the electorate, they deprive parties of sources of voting support that may previously have been important to them. If some voters re-enter the electorate after one or more elections of non-participation, they introduce into the calculus a new short-term source of variation. Thus, a party such as the Conservatives could win an election by gaining the support of some voters who identify with other parties, by appealing to those who have not previously voted because of a perceived lack of choice, or by gaining advantage when previous supporters of other parties choose not to vote. In reality, *every* election involves some combination of these forces, as the patterns of switching displayed in Figure 14.5 clearly suggest. No matter which party is in power, electoral volatility remains a central fact of Canadian political life.

The Future of Canadian Electoral Politics

The image of Canadian politics portrayed throughout this book is that of a highly volatile or "dealigned" electorate to which parties and leaders must continually present new electoral appeals based on relatively short-term political calculations. As history shows us, that state of affairs can continue to sustain a government with relatively little apparent change if a leader proves adept at managing the many competing forces at work in the Canadian polity.

In considering the political dynasties that have been most successful over the course of Canadian history, it does not escape notice that four of the five (see Figure 14.1) have been Liberal dynasties. Following John A. Macdonald's dominance of the Canadian political arena in the nineteenth century, no Conservative leader has succeeded in constructing an enduring period of political success, although several have won decisive electoral victories. The Liberal Party has been in power federally through much of Canada's modern history, and has been extraordinarily successful at adapting to a variety of political and social changes that have occurred. The durability of the King/St. Laurent, Pearson/Trudeau, and Chrétien/Martin dynasties is often explained in terms of the leaders' ability to read the political signals of their time and to adapt to new political circumstances as they arose. But these dynasties ended suddenly and unexpectedly in 1957, 1984, and 2006 respectively at the hands of the Conservatives. Does the current period resemble these previous situations, or might the political balance at last be shifting in the Conservatives' direction?

One might argue that, despite the minority outcome of 2004 and their losses in 2006 and 2008, the present period still bears some resemblance to the interludes between other long periods of Liberal hegemony in Canadian federal politics. Even with the weight of the sponsorship scandal and an inept campaign, the Liberals nevertheless managed to win 103 seats and 30 percent of the vote in 2006, and they won seats in that election in every province except Alberta. Despite an unpopular leader, a disastrous issue choice, and another inept campaign, the Liberals managed to retain 77 seats in 2008. Surveys of the electorate still show that a substantial number of Canadians identify with the Liberal Party, in spite of these setbacks.

Analysts of the 1958 and 1984 landslide elections, or even of Joe Clark's defeat of Trudeau in 1979, might easily have misread those events at the time as portending the demise of the Liberals. But in each instance they were back in power within a few years. In our attempt to track the course of changing political alignments, we sometimes ignore the ability of established political parties to adapt to new political circumstances. Parties that are primarily "power seeking," as the Liberals have tended to be, are often particularly good at such adaptation.[20] Those who have seen the Liberal Party come back time and again from electoral defeat throughout Canadian history would not be surprised to see yet another rebirth of "Canada's natural governing party."[21]

However, it is also possible that the present period *is* different than the past, and that the dominance of the Liberals over the period following Jean Chrétien's 1993 election victory has been deceptive. At first, the post-1993 world seemed very different than the traditional brokerage model of party politics that Canadians had long become accustomed to, and that we have discussed throughout this book. After 1993, Canadian federal politics became segmented into parties and groups representing much narrower and more specific ideological, interest, or issue positions than had been the case in the past.[22] Even the Liberals, with weaker representation from Quebec and the West, appeared increasingly to speak largely for the interests of Ontario or the major urban centres.

Now, with five further federal elections producing broadly similar electoral patterns, it becomes increasingly difficult to argue that 1993 was a temporary aberration or a transient phenomenon similar to those of 1962 or 1979. The Bloc Québécois has retained its appeal among Quebec voters, and the new Conservative Party of Canada has captured most of the electoral support won by two of its predecessors — Reform and the Canadian Alliance. The Liberals' share of the vote has declined from a high of 41 percent in the 1993 and 2000 elections to lows of 30 percent in 2006 and 26 percent in 2008.

This newer and more highly regionalized alignment makes it increasingly difficult for *any* party to win a majority of seats across the country. Minority governments may well become the new norm, heralding more frequent elections and weaker, more unstable federal governments. Partisan attachment in such a system could harden, reinforcing regional alignments and increasing heretofore weak ideological differences between the parties. Such a situation could, in turn, cause portions of the eligible electorate to withdraw from politics altogether, in a vicious circle of turnout decline and political reaction.

Despite the surface plausibility of both of these interpretations, neither the "Liberal hegemony" hypothesis nor the "new party system" line of argument stands up well when examined in the light of the evidence presented throughout this book regarding the attitudes and attachments of Canadian voters and the ways in which successful Canadian political leaders have operated.

While nearly a third of Canadian voters still identify themselves as "Liberals," such attachments are weak, and may well be growing weaker. The numbers of Canadians who do not identify with *any* of the federal political parties continues to increase. Given the right electoral circumstances, significant numbers of Canadian voters can still be moved by short-term appeals emanating from an election campaign or other sources. The volatility of public opinion polls over relatively short periods, such as an election campaign, further demonstrates this.

We have also seen that the ideological underpinnings of the Canadian party system are very weak (see Figure 14.2). This relative lack of ideological fervor does not appear to favour the prospects of those who believe that the future of the Canadian party system lies in presenting voters with more polarized choices. Neither a united right nor a more radical left would appear to be well placed to win the allegiance of a large cross-section of Canadian voters on any continuing basis. Stephen Harper fashioned his 2006 victory not by uniting the right but by deliberately positioning his new party closer to the centre of the ideological spectrum and appealing more directly to interests outside of his secure western base. It is therefore reasonable to expect more of the same in future elections.

However, in a dealigned electorate with weak party ties, the potential for sudden and unpredictable change is also high. In the past, leaders such as Diefenbaker, Trudeau, and Mulroney have burst onto the scene suddenly, and swept to landslide victories. The conditions under which this scenario might occur continue to be present in the Canadian electorate. A new party, political leader, or a compelling issue could easily ignite such a process of rapid change. It has happened before in the elections of 1911, 1930, 1958, 1984, and 1993.

Such a reversal of fortune can be precipitated by changing economic conditions, political miscalculations, or changes in the leadership of one or more parties. Given the nature of the Canadian electorate and the Canadian political environment as profiled throughout this book, there is no reason to believe that these traditional patterns will not occur again, perhaps in the not too distant future.

Notes

1. See Michael Bliss, *Right Honourable Men* (HarperCollins, 1995), Chapter 8.
2. Peter Russell, *Two Cheers for Minority Government: The Evolution of Canadian Parliamentary Democracy* (Toronto: Emond Montgomery, 2008).
3. Alan Cairns, "The Electoral System and the Party System in Canada," *Canadian Journal of Political Science* 1 (1968), 55–80.
4. A large and active lobbying organization, Fair Vote Canada, continues to press for changes in the electoral system, as does an important women's organization, Equal Voice. For some of the background of this issue, and a critical discussion of various reform proposals, see Henry Milner, ed., *Making Every Vote Count* (Toronto: Broadview Press, 1999). See

also *Voting Counts: Electoral Reform for Canada*, the report of the Law Commission of Canada (Ottawa, 2004).

5. Ronald D. Lambert, James Curtis, Steven Brown, and Barry Kay, "In Search of Left/Right Beliefs in the Canadian Electorate," *Canadian Journal of Political Science* 19 (1986), 542–63.
6. Robert Alford, *Party and Society* (Chicago: Rand McNally, 1963); Richard Rose, ed., *Electoral Behavior: A Comparative Handbook* (New York: Free Press, 1974).
7. See Kaare Strøm, "A Behavioral Theory of Competitive Political Parties," *American Journal of Political Science* 34 (1990), 565–97.
8. J.A. Corry, *Democratic Government and Politics* (Toronto: University of Toronto Press, 1946). On the theory and practice of brokerage politics, see, among other sources, David Smith, "Party Government, Representation and National Integration in Canada," in Peter Aucoin, ed., *Party Government and Regional Representation in Canada*, Vol. 36 of the Research Studies for The Royal Commission on the Economic Union and Development Prospects for Canada (Toronto: University of Toronto Press, 1985), and Janine Brodie and Jane Jenson, "Piercing the Smokescreen: Stability and Change in Brokerage Politics," in A. Brian Tanguay and Alain-G. Gagnon, eds., *Canadian Parties in Transition*, second edition (Toronto: Nelson, 1996). See also Janine Brodie and Jane Jenson, *Crisis, Challenge and Change: Party and Class in Canada Revisited* (Ottawa: Carleton University Press, 1988).
9. The policy implications of brokerage politics are developed in some detail in Harold D. Clarke, Jane Jenson, Lawrence LeDuc, and Jon H Pammett, *Absent Mandate: Canadian Electoral Politics in an Era of Restructuring* (Toronto: Gage, 1996). See especially Chapters 1 and 2.
10. André Siegfried, *The Race Question in Canada* (London: Eveleigh Nash, 1907). As cited in Chapter 1.
11. The others were a 1 percent reduction in the GST, a $100/month child care tax credit, a federal accountability act, and an anti-crime package.
12. See Lawrence LeDuc, Harold D. Clarke, Jane Jenson, and Jon H. Pammett, "Partisan Instability in Canada: Evidence from a New Panel Study," *American Political Science Review* 78 (1984), 470–84.
13. Herman Bakvis, "The Canadian Paradox: Party System Stability in the Face of a Weakly Aligned Electorate," in Steven Wolinetz, ed., *Parties and Party Systems in Liberal Democracies* (London: Routledge, 1988).
14. In the 1974 Canadian National Election Study, for example, 12 percent of those sampled held no identification with any political party. See Harold D. Clarke, Jane Jenson, Lawrence LeDuc, and Jon H Pammett, *Political Choice in Canada*, abridged edition (Toronto: McGraw-Hill Ryerson, 1980), 111.
15. In 1979, for example, about 29 percent of the electorate identified their partisan allegiance as Progressive Conservative. In 1984, the comparable figure was about 40 percent. See Harold D. Clarke, Jane Jenson, Lawrence LeDuc,

and Jon H. Pammett, *Absent Mandate: Canadian Electoral Politics in an Era of Restructuring* (Toronto: Gage, 1996), 51.

16. In 1993, for example, the turnover figure would have been considerably higher because of the collapse in support for the Conservatives and the shift of votes toward the new parties. In 1979, by contrast, only about 18 percent of the electorate changed their vote from that of 1974. For comparisons with other elections, see Harold D. Clarke, Jane Jenson, Lawrence LeDuc, and Jon H. Pammett, *Absent Mandate: Interpreting Change in Canadian Elections* (Toronto: Gage, 1991), 117–21.
17. André Blais et al., *Anatomy of a Liberal Victory* (Toronto: Broadview Press, 2002), 45–63. See also Jon H. Pammett and Lawrence LeDuc, *Explaining the Turnout Decline in Canadian Federal Elections: A New Survey of Non-Voters* (Ottawa: Elections Canada, 2002).
18. Jon H. Pammett and Lawrence LeDuc, "Behind the Turnout Decline," in Jon H. Pammett and Christopher Dornan, eds., *The Canadian General Election of 2004* (Toronto: Dundurn Press, 2004), Chapter 12.
19. On turnout in the 2006 election and its relationship to some of the longer term trends discussed here, see Lawrence LeDuc and Jon H. Pammett, "Voter Turnout in 2006: More Than Just the Weather," in Jon H. Pammett and Christopher Dornan, eds., *The Canadian General Election of 2006* (Toronto: Dundurn Press, 2006), Chapter 12.
20. Peter Mair, "Myths of Electoral Change and the Survival of Traditional Parties," *European Journal of Political Research* 24 (1993), 121–33.
21. For a more detailed exposition of this argument, with references to many of the elections discussed in detail in this book, see Stephen Clarkson, *The Big Red Machine: How the Liberal Party Dominates Canadian Politics* (Vancouver: University of British Columbia Press, 2005). See also André Blais, "Accounting for the Electoral Success of the Liberal Party in Canada," *Canadian Journal of Political Science* 38 (2005), 821–40.
22. This interpretation is explored in detail in R. Kenneth Carty, William Cross, and Lisa Young, *Rebuilding Canadian Party Politics* (Vancouver: University of British Columbia Press, 2000).

BIBLIOGRAPHY

Alford, Robert. *Party and Society.* Chicago: Rand McNally, 1963.

Armstrong, Elizabeth. *The Crisis of Quebec, 1914–1918.* Toronto: McClelland & Stewart, 1974. First published in 1937.

Aucoin, Peter. "Organizational Change in the Machinery of Canadian Government: From Rational Management to Brokerage Politics." *Canadian Journal of Political Science* 19 (1986): 3–27.

Aucoin, Peter, ed. *Party Government and Regional Representation in Canada.* Toronto: University of Toronto Press, 1985.

Avakumovic, Ivan. *Socialism in Canada: A Study of the CCF-NDP in Federal and Provincial Politics.* Toronto: McClelland & Stewart, 1978.

Bakvis, Herman. "The Canadian Paradox: Party System Stability in the Face of a Weakly Aligned Electorate." In Steven Wolinetz, *Parties and Party Systems in Liberal Democracies.* London: Routledge, 1988.

____. *Regional Ministers: Power and Influence in the Canadian Cabinet.* Toronto: University of Toronto Press, 1991.

Banting, Keith, and Richard Simeon, eds. *And No One Cheered: Federalism, Democracy and the Constitution Act.* Toronto: Methuen, 1983.

Beck, J. Murray. *The Government of Nova Scotia.* Toronto: University of Toronto Press, 1957.

____. *Pendulum of Power: Canada's Federal Elections.* Toronto: Prentice-Hall, 1968.

Bercuson, David, Jack Granatstein, and W.R. Young. *Sacred Trust? Brian Mulroney and the Conservatives in Power.* Toronto: Doubleday, 1986.

Bernard, André. "The Bloc Québécois." In *The Canadian General Election of 1993*, edited by Alan Frizzell, Jon H. Pammett, and Anthony Westell. Ottawa: Carleton University Press, 1994.

_____. "The Bloc Quebecois." In *The Canadian General Election of 1997*, edited by Alan Frizzell and Jon H. Pammett. Toronto: Dundurn Press, 1998.

Bernard, Paul. "Canada as a Social Experiment." *Canadian Journal of Sociology* 21 (1996): 245–58.

Betcherman, Lita-Rose. *Ernest Lapointe: Mackenzie King's Great Quebec Lieutenant*. Toronto: University of Toronto Press, 2002.

Bickerton, James, and Alain Gagnon, eds. *Canadian Politics*, 4th edition. Toronto: Broadview, 2004.

Blais, André. "The Debate Over Electoral Systems." *International Political Science Review* 12 (1991): 239–60.

_____. "Accounting for the Electoral Success of the Liberal Party in Canada." *Canadian Journal of Political Science* 38 (2005): 821–40.

Blais, André, and Louis Massicotte. "Electoral Systems." In *Comparing Democracies: Elections and Voting in Global Perspective*, edited by Lawrence LeDuc, Richard G. Niemi, and Pippa Norris. Thousand Oaks, CA: Sage, 1996.

Blais, André, Elisabeth Gidengil, Richard Nadeau, and Neil Nevitte. *Anatomy of a Liberal Victory: Making Sense of the Vote in the 2000 Canadian Election*. Toronto: Broadview, 2002.

Blake, Donald E. "1896 and All That: Critical Elections in Canada." *Canadian Journal of Political Science* 12 (1979): 259–80.

Blake, Raymond B., Penny E. Bryden, and J. Frank Strain, eds. *The Welfare State in Canada: Past, Present and Future*. Concord, ON: Irwin, 1997.

Bliss, Michael. *Right Honourable Men*. Toronto: HarperCollins, 1995.

Bothwell, Robert. *C.D. Howe: A Biography*. Toronto: McClelland & Stewart, 1979.

Bothwell, Robert, Ian Drummond, and John English. *Canada Since 1945: Power, Politics and Provincialism*. Toronto: University of Toronto Press, 1981.

Bouchard, Lucien. *A visage découvert*. Montréal: Boréal, 1992.

Boyer, Patrick. *The People's Mandate: Referendums and a More Democratic Canada*. Toronto: Dundurn Press, 1992.

_____. *Direct Democracy in Canada: The History and Future of Referendums*. Toronto: Dundurn Press, 1992.

Brodie, Janine, and Jane Jenson. *Crisis, Challenge and Change: Party and Class in Canada Revisited*. Ottawa: Carleton University Press, 1988.

_____. "Piercing the Smokescreen: Stability and Change in Brokerage Politics." In *Canadian Parties in Transition*, edited by A. Brian Tanguay and Alain G. Gagnon, 2nd edition. Toronto: Nelson, 1996.

Brown, Craig, and Paul-André Linteau. *Histoire générale du Canada*. Montréal: Boréal, 1990.

Burnham, Walter Dean. *Critical Elections and the Mainsprings of American Politics*. New York: Norton, 1970.

Cahill, Jack. *John Turner: The Long Run*. Toronto: McClelland & Stewart, 1984.

Cairns, Alan. "The Electoral System and the Party System in Canada." *Canadian Journal of Political Science* 1 (1968): 55–80.

Cameron, Duncan, ed. *The Free Trade Deal*. Toronto: Lorimer, 1988.

Camp, Dalton. *Gentlemen, Players and Politicians*. Toronto: McClelland & Stewart, 1970.

Campbell, Angus, Philip Converse, Warren Miller, and Donald Stokes. *The American Voter*. New York: Wiley, 1960.

Campbell, Colin, and William Christian. *Parties, Leaders and Ideologies in Canada*. Toronto: McGraw-Hill, 1996.

Caplan, Gerald. *The Dilemma of Canadian Socialism: The CCF in Ontario* Toronto: McClelland & Stewart, 1973.

Caplan, Gerald, Michael Kirby, and Hugh Segal. *Election: The Issues, the Strategies, the Aftermath*. Toronto: Prentice-Hall, 1989.

Careless, J.M.S., and R. Craig Brown. *The Canadians 1867–1967*. Toronto: Macmillan, 1967.

Carisse, Jean-Marc, and Mark Bell. *Privileged Access With Trudeau, Turner and Chrétien*. Toronto: Warwick Publishing, 2000.

Carrigan, Owen D. *Canadian Party Programs, 1867–1968*. Toronto: Clark, 1968.

Carty, R.K. "Three Canadian Party Systems." In *Canadian Political Party Systems: A Reader*, edited by R.K. Carty. Toronto: Broadview, 1992.

Carty, R.K., ed. *Canadian Political Party Systems: A Reader*. Toronto: Broadview, 1992.

Carty, R.K., and Munroe Eagles. "Do Local Campaigns Matter? Campaign Spending, the Local Canvass and Party Support in Canada." *Electoral Studies* 18 (1999): 69–87.

Carty, R.K., William Cross, and Lisa Young. *Rebuilding Canadian Party Politics*. Vancouver: University of British Columbia Press, 2000.

Chrétien, Jean. *Straight from the Heart*. Toronto: Key Porter, 1985.

____. *My Years as Prime Minister*. Toronto: Alfred A. Knopf, 2007.

Christian, William, and Colin Campbell. *Political Parties and Ideologies in Canada*, 3rd edition. Toronto: McGraw-Hill Ryerson, 1990.

Clarke, Harold D., Jane Jenson, Lawrence LeDuc, and Jon H. Pammett. *Political Choice in Canada*. Toronto: McGraw-Hill Ryerson, 1979.

____. "Voting Behaviour and the Outcome of the 1979 Election: The Impact of Leaders and Issues." *Canadian Journal of Political Science* 15 (1982): 517–52.

____. *Absent Mandate: The Politics of Discontent in Canada*. Toronto: Gage, 1984.

____. *Absent Mandate: Interpreting Change in Canadian Elections*. Toronto: Gage, 1991.

____. *Absent Mandate: Canadian Electoral Politics in an Era of Restructuring*. Toronto: Gage, 1996.

Clarke, Harold D., Allan Kornberg, and Peter Wearing. *A Polity on the Edge: Canada and the Politics of Fragmentation*. Toronto: Broadview, 2000.

Clarke, Harold D., Allan Kornberg, and Thomas J. Scotto. *Making Political Choices: Canada and the United States*. Toronto: University of Toronto Press, 2009.

_____. "None of the Above: Voters in the 2008 Federal Election." In *The Canadian General Election of 2008*, edited by Jon H. Pammett and Christopher Dornan. Toronto: Dundurn Press, 2009.

Clarkson, Stephen. *The Big Red Machine: How the Liberal Party Dominates Canadian Politics*. Vancouver: University of British Columbia Press, 2005.

Clarkson, Stephen, and Christina McCall. *Trudeau and Our Times*. Vol. 1. *The Magnificent Obsession*. Toronto: McClelland & Stewart, 1990.

Cleverdon, Catherine Lyle. *The Woman Suffrage Movement in Canada*. Toronto: University of Toronto Press, 1950.

Coates, Robert. *The Night of the Knives*. Fredericton, NB: Brunswick Press, 1969.

Cook, Ramsay, and Réal Bélanger, eds. *Canada's Prime Ministers: Macdonald to Trudeau*. Toronto: University of Toronto Press, 2007.

Cornellier, Manon. *The Bloc*. Toronto: Lorimer, 1995.

Corry, J.A. *Democratic Government and Politics*. Toronto: University of Toronto Press, 1946.

Courtney, John C. *The Selection of National Party Leaders in Canada*. Toronto: Macmillan, 1973.

_____. "Prime Ministerial Character: An Examination of Mackenzie King's Political Leadership." *Canadian Journal of Political Science* 9 (1976): 77–100.

_____. *Do Conventions Matter? Choosing National Party Leaders in Canada*. Montreal: McGill-Queen's University Press, 1995.

Courtney, John C., ed. *Voting in Canada*. Toronto: Prentice-Hall, 1967.

Cox, Gary. *Making Votes Count: Strategic Coordination in the World's Electoral Systems*. New York: Cambridge University Press, 1997.

Creighton, Donald. *John A. Macdonald*. 2 vols. Toronto: Macmillan, 1955.

Cutler, Fred. "The Simplest Shortcut of All: Sociodemographic Characteristics and Electoral Choice." *Journal of Politics* 64 (2002): 466–90.

Dabbs, Frank. *Preston Manning: The Roots of Reform*. Vancouver: Greystone, 1997.

Dafoe, J. W. *Laurier: A Study in Canadian Politics*. Toronto: Thomas Allan, 1922.

Dale, Ann, and Ted Naylor. "Dialogue and Public Space: An Exploration of Radio and Information Communication Technologies." *Canadian Journal of Political Science* 38 (2005): 203–25.

Dalton, Russell J. *Citizen Politics: Public Opinion and Political Parties in Advanced Industrial Democracies*, 5th edition. Washington, DC: CQ Press, 2008.

Davey, Keith. *The Rainmaker: A Passion for Politics*. Toronto: Stoddart, 1986.

Dawson, R. MacGregor. *William Lyon Mackenzie King: A Political Biography*. Toronto: University of Toronto Press, 1958.

Delacourt, Susan. *Juggernaut: Paul Martin's Campaign for Chrétien's Crown*. Toronto: McClelland & Stewart, 2003.

Diefenbaker, John G. *One Canada*. Toronto: Macmillan, 1977.

Dobbin, Murray. *The Politics of Kim Campbell: From School Trustee to Prime Minister*. Toronto: Lorimer, 1993.

Doern, G. Bruce, and Glen Toner. *The Politics of Energy: The Development and Implementation of the NEP*. Toronto: Methuen, 1985.

Duffy, John. *Fights of Our Lives: Elections, Leadership and the Making of Canada*. Toronto: HarperCollins, 2002.

Eagles, Munroe, James P. Bickerton, Alain G. Gagnon, and Patrick J. Smith. *The Almanac of Canadian Politics*, 2nd edition. Toronto: Oxford University Press, 1995.

Eijk, Cees van der, and Mark N. Franklin. *Elections and Voters*. London: Palgrave Macmillan, 2009.

Elections Canada. *A History of the Vote in Canada*. Ottawa: Minister of Public Works and Government Services, 1997.

Endersby J.W., S.E. Galatas, and C.B. Rackaway. "Closeness Counts in Canada: Voter Participation in the 1993 and 1997 Federal Elections." *Journal of Politics* 64 (2002): 610–31.

Engelman, Fred C., and Mildred A. Schwartz. *Political Parties and the Canadian Social Structure*. Toronto: Prentice-Hall, 1967.

____. *Canadian Political Parties: Origin, Character, Impact*. Toronto: Prentice-Hall, 1975.

English, John. *The Decline of Politics: The Conservatives and the Party System: 1901–1920*. Toronto: University of Toronto Press, 1977.

____. *The Worldly Years: The Life of Lester Pearson, Volume II, 1949–72*. Toronto: Random House, 1992.

English, John, and J.O. Stubbs, eds. *Mackenzie King: Widening the Debate*. Toronto: Macmillan, 1977.

Epstein, Leon D., *Political Parties in Western Democracies*, 2nd edition. New Brunswick, NJ: Transaction Books, 1980.

Evans, Geoffrey, and Pippa Norris. *Critical Elections: British Parties and Voters in Long-Term Perspective*. London: Sage, 1999.

Farrell, David M. "Campaign Strategies and Tactics." In *Comparing Democracies: Elections and Voting in Global Perspective*, edited by Lawrence LeDuc, Richard G. Niemi, and Pippa Norris. Thousand Oaks, CA: Sage, 1996.

Farrell, David M., and Rüdiger Schmitt-Beck, eds. *Do Political Campaigns Matter: Campaign Effects in Elections and Referendums*. London: Routledge, 2002.

Feigert, Frank. *Canada Votes: 1935–1988*. Durham, NC: Duke University Press, 1989.

Ferns, Henry, and Bernard Ostry. *The Age of Mackenzie King*. Toronto: J. Lorimer, 1976.

Fiorina, Morris. *Retrospective Voting in American National Elections*. New Haven, CT: Yale University Press, 1981.

Flanagan, Tom. *Waiting for the Wave: The Reform Party and Preston Manning*. Toronto: Stoddart, 1995.

____. *Harper's Team*. Montreal: McGill-Queen's University Press, 2007.

Flanagan, Tom, and Harold J. Jansen. "Election Campaigns Under Canada's Party Finance Laws." In *The Canadian General Election of 2008*, edited by Jon H. Pammett and Christopher Dornan. Toronto: Dundurn Press, 2009.

Franklin, Mark. *Voter Turnout and the Dynamics of Electoral Competition in Western Democracies Since 1945*. New York: Cambridge University Press, 2004.

Franklin, Mark, T.T. Mackie, and Henry Valen. *Electoral Change: Responses to Evolving Social and Attitudinal Structures in Western Democracies*. New York: Cambridge University Press, 1992.

Fraser, Graham. *Playing for Keeps: The Making of the Prime Minister, 1988*. Toronto: McClelland & Stewart, 1989.

Frizzell, Alan, and Anthony Westell, eds. *The Canadian General Election of 1984*. Ottawa: Carleton University Press, 1985.

Frizzell, Alan, and Jon H. Pammett, eds. *The Canadian General Election of 1997*. Toronto: Dundurn Press, 1997.

Frizzell, Alan, Jon H. Pammett, and Anthony Westell, eds. *The Canadian General Election of 1988*. Ottawa: Carleton University Press, 1989.

____. *The Canadian General Election of 1993*. Ottawa: Carleton University Press, 1994.

Gagnon, Alain G., and Daniel Latouche. *Allaire, Bélanger, Campeau et les autres: Les Québécois s'interrogent sur leur avenir*. Montréal: Editions Québec/Amérique, 1991.

Gagnon, Alain G., and Jacques Hérivault. "The Bloc Québécois: The Dynamics of a Distinct Electorate." In *The Canadian General Election of 2004*, edited by Jon H. Pammett and Christopher Dornan. Toronto: Dundurn Press, 2004.

Gagnon, Alain G., and Brian Tanguay, eds. *Canadian Parties in Transition*, 3rd edition. Toronto: Broadview, 2007.

Garner, John. *The Franchise and Politics in British North America, 1755–1867*. Toronto: University of Toronto Press, 1969.

Godin, Pierre. *La révolution tranquille*. Montréal: Boréal, 1991.

____. *René Lévesque: L'espoir et le chagrin*. Montréal: Boréal, 2001.

____. *René Lévesque: L'homme brisé*. Montréal: Boréal, 2005.

Goldenberg, Eddie. *The Way It Works: Inside Ottawa*. Toronto: Douglas Gibson Books, 2006.

Gollner, Andrew, and Daniel Salee, eds. *Canada under Mulroney: An End-of-Term Report*. Montreal: Véhicule Press, 1988.

Gordon, Walter. *A Political Memoir*. Toronto: McClelland & Stewart, 1977.

Gossage, Patrick. *Close to Charisma: My Years Between the Press and Pierre Elliot Trudeau*. Toronto: McClelland & Stewart, 1986.

Graham, Roger. *Arthur Meighen: A Biography*. Toronto: Clarke Irwin, 1963.

____. *One-Eyed Kings: Promise and Illusion in Canadian Politics*. Toronto: Collins, 1986.

Granatstein, J.L. *Canada 1957–1967: The Years of Uncertainty and Innovation*. The Canadian Centenary Series. Vol. 19. Toronto: McClelland & Stewart, 1986.

Gratton, Michel. *So What Are the Boys Saying? An Inside Look at Brian Mulroney in Power*. Toronto: McGraw-Hill Ryerson, 1987.

Gray, John. *Paul Martin: The Power of Ambition*. Toronto: Key Porter, 2003.

Greenspon, Edward, and Anthony Wilson-Smith. *Double Vision: The Inside Story of the Liberals in Power*. Toronto: Doubleday, 1996.

Grofman, Bernard, and Arend Lijphart. *Electoral Laws and Their Political Consequences*. New York: Agathon, 1986.

Gwyn, Richard. *The Northern Magus: Pierre Trudeau and Canadians*. Toronto: McClelland & Stewart, 1980.

Harmel, Robert, and Kenneth Janda. "Party Goals and Party Change." *Journal of Theoretical Politics* 6 (1994): 269–87.

Held, David. *Models of Democracy*. Stanford: Stanford University Press, 1987.

Hogg, Peter. 1988. *The Meech Lake Constitutional Accord: Annotated*. Toronto: Carswell

Hoy, Claire. *Friends in High Places: Politics and Patronage in the Mulroney Government*. Toronto: Key Porter, 1987.

Humphreys, David L. *Joe Clark: A Portrait*. Ottawa: Deneau and Greenberg, 1978.

Hutchison, Bruce. *The Incredible Canadian*. Toronto: Longmans, Green, 1952.

Inglehart, Ronald F., Neil Nevitte, and Miguel Basanez. *The North American Trajectory: Cultural, Economic and Political Ties Among the United States, Canada, and Mexico*. New York: de Gruyter, 1996.

Irvine, William. "Explaining the Religious Basis of Canadian Partisan Identity," *Canadian Journal of Political Science* 7 (1974): 560–63.

Irving, John. *The Social Credit Movement in Alberta*. Toronto: University of Toronto Press, 1959.

Jackson, Robert J., and Doreen Jackson. *Politics in Canada: Culture, Institutions, Behaviour and Public Policy*, 3rd edition. Toronto: Prentice-Hall, 1994.

Jenson, Jane. "Party Loyalty in Canada: the Question of Party Identification." *Canadian Journal of Political Science* 8 (1975): 543–53.

Jewett, Pauline. "Voting in the 1960 Federal By-Elections at Peterborough and Niagara Falls: Who Voted New Party and Why?" *Canadian Journal of Economics and Political Science* 28 (1962): 35–53.

Johnston, James. *The Party's Over*. Toronto: Longmans, 1971.

Johnston, J. Paul, and Harvey E. Pasis, eds. *Representation and Electoral Systems: Canadian Perspectives*. Toronto: Prentice-Hall, 1990.

Johnston, Richard. "The Reproduction of the Religious Cleavage in Canadian Elections," *Canadian Journal of Political Science* 18 (1985): 99–113.

Johnston, Richard, André Blais, Elisabeth Gidengil, and Neil Nevitte. *The Challenge of Direct Democracy: The 1992 Canadian Referendum*. Montreal: McGill-Queen's University Press, 1996.

Johnston, Richard, André Blais, Henry Brady, and Jean Crête. "Free Trade and the Dynamics of the 1988 Election." In Joseph Wearing, *The Ballot and Its Message*. Toronto: Copp Clark, 1991.

____. *Letting the People Decide*. Montreal: McGill-Queen's University Press, 1992.

Johnston, William. *Stephen Harper and the Future of Canada*. Toronto: McClelland & Stewart, 2006.

Kay, Barry J., Steven D. Brown, James E. Curtis, Ronald D. Lambert, and John M. Wilson. "The Character of Electoral Change: A Preliminary Report from the 1984 Election Study." In *The Ballot and Its Message: Voting in Canada*, edited by Joseph Wearing. Toronto: Copp Clark Pitman, 1991.

____. "The Character of Electoral Change: A Preliminary Report from the 1984 Election Study." In *The Ballot and Its Message: Voting in Canada*, edited by Joseph Wearing. Toronto: Copp Clark Pitman, 1991.

Kendle, John. *John Bracken: A Political Biography*. Toronto: University of Toronto Press, 1979.

Kesterton, W.H. *A History of Journalism in Canada*. Toronto: McClelland & Stewart, 1967.

Key, V.O. "A Theory of Critical Elections," *Journal of Politics* 17 (1955): 3–18.

Kilbourn, William. *Pipeline*. Toronto: Clark Irwin, 1970.

King, William Lyon Mackenzie. *Industry and Humanity*. Boston: Houghton Mifflin, 1918.

Krause, Robert, and Lawrence LeDuc. "Voting Behaviour and Electoral Strategies in the 1976 Progressive-Conservative Leadership Convention." *Canadian Journal of Political Science* 12 (1979): 97–136.

LaMarsh, Judy. *Memoirs of a Bird in a Gilded Cage*. Toronto: McClelland & Stewart, 1969.

Lambert, Ronald D., James Curtis, Steven Brown, and Barry Kay. "In Search of Left/Right Beliefs in the Canadian Electorate." *Canadian Journal of Political Science* 19 (1986): 542–63.

Law Commission of Canada. *Voting Counts: Electoral Reform for Canada*. Ottawa: Public Works and Government Services, 2004.

LeDuc, Lawrence. "Canada: the Politics of Stable Dealignment." In *Electoral Change in Advanced Industrial Democracies*, edited by Russell Dalton, Scott Flanagan, and Paul Allen Beck. Princeton, NJ: Princeton University Press, 1984.

____. "Partisan Change and Dealignment in Canada, Great Britain, and the United States." *Comparative Politics* 17 (1985): 379–98.

____. "Party Strategies and the Use of Televised Campaign Debates." *European Journal of Political Research* 18 (1990): 121–41.

____. "Voting for Free Trade? The Canadian Voter and the 1988 Federal Election." In *Politics: Canada*, 7th edition, edited by Paul Fox and Graham White. Toronto: McGraw-Hill Ryerson, 1991.

____. "Leaders and Voters: The Public Images of Canadian Political Leaders." In *Leaders and Leadership in Canada*, edited by Maureen Mancuso et al. Toronto: Oxford University Press, 1994.

____. "Citizens; Revenge: the Canadian Voter and the 1993 Federal Election." In *Politics: Canada*, 8th edition, edited by Paul Fox and Graham White. Toronto: McGraw-Hill Ryerson, 1995.

____. "Elections and Democratic Governance." In *Comparing Democracies: Elections and Voting in Global Perspective*, edited by Lawrence LeDuc, Richard G. Niemi, and Pippa Norris. Thousand Oaks, CA: Sage, 1996.

____. "The Leaders' Debates … And the Winner Is …" In *The Canadian General Election of 1997*, edited by Alan Frizzell and Jon H. Pammett. Toronto: Dundurn Press, 1997.

____. "The Canadian Federal Election of 1997." *Electoral Studies* 17 (1998): 132–37.

____. "New Challenges Demand New Thinking About Our Antiquated Electoral System." In *Making Every Vote Count: Reassessing Canada's Electoral System*, edited by Henry Milner. Toronto: Broadview, 1999.

____. "Democratizing Party Leadership Selection." *Party Politics* 7 (2001): 323–41.

____. "The Canadian Federal Election, November 2000." *Electoral Studies* 21 (2002): 655–59.

____. "The Federal Election in Canada: June 2004." *Electoral Studies* 24 (2005): 338–44.

____. "The Federal Election in Canada: January 2006." *Electoral Studies* 26 (2007): 716–20.

____. "The Federal Election in Canada: October 2008." *Electoral Studies* 28 (2009): 322–29.

LeDuc, Lawrence, Harold D. Clarke, Jane Jenson, and Jon H Pammett. "Partisan Instability in Canada: Evidence from a New Panel Study." *American Political Science Review* 78 (1984): 470–84.

LeDuc, Lawrence, Richard G. Niemi, and Pippa Norris, eds. *Comparing Democracies: Elections and Voting in Global Perspective*. Thousand Oaks, CA: Sage, 1996.

____. *Comparing Democracies 2: New Challenges in the Study of Elections and Voting*. London: Sage, 2002.

____. *Comparing Democracies 3: Elections and Voting in the 21st Century*. London: Sage, 2010.

LeDuc, Lawrence, and Jon H. Pammett. "Referendum Voting: Attitudes and Behaviour in the October 1992 Referendum." *Canadian Journal of Political Science* 28 (1995): 1–31.

____. "Sovereignty, Leadership and Voting in the Quebec Referendums." *Electoral Studies* 20 (2001): 265–80.

____. "Voter Turnout in 2006: More Than Just the Weather." In *The Canadian General Election of 2006*, edited by Jon H. Pammett and Christopher Dornan. Toronto: Dundurn Press, 2006.

____. "The 2008 Election: Long-Term and Short-Term Assessments." In *The Canadian General Election of 2008*, edited by Jon H. Pammett and Christopher Dornan. Toronto: Dundurn Press, 2009.

____. "Voter Turnout." In *Election*, edited by Heather MacIvor. Toronto: Emond Montgomery, 2010.

LeDuc, Lawrence, and Richard Price. "Great Debates: the Televised Leadership Debates of 1979." *Canadian Journal of Political Science* 18 (1983): 135–54.

Lee, Robert Mason. *One Hundred Monkeys*. Toronto: Macfarlane and Ross, 1989.

Liberal Party of Canada. *Creating Opportunity: The Liberal Plan for Canada* (aka "The Red Book"). Ottawa: Liberal Party of Canada, 1993.

Lipset, Seymour Martin. *Agrarian Socialism*. Berkeley: University of California Press, 1950.

Lipset, Seymour Martin, and Stein Rokkan. *Party Systems and Voter Alignments: Cross-National Perspectives*. New York: Free Press, 1967.

Lisée, Jean-François. *Le Tricheur: Robert Bourassa et les Québécois 1990–1991*. Montréal: Boréal, 1994.

____. *Le Naufrageur: Robert Bourassa et les Québécois 1991–1992*. Montréal: Boréal, 1994.

MacDonald, L. Ian. *Mulroney: The Making of the Prime Minister*. Toronto: McClelland & Stewart, 1984.

MacIvor, Heather, ed. *Election*. Toronto: Emond Montgomery, 2010.

Macpherson, C.B. *Democracy in Alberta: Social Credit and the Party System*. Toronto: University of Toronto Press, 1953.

Macpherson, C.B. *The Life and Times of Liberal Democracy*. Oxford: Oxford University Press, 1977.

Mair, Peter. "Myths of Electoral Change and the Survival of Traditional Parties." *European Journal of Political Research* 24 (1993): 121–33.

____. "Party Systems and Structures of Competition." In *Comparing Democracies: Elections and Voting in Global Perspective*, edited by Lawrence LeDuc, Richard G. Niemi, and Pippa Norris. Thousand Oaks, CA: Sage, 1996.

Mancuso, Maureen, et al., eds. *Leaders and Leadership in Canada*. Toronto: Oxford University Press Canada, 1994.

Manning, Preston. *The New Canada*. Toronto: MacMillan, 1992.

____. *Think Big: My Adventures in Life and Democracy*. Toronto: McClelland & Stewart, 2002.

Martin, Lawrence. *Chrétien: The Will to Win*. Toronto: Lester, 1995.

____. *The Antagonist: Lucien Bouchard and the Politics of Delusion*. Toronto: Viking, 1997.

____. *Iron Man: The Defiant Reign of Jean Chrétien*. Toronto: Viking, 2003.

Martin, Patrick, Allan Gregg, and George Perlin. *Contenders: The Tory Quest for Power*. Toronto: Prentice-Hall, 1983.

Martin, Paul. *Hell or High Water: My Life In and Out of Politics*. Toronto: McClelland & Stewart, 2008.

Martin, Paul Sr. *A Very Public Life*. Toronto: Deneau, 1985.

Marzolini, Michael. "The Politics of Values." In *The Canadian General Election of 2000*, edited by Jon H. Pammett and Christopher Dornan. Toronto: Dundurn Press, 2001.

McCall, Christina, and Stephen Clarkson. *Trudeau and Our Times. Volume 2: The Heroic Delusion*. Toronto: McClelland & Stewart, 1994.

McCall-Newman, Christina. *Grits: An Intimate Portrait of the Liberal Party.* Toronto: Macmillan, 1982.

McGregor, F.A. *The Fall and Rise of Mackenzie King: 1911–1919.* Toronto: Macmillan, 1962.

McKie, Craig, and Keith Thompson. *Canadian Social Trends.* Toronto: Thompson Educational Publishing, 1990.

McLaughlin, David. *Poisoned Chalice: The Last Campaign of the Progressive Conservative Party?* Toronto: Dundurn Press, 1994.

McNaught, Kenneth. *A Prophet in Politics: A Biography of J.S. Woodsworth.* Toronto: University of Toronto Press, 1959.

McRoberts, Kenneth, and Dale Posgate. *Quebec: Social Change and Political Crisis.* Toronto: McClelland & Stewart, 1980.

Meisel, John. "Religious Affiliation and Electoral Behaviour: A Case Study." *Canadian Journal of Economics and Political Science* 22 (1956): 481–96.

____. *The Canadian General Election of 1957.* Toronto: University of Toronto Press, 1962.

____. "The 1962 Election: Break-Up of our Party System?" *Queen's Quarterly* 69 (1962): 329–46.

____. "The Stalled Omnibus: Canadian Parties in the 1960s," *Social Research* 30 (1962): 367–90.

____. "Cleavages, Parties and Values in Canada." *Sage Papers in Contemporary Political Sociology.* Beverley Hills, CA: Sage, 1974.

____. *Working Papers on Canadian Politics.* Montreal: McGill-Queen's University Press, 1975.

Meisel, John, ed. *Papers on the 1962 Election.* Toronto: University of Toronto Press, 1964.

Meisel, John, and Matthew Mendelsohn. "Meteor? Phoenix? Chameleon? The Decline and Transformation of Party in Canada." In *Party Politics in Canada,* 8th edition, edited by Hugh Thorburn and Alan Whitehorn. Toronto: Prentice-Hall, 2001.

Miller, William L., and Richard G. Niemi. "Voting Choice, Conditioning, and Constraint." In *Comparing Democracies 2: New Challenges in the Study of Elections and Voting,* edited by Lawrence LeDuc, Richard G. Niemi, and Pippa Norris. London: Sage, 2002.

Milne David. *The Canadian Constitution.* Toronto: Lorimer, 1991.

Milner, Henry, ed. *Making Every Vote Count: Reassessing Canada's Electoral System.* Toronto: Broadview, 1999.

Morton, Desmond. *The New Democrats: 1961–1986.* Toronto: Copp Clark Pitman, 1986.

Morton, W.L. *The Progressive Party in Canada.* Toronto: University of Toronto Press, 1950.

Mulroney, Brian. *Memoirs: 1939–1993.* Toronto: McClelland & Stewart, 2007.

Murphy, Rae, Robert Chodos, and Nick Auf der Maur. *Brian Mulroney: The Boy from Baie Comeau.* Toronto: Lorimer, 1984.

Neatby, H. Blair. *William Lyon Mackenzie King, 1924–1932: The Lonely Heights.* Toronto: University of Toronto Press, 1963.

_____. *Laurier and a Liberal Quebec: A Study in Political Management.* Toronto: McClelland & Stewart, 1973.

_____. *William Lyon Mackenzie King, 1932–1939: The Prism of Unity.* Toronto: University of Toronto Press, 1976.

Nevitte, Neil. *The Decline of Deference: Canadian Value Change in Cross-National Perspective.* Toronto: Broadview, 1996.

Nevitte, Neil, ed. *Value Change and Governance in Canada.* Toronto: University of Toronto Press, 2002.

Nevitte, Neil, André Blais, Elisabeth Gidengil, and Richard Nadeau. *Unsteady State: The 1997 Canadian Federal Election.* Toronto: Oxford University Press Canada, 2000.

Nevitte, Neil, Richard Johnston, André Blais, and Elisabeth Gidengil. "The People and the Charlottetown Accord." In *Canada: The State of the Federation,* edited by Ronald L. Watts and Douglas M. Brown. Kingston, ON: Institute of Intergovernmental Relations, 1993.

Newman, Peter C. *Renegade in Power.* Toronto: McClelland & Stewart, 1963.

_____. *The Distemper of Our Times.* Toronto: McClelland & Stewart, 1968.

_____. *The Canadian Revolution 1985–1995: From Deference to Defiance.* Toronto: Viking, 1995.

_____. *The Secret Mulroney Tapes: Unguarded Confessions of a Prime Minister.* Toronto: Random House Canada, 2005.

Noel, S.J.R. *Patrons, Clients and Brokers: Ontario Society and Politics, 1791–1896.* Toronto: University of Toronto Press, 1990.

Nolan, Michael. *Joe Clark: The Emerging Leader.* Toronto: Fitzhenry & Whiteside, 1978.

Norris, Pippa, et al. *On Message: Communicating the Campaign.* London: Sage, 1999.

O'Leary, Grattan. *Recollections of People, Press and Politics.* Toronto: Macmillan, 1977.

Pammett, Jon H. "Class Voting and Class Consciousness in Canada," *Canadian Review of Sociology and Anthropology* 24 (1987): 269–90.

_____. "A Framework for the Comparative Analysis of Elections Across Time and Space," *Electoral Studies* 7 (1988): 125–42.

_____. "Voting Turnout in Canada." In *Voter Turnout in Canada,* edited by Herman Bakvis. Toronto: Dundurn Press, 1991.

_____. "The Voters Decide." In *The Canadian General Election of 1997,* edited by Alan Frizzell and Jon H. Pammett. Toronto: Dundurn Press, 1997.

Pammett, Jon H., and Christopher Dornan, eds. *The Canadian General Election of 2000.* Toronto: Dundurn Press, 2001.

_____. *The Canadian General Election of 2004.* Toronto: Dundurn Press, 2004.

_____. *The Canadian Federal Election of 2006.* Toronto: Dundurn Press, 2006.

_____. *The Canadian Federal Election of 2008.* Toronto: Dundurn Press, 2008.

Pammett, Jon H., and Lawrence LeDuc. *Explaining the Turnout Decline in Canadian Federal Elections: A New Survey of Non-Voters*. Ottawa: Elections Canada, 2003.

____. "Behind the Turnout Decline." In *The Canadian General Election of 2006*, edited by Jon H. Pammett and Christopher Dornan. Toronto: Dundurn Press, 2004.

Pammett, Jon H., and Brian Tomlin, eds. *The Integration Question: Political Economy and Public Policy in Canada and North America*. Toronto: Addison-Wesley, 1984.

Peacock, Donald. *Journey to Power: The Story of a Canadian Election*. Toronto: Ryerson, 1968.

Pearson, Lester B. *Mike: The Memoirs of the Right Honourable Lester B. Pearson*. Toronto: University of Toronto Press, 1973.

Penniman, Howard, ed. *Canada at the Polls: The General Election of 1974*. Washington, DC: American Enterprise Institute for Public Policy Research, 1975.

____. *Canada at the Polls 1979 and 1980: A Study of the General Elections*. Washington DC: American Enterprise Institute for Public Policy Research, 1981.

____. *Canada at the Polls, 1984*. Washington, DC: American Enterprise Institute for Public Policy Research, 1988.

Perlin, George C. *The Tory Syndrome: Leadership Politics in the Progressive Conservative Party*. Montreal: McGill-Queen's University Press, 1980.

Phillips, Harry C. "Challenges to the Voting System in Canada: 1874–1974." Ph.D. dissertation, University of Western Ontario, 1976.

Pickersgill, J.W. *My Years with Louis St. Laurent: A Political Memoir*. Toronto: University of Toronto Press, 1975.

Pilon, Dennis. *The Politics of Voting: Reforming Canada's Electoral System*. Toronto: Emond Montgomery Publications, 2007.

Pinard, Maurice. *The Rise of a Third Party: A Study in Crisis Politics*. Englewood Cliffs, NJ: Prentice Hall, 1971.

Pinard, Maurice, Robert Bernier, and Vincent Lemieux. *Un Combat Inachevé*. Québec: Presses de l'Université du Québec, 1997.

Plamondon, Robert. *Full Circle: Death and Resurrection in Canadian Conservative Politics*. Toronto: Key Porter, 2006.

Porter, John. *The Vertical Mosaic*. Toronto: University of Toronto Press, 1965.

Radwanski, George. *Trudeau*. Toronto: Macmillan, 1978.

Regenstreif, Peter. "Some Aspects of National Party Support in Canada." *Canadian Journal of Economics and Political Science* 29 (1963): 59–74.

____. *The Diefenbaker Interlude: Parties and Voting in Canada*. Toronto: University of Toronto Press, 1965.

Reid, Escott M. "The Rise of National Political Parties in Canada." *Proceedings of the Canadian Political Science Association*, Vol. 4, 1932.

Robinson, Daniel J. *The Measure of Democracy: Polling, Market Research and Public Life, 1930–1945*. Toronto: University of Toronto Press, 1999.

Romanow, Roy, John White, and Howard Leeson. *Canada ... Notwithstanding: The Making of the Constitution, 1976–1982.* Toronto: Carswell-Methuen, 1984.

Rose, Richard, ed. *Electoral Behavior: A Comparative Handbook.* New York: Free Press, 1974.

Royal Commission on the Economic Union and Developments Prospects for Canada. *Report.* Toronto: University of Toronto Press, 1985.

Royal Commission on Electoral Reform and Party Financing. *Reforming Electoral Democracy.* Ottawa: Government Publications, 1991.

Russell, Peter. *Constitutional Odyssey,* 2nd edition. Toronto: University of Toronto Press, 1993.

——. *Two Cheers for Minority Government: The Evolution of Canadian Parliamentary Democracy.* Toronto: Emond Montgomery Publications, 2008.

Russell, Peter, and Lorne Sossin, eds. *Parliamentary Democracy in Crisis.* Toronto: University of Toronto Press, 2009.

Sawatsky, John. *Mulroney: the Politics of Ambition.* Toronto: Macfarlane, Walter & Ross, 1991.

Scarrow, Howard. *Canada Votes.* New Orleans, LA: Hauser Press, 1963.

Schlesinger, Arthur. *A Thousand Days: John F. Kennedy in the White House.* New York: Houghton Mifflin, 1965.

Schumpeter, Joseph. *Capitalism, Socialism and Democracy.* New York: Harper, 1942.

Schull, Joseph. *Laurier: The First Canadian.* Toronto: Macmillan, 1965.

Schwartz, Mildred. "Canadian Voting Behavior." In *Electoral Behavior: A Comparative Handbook,* edited by Richard Rose. New York: Free Press, 1974.

Segal, Hugh. *The Long Road Back.* Toronto: HarperCollins, 2006.

Siegfried, André. *The Race Question in Canada.* London: Eveleigh Nash, 1907.

Simpson, Jeffrey. *Discipline of Power: The Conservative Interlude and the Liberal Restoration.* Toronto: Personal Library Publishers, 1980.

——. *Spoils of Power: The Politics of Patronage.* Toronto: HarperCollins, 1988.

——. *The Friendly Dictatorship.* Toronto: McClelland & Stewart, 2001.

Skelton, O.D. *General Economic History of the Dominion 1967–1912.* Toronto: Publishers Association of Canada, 1913.

——. *The Life and Letters of Sir Wilfrid Laurier.* Toronto: McClelland & Stewart, 1965.

Smiley, Donald V. "Canada's Poujadists: A New Look at Social Credit." *The Canadian Forum* 62 (1962): 121–23.

Smith, David E. *The Regional Decline of a National Party: Liberals on the Prairies.* Toronto: University of Toronto Press, 1981.

——. "Party Government, Representation and National Integration in Canada." In *Party Government and Regional Representation in Canada,* edited by Peter Aucoin. Toronto: University of Toronto Press, 1985.

Smith, Denis. *Rogue Tory.* Toronto: Macfarlane, Walter & Ross, 1995.

Sniderman, Paul, H.D. Forbes, and Ian Melzer. "Party Loyalty and Electoral Volatility: a Study of the Canadian Party System." *Canadian Journal of Political Science* 7 (1974): 268–88.

Spicer, Keith. *Citizens' Forum on Canada's Future.* Ottawa: Supply and Services, 1991.

Stacey, C.P. *A Very Double Life: The Private World of Mackenzie King.* Toronto: Macmillan, 1976.

Stevens, Geoffrey. *Stanfield.* Toronto: McClelland & Stewart, 1973.

____. *The Player: The Life and times of Dalton Camp.* Toronto: Key Porter, 2003.

Stevenson, H. Michael. "Ideology and Unstable Party Identification in Canada: Limited Rationality in a Brokerage Party System." *Canadian Journal of Political Science* 20 (1987): 813–50.

Stewart, Gordon T. "John A. Macdonald's Greatest Triumph." *Canadian Historical Review* 33 (1982): 3–33.

____. *The Origins of Canadian Politics: A Comparative Approach.* Vancouver: University of British Columbia Press, 1986.

Stewart, Walter. *The Life and Times of M.J. Coldwell.* Toronto: Stoddart, 2000.

Story, D.C., and R. Bruce Shephard, eds. *The Diefenbaker Legacy: Canadian Politics, Law and Society Since 1957.* Regina: Canadian Plains Research Centre, 1998.

Strøm, Kaare. "A Behavioral Theory of Competitive Political Parties." *American Journal of Political Science* 34 (1990): 565–98.

Studlar, Donley T. "Canadian Exceptionalism: Explaining Differences Over Time in Provincial and Federal Voter Turnout." *Canadian Journal of Political Science*, 34 (2001): 299–319.

Stursberg, Peter. *Diefenbaker: Leadership Gained, 1956–62.* Toronto: University of Toronto Press, 1975.

Sullivan, Martin. *Mandate '68: The Year of Pierre Elliott Trudeau.* Toronto: Doubleday, 1968.

Thomson, Dale. *Alexander Mackenzie: Clear Grit.* Toronto: Macmillan, 1960.

____. *Louis St. Laurent: Canadian.* Toronto: Macmillan, 1967.

Thorburn, Hugh. "Parliament and Policy-Making: The Case of the Trans-Canada Gas Pipeline," *Canadian Journal of Economics and Political Science* 23 (1957): 516–31.

Thorburn, Hugh G., and Alan Whitehorn, eds. *Party Politics in Canada*, 8th edition. Toronto: Prentice Hall, 2001.

Thordarson, Bruce. *Lester Pearson: Diplomat and Politician.* Toronto: Oxford University Press Canada, 1974.

Troyer, Warner. *200 Days: Joe Clark in Power.* Toronto: Personal Library Publishers, 1980.

Trudeau, Pierre Elliott. *Federalism and the French Canadians.* Toronto: Macmillan, 1968.

____. *Approaches to Politics.* Toronto: Oxford University Press Canada, 1970.

____. *Memoirs.* Toronto: McClelland & Stewart, 1990.

____. *Against the Current: Selected Writings, 1939–1996* (edited by Gérard Pelletier). Toronto: McClelland & Stewart, 1996.

Turcotte, André. "A la prochaine … again: The Québec Referendum of 1995." *Electoral Studies* 15 (1996): 399–403.

____. "Different Strokes: Why Young Canadians Don't Vote." *Electoral Insight* 7 (January 2005).

____. "What Do You Mean I Cannot Have A Say?" Ottawa: Canadian Public Research Networks, no. 48799, 2007.

Vastel, Michel. *Trudeau le Québécois*. Montréal: Les Editions de l'Homme, 1989.

____. *The Outsider: The Life of Pierre Elliott Trudeau*. Toronto: Macmillan, 1990.

Von Beyme, Klaus. *Political Parties in Western Democracies*. Aldershot, ON: Gower, 1985.

Waite, Peter B. *Canada 1874–1896*. Toronto: McClelland & Stewart, 1971.

____. *Macdonald: His Life and World*. Toronto: McGraw-Hill Ryerson, 1975.

Ward, Norman. *The Canadian House of Commons Representation*. Toronto: University of Toronto Press, 1950.

Ward, Norman, ed. *A Party Politician: The Memoirs of Chubby Power*. Toronto: Macmillan, 1966.

Wardhaugh, Robert A. *Mackenzie King and the Prairie West*. Toronto: University of Toronto Press, 2000.

Ware, Alan. *Political Parties and Party Systems*. Oxford: Oxford University Press, 1996.

Watts, Ronald L., and Douglas M. Brown, eds. *Canada: The State of the Federation*. Kingston, ON: Institute of Intergovernmental Relations, 1993.

Wearing, Joseph. *The L-Shaped Party: The Liberal Party of Canada, 1958–1980*. Toronto: McGraw-Hill Ryerson, 1981.

____. *Strained Relations: Canadian Parties and Voters*. Toronto: McClelland & Stewart, 1988.

Wearing, Joseph, ed. *The Ballot and Its Message*. Toronto: Copp Clark, 1991.

Wells, Paul. *Right Side Up*. Toronto: McClelland & Stewart, 2006.

Westell, Anthony. *Paradox: Trudeau as Prime Minister*. Toronto: Prentice-Hall, 1972.

Weston, Gregg. *Reign of Error: The Inside Story of John Turner's Troubled Leadership*. Toronto: McGraw-Hill Ryerson, 1988.

Whitaker, Reginald. *The Government Party: Organizing and Financing the Liberal Party of Canada, 1930–1958*. Toronto: University of Toronto Press, 1977.

Whitehorn, Alan. *Canadian Socialism: Essays on the CCF-NDP*. Toronto: Oxford University Press Canada, 1992.

____. "The NDP and the Enigma of Strategic Voting." In *The Canadian General Election of 2006*, edited by Jon H. Pammett and Christopher Dornan. Toronto: Dundurn Press, 2006.

Wilbur, Richard. *H.H. Stevens*. Toronto: University of Toronto Press, 1977.

Williams, John R. *The Conservative Party of Canada, 1920–1949*. Durham, NC: Duke University Press, 1956.

Winn, Conrad, and John McMenemy. *Political Parties in Canada*. Toronto: McGraw-Hill Ryerson, 1976.

Wolinetz, Steven. *Parties and Party Systems in Liberal Democracies*. London: Routledge, 1988.

Young, Robert A. *The Struggle for Quebec: From Referendum to Referendum?* Montreal: McGill-Queen's University Press, 1999.

Young, Walter D. *The Anatomy of a Party: The National CCF, 1932–61*. Toronto: University of Toronto Press, 1969.

____. *Democracy and Discontent*, 2nd edition. Toronto: McGraw-Hill Ryerson, 1978.

INDEX

ABOUT THE AUTHORS

Lawrence LeDuc is professor of political science at the University of Toronto. His publications include *Comparing Democracies 3: Elections and Voting in the 21st Century* (Sage, 2010), *The Politics of Direct Democracy* (Broadview, 2003), *Absent Mandate: Canadian Electoral Politics in an Era of Restructuring* (Gage, 1996), *How Voters Change: the 1987 British Election Campaign in Perspective* (Oxford, 1990), and *Political Choice in Canada* (McGraw-Hill Ryerson, 1979, 1980), as well as numerous book chapters and articles on political parties, elections, and voting. He currently serves on the editorial boards of the *Journal of Elections, Public Opinion, and Parties* and *Electoral Studies.*

Jon H. Pammett is professor of political science at Carleton University in Ottawa. He is co-author of *Political Choice in Canada* (McGraw-Hill Ryerson, 1979, 1980) and *Absent Mandate* (Gage, 1984, 1991, 1996). He has edited and contributed to several books about specific Canadian federal elections, the most recent of which is *The Canadian Federal Election of 2008* (Dundurn Press, 2009). He has published journal articles on public opinion and voting behaviour in Canada and other countries, and has also worked in the field of political education. His current research involves the reasons for the decline in electoral participation.

Judith I. McKenzie is associate professor in the Department of Political Science at the University of Guelph. She has written *Environmental Politics in Canada: Managing the Commons Into the Twenty-First Century* (Oxford University Press, 2002) and *Pauline Jewett: A Passion for Canada* (McGill-Queen's University Press, 1999). She has also published articles in several journals, including the *Journal of Legislative Studies* and the *International Journal of Environment and Pollution*. She is currently working on a project funded by the Canadian Institutes of Health Research, studying urban poverty in Canada.

André Turcotte is assistant professor in Communication at Carleton University's School of Journalism and Communication. He specializes in Image, Politics, and Persuasion and advanced research methods. He has contributed to several books, most recently *The Canadian General Election of 2006* (Dundurn Press, 2006) and *Elections* (Emond Montgomery Publications, 2010). Between 1994 and 2000, Dr. Turcotte was the official pollster of the Reform Party of Canada and its leader, Preston Manning.

BY THE SAME AUTHORS

The Canadian Federal Election of 2008
edited by Jon H. Pammett
and Christopher Dornan
978-1-55488-407-0
$36.99

A comprehensive analysis of all aspects of the 2008 campaign and election outcome, written by leading professors of political science, journalism, and communications. It examines the strategies, successes, and failures of the major political parties, includes chapters on the media coverage and the way Canada's party finance laws affected the campaign, and concludes with a detailed analysis of the voting behaviour of Canadians and an overview of the long- and short-term forces influencing the future of Canadian electoral politics.

OF RELATED INTEREST

Doing the Continental
A New Canadian-American Relationship
by David Dyment
978-1-55488-758-3
$19.99

Canada's relations with the United States are broad and deep, and with Obama in the White House, the two countries are about to enter what could be a new era of hope and renewal. From water and energy policy to defence, environmental strategy, and Arctic sovereignty, David Dyment provides an astute, pithy analysis of the past, present, and future continental dance between two countries that have much in common, yet often step on each other's feet.